Ian Allan abc

MILITARY AIRCRAFT MARKINGS 2005

Peter R. March &
Howard J. Curtis

Contents

Photographs by Peter R. March (PRM) unless otherwise credited

This twenty-sixth edition published 2005

ISBN 0 7110 3052 9

Published by Ian Allan Publishing

an imprint of Ian Allan Publishing Ltd,
Hersham, Surrey KT12 4RG.

Printed in England by Ian Allan Printing Ltd,
Hersham, Surrey KT12 4RG

Code: 0503/

Front cover: Tornado GR4 of the RAF Coningsby Fast Jet Weapons OEU. *R. Cooper*

Back cover: Eurofighter EF.2000 98+29 WTD-61. *R. Cooper*

Introduction

This twenty-sixth annual edition of the *abc Military Aircraft Markings*, jointly edited by Peter R. March and Howard J Curtis, lists in alphabetical and numerical order all of the aircraft that carry a United Kingdom military serial, and which are based, or might be seen, in the UK. It also includes airworthy and current RAF/RN/Army aircraft that are based permanently or temporarily overseas. The term *aircraft* used here covers powered, manned aeroplanes, helicopters, airships and gliders. Included are all the current Royal Air Force, Royal Navy, Army Air Corps, Defence Procurement Agency, QinetiQ operated, manufacturers' test aircraft and civilian-owned aircraft with military markings or operated for the Ministry of Defence.

Aircraft withdrawn from operational use but which are retained in the UK for ground training purposes or otherwise preserved by the Services and in the numerous museums and collections are listed. The serials of some incomplete aircraft have been included, such as the cockpit sections of machines displayed by the RAF, aircraft used by airfield fire sections and for service battle damage repair training (BDRT), together with significant parts of aircraft held by preservation groups and societies. Where only part of the aircraft fuselage remains the abbreviation <ff> for front fuselage/cockpit section or <rf> for rear fuselage is shown after the type. Many of these aircraft are allocated, and sometimes wear, a secondary identity, such as an RAF 'M' maintenance number. These numbers are listed against those aircraft to which they have been allocated.

A serial 'missing' from a sequence is either because it was never issued as it formed part of a 'black-out block' or because the aircraft is written off, scrapped, sold abroad or allocated an alternative marking. Aircraft used as targets on MoD ranges to which access is restricted, and UK military aircraft that have been permanently grounded and are based overseas and unlikely to return to Britain have generally been omitted. With the appearance of some military registered UAVs, drones and small target aircraft at public events and ground displays, these have now been included if they are likely to be seen.

In the main, the serials listed are those markings presently displayed on the aircraft. Where an aircraft carries a false serial it is quoted in *italic type*. Very often these serials are carried by replicas, that are denoted by <R> after the type. The manufacturer and aircraft type are given, together with recent alternative, previous, secondary or civil identity shown in round brackets. Complete records of multiple previous identities are only included where space permits. The operating unit and its based location, along with any known unit and base code markings in square brackets, are given as accurately as possible. The unit markings are normally carried boldly on the sides of the fuselage or on the aircraft's fin. In the case of RAF and AAC machines currently in service, they are usually one or two letters or numbers, while the RN continues to use a well-established system of three-figure codes between 000 and 999 together with a fin letter code denoting the aircraft's operational base. RN squadrons, units and bases are allocated blocks of numbers from which individual aircraft codes are issued. To help identification of RN bases and landing platforms on ships, a list of tail-letter codes with their appropriate name, helicopter code number, ship pennant number and type of vessel, is included; as is a helicopter code number/ships' tail-letter code grid cross-reference.

Code changes, for example when aircraft move between units, and therefore the markings currently painted on a particular aircraft might not be those shown in this edition because of subsequent events. Aircraft currently under manufacture or not yet delivered to the Service, such as Eurofighter Typhoons, Hawk 128s and Airbus A400Ms are listed under their allocated serial number. Likewise there are a number of newly built aircraft for overseas air arms that carry British serials for their UK test and delivery flights. The airframes which will not appear in the next edition because of sale, accident, etc, have their fates, where known, given in italic type in the *locations* column.

The Irish Army Air Corps fleet is listed, together with the serials of other overseas air arms whose aircraft might be seen visiting the UK from time to time. The serial numbers are as usually presented on the individual machine or as they are normally identified. Where possible, the aircraft's base and operating unit have been shown.

USAF, US Army and US Navy aircraft based in the UK and in Western Europe, and types that regularly visit the UK from the USA, are each listed in separate sections by aircraft type. The serial number actually displayed on the aircraft is shown in full, with additional Fiscal Year (FY) or full serial information also provided. Where appropriate, details of the operating wing, squadron allocation and base are added. The USAF is, like the RAF, in a continuing period of change, resulting in the adoption of new unit titles, squadron and equipment changes and the closure of bases. Only details that concern changes effected by January 2005 are shown.

Veteran and vintage aircraft which carry overseas military markings but which are based in the UK or regularly visit from mainland Europe, have been separately listed showing their principal means of identification. The growing list of aircraft in government or military service, often under contract to private operating companies, that carry civil registrations has again been included at the end of the respective country.

With the use of the Internet now very well established as a rich source of information, the section listing a selection of military aviation 'world wide web' sites, has again been expanded and up-dated this year. Although only a few of these provide details of aircraft serials and markings, they do give interesting insights into air arms and their operating units, aircraft, museums and a broad range of associated topics.

Information shown is believed to be correct at 31 January 2005, and significant changes can be monitored through the monthly 'Military Markings' and 'Vintage Serials' columns in *Aircraft Illustrated* and for Internet up-dates see the 'A Guide' column.

Acknowledgements

The compilers wish to thank the many people who have taken trouble to send comments, additions, deletions and other useful information since the publication of the previous edition of *abc Military Aircraft Markings*. In particular the following individuals: Dave Albrecht, Alan Allen, Bob Archer, Alan Barley, Lee Barton, Derek Bower, Nigel Burch, Richard Cawsey, Dale Clarke, Barry Clay, Glyn Coney, Dougie Couch, Paul Davies, Jean-Luc Debroux, Andy Donovan, Dale Donovan, Ben Dunnell, John Dyer, Dylan Eklund, Keith Ella, Ray Fitton, Wal Gandy, Peter Gerhardt, Kevin Hart, Howard Heeley, Nigel Hitchman, Bill Hodges, Geoff Hooper, Lee Howard, Paul van den Hurk, Wilgert Ijlst, Paul Jackson, Tommy Johansson, Phil Jones, Tim Jones, Ian Joslin, Martin Keen, Nigel Lees, Paul van der Linden, Daniel March, Andy Marden, Bram Marijnissen, Tom McGhee, Gavin McLean, Julian Moody, Lars Olausson, Martin Pole, Doug Pritchard, Colin Rossiter, Stuart Richardson, Brian Rogers, Kev Storer, David Stretton, David Thompson and Bob Turner.

This compilation has also relied heavily on the publications/editors, aviation groups and societies as follows: Aerodata Quantum+, Pacific Aviation Database, Air-Britain Information Exchange, 'Air-Britain News', Airfields e-mail group, BAEG e-mail group, Graham Gaff/East London Aviation Society, Brian Pickering/'Military Aviation Review', Military Spotter's Forum, NAMAR e-mail group, P-3 Orion Research Group, Andrew & Mervyn Thomas/St Athan Aviation Group, SAAB Viggen E-mail group, Mark Walton/'Scottish Air News', 'Scramble', Spotter's Nest web site, Keith Preen/Wales Aviation Research Centre, Geoff Goodall/Warbirds Directory 4 and Mick Boulanger/Wolverhampton Aviation Group.

PRM & HJC **January 2005**

Abbreviations

AAC Army Air Corps
AACS Airborne Air Control Squadron
AACTS Airborne Air Control Training Squadron
ACC Air Combat Command
ACCGS Air Cadets Central Gliding School
ACW Airborne Control Wing
AD&StA Aberdeen, Dundee & St Andrews
AEF Air Experience Flight
AESS Air Engineering & Survival School
AEW Airborne Early Warning
AF Arméflyget (Army Air Battalion)
AFB Air Force Base
AFD Air Fleet Department
AFRC Air Force Reserve Command
AFSC Air Force Systems Command
AFSK Armeflygskolan (Army Flying School)
AFWF Advanced Fixed Wing Flight
AG Airlift Group
AGA Academia General del Aire (General Air Academy)
AkG Aufklärungsgeschwader (Reconnaissance Wing)
AMC Air Mobility Command
AMD-BA Avions Marcel Dassault-Breguet Aviation
AMF Aircraft Maintenance Flight
AMG Aircraft Maintenance Group
AMIF Aircraft Maintenance Instruction Flight
AMS Air Movements School
AMW Air Mobility Wing
ANG Air National Guard
APS Aircraft Preservation Society
ARS Air Refuelling Squadron
ARW Air Refuelling Wing
ARWS Advanced Rotary Wing Squadron
AS Airlift Squadron/Air Squadron
ASF Aircraft Servicing Flight
AS&RU Aircraft Salvage and Repair Unit
ATC Air Training Corps
ATCC Air Traffic Control Centre
AVDEF Aviation Defence Service
Avn Aviation
Avn Co Aviation Company
AW Airlift Wing/Armstrong Whitworth Aircraft
AWC Air Warfare Centre
BAC British Aircraft Corporation
BAe British Aerospace PLC
BAPC British Aviation Preservation Council
BATSUB British Army Training Support Unit Belize
BATUS British Army Training Unit Suffield
BBMF Battle of Britain Memorial Flight
BDRF Battle Damage Repair Flight
BDRT Battle Damage Repair Training
Be Beech
Bf Bayerische Flugzeugwerke
BFWF Basic Fixed Wing Flight
BG Bomber Group
BGA British Gliding & Soaring Association
bk black (squadron colours and markings)
bl blue (squadron colours and markings)
BNFL British Nuclear Fuels Ltd
BnHATk Helicopter Attack Battalion
BnHLn Liaison Battalion
BP Boulton & Paul
br brown (squadron colours and markings)
BS Bomber Squadron
B-V Boeing-Vertol
BW Bomber Wing
CAARP Co-operative des Ateliers Air de la Région Parisienne
CAC Commonwealth Aircraft Corporation
CARG Cotswold Aircraft Restoration Group
CASA Construcciones Aeronautics SA
Cav Cavalry
CC County Council
CCF Combined Cadet Force/Canadian Car & Foundry Company
CDE Chemical Defence Establishment
CEAM Centre d'Expérimentation Aériennes Militaires (Military Air Experimental Centre)
CEPA Centre d'Expérimentation Pratique de l'Aéronautique Navale
CEV Centre d'Essais en Vol (Flight Test Centre)
CFS Central Flying School
CGMF Central Glider Maintenance Flight
CIFAS Centre d'Instruction des Forces Aériennes Stratégiques (Air Strategic Training Centre)
CinC Commander in Chief
CinCLANT Commander in Chief Atlantic
CITac Centre d'Instruction Tactique (Tactical Training Centre)
Co Company
Comp Composite with
CT College of Technology
CTE Central Training Establishment
CV Chance-Vought
D-BA Daimler-Benz Aerospace
D-BD Dassault-Breguet Dornier
D&G Dumfries and Galloway
DARA Defence Aviation Repair Agency
DEFTS Defence Elementary Flying Training School
DEODS Defence Explosives Ordnance Disposal School
Det Detachment
DH de Havilland
DHC de Havilland Canada
DHFS Defence Helicopter Flying School
DLMW Dywizjon Lotniczy Marynarki Wojennej
DLO Defence Logistics Organisation
DPA Defence Procurement Agency
DS&DC Defence Storage & Disposition Centre
DS&TL Defence Science & Technology Laboratory
DTI Department of Trade and Industry
EA Escadron Aérien (Air Squadron)
EAAT Escadrille Avions de l'Armée de Terre
EAC Ecole de l'Aviation de Chasse (Fighter Aviation School)
EAP European Aircraft Project
EAT Ecole de l'Aviation de Transport (Transport Aviation School)
EC Escadre de Chasse (Fighter Wing)
ECM Electronic Counter Measures
ECS Electronic Countermeasures Squadron
EDA Escadre de Detection Aéroportée (Air Detection Wing)
EdC Escadron de Convoyage
EDCA Escadron de Détection et de Control Aéroportée (Airborne Detection & Control Sqn)
EE English Electric/Escadrille Electronique
EET Escadron Electronique Tactique (Tactical Electronics Flight)
EFTS Elementary Flying Training School
EH Escadron d'Helicoptères (Helicopter Flight)
EHI European Helicopter Industries
EKW Eidgenössiches Konstruktionswerkstätte
EL Escadre de Liaison (Liaison Wing)
ELT Eskadra Lotnictwa Taktycznego (Tactical Air Squadron)
ELTR Eskadra Lotnictwa Transportowego (Air Transport Squadron)
EMA East Midlands Airport
EMVO Elementaire Militaire Vlieg Opleiding (Elementary Flying Training)
ENOSA Ecole des Navigateurs Operationales Systemes d'Armees (Navigation School)
EoN Elliot's of Newbury
EPAA Ecole de Pilotage Elementaire de l'Armée de l'Air (Air Force Elementary Flying School)
EPE Ecole de Pilotage Elementaire (Elementary Flying School)

EPNER Ecole du Personnel Navigant d'Essais et de Reception
ER Escadre de Reconnaissance (Reconnaissance Wing)
ERS Escadron de Reconnaissance Stratégique (Strategic Reconnaissance Squadron)
ERV Escadre de Ravitaillement en Vol (Air Refuelling Wing)
ES Escadrille de Servitude
Esc Escuadron (Squadron)
Esk Eskadrille (Squadron)
Eslla Escuadrilla (Squadron)
Esq Esquadra (Squadron)
ET Escadre de Transport (Transport Squadron)
ETE Escadron de Transport et Entrainment (Transport Training Squadron)
ETEC Escadron de Transport d'Entrainement et de Calibration (Transport Training & Calibration Sqn)
ETL Escadron de Transport Légère (Light Transport Squadron)
ETO Escadron de Transition Operationnelle
ETOM Escadron de Transport Outre Mer (Overseas Transport Squadron)
ETPS Empire Test Pilots' School
ETS Engineering Training School
FAA Fleet Air Arm/Federal Aviation Administration
FBS Flugbereitschaftstaffel
FBW Fly by wire
FC Forskokcentralen (Flight Centre)
FE Further Education
FETC Fire and Emergency Training Centre
ff Front fuselage
FG Fighter Group
FH Fairchild-Hiller
FI Falkland Islands
FJWOEU Fast Jet & Guided Weapon Operational Evaluation Unit
FISt Flieger Staffel (Flight Squadron)
Flt Flight
FMA Fabrica Militar de Aviones
FMT Flotila Militara de Transport (Transport Regiment)
FMV Forsvarets Materielwerk
FONA Flag Officer Naval Aviation
FRADU Fleet Requirements and Air Direction Unit
FRA FR Aviation
FS Fighter Squadron
FSAIU Flight Safety & Accident Investigation Unit
FSCTE Fire Services Central Training Establishment
FTS Flying Training School
FTW Flying Training Wing
Fw Focke Wulf
FW Fighter Wing/Foster Wickner
FWTS Fixed Wing Test Squadron
FY Fiscal Year
F3 OCU Tornado F3 Operational Conversion Unit
GAF Government Aircraft Factory
GAL General Aircraft Ltd
GAM Groupe Aerien Mixte (Composite Air Group)
gd gold (squadron colours and markings)
GD General Dynamics
GHL Groupe d'Helicopteres Legeres (Light Helicopter Group)
GI Ground Instruction/Groupement d'Instruction (Instructional Group)
gn green (squadron colours and markings)
GRD Gruppe fur Rustunggdienste (Group for Service Preparation)
GT Grupo de Transporte (Transport Wing)
GTT Grupo de Transporte de Tropos (Troop Carrier Wing)
gy grey (squadron colours and markings)
H&W Hereford and Worcester
HAF Historic Aircraft Flight
HC Helicopter Combat Support Squadron
HCS Hunting Contract Services
HF Historic Flying Ltd
HFUS Heeresfliegerunterstützungsstaffel
HFVAS Heeresfliegerverbindungs/Aufklärungsstaffel
HFVS Heeresfliegerversuchstaffel
HFWS Heeresflieger Waffenschule (Army Air Weapons School)
Hkp.Bat Helikopter Bataljon (Helicopter Battalion)
HMA Helicopter Maritime Attack
HMF Harrier Maintenance Flight/Helicopter Maintenance Flight
HMS Her Majesty's Ship
HOCU Harrier OCU
HP Handley-Page
HQ Headquarters
HRO Harcàszati Repülö Ezred
HS Hawker Siddeley
IAF Israeli Air Force
IAP International Airport
INTA Instituto Nacional de Tecnica Aerospacial
IOW Isle Of Wight
IWM Imperial War Museum
JATE Joint Air Transport Establishment
JbG Jagdbombergeschwader (Fighter Bomber Wing)
JFACTSU Joint Forward Air Control Training & Standards Unit
JG Jagdgeschwader (Fighter Wing)
JHF Joint Helicopter Force
KHR Kampfhubschrauberregiment
Kridlo Wing
lbvr letka Bitevnich Vrtulníkù (Attack Helicopter Squadron)
Letka Squadron
LS Letistni Sprava
LTG Lufttransportgeschwader (Air Transport Wing)
LTV Ling-Temco-Vought
LVG Luftwaffen Versorgungs Geschwader (Air Force Maintenance Wing)/Luft Verkehrs Gesellschaft
LZO Letecky Zku ební Odbor (Aviation Test Department)
m multi-coloured (squadron colours and markings)
MAPK Mira Anachestisis Pantos Kerou (All Weather Interception Sqn)
MASD Marine Air Support Detachment
MASU Mobile Aircraft Support Unit
MBB Messerschmitt Bolkow-Blohm
MCAS Marine Corps Air Station
McD McDonnell Douglas
Med Medical
MFG Marine Flieger Geschwader (Naval Air Wing)
MH Max Holste
MIB Military Intelligence Battalion
MiG Mikoyan – Gurevich
Mod Modified
MR Maritime Reconnaissance
M&RU Marketing & Recruitment Unit
MS Morane-Saulnier
MTHR Mittlerer Transporthubschrauber Regiment (Medium Transport Helicopter Regiment)
MTM Mira Taktikis Metaforon (Tactical Transport Sqn)
MU Maintenance Unit
NA North American
NACDS Naval Air Command Driving School
NAEW&CF NATO Airborne Early Warning & Control Force
NAF Naval Air Facility
NAS Naval Air Station
NASU Naval Air Support Unit
NATO North Atlantic Treaty Organisation
NAWC Naval Air Warfare Center
NAWC-AD Naval Air Warfare Center Aircraft Division
NBC Nuclear, Biological and Chemical
NE North-East
NFATS Naval Force Aircraft Test Squadron
NI Northern Ireland
NMSU Nimrod Major Servicing Unit
NOCU Nimrod Operational Conversion Unit
NTOCU National Tornado Operational Conversion Unit
NWTSPM United States Navy Test Pilots School
NYARC North Yorks Aircraft Restoration Centre

OCU	Operational Conversion Unit
OEU	Operation Evaluation Unit
OFMC	Old Flying Machine Company
OGMA	Oficinas Gerais de Material Aeronautico
or	orange (squadron colours and markings)
OSAC	Operational Support Airlift Command
OVH Kmp	Observations-Helicopter Kompagni
PAT	Priority Air Transport Detachment
PBN	Pilatus Britten-Norman
PLM	Pulk Lotnictwa Mysliwskiego (Fighter Regiment)
pr	purple (squadron colours and markings)
PRU	Photographic Reconnaissance Unit
PVH Kmp	Panservaerns-Helicopter Kompagni
r	red (squadron colours and markings)
R	Replica
RAeS	Royal Aeronautical Society
RAF	Royal Aircraft Factory/Royal Air Force
RAFC	Royal Air Force College
RAFM	Royal Air Force Museum
RAFGSA	Royal Air Force Gliding and Soaring Association
RE	Royal Engineers
Regt	Regiment
REME	Royal Electrical & Mechanical Engineers
rf	Rear fuselage
RFA	Royal Fleet Auxiliary
RJAF	Royal Jordanian Air Force
RM	Royal Marines
RMB	Royal Marines Base
RMC of S	Royal Military College of Science
RN	Royal Navy
RNAS	Royal Naval Air Station
RNGSA	Royal Navy Gliding and Soaring Association
ROF	Royal Ordnance Factory
RQS	Rescue Squadron
R-R	Rolls-Royce
RS	Reid & Sigrist/Reconnaissance Squadron
RSV	Reparto Sperimentale Volo (Experimental Flight School)
RW	Reconnaissance Wing
SA	Scottish Aviation
SAAB	Svenska Aeroplan Aktieboleg
SAH	School of Air Handling
SAL	Scottish Aviation Limited
SAR	Search and Rescue
Saro	Saunders-Roe
SARTU	Search and Rescue Training Unit
SBoLK	Stíhacie Bombardovacie Letecké Kridlo (Fighter Bomber Air Wing)
SCW	Strategic Communications Wing
SEAE	School of Electrical & Aeronautical Engineering
SEPECAT	Société Européenne de Production de l'avion Ecole de Combat et d'Appui Tactique
SFDO	School of Flight Deck Operations
SHAPE	Supreme Headquarters Allied Forces Europe
SHOPS	Sea Harrier Operational Support Unit
si	silver (squadron colours and markings)
SIET	Section d'Instruction et d'Etude du Tir
SKTU	Sea King Training Unit
Skv	Skvadron (Squadron)
SLK	Stíhacie Letecké Kridlo (Fighter Air Wing)
slt	stíhací letka (Fighter Squadron)
SLV	School Licht Vliegwezen (Flying School)
Sm	Smaldeel (Squadron)
smdl	Smisena Dopravní Letka
SNCAN	Société Nationale de Constructions Aéronautiques du Nord
SOG	Special Operations Group
SOS	Special Operations Squadron
SoTT	School of Technical Training
SOW	Special Operations Wing
SPAD	Société Pour les Appareils Deperdussin
SPP	Strojirny Prvni Petilesky
Sqn	Squadron
SWWAPS	Second World War Aircraft Preservation Society
TA	Territorial Army
TAP	Transporten Avio Polk (Air Transport Regiment)
TFC	The Fighter Collection
TGp	Test Groep
TIARA	Tornado Integrated Avionics Research Aircraft
TL	Taktická Letka (Tactical Squadron)
tlt	taktická letka (Tactical Squadron)
TMF	Tornado Maintenance Flight
TMTS	Trade Management Training School
TOCU	Typhoon Operational Conversion Unit
tpzlt	taktická a prùzkumná letka (Tactical & Reconnaissance Squadron)
TS	Test Squadron
TsAGI	Tsentral'ny Aerogidrodinamicheski Instut (Central Aero & Hydrodynamics Institute)
TsLw	Technische Schule der Luftwaffe (Luftwaffe Technical School)
TW	Test Wing
UAS	University Air Squadron
UAV	Unmanned Air Vehicle
Uberwg	Uberwachunggeschwader (Surveillance Wing)
UK	United Kingdom
UKAEA	United Kingdom Atomic Energy Authority
UNFICYP	United Nations' Forces in Cyprus
US	United States
USAF	United States Air Force
USAFE	United States Air Forces in Europe
USAREUR	US Army Europe
USCGS	US Coast Guard Station
USEUCOM	United States European Command
USMC	United States Marine Corps
USN	United States Navy
VAAC	Vectored thrust Advanced Aircraft flight Control
VFW	Vereinigte Flugtechnische Werke
VGS	Volunteer Gliding School
VLA	Vojenska Letecka Akademia
vlt	vycviková letka (Training Squadron)
VMGR	Marine Aerial Refuelling/Transport Squadron
VMGRT	Marine Aerial Refuelling/Transport Training Squadron
VQ	Fleet Air Reconnaissance Squadron
VR	Fleet Logistic Support Squadron
VS	Vickers-Supermarine
VSD	Vegyes Szàllitorepülö Dandàr (Aircraft Transport Brigade)
w	white (squadron colours and markings)
Wg	Wing
WHL	Westland Helicopters Ltd
WLT	Weapons Loading Training
WRS	Weather Reconnaissance Squadron
WS	Westland
WSK	Wytwornia Sprzetu Kominikacyjnego
WTD	Wehrtechnische Dienstelle (Technical Support Unit)
WW2	World War II
y	yellow (squadron colours and markings)
zDL	základna Dopravního Letectva (Air Transport Base)
zL	základna Letectva
ZmDK	Zmie an˝ Dopravn˝ Kridlo (Mixed Transport Wing)
zSL	základna Speciálního Letectva (Training Air Base)
zTL	základna Taktického Letectva (Tactical Air Base)
zVrL	základna Vrtulníkového Letectva (Helicopter Air Base)

A Guide to the Location of Operational Military Bases in the UK

This section is to assist the reader to locate the places in the United Kingdom where operational military aircraft are based. The term *aircraft* also includes helicopters and gliders.

The alphabetical order listing gives each location in relation to its county and to its nearest classified road(s) (*by* means adjoining; *of* means proximate to), together with its approximate direction and mileage from the centre of a nearby major town or city. Some civil airports are included where active military units are also based, but **excluded** are MoD sites with non-operational aircraft (eg *gate guardians*), the bases of privately-owned civil aircraft that wear military markings and museums.

User	*Base name*	*County/Region*	*Location*	*Distance/direction from (town)*
QinetiQ	Aberporth	Dyfed	N of A487	6m ENE of Cardigan
Army	Abingdon	Oxfordshire	W by B4017, W of A34	5m SSW of Oxford
RAF	Aldergrove/Belfast Airport	Co Antrim	W by A26	13m W of Belfast
RM	Arbroath	Angus	E of A933	2m NW of Arbroath
RAF/HCS	Barkston Heath	Lincolnshire	W by B6404, S of A153	5m NNE of Grantham
RAF	Benson	Oxfordshire	E by A423	1m NE of Wallingford
QinetiQ/ RAF	Boscombe Down	Wiltshire	S by A303, W of A338	6m N of Salisbury
RAF	Boulmer	Northumberland	E of B1339	4m E of Alnwick
RAF	Brize Norton	Oxfordshire	W of A4095	5m SW of Witney
Marshall	Cambridge Airport/ Teversham	Cambridgeshire	S by A1303	2m E of Cambridge
RM/RAF	Chivenor	Devon	S of A361	4m WNW of Barnstaple
RAF	Church Fenton	Yorkshire North	S of B1223	7m WNW of Selby
RAF	Colerne	Wiltshire	S of A420, E of Fosse Way	5m NE of Bath
RAF	Coltishall	Norfolk	W of B1150	9m NNE of Norwich
RAF	Coningsby	Lincolnshire	S of A153, W by B1192	10m NW of Boston
RAF	Cosford	Shropshire	W of A41, N of A464	9m WNW of Wolverhampton
RAF	Cottesmore	Rutland	W of A1, N of B668	9m NW of Stamford
RAF	Cranwell	Lincolnshire	N by A17, S by B1429	5m WNW of Sleaford
RN	Culdrose	Cornwall	E by A3083	1m SE of Helston
Army	Dishforth	Yorkshire North	E by A1	4m E of Ripon
USAF	Fairford	Gloucestershire	S of A417	9m ESE of Cirencester
RN	Fleetlands	Hampshire	E by A32	2m SE of Fareham
RAF	Halton	Buckinghamshire	N of A4011, S of B4544	4m ESE of Aylesbury
RAF	Henlow	Bedfordshire	E of A600, W of A6001	1m SW of Henlow
RAF	Honington	Suffolk	E of A134, W of A1088	6m S of Thetford
Army	Hullavington	Wiltshire	W of A429	1m N of M4 jn 17
RAF	Kenley	Greater London	W of A22	1m W of Warlingham
RAF	Kinloss	Grampian	E of B9011, N of B9089	3m NE of Forres
RAF	Kirknewton	Lothian	E by B7031, N by A70	8m SW of Edinburgh
USAF	Lakenheath	Suffolk	W by A1065	8m W of Thetford
RAF	Leeming	Yorkshire North	E by A1	5m SW of Northallerton
RAF	Leuchars	Fife	E of A919	7m SE of Dundee
RAF	Linton-on-Ouse	Yorkshire North	E of B6265	10m NW of York
RAF	Lossiemouth	Grampian	W of B9135, S of B9040	4m N of Elgin
RAF	Lyneham	Wiltshire	W of A3102, S of A420	10m WSW of Swindon
RAF	Marham	Norfolk	N by A1122	6m W of Swaffham
Army	Middle Wallop	Hampshire	S by A343	6m SW of Andover
USAF	Mildenhall	Suffolk	S by A1101	9m NNE of Newmarket
RAF	Northolt	Greater London	N by A40	3m E of M40 jn 1
RAF	Odiham	Hampshire	E of A32	2m S of M3 jn 5
RN	Predannack	Cornwall	W by A3083	7m S of Helston
RAF	St Athan	South Glamorgan	N of B4265	13m WSW of Cardiff
RAF	St Mawgan/Newquay	Cornwall	N of A3059	4m ENE of Newquay
RAF	Scampton	Lincolnshire	W by A15	6m N of Lincoln
RAF	Sealand	Flint	W by A550	6m WNW of Chester
RAF	Shawbury	Shropshire	W of B5063	7m NNE of Shrewsbury
RAF	Syerston	Nottinghamshire	W by A46	5m SW of Newark
RAF	Ternhill	Shropshire	SW by A41	3m SW of Market Drayton

User	*Base name*	*County/Region*	*Location*	*Distance/direction from (town)*
RAF/ Army	Topcliffe	Yorkshire North	E of A167, W of A168	3m SW of Thirsk
RAF	Valley	Gwynedd	S of A5 on Anglesey	5m SE of Holyhead
RAF	Waddington	Lincolnshire	E by A607, W by A15	5m S of Lincoln
Army/ RAF	Wattisham	Suffolk	N of B1078	5m SSW of Stowmarket
RAF	Weston-on-the-Green	Oxfordshire	E by A43	9m N of Oxford
RAF	Wittering	Cambridgeshire	W by A1, N of A47	3m S of Stamford
RAF	Woodvale	Merseyside	W by A565	5m SSW of Southport
RAF	Wyton	Cambridgeshire	E of A141, N of B1090	3m NE of Huntingdon
RN	Yeovilton	Somerset	S by B3151, S of A303	5m N of Yeovil

This Royal Aircraft Factory SE 5A F904 is owned by the Shuttleworth Trust at Old Warden.

Hawker Hart J9941 features in the Milestones of Flight Exhibition at the RAF Museum.

British Military Aircraft Serials

The Committee of Imperial Defence through its Air Committee introduced a standardised system of numbering aircraft in November 1912. The Air Department of the Admiralty was allocated the first batch 1-200 and used these to cover aircraft already in use and those on order. The Army was issued with the next block from 201-800, which included the number 304 which was given to the Cody Biplane now preserved in the Science Museum. By the outbreak of World War 1 the Royal Navy was on its second batch of serials 801-1600 and this system continued with alternating allocations between the Army and Navy until 1916 when number 10000, a Royal Flying Corps BE2C, was reached.

It was decided not to continue with five digit numbers but instead to start again from 1, prefixing RFC aircraft with the letter A and RNAS aircraft with the prefix N. The RFC allocations commenced with A1 an FE2D and before the end of the year had reached A9999 an Armstrong Whitworth FK8. The next group commenced with B1 and continued in logical sequence through the C, D, E and F prefixes. G was used on a limited basis to identify captured German aircraft, while H was the last block of wartime-ordered aircraft. To avoid confusion I was not used, so the new postwar machines were allocated serials in the J range. A further minor change was made in the serial numbering system in August 1929 when it was decided to maintain four numerals after the prefix letter, thus omitting numbers 1 to 999. The new K series therefore commenced at K1000, which was allocated to an AW Atlas.

The Naval N prefix was not used in such a logical way. Blocks of numbers were allocated for specific types of aircraft such as seaplanes or flying-boats. By the late 1920s the sequence had largely been used up and a new series using the prefix S was commenced. In 1930 separate naval allocations were stopped and subsequent serials were issued in the 'military' range which had by this time reached the K series. A further change in the pattern of allocations came in the L range. Commencing with L7272 numbers were issued in blocks with smaller blocks of serials between not used. These were known as blackout blocks. As M had already been used as a suffix for Maintenance Command instructional airframes it was not used as a prefix. Although N had previously been used for naval aircraft it was used again for serials allocated from 1937.

With the build-up to World War 2 the rate of allocations quickly accelerated and the prefix R was being used when war was declared. The letters O and Q were not allotted, and nor was S which had been used up to S1865 for naval aircraft before integration into the RAF series. By 1940 the serial Z9999 had been reached, as part of a blackout block, with the letters U and Y not used to avoid confusion. The option to recommence serial allocation at A1000 was not taken up; instead it was decided to use an alphabetical two-letter prefix with three numerals running from 100 to 999. Thus AA100 was allocated to a Blenheim IV.

This two-letter, three-numeral serial system which started in 1940 continues today. The letters C, I, O, Q, U and Y were, with the exception of NC, not used. For various reasons the following letter combinations were not issued: DA, DB, DH, EA, GA to GZ, HA, HT, JE, JH, JJ, KR to KT, MR, NW, NZ, SA to SK, SV, TN, TR and VE. The first postwar serials issued were in the VP range while the end of the WZs had been reached by the Korean War. In January 1952 a civil servant at the then Air Ministry penned a memo to his superiors alerting them to the fact that a new military aircraft serial system would soon have to be devised. With allocations accelerating to accommodate a NATO response to the Korean War and a perceived Soviet threat building, he estimated that ZZ999 would quickly be reached. How wrong can you be. Over five decades later the allocations are only at the start of the ZKs and at the present rate are unlikely to reach the end of the ZZs until the end of this century!

Military aircraft serials are allocated by the Defence Procurement Agency, where the Military Aircraft Register is maintained. A change in policy in 2003 has resulted in the use of the first 99 digits in the ZK sequence (ZK001 to ZK099), following on from ZJ999. The latest allocation is ZK010 to ZK044, a block reserved for the BAE Systems Hawk 128s due for delivery to the RAF in a few years time. There is also a growing trend for 'out-of-sequence' serial numbers to be issued. At first this was to a manufacturer's prototype or development aircraft. However, following the Boeing C-17 Globemasters leased from Boeing (ZZ171-ZZ174), more allocations have been noted, including the reservation of ZM400 to ZM424 for the RAF's prospective Airbus A400Ms and ZK201 to ZK204 on a batch of Army UAVs.

Since 2002 there has also been a new official policy concerning the use of military serial numbers on some types of UAV. 'Where a UAV is of modular construction the nationality and registration mark shall be applied to the fuselage of the vehicle or on the assembly forming the main part of the fuselage. To prevent the high usage of numbers for target drones which are eventually destroyed, a single registration mark (prefix) should be issued relating to the UAV type. The agency or service operating the target drone will be responsible for the identification of each individual UAV covered by that registration mark by adding a suffix.' This has resulted in the use of the same serial on a number of UAVs with a letter following it. Hence the appearance of ZK201A, ZK201B, ZK201C et seq on Army Meggitt Banshee drones.

Note: The compilers will be pleased to receive comments, corrections and further information for inclusion in subsequent editions of *Military Aircraft Markings* and the monthly up-date of additions and amendments that is published in *Aircraft Illustrated*. Please send your information to Military Aircraft Markings, 25 Sabrina Way, Stoke Bishop, Bristol BS9 1ST; or fax to 0117 968 3928 or e-mail to HJCurtis@aol.com.

British Military Aircraft Markings

A serial in *italics* denotes that it is not the genuine marking for that airframe.

Serial	Type (other identity) [code]	Owner/operator, location or fate	Notes
168	Sopwith Tabloid Scout <R> (G-BFDE)	RAF Museum, Hendon	
304	Cody Biplane (BAPC 62)	Science Museum, South Kensington	
687	RAF BE2b <R> (BAPC 181)	RAF Museum, Hendon	
1701	RAF BE2c <R> (BAPC 117)	*Scrapped*	
2345	Vickers FB5 Gunbus <R> (G-ATVP)	RAF Museum, Hendon	
2699	RAF BE2c	Imperial War Museum, Lambeth	
3066	Caudron GIII (G-AETA/9203M)	RAF Museum, Hendon	
5964	DH2 <R> (BAPC 112)	Privately owned, Stretton on Dunsmore	
5964	DH2 <R> (G-BFVH)	Privately owned, Withybush	
6232	RAF BE2c <R> (BAPC 41)	Yorkshire Air Museum, stored Elvington	
8359	Short 184 <ff>	FAA Museum, RNAS Yeovilton	
A301	Morane BB (frame)	RAF Museum Reserve Collection, Stafford	
A1325	RAF BE2e (G-BVGR)	*Sold to New Zealand*	
A1742	Bristol Scout D <R> (BAPC 38)	Bristol Aero Collection, Kemble	
A7317	Sopwith Pup <R> (BAPC 179)	Midland Air Museum, Coventry	
A8226	Sopwith 1½ Strutter <R> (G-BIDW)	RAF Museum, Hendon	
B595	RAF SE5a <R> (G-BUOD) [W]	Privately owned, Kemble	
B1807	Sopwith Pup (G-EAVX) [A7]	*Broken up*	
B2458	Sopwith 1F.1 Camel <R> (G-BPOB/*F542*) [R]	Privately owned, Booker	
B3459	Nieuport Scout 17/23 <R> (G-BWMJ) [21]	Privately owned, Fairoaks	
B5539	Sopwith 1F.1 Camel <R>	Privately owned, Compton Abbas	
B5577	Sopwith 1F.1 Camel <R> (*D3419*/ BAPC 59) [W]	RAF Museum, Cosford	
B6401	Sopwith 1F.1 Camel <R> (G-AWYY/C1701)	FAA Museum, RNAS Yeovilton	
B7270	Sopwith 1F.1 Camel <R> (G-BFCZ)	Brooklands Museum, Weybridge	
C1904	RAF SE5a <R> (G-PFAP) [Z]	Privately owned, Castle Bytham, Leics	
C3011	Phoenix Currie Super Wot (G-SWOT) [S]	Privately owned, Sibson	
C4451	Avro 504J <R> (BAPC 210)	Solent Sky, Southampton	
C4918	Bristol M1C <R> (G-BWJM)	The Shuttleworth Collection, Old Warden	
C4994	Bristol M1C <R> (G-BLWM)	RAF Museum, Hendon	
C9533	RAF SE5a <R> (G-BUWE) [M]	Privately owned, Boscombe Down	
D276	RAF SE5a <R> (BAPC 208) [A]	Prince's Mead Shopping Centre, Farnborough	
D5329	Sopwith 5F.1 Dolphin	RAF Museum Restoration Centre, Cosford	
D5649	Airco DH9	Aero Vintage, St Leonards-on-Sea	
D7560	Avro 504K	Science Museum, South Kensington	
D7889	Bristol F2b Fighter (G-AANM/ BAPC 166)	Privately owned, Old Warden	
D8084	Bristol F2b Fighter (G-ACAA/ F4516) [S]	The Fighter Collection, Duxford	
D8096	Bristol F2b Fighter (G-AEPH) [D]	The Shuttleworth Collection, Old Warden	
E373	Avro 504K <R> (BAPC 178)	Privately owned	
E449	Avro 504K (G-EBJE/9205M)	RAF Museum, Hendon	
E2466	Bristol F2b Fighter (BAPC 165) [I]	RAF Museum, Hendon	
E2581	Bristol F2b Fighter [13]	Imperial War Museum, Duxford	
F141	RAF SE5a <R> (G-SEVA) [G]	Privately owned, Boscombe Down	
F235	RAF SE5a <R> (G-BMDB) [B]	Privately owned, Boscombe Down	
F904	RAF SE5a (G-EBIA)	The Shuttleworth Collection, Old Warden	
F938	RAF SE5a (G-EBIC/9208M)	RAF Museum, Hendon	
F943	RAF SE5a <R> (G-BIHF) [S]	Museum of Army Flying, Middle Wallop	
F943	RAF SE5a <R> (G-BKDT)	Yorkshire Air Museum, Elvington	
F1010	Airco DH9A [C]	RAF Museum, Hendon	

Notes	Serial	Type (other identity) [code]	Owner/operator, location or fate
	F3556	RAF RE8	Imperial War Museum, Duxford
	F5447	RAF SE5a <R> (G-BKER) [N]	Privately owned, Bridge of Weir
	F5459	RAF SE5a <R> (G-INNY) [Y]	Privately owned, Lee-on-Solent
	F5475	RAF SE5a <R> (BAPC 250)	Brooklands Museum, Weybridge
	F6314	Sopwith 1F.1 Camel (9206M) [B]	RAF Museum Restoration Centre, Cosford
	F8010	RAF SE5a <R> (G-BDWJ) [Z]	Privately owned, Langport, Somerset
	F8614	Vickers FB27A Vimy IV <R> (G-AWAU)	RAF Museum, Hendon
	H1968	Avro 504K <R> (BAPC 42)	Yorkshire Air Museum, stored Elvington
	H2311	Avro 504K (G-ABAA)	Gr Manchester Mus of Science & Industry
	H3426	Hawker Hurricane <R> (BAPC 68)	NW Aviation Heritage Group, Hooton Park
	H5199	Avro 504K (BK892/3118M/ G-ACNB/G-ADEV)	The Shuttleworth Collection, Old Warden
	J7326	DH53 Humming Bird (G-EBQP)	Mosquito Aircraft Museum, London Colney
	J8067	Westland Pterodactyl 1a	Science Museum, South Kensington
	J9941	Hawker Hart 2 (G-ABMR)	RAF Museum, Hendon
	K1786	Hawker Tomtit (G-AFTA)	The Shuttleworth Collection, Old Warden
	K1930	Hawker Fury <R> (G-BKBB/ OO-HFU)	Privately owned, Wevelgem, Belgium
	K2048	Isaacs Fury II (G-BZNW)	Privately owned, Fishburn
	K2050	Isaacs Fury II (G-ASCM)	Privately owned, Brize Norton
	K2059	Isaacs Fury II (G-PFAR)	Privately owned, Netherthorpe
	K2060	Isaacs Fury II (G-BKZM)	Privately owned, Haverfordwest
	K2075	Isaacs Fury II (G-BEER)	Privately owned, Shennington
	K2227	Bristol 105 Bulldog IIA (G-ABBB)	RAF Museum, Hendon
	K2567	DH82A Tiger Moth (DE306/ 7035M/G-MOTH)	Privately owned, Tadlow
	K2572	DH82A Tiger Moth (NM129/ G-AOZH)	Privately owned, Redhill
	K2572	DH82A Tiger Moth <R>	*Repainted as DE998*
	K2587	DH82A Tiger Moth <R> (G-BJAP)	Privately owned, Shobdon
	K3215	Avro 621 Tutor (G-AHSA)	*Repainted as K3241*
	K3241	Avro 621 Tutor (K3215/G-AHSA)	The Shuttleworth Collection, Old Warden
	K3661	Hawker Nimrod II (G-BURZ)	Aero Vintage, St Leonards-on-Sea
	K3731	Isaacs Fury <R> (G-RODI)	Privately owned, Hailsham
	K4232	Avro 671 Rota I (SE-AZB)	RAF Museum, Hendon
	K4259	DH82A Tiger Moth (G-ANMO) [71]	Privately owned, White Waltham
	K4672	Hawker Hind (BAPC 82)	RAF Museum, Cosford
	K4972	Hawker Hart Trainer IIA (1764M)	RAF Museum, Hendon
	K5054	Supermarine Spitfire <R> (BAPC 190/*EN398*)	Privately owned, Hawkinge
	K5054	Supermarine Spitfire <R> (BAPC 214)	Tangmere Military Aviation Museum
	K5054	Supermarine Spitfire <R> (G-BRDV)	Solent Sky, stored
	K5054	Supermarine Spitfire <R>	Kent Battle of Britain Museum, Hawkinge
	K5054	Supermarine Spitfire <R>	Southampton Airport, on display
	K5414	Hawker Hind (G-AENP/BAPC 78) [XV]	The Shuttleworth Collection, Old Warden
	K5600	Hawker Audax I (2015M/G-BVVI)	Aero Vintage, St Leonards-on-Sea
	K5673	Isaacs Fury II (G-BZAS)	Bournemouth Aviation Museum
	K5673	Hawker Fury I <R> (BAPC 249)	Brooklands Museum, Weybridge
	K5674	Hawker Fury I (G-CBZP)	Aero Vintage, St Leonards-on-Sea
	K6035	Westland Wallace II (2361M)	RAF Museum, Hendon
	K7271	Hawker Fury II <R> (BAPC 148)	Shropshire Wartime Aircraft Recovery Grp Mus, Sleap
	K8042	Gloster Gladiator II (8372M)	RAF Museum, Hendon
	K8203	Hawker Demon I (G-BTVE/2292M)	Demon Displays, Hatch
	K8303	Isaacs Fury II (G-BWWN) [D]	Privately owned, Wisbech St Mary
	K9926	VS300 Spitfire I <R> (BAPC 217) [JH-C]	RAF Bentley Priory, on display
	K9942	VS300 Spitfire I (8383M) [SD-D]	RAF Museum Restoration Centre, Cosford
	K9962	VS300 Spitfire I <R> [JH-C]	Privately owned
	L1070	VS300 Spitfire I <R> (BAPC 227) [XT-A]	Edinburgh airport, on display
	L1592	Hawker Hurricane I [KW-Z]	Science Museum, South Kensington
	L1639	Hawker Hurricane I	Cambridge Fighter & Bomber Society
	L1679	Hawker Hurricane I <R> (BAPC 241) [JX-G]	Tangmere Military Aviation Museum

Serial	Type (other identity) [code]	Owner/operator, location or fate	Notes
L1710	Hawker Hurricane I <R> (BAPC 219) [AL-D]	RAF Biggin Hill, on display	
L2301	VS Walrus I (G-AIZG)	FAA Museum, RNAS Yeovilton	
L2940	Blackburn Skua I	FAA Museum, RNAS Yeovilton	
L5343	Fairey Battle I [VO-S]	RAF Museum, Hendon	
L6906	Miles M14A Magister I (G-AKKY/ T9841/BAPC 44)	Museum of Berkshire Aviation, Woodley	
L7005	Boulton Paul P82 Defiant I <R> [PS-B]	Boulton Paul Association, Wolverhampton	
L7181	Hawker Hind (G-CBLK)	Aero Vintage, Duxford	
L8756	Bristol 149 Bolingbroke IVT (RCAF 10001) [XD-E]	RAF Museum, Hendon	
N248	Supermarine S6A (*S1596*)	Solent Sky, Southampton	
N500	Sopwith LC-1T Triplane <R> (G-PENY/G-BWRA)	Privately owned, Yarcombe/RNAS Yeovilton	
N546	Wright Quadruplane 1 <R> (BAPC 164)	Solent Sky, Southampton	
N1671	Boulton Paul P82 Defiant I (8370M) [EW-D]	RAF Museum, Hendon	
N1854	Fairey Fulmar II (G-AIBE)	FAA Museum, RNAS Yeovilton	
N2078	Sopwith Baby (8214/8215)	FAA Museum, RNAS Yeovilton	
N2532	Hawker Hurricane I <R> (BAPC 272) [GZ-H]	Kent Battle of Britain Museum, Hawkinge	
N2980	Vickers Wellington IA [R]	Brooklands Museum, Weybridge	
N3194	VS300 Spitfire I <R> (BAPC 220) [GR-Z]	RAF Biggin Hill, on display	
N3200	VS300 Spitfire IA (wreck)	Privately owned, Braintree	
N3289	VS300 Spitfire I <R> (BAPC 65) [DW-K]	Kent Battle of Britain Museum, Hawkinge	
N3313	VS300 Spitfire I <R> (*MH314*/ BAPC 69) [KL-B]	Kent Battle of Britain Museum, Hawkinge	
N3317	VS361 Spitfire IX <R> (BAPC 268)	Privately owned, St Mawgan	
N3320	VS361 Spitfire IX <R>	Privately owned, Wellesbourne Mountford	
N3378	Boulton Paul P82 Defiant I	Boulton Paul Association, Wolverhampton	
N4389	Fairey Albacore (N4172) [4M]	FAA Museum, RNAS Yeovilton	
N4877	Avro 652A Anson I (G-AMDA) [MK-V]	Imperial War Museum, Duxford	
N5177	RAF BE2e <R>	Privately owned, Wingates, Lancs	
N5182	Sopwith Pup <R> (G-APUP/9213M)	RAF Museum, Hendon	
N5195	Sopwith Pup (G-ABOX)	Museum of Army Flying, Middle Wallop	
N5492	Sopwith Triplane <R> (BAPC 111)	FAA Museum, RNAS Yeovilton	
N5579	Gloster Sea Gladiator	FAA Museum, RNAS Yeovilton	
N5628	Gloster Gladiator II	RAF Museum, Hendon	
N5719	Gloster Gladiator II (G-CBHO)	Privately owned, Dursley, Glos	
N5903	Gloster Gladiator II (*N2276*/ G-GLAD) [H]	The Fighter Collection, Duxford	
N5912	Sopwith Triplane (8385M)	RAF Museum, Hendon	
N6181	Sopwith Pup (G-EBKY/N5180)	The Shuttleworth Collection, Old Warden	
N6290	Sopwith Triplane <R> (G-BOCK)	The Shuttleworth Collection, Old Warden	
N6452	Sopwith Pup <R> (G-BIAU)	FAA Museum, RNAS Yeovilton	
N6466	DH82A Tiger Moth (G-ANKZ)	Privately owned, Winchester	
N6537	DH82A Tiger Moth (G-AOHY)	AAC Historic Aircraft Flt, Middle Wallop	
N6720	DH82A Tiger Moth (G-BYTN/ 7014M) [RUO-B]	Privately owned, Hatch	
N6797	DH82A Tiger Moth (G-ANEH)	Privately owned, Swyncombe	
N6812	Sopwith 2F.1 Camel	Imperial War Museum, Lambeth	
N6847	DH82A Tiger Moth (G-APAL)	Privately owned, Leicester	
N6965	DH82A Tiger Moth (G-AJTW) [FL-J] (wreck)	Privately owned, Tibenham	
N7033	Noorduyn AT-16 Harvard IIB (FX442)	Kent Battle of Britain Museum, Hawkinge	
N9191	DH82A Tiger Moth (G-ALND)	Privately owned, Pontypool	
N9192	DH82A Tiger Moth (G-DHZF) [RCO-N]	Privately owned, Sywell	
N9389	DH82A Tiger Moth (G-ANJA)	Privately owned, Seething	
N9899	Supermarine Southampton I (fuselage)	RAF Museum, Hendon	
P1344	HP52 Hampden I (9175M) [PL-K]	RAF Museum Restoration Centre, Cosford	
P1344	HP52 Hampden I <rf> (parts Hereford L6012)	RAF Museum, Hendon	
P2617	Hawker Hurricane I (8373M) [AF-A]	RAF Museum, Hendon	

Notes	*Serial*	*Type (other identity) [code]*	*Owner/operator, location or fate*
	P2725	Hawker Hurricane I (wreck)	Imperial War Museum, Lambeth
	P2793	Hawker Hurricane I <R> (BAPC 236) [SD-M]	Eden Camp Theme Park, Malton, North Yorkshire
	P2902	Hawker Hurricane I (G-ROBT)	Privately owned, Billingshurst
	P2921	Hawker Hurricane I <R> (BAPC 273) [GZ-L]	Kent Battle of Britain Museum, Hawkinge
	P2970	Hawker Hurricane I <R> [US-X]	Battle of Britain Memorial, Capel le Ferne, Kent
	P3059	Hawker Hurricane I <R> (BAPC 64) [SD-N]	Kent Battle of Britain Museum, Hawkinge
	P3175	Hawker Hurricane I (wreck)	RAF Museum, Hendon
	P3179	Hawker Hurricane I <ff>	Tangmere Military Aviation Museum
	P3208	Hawker Hurricane I <R> (BAPC 63/*L1592*) [SD-T]	Kent Battle of Britain Museum, Hawkinge
	P3386	Hawker Hurricane I <R> (BAPC 218) [FT-A]	RAF Bentley Priory, on display
	P3395	Hawker Hurricane IV (KX829) [JX-B]	Millennium Discovery Centre, Birmingham
	P3554	Hawker Hurricane I (composite)	The Air Defence Collection, Salisbury
	P3679	Hawker Hurricane I <R> (BAPC 278) [GZ-K]	Kent Battle of Britain Museum, Hawkinge
	P3717	Hawker Hurricane I (composite) (DR348)	Privately owned, Milden
	P3873	Hawker Hurricane I <R> (BAPC 265) [YO-H]	Yorkshire Air Museum, Elvington
	P4139	Fairey Swordfish II (HS618) [5H]	FAA Museum, RNAS Yeovilton
	P6382	Miles M14A Hawk Trainer 3 (G-AJRS) [C]	The Shuttleworth Collection, Old Warden
	P7350	VS329 Spitfire IIA (G-AWIJ) [XT-D]	RAF BBMF, Coningsby
	P7540	VS329 Spitfire IIA [DU-W]	Dumfries & Galloway Avn Mus, Dumfries
	P7966	VS329 Spitfire II <R> [D-B]	Manx Aviation & Military Museum, Ronaldsway
	P8140	VS329 Spitfire II <R> (*P9390*/ BAPC 71) [ZF-K]	Norfolk & Suffolk Avn Museum, Flixton
	P8448	VS329 Spitfire II <R> (BAPC 225) [UM-D]	RAF Cranwell, on display
	P9374	VS300 Spitfire IA (G-MKIA)	Privately owned, Braintree
	P9444	VS300 Spitfire IA [RN-D]	Science Museum, South Kensington
	R1914	Miles M14A Magister (G-AHUJ)	Privately owned, Strathallan
	R3821	Bristol 149 Bolingbroke IVT (G-BPIV/*Z5722*) [UX-N]	The Aircraft Restoration Company, Duxford (damaged)
	R4115	Hawker Hurricane I <R> (BAPC 267) [LE-X]	Imperial War Museum, Duxford
	R4118	Hawker Hurricane I (G-HUPW) [UP-W]	Privately owned, Cambridge
	R4922	DH82A Tiger Moth II (G-APAO)	Privately owned, Duxford
	R4959	DH82A Tiger Moth II (G-ARAZ) [59]	Privately owned, Temple Bruer
	R5136	DH82A Tiger Moth II (G-APAP)	Privately owned, Henlow
	R5172	DH82A Tiger Moth II (G-AOIS) [FIJ-E]	Privately owned, Sherburn-in-Elmet
	R5250	DH82A Tiger Moth II (G-AODT)	*Repainted as G-AODT*
	R5868	Avro 683 Lancaster I (7325M) [PO-S]	RAF Museum, Hendon
	R6690	VS300 Spitfire I <R> (BAPC 254) [PR-A]	Yorkshire Air Museum, Elvington
	R6915	VS300 Spitfire I	Imperial War Museum, Lambeth
	R9125	Westland Lysander III (8377M) [LX-L]	RAF Museum, Hendon
	R9371	HP59 Halifax II <ff>	Privately owned, Charlton Kings
	S1287	Fairey Flycatcher <R> (G-BEYB)	FAA Museum, RNAS Yeovilton
	S1579	Hawker Nimrod I <R> (G-BBVO) [571]	Privately owned, Wreningham
	S1581	Hawker Nimrod I (G-BWWK) [573]	The Fighter Collection, Duxford
	S1595	Supermarine S6B	Science Museum, South Kensington
	T5298	Bristol 156 Beaufighter I (4552M) <ff>	Midland Air Museum, Coventry
	T5424	DH82A Tiger Moth II (G-AJOA)	Privately owned, Swindon
	T5672	DH82A Tiger Moth II (G-ALRI)	Privately owned, Netheravon
	T5854	DH82A Tiger Moth II (G-ANKK)	Privately owned, Baxterley

Serial	*Type (other identity) [code]*	*Owner/operator, location or fate*	*Notes*
T5879	DH82A Tiger Moth II (G-AXBW) [RUC-W]	Privately owned, Frensham	
T6296	DH82A Tiger Moth II (8387M)	RAF Museum, Hendon	
T6313	DH82A Tiger Moth II (G-AHVU)	Privately owned, West Meon	
T6562	DH82A Tiger Moth II (G-ANTE)	Privately owned, Sywell	
T6818	DH82A Tiger Moth II (G-ANKT) [91]	The Shuttleworth Collection, Old Warden	
T6953	DH82A Tiger Moth II (G-ANNI)	Privately owned, Goodwood	
T6991	DH82A Tiger Moth II (HB-UPY/ DE694)	Privately owned, Switzerland	
T7230	DH82A Tiger Moth II (G-AFVE)	Privately owned, Booker	
T7281	DH82A Tiger Moth II (G-ARTL)	Privately owned, Egton, nr Whitby	
T7404	DH82A Tiger Moth II (G-ANMV) [04]	Privately owned, stored Booker	
T7793	DH82A Tiger Moth II (G-ANKV)	Privately owned, Croydon, on display	
T7842	DH82A Tiger Moth II (G-AMTF)	Privately owned, RAF Marham	
T7909	DH82A Tiger Moth II (G-ANON)	Privately owned, Sherburn-in-Elmet	
T7997	DH82A Tiger Moth II (NL750/ G-AHUF)	Privately owned, Edburton	
T8191	DH82A Tiger Moth II (G-BWMK)	Privately owned,	
T9707	Miles M14A Magister I (G-AKKR/ 8378M/T9708)	Museum of Army Flying, Middle Wallop	
T9738	Miles M14A Magister I (G-AKAT)	Privately owned, Breighton	
V1075	Miles M14A Magister I (G-AKPF)	Privately owned, Old Warden	
V3388	Airspeed AS10 Oxford I (G-AHTW)	Imperial War Museum, Duxford	
V6028	Bristol 149 Bolingbroke IVT (G-MKIV) [GB-D] <rf>	The Aircraft Restoration Co, stored Duxford	
V6799	Hawker Hurricane I <R> (BAPC 72/*V7767*) [SD-X]	Gloucestershire Avn Coll, stored Gloucester	
V7350	Hawker Hurricane I (fuselage)	Brenzett Aeronautical Museum	
V7467	Hawker Hurricane I <R> (BAPC 223) [LE-D]	RAF Coltishall, on display	
V7467	Hawker Hurricane I <R> [LE-D]	Wonderland Pleasure Park, Farnsfield, Notts	
V7497	Hawker Hurricane I (G-HRLI)	Hawker Restorations, Milden	
V9367	Westland Lysander IIIA (G-AZWT) [MA-B]	The Shuttleworth Collection, Old Warden	
V9673	Westland Lysander IIIA (V9300/ G-LIZY) [MA-J]	Imperial War Museum, Duxford	
V9723	Westland Lysander IIIA (2442/ OO-SOT) [MA-D]	SABENA Old Timers, Brussels, Belgium	
V9312	Westland Lysander IIIA (G-CCOM)	The Aircraft Restoration Co, Duxford	
W1048	HP59 Halifax II (8465M) [TL-S]	RAF Museum, Hendon	
W2068	Avro 652A Anson I (9261M/ VH-ASM) [68]	RAF Museum, Hendon	
W2718	VS Walrus I (G-RNLI)	Dick Melton Aviation, Great Yarmouth	
W4041	Gloster E28/39 [G]	Science Museum, South Kensington	
W4050	DH98 Mosquito	Mosquito Aircraft Museum, London Colney	
W5856	Fairey Swordfish II (G-BMGC) [A2A]	RN Historic Flight, Yeovilton	
W9385	DH87B Hornet Moth (G-ADND) [YG-L,3]	The Shuttleworth Collection, Old Warden	
X4590	VS300 Spitfire I (8384M) [PR-F]	RAF Museum, Hendon	
X7688	Bristol 156 Beaufighter I (3858M/ G-DINT)	Privately owned, Hatch	
Z1206	Vickers Wellington IV (fuselage)	Midland Warplane Museum, Baxterley	
Z2033	Fairey Firefly I (G-ASTL) [275]	FAA Museum, RNAS Yeovilton	
Z2186	Douglas Boston III	Privately owned, Hinckley, Leics	
Z2315	Hawker Hurricane IIA [JU-E]	Imperial War Museum, Duxford	
Z2389	Hawker Hurricane IIA	Brooklands Museum, Weybridge	
Z5140	Hawker Hurricane XIIA (*Z7381*/ G-HURI) [HA-C]	Historic Aircraft Collection, Duxford	
Z5207	Hawker Hurricane IIB (G-BYDL)	Privately owned, Dursley, Glos	
Z5252	Hawker Hurricane IIB (G-BWHA/ Z5053) [GO-B]	Privately owned, Milden	
Z7015	Hawker Sea Hurricane IB (G-BKTH) [7-L]	The Shuttleworth Collection, Old Warden	
Z7197	Percival P30 Proctor III (G-AKZN/ 8380M)	RAF Museum Reserve Collection, Stafford	
Z7258	DH89A Dragon Rapide (NR786/ G-AHGD)	Privately owned, Membury (wreck)	

Notes	*Serial*	*Type (other identity) [code]*	*Owner/operator, location or fate*
	Z7381	Hawker Hurricane XIIA (G-HURI) [XR-T]	*Repainted as Z5140*
	AA550	VS349 Spitfire VB <R> (BAPC 230/*AA908*) [GE-P]	Eden Camp Theme Park, Malton, North Yorkshire
	AB910	VS349 Spitfire VB (G-AISU) [IR-C]	RAF BBMF, Coningsby
	AD540	VS349 Spitfire VB (wreck)	Kennet Aviation, North Weald
	AE436	HP52 Hampden I [PL-J] (parts)	Lincolnshire Avn Heritage Centre, E Kirkby
	AL246	Grumman Martlet I	FAA Museum, RNAS Yeovilton
	AP506	Cierva C30A (G-ACWM)	The Helicopter Museum, Weston-super-Mare
	AP507	Cierva C30A (G-ACWP) [KX-P]	Science Museum, South Kensington
	AR213	VS300 Spitfire IA (*K9853*/G-AIST) [PR-D]	Privately owned, Booker
	AR501	VS349 Spitfire LF VC (G-AWII/ *AR4474*) [NN-A]	The Shuttleworth Collection, Old Warden
	BB807	DH82A Tiger Moth (G-ADWO)	Solent Sky, Southampton
	BE417	Hawker Hurricane XIIB (G-HURR) [LK-A]	The Real Aeroplane Company, Breighton
	BE421	Hawker Hurricane IIC <R> (BAPC 205) [XP-G]	RAF Museum, Hendon
	BL614	VS349 Spitfire VB (4354M) [ZD-F]	RAF Museum, Hendon
	BL655	VS349 Spitfire VB (wreck)	Lincolnshire Avn Heritage Centre, East Kirkby
	BL924	VS349 Spitfire VB <R> (BAPC 242) [AZ-G]	Tangmere Military Aviation Museum
	BM361	VS349 Spitfire VB <R> [XR-C]	RAF Lakenheath, on display
	BM593	VS349 Spitfire VB <R> [JH-O]	RAF Halton
	BM597	VS349 Spitfire LF VB (5718M/ G-MKVB) [JH-C]	Historic Aircraft Collection, Duxford
	BN230	Hawker Hurricane IIC (LF751/ 5466M) [FT-A]	RAF Manston, Memorial Pavilion
	BR600	VS361 Spitfire IX <R> (BAPC 222) [SH-V]	RAF Uxbridge, on display
	BR600	VS361 Spitfire IX <R> (fuselage)	Privately owned,
	BW881	Hawker Hurricane XIIA (G-KAMM)	Privately owned, Milden
	CB733	SA122 Bulldog (G-BCUV/G-112)	Privately owned, Old Sarum
	DD931	Bristol 152 Beaufort VIII (9131M) [L]	RAF Museum, Hendon
	DE208	DH82A Tiger Moth II (G-AGYU)	Privately owned, Ronaldsway
	DE470	DH82A Tiger Moth II (G-ANMY)	Privately owned, Swindon
	DE623	DH82A Tiger Moth II (G-ANFI)	Privately owned, Withybush
	DE673	DH82A Tiger Moth II (6948M/ G-ADNZ)	Privately owned, Old Buckenham
	DE992	DH82A Tiger Moth II (G-AXXV)	Privately owned, Upavon
	DE998	DH82A Tiger Moth (comp G-APAO & G-APAP) [RCU-T]	Imperial War Museum, Duxford
	DF112	DH82A Tiger Moth II (G-ANRM)	Privately owned, Clacton
	DF128	DH82A Tiger Moth II (G-AOJJ) [RCO-U]	Privately owned, White Waltham
	DF155	DH82A Tiger Moth II (G-ANFV)	Privately owned, Shempston Farm, Lossiemouth
	DF198	DH82A Tiger Moth II (G-BBRB)	Privately owned, Biggin Hill
	DG202	Gloster F9/40 (5758M) [G]	RAF Museum, Cosford
	DG590	Miles M2H Hawk Major (8379M/ G-ADMW)	RAF Museum Reserve Collection, Stafford
	DP872	Fairey Barracuda II (fuselage)	FAA Museum, RNAS Yeovilton
	DR613	Foster-Wikner GM1 Wicko (G-AFJB)	*Repainted as G-AFJB*
	DV372	Avro 683 Lancaster I <ff>	Imperial War Museum, Lambeth
	EE416	Gloster Meteor F3 <ff>	Martin Baker Aircraft, Chalgrove, fire section
	EE425	Gloster Meteor F3 <ff>	Gloucestershire Avn Coll, stored Gloucester
	EE531	Gloster Meteor F4 (7090M)	Midland Air Museum, Coventry
	EE549	Gloster Meteor F4 (7008M) [A]	Tangmere Military Aviation Museum
	EJ693	Hawker Tempest V (N7027E) [SA-J]	Privately owned, Booker
	EJ922	Hawker Typhoon IB <ff>	Privately owned, Hawkinge
	EM720	DH82A Tiger Moth II (G-AXAN)	Privately owned, Little Gransden

Serial	Type (other identity) [code]	Owner/operator, location or fate	Notes
EM727	DH82A Tiger Moth II (G-AOXN)	*Repainted as G-AOXN*	
EN224	VS366 Spitfire F XII (G-FXII)	Privately owned, Newport Pagnell	
EN343	VS365 Spitfire PR XI <R> (BAPC 226)	RAF Benson, on display	
EN398	VS361 Spitfire F IX <R> [JE-J]	Shropshire Wartime Aircraft Recovery Grp Mus, Sleap	
EN398	VS361 Spitfire F IX <R> (BAPC 184)	Privately owned, North Weald	
EP120	VS349 Spitfire LF VB (5377M/ 8070M/G-LFVB) [AE-A]	The Fighter Collection, Duxford	
EX976	NA AT-6D Harvard III (FAP.1657)	FAA Museum, RNAS Yeovilton	
EZ259	NA AT-6D Harvard III (G-BMJW) <ff>	*Sold to The Netherlands, 2003*	
FB226	Bonsall Mustang <R> (G-BDWM) [MT-A]	Privately owned, Gamston	
FE695	Noorduyn AT-16 Harvard IIB (G-BTXI) [94]	The Fighter Collection, Duxford	
FE788	CCF Harvard IV (MM54137/ G-CTKL)	Privately owned, Rochester	
FE905	Noorduyn AT-16 Harvard IIB (LN-BNM)	RAF Museum, Hendon	
FE992	Noorduyn AT-16 Harvard IIB (G-BDAM) [K-T]	*Sold as C-GFLR, 2003*	
FJ992	Boeing-Stearman PT-17 Kaydet (OO-JEH) [44]	Privately owned, Wevelgem, Belgium	
FL586	Douglas C-47B Dakota (OO-SMA) [AI-N] (fuselage)	Privately owned, North Weald	
FR886	Piper L-4J Cub (G-BDMS)	Privately owned, Old Sarum	
FR887	Piper J-3C Cub 85 (G-BWEZ)	Privately owned, Cumbernauld	
FS628	Fairchild Argus 2 (43-14601/ G-AIZE)	RAF Museum, Cosford	
FS668	Noorduyn AT-16 Harvard IIB (PH-TBR)	Privately owned, Gilze-Rijen, The Netherlands	
FS728	Noorduyn AT-16 Harvard IIB (HB-RCP)	Privately owned, Gelnhausen, Germany	
FT118	Noorduyn AT-16 Harvard IIB (G-BZHL)	Privately owned, Hemswell	
FT323	NA AT-6D Harvard III (FAP 1513)	Air Engineering Services, Swansea	
FT391	Noorduyn AT-16 Harvard IIB (G-AZBN)	Privately owned, Goodwood	
FX301	NA AT-6D Harvard III (EX915/ G-JUDI) [FD-NQ]	Privately owned, Bryngwyn Bach, Clwyd	
FX322	Noorduyn AT-16 Harvard IIB <ff>	Privately owned, Doncaster	
FX760	Curtiss P-40N Kittyhawk IV (9150M) [GA-?]	RAF Museum, Hendon	
FZ626	Douglas Dakota III (KN566/ G-AMPO) [YS-DH]	RAF Lyneham, on display	
HB275	Beech C-45 Expeditor II (G-BKGM)	Privately owned, Exeter	
HB751	Fairchild Argus III (G-BCBL)	Privately owned, Woolsery, Devon	
HG691	DH89A Dragon Rapide (G-AIYR)	Privately owned, Duxford	
HH268	GAL48 Hotspur II (HH379/ BAPC 261) [H]	Museum of Army Flying, AAC Middle Wallop	
HJ711	DH98 Mosquito NF II [VI-C]	Night-Fighter Preservation Tm, Elvington	
HM354	Percival P34 Proctor III (G-ANPP)	*Broken up*	
HM503	Miles M12 Mohawk (G-AEKW)	RAF Museum Restoration Centre, Cosford	
HM580	Cierva C-30A (G-ACUU) [KX-K]	Imperial War Museum, Duxford	
HS503	Fairey Swordfish IV (BAPC 108)	RAF Museum Reserve Collection, Stafford	
JF343	Pearson Spitfire 26 (G-CCZP) [WP-J]	Privately owned, Elstree	
JG891	VS349 Spitfire LF VC (A58-178/ G-LFVC)	Historic Flying Ltd, Duxford	
JP843	Hawker Typhoon IB [Y]	Privately owned, Shrewsbury	
JR505	Hawker Typhoon IB <ff>	Midland Air Museum, Coventry	
JV482	Grumman Wildcat V	Ulster Aviation Society, Langford Lodge	
JV579	Grumman FM-2 Wildcat (N4845V/ G-RUMW) [F]	The Fighter Collection, Duxford	
JV928	Consolidated PBY-5A Catalina (N423RS) [Y]	Super Catalina Restoration, Lee-on-Solent	

Notes	Serial	Type (other identity) [code]	Owner/operator, location or fate
	KB889	Avro 683 Lancaster B X (G-LANC) [NA-I]	Imperial War Museum, Duxford
	KB976	Avro 683 Lancaster B X <ff>	Privately owned, Lee-on-Solent, Hants
	KB976	Avro 683 Lancaster B X (G-BCOH) <rf>	Aeroventure, Doncaster
	KB994	Avro 683 Lancaster B X (G-BVBP) <ff>	Privately owned, Greenham Common
	KD345	Goodyear FG-1D Corsair (88297/ G-FGID) [130-A]	The Fighter Collection, Duxford
	KD431	CV Corsair IV [E2-M]	FAA Museum, RNAS Yeovilton
	KE209	Grumman Hellcat II	FAA Museum, RNAS Yeovilton
	KE418	Hawker Tempest <rf>	RAF Museum Restoration Centre, Cosford
	KF183	Noorduyn AT-16 Harvard IIB [3]	DPA/AFD/QinetiQ, Boscombe Down
	KF435	Noorduyn AT-16 Harvard IIB <ff>	Privately owned, Swindon
	KF488	Noorduyn AT-16 Harvard IIB <ff>	Bournemouth Aviation Museum
	KF532	Noorduyn AT-16 Harvard IIB <ff>	Newark Air Museum, Winthorpe
	KF584	CCF T-6J Texan (*FT239*/G-BIWX/ G-RAIX) [RAI-X]	Privately owned, Lee-on-Solent
	KF729	CCF T-6J Texan (G-BJST)	Privately owned, Thruxton
	KG374	Douglas Dakota IV (KN645/ 8355M) [YS]	RAF Museum, Cosford
	KG651	Douglas Dakota III (G-AMHJ)	Assault Glider Trust, Shawbury
	KJ351	Airspeed AS58 Horsa II (TL659/ BAPC 80) [23]	Museum of Army Flying, Middle Wallop
	KK995	Sikorsky Hoverfly I [E]	RAF Museum, Hendon
	KL216	Republic P-47D Thunderbolt (45-49295/9212M) [RS-L]	RAF Museum, Hendon
	KN353	Douglas Dakota IV (G-AMYJ)	Yorkshire Air Museum, Elvington
	KN448	Douglas Dakota IV <ff>	Science Museum, South Kensington
	KN751	Consolidated Liberator C VI (IAF HE807) [F]	RAF Museum, Cosford
	KP208	Douglas Dakota IV [YS]	Airborne Forces Museum, Aldershot
	KZ191	Hawker Hurricane IV (frame only)	Privately owned, East Garston, Bucks
	KZ321	Hawker Hurricane IV (G-HURY) [JV-N]	The Fighter Collection, Duxford
	LA198	VS356 Spitfire F21 (7118M) [RAI-G]	Glasgow Museum of Transport
	LA226	VS356 Spitfire F21 (7119M)	RAF Museum Reserve Collection, Stafford
	LA255	VS356 Spitfire F21 (6490M) [JX-U]	RAF No 1 Sqn, Cottesmore (preserved)
	LB264	Taylorcraft Plus D (G-AIXA)	RAF Museum, Hendon
	LB294	Taylorcraft Plus D (G-AHWJ)	Museum of Army Flying, Whitchurch, Hants
	LB312	Taylorcraft Plus D (*HH982*/ G-AHXE)	Privately owned, Netheravon
	LB367	Taylorcraft Plus D (G-AHGZ)	Privately owned, Henstridge
	LB375	Taylorcraft Plus D (G-AHGW)	Privately owned, Coventry
	LF363	Hawker Hurricane IIC [US-C]	RAF BBMF, Coningsby
	LF738	Hawker Hurricane IIC (5405M) [UH-A]	RAF Museum, Cosford
	LF789	DH82 Queen Bee (K3584/ BAPC 186) [R2-K]	Mosquito Aircraft Museum, London Colney
	LF858	DH82 Queen Bee (G-BLUZ)	Privately owned, Henlow
	LS326	Fairey Swordfish II (G-AJVH) [L2]	RN Historic Flight, Yeovilton
	LV907	HP59 Halifax III (HR792) [NP-F]	Yorkshire Air Museum, Elvington
	LZ551	DH100 Vampire	FAA Museum, RNAS Yeovilton
	LZ766	Percival P34 Proctor III (G-ALCK)	Imperial War Museum, Duxford
	MB293	VS357 Seafire IIC (wreck)	Privately owned, Braintree
	MD338	VS359 Spitfire LF VIII	Privately owned, Sandown
	MF628	Vickers Wellington T10 (9210M)	RAF Museum, Hendon
	MH434	VS361 Spitfire LF IXB (G-ASJV) [SZ-G]	The Old Flying Machine Company, Duxford
	MH486	VS361 Spitfire LF IX <R> (BAPC 206) [FF-A]	RAF Museum, Hendon
	MH415	VS361 Spitfire IX <R> (*MJ751*/ BAPC 209) [DU-V]	The Aircraft Restoration Co, Duxford
	MH777	VS361 Spitfire IX <R> (BAPC 221) [RF-N]	RAF Northolt, on display
	MJ147	VS361 Spitfire LF IX	Privately owned, Kent
	MJ627	VS509 Spitfire T9 (G-BMSB) [9G-P]	Privately owned, East Kirkby

Serial	*Type (other identity) [code]*	*Owner/operator, location or fate*	*Notes*
MJ832	VS361 Spitfire IX <R> (*L1096*/ BAPC 229) [DN-Y]	RAF Digby, on display	
MK356	VS361 Spitfire LF IXC (5690M) [2I-V]	RAF BBMF, Coningsby	
MK356	VS361 Spitfire LF IXC <R> [2I-V]	Kent Battle of Britain Museum, Hawkinge	
MK356	VS361 Spitfire LF IXC <R>	RAF Cosford, on display	
ML407	VS509 Spitfire T9 (G-LFIX) [OU-V]	Privately owned, Duxford	
ML411	VS361 Spitfire LF IXE (G-CBNU)	Privately owned, Ashford, Kent	
ML427	VS361 Spitfire IX (6457M) [HK-A]	Millennium Discovery Centre, Birmingham	
ML796	Short S25 Sunderland V	Imperial War Museum, Duxford	
ML824	Short S25 Sunderland V [NS-Z]	RAF Museum, Hendon	
MN235	Hawker Typhoon IB	RAF Museum, Hendon	
MP425	Airspeed AS10 Oxford I (G-AITB) [G]	RAF Museum, Hendon	
MS902	Miles M25 Martinet TT1 (TF-SHC)	Museum of Berkshire Aviation, Woodley	
MT197	Auster IV (G-ANHS)	Privately owned, Spanhoe	
MT438	Auster III (G-AREI)	Privately owned, Eggesford	
MT847	VS379 Spitfire FR XIVE (6960M) [AX-H]	Gr Manchester Mus of Science & Industry	
MT928	VS359 Spitfire HF VIIIC (G-BKMI/ MV154/*AR654*)[ZX-M]	Privately owned, East Garston, Berks	
MV262	VS379 Spitfire FR XIV (G-CCVV)	Privately owned, Booker	
MV268	VS379 Spitfire FR XIVE (MV293/ G-SPIT) [JE-J]	The Fighter Collection, Duxford	
MW401	Hawker Tempest II (IAF HA604/ G-PEST)	Privately owned, Hemswell, Lincs	
MW763	Hawker Tempest II (IAF HA586/ G-TEMT) [HF-A]	Privately owned, Gamston	
NF370	Fairey Swordfish III	Imperial War Museum, Duxford	
NF389	Fairey Swordfish III [D]	RN Historic Flight, Yeovilton	
NJ633	Auster 5D (G-AKXP)	Privately owned, Keevil	
NJ673	Auster 5D (G-AOCR)	Privately owned, Bagby	
NJ695	Auster 4 (G-AJXV)	Privately owned, Newark	
NJ703	Auster 5 (G-AKPI)	Privately owned, Croft, Lincs	
NJ719	Auster 5 (TW385/G-ANFU)	Newcastle Motor Museum	
NL750	DH82A Tiger Moth II (T7997/ G-AOBH)	Privately owned, Thruxton	
NL985	DH82A Tiger Moth I (7015M/ G-BWIK)	Privately owned, Sywell	
NM181	DH82A Tiger Moth I (G-AZGZ)	Privately owned, Dunkeswell	
NP294	Percival P31 Proctor IV [TB-M]	Lincolnshire Avn Heritage Centre, E Kirkby	
NP303	Percival P31 Proctor IV (G-ANZJ)	*Scrapped*	
NV778	Hawker Tempest TT5 (8386M)	RAF Museum, Hendon	
NX534	Auster III (G-BUDL)	Privately owned, Netheravon	
NX611	Avro 683 Lancaster B VII (8375M/ G-ASXX) [DE-C,LE-C]	Lincolnshire Avn Heritage Centre, E Kirkby	
PA474	Avro 683 Lancaster B I [QR-M]	RAF BBMF, Coningsby	
PD685	Slingsby T7 Cadet TX1	Boulton Paul Association, Wolverhampton	
PF179	HS Gnat T1 (XR541/8602M)	*Currently not known*	
PK624	VS356 Spitfire F22 (8072M) [RAU-T]	The Fighter Collection, Duxford	
PK664	VS356 Spitfire F22 (7759M) [V6-B]	RAF Museum Reserve Collection, Stafford	
PK683	VS356 Spitfire F24 (7150M)	Solent Sky, Southampton	
PK724	VS356 Spitfire F24 (7288M)	RAF Museum, Hendon	
PL965	VS365 Spitfire PR XI (N965RF/ G-MKXI) [R]	Privately owned, North Weald	
PM631	VS390 Spitfire PR XIX	RAF BBMF, Coningsby	
PM651	VS390 Spitfire PR XIX (7758M) [X]	RAF Museum Reserve Collection, Stafford	
PN323	HP Halifax VII <ff>	Imperial War Museum, Lambeth	
PP972	VS358 Seafire LF IIIC (G-BUAR)	Privately owned, stored Greenham Common	
PR536	Hawker Tempest II (IAF HA457) [OQ-H]	RAF Museum, Hendon	
PS853	VS390 Spitfire PR XIX (G-MXIX/ G-RRGN) [C]	Rolls-Royce, Filton	
PS915	VS390 Spitfire PR XIX (7548M/ 7711M)	RAF BBMF, Coningsby	
PT462	VS509 Spitfire T9 (G-CTIX/ N462JC) [SW-A]	Privately owned, Caernarfon/Duxford	
PZ865	Hawker Hurricane IIC (G-AMAU) [Q]	RAF BBMF, Coningsby	

Notes	Serial	Type (other identity) [code]	Owner/operator, location or fate
	RA848	Slingsby T7 Cadet TX1	The Aeroplane Collection, stored Wigan
	RA854	Slingsby T7 Cadet TX1	Yorkshire Air Museum, Elvington
	RA897	Slingsby T7 Cadet TX1	Newark Air Museum, Winthorpe
	RA905	Slingsby T7 Cadet TX1 (BGA1143)	Trenchard Museum, RAF Halton
	RD220	Bristol 156 Beaufighter TF X	Royal Scottish Mus'm of Flight, E Fortune
	RD253	Bristol 156 Beaufighter TF X (7931M)	RAF Museum, Hendon
	RF342	Avro 694 Lincoln B II (G-29-1/ G-APRJ)	Privately owned, stored Sandtoft
	RF398	Avro 694 Lincoln B II (8376M)	RAF Museum, Cosford
	RG333	Miles M38 Messenger IIA (G-AIEK)	Privately owned, Felton, Bristol
	RH377	Miles M38 Messenger 4A (G-ALAH)	*Sold to Spain*
	RH746	Bristol 164 Brigand TF1 (fuselage)	Bristol Aero Collection, Kemble
	RL962	DH89A Dominie II (G-AHED)	RAF Museum Reserve Collection, Stafford
	RM221	Percival P31 Proctor IV (G-ANXR)	Privately owned, Biggin Hill
	RM689	VS379 Spitfire F XIV (G-ALGT)	Rolls-Royce, Filton (rebuild)
	RM694	VS379 Spitfire F XIV (6640M)	Privately owned, High Wycombe
	RM927	VS379 Spitfire F XIV	Privately owned, High Wycombe
	RN201	VS379 Spitfire FR XIV (SG-31/ *SG-3*/G-BSKP)	Historic Flying Ltd, Duxford
	RN218	Isaacs Spitfire <R> (G-BBJI) [N]	Privately owned, Builth Wells
	RR232	VS361 Spitfire HF IXC (G-BRSF)	Privately owned, Sandown
	RT486	Auster 5 (G-AJGJ) [PF-A]	Privately owned, Lee-on-Solent
	RT520	Auster 5 (G-ALYB)	Aeroventure, Doncaster
	RT610	Auster 5A-160 (G-AKWS)	Privately owned, Crowfield
	RW382	VS361 Spitfire LF XVIE (7245M/ 8075M/N382RW) (wreck)	Privately owned, Sandown
	RW386	VS361 Spitfire LF XVIE (6944M/ G-BXVI)	Privately owned, Greenham Common
	RW388	VS361 Spitfire LF XVIE (6946M) [U4-U]	Stoke-on-Trent City Museum, Hanley
	RW393	VS361 Spitfire LF XVIE (7293M) [XT-A]	RAF Museum Reserve Collection, Stafford
	RX168	VS358 Seafire L IIIC (IAC 157/ G-BWEM)	Privately owned, Exeter
	SL611	VS361 Spitfire LF XVIE	Supermarine Aero Engineering, Stoke-on-Trent
	SL674	VS361 Spitfire LF IX (8392M) [RAS-H]	RAF Museum Reserve Collection, Stafford
	SM520	VS361 Spitfire LF IX (G-BXHZ/ G-ILDA)	Privately owned, Thruxton
	SM832	VS379 Spitfire F XIVE (G-WWII) [YB-A]	*Sold as N54SF, 2004*
	SM845	VS394 Spitfire FR XVIII (G-BUOS) [GZ-J]	Silver Victory Collection, Duxford
	SX137	VS384 Seafire F XVII	FAA Museum, RNAS Yeovilton
	SX336	VS384 Seafire F XVII (G-KASX)	Kennet Aviation, North Weald
	TA122	DH98 Mosquito FB VI [UP-G]	Mosquito Aircraft Museum, London Colney
	TA634	DH98 Mosquito TT35 (G-AWJV) [8K-K]	Mosquito Aircraft Museum, London Colney
	TA639	DH98 Mosquito TT35 (7806M) [AZ-E]	RAF Museum, Cosford
	TA719	DH98 Mosquito TT35 (G-ASKC)	Imperial War Museum, Duxford
	TA805	VS361 Spitfire HF IX (G-PMNF)	Privately owned, Duxford
	TB252	VS361 Spitfire LF XVIE (G-XVIE) [GW-H]	*Sold as N752TB, 2001*
	TB382	VS361 Spitfire LF XVIE (*X4277/ MK673*)	RAF BBMF, stored Coningsby
	TB752	VS361 Spitfire LF XVIE (8086M) [KH-Z]	RAF Manston, Memorial Pavilion
	TD248	VS361 Spitfire LF XVIE (7246M/ G-OXVI) [D]	Silver Victory Collection, Duxford
	TD248	VS361 Spitfire LF XVIE [8Q-T] (fuselage)	Norfolk & Suffolk Avn Mus'm, Flixton
	TD314	VS361 Spitfire LF IX (*N601DA*)	Privately owned, Norwich
	TE184	VS361 Spitfire LF XVIE (6850M/ G-MXVI) [D]	Privately owned, Duxford
	TE311	VS361 Spitfire LF XVIE (*MK178/* 7241M)	RAF BBMF, Coningsby (on rebuild)
	TE462	VS361 Spitfire LF XVIE (7243M)	Royal Scottish Mus'm of Flight, E Fortune

Serial	*Type (other identity) [code]*	*Owner/operator, location or fate*	*Notes*
TE517	VS361 Spitfire LF IXE (G-CCIX) [HL-K]	Privately owned, stored Booker	
TG263	Saro SR A1 (G-12-1)	Solent Sky, Southampton	
TG511	HP67 Hastings C1 (8554M)	RAF Museum, Cosford	
TG517	HP67 Hastings T5	Newark Air Museum, Winthorpe	
TG528	HP67 Hastings C1A	Imperial War Museum, Duxford	
TJ118	DH98 Mosquito TT35 <ff>	Mosquito Aircraft Museum, stored London Colney	
TJ138	DH98 Mosquito B35 (7607M) [VO-L]	RAF Museum, Hendon	
TJ343	Auster 5 (G-AJXC)	Privately owned, Hook	
TJ398	Auster AOP6 (BAPC 70)	Aircraft Pres'n Soc of Scotland, E Fortune	
TJ534	Auster 5 (G-AKSY)	Privately owned, Breighton	
TJ569	Auster 5 (G-AKOW)	Museum of Army Flying, Middle Wallop	
TJ652	Auster 5D (G-AMVD)	Privately owned, Hardwick, Norfolk	
TJ672	Auster 5D (G-ANIJ) [TS-D]	Privately owned, Whitchurch, Hants	
TJ704	Beagle A61 Terrier 2 (VW993/ G-ASCD) [JA]	Yorkshire Air Museum, Elvington	
TK718	GAL59 Hamilcar I	National Tank Museum, Bovington	
TK777	GAL59 Hamilcar I (fuselage)	Museum of Army Flying, Middle Wallop	
TS291	Slingsby T7 Cadet TX1 (BGA852)	Royal Scottish Mus'm of Flight, E Fortune	
TS798	Avro 685 York C1 (G-AGNV)	RAF Museum, Cosford	
TV959	DH98 Mosquito T III [AF-V]	The Fighter Collection, stored Duxford	
TV959	DH98 Mosquito T III <R>	*Currently not known*	
TW439	Auster 5 (G-ANRP)	The Real Aeroplane Company, Breighton	
TW467	Auster 5 (G-ANIE)	Privately owned, Kemble	
TW511	Auster 5 (G-APAF)	Privately owned, Henstridge	
TW536	Auster AOP6 (7704M/G-BNGE) [TS-V]	Privately owned, Netheravon	
TW591	Auster 6A (G-ARIH) [N]	Privately owned, Compton Abbas	
TW641	Beagle A61 Terrier 2 (G-ATDN)	Privately owned, Biggin Hill	
TX213	Avro 652A Anson C19 (G-AWRS)	North-East Aircraft Museum, Usworth	
TX214	Avro 652A Anson C19 (7817M)	RAF Museum, Cosford	
TX226	Avro 652A Anson C19 (7865M)	Air Atlantique Classic Flight, Coventry	
TX235	Avro 652A Anson C19	Air Atlantique Classic Flight, Coventry	
VF301	DH100 Vampire F1 (7060M) [RAL-G]	Midland Air Museum, Coventry	
VF512	Auster 6A (G-ARRX) [PF-M]	Privately owned, Popham	
VF516	Beagle A61 Terrier 2 (G-ASMZ) [T]	Privately owned, Eggesford	
VF526	Auster 6A (G-ARXU) [T]	Privately owned, Netheravon	
VF548	Beagle A61 Terrier 1 (G-ASEG)	*Sold to Denmark*	
VF560	Auster 6A (frame)	Aeroventure, Doncaster	
VF581	Beagle A61 Terrier 1 (G-ARSL)	Privately owned, Eggesford	
VH127	Fairey Firefly TT4 [200/R]	FAA Museum, RNAS Yeovilton	
VL348	Avro 652A Anson C19 (G-AVVO)	Newark Air Museum, Winthorpe	
VL349	Avro 652A Anson C19 (G-AWSA) [V7-Q]	Norfolk & Suffolk Avn Mus'm, Flixton	
VM325	Avro 652A Anson C19	Privately owned, stored Gloucester	
VM360	Avro 652A Anson C19 (G-APHV)	Royal Scottish Mus'm of Flight, E Fortune	
VM684	Slingsby Cadet T2 (BGA791)	NW Aviation Heritage Museum, Hooton Park	
VM687	Slingsby T8 Tutor (BGA794)	Privately owned, Lee-on-Solent	
VM791	Slingsby Cadet TX3 (XA312/ 8876M)	RAF Manston History Museum	
VN485	VS356 Spitfire F24 (7326M)	Imperial War Museum, Duxford	
VN799	EE Canberra T4 (WJ874)	RAF No 39(1 PRU) Sqn, Marham	
VP293	Avro 696 Shackleton T4 [A] <ff>	Newark Air Museum, Winthorpe	
VP519	Avro 652A Anson C19 (G-AVVR) <ff>	Privately owned, Wolverhampton	
VP952	DH104 Devon C2 (8820M)	RAF Museum, Cosford	
VP955	DH104 Devon C2 (G-DVON)	Privately owned, Kemble	
VP957	DH104 Devon C2 (8822M) <ff>	No 1137 Sqn ATC, Belfast	
VP967	DH104 Devon C2 (G-KOOL)	Privately owned, Redhill	
VP975	DH104 Devon C2 [M]	Science Museum, Wroughton	
VP981	DH104 Devon C2 (G-DHDV)	Air Atlantique Classic Flight, Coventry	
VR137	Westland Wyvern TF1	FAA Museum, RNAS Yeovilton	
VR192	Pervical P40 Prentice T1 (G-APIT)	SWWAPS, Lasham	
VR249	Percival P40 Prentice T1 (G-APIY) [FA-EL]	Newark Air Museum, Winthorpe	
VR259	Percival P40 Prentice T1 (G-APJB) [M]	Air Atlantique Classic Flight, Coventry	

Notes	Serial	Type (other identity) [code]	Owner/operator, location or fate
	VR930	Hawker Sea Fury FB11 (8382M) [110/O]	RN Historic Flight, Yeovilton
	VS356	Percival P40 Prentice T1 (G-AOLU)	Privately owned, Montrose
	VS562	Avro 652A Anson T21 (8012M)	Maes Artro Craft Village, Llanbedr
	VS610	Percival P40 Prentice T1 (G-AOKL) [K-L]	The Shuttleworth Collection, Old Warden
	VS623	Percival P40 Prentice T1 (G-AOKZ) [KQ-F]	Midland Air Museum, Coventry
	VT409	Fairey Firefly AS5 <rf>	North-East Aircraft Museum, stored Usworth
	VT812	DH100 Vampire F3 (7200M) [N]	RAF Museum, Hendon
	VT871	DH100 Vampire FB6 (J-1173/*LZ551*/G-DHXX) [G]	Source Classic Jet Flight, Bournemouth
	VT935	Boulton Paul P111A (VT769)	Midland Air Museum, Coventry
	VT987	Auster AOP6 (G-BKXP)	Privately owned, Thruxton
	VV106	Supermarine 510 (7175M)	FAA Museum, stored RNAS Yeovilton
	VV217	DH100 Vampire FB5 (7323M)	North-East Aircraft Museum, stored Usworth
	VV612	DH112 Venom FB50 (J-1523/*WE402*/G-VENI)	Source Classic Jet Flight, Bournemouth
	VV901	Avro 652A Anson T21	Yorkshire Air Museum, Elvington
	VW453	Gloster Meteor T7 (8703M) [Z]	RAF Innsworth, on display
	VW957	DH103 Sea Hornet NF21 <rf>	Privately owned, Fyvie, Grampian Region
	VX113	Auster AOP6 (G-ARNO)	Privately owned, Eggesford
	VX118	Auster AOP6 (G-ASNB)	Privately owned, Shotteswell
	VX147	Alon A2 Aircoupe (G-AVIL)	Privately owned, Kent
	VX185	EE Canberra B(I)8 (7631M) <ff>	Royal Scottish Mus'm of Flight, E Fortune
	VX250	DH103 Sea Hornet NF21 [48] <rf>	Mosquito Aircraft Museum, London Colney
	VX272	Hawker P.1052 (7174M)	FAA Museum, stored RNAS Yeovilton
	VX275	Slingsby T21B Sedbergh TX1 (8884M/BGA572)	RAF Museum Reserve Collection, Stafford
	VX573	Vickers Valetta C2 (8389M)	RAF Museum, stored Cosford
	VX580	Vickers Valetta C2	Norfolk & Suffolk Avn Museum, Flixton
	VX595	WS51 Dragonfly HR1	FAA Museum, stored RNAS Yeovilton
	VX665	Hawker Sea Fury FB11 <rf>	RN Historic Flight, at BAE Systems Brough
	VX926	Auster T7 (G-ASKJ)	Privately owned,
	VX927	Auster T7 (G-ASYG)	Privately owned, Hemswell
	VZ345	Hawker Sea Fury T20S	RN Historic Flight, stored Yeovilton
	VZ477	Gloster Meteor F8 (7741M) <ff>	Midland Air Museum, Coventry
	VZ608	Gloster Meteor FR9	Newark Air Museum, Winthorpe
	VZ634	Gloster Meteor T7 (8657M)	Newark Air Museum, Winthorpe
	VZ638	Gloster Meteor T7 (G-JETM) [HF]	Gatwick Aviation Museum, Charlwood, Surrey
	VZ728	RS4 Desford Trainer (G-AGOS)	Snibston Discovery Park, stored Coalville
	VZ962	WS51 Dragonfly HR1 [904]	The Helicopter Museum, Weston-super-Mare
	WA346	DH100 Vampire FB5	RAF Museum Restoration Centre, Cosford
	WA473	VS Attacker F1 [102/J]	FAA Museum, RNAS Yeovilton
	WA576	Bristol 171 Sycamore 3 (7900M/G-ALSS)	Dumfries & Galloway Avn Mus, Dumfries
	WA577	Bristol 171 Sycamore 3 (7718M/G-ALST)	North-East Aircraft Museum, Usworth
	WA591	Gloster Meteor T7 (7917M/G-BWMF) [W]	Meteor Flight, Yatesbury
	WA630	Gloster Meteor T7 [69] <ff>	Robertsbridge Aviation Society, Newhaven
	WA634	Gloster Meteor T7/8	RAF Museum, Cosford
	WA638	Gloster Meteor T7(mod)	Martin Baker Aircraft, Chalgrove
	WA662	Gloster Meteor T7	Aeroventure, Doncaster
	WA829	Gloster Meteor F8 (WA984) [A]	Tangmere Military Aviation Museum
	WB188	Hawker Hunter F3 (7154M)	Tangmere Military Aviation Museum
	WB188	Hawker Hunter GA11 (WV256/G-BZPB)	Hunter Flying Club, Exeter (duck egg green)
	WB188	Hawker Hunter GA11 (XF300/G-BZPC)	Hunter Flying Club, Exeter (red)
	WB440	Fairey Firefly AS6 <ff>	Privately owned, Newton-le-Willows
	WB491	Avro 706 Ashton 2 (TS897/G-AJJW) <ff>	Newark Air Museum, Winthorpe
	WB556	DHC1 Chipmunk T10	*Currently not known*
	WB560	DHC1 Chipmunk T10 (comp WG403)	Aeroventure, stored Doncaster
	WB565	DHC1 Chipmunk T10 (G-PVET) [X]	Privately owned, Kemble

Serial	Type (other identity) [code]	Owner/operator, location or fate	Notes
WB569	DHC1 Chipmunk T10 (G-BYSJ) [R]	Privately owned, Duxford	
WB584	DHC1 Chipmunk T10 (7706M) <ff>	Royal Scottish Museum of Flight, East Fortune	
WB585	DHC1 Chipmunk T10 (G-AOSY) [M]	Privately owned, Seething	
WB588	DHC1 Chipmunk T10 (G-AOTD) [D]	Privately owned, Old Sarum	
WB615	DHC1 Chipmunk T10 (G-BXIA) [E]	Privately owned, Blackpool	
WB624	DHC1 Chipmunk T10 <ff>	Newark Air Museum, Winthorpe	
WB626	DHC1 Chipmunk T10 <ff>	Privately owned, Aylesbury	
WB627	DHC1 Chipmunk T10 (9248M) [N]	Dulwich College CCF	
WB645	DHC1 Chipmunk T10 (8218M)	*Currently not known*	
WB652	DHC1 Chipmunk T10 (G-CHPY) [V]	Privately owned, Portimao, Portugal	
WB654	DHC1 Chipmunk T10 (G-BXGO) [U]	Privately owned, Booker	
WB657	DHC1 Chipmunk T10 [908]	RN Historic Flight, Yeovilton	
WB660	DHC1 Chipmunk T10 (G-ARMB)	*Sold as ZK-CHP, August 2004*	
WB670	DHC1 Chipmunk T10 (8361M)	Privately owned, East Fortune	
WB671	DHC1 Chipmunk T10 (G-BWTG) [910]	Privately owned, Epse, The Netherlands	
WB685	DHC1 Chipmunk T10 <rf>	North-East Aircraft Museum, stored Usworth	
WB697	DHC1 Chipmunk T10 (G-BXCT) [95]	Privately owned, Wickenby	
WB702	DHC1 Chipmunk T10 (G-AOFE)	Privately owned, Kindford	
WB703	DHC1 Chipmunk T10 (G-ARMC)	Privately owned, White Waltham	
WB711	DHC1 Chipmunk T10 (G-APPM)	Privately owned, Turweston	
WB726	DHC1 Chipmunk T10 (G-AOSK) [E]	Privately owned, Audley End	
WB733	DHC1 Chipmunk T10 (comp WG422)	Aeroventure, Doncaster	
WB758	DHC1 Chipmunk T10 (7729M) [P]	Privately owned,	
WB763	DHC1 Chipmunk T10 (G-BBMR) [14]	Privately owned, Tollerton	
WB922	Slingsby T21B Sedbergh TX1 (BGA4366)	Privately owned, Hullavington	
WB924	Slingsby T21B Sedbergh TX1 (BGA3901)	Privately owned, Dunstable	
WB938	Slingsby T21B Sedbergh TX1	*Sold as ZS-GSO*	
WB943	Slingsby T21B Sedbergh TX1 (BGA2941)	Privately owned, Rufforth	
WB944	Slingsby T21B Sedbergh TX1 (BGA3160)	Privately owned, Bicester	
WB969	Slingsby T21B Sedbergh TX1	*To BGA2036*	
WB971	Slingsby T21B Sedbergh TX1 (BGA 3324)	Privately owned, Tibenham	
WB975	Slingsby T21B Sedbergh TX1 (BGA 3288)	Privately owned, Drumshade, Fife	
WB981	Slingsby T21B Sedbergh TX1 (BGA 3238)	Privately owned, Keevil	
WD286	DHC1 Chipmunk T10 (G-BBND)	Privately owned, Oaksey Park	
WD288	DHC1 Chipmunk T10 (G-AOSO) [38]	*Sold as N122DH, July 2004*	
WD292	DHC1 Chipmunk T10 (G-BCRX)	Privately owned, White Waltham	
WD293	DHC1 Chipmunk T10 (7645M) <ff>	No 30F Sqn ATC, Cardiff	
WD305	DHC1 Chipmunk T10 (G-ARGG)	Privately owned, Prestwick	
WD310	DHC1 Chipmunk T10 (G-BWUN) [B]	Privately owned, Deanland	
WD318	DHC1 Chipmunk T10 (8207M) <ff>	*Currently not known*	
WD325	DHC1 Chipmunk T10 [N]	AAC Historic Aircraft Flight, Middle Wallop	
WD331	DHC1 Chipmunk T10 (G-BXDH) [J]	Privately owned, Enstone	
WD347	DHC1 Chipmunk T10 (G-BBRV)	Privately owned, Sheffield	
WD355	DHC1 Chipmunk T10 (WD335/ G-CBAJ)	Privately owned, Solihull	
WD363	DHC1 Chipmunk T10 (G-BCIH) [5]	Privately owned, Audley End	
WD370	DHC1 Chipmunk T10 <ff>	No 225 Sqn ATC, Brighton	
WD373	DHC1 Chipmunk T10 (G-BXDI) [12]	Privately owned, Duxford	
WD377	DHC1 Chipmunk T10 <ff>	RAF Millom Museum, Haverigg	
WD379	DHC1 Chipmunk T10 (WB696/ G-APLO) [K]	Privately owned, Jersey	

Notes	*Serial*	*Type (other identity) [code]*	*Owner/operator, location or fate*
	WD386	DHC1 Chipmunk T10 (comp WD377)	Dumfries & Galloway Avn Mus, Prestwick
	WD390	DHC1 Chipmunk T10 (G-BWNK) [68]	Privately owned, Breighton
	WD413	Avro 652A Anson T21 (7881M/ G-VROE)	Air Atlantique Classic Flight, Coventry
	WD615	Gloster Meteor TT20 (WD646/ 8189M) [R]	RAF Manston History Museum
	WD686	Gloster Meteor NF11	Muckleburgh Collection, Weybourne
	WD790	Gloster Meteor NF11 (8743M)<ff>	North-East Aircraft Museum, Usworth
	WD889	Fairey Firefly AS5 <ff>	North-East Aircraft Museum, Usworth
	WD931	EE Canberra B2 <ff>	RAF Museum, stored Cosford
	WD935	EE Canberra B2 (8440M) <ff>	Aeroventure, Doncaster
	WD954	EE Canberra B2 <ff>	Privately owned, St Mawgan
	WE113	EE Canberra B2 <ff>	Privately owned, Woodhurst, Cambridgeshire
	WE122	EE Canberra TT18 [845] <ff>	Blyth Valley Aviation Collection, Walpole, Suffolk
	WE139	EE Canberra PR3 (8369M)	RAF Museum, Hendon
	WE168	EE Canberra PR3 (8049M) <ff>	Norfolk & Suffolk Avn Museum, Flixton
	WE173	EE Canberra PR3 (8740M) <ff>	Robertsbridge Aviation Society, Mayfield
	WE188	EE Canberra T4	Solway Aviation Society, Carlisle
	WE192	EE Canberra T4 <ff>	Blyth Valley Aviation Collection, Walpole, Suffolk
	WE275	DH112 Venom FB50 (J-1601/ G-VIDI)	BAE Systems Hawarden, Fire Section
	WE569	Auster T7 (G-ASAJ)	Privately owned, Bassingbourn
	WE591	Auster T7 (G-ASAK) [Y]	Privately owned, Biggin Hill
	WE600	Auster T7 Antarctic (7602M)	RAF Museum, Cosford
	WE724	Hawker Sea Fury FB11 (VX653/ G-BUCM) [062]	The Fighter Collection, Duxford
	WE982	Slingsby T30B Prefect TX1 (8781M)	RAF Museum, stored Cosford
	WE987	Slingsby T30B Prefect TX1	Aeroventure, Doncaster
	WE990	Slingsby T30B Prefect TX1 (BGA2583)	Privately owned, stored Beds
	WE992	Slingsby T30B Prefect TX1 (BGA2692)	Privately owned, Keevil
	WF118	Percival P57 Sea Prince T1 (G-DACA)	Gatwick Aviation Museum, Charlwood, Surrey
	WF122	Percival P57 Sea Prince T1 [575/CU]	Aeroventure, Doncaster
	WF128	Percival P57 Sea Prince T1 (8611M)	Norfolk & Suffolk Avn Museum, Flixton
	WF137	Percival P57 Sea Prince C1	SWWAPS, Lasham
	WF145	Hawker Sea Hawk F1 <ff>	Privately owned, Ingatestone, Essex
	WF225	Hawker Sea Hawk F1 [CU]	RNAS Culdrose, at main gate
	WF259	Hawker Sea Hawk F2 [171/A]	Royal Scottish Mus'm of Flight,E Fortune
	WF369	Vickers Varsity T1 [F]	Newark Air Museum, Winthorpe
	WF372	Vickers Varsity T1 [A]	Brooklands Museum, Weybridge
	WF376	Vickers Varsity T1	Bristol Airport Fire Section
	WF408	Vickers Varsity T1 (8395M)	Privately owned, East Grinstead
	WF410	Vickers Varsity T1 [F]	Brunel Technical College, Lulsgate
	WF643	Gloster Meteor F8 [P]	Norfolk & Suffolk Avn Museum, Flixton
	WF714	Gloster Meteor F8 (WK914)	Hooton Park Trust, Cheshire
	WF784	Gloster Meteor T7 (7895M)	Gloucestershire Avn Coll, stored Gloucester
	WF825	Gloster Meteor T7 (8359M) [A]	Meteor Flight, Yatesbury
	WF877	Gloster Meteor T7 (G-BPOA)	*Sold to the USA*
	WF911	EE Canberra B2 [CO] <ff>	The Griffin Trust, Hooton Park, Cheshire
	WF922	EE Canberra PR3	Midland Air Museum, Coventry
	WG300	DHC1 Chipmunk T10 <ff>	*Currently not known*
	WG303	DHC1 Chipmunk T10 (8208M) <ff>	RAFGSA, Bicester
	WG308	DHC1 Chipmunk T10 (G-BYHL) [71]	Privately owned, Newton
	WG316	DHC1 Chipmunk T10 (G-BCAH)	Privately owned, Leicester
	WG321	DHC1 Chipmunk T10 (G-DHCC)	Privately owned, Wevelgem, Belgium
	WG348	DHC1 Chipmunk T10 (G-BBMV)	Privately owned, Sywell
	WG350	DHC1 Chipmunk T10 (G-BPAL)	Privately owned, Cascais, Portugal

Serial	Type (other identity) [code]	Owner/operator, location or fate	Notes
WG362	DHC1 Chipmunk T10 (8437M/ 8630M/*WX643*) <ff>	No 1094 Sqn ATC, Ely	
WG407	DHC1 Chipmunk T10 (G-BWMX)	Privately owned, Croydon, Cambs	
WG418	DHC1 Chipmunk T10 (8209M/ G-ATDY) <ff>	No 1940 Sqn ATC, Levenshulme, Gr Manchester	
WG419	DHC1 Chipmunk T10 (8206M) <ff>	No 1053 Sqn ATC, Armthorpe	
WG422	DHC1 Chipmunk T10 (8394M/ G-BFAX) [116]	Privately owned, Eggesford	
WG432	DHC1 Chipmunk T10 [L]	Museum of Army Flying, Middle Wallop	
WG458	DHC1 Chipmunk T10 (N458BG) [2]	Privately owned, Breighton	
WG465	DHC1 Chipmunk T10 (G-BCEY)	Privately owned, White Waltham	
WG469	DHC1 Chipmunk T10 (G-BWJY) [72]	Privately owned, Newtownards	
WG471	DHC1 Chipmunk T10 (8210M) <ff>	Thameside Aviation Museum, East Tilbury	
WG472	DHC1 Chipmunk T10 (G-AOTY)	Privately owned, Bryngwyn Bach, Clwyd	
WG477	DHC1 Chipmunk T10 (8362M/ G-ATDP) <ff>	No 281 Sqn ATC, Birkdale, Merseyside	
WG482	DHC1 Chipmunk T10 (VH-ZOT) [01]	*Returned to Australia*	
WG483	DHC1 Chipmunk T10 (WG393/ VH-ZIT)	*Returned to Australia*	
WG486	DHC1 Chipmunk T10 [G]	RAF BBMF, Coningsby	
WG498	Slingsby T21B Sedbergh TX1 (BGA3245)	Privately owned, Aston Down	
WG511	Avro 696 Shackleton T4 (fuselage)	Flambards Village Theme Park, Helston	
WG718	WS51 Dragonfly HR3 [934]	*Broken up for spares at Elvington*	
WG719	WS51 Dragonfly HR5 (G-BRMA)	The Helicopter Museum, Weston-super-Mare	
WG724	WS51 Dragonfly HR5 [932]	North-East Aircraft Museum, Usworth	
WG751	WS51 Dragonfly HR5 [710/GJ]	World Naval Base, Chatham	
WG760	EE P1A (7755M)	RAF Museum, Cosford	
WG763	EE P1A (7816M)	Gr Manchester Mus of Science & Industry	
WG768	Short SB5 (8005M)	RAF Museum, Cosford	
WG774	BAC 221	Science Museum, at FAA Museum, RNAS Yeovilton	
WG777	Fairey FD2 (7986M)	RAF Museum, Cosford	
WG789	EE Canberra B2/6 <ff>	Norfolk & Suffolk Avn Museum, Flixton	
WH132	Gloster Meteor T7 (7906M) [J]	No 276 Sqn ATC, Chelmsford	
WH166	Gloster Meteor T7 (8052M) [A]	Privately owned, Birlingham, Worcs	
WH291	Gloster Meteor F8	SWWAPS, Lasham	
WH301	Gloster Meteor F8 (7930M) [T]	RAF Museum, Hendon	
WH364	Gloster Meteor F8 (8169M)	Gloucestershire Avn Coll, stored Gloucester	
WH453	Gloster Meteor D16 [L]	DPA/QinetiQ, stored Llanbedr	
WH646	EE Canberra T17A <ff>	Midland Air Museum, Coventry	
WH657	EE Canberra B2	Brenzett Aeronautical Museum	
WH665	EE Canberra T17 (8763M) [J]	BAE Systems Filton, Fire Section	
WH725	EE Canberra B2	Imperial War Museum, Duxford	
WH734	EE Canberra B2(mod)	DPA/QinetiQ, Llanbedr	
WH739	EE Canberra B2 <ff>	No 2475 Sqn ATC, Ammanford, Dyfed	
WH740	EE Canberra T17 (8762M) [K]	East Midlands Airport Aeropark	
WH773	EE Canberra PR7 (8696M)	Gatwick Aviation Museum, Charlwood, Surrey	
WH775	EE Canberra PR7 (8128M/8868M) <ff>	Privately owned, Welshpool	
WH779	EE Canberra PR7 <ff>	Boscombe Down Aviation Collection	
WH779	EE Canberra PR7 [BP] <rf>	RAF, stored Shawbury	
WH791	EE Canberra PR7 (8165M/8176M/ 8187M)	Newark Air Museum, Winthorpe	
WH803	EE Canberra T22 <ff>	*Scrapped, 2003*	
WH840	EE Canberra T4 (8350M)	Privately owned, Flixton	
WH846	EE Canberra T4	Yorkshire Air Museum, Elvington	
WH849	EE Canberra T4	RAF, stored Shawbury	
WH850	EE Canberra T4 <ff>	Privately owned, Narborough	
WH863	EE Canberra T17 (8693M) [CP] <ff>	Newark Air Museum, Winthorpe	
WH876	EE Canberra B2(mod) <ff>	Boscombe Down Aviation Collection	
WH887	EE Canberra TT18 [847] <ff>	Privately owned, Booker	
WH903	EE Canberra B2 <ff>	Yorkshire Air Museum, Elvington	
WH904	EE Canberra T19	Newark Air Museum, Winthorpe	
WH946	EE Canberra B6(mod) (8185M) <ff>	*Scrapped*	

Notes	Serial	Type (other identity) [code]	Owner/operator, location or fate
	WH953	EE Canberra B6(mod) <ff>	Blyth Valley Aviation Collection, Walpole, Suffolk
	WH957	EE Canberra E15 (8869M) <ff>	Lincolnshire Avn Heritage Centre, East Kirkby
	WH960	EE Canberra B15 (8344M) <ff>	Rolls-Royce Heritage Trust, Derby
	WH964	EE Canberra E15 (8870M) <ff>	Privately owned, Lewes
	WH984	EE Canberra B15 (8101M) <ff>	Privately owned, Mold
	WH991	WS51 Dragonfly HR3	Yorkshire Helicopter Preservation Group, Elvington
	WJ231	Hawker Sea Fury FB11 (*WE726*) [115/O]	FAA Museum, Yeovilton
	WJ358	Auster AOP6 (G-ARYD)	Museum of Army Flying, Middle Wallop
	WJ565	EE Canberra T17 (8871M) <ff>	Aeroventure, Doncaster
	WJ567	EE Canberra B2 <ff>	Privately owned, Houghton, Cambs
	WJ576	EE Canberra T17 <ff>	Boulton Paul Association, Wolverhampton
	WJ581	EE Canberra PR7 <ff>	Privately owned, Canterbury
	WJ633	EE Canberra T17 [EF] <ff>	RAF Wyton
	WJ639	EE Canberra TT18 [39]	North-East Aircraft Museum, Usworth
	WJ640	EE Canberra B2 (8722M) <ff>	Privately owned,
	WJ676	EE Canberra B2 (7796M) <ff>	North-West Aviation Heritage, Hooton Park, Cheshire
	WJ677	EE Canberra B2 <ff>	Privately owned, Redruth
	WJ717	EE Canberra TT18 (9052M) <ff>	RAF St Athan, Fire Section
	WJ721	EE Canberra TT18 [21] <ff>	Privately owned, Oban
	WJ731	EE Canberra B2T [BK] <ff>	Privately owned, Golders Green
	WJ821	EE Canberra PR7 (8668M)	Army, Bassingbourn, on display
	WJ863	EE Canberra T4 <ff>	*Burnt at Cambridge Airport*
	WJ865	EE Canberra T4	Privately owned, Bromsgrove
	WJ866	EE Canberra T4	*Crashed 2 September 2004, Marham*
	WJ880	EE Canberra T4 (8491M) <ff>	Dumfries & Galloway Avn Mus, Dumfries
	WJ903	Vickers Varsity T1 <ff>	Aeroventure, Doncaster
	WJ945	Vickers Varsity T1 (G-BEDV) [21]	Imperial War Museum, Duxford
	WJ975	EE Canberra T19 [S]	Bomber County Aviation Museum, Hemswell
	WJ992	EE Canberra T4	Bournemouth Int'l Airport, Fire Section
	WK102	EE Canberra T17 (8780M) <ff>	Privately owned, Welshpool
	WK118	EE Canberra TT18 <ff>	Privately owned, Chipperfield, Herts
	WK122	EE Canberra TT18 <ff>	Privately owned, Chipperfield, Herts
	WK124	EE Canberra TT18 (9093M) [CR]	MoD FSCTE, Manston
	WK126	EE Canberra TT18 (N2138J) [843]	Gloucestershire Avn Coll, stored Gloucester
	WK127	EE Canberra TT18 (8985M) <ff>	No 2484 Sqn ATC, Bassingbourn
	WK128	EE Canberra B2	DPA/QinetiQ, Llanbedr
	WK146	EE Canberra B2 <ff>	Gatwick Aviation Museum, Charlwood, Surrey
	WK163	EE Canberra B2/6 (G-BVWC)	Air Atlantique Classic Flight, Coventry
	WK198	VS Swift F4 (7428M) (fuselage)	North-East Aircraft Museum, Usworth
	WK275	VS Swift F4	Privately owned, Upper Hill, nr Leominster
	WK277	VS Swift FR5 (7719M) [N]	Newark Air Museum, Winthorpe
	WK281	VS Swift FR5 (7712M) [S]	Tangmere Military Aviation Museum
	WK393	DH112 Venom FB1 <ff>	Aeroventure, Doncaster
	WK436	DH112 Venom FB50 (J-1614/ G-VENM)	Kennet Aviation, North Weald
	WK512	DHC1 Chipmunk T10 (G-BXIM) [A]	Privately owned, Brize Norton
	WK514	DHC1 Chipmunk T10 (G-BBMO)	Privately owned, Wellesbourne Mountford
	WK517	DHC1 Chipmunk T10 (G-ULAS) [84]	Privately owned, Denham
	WK518	DHC1 Chipmunk T10 [K]	RAF BBMF, Coningsby
	WK522	DHC1 Chipmunk T10 (G-BCOU)	Privately owned, Duxford
	WK549	DHC1 Chipmunk T10 (G-BTWF)	Privately owned, Breighton
	WK570	DHC1 Chipmunk T10 (8211M) <ff>	No 424 Sqn ATC, Solent Sky, Southampton
	WK576	DHC1 Chipmunk T10 (8357M) <ff>	No 1206 Sqn ATC, Lichfield
	WK577	DHC1 Chipmunk T10 (G-BCYM)	Privately owned, Kemble
	WK584	DHC1 Chipmunk T10 (7556M) <ff>	No 2008 Sqn ATC, Bawtry
	WK585	DHC1 Chipmunk T10 (9265M/ G-BZGA)	Privately owned, Duxford
	WK586	DHC1 Chipmunk T10 (G-BXGX) [V]	Privately owned, Slinfold
	WK590	DHC1 Chipmunk T10 (G-BWVZ) [69]	Privately owned, Spanhoe

Serial	*Type (other identity) [code]*	*Owner/operator, location or fate*	*Notes*
WK608	DHC1 Chipmunk T10 [906]	RN Historic Flight, Yeovilton	
WK609	DHC1 Chipmunk T10 (G-BXDN) [B]	Privately owned, Booker	
WK611	DHC1 Chipmunk T10 (G-ARWB)	Privately owned, Thruxton	
WK620	DHC1 Chipmunk T10 [T] (fuselage)	Privately owned, Twyford, Bucks	
WK622	DHC1 Chipmunk T10 (G-BCZH)	Privately owned, Horsford	
WK624	DHC1 Chipmunk T10 (G-BWHI)	Privately owned, Hawarden	
WK626	DHC1 Chipmunk T10 (8213M) <ff>	Aeroventure, stored Doncaster	
WK628	DHC1 Chipmunk T10 (G-BBMW)	Privately owned, Goodwood	
WK630	DHC1 Chipmunk T10 (G-BXDG) [11]	Privately owned, Felthorpe	
WK633	DHC1 Chipmunk T10 (G-BXEC) [A]	Privately owned, Redhill	
WK638	DHC1 Chipmunk T10 (G-BWJZ) (fuselage)	Privately owned, Eccleshall, Staffs	
WK640	DHC1 Chipmunk T10 (G-BWUV) [C]	Privately owned, Wombleton	
WK642	DHC1 Chipmunk T10 (G-BXDP) [94]	Privately owned, Kilrush, Eire	
WK654	Gloster Meteor F8 (8092M) [B]	City of Norwich Aviation Museum	
WK800	Gloster Meteor D16 [Z]	DPA/QinetiQ, Boscombe Down, wfu	
WK864	Gloster Meteor F8 (WL168/7750M) [C]	Yorkshire Air Museum, Elvington	
WK914	Gloster Meteor F8 (*WF714)*	Hooton Park Trust, Cheshire	
WK935	Gloster Meteor Prone Pilot (7869M)	RAF Museum, Cosford	
WK991	Gloster Meteor F8 (7825M)	Imperial War Museum, Duxford	
WL131	Gloster Meteor F8 (7751M) <ff>	Aeroventure, Doncaster	
WL181	Gloster Meteor F8 [X]	North-East Aircraft Museum, Usworth	
WL332	Gloster Meteor T7 [888]	Privately owned, Long Marston	
WL345	Gloster Meteor T7	St Leonard's Motors, Hollington, E Sussex	
WL349	Gloster Meteor T7 [Z]	Gloucestershire Airport, Staverton, on display	
WL360	Gloster Meteor T7 (7920M) [G]	Meteor Flight, Yatesbury	
WL375	Gloster Meteor T7(mod)	Dumfries & Galloway Avn Mus, Dumfries	
WL405	Gloster Meteor T7	Meteor Flight, Yatesbury	
WL419	Gloster Meteor T7	Martin Baker Aircraft, Chalgrove	
WL505	DH100 Vampire FB9 (7705M/ G-FBIX)	Vampire Preservation Society, Bournemouth	
WL505	DH100 Vampire FB6 (J-1167/ *VZ304*/G-MKVI)	Privately owned, Hibaldstow	
WL626	Vickers Varsity T1 (G-BHDD) [P]	East Midlands Airport Aeropark	
WL627	Vickers Varsity T1 (8488M) [D] <ff>	Privately owned, Preston, E Yorkshire	
WL679	Vickers Varsity T1 (9155M)	RAF Museum, Cosford	
WL732	BP P108 Sea Balliol T21	RAF Museum, Cosford	
WL795	Avro 696 Shackleton MR2C (8753M) [T]	RAF St Mawgan, on display	
WL798	Avro 696 Shackleton MR2C (8114M) <ff>	Privately owned, Elgin	
WL925	Slingsby T31B Cadet TX3 (WV925) <ff>	*Currently not known*	
WM145	AW Meteor NF11 <ff>	Highland Aircraft Preservation Society, Inverness	
WM167	AW Meteor NF11 (G-LOSM)	Air Atlantique Classic Flight, Coventry	
WM267	Gloster Meteor NF11 <ff>	Blyth Valley Aviation Collection, Walpole, Suffolk	
WM292	AW Meteor TT20 [841]	FAA Museum, stored RNAS Yeovilton	
WM311	AW Meteor TT20 (WM224/8177M)	East Midlands Airport Aeropark	
WM366	AW Meteor NF13 (4X-FNA) (comp VZ462)	SWWAPS, Lasham	
WM367	AW Meteor NF13 <ff>	Jet Avn Preservation Grp, Long Marston	
WM571	DH112 Sea Venom FAW21 [VL]	Solent Sky, stored	
WM729	DH113 Vampire NF10 <ff>	Mosquito Aircraft Museum, London Colney	
WM913	Hawker Sea Hawk FB5 (8162M) [456/J]	Newark Air Museum, Winthorpe	
WM961	Hawker Sea Hawk FB5 [J]	Caernarfon Air World	
WM969	Hawker Sea Hawk FB5 [10/Z]	Imperial War Museum, Duxford	
WN105	Hawker Sea Hawk FB3 (WF299/ 8164M)	Privately owned, Birlingham, Worcs	
WN108	Hawker Sea Hawk FB5 [033]	Ulster Aviation Society, Langford Lodge	

Notes	Serial	Type (other identity) [code]	Owner/operator, location or fate
	WN149	BP P108 Balliol T2	Boulton Paul Association, Wolverhampton
	WN411	Fairey Gannet AS1 (fuselage)	Privately owned, Sholing, Hants
	WN493	WS51 Dragonfly HR5	FAA Museum, RNAS Yeovilton
	WN499	WS51 Dragonfly HR5 [Y]	Caernarfon Air World
	WN516	BP P108 Balliol T2 <ff>	North-East Aircraft Museum, Usworth
	WN534	BP P108 Balliol T2 <ff>	Boulton Paul Association, Wolverhampton
	WN890	Hawker Hunter F2 <ff>	Aeroventure, Doncaster
	WN904	Hawker Hunter F2 (7544M) [3]	RE 39 Regt, Waterbeach, on display
	WN907	Hawker Hunter F2 (7416M) <ff>	Robertsbridge Aviation Society, Newhaven
	WN957	Hawker Hunter F5 <ff>	Privately owned, Llanbedr
	WP185	Hawker Hunter F5 (7583M)	Privately owned, Great Dunmow, Essex
	WP190	Hawker Hunter F5 (7582M/8473M/ *WP180*) [K]	Tangmere Military Aviation Museum
	WP250	DH113 Vampire NF10 <ff>	Privately owned, Tamworth
	WP255	DH113 Vampire NF10 <ff>	Aeroventure, Doncaster
	WP270	EoN Eton TX1 (8598M)	Gr Manchester Mus of Science & Industry, stored
	WP308	Percival P57 Sea Prince T1 (G-GACA) [572/CU]	Gatwick Aviation Museum, Charlwood, Surrey
	WP313	Percival P57 Sea Prince T1 [568/CU]	FAA Museum, stored RNAS Yeovilton
	WP314	Percival P57 Sea Prince T1 (8634M) [573/CU]	Privately owned, Carlisle Airport
	WP321	Percival P57 Sea Prince T1 (N7SY)	Bournemouth Aviation Museum
	WP515	EE Canberra B2 <ff>	Privately owned, Scampton
	WP772	DHC1 Chipmunk T10 [Q] (wreck)	RAF Manston History Museum
	WP784	DHC1 Chipmunk T10 <ff>	Jet Avn Preservation Grp, Long Marston
	WP788	DHC1 Chipmunk T10 (G-BCHL)	Privately owned, Sleap
	WP790	DHC1 Chipmunk T10 (G-BBNC) [T]	Mosquito Aircraft Museum, London Colney
	WP795	DHC1 Chipmunk T10 (G-BVZZ) [901]	Privately owned, Lee-on-Solent
	WP800	DHC1 Chipmunk T10 (G-BCXN) [2]	Privately owned, Halton
	WP803	DHC1 Chipmunk T10 (G-HAPY) [G]	Privately owned, Booker
	WP805	DHC1 Chipmunk T10 (G-MAJR) [D]	Privately owned, Lee-on-Solent
	WP808	DHC1 Chipmunk T10 (G-BDEU)	Privately owned, Hurstbourne Tarrant
	WP809	DHC1 Chipmunk T10 (G-BVTX) [78]	Privately owned, Husbands Bosworth
	WP833	DHC1 Chipmunk T10 (G-BZDU) [H]	Privately owned, Newcastle
	WP835	DHC1 Chipmunk T10 (D-ERTY)	Privately owned, The Netherlands
	WP839	DHC1 Chipmunk T10 (G-BZXE) [A]	Privately owned, Blackpool
	WP840	DHC1 Chipmunk T10 (G-BXDM) [9]	Privately owned, Halton
	WP844	DHC1 Chipmunk T10 (G-BWOX) [85]	Privately owned, Shobdon
	WP856	DHC1 Chipmunk T10 (G-BVWP) [904]	Privately owned, Horsham
	WP857	DHC1 Chipmunk T10 (G-BDRJ) [24]	Privately owned, Prestwick
	WP859	DHC1 Chipmunk T10 (G-BXCP) [E]	Privately owned, Spanhoe Lodge
	WP860	DHC1 Chipmunk T10 (G-BXDA) [6]	Privately owned, Perth
	WP863	DHC1 Chipmunk T10 (8360M/ G-ATJI) <ff>	No 1011 Sqn ATC, Boscombe Down
	WP869	DHC1 Chipmunk T10 (8215M) <ff>	Privately owned, Rush Green
	WP870	DHC1 Chipmunk T10 (G-BCOI) [12]	Privately owned, Rayne Hall Farm, Essex
	WP871	DHC1 Chipmunk T10 [W]	Privately owned, Duxford
	WP896	DHC1 Chipmunk T10 (G-BWVY) [M]	Privately owned, White Waltham
	WP901	DHC1 Chipmunk T10 (G-BWNT) [B]	Privately owned, East Midlands Airport
	WP903	DHC1 Chipmunk T10 (G-BCGC)	Privately owned, Henlow
	WP912	DHC1 Chipmunk T10 (8467M)	RAF Museum, Cosford
	WP921	DHC1 Chipmunk T10 (G-ATJJ) <ff>	Privately owned, Brooklands

Serial	*Type (other identity) [code]*	*Owner/operator, location or fate*	*Notes*
WP925	DHC1 Chipmunk T10 (G-BXHA) [C]	Privately owned, Seppe, The Netherlands	
WP927	DHC1 Chipmunk T10 (8216M/ G-ATJK) <ff>	Mosquito Aircraft Museum, London Colney	
WP928	DHC1 Chipmunk T10 (G-BXGM) [D]	Privately owned, Shoreham	
WP929	DHC1 Chipmunk T10 (G-BXCV) [F]	Privately owned, Duxford	
WP930	DHC1 Chipmunk T10 (G-BXHF) [J]	Privately owned, Redhill	
WP962	DHC1 Chipmunk T10 [C]	RAF Museum, Hendon	
WP964	DHC1 Chipmunk T10 [Y]	Privately owned, Duxford	
WP969	DHC1 Chipmunk T10 (comp WB685/G-ATHC) [C]	North-East Aircraft Museum, Usworth	
WP971	DHC1 Chipmunk T10 (G-ATHD)	Privately owned, Denham	
WP977	DHC1 Chipmunk T10 (G-BHRD) <ff>	Privately owned, Yateley, Hants	
WP983	DHC1 Chipmunk T10 (G-BXNN) [B]	Privately owned, Eggesford	
WP984	DHC1 Chipmunk T10 (G-BWTO) [H]	Privately owned, Little Gransden	
WR360	DH112 Venom FB50 (J-1626/ G-DHSS) [K]	Source Classic Jet Flight, Bournemouth	
WR410	DH112 Venom FB50 (J-1539/ G-DHUU/*WE410*)	Source Classic Jet Flight, Bournemouth	
WR410	DH112 Venom FB54 (J-1790/ G-BLKA) [N]	Mosquito Aircraft Museum, London Colney	
WR421	DH112 Venom FB50 (J-1611/ G-DHTT)	Bournemouth Aviation Museum	
WR470	DH112 Venom FB50 (J-1542/ G-DHVM)	Air Atlantique Classic Flight, Coventry	
WR539	DH112 Venom FB4 (8399M) <ff>	Mosquito Aircraft Museum, London Colney	
WR960	Avro 696 Shackleton AEW2 (8772M)	Gr Manchester Mus of Science & Industry	
WR963	Avro 696 Shackleton AEW2	Air Atlantique Classic Flight, Coventry	
WR971	Avro 696 Shackleton MR3 (8119M) [Q]	Fenland & W Norfolk Aviation Museum, Wisbech	
WR974	Avro 696 Shackleton MR3 (8117M) [K]	Gatwick Aviation Museum, Charlwood, Surrey	
WR977	Avro 696 Shackleton MR3 (8186M)	Newark Air Museum, Winthorpe	
WR982	Avro 696 Shackleton MR3 (8106M) [J]	Gatwick Aviation Museum, Charlwood, Surrey	
WR985	Avro 696 Shackleton MR3 (8103M) [H]	Privately owned, Long Marston	
WS103	Gloster Meteor T7 [709/VL]	FAA Museum, stored RNAS Yeovilton	
WS692	Gloster Meteor NF12 (7605M) [C]	Newark Air Museum, Winthorpe	
WS726	Gloster Meteor NF14 (7960M) [G]	No 1855 Sqn ATC, Royton, Gr Manchester	
WS739	Gloster Meteor NF14 (7961M)	Newark Air Museum, Winthorpe	
WS760	Gloster Meteor NF14 (7964M)	Meteor Flight, stored Yatesbury	
WS774	Gloster Meteor NF14 (7959M)	Privately owned, Quedgeley, Glos	
WS776	Gloster Meteor NF14 (7716M) [K]	Privately owned, Armthorpe	
WS788	Gloster Meteor NF14 (7967M) [Z]	Yorkshire Air Museum, Elvington	
WS792	Gloster Meteor NF14 (7965M) [K]	Brighouse Bay Caravan Park, Borgue, D&G	
WS807	Gloster Meteor NF14 (7973M) [N]	Gloucestershire Avn Coll, stored Gloucester	
WS832	Gloster Meteor NF14 [W]	Solway Aviation Society, Carlisle	
WS838	Gloster Meteor NF14	Midland Air Museum, Coventry	
WS843	Gloster Meteor NF14 (7937M) [Y]	RAF Museum Restoration Centre, Cosford	
WT121	Douglas Skyraider AEW1 [415/CU]	FAA Museum, stored RNAS Yeovilton	
WT205	EE Canberra B15 <ff>	RAF Manston History Museum	
WT308	EE Canberra B(I)6	RN, Predannack Fire School	
WT309	EE Canberra B(I)6 <ff>	Farnborough Air Sciences Trust, Farnborough	
WT319	EE Canberra B(I)6 <ff>	Privately owned, Lavendon, Bucks	
WT333	EE Canberra B6(mod) (G-BVXC)	Privately owned, Bruntingthorpe	
WT339	EE Canberra B(I)8 (8198M)	RAF Barkston Heath Fire Section	
WT480	EE Canberra T4 [AT]	RAF, stored Shawbury	
WT482	EE Canberra T4 <ff>	Privately owned	
WT483	EE Canberra T4 [83]	Privately owned, Long Marston	

Notes	Serial	Type (other identity) [code]	Owner/operator, location or fate
	WT486	EE Canberra T4 (8102M) <ff>	Privately owned, Gilnahirk, Belfast
	WT507	EE Canberra PR7 (8131M/8548M) [44] <ff>	No 384 Sqn ATC, Mansfield
	WT509	EE Canberra PR7 [BR]	RAF Marham Fire Section
	WT510	EE Canberra T22 <ff>	*Scrapped at Stock*
	WT519	EE Canberra PR7 [CH]	RAF Wyton, Fire Section
	WT520	EE Canberra PR7 (8094M/8184M) <ff>	No 967 Sqn ATC, Warton
	WT525	EE Canberra T22 <ff>	Privately owned, South Woodham Ferrers
	WT532	EE Canberra PR7 (8728M/8890M) <ff>	Bournemouth Aviation Museum
	WT534	EE Canberra PR7 (8549M) [43] <ff>	Aeroventure, Doncaster
	WT536	EE Canberra PR7 (8063M) <ff>	Privately owned, Shirrell Heath, Hants
	WT537	EE Canberra PR7	BAE Systems Samlesbury, on display
	WT555	Hawker Hunter F1 (7499M)	Vanguard Haulage, Greenford, London
	WT569	Hawker Hunter F1 (7491M)	No 2117 Sqn ATC, Kenfig Hill, Mid-Glamorgan
	WT612	Hawker Hunter F1 (7496M)	RAF Henlow, on display
	WT619	Hawker Hunter F1 (7525M)	Gr Manchester Mus of Science & Industry
	WT648	Hawker Hunter F1 (7530M) <ff>	Boscombe Down Aviation Collection
	WT651	Hawker Hunter F1 (7532M) [C]	Newark Air Museum, Winthorpe
	WT660	Hawker Hunter F1 (7421M) [C]	Highland Aircraft Preservation Society, Inverness
	WT680	Hawker Hunter F1 (7533M) [J]	Privately owned, Holbeach, Lincs
	WT684	Hawker Hunter F1 (7422M) <ff>	Privately owned, Lavendon, Bucks
	WT694	Hawker Hunter F1 (7510M)	Caernarfon Air World
	WT711	Hawker Hunter GA11 [833/DD]	Air Atlantique Classic Flight, Coventry
	WT720	Hawker Hunter F51 (RDAF E-408/ 8565M) [B]	RAF Sealand, on display
	WT722	Hawker Hunter T8C (G-BWGN) [878/VL]	Hunter Flying Club, Exeter
	WT723	Hawker Hunter PR11 (G-PRII) [866/VL,3]	Privately owned, Exeter
	WT744	Hawker Hunter GA11 [868/VL]	South West Aviation Heritage, Eaglescott
	WT799	Hawker Hunter T8C [879]	Hunter Flying Club, Exeter
	WT804	Hawker Hunter GA11 [831/DD]	FETC, Moreton-in-Marsh, Glos
	WT806	Hawker Hunter GA11	Northbrook College, Shoreham Airport
	WT859	Supermarine 544 <ff>	Boscombe Down Aviation Collection
	WT867	Slingsby T31B Cadet TX3	Privately owned, Eaglescott
	WT871	Slingsby T31B Cadet TX3 (BGA3149)	Privately owned, Marham
	WT877	Slingsby T31B Cadet TX3	Boulton Paul Association, Wolverhampton
	WT898	Slingsby T31B Cadet TX3 (BGA3284/BGA4412)	*To BGA4412*
	WT899	Slingsby T31B Cadet TX3	Privately owned, stored Swindon
	WT905	Slingsby T31B Cadet TX3	Privately owned, Keevil
	WT908	Slingsby T31B Cadet TX3 (BGA3487)	Privately owned, Dunstable
	WT910	Slingsby T31B Cadet TX3 (BGA3953)	Privately owned, Swansea
	WT914	Slingsby T31B Cadet TX3 (BGA3194) (fuselage)	Privately owned, Tibenham
	WT933	Bristol 171 Sycamore 3 (G-ALSW/ 7709M)	Newark Air Museum, Winthorpe
	WV106	Douglas Skyraider AEW1 [427/C]	FAA Museum, stored Yeovilton
	WV198	Sikorsky S55 Whirlwind HAR21 (G-BJWY) [K]	Solway Aviation Society, Carlisle
	WV276	Hawker Hunter F4 (7847M) [D]	Privately owned, stored Scampton
	WV318	Hawker Hunter T7B (9236M/ G-FFOX)	Delta Jets, Kemble
	WV322	Hawker Hunter T8C (G-BZSE/ 9096M) [Y]	Privately owned, Kemble
	WV332	Hawker Hunter F4 (7673M) <ff>	Tangmere Military Aircraft Museum
	WV372	Hawker Hunter T7 (G-BXFI) [R]	Privately owned, Kemble
	WV381	Hawker Hunter GA11 [732/VL] (fuselage)	UKAEA, Culham, Oxon
	WV382	Hawker Hunter GA11 [830/VL]	Jet Avn Preservation Grp, Long Marston
	WV383	Hawker Hunter T7	Farnborough Air Sciences Trust, Farnborough
	WV396	Hawker Hunter T8C (9249M) [91]	RAF Valley, at main gate

Serial	Type (other identity) [code]	Owner/operator, location or fate	Notes
WV483	Percival P56 Provost T1 (7693M) [N-E]	Privately owned	
WV486	Percival P56 Provost T1 (7694M) [N-D]	Privately owned, Thatcham, Berks	
WV493	Percival P56 Provost T1 (G-BDYG/ 7696M) [29]	Royal Scottish Mus'm of Flight, stored E Fortune	
WV499	Percival P56 Provost T1 (G-BZRF/ 7698M) [P-G]	Privately owned, Booker	
WV562	Percival P56 Provost T1 (7606M) [P-C]	RAF Museum, Cosford	
WV605	Percival P56 Provost T1 [T-B]	Norfolk & Suffolk Avn Museum, Flixton	
WV606	Percival P56 Provost T1 (7622M) [P-B]	Newark Air Museum, Winthorpe	
WV679	Percival P56 Provost T1 (7615M) [O-J]	Wellesbourne Wartime Museum	
WV703	Percival P66 Pembroke C1 (8108M/*G-IIIM*)	*Scrapped at Tattershall Thorpe*	
WV705	Percival P66 Pembroke C1 <ff>	Privately owned, Awbridge, Hants	
WV740	Percival P66 Pembroke C1 (G-BNPH)	Privately owned, Bournemouth	
WV746	Percival P66 Pembroke C1 (8938M)	RAF Museum, Cosford	
WV753	Percival P66 Pembroke C1 (8113M)	*Burnt at Cardiff International Airport*	
WV781	Bristol 171 Sycamore HR12 (G-ALTD/7839M)	Caernarfon Air World	
WV783	Bristol 171 Sycamore HR12 (G-ALSP/7841M)	RAF Museum, Hendon	
WV787	EE Canberra B2/8 (8799M)	Newark Air Museum, Winthorpe	
WV795	Hawker Sea Hawk FGA6 (8151M)	Farnborough Air Sciences Trust, Farnborough	
WV797	Hawker Sea Hawk FGA6 (8155M) [491/J]	Midland Air Museum, Coventry	
WV798	Hawker Sea Hawk FGA6 [026/CU]	SWWAPS, Lasham	
WV838	Hawker Sea Hawk FGA4 <ff>	Privately owned, Liverpool	
WV856	Hawker Sea Hawk FGA6 [163]	FAA Museum, RNAS Yeovilton	
WV903	Hawker Sea Hawk FGA4 (8153M) [128/C]	RNAS Yeovilton Fire Section	
WV908	Hawker Sea Hawk FGA6 (8154M) [188/A]	RN Historic Flight, Yeovilton	
WV910	Hawker Sea Hawk FGA6 <ff>	Boscombe Down Aviation Collection	
WV911	Hawker Sea Hawk FGA4 [115/C]	RN Historic Flight, Yeovilton	
WW138	DH112 Sea Venom FAW22 [227/Z]	FAA Museum, stored RNAS Yeovilton	
WW145	DH112 Sea Venom FAW22 [680/LM]	Royal Scottish Mus'm of Flight, E Fortune	
WW217	DH112 Sea Venom FAW22 [351]	Newark Air Museum, Winthorpe	
WW388	Percival P56 Provost T1 (7616M) [O-F]	Bomber County Aviation Museum, Hemswell	
WW421	Percival P56 Provost T1 (G-BZRE/ 7688M) [P-B]	Privately owned, Armthorpe	
WW442	Percival P56 Provost T1 (7618M) [N]	Gatwick Aviation Museum, Charlwood, Surrey	
WW444	Percival P56 Provost T1 [D]	Privately owned, Brownhills, Staffs	
WW447	Percival P56 Provost T1	Privately owned, Grazeley, Berks	
WW453	Percival P56 Provost T1 (G-TMKI) [W-S]	Privately owned, Clevedon	
WW654	Hawker Hunter GA11 [834/DD]	Privately owned, Ford, W Sussex	
WX788	DH112 Venom NF3	Aeroventure, Doncaster	
WX853	DH112 Venom NF3 (7443M)	Mosquito Aircraft Museum, London Colney	
WX905	DH112 Venom NF3 (7458M)	Newark Air Museum, Winthorpe	
WZ425	DH115 Vampire T11	Privately owned, Birlingham, Worcs	
WZ450	DH115 Vampire T11 <ff>	Lashenden Air Warfare Museum, Headcorn	
WZ507	DH115 Vampire T11 (G-VTII) [74]	De Havilland Aviation, Bournemouth	
WZ515	DH115 Vampire T11 [60]	Solway Aviation Society, Carlisle	
WZ518	DH115 Vampire T11	North-East Aircraft Museum, Usworth	
WZ549	DH115 Vampire T11 (8118M) [F]	Ulster Aviation Society, Langford Lodge	
WZ553	DH115 Vampire T11 (G-DHYY) [40]	Air Atlantique Classic Flight, Coventry	
WZ557	DH115 Vampire T11	Highland Aircraft Preservation Society, Inverness	

Notes	Serial	Type (other identity) [code]	Owner/operator, location or fate
	WZ572	DH115 Vampire T11 (8124M) [65] <ff>	Privately owned, Sholing, Hants
	WZ581	DH115 Vampire T11 <ff>	The Vampire Collection, Hemel Hempstead
	WZ584	DH115 Vampire T11 (G-BZRC) [K]	Privately owned, Armthorpe
	WZ589	DH115 Vampire T11 [19]	Privately owned, Rochester
	WZ589	DH115 Vampire T55 (U-1230/ G-DHZZ)	Source Classic Jet Flight, Bournemouth
	WZ590	DH115 Vampire T11 [19]	Imperial War Museum, Duxford
	WZ620	DH115 Vampire T11 [68]	*Currently not known*
	WZ662	Auster AOP9 (G-BKVK)	Privately owned, Eggesford
	WZ706	Auster AOP9 (7851M/G-BURR)	Privately owned, Middle Wallop
	WZ711	Auster AOP9/Beagle E3 (G-AVHT)	Privately owned, Spanhoe Lodge
	WZ721	Auster AOP9	Museum of Army Flying, Middle Wallop
	WZ724	Auster AOP9 (7432M)	AAC Middle Wallop, at main gate
	WZ729	Auster AOP9 (G-BXON)	Privately owned, Newark-on-Trent
	WZ736	Avro 707A (7868M)	Gr Manchester Mus of Science & Industry
	WZ744	Avro 707C (7932M)	RAF Museum, Cosford
	WZ753	Slingsby T38 Grasshopper TX1	Solent Sky, Southampton
	WZ755	Slingsby T38 Grasshopper TX1 (BGA3481)	Boulton Paul Association, Wolverhampton
	WZ757	Slingsby T38 Grasshopper TX1 (comp XK820)	Privately owned, Kirton-in-Lindsey, Lincs
	WZ767	Slingsby T38 Grasshopper TX1	North-East Aircraft Museum, stored Usworth
	WZ772	Slingsby T38 Grasshopper TX1	Museum of Army Flying, Middle Wallop
	WZ773	Slingsby T38 Grasshopper TX1	Edinburgh Academy
	WZ779	Slingsby T38 Grasshopper TX1	Privately owned,
	WZ784	Slingsby T38 Grasshopper TX1	Solway Aviation Society, Carlisle
	WZ791	Slingsby T38 Grasshopper TX1 (8944M)	RAF Museum, Hendon
	WZ792	Slingsby T38 Grasshopper TX1	Privately owned, Sproughton
	WZ793	Slingsby T38 Grasshopper TX1	Privately owned, Keevil
	WZ796	Slingsby T38 Grasshopper TX1	*Broken up*
	WZ798	Slingsby T38 Grasshopper TX1	Bournemouth Aviation Museum
	WZ816	Slingsby T38 Grasshopper TX1 (BGA3979)	Privately owned, Redhill
	WZ819	Slingsby T38 Grasshopper TX1 (BGA3498)	Privately owned, Halton
	WZ820	Slingsby T38 Grasshopper TX1	Sywell Aviation Museum
	WZ822	Slingsby T38 Grasshopper TX1	Aeroventure, stored Doncaster
	WZ824	Slingsby T38 Grasshopper TX1	Privately owned, stored Strathaven, Strathclyde
	WZ826	Vickers Valiant B(K)1 (XD826/ 7872M) <ff>	Privately owned, Rayleigh, Essex
	WZ827	Slingsby T38 Grasshopper TX1	Privately owned, Keevil
	WZ828	Slingsby T38 Grasshopper TX1 (BGA4421)	Privately owned, Bicester
	WZ831	Slingsby T38 Grasshopper TX1	Privately owned, stored Nympsfield, Glos
	WZ846	DHC1 Chipmunk T10 (G-BCSC/ 8439M)	No 2427 Sqn ATC, Biggin Hill
	WZ847	DHC1 Chipmunk T10 (G-CPMK) [F]	Privately owned, Sleap
	WZ872	DHC1 Chipmunk T10 (G-BZGB) [E]	Privately owned, Newcastle
	WZ876	DHC1 Chipmunk T10 (G-BBWN) <ff>	Privately owned, Yateley, Hants
	WZ879	DHC1 Chipmunk T10 (G-BWUT) [X]	Privately owned, Duxford
	WZ882	DHC1 Chipmunk T10 (G-BXGP) [K]	Privately owned, Eaglescott
	XA109	DH115 Sea Vampire T22	Royal Scottish Mus'm of Flight, E Fortune
	XA127	DH115 Sea Vampire T22 <ff>	FAA Museum, RNAS Yeovilton
	XA129	DH115 Sea Vampire T22	FAA Museum, stored RNAS Yeovilton
	XA225	Slingsby T38 Grasshopper TX1	Privately owned, Upavon
	XA226	Slingsby T38 Grasshopper TX1	Norfolk & Suffolk Avn Museum, Flixton
	XA228	Slingsby T38 Grasshopper TX1	Royal Scottish Mus'm of Flight, E Fortune
	XA230	Slingsby T38 Grasshopper TX1 (BGA4098)	Privately owned, Henlow
	XA231	Slingsby T38 Grasshopper TX1 (8888M)	RAF Manston History Museum

Serial	Type (other identity) [code]	Owner/operator, location or fate	Notes
XA240	Slingsby T38 Grasshopper TX1 (BGA4556)	Privately owned, Keevil	
XA241	Slingsby T38 Grasshopper TX1	Shuttleworth Collection, Old Warden	
XA243	Slingsby T38 Grasshopper TX1 (8886M)	Privately owned, Gransden Lodge, Cambs	
XA244	Slingsby T38 Grasshopper TX1	Privately owned, Keevil	
XA282	Slingsby T31B Cadet TX3	Caernarfon Air World	
XA286	Slingsby T31B Cadet TX3	*Sold to Holland*	
XA289	Slingsby T31B Cadet TX3	Privately owned, Eaglescott	
XA290	Slingsby T31B Cadet TX3	Privately owned, stored Rufforth	
XA293	Slingsby T31B Cadet TX3 <ff>	Privately owned, Breighton	
XA302	Slingsby T31B Cadet TX3 (BGA3786)	Privately owned, Syerston	
XA310	Slingsby T31B Cadet TX3 (BGA4963)	Privately owned, Keevil	
XA459	Fairey Gannet ECM6 [E]	Privately owned, Lambourn, Berks	
XA460	Fairey Gannet ECM6 [768/BY]	Aeroventure, Doncaster	
XA466	Fairey Gannet COD4 [777/LM]	FAA Museum, stored Yeovilton	
XA508	Fairey Gannet T2 [627/GN]	FAA Museum, at Midland Air Museum, Coventry	
XA564	Gloster Javelin FAW1 (7464M)	RAF Museum, Cosford	
XA634	Gloster Javelin FAW4 (7641M)	RAF Leeming, on display	
XA699	Gloster Javelin FAW5 (7809M)	Midland Air Museum, Coventry	
XA847	EE P1B (8371M)	Privately owned, Stowmarket, Suffolk	
XA862	WS55 Whirlwind HAR1 (G-AMJT) [9]	The Helicopter Museum, Weston-super-Mare	
XA864	WS55 Whirlwind HAR1	FAA Museum, stored Yeovilton	
XA870	WS55 Whirlwind HAR1 [911]	Aeroventure, Doncaster	
XA880	DH104 Devon C2 (G-BVXR)	Privately owned, Kemble	
XA893	Avro 698 Vulcan B1 (8591M) <ff>	RAF Museum, Cosford	
XA903	Avro 698 Vulcan B1 <ff>	Privately owned, Wellesbourne Mountford	
XA917	HP80 Victor B1 (7827M) <ff>	Privately owned, Pitscottie, Fife	
XB259	Blackburn B101 Beverley C1 (G-AOAI)	Fort Paull Armoury	
XB261	Blackburn B101 Beverley C1 <ff>	Newark Air Museum, Winthorpe	
XB446	Grumman TBM-3 Avenger ECM6B	FAA Museum, Yeovilton	
XB480	Hiller HT1 [537]	FAA Museum, stored Yeovilton	
XB812	Canadair CL-13 Sabre F4 (9227M) [U]	RAF Museum, Hendon	
XD145	Saro SR53	RAF Museum, Cosford	
XD163	WS55 Whirlwind HAR10 (8645M)	The Helicopter Museum, Weston-super-Mare	
XD165	WS55 Whirlwind HAR10 (8673M) [B]	Yorkshire Helicopter Pres Grp, stored Doncaster	
XD215	VS Scimitar F1 <ff>	Privately owned, Cheltenham	
XD235	VS Scimitar F1 <ff>	Privately owned, Ingatestone, Essex	
XD317	VS Scimitar F1 [112/R]	FAA Museum, RNAS Yeovilton	
XD332	VS Scimitar F1 [194/C]	Solent Sky, stored	
XD377	DH115 Vampire T11 (8203M) <ff>	Aeroventure, stored Doncaster	
XD382	DH115 Vampire T11 (8033M)	East Midlands Airport Aeropark	
XD425	DH115 Vampire T11 <ff>	RAF Millom Museum, Haverigg	
XD434	DH115 Vampire T11 [25]	Fenland & W Norfolk Aviation Museum, Wisbech	
XD445	DH115 Vampire T11	Bomber County Aviation Museum, Hemswell	
XD447	DH115 Vampire T11 [50]	Jet Avn Preservation Grp, Long Marston	
XD452	DH115 Vampire T11 (7990M) [66] <ff>	Privately owned, Chester	
XD459	DH115 Vampire T11 [63] <ff>	Aeroventure, stored Doncaster	
XD506	DH115 Vampire T11 (7983M)	Gloucestershire Avn Coll, stored Gloucester	
XD515	DH115 Vampire T11 (7998M/ *XM515*)	Privately owned, Rugeley, Staffs	
XD525	DH115 Vampire T11 (7882M) <ff>	Campbell College, Belfast	
XD528	DH115 Vampire T11 (8159M) <ff>	*Scrapped at Gamston*	
XD534	DH115 Vampire T11 [41]	East Midlands Airport Aeropark	
XD536	DH115 Vampire T11 (7734M) [H]	*Scrapped*	
XD542	DH115 Vampire T11 (7604M) [N]	Montrose Air Station Museum	
XD547	DH115 Vampire T11 [Z] (composite)	Dumfries & Galloway Avn Mus, Dumfries	
XD593	DH115 Vampire T11 [50]	Newark Air Museum, Winthorpe	

Notes	Serial	Type (other identity) [code]	Owner/operator, location or fate
	XD595	DH115 Vampire T11 <ff>	Privately owned, Glentham, Lincs
	XD596	DH115 Vampire T11 (7939M)	Southampton Hall of Aviation
	XD599	DH115 Vampire T11 [A] <ff>	Sywell Aviation Museum
	XD602	DH115 Vampire T11 (7737M) (composite)	Privately owned, South Shields
	XD616	DH115 Vampire T11 [56]	Mosquito Aircraft Museum, stored Gloucester
	XD622	DH115 Vampire T11 (8160M)	No 2214 Sqn ATC, Usworth
	XD624	DH115 Vampire T11 [O]	Manchester Airport, on display
	XD626	DH115 Vampire T11 [Q]	Midland Air Museum, Coventry
	XD674	Hunting Jet Provost T1 (7570M) [T]	RAF Museum, stored Cosford
	XD693	Hunting Jet Provost T1 (XM129/ G-AOBU) [Z-Q]	Kennet Aviation, North Weald
	XD816	Vickers Valiant B(K)1 <ff>	Brooklands Museum, Weybridge
	XD818	Vickers Valiant B(K)1 (7894M)	RAF Museum, Hendon
	XD857	Vickers Valiant B(K)1 <ff>	RAF Manston History Museum
	XD875	Vickers Valiant B(K)1 <ff>	Highland Aircraft Preservation Group, Dalcross
	XE317	Bristol 171 Sycamore HR14 (G-AMWO) [S-N]	Aeroventure, stored Doncaster
	XE339	Hawker Sea Hawk FGA6 (8156M) [149/E]	RNAS Yeovilton Fire Section
	XE340	Hawker Sea Hawk FGA6 [131/Z]	FAA Museum, at Montrose Air Station Museum
	XE368	Hawker Sea Hawk FGA6 [200/J]	Phoenix Aviation, Bruntingthorpe
	XE489	Hawker Sea Hawk FGA6 (G-JETH)	Gatwick Aviation Museum, Charlwood, Surrey
	XE521	Fairey Rotodyne Y (parts)	The Helicopter Museum, Weston-super-Mare
	XE584	Hawker Hunter FGA9 <ff>	NW Aviation Heritage Group, Hooton Park
	XE597	Hawker Hunter FGA9 (8874M) <ff>	Privately owned, Bromsgrove
	XE601	Hawker Hunter FGA9 (G-ETPS)	Privately owned, Exeter
	XE606	Hawker Hunter F6A (*XJ673*/ 8841M)	RAF Cottesmore, preserved
	XE624	Hawker Hunter FGA9 (8875M) [G]	Privately owned,
	XE627	Hawker Hunter F6A [T]	Imperial War Museum, Duxford
	XE643	Hawker Hunter FGA9 (8586M) <ff>	RAF M&RU, Aldergrove
	XE664	Hawker Hunter F4 <ff>	Gloucestershire Avn Coll, stored Gloucester
	XE665	Hawker Hunter T8C (G-BWGM) [876/VL]	Hunter Flying Club, Exeter
	XE668	Hawker Hunter GA11 [832/DD]	RN, Predannack Fire School
	XE670	Hawker Hunter F4 (7762M/8585M) <ff>	RAF Museum, Cosford
	XE683	Hawker Hunter F51 (RDAF E-409) [G]	City of Norwich Aviation Museum
	XE685	Hawker Hunter GA11 (G-GAII) [861/VL]	Privately owned, Exeter
	XE689	Hawker Hunter GA11 (G-BWGK) [864/VL]	Hunter Flying Club, Exeter
	XE786	Slingsby T31B Cadet TX3 (BGA4033)	Privately owned, Arbroath
	XE793	Slingsby T31B Cadet TX3 (8666M)	Privately owned, Tamworth
	XE796	Slingsby T31B Cadet TX3 (BGA4746)	Privately owned, stored North Weald
	XE799	Slingsby T31B Cadet TX3 (8943M) [R]	Boulton Paul Association, Wolverhampton
	XE802	Slingsby T31B Cadet TX3	Privately owned, stored Cupar, Fife
	XE849	DH115 Vampire T11 (7928M) [V3]	Privately owned, Corby
	XE852	DH115 Vampire T11 [H]	No 2247 Sqn ATC, Hawarden
	XE855	DH115 Vampire T11	Midland Air Museum, Coventry
	XE856	DH115 Vampire T11 (G-DUSK)	Privately owned, Henlow
	XE864	DH115 Vampire T11(comp XD435) <ff>	Privately owned, Ingatstone, Essex
	XE872	DH115 Vampire T11 [62]	Midland Air Museum, Coventry
	XE874	DH115 Vampire T11 (8582M)	Montrose Air Station Museum
	XE897	DH115 Vampire T11 (XD403)	Privately owned, Errol, Tayside
	XE897	DH115 Vampire T55 (U-1214/ G-DHVV)	Source Classic Jet Flight, Bournemouth
	XE920	DH115 Vampire T11 (8196M/ G-VMPR) [A]	The Jet Fighter Experience, Swansea
	XE921	DH115 Vampire T11 [64] <ff>	Privately owned, Yarmouth, IoW

Serial	Type (other identity) [code]	Owner/operator, location or fate	Notes
XE935	DH115 Vampire T11	Aeroventure, Doncaster	
XE946	DH115 Vampire T11 (7473M) <ff>	RAF Cranwell Aviation Heritage Centre	
XE956	DH115 Vampire T11 (G-OBLN)	De Havilland Aviation, stored Rochester	
XE979	DH115 Vampire T11 [54]	Privately owned, Birlingham, Worcs	
XE982	DH115 Vampire T11 (7564M) [01]	Privately owned, Weston, Eire	
XE985	DH115 Vampire T11 (*WZ476*)	De Havilland Aviation, Bridgend	
XE993	DH115 Vampire T11 (8161M)	Privately owned, Cosford	
XE995	DH115 Vampire T11 [53]	*Scrapped*	
XE998	DH115 Vampire T11 (*U-1215*)	Solent Sky, Southampton	
XF113	VS Swift F7 [19] <ff>	Boscombe Down Aviation Collection	
XF114	VS Swift F7 (G-SWIF)	Southampton Hall of Aviation, stored	
XF303	Hawker Hunter F58A (J-4105/ G-BWOU) [105,A]	The Old Flying Machine Company, Scampton	
XF314	Hawker Hunter F51 (RDAF E-412) [N]	Privately owned, Bruntingthorpe	
XF321	Hawker Hunter T7	Phoenix Aviation, Bruntingthorpe	
XF324	Hawker Hunter F51 (RDAF E-427) [D]	British Aviation Heritage, Bruntingthorpe	
XF358	Hawker Hunter T8C [870/VL] <rf>	Privately owned, Exeter	
XF375	Hawker Hunter F6A (8736M/ G-BUEZ) [05]	Privately owned, Spanhoe	
XF382	Hawker Hunter F6A [15]	Midland Air Museum, Coventry	
XF383	Hawker Hunter F6 (8706M) <ff>	Privately owned, Kidlington	
XF418	Hawker Hunter F51 (RDAF E-430)	Gatwick Aviation Museum, Charlwood, Surrey	
XF506	Hawker Hunter F4 (WT746/7770M) [A]	Dumfries & Galloway Avn Mus, Dumfries	
XF509	Hawker Hunter F6 (8708M)	Humbrol Paints, Marfleet, E Yorkshire	
XF515	Hawker Hunter F6A (8830M/ G-KAXF) [R]	Kennet Aviation, North Weald	
XF522	Hawker Hunter F6 <ff>	No 2352 Sqn ATC, Milton Keynes	
XF526	Hawker Hunter F6 (8679M) [78/E]	Privately owned, Birlingham, Worcs	
XF527	Hawker Hunter F6 (8680M)	RAF Halton, on display	
XF545	Percival P56 Provost T1 (7957M) [O-K]	Privately owned, Thatcham	
XF597	Percival P56 Provost T1 (G-BKFW) [AH]	Privately owned, Thatcham	
XF603	Percival P56 Provost T1 (G-KAPW)	Kennet Aviation, North Weald	
XF690	Percival P56 Provost T1 (8041M/ G-MOOS)	Kennet Aviation, North Weald	
XF708	Avro 716 Shackleton MR3 [203/C]	Imperial War Museum, Duxford	
XF785	Bristol 173 (7648M/G-ALBN)	Bristol Aero Collection, Kemble	
XF836	Percival P56 Provost T1 (8043M/ G-AWRY) [JG]	Privately owned, Thatcham	
XF844	Percival P56 Provost T1 [70]	British Aviation Heritage, Bruntingthorpe	
XF877	Percival P56 Provost T1 (G-AWVF) [JX]	Privately owned, Brimpton, Berks	
XF926	Bristol 188 (8368M)	RAF Museum, Cosford	
XF994	Hawker Hunter T8C [873/VL]	Boscombe Down Aviation Collection	
XF995	Hawker Hunter T8B (G-BZSF/ 9237M) [K]	Delta Jets, Kemble	
XG154	Hawker Hunter FGA9 (8863M) [54]	RAF Museum, Hendon	
XG160	Hawker Hunter F6A (8831M/ G-BWAF) [U]	Bournemouth Aviation Museum	
XG164	Hawker Hunter F6 (8681M)	Privately owned, Wellington, Somerset	
XG168	Hawker Hunter F6A (XG172/ 8832M) [A]	City of Norwich Aviation Museum	
XG172	Hawker Hunter F6A (8832M) [A]	*Repainted as XG168*	
XG190	Hawker Hunter F51 (RDAF E-425) [C]	Midland Air Museum, Coventry	
XG193	Hawker Hunter FGA9 (XG297) (comp with WT741)	Bomber County Aviation Museum, Hemswell	
XG195	Hawker Hunter FGA9 <ff>	Privately owned, Lewes	
XG196	Hawker Hunter F6A (8702M) [31]	Army, Mytchett, Surrey, on display	
XG209	Hawker Hunter F6 (8709M) <ff>	*Currently not known*	
XG210	Hawker Hunter F6	Privately owned, Beck Row, Suffolk	
XG225	Hawker Hunter F6A (8713M) [S]	RAF Cosford, at main gate	
XG226	Hawker Hunter F6A (8800M) [28] <ff>	RAF Manston History Museum	
XG252	Hawker Hunter FGA9 (8840M) [U]	Privately owned, Bosbury, Hereford	
XG254	Hawker Hunter FGA9 (8881M)	Norfolk & Suffolk Avn Museum, Flixton	

Notes	Serial	Type (other identity) [code]	Owner/operator, location or fate
	XG274	Hawker Hunter F6 (8710M) [71]	Privately owned, Newmarket
	XG290	Hawker Hunter F6 (8711M) <ff>	Boscombe Down Aviation Collection
	XG297	Hawker Hunter FGA9 <ff>	Aeroventure, Doncaster
	XG325	EE Lightning F1 <ff>	No 1476 Sqn ATC, Southend
	XG329	EE Lightning F1 (8050M)	Privately owned, Flixton
	XG331	EE Lightning F1 <ff>	Gloucestershire Avn Coll, stored Gloucester
	XG337	EE Lightning F1 (8056M) [M]	RAF Museum, Cosford
	XG452	Bristol 192 Belvedere HC1 (7997M/G-BRMB)	The Helicopter Museum, Weston-super-Mare
	XG454	Bristol 192 Belvedere HC1 (8366M)	Gr Manchester Mus of Science & Industry
	XG462	Bristol 192 Belvedere HC1 <ff>	The Helicopter Museum, stored Weston-super-Mare
	XG474	Bristol 192 Belvedere HC1 (8367M) [O]	RAF Museum, Hendon
	XG502	Bristol 171 Sycamore HR14	Museum of Army Flying, Middle Wallop
	XG506	Bristol 171 Sycamore HR14 (7852M) <ff>	*Scrapped*
	XG518	Bristol 171 Sycamore HR14 (8009M) [S-E]	Norfolk & Suffolk Avn Museum, Flixton
	XG523	Bristol 171 Sycamore HR14 <ff> [K]	Norfolk & Suffolk Avn Museum, Flixton
	XG544	Bristol 171 Sycamore HR14	Privately owned,
	XG547	Bristol 171 Sycamore HR14 (G-HAPR) [S-T]	The Helicopter Museum, Weston-super-Mare
	XG574	WS55 Whirlwind HAR3 [752/PO]	FAA Museum, stored RNAS Yeovilton
	XG577	WS55 Whirlwind HAR3 (9050M)	*Scrapped at Leconfield*
	XG588	WS55 Whirlwind HAR3 (G-BAMH/ VR-BEP)	East Midlands Airport Aeropark
	XG592	WS55 Whirlwind HAS7	*Task Force* Adventure Park, Cowbridge, S Glam
	XG594	WS55 Whirlwind HAS7 [517/PO]	FAA Museum, stored Yeovilton
	XG596	WS55 Whirlwind HAS7 [66]	The Helicopter Museum, Weston-super-Mare
	XG613	DH112 Sea Venom FAW21	Imperial War Museum, Duxford
	XG629	DH112 Sea Venom FAW22	Privately owned, Stone, Staffs
	XG680	DH112 Sea Venom FAW22 [438]	North-East Aircraft Museum, Usworth
	XG691	DH112 Sea Venom FAW22 [93/J]	Gloucestershire Avn Coll, stored Gloucester
	XG692	DH112 Sea Venom FAW22 [668/LM]	Privately owned, Stone, Staffs
	XG730	DH112 Sea Venom FAW22 [499/A]	Mosquito Aircraft Museum, London Colney
	XG736	DH112 Sea Venom FAW22	Ulster Aviation Society, Newtownards
	XG737	DH112 Sea Venom FAW22 [220/Z]	Jet Avn Preservation Grp, stored Long Marston
	XG743	DH115 Sea Vampire T22 [597/LM]	Imperial War Museum, Duxford
	XG775	DH115 Vampire T55 (U-1219/ G-DHWW) [VL]	Source Classic Jet Flight, Bournemouth
	XG797	Fairey Gannet ECM6 [277]	Imperial War Museum, Duxford
	XG831	Fairey Gannet ECM6 [396]	Flambards Village Theme Park, Helston
	XG882	Fairey Gannet T5 (8754M) [771/LM]	Privately owned, Errol, Tayside
	XG883	Fairey Gannet T5 [773/BY]	FAA Museum, at Museum of Berkshire Aviation, Woodley
	XG900	Short SC1	Science Museum, South Kensington
	XG905	Short SC1	Ulster Folk & Transpt Mus, Holywood, Co Down
	XH131	EE Canberra PR9	RAF No 39(1 PRU) Sqn, Marham
	XH134	EE Canberra PR9	RAF No 39(1 PRU) Sqn, Marham
	XH135	EE Canberra PR9	RAF No 39(1 PRU) Sqn, Marham
	XH136	EE Canberra PR9 (8782M) [W] <ff>	Phoenix Aviation, Bruntingthorpe
	XH165	EE Canberra PR9 <ff>	Blyth Valley Aviation Collection, Walpole
	XH168	EE Canberra PR9	RAF Marham (damaged)
	XH169	EE Canberra PR9	RAF No 39(1 PRU) Sqn, Marham
	XH170	EE Canberra PR9 (8739M)	RAF Wyton, on display
	XH171	EE Canberra PR9 (8746M) [U]	RAF Museum, Cosford
	XH174	EE Canberra PR9 <ff>	RAF, stored Shawbury
	XH175	EE Canberra PR9 <ff>	Privately owned, Stock, Essex
	XH177	EE Canberra PR9 <ff>	Newark Air Museum, Winthorpe
	XH278	DH115 Vampire T11 (8595M/ 7866M) [42]	Yorkshire Air Museum, Elvington

Serial	*Type (other identity) [code]*	*Owner/operator, location or fate*	*Notes*
XH312	DH115 Vampire T11 [18]	Privately owned, Dodleston, Cheshire	
XH313	DH115 Vampire T11 (G-BZRD) [E]	Privately owned, Booker	
XH318	DH115 Vampire T11 (7761M) [64]	Privately owned, Sholing, Hants	
XH328	DH115 Vampire T11 <ff>	Mosquito Aircraft Museum, London Colney	
XH330	DH115 Vampire T11 [73]	Privately owned, Camberley, Surrey	
XH537	Avro 698 Vulcan B2MRR (8749M) <ff>	Bournemouth Aviation Museum	
XH558	Avro 698 Vulcan B2 (G-VLCN)	British Aviation Heritage, Bruntingthorpe	
XH560	Avro 698 Vulcan K2 <ff>	Privately owned, Foulness	
XH563	Avro 698 Vulcan B2MRR <ff>	Privately owned, Bruntingthorpe	
XH568	EE Canberra B6(mod) (G-BVIC)	Classic Aviation Projects, Bruntingthorpe	
XH584	EE Canberra T4 (G-27-374) <ff>	Aeroventure, Doncaster	
XH592	HP80 Victor K1A (8429M) <ff>	Phoenix Aviation, Bruntingthorpe	
XH648	HP80 Victor K1A	Imperial War Museum, Duxford	
XH669	HP80 Victor K2 (9092M) <ff>	Privately owned, Foulness	
XH670	HP80 Victor SR2 <ff>	Privately owned, Foulness	
XH672	HP80 Victor K2 (9242M)	RAF Museum, Cosford	
XH673	HP80 Victor K2 (8911M)	RAF Marham, on display	
XH767	Gloster Javelin FAW9 (7955M) [A]	Yorkshire Air Museum, Elvington	
XH783	Gloster Javelin FAW7 (7798M) <ff>	Privately owned, Catford	
XH837	Gloster Javelin FAW7 (8032M) <ff>	Caernarfon Air World	
XH892	Gloster Javelin FAW9R (7982M) [J]	Norfolk & Suffolk Avn Museum, Flixton	
XH897	Gloster Javelin FAW9	Imperial War Museum, Duxford	
XH903	Gloster Javelin FAW9 (7938M)	Gloucestershire Avn Coll, stored Gloucester	
XH992	Gloster Javelin FAW8 (7829M) [P]	Newark Air Museum, Winthorpe	
XJ314	RR Thrust Measuring Rig	Science Museum, South Kensington	
XJ380	Bristol 171 Sycamore HR14 (8628M)	Montrose Air Station Museum	
XJ389	Fairey Jet Gyrodyne (XD759/ G-AJJP)	Museum of Berkshire Aviation, Woodley	
XJ398	WS55 Whirlwind HAR10 (XD768/ G-BDBZ)	Aeroventure, stored Doncaster	
XJ409	WS55 Whirlwind HAR10 (XD779)	Maes Artro Craft Village, Llanbedr	
XJ435	WS55 Whirlwind HAR10 (XD804/ 8671M) [V]	RAF Manston History Museum, spares use	
XJ476	DH110 Sea Vixen FAW1 <ff>	No 424 Sqn ATC, Southampton Hall of Avn	
XJ481	DH110 Sea Vixen FAW1 [VL]	FAA Museum, stored RNAS Yeovilton	
XJ482	DH110 Sea Vixen FAW1 [713/VL]	Norfolk & Suffolk Avn Museum, Flixton	
XJ488	DH110 Sea Vixen FAW1 <ff>	Robertsbridge Aviation Society, Mayfield	
XJ494	DH110 Sea Vixen FAW2	Privately owned, Bruntingthorpe	
XJ560	DH110 Sea Vixen FAW2 (8142M) [242]	Newark Air Museum, Winthorpe	
XJ565	DH110 Sea Vixen FAW2 [127/E]	Mosquito Aircraft Museum, London Colney	
XJ571	DH110 Sea Vixen FAW2 (8140M) [242/R]	Southampton Hall of Aviation	
XJ575	DH110 Sea Vixen FAW2 <ff> [SAH-13]	Wellesbourne Wartime Museum	
XJ579	DH110 Sea Vixen FAW2 <ff>	Midland Air Museum, Coventry	
XJ580	DH110 Sea Vixen FAW2 [131/E]	Tangmere Military Aviation Museum	
XJ615	Hawker Hunter T8C(mod) (XF357/ G-BWGL)	Privately owned, Cranwell	
XJ639	Hawker Hunter F6A (8687M) [H]	Hunter Flying Club, Exeter	
XJ714	Hawker Hunter FR10 (comp XG226)	Jet Avn Preservation Grp, Long Marston	
XJ723	WS55 Whirlwind HAR10	Montrose Air Station Museum	
XJ726	WS55 Whirlwind HAR10 [F]	Caernarfon Air World	
XJ727	WS55 Whirlwind HAR10 (8661M) [L]	RAF Manston History Museum	
XJ758	WS55 Whirlwind HAR10 (8464M) <ff>	Privately owned, Welshpool	
XJ771	DH115 Vampire T55 (U-1215/ G-HELV)	Air Atlantique Classic Flight, Coventry	
XJ772	DH115 Vampire T11 [H]	Mosquito Aircraft Museum, London Colney	
XJ823	Avro 698 Vulcan B2A	Solway Aviation Society, Carlisle	
XJ824	Avro 698 Vulcan B2A	Imperial War Museum, Duxford	
XJ917	Bristol 171 Sycamore HR14 [H-S]	Bristol Sycamore Group, stored Kemble	
XJ918	Bristol 171 Sycamore HR14 (8190M)	RAF Museum, Cosford	

Notes	Serial	Type (other identity) [code]	Owner/operator, location or fate
	XK149	Hawker Hunter F6A (8714M) [L]	*Sold to the USA, 2001*
	XK416	Auster AOP9 (7855M/G-AYUA)	Privately owned, Widmerpool
	XK417	Auster AOP9 (G-AVXY)	Privately owned, Widmerpool
	XK418	Auster AOP9 (7976M)	SWWAPS, Lasham
	XK421	Auster AOP9 (8365M) (frame)	Privately owned, Eggesford
	XK488	Blackburn NA39 Buccaneer S1	FAA Museum, stored RNAS Yeovilton
	XK526	Blackburn NA39 Buccaneer S2 (8648M)	RAF Honington, at main gate
	XK527	Blackburn NA39 Buccaneer S2D (8818M) <ff>	Privately owned, North Wales
	XK532	Blackburn NA39 Buccaneer S1 (8867M) [632/LM]	Highland Aircraft Preservation Group, Dalcross
	XK533	Blackburn NA39 Buccaneer S1 <ff>	Royal Scottish Mus'm of Flight, E Fortune
	XK590	DH115 Vampire T11 [V]	Wellesbourne Wartime Museum
	XK623	DH115 Vampire T11 (*G-VAMP*) [56]	Caernarfon Air World
	XK624	DH115 Vampire T11 [32]	Norfolk & Suffolk Avn Museum, Flixton
	XK625	DH115 Vampire T11 [14]	Brenzett Aeronautical Museum
	XK627	DH115 Vampire T11	Privately owned, Lavendon, Bucks
	XK632	DH115 Vampire T11 [67]	*Scrapped*
	XK637	DH115 Vampire T11 [56]	RAF Millom Museum, Haverigg
	XK655	DH106 Comet C2(RC) (G-AMXA) <ff>	*Currently not known*
	XK695	DH106 Comet C2(RC) (G-AMXH/ 9164M) <ff>	Mosquito Aircraft Museum, London Colney
	XK699	DH106 Comet C2 (7971M)	RAF Lyneham on display
	XK724	Folland Gnat F1 (7715M)	RAF Museum, Cosford
	XK740	Folland Gnat F1 (8396M)	Southampton Hall of Aviation
	XK741	Folland Gnat F1 (fuselage)	*Repainted in Finnish marks, 2004*
	XK776	ML Utility 1	Museum of Army Flying, Middle Wallop
	XK788	Slingsby T38 Grasshopper TX1	Privately owned, Sproughton
	XK789	Slingsby T38 Grasshopper TX1	Midland Air Museum, stored Coventry
	XK790	Slingsby T38 Grasshopper TX1	Privately owned, stored Husbands Bosworth
	XK819	Slingsby T38 Grasshopper TX1	Privately owned, Selby
	XK822	Slingsby T38 Grasshopper TX1	Privately owned, Kenley
	XK895	DH104 Sea Devon C20 (G-SDEV) [19/CU]	Privately owned, Shoreham
	XK896	DH104 Sea Devon C20 (G-RNAS) (fuselage)	Privately owned, Filton (spares use)
	XK907	WS55 Whirlwind HAS7 [U]	Midland Air Museum, Coventry
	XK911	WS55 Whirlwind HAS7 [519/PO]	Privately owned, Chipping Sodbury
	XK936	WS55 Whirlwind HAS7 [62]	Imperial War Museum, Duxford
	XK940	WS55 Whirlwind HAS7 (G-AYXT) [911]	The Helicopter Museum, Weston-super-Mare
	XK944	WS55 Whirlwind HAS7	*Scrapped*
	XK970	WS55 Whirlwind HAR10 (8789M)	Army, Bramley, Hants
	XL149	Blackburn B101 Beverley C1 (7988M) <ff>	Newark Air Museum, Winthorpe
	XL160	HP80 Victor K2 (8910M) <ff>	HP Victor Association, Walpole
	XL164	HP80 Victor K2 (9215M) <ff>	Gatwick Aviation Museum, Charlwood, Surrey
	XL188	HP80 Victor K2 (9100M) (fuselage)	*Scrapped at Kinloss*
	XL190	HP80 Victor K2 (9216M) <ff>	RAF Manston History Museum
	XL231	HP80 Victor K2	Yorkshire Air Museum, Elvington
	XL318	Avro 698 Vulcan B2 (8733M)	RAF Museum, Hendon
	XL319	Avro 698 Vulcan B2	North-East Aircraft Museum, Usworth
	XL360	Avro 698 Vulcan B2A	Midland Air Museum, Coventry
	XL388	Avro 698 Vulcan B2 <ff>	Aeroventure, Doncaster
	XL391	Avro 698 Vulcan B2	Privately owned, Blackpool
	XL426	Avro 698 Vulcan B2 (G-VJET)	Vulcan Restoration Trust, Southend
	XL445	Avro 698 Vulcan K2 (8811M) <ff>	Blyth Valley Aviation Collection, Walpole
	XL449	Fairey Gannet AEW3 <ff>	Privately owned, Camberley, Surrey
	XL472	Fairey Gannet AEW3 [044/R]	Gatwick Aviation Museum, Charlwood, Surrey
	XL497	Fairey Gannet AEW3 [041/R]	RN, Prestwick
	XL500	Fairey Gannet AEW3 (G-KAEW) [CU]	Kennet Aviation, North Weald
	XL502	Fairey Gannet AEW3 (8610M/ G-BMYP)	Privately owned, Sandtoft
	XL503	Fairey Gannet AEW3 [070/E]	FAA Museum, RNAS Yeovilton
	XL563	Hawker Hunter T7 (9218M)	Privately owned, Bosbury, Hereford

Serial	*Type (other identity) [code]*	*Owner/operator, location or fate*	*Notes*
XL564	Hawker Hunter T7 (fuselage)	Boscombe Down Aviation Collection	
XL565	Hawker Hunter T7 (parts of WT745)	Privately owned, Bruntingthorpe	
XL568	Hawker Hunter T7A (9224M) [C]	RAF Museum, Cosford	
XL569	Hawker Hunter T7 (8833M)	East Midlands Airport Aeropark	
XL571	Hawker Hunter T7 (XL572/8834M/ G-HNTR) [V]	Yorkshire Air Museum, Elvington	
XL573	Hawker Hunter T7 (G-BVGH)	Privately owned, Humberside	
XL577	Hawker Hunter T7 (G-BXKF/ 8676M)	Delta Jets, Kemble	
XL578	Hawker Hunter T7 (fuselage) [77]	Privately owned, Kemble	
XL580	Hawker Hunter T8M [723]	FAA Museum, RNAS Yeovilton	
XL586	Hawker Hunter T7 <rf>	Delta Jets, Kemble	
XL587	Hawker Hunter T7 (8807M/ G-HPUX) [Z]	The Old Flying Machine Company, stored Scampton	
XL591	Hawker Hunter T7	Gatwick Aviation Museum, Charlwood, Surrey	
XL592	Hawker Hunter T7 (8836M) [Y]	Hunter Flying Club, Exeter	
XL601	Hawker Hunter T7 (G-BZSR) [874/VL]	Classic Fighters, Brustem, Belgium	
XL602	Hawker Hunter T8M (G-BWFT)	Hunter Flying Club, Exeter	
XL609	Hawker Hunter T7 <ff>	Boscombe Down Aviation Collection	
XL612	Hawker Hunter T7 [2]	Privately owned, Exeter	
XL618	Hawker Hunter T7 (8892M) [05]	Caernarfon Air World	
XL621	Hawker Hunter T7 (G-BNCX)	Privately owned, Brooklands Museum	
XL623	Hawker Hunter T7 (8770M)	The Planets Leisure Centre, Woking	
XL629	EE Lightning T4	DPA/QinetiQ Boscombe Down, at main gate	
XL703	SAL Pioneer CC1 (8034M)	RAF Museum, Cosford	
XL714	DH82A Tiger Moth II (T6099/ G-AOGR)	Privately owned, Boughton, Lincs	
XL716	DH82A Tiger Moth II (T7363/ G-AOIL)	Privately owned, Compton Abbas	
XL735	Saro Skeeter AOP12	*Currently not known*	
XL738	Saro Skeeter AOP12 (7860M)	Privately owned, Leeds	
XL739	Saro Skeeter AOP12	AAC Wattisham, on display	
XL762	Saro Skeeter AOP12 (8017M)	Royal Scottish Mus'm of Flight, E Fortune	
XL763	Saro Skeeter AOP12	Privately owned, Leeds	
XL764	Saro Skeeter AOP12 (7940M) [J]	Newark Air Museum, Winthorpe	
XL765	Saro Skeeter AOP12	Privately owned, Melksham, Wilts	
XL770	Saro Skeeter AOP12 (8046M)	Southampton Hall of Aviation	
XL809	Saro Skeeter AOP12 (G-BLIX)	Privately owned, Wilden, Beds	
XL811	Saro Skeeter AOP12	The Helicopter Museum, Weston-super-Mare	
XL812	Saro Skeeter AOP12 (G-SARO)	AAC Historic Aircraft Flt, stored Middle Wallop	
XL813	Saro Skeeter AOP12	Museum of Army Flying, Middle Wallop	
XL814	Saro Skeeter AOP12	AAC Historic Aircraft Flight, Middle Wallop	
XL824	Bristol 171 Sycamore HR14 (8021M)	Gr Manchester Mus of Science & Industry	
XL829	Bristol 171 Sycamore HR14	Bristol Industrial Museum	
XL840	WS55 Whirlwind HAS7	Privately owned, Bawtry	
XL847	WS55 Whirlwind HAS7 [83]	*Scrapped at Middle Wallop*	
XL853	WS55 Whirlwind HAS7 [PO]	FAA Museum, stored RNAS Yeovilton	
XL875	WS55 Whirlwind HAR9	Perth Technical College	
XL929	Percival P66 Pembroke C1 (G-BNPU)	Air Atlantique Classic Flight, stored Coventry	
XL954	Percival P66 Pembroke C1 (9042M/N4234C/G-BXES)	Air Atlantique Classic Flight, Coventry	
XL993	SAL Twin Pioneer CC1 (8388M)	RAF Museum, Cosford	
XM135	BAC Lightning F1 [B]	Imperial War Museum, Duxford	
XM144	BAC Lightning F1 (8417M) <ff>	Privately owned, Pershore	
XM169	BAC Lightning F1A (8422M) <ff>	Highland Aircraft Preservation Group, Dalcross	
XM172	BAC Lightning F1A (8427M)	Privately owned, Booker	
XM173	BAC Lightning F1A (8414M) [A]	RAF Bentley Priory, at main gate	
XM191	BAC Lightning F1A (7854M/ 8590M) <ff>	RAF M&RU, Bottesford	
XM192	BAC Lightning F1A (8413M) [K]	Bomber County Aviation Museum, Hemswell	
XM223	DH104 Devon C2 (G-BWWC) [J]	Air Atlantique Classic Flight, Coventry	
XM279	EE Canberra B(I)8 <ff>	Privately owned, Flixton	

Notes	Serial	Type (other identity) [code]	Owner/operator, location or fate
	XM300	WS58 Wessex HAS1	Welsh Industrial & Maritime Mus'm, stored Cardiff
	XM328	WS58 Wessex HAS3 [653/PO]	The Helicopter Museum, Weston-super-Mare
	XM330	WS58 Wessex HAS1	The Helicopter Museum, Weston-super-Mare
	XM349	Hunting Jet Provost T3A (9046M) [T]	Global Aviation, Binbrook
	XM350	Hunting Jet Provost T3A (9036M) [89]	Aeroventure, Doncaster
	XM351	Hunting Jet Provost T3 (8078M) [Y]	RAF Museum, Cosford
	XM355	Hunting Jet Provost T3 (8229M) [D]	Privately owned, Bruntingthorpe
	XM358	Hunting Jet Provost T3A (8987M) [53]	Privately owned, Newbridge, Powys
	XM362	Hunting Jet Provost T3 (8230M)	RAF No 1 SoTT, Cosford
	XM365	Hunting Jet Provost T3A (G-BXBH) [37]	Privately owned, Norwich
	XM369	Hunting Jet Provost T3 (8084M) [C]	Privately owned, Rossendale, Lancs
	XM370	Hunting Jet Provost T3A (G-BVSP) [10]	Privately owned, Long Marston
	XM383	Hunting Jet Provost T3A [90]	Newark Air Museum, Winthorpe
	XM402	Hunting Jet Provost T3 (8055AM) [J]	Fenland & W Norfolk Aviation Museum, Wisbech
	XM404	Hunting Jet Provost T3 (8055BM)	FETC, Moreton-in-Marsh, Glos
	XM409	Hunting Jet Provost T3 (8082M) <ff>	Air Scouts, Guernsey Airport
	XM410	Hunting Jet Provost T3 (8054AM) [B]	DEODS, Chattenden, Kent
	XM411	Hunting Jet Provost T3 (8434M) <ff>	Aeroventure, Doncaster
	XM412	Hunting Jet Provost T3A (9011M) [41]	Privately owned, Kinross, Scotland
	XM414	Hunting Jet Provost T3A (8996M)	Ulster Aviation Society, Langford Lodge
	XM417	Hunting Jet Provost T3 (8054BM) [D] <ff>	Privately owned, Cannock
	XM419	Hunting Jet Provost T3A (8990M) [102]	DARA Training School, RAF St Athan
	XM424	Hunting Jet Provost T3A (G-BWDS)	*Repainted as G-BWDS, 2004*
	XM425	Hunting Jet Provost T3A (8995M) [88]	Privately owned, Longton, Staffs
	XM463	Hunting Jet Provost T3A [38] (fuselage)	RAF Museum, Hendon
	XM468	Hunting Jet Provost T3 (8081M)	Fenland & W Norfolk Aviation Museum, stored Wisbech
	XM470	Hunting Jet Provost T3A (G-BWZZ) [12]	*Sold as ZU-JPR, June 2004*
	XM473	Hunting Jet Provost T3A (8974M/ *G-TINY*)	Bedford College, instructional use
	XM474	Hunting Jet Provost T3 (8121M) <ff>	No 2517 Sqn ATC, Levenshulme
	XM478	Hunting Jet Provost T3A (8983M/ G-BXDL)	Privately owned, Swansea
	XM479	Hunting Jet Provost T3A (G-BVEZ) [54]	Privately owned, Newcastle
	XM480	Hunting Jet Provost T3 (8080M)	4x4 Car Centre, Chesterfield
	XM496	Bristol 253 Britannia C1 (EL-WXA)	Britannia Preservation Society, Kemble
	XM529	Saro Skeeter AOP12 (7979M/ G-BDNS)	Privately owned, Handforth
	XM553	Saro Skeeter AOP12 (G-AWSV)	Privately owned, Middle Wallop
	XM555	Saro Skeeter AOP12 (8027M)	RAF Museum, Cosford
	XM561	Saro Skeeter AOP12 (7980M)	Aeroventure, Doncaster
	XM564	Saro Skeeter AOP12	National Tank Museum, Bovington
	XM569	Avro 698 Vulcan B2 <ff>	Gloucestershire Avn Coll, stored Gloucester
	XM575	Avro 698 Vulcan B2A (G-BLMC)	East Midlands Airport Aeropark
	XM594	Avro 698 Vulcan B2	Newark Air Museum, Winthorpe
	XM597	Avro 698 Vulcan B2	Royal Scottish Mus'm of Flight, E Fortune
	XM598	Avro 698 Vulcan B2 (8778M)	RAF Museum, Cosford
	XM602	Avro 698 Vulcan B2 (8771M) <ff>	Avro Aircraft Heritage Society, Woodford
	XM603	Avro 698 Vulcan B2	Avro Aircraft Heritage Society, Woodford
	XM607	Avro 698 Vulcan B2 (8779M)	RAF Waddington, on display
	XM612	Avro 698 Vulcan B2	City of Norwich Aviation Museum

Serial	Type (other identity) [code]	Owner/operator, location or fate	Notes
XM652	Avro 698 Vulcan B2 <ff>	Privately owned, Welshpool	
XM655	Avro 698 Vulcan B2 (G-VULC)	Privately owned, Wellesbourne Mountford	
XM660	WS55 Whirlwind HAS7	RAF Millom Museum, Haverigg	
XM685	WS55 Whirlwind HAS7 (G-AYZJ) [513/PO]	Newark Air Museum, Winthorpe	
XM692	HS Gnat T1 <ff>	Thameside Aviation Museum, East Tilbury	
XM693	HS Gnat T1 (7891M)	BAE Systems Hamble, on display	
XM693	HS Gnat T1 (8618M/XP504/ G-TIMM) [04]	*Repainted as XS111*	
XM697	HS Gnat T1 (G-NAAT)	Privately owned, Exeter	
XM708	HS Gnat T1 (8573M)	Privately owned, Lytham St Annes	
XM715	HP80 Victor K2	British Aviation Heritage, Bruntingthorpe	
XM717	HP80 Victor K2 <ff>	RAF Museum, Hendon	
XM819	Lancashire EP9 Prospector (G-APXW)	Museum of Army Flying, Middle Wallop	
XM833	WS58 Wessex HAS3	SWWAPS, Lasham	
XM870	WS58 Wessex HAS3 [PO]	RN, Predannack Fire School	
XN126	WS55 Whirlwind HAR10 (8655M) [S]	Pinewood Studios, Elstree	
XN157	Slingsby T21B Sedbergh TX1 (BGA3255)	Privately owned, stored Long Mynd	
XN185	Slingsby T21B Sedbergh TX1 (8942M/BGA4077)	RAFGSA, Syerston	
XN187	Slingsby T21B Sedbergh TX1 (BGA3903)	Privately owned, Seighford	
XN198	Slingsby T31B Cadet TX3	Privately owned, Challock Lees	
XN238	Slingsby T31B Cadet TX3 <ff>	Aeroventure, stored Doncaster	
XN239	Slingsby T31B Cadet TX3 (8889M) [G]	Imperial War Museum, Duxford	
XN243	Slingsby T31B Cadet TX3 (BGA3145)	*To BGA3145*	
XN246	Slingsby T31B Cadet TX3	Southampton Hall of Aviation	
XN258	WS55 Whirlwind HAR9 [589/CU]	North-East Aircraft Museum, Usworth	
XN263	WS55 Whirlwind HAS7	Privately owned, Bosham, W Sussex	
XN297	WS55 Whirlwind HAR9 (XN311) [12]	Privately owned, Hull	
XN298	WS55 Whirlwind HAR9 [810/LS]	International Fire Training Centre, Chorley	
XN299	WS55 Whirlwind HAS7 [758]	Tangmere Military Aviation Museum	
XN304	WS55 Whirlwind HAS7 [64]	Norfolk & Suffolk Avn Museum, Flixton	
XN332	Saro P531 (G-APNV) [759]	FAA Museum, stored RNAS Yeovilton	
XN334	Saro P531	FAA Museum, stored RNAS Yeovilton	
XN341	Saro Skeeter AOP12 (8022M)	Stondon Transport Mus & Garden Centre, Beds	
XN344	Saro Skeeter AOP12 (8018M)	Science Museum, South Kensington	
XN351	Saro Skeeter AOP12 (G-BKSC)	Privately owned, Ipswich	
XN380	WS55 Whirlwind HAS7	RAF Manston History Museum	
XN385	WS55 Whirlwind HAS7	Privately owned, Wingates, Lancs	
XN386	WS55 Whirlwind HAR9 [435/ED]	Aeroventure, Doncaster	
XN412	Auster AOP9	Auster 9 Group, Melton Mowbray	
XN435	Auster AOP9 (G-BGBU)	Privately owned,	
XN437	Auster AOP9 (G-AXWA)	Privately owned, North Weald	
XN441	Auster AOP9 (G-BGKT)	Privately owned, Eggesford	
XN459	Hunting Jet Provost T3A (G-BWOT)	Transair(UK) Ltd, North Weald	
XN462	Hunting Jet Provost T3A [17]	FAA Museum, stored RNAS Yeovilton	
XN466	Hunting Jet Provost T3A [29] <ff>	No 1005 Sqn ATC, Radcliffe, Gtr Manchester	
XN492	Hunting Jet Provost T3 (8079M) <ff>	*Scrapped, 2004*	
XN493	Hunting Jet Provost T3 (XN137) <ff>	Privately owned, Camberley	
XN494	Hunting Jet Provost T3A (9012M) [43]	Crawley Technical College	
XN497	Hunting Jet Provost T3A [52]	Privately owned, Newby Wiske	
XN500	Hunting Jet Provost T3A [48]	East Midlands Airport Aeropark	
XN501	Hunting Jet Provost T3A (8958M) [G]	Privately owned, Billockby, Norfolk	
XN503	Hunting Jet Provost T3 <ff>	Boscombe Down Aviation Collection	
XN508	Hunting Jet Provost T3A <ff>	RAF/DARA, St Athan	
XN510	Hunting Jet Provost T3A (G-BXBI) [40]	Privately owned, Sproughton	
XN511	Hunting Jet Provost T3 [64] <ff>	Aeroventure, Doncaster	

Notes	Serial	Type (other identity) [code]	Owner/operator, location or fate
	XN549	Hunting Jet Provost T3 (8235M) [32,P]	RAF Shawbury Fire Section
	XN550	Hunting Jet Provost T3 <ff>	Privately owned, Stone, Staffs
	XN551	Hunting Jet Provost T3A (8984M)	DARA Training School, RAF St Athan
	XN554	Hunting Jet Provost T3 (8436M) [K]	Privately owned, Sproughton
	XN573	Hunting Jet Provost T3 [E] <ff>	Newark Air Museum, Winthorpe
	XN577	Hunting Jet Provost T3A (8956M) [89,F]	*Sold to the USA*
	XN579	Hunting Jet Provost T3A (9137M) [14]	Privately owned, Sproughton
	XN582	Hunting Jet Provost T3A (8957M) [95,H]	Arbury College, Cambridge
	XN584	Hunting Jet Provost T3A (9014M) [E]	Phoenix Aviation, Bruntingthorpe
	XN586	Hunting Jet Provost T3A (9039M) [91,S]	Brooklands Technical College
	XN589	Hunting Jet Provost T3A (9143M) [46]	RAF Linton-on-Ouse, on display
	XN593	Hunting Jet Provost T3A (8988M) [97,Q]	*Sold to the USA*
	XN594	Hunting Jet Provost T3 (8234M/ XN458)	Privately owned, Ashington, W Sussex
	XN597	Hunting Jet Provost T3 (7984M) <ff>	RAF Millom Museum, Haverigg
	XN607	Hunting Jet Provost T3 <ff>	Highland Aircraft Preservation Group, Dalcross
	XN623	Hunting Jet Provost T3 (XN632/ 8352M)	Privately owned, Birlingham, Worcs
	XN629	Hunting Jet Provost T3A (G-BVEG/ G-KNOT) [49]	Privately owned, North Weald
	XN634	Hunting Jet Provost T3A <ff>	Privately owned, Preston, Lancs
	XN634	Hunting Jet Provost T3A [53] <rf>	BAE Systems Warton Fire Section
	XN636	Hunting Jet Provost T3A (9045M) [15]	Privately owned
	XN637	Hunting Jet Provost T3 (G-BKOU) [03]	Privately owned, North Weald
	XN647	DH110 Sea Vixen FAW2 <ff>	Privately owned, Bicester
	XN650	DH110 Sea Vixen FAW2 <ff>	Privately owned, Newton Abbot
	XN651	DH110 Sea Vixen FAW2 <ff>	Privately owned, stored Lavendon, Bucks
	XN657	DH110 Sea Vixen D3 [TR-1]	*Currently not known*
	XN685	DH110 Sea Vixen FAW2 (8173M) [03/VL]	Midland Air Museum, Coventry
	XN696	DH110 Sea Vixen FAW2 <ff>	Blyth Valley Aviation Collection, stored Walpole
	XN714	Hunting H126	RAF Museum, Cosford
	XN726	EE Lightning F2A (8545M) <ff>	Boscombe Down Aviation Collection
	XN728	EE Lightning F2A (8546M) [V]	Privately owned, Balderton, Notts
	XN734	EE Lightning F3A (8346M/ G-BNCA) <ff>	*Scrapped*
	XN774	EE Lightning F2A (8551M) <ff>	Privately owned, Boston
	XN776	EE Lightning F2A (8535M) [C]	Royal Scottish Mus'm of Flight, E Fortune
	XN795	EE Lightning F2A <ff>	Privately owned, Foulness
	XN817	AW660 Argosy C1	QinetiQ West Freugh Fire Section
	XN819	AW660 Argosy C1 (8205M) <ff>	Newark Air Museum, Winthorpe
	XN923	HS Buccaneer S1 [13]	Gatwick Aviation Museum, Charlwood, Surrey
	XN928	HS Buccaneer S1 (8179M) <ff>	Privately owned, Gravesend
	XN957	HS Buccaneer S1 [630/LM]	FAA Museum, RNAS Yeovilton
	XN964	HS Buccaneer S1 [613/LM]	Newark Air Museum, Winthorpe
	XN967	HS Buccaneer S1 <ff>	Muckleburgh Collection, Weybourne, Norfolk
	XN972	HS Buccaneer S1 (8183M/XN962) <ff>	RAF Museum, Hendon
	XN974	HS Buccaneer S2A	Yorkshire Air Museum, Elvington
	XN981	HS Buccaneer S2B (fuselage)	Privately owned, Errol
	XN983	HS Buccaneer S2B <ff>	Fenland & W Norfolk Aviation Museum, Wisbech
	XP110	WS58 Wessex HAS3 [55/FL]	RN AESS, *HMS Sultan*, Gosport, BDRT
	XP137	WS58 Wessex HAS3 [711/DD]	RN, Predannack Fire School
	XP142	WS58 Wessex HAS3	FAA Museum, Yeovilton
	XP150	WS58 Wessex HAS3 [LS]	FETC, Moreton-in-Marsh, Glos
	XP160	WS58 Wessex HAS1	*Scrapped at Predannack*

Serial	Type (other identity) [code]	Owner/operator, location or fate	Notes
XP165	WS Scout AH1	The Helicopter Museum, Weston-super-Mare	
XP190	WS Scout AH1	Aeroventure, Doncaster	
XP191	WS Scout AH1	Privately owned, Dunkeswell	
XP226	Fairey Gannet AEW3 [073/E]	Newark Air Museum, Winthorpe	
XP241	Auster AOP9	Privately owned, Eggesford	
XP242	Auster AOP9 (G-BUCI)	AAC Historic Aircraft Flight, Middle Wallop	
XP244	Auster AOP9 (7864M/*M7922*)	Privately owned, Stretton on Dunsmore	
XP248	Auster AOP9 (7863M/WZ679)	Privately owned, Sandy, Beds	
XP254	Auster AOP11 (G-ASCC)	Privately owned, Widmerpool	
XP279	Auster AOP9 (G-BWKK)	Privately owned, Popham	
XP280	Auster AOP9	Snibston Discovery Park, Coalville	
XP281	Auster AOP9	Imperial War Museum, Duxford	
XP283	Auster AOP9 (7859M) (frame)	Privately owned,	
XP286	Auster AOP9	Privately owned, Eggesford	
XP299	WS55 Whirlwind HAR10 (8726M)	RAF Museum, Hendon	
XP330	WS55 Whirlwind HAR10	CAA Fire School, Teesside Airport	
XP344	WS55 Whirlwind HAR10 (8764M) [H723]	RAF North Luffenham Training Area	
XP345	WS55 Whirlwind HAR10 (8792M) [UN]	Aeroventure, Doncaster	
XP346	WS55 Whirlwind HAR10 (8793M)	Privately owned, Long Marston	
XP350	WS55 Whirlwind HAR10	Privately owned,	
XP351	WS55 Whirlwind HAR10 (8672M) [Z]	Gatwick Aviation Museum, Charlwood, Surrey	
XP355	WS55 Whirlwind HAR10 (8463M/ G-BEBC)	City of Norwich Aviation Museum	
XP360	WS55 Whirlwind HAR10 [V]	Privately owned, Upper Hill, nr Leominster	
XP398	WS55 Whirlwind HAR10 (8794M)	Gatwick Aviation Museum, Charlwood, Surrey	
XP399	WS55 Whirlwind HAR10	*Currently not known*	
XP404	WS55 Whirlwind HAR10 (8682M)	The Helicopter Museum, Weston-super-Mare	
XP411	AW660 Argosy C1 (8442M) [C]	RAF Museum, Cosford	
XP454	Slingsby T38 Grasshopper TX1	Privately owned, Sywell	
XP463	Slingsby T38 Grasshopper TX1 (BGA4372)	Privately owned, Lasham	
XP488	Slingsby T38 Grasshopper TX1	Fenland & W Norfolk Aviation Museum, stored Wisbech	
XP490	Slingsby T38 Grasshopper TX1 (BGA4552)	Privately owned, stored Watton	
XP492	Slingsby T38 Grasshopper TX1 (BGA3480)	Privately owned, Gallows Hill, Dorset	
XP493	Slingsby T38 Grasshopper TX1	Privately owned, stored Aston Down	
XP494	Slingsby T38 Grasshopper TX1	Privately owned, Rattlesden, Suffolk	
XP502	HS Gnat T1 (8576M)	Privately owned, Kemble	
XP505	HS Gnat T1	Science Museum, Wroughton	
XP516	HS Gnat T1 (8580M) [16]	Farnborough Air Sciences Trust, Farnborough	
XP540	HS Gnat T1 (8608M) [62]	Privately owned, North Weald	
XP542	HS Gnat T1 (8575M)	Solent Sky, Southampton	
XP556	Hunting Jet Provost T4 (9027M) [B]	RAF Cranwell Aviation Heritage Centre	
XP557	Hunting Jet Provost T4 (8494M) [72]	Bomber County Aviation Museum, Hemswell	
XP558	Hunting Jet Provost T4 (8627M) <ff>	Privately owned, Northants	
XP558	Hunting Jet Provost T4 (8627M) [20] <rf>	Privately owned, Sproughton	
XP563	Hunting Jet Provost T4 (9028M) [C]	Privately owned, Sproughton	
XP568	Hunting Jet Provost T4	Jet Avn Preservation Grp, Long Marston	
XP573	Hunting Jet Provost T4 (8236M) [19]	Jersey Airport Fire Section	
XP585	Hunting Jet Provost T4 (8407M) [24]	NE Wales Institute, Wrexham	
XP627	Hunting Jet Provost T4	North-East Aircraft Museum, Usworth	
XP629	Hunting Jet Provost T4 (9026M) [P]	Privately owned, Sproughton	
XP638	Hunting Jet Provost T4 (9034M) [A]	*Scrapped, 2004*	
XP640	Hunting Jet Provost T4 (8501M) [27]	Yorkshire Air Museum, Elvington	
XP642	Hunting Jet Provost T4 <ff>	Privately owned, Lavendon, Bucks	

Notes	Serial	Type (other identity) [code]	Owner/operator, location or fate
	XP672	Hunting Jet Provost T4 (8458M/ G-RAFI) [03]	Privately owned, Sproughton
	XP680	Hunting Jet Provost T4 (8460M)	FETC, Moreton-in-Marsh, Glos
	XP686	Hunting Jet Provost T4 (8401M/ 8502M) [G]	Privately owned, Sproughton
	XP688	Hunting Jet Provost T4 (9031M)	Privately owned, Wingates, Lancs
	XP701	BAC Lightning F3 (8924M) <ff>	Robertsbridge Aviation Society, Mayfield
	XP703	BAC Lightning F3 <ff>	The Cockpit Collection, RAF Coltishall
	XP706	BAC Lightning F3 (8925M)	Aeroventure, Doncaster
	XP743	BAC Lightning F3 <ff>	No 351 Sqn ATC, Burton-upon-Trent
	XP745	BAC Lightning F3 (8453M) <ff>	Greenford Haulage, West London
	XP772	DHC2 Beaver AL1 (G-BUCJ)	AAC Historic Aircraft Flight, stored Duxford
	XP775	DHC2 Beaver AL1	Privately owned
	XP820	DHC2 Beaver AL1	AAC Historic Aircraft Flight, Middle Wallop
	XP821	DHC2 Beaver AL1 [MCO]	Museum of Army Flying, Middle Wallop
	XP822	DHC2 Beaver AL1	Museum of Army Flying, Middle Wallop
	XP831	Hawker P.1127 (8406M)	Science Museum, South Kensington
	XP841	Handley-Page HP115	FAA Museum, RNAS Yeovilton
	XP846	WS Scout AH1 [B,H] (fuselage)	*Currently not known*
	XP847	WS Scout AH1	Museum of Army Flying, Middle Wallop
	XP848	WS Scout AH1	AAC Arborfield, on display
	XP853	WS Scout AH1	Privately owned, Dunkeswell
	XP854	WS Scout AH1 (7898M/TAD043)	Bedford College
	XP855	WS Scout AH1	Army SEAE, Arborfield
	XP856	WS Scout AH1	Privately owned, Dunkeswell
	XP883	WS Scout AH1	Privately owned, Oaksey Park, Wilts
	XP884	WS Scout AH1	AAC Middle Wallop, instructional use
	XP885	WS Scout AH1	AAC Wattisham, instructional use
	XP886	WS Scout AH1	Yeovil College
	XP888	WS Scout AH1	Privately owned, Sproughton
	XP890	WS Scout AH1 [G] (fuselage)	Privately owned, Ipswich
	XP893	WS Scout AH1	AAC Middle Wallop, BDRT
	XP899	WS Scout AH1 [D]	Army SEAE, Arborfield
	XP900	WS Scout AH1	AAC Wattisham, instructional use
	XP902	WS Scout AH1 <ff>	Aeroventure, stored Doncaster
	XP905	WS Scout AH1	Privately owned, Sproughton
	XP907	WS Scout AH1 (G-SROE)	Privately owned, Wattisham
	XP910	WS Scout AH1	Museum of Army Flying, Middle Wallop
	XP919	DH110 Sea Vixen FAW2 (8163M) [706/VL]	Blyth Valley Aviation Collection, Walpole
	XP925	DH110 Sea Vixen FAW2 [752] <ff>	No 1268 Sqn ATC, Haslemere, Surrey
	XP980	Hawker P.1127	FAA Museum, RNAS Yeovilton
	XP984	Hawker P.1127	Brooklands Museum, Weybridge
	XR220	BAC TSR2 (7933M)	RAF Museum, Cosford
	XR222	BAC TSR2	Imperial War Museum, Duxford
	XR232	Sud Alouette AH2 (F-WEIP)	Museum of Army Flying, Middle Wallop
	XR239	Auster AOP9	Privately owned, Stretton on Dunsmore
	XR240	Auster AOP9 (G-BDFH)	Privately owned, Eggesford
	XR241	Auster AOP9 (G-AXRR)	Privately owned, Eggesford
	XR244	Auster AOP9	AAC Historic Aircraft Flight, Middle Wallop
	XR246	Auster AOP9 (7862M/G-AZBU)	Privately owned, North Coates
	XR267	Auster AOP9 (G-BJXR)	Privately owned, Widmerpool
	XR271	Auster AOP9	Royal Artillery Experience, Woolwich
	XR371	SC5 Belfast C1	RAF Museum, Cosford
	XR379	Sud Alouette AH2	AAC Historic Aircraft Flight, Middle Wallop
	XR453	WS55 Whirlwind HAR10 (8873M) [A]	RAF Odiham, on gate
	XR458	WS55 Whirlwind HAR10 (8662M) [H]	Privately owned, Chipping Sodbury
	XR485	WS55 Whirlwind HAR10 [Q]	Norfolk & Suffolk Avn Museum, Flixton
	XR486	WS55 Whirlwind HCC12 (8727M/ G-RWWW)	The Helicopter Museum, Weston-super-Mare
	XR498	WS58 Wessex HC2 (9342M) [X]	RAF No 1 SoTT, Cosford
	XR499	WS58 Wessex HC2 [W]	*Scrapped at Hitchin, April 2004*
	XR501	WS58 Wessex HC2	Army, Keogh Barracks, Aldershot, instructional use
	XR502	WS58 Wessex HC2 (G-CCUP) [Z]	Privately owned, Redhill
	XR503	WS58 Wessex HC2	MoD FSCTE, Manston
	XR506	WS58 Wessex HC2 (9343M) [V]	RAF No 1 SoTT, Cosford
	XR507	WS58 Wessex HC2	Privately owned, Hixon, Staffs
	XR508	WS58 Wessex HC2 [B]	RN AESS, *HMS Sultan*, Gosport
	XR511	WS58 Wessex HC2 [L]	*Sold to New Zealand, January 2004*

Serial	Type (other identity) [code]	Owner/operator, location or fate	Notes
XR516	WS58 Wessex HC2 [V]	RAF Shawbury, for display	
XR517	WS58 Wessex HC2 [N]	Ulster Aviation Society, Langford Lodge	
XR518	WS58 Wessex HC2 [J]	RN AESS, *HMS Sultan*, Gosport	
XR520	WS58 Wessex HC2	*Scrapped at Hitchin, April 2004*	
XR523	WS58 Wessex HC2 [M]	RN *HMS Raleigh*, Torpoint, instructional use	
XR525	WS58 Wessex HC2 [G]	RAF Museum, Cosford	
XR526	WS58 Wessex HC2 (8147M)	The Helicopter Museum, Weston-super-Mare	
XR528	WS58 Wessex HC2	SFDO, RNAS Culdrose	
XR529	WS58 Wessex HC2 (9268M) [E]	RAF Aldergrove, on display	
XR534	HS Gnat T1 (8578M) [65]	Newark Air Museum, Winthorpe	
XR537	HS Gnat T1 (8642M/G-NATY) [T]	Bournemouth Aviation Museum	
XR538	HS Gnat T1 (8621M/G-RORI) [01]	Privately owned, Kemble	
XR571	HS Gnat T1 (8493M)	RAF *Red Arrows*, Scampton, on display	
XR574	HS Gnat T1 (8631M) [72]	RAF No 1 SoTT, Cosford	
XR588	WS58 Wessex HC2 [*Hearts*]	*Sold to New Zealand, January 2004*	
XR595	WS Scout AH1 (G-BWHU) [M]	Privately owned, Staddon Heights, Devon	
XR597	WS Scout AH1 (fuselage)	Privately owned, Sproughton	
XR601	WS Scout AH1	Army SEAE, Arborfield	
XR627	WS Scout AH1 [X]	Privately owned, Sproughton	
XR628	WS Scout AH1	Privately owned, Ipswich	
XR629	WS Scout AH1 (fuselage)	Privately owned, Ipswich	
XR635	WS Scout AH1	Coventry University, instructional use	
XR650	Hunting Jet Provost T4 (8459M) [28]	Boscombe Down Aviation Collection	
XR654	Hunting Jet Provost T4 <ff>	Privately owned, Chester	
XR658	Hunting Jet Provost T4 (8192M)	Deeside College, Connah's Quay, Clwyd	
XR662	Hunting Jet Provost T4 (8410M) [25]	Boulton Paul Association, Wolverhampton	
XR672	Hunting Jet Provost T4 (8495M) [50]	RAF Halton, Fire Section	
XR673	Hunting Jet Provost T4 (G-BXLO/ 9032M) [L]	Privately owned, North Weald	
XR681	Hunting Jet Provost T4 (8588M) <ff>	Robertsbridge Aviation Society, Mayfield	
XR700	Hunting Jet Provost T4 (8589M) <ff>	RAF Cosford	
XR713	BAC Lightning F3 (8935M) [C]	RAF Leuchars, on display	
XR718	BAC Lightning F6 (8932M) [DA]	Blyth Valley Aviation Collection, Walpole	
XR724	BAC Lightning F6 (G-BTSY)	The Lightning Association, Binbrook	
XR725	BAC Lightning F6	Privately owned, Binbrook	
XR726	BAC Lightning F6 <ff>	Privately owned, Harrogate	
XR728	BAC Lightning F6 [JS]	Lightning Preservation Grp, Bruntingthorpe	
XR747	BAC Lightning F6 <ff>	Privately owned, Cubert, Cornwall	
XR749	BAC Lightning F3 (8934M) [DA]	Highland Aircraft Preservation Group, Dalcross	
XR751	BAC Lightning F3	Privately owned, Tremar, Cornwall	
XR753	BAC Lightning F6 (8969M) [BP]	RAF Leeming on display	
XR753	BAC Lightning F53 (ZF578)	Tangmere Military Aviation Museum	
XR754	BAC Lightning F6 (8972M) <ff>	Aeroventure, Doncaster	
XR755	BAC Lightning F6	Privately owned, Callington, Cornwall	
XR757	BAC Lightning F6 <ff>	Privately owned, Grainthorpe, Lincs	
XR759	BAC Lightning F6 <ff>	Privately owned, Haxey, Lincs	
XR770	BAC Lightning F6 [AA]	Privately owned, Grainthorpe, Lincs	
XR771	BAC Lightning F6 [BM]	Midland Air Museum, Coventry	
XR806	BAC VC10 C1K <ff>	RAF Brize Norton, BDRT	
XR807	BAC VC10 C1K	RAF No 10 Sqn, Brize Norton	
XR808	BAC VC10 C1K	RAF No 10 Sqn, Brize Norton	
XR810	BAC VC10 C1K	RAF No 10 Sqn, Brize Norton	
XR944	Wallis WA116 (G-ATTB)	RAF Museum, Hendon	
XR954	HS Gnat T1 (8570M) [30]	Source Classic Jet Flight, stored Bournemouth	
XR977	HS Gnat T1 (8640M) [3]	RAF Museum, Cosford	
XR991	HS Gnat T1 (8624M/XS102/ G-MOUR)	Delta Jets, Kemble	
XR993	HS Gnat T1 (8620M/XP534/ G-BVPP)	Kennet Aviation, North Weald	
XS100	HS Gnat T1 (8561M) <ff>	Privately owned, London SW3	
XS101	HS Gnat T1 (8638M) (G-GNAT)	*Sold as VH-XSO, October 2003*	

Notes	Serial	Type (other identity) [code]	Owner/operator, location or fate
	XS111	HS Gnat T1 (8618M/XP504/ G-TIMM)	Kennet Aviation, North Weald
	XS122	WS58 Wessex HAS3 [655/PO]	RN AESS, *HMS Sultan*, Gosport
	XS149	WS58 Wessex HAS3 [661/GL]	The Helicopter Museum, Weston-super-Mare
	XS165	Hiller UH12E (G-ASAZ) [37]	Privately owned, Sherburn-in-Elmet
	XS176	Hunting Jet Provost T4 (8514M) <ff>	Privately owned, Stamford
	XS177	Hunting Jet Provost T4 (9044M) [N]	RAF No 1 SoTT, Cosford
	XS179	Hunting Jet Provost T4 (8237M) [20]	Gr Manchester Mus of Science & Industry
	XS180	Hunting Jet Provost T4 (8238M) [21]	RAF St Athan, Fire Section
	XS181	Hunting Jet Provost T4 (9033M) <ff>	No 1084 Sqn ATC, Market Harborough
	XS183	Hunting Jet Provost T4 <ff>	Privately owned, Plymouth
	XS186	Hunting Jet Provost T4 (8408M) [M]	Metheringham Airfield Visitors Centre
	XS209	Hunting Jet Provost T4 (8409M)	Privately owned, Bruntingthorpe
	XS215	Hunting Jet Provost T4 (8507M) [17]	RAF Halton
	XS216	Hunting Jet Provost T4 <ff>	No 2357 Sqn ATC, Goole
	XS217	Hunting Jet Provost T4 (9029M)	Privately owned, Bruntingthorpe
	XS218	Hunting Jet Provost T4 (8508M) <ff>	No 447 Sqn ATC, Henley-on-Thames, Berks
	XS231	BAC Jet Provost T5 (G-ATAJ)	Privately owned, Barnstaple
	XS235	DH106 Comet 4C (G-CPDA)	British Aviation Heritage, Bruntingthorpe
	XS416	BAC Lightning T5	Privately owned, Grainthorpe, Lincs
	XS417	BAC Lightning T5 [DZ]	Newark Air Museum, Winthorpe
	XS420	BAC Lightning T5	Farnborough Air Sciences Trust, Farnborough
	XS421	BAC Lightning T5 <ff>	Privately owned, Foulness
	XS456	BAC Lightning T5 [DX]	Privately owned, Wainfleet
	XS457	BAC Lightning T5 <ff>	Privately owned, Grainthorpe, Lincs
	XS458	BAC Lightning T5 [T]	T5 Projects, Cranfield
	XS459	BAC Lightning T5 [AW]	Fenland & W Norfolk Aviation Museum, Wisbech
	XS463	WS Wasp HAS1 (comp XT431)	Crawley College, West Sussex
	XS481	WS58 Wessex HU5	Aeroventure, Doncaster
	XS482	WS58 Wessex HU5	RAF Manston History Museum
	XS486	WS58 Wessex HU5 (9272M) [524/CU,F]	The Helicopter Museum, Weston-super-Mare
	XS488	WS58 Wessex HU5 (9056M) [XK]	RN AESS, *HMS Sultan*, Gosport
	XS489	WS58 Wessex HU5 [R]	Privately owned, Redhill
	XS493	WS58 Wessex HU5	RN/DARA, stored Fleetlands
	XS496	WS58 Wessex HU5 [625/PO]	RN AESS, *HMS Sultan*, Gosport
	XS498	WS58 Wessex HC5C (comp XS677) [WK]	Privately owned, Hixon, Staffs
	XS507	WS58 Wessex HU5	RN AESS, *HMS Sultan*, Gosport
	XS508	WS58 Wessex HU5	FAA Museum, stored RNAS Yeovilton
	XS510	WS58 Wessex HU5 [626/PO]	Privately owned, Hixon, Staffs
	XS511	WS58 Wessex HU5 [M]	Tangmere Military Aircraft Museum
	XS513	WS58 Wessex HU5 [419/CU]	RNAS Yeovilton Fire Section
	XS514	WS58 Wessex HU5 [L]	RN AESS, *HMS Sultan*, Gosport
	XS515	WS58 Wessex HU5 [N]	Army, Keogh Barracks, Aldershot, instructional use
	XS516	WS58 Wessex HU5 [Q]	RN, Predannack Fire School
	XS520	WS58 Wessex HU5 [F]	RN AESS, *HMS Sultan*, Gosport
	XS522	WS58 Wessex HU5 [ZL]	RN, Predannack Fire School
	XS527	WS Wasp HAS1	FAA Museum, stored RNAS Yeovilton
	XS529	WS Wasp HAS1	RN, Predannack Fire School
	XS539	WS Wasp HAS1 [435]	DARA Fleetlands Apprentice School
	XS567	WS Wasp HAS1 [434/E]	Imperial War Museum, Duxford
	XS568	WS Wasp HAS1 [441]	RN AESS, *HMS Sultan*, Gosport
	XS569	WS Wasp HAS1	DARA Fleetlands Apprentice School
	XS570	WS Wasp HAS1 [445/P]	Warship Preservation Trust, Birkenhead
	XS576	DH110 Sea Vixen FAW2 [125/E]	Imperial War Museum, Duxford
	XS587	DH110 Sea Vixen FAW(TT)2 (8828M/G-VIXN)	Gatwick Aviation Museum, Charlwood, Surrey
	XS590	DH110 Sea Vixen FAW2 [131/E]	FAA Museum, RNAS Yeovilton
	XS596	HS Andover C1(PR)	DPA/AFD/*Open Skies*, Boscombe Down
	XS598	HS Andover C1 (fuselage)	FETC, Moreton-in-Marsh, Glos

Serial	Type (other identity) [code]	Owner/operator, location or fate	Notes
XS606	HS Andover C1	DPA/ETPS, Boscombe Down	
XS639	HS Andover E3A (9241M)	RAF Museum, Cosford	
XS641	HS Andover C1(PR) (9198M) [Z]	MoD HQ DLO, Andover, on display	
XS643	HS Andover E3A (9278M) <ff>	Privately owned, Stock, Essex	
XS646	HS Andover C1(mod)	DPA/AFD/QinetiQ, Boscombe Down	
XS652	Slingsby T45 Swallow TX1 (BGA1107)	Privately owned, Rufforth	
XS674	WS58 Wessex HC2 [R]	Privately owned, Hixon, Staffs	
XS675	WS58 Wessex HC2 [*Spades*]	*Sold to New Zealand, January 2004*	
XS695	HS Kestrel FGA1	RAF Museum Restoration Centre, Cosford	
XS709	HS125 Dominie T1 [M]	RAF No 3 FTS/55(R) Sqn, Cranwell	
XS710	HS125 Dominie T1 (9259M) [O]	RAF No 1 SoTT, Cosford	
XS711	HS125 Dominie T1 [L]	RAF No 3 FTS/55(R) Sqn, Cranwell	
XS712	HS125 Dominie T1 [A]	RAF No 3 FTS/55(R) Sqn, Cranwell	
XS713	HS125 Dominie T1 [C]	RAF No 3 FTS/55(R) Sqn, Cranwell	
XS714	HS125 Dominie T1 (9246M) [P]	MoD FSCTE, Manston	
XS726	HS125 Dominie T1 (9273M) [T]	RAF No 1 SoTT, Cosford	
XS727	HS125 Dominie T1 [D]	RAF No 3 FTS/55(R) Sqn, Cranwell	
XS728	HS125 Dominie T1 [E]	RAF No 3 FTS/55(R) Sqn, Cranwell	
XS729	HS125 Dominie T1 (9275M) [G]	RAF No 1 SoTT, Cosford	
XS730	HS125 Dominie T1 [H]	RAF No 3 FTS/55(R) Sqn, Cranwell	
XS731	HS125 Dominie T1 [J]	RAF No 3 FTS/55(R) Sqn, Cranwell	
XS733	HS125 Dominie T1 (9276M) [Q]	RAF No 1 SoTT, Cosford	
XS734	HS125 Dominie T1 (9260M) [N]	RAF No 1 SoTT, Cosford	
XS735	HS125 Dominie T1 (9264M) [R]	DARA Training School, RAF St Athan	
XS736	HS125 Dominie T1 [S]	RAF No 3 FTS/55(R) Sqn, Cranwell	
XS737	HS125 Dominie T1 [K]	RAF No 3 FTS/55(R) Sqn, Cranwell	
XS738	HS125 Dominie T1 (9274M) [U]	RAF No 1 SoTT, Cosford	
XS739	HS125 Dominie T1 [F]	RAF No 3 FTS/55(R) Sqn, Cranwell	
XS743	Beagle B206Z Basset CC1	DPA/ETPS, Boscombe Down	
XS765	Beagle B206Z Basset CC1 (G-BSET)	DPA, QinetiQ, Boscombe Down (spares use)	
XS770	Beagle B206Z Basset CC1 (G-HRHI)	Privately owned, Cranfield	
XS790	HS748 Andover CC2 <ff>	Boscombe Down Aviation Collection	
XS791	HS748 Andover CC2 (fuselage)	Privately owned, Ely	
XS862	WS58 Wessex HAS3	Privately owned, Hixon, Staffs	
XS863	WS58 Wessex HAS1	Imperial War Museum, Duxford	
XS866	WS58 Wessex HAS1 [520/CU]	*Burnt at Predannack, 2004*	
XS868	WS58 Wessex HAS1	*Burnt at Predannack, 2004*	
XS871	WS58 Wessex HAS1 (8457M) [265]	*Scrapped at Chippenham, 1999*	
XS876	WS58 Wessex HAS1 [523/PO]	East Midlands Airport Aeropark	
XS881	WS58 Wessex HAS1	*Scrapped at Predannack*	
XS885	WS58 Wessex HAS1 [512/DD]	SFDO, RNAS Culdrose	
XS886	WS58 Wessex HAS1 [527/CU]	Sea Scouts, Evesham, Worcs	
XS887	WS58 Wessex HAS1 [403/FI]	Flambards Village Theme Park, Helston	
XS888	WS58 Wessex HAS1 [521]	Guernsey Airport Fire Section	
XS897	BAC Lightning F6	Aeroventure, Doncaster	
XS898	BAC Lightning F6 <ff>	Privately owned, Lavendon, Bucks	
XS899	BAC Lightning F6 <ff>	The Cockpit Collection, RAF Coltishall	
XS903	BAC Lightning F6 [BA]	Yorkshire Air Museum, Elvington	
XS904	BAC Lightning F6 [BQ]	Lightning Preservation Grp, Bruntingthorpe	
XS919	BAC Lightning F6	Wonderland Pleasure Park, Farnsfield, Notts	
XS922	BAC Lightning F6 (8973M) <ff>	The Air Defence Collection, Salisbury	
XS923	BAC Lightning F6 <ff>	Privately owned, Welshpool	
XS925	BAC Lightning F6 (8961M) [BA]	RAF Museum, Hendon	
XS928	BAC Lightning F6 [D]	BAE Systems Warton, on display	
XS932	BAC Lightning F6 <ff>	Farnborough Air Sciences Trust, Farnborough	
XS933	BAC Lightning F6 <ff>	Privately owned, Farnham	
XS936	BAC Lightning F6	Castle Motors, Liskeard, Cornwall	
XT108	Agusta-Bell 47G-3 Sioux AH1 [U]	Museum of Army Flying, Middle Wallop	
XT123	WS Sioux AH1 (XT827) [D]	AAC Middle Wallop, at main gate	
XT131	Agusta-Bell 47G-3 Sioux AH1 [B]	AAC Historic Aircraft Flight, Middle Wallop	
XT133	Agusta-Bell 47G-3 Sioux AH1 (7923M)	Royal Engineers' Museum, stored Chattenden	
XT140	Agusta-Bell 47G-3 Sioux AH1	Perth Technical College	
XT141	Agusta-Bell 47G-3 Sioux AH1	Privately owned, Dunkeswell	

Notes	Serial	Type (other identity) [code]	Owner/operator, location or fate
	XT150	Agusta-Bell 47G-3 Sioux AH1 (7883M) [R]	AAC Netheravon, at main gate
	XT151	WS Sioux AH1 [W]	Museum of Army Flying, stored Middle Wallop
	XT175	WS Sioux AH1 (TAD175)	Privately owned, Cambs
	XT176	WS Sioux AH1 [U]	FAA Museum, stored RNAS Yeovilton
	XT190	WS Sioux AH1	The Helicopter Museum, Weston-super-Mare
	XT200	WS Sioux AH1 [F]	Newark Air Museum, Winthorpe
	XT223	WS Sioux AH1 (G-XTUN)	Privately owned, Sherburn-in-Elmet
	XT236	WS Sioux AH1 (frame only)	North-East Aircraft Museum, stored Usworth
	XT242	WS Sioux AH1 (composite) [12]	Aeroventure, Doncaster
	XT257	WS58 Wessex HAS3 (8719M)	Bournemouth Aviation Museum
	XT277	HS Buccaneer S2A (8853M) <ff>	Privately owned, Welshpool
	XT280	HS Buccaneer S2A <ff>	Dumfries & Galloway Avn Mus, Dumfries
	XT284	HS Buccaneer S2A (8855M) <ff>	Privately owned, Felixstowe
	XT288	HS Buccaneer S2B (9134M)	Royal Scottish Museum of Flight, stored E Fortune
	XT420	WS Wasp HAS1 (G-CBUI) [606]	Privately owned, Thruxton
	XT427	WS Wasp HAS1 [606]	FAA Museum, stored RNAS Yeovilton
	XT434	WS Wasp HAS1 [455]	DARA Fleetlands Apprentice School
	XT435	WS Wasp HAS1 (NZ3907/ G-RIMM) [430]	Privately owned, Cranfield
	XT437	WS Wasp HAS1 [423]	Boscombe Down Aviation Collection
	XT439	WS Wasp HAS1 [605]	Privately owned, Hemel Hempstead
	XT443	WS Wasp HAS1 [422/AU]	The Helicopter Museum, Weston-super-Mare
	XT453	WS58 Wessex HU5 [A/B]	Privately owned, Hixon, Staffs
	XT455	WS58 Wessex HU5 [U]	RN AESS, *HMS Sultan*, Gosport
	XT456	WS58 Wessex HU5 (8941M) [XZ]	RAF Aldergrove, BDRT
	XT458	WS58 Wessex HU5 [622]	RN AESS, *HMS Sultan*, Gosport
	XT460	WS58 Wessex HU5	*Scrapped at Gosport*
	XT463	WS58 Wessex HC5C (comp XR508) [*Clubs*]	Privately owned, Hixon, Staffs
	XT466	WS58 Wessex HU5 (8921M) [XV]	RN AESS, *HMS Sultan*, Gosport
	XT467	WS58 Wessex HU5 (8922M) [BF]	Privately owned, Sproughton
	XT468	WS58 Wessex HU5 (comp XT460) [628]	RN, Predannack Fire School
	XT469	WS58 Wessex HU5 (8920M)	RAF No 16 MU, Stafford, ground instruction
	XT472	WS58 Wessex HU5 [XC]	The Helicopter Museum, Weston-super-Mare
	XT474	WS58 Wessex HU5 [820]	*Scrapped at Hitchin, April 2004*
	XT480	WS58 Wessex HU5 [468/RG]	East Midlands Airport Aeropark
	XT482	WS58 Wessex HU5 [ZM/VL]	FAA Museum, RNAS Yeovilton
	XT484	WS58 Wessex HU5 [H]	RN AESS, *HMS Sultan*, Gosport
	XT485	WS58 Wessex HU5	RN AESS, *HMS Sultan*, Gosport
	XT575	Vickers Viscount 837 <ff>	Brooklands Museum, Weybridge
	XT596	McD F-4K Phantom FG1	FAA Museum, RNAS Yeovilton
	XT597	McD F-4K Phantom FG1	Boscombe Down Aviation Collection
	XT601	WS58 Wessex HC2 (9277M) (composite)	RAF Odiham, BDRT
	XT604	WS58 Wessex HC2	East Midlands Airport Aeropark
	XT607	WS58 Wessex HC2 [P]	RN AESS, *HMS Sultan*, Gosport
	XT617	WS Scout AH1	AAC Wattisham, on display
	XT621	WS Scout AH1	R. Military College of Science, Shrivenham
	XT623	WS Scout AH1	Army SEAE, Arborfield
	XT626	WS Scout AH1 [Q]	AAC Historic Aircraft Flt, Middle Wallop
	XT630	WS Scout AH1 (G-BXRL) [X]	Privately owned, Bruntingthorpe
	XT631	WS Scout AH1 [D]	Privately owned, Ipswich
	XT632	WS Scout AH1 (G-BZBD)	Privately owned, North Weald (spares use)
	XT633	WS Scout AH1	Army SEAE, Arborfield
	XT634	WS Scout AH1 (G-BYRX) [T]	Privately owned, Tollerton
	XT638	WS Scout AH1 [N]	AAC Middle Wallop, at gate
	XT640	WS Scout AH1	Privately owned, Sproughton
	XT643	WS Scout AH1 [Z]	Army, Thorpe Camp, East Wretham
	XT645	WS Scout AH1 (fuselage)	Privately owned, Ipswich
	XT670	WS58 Wessex HC2	*To Germany for preservation*
	XT671	WS58 Wessex HC2 (G-BYRC) [D]	Privately owned, Redhill
	XT672	WS58 Wessex HC2 [WE]	RAF Shawbury, on display
	XT677	WS58 Wessex HC2 (8016M)	Privately owned, Stock, Essex

Serial	Type (other identity) [code]	Owner/operator, location or fate	Notes
XT680	WS58 Wessex HC2 [*Diamonds*]	*Sold to New Zealand, January 2004*	
XT681	WS58 Wessex HC2 (9279M) [U]	RAF Benson, BDRT	
XT761	WS58 Wessex HU5	RN AESS, *HMS Sultan*, Gosport	
XT762	WS58 Wessex HU5	RN, Predannack Fire School	
XT765	WS58 Wessex HU5 [J]	RNAS Yeovilton, on display	
XT769	WS58 Wessex HU5 [823]	FAA Museum, RNAS Yeovilton	
XT770	WS58 Wessex HU5 (9055M) [P]	Privately owned, Shawell, Leics	
XT771	WS58 Wessex HU5 [620/PO]	RN AESS, *HMS Sultan*, Gosport	
XT772	WS58 Wessex HU5 (8805M)	SARTU RAF Valley, ground instruction	
XT773	WS58 Wessex HU5 (9123M) [822/CU]	RAF No 1 SoTT, Cosford	
XT778	WS Wasp HAS1 [430]	FAA Museum, stored Yeovilton	
XT780	WS Wasp HAS1 [636]	DARA Fleetlands Apprentice School	
XT781	WS Wasp HAS1 (NZ3908/ G-KAWW) [426]	Privately owned, Sandtoft	
XT787	WS Wasp HAS1 (NZ3905/ G-KAXT)	Kennet Aviation, North Weald	
XT788	WS Wasp HAS1 (G-BMIR) [316] (painted as XT78?)	Privately owned, Dunkeswell	
XT793	WS Wasp HAS1 (G-BZPP) [456]	Privately owned, Otley	
XT803	WS Sioux AH1 [Y]	*Scrapped*	
XT852	McD YF-4M Phantom FGR2	QinetiQ West Freugh Fire Section	
XT863	McD F-4K Phantom FG1 <ff>	Privately owned, Cowes, IOW	
XT864	McD F-4K Phantom FG1 (8998M/ *XT684*) [BJ]	RAF Leuchars on display	
XT891	McD F-4M Phantom FGR2 (9136M) [Z]	RAF Coningsby, at main gate	
XT903	McD F-4M Phantom FGR2 <ff>	RAF Museum Restoration Centre, Cosford	
XT905	McD F-4M Phantom FGR2 [P]	RAF North Luffenham Training Area	
XT907	McD F-4M Phantom FGR2 (9151M) [W]	DEODS, Chattenden, Kent	
XT914	McD F-4M Phantom FGR2 (9269M) [Z]	RAF Brampton, Cambs, on display	
XV101	BAC VC10 C1K	RAF No 10 Sqn, Brize Norton	
XV102	BAC VC10 C1K	RAF No 10 Sqn, Brize Norton	
XV104	BAC VC10 C1K	RAF No 10 Sqn, Brize Norton	
XV105	BAC VC10 C1K	RAF No 10 Sqn, Brize Norton	
XV106	BAC VC10 C1K	RAF No 10 Sqn, Brize Norton	
XV107	BAC VC10 C1K	RAF No 10 Sqn, Brize Norton	
XV108	BAC VC10 C1K	RAF No 10 Sqn, Brize Norton	
XV109	BAC VC10 C1K	RAF No 10 Sqn, Brize Norton	
XV118	WS Scout AH1 (9141M)	Privately owned, North Weald	
XV122	WS Scout AH1 [D]	R. Military College of Science, Shrivenham	
XV123	WS Scout AH1	RAF Shawbury, on display	
XV124	WS Scout AH1 [W]	Army SEAE, Arborfield	
XV127	WS Scout AH1	Museum of Army Flying, Middle Wallop	
XV130	WS Scout AH1 (G-BWJW) [R]	Privately owned, Bournemouth	
XV131	WS Scout AH1 [Y]	AAC 70 Aircraft Workshops, Middle Wallop, BDRT	
XV136	WS Scout AH1 [X]	AAC Netheravon, on display	
XV137	WS Scout AH1 (G-CRUM)	Privately owned, Chiseldon, Wilts	
XV137	WS Scout AH1 (XV139)	AAC, Wattisham	
XV138	WS Scout AH1	Privately owned, East Dereham, Norfolk	
XV140	WS Scout AH1 (G-KAXL) [K]	Kennet Aviation, North Weald	
XV141	WS Scout AH1	REME Museum, Arborfield	
XV147	HS Nimrod MR1(mod) (fuselage)	*Scrapped at Warton, March 2003*	
XV148	HS Nimrod MR1(mod) <ff>	Privately owned, Malmesbury	
XV161	HS Buccaneer S2B (9117M) <ff>	Dundonald Aviation Centre	
XV165	HS Buccaneer S2B <ff>	Farnborough Air Sciences Trust, Farnborough	
XV168	HS Buccaneer S2B	BAE Systems Brough, on display	
XV177	Lockheed C-130K Hercules C3	RAF Lyneham Transport Wing	
XV179	Lockheed C-130K Hercules C1	RAF Lyneham Transport Wing	
XV184	Lockheed C-130K Hercules C3	RAF Lyneham Transport Wing	
XV188	Lockheed C-130K Hercules C3	RAF Lyneham Transport Wing	
XV196	Lockheed C-130K Hercules C1	RAF Lyneham Transport Wing	
XV197	Lockheed C-130K Hercules C3	RAF Lyneham Transport Wing	
XV199	Lockheed C-130K Hercules C3	RAF Lyneham Transport Wing	
XV200	Lockheed C-130K Hercules C1	RAF Lyneham Transport Wing	
XV201	Lockheed C-130K Hercules C1K (fuselage)	Marshalls, Cambridge	
XV202	Lockheed C-130K Hercules C3	RAF Lyneham Transport Wing	

Notes	Serial	Type (other identity) [code]	Owner/operator, location or fate
	XV205	Lockheed C-130K Hercules C1	RAF Lyneham Transport Wing
	XV206	Lockheed C-130K Hercules C1	RAF Lyneham Transport Wing
	XV208	Lockheed C-130K Hercules W2	*Sold to the Dutch Air Force, October 2004*
	XV209	Lockheed C-130K Hercules C3	RAF Lyneham Transport Wing
	XV212	Lockheed C-130K Hercules C3	RAF Lyneham Transport Wing
	XV214	Lockheed C-130K Hercules C3	RAF Lyneham Transport Wing
	XV217	Lockheed C-130K Hercules C3	RAF Lyneham Transport Wing
	XV220	Lockheed C-130K Hercules C3	RAF Lyneham Transport Wing
	XV221	Lockheed C-130K Hercules C3	RAF Lyneham Transport Wing
	XV226	HS Nimrod MR2	RAF Kinloss MR Wing
	XV227	HS Nimrod MR2	RAF Kinloss MR Wing
	XV228	HS Nimrod MR2	RAF Kinloss MR Wing
	XV229	HS Nimrod MR2	RAF Kinloss MR Wing
	XV230	HS Nimrod MR2	RAF Kinloss MR Wing
	XV231	HS Nimrod MR2	RAF Kinloss MR Wing
	XV232	HS Nimrod MR2	RAF Kinloss MR Wing
	XV235	HS Nimrod MR2	RAF Kinloss MR Wing
	XV236	HS Nimrod MR2	RAF Kinloss MR Wing
	XV237	HS Nimrod MR2 <ff>	*Scrapped*
	XV238	HS Nimrod <R> (parts of G-ALYW)	RAF M&RU, Bottesford
	XV240	HS Nimrod MR2	RAF Kinloss MR Wing
	XV241	HS Nimrod MR2	RAF Kinloss MR Wing
	XV243	HS Nimrod MR2	RAF Kinloss MR Wing
	XV244	HS Nimrod MR2	RAF Kinloss MR Wing
	XV245	HS Nimrod MR2	RAF Kinloss MR Wing
	XV246	HS Nimrod MR2	RAF Kinloss MR Wing
	XV248	HS Nimrod MR2	RAF Kinloss MR Wing
	XV249	HS Nimrod R1	RAF No 51 Sqn, Waddington
	XV250	HS Nimrod MR2	RAF Kinloss MR Wing
	XV252	HS Nimrod MR2	RAF Kinloss MR Wing
	XV253	HS Nimrod MR2 (9118M)	DPA/BAE Systems, Woodford
	XV254	HS Nimrod MR2	RAF Kinloss MR Wing
	XV255	HS Nimrod MR2	RAF Kinloss MR Wing
	XV259	BAe Nimrod AEW3 <ff>	Privately owned, Carlisle
	XV260	HS Nimrod MR2	RAF Kinloss MR Wing
	XV263	BAe Nimrod AEW3P (8967M) <ff>	BAE Systems, Warton, instructional use
	XV263	BAe Nimrod AEW3P (8967M) <rf>	DPA/BAE Systems, Woodford
	XV268	DHC2 Beaver AL1 (G-BVER)	Privately owned, Cumbernauld
	XV277	HS P.1127(RAF)	Royal Scottish Mus'm of Flight, E Fortune
	XV279	HS P.1127(RAF) (8566M)	RAF Harrier Maintenance School, Wittering
	XV280	HS P.1127(RAF) <ff>	RNAS Yeovilton Fire Section
	XV290	Lockheed C-130K Hercules C3	RAF Lyneham Transport Wing
	XV291	Lockheed C-130K Hercules C1	*To Austria as 8T-CB, 18 February 2004*
	XV294	Lockheed C-130K Hercules C3	RAF Lyneham Transport Wing
	XV295	Lockheed C-130K Hercules C1	RAF Lyneham Transport Wing
	XV299	Lockheed C-130K Hercules C3	RAF Lyneham Transport Wing
	XV301	Lockheed C-130K Hercules C3	RAF Lyneham Transport Wing
	XV302	Lockheed C-130K Hercules C3	Marshalls, Cambridge, fatigue test airframe
	XV303	Lockheed C-130K Hercules C3	RAF Lyneham Transport Wing
	XV304	Lockheed C-130K Hercules C3	RAF Lyneham Transport Wing
	XV305	Lockheed C-130K Hercules C3	RAF Lyneham Transport Wing
	XV307	Lockheed C-130K Hercules C3	RAF Lyneham Transport Wing
	XV328	BAC Lightning T5 <ff>	Phoenix Aviation, Bruntingthorpe
	XV333	HS Buccaneer S2B [234/H]	FAA Museum, RNAS Yeovilton
	XV337	HS Buccaneer S2C (8852M) <ff>	Privately owned, Diseworth, Leics
	XV344	HS Buccaneer S2C	QinetiQ Farnborough, on display
	XV350	HS Buccaneer S2B	East Midlands Airport Aeropark
	XV352	HS Buccaneer S2B <ff>	RAF Manston History Museum
	XV353	HS Buccaneer S2B (9144M) <ff>	Privately owned, Dalkeith
	XV359	HS Buccaneer S2B [035/R]	RNAS Culdrose, on display
	XV361	HS Buccaneer S2B	Ulster Aviation Society, Langford Lodge
	XV370	Sikorsky SH-3D [260]	RN AESS, *HMS Sultan*, Gosport
	XV371	WS61 Sea King HAS1(DB) [261]	SFDO, RNAS Culdrose
	XV372	WS61 Sea King HAS1	RAF HMF, St Mawgan
	XV399	McD F-4M Phantom FGR2 <ff>	*Scrapped*
	XV401	McD F-4M Phantom FGR2 [I]	Boscombe Down Aviation Collection
	XV402	McD F-4M Phantom FGR2 <ff>	Robertsbridge Aviation Society, Mayfield
	XV406	McD F-4M Phantom FGR2 (9098M) [CK]	Solway Aviation Society, Carlisle
	XV408	McD F-4M Phantom FGR2 (9165M) [Z]	RAF Fairford, derelict

Serial	Type (other identity) [code]	Owner/operator, location or fate	Notes
XV411	McD F-4M Phantom FGR2 (9103M) [L]	MoD FSCTE, Manston	
XV415	McD F-4M Phantom FGR2 (9163M) [E]	RAF Boulmer, on display	
XV420	McD F-4M Phantom FGR2 (9247M) [BT]	RAF Neatishead, at main gate	
XV424	McD F-4M Phantom FGR2 (9152M) [I]	RAF Museum, Hendon	
XV426	McD F-4M Phantom FGR2 <ff>	The Cockpit Collection, RAF Coltishall	
XV426	McD F-4M Phantom FGR2 [P] <rf>	RAF Coningsby, BDRT	
XV435	McD F-4M Phantom FGR2 [R]	QinetiQ Llanbedr Fire Section	
XV460	McD F-4M Phantom FGR2 <ff>	No 2214 Sqn ATC, Usworth	
XV474	McD F-4M Phantom FGR2 [T]	The Old Flying Machine Company, Duxford	
XV490	McD F-4M Phantom FGR2 <ff>	Privately owned, Nantwich	
XV497	McD F-4M Phantom FGR2 [D]	RAF No 23 Sqn Waddington, (preserved)	
XV498	McD F-4M Phantom FGR2 (XV500/9113M) [U]	RAF St Athan, on display	
XV499	McD F-4M Phantom FGR2	RAF Leeming, WLT	
XV581	McD F-4K Phantom FG1 (9070M) <ff>	No 2481 Sqn ATC, Bridge of Don	
XV582	McD F-4K Phantom FG1 (9066M) [M]	RAF Leuchars, on display	
XV586	McD F-4K Phantom FG1 (9067M) [AJ]	RAF Leuchars, on display	
XV591	McD F-4K Phantom FG1 <ff>	RAF Museum, Cosford	
XV625	WS Wasp HAS1 [471]	RN, stored *HMS Sultan*, Gosport	
XV631	WS Wasp HAS1 (fuselage)	QinetiQ Acoustics Dept, Farnborough	
XV642	WS61 Sea King HAS2A [259]	RN AESS, *HMS Sultan*, Gosport	
XV643	WS61 Sea King HAS6 [262]	RAF St Athan, BDRT	
XV647	WS61 Sea King HU5 [707]	RN AMG, Culdrose	
XV648	WS61 Sea King HU5 [818/CU]	RN No 771 Sqn, Culdrose	
XV649	WS61 Sea King AEW7 [180/CU]	RN No 849 Sqn, HQ Flt, Culdrose	
XV651	WS61 Sea King HU5 [824/CU]	RN No 771 Sqn, Culdrose	
XV653	WS61 Sea King HAS6 (9326M) [63/CU]	RAF No 1 SoTT, Cosford	
XV654	WS61 Sea King HAS6 [705] (wreck)	SFDO, RNAS Culdrose	
XV655	WS61 Sea King HAS6 [270/N]	RN, stored *HMS Sultan*, Gosport	
XV656	WS61 Sea King AEW7 [185/N]	RN No 849 Sqn, B Flt, Culdrose	
XV657	WS61 Sea King HAS5 (*ZA135*) [32/DD]	SFDO, RNAS Culdrose	
XV659	WS61 Sea King HAS6 (9324M) [62/CU]	RAF No 1 SoTT, Cosford	
XV660	WS61 Sea King HAS6 [69]	RN, stored *HMS Sultan*, Gosport	
XV661	WS61 Sea King HU5 [821]	RN AMG, Culdrose	
XV663	WS61 Sea King HAS6	RN, stored *HMS Sultan*, Gosport	
XV664	WS61 Sea King AEW7 [187/R]	RN No 849 Sqn, A Flt, Culdrose	
XV665	WS61 Sea King HAS6 [507/CU]	RN, stored *HMS Sultan*, Gosport	
XV666	WS61 Sea King HU5 [823]	RN No 771 Sqn, Culdrose	
XV669	WS61 Sea King HAS1 [10]	*Scrapped at Fleetlands*	
XV670	WS61 Sea King HU5 [588]	RN/Westland Helicopters, Yeovil	
XV671	WS61 Sea King AEW7 [183/N]	RN No 849 Sqn, B Flt, Culdrose	
XV672	WS61 Sea King AEW7	RN/DARA, Fleetlands	
XV673	WS61 Sea King HU5 [827/CU]	RN No 771 Sqn, Culdrose	
XV674	WS61 Sea King HAS6 [015/L]	RN, stored *HMS Sultan*, Gosport	
XV675	WS61 Sea King HAS6 [701/PW]	RN, stored *HMS Sultan*, Gosport	
XV676	WS61 Sea King HAS6 [ZE]	RN/DARA, Fleetlands (under conversion)	
XV677	WS61 Sea King HAS6 [269]	RN, stored *HMS Sultan*, Gosport	
XV696	WS61 Sea King HAS6 [267/N]	RN, stored *HMS Sultan*, Gosport	
XV697	WS61 Sea King AEW7 [181/CU]	RN No 849 Sqn, HQ Flt, Culdrose	
XV699	WS61 Sea King HU5 [823/CU]	RN No 771 Sqn, Culdrose	
XV700	WS61 Sea King HAS6 [ZC]	RN No 846 Sqn, Yeovilton	
XV701	WS61 Sea King HAS6 [268/N]	RN, stored *HMS Sultan*, Gosport	
XV703	WS61 Sea King HAS6 [ZD]	RN No 846 Sqn, Yeovilton	
XV705	WS61 Sea King HAR5 [821/CU]	RN/DARA, stored Fleetlands	
XV706	WS61 Sea King HAS6 [017/L]	RN ETS, Culdrose	
XV707	WS61 Sea King AEW7 [184/N]	RN No 849 Sqn, B Flt, Culdrose	
XV708	WS61 Sea King HAS6 [501/CU]	RN, stored *HMS Sultan*, Gosport	
XV709	WS61 Sea King HAS6 (9303M) [263]	RAF St Mawgan, instructional use	
XV710	WS61 Sea King HAS6 (9325M) [64/CU]	RAF No 1 SoTT, Cosford	

Notes	*Serial*	*Type (other identity) [code]*	*Owner/operator, location or fate*
	XV711	WS61 Sea King HAS6 [515/CT]	RN, stored *HMS Sultan*, Gosport
	XV712	WS61 Sea King HAS6 [269]	RN AESS, *HMS Sultan*, Gosport
	XV713	WS61 Sea King HAS6 [018]	RN, stored *HMS Sultan*, Gosport
	XV714	WS61 Sea King AEW7 [188/R]	RN No 849 Sqn, A Flt, Culdrose
	XV720	WS58 Wessex HC2	RN, stored *HMS Sultan*, Gosport
	XV722	WS58 Wessex HC2 [WH]	Privately owned, Hixon, Staffs
	XV724	WS58 Wessex HC2	RN AESS, *HMS Sultan*, Gosport
	XV725	WS58 Wessex HC2 [C]	RN AESS, *HMS Sultan*, Gosport
	XV726	WS58 Wessex HC2 [J]	RAF, stored Shawbury
	XV728	WS58 Wessex HC2 [A]	Newark Air Museum, Winthorpe
	XV730	WS58 Wessex HC2 [*Clubs*]	*Sold to New Zealand, January 2004*
	XV731	WS58 Wessex HC2 [Y]	Privately owned, stored Redhill
	XV732	WS58 Wessex HCC4	RAF Museum, Hendon
	XV733	WS58 Wessex HCC4	The Helicopter Museum, Weston-super-Mare
	XV741	HS Harrier GR3 [41]	SFDO, RNAS Culdrose
	XV744	HS Harrier GR3 (9167M) [3K]	R. Military College of Science, Shrivenham
	XV748	HS Harrier GR3 [3D]	Yorkshire Air Museum, Elvington
	XV751	HS Harrier GR3	Gatwick Aviation Museum, Charlwood
	XV752	HS Harrier GR3 (9078M) [B,HF]	RAF No 1 SoTT, Cosford
	XV753	HS Harrier GR3 (9075M) [53]	SFDO, RNAS Culdrose
	XV755	HS Harrier GR3 [M]	RNAS Yeovilton Fire Section
	XV759	HS Harrier GR3 [O] <ff>	Privately owned, Hitchin, Herts
	XV760	HS Harrier GR3 <ff>	Privately owned, Sussex
	XV779	HS Harrier GR3 (8931M)	RAF Wittering on display
	XV783	HS Harrier GR3 [83]	SFDO, RNAS Culdrose
	XV784	HS Harrier GR3 (8909M) <ff>	Boscombe Down Aviation Collection
	XV786	HS Harrier GR3 <ff>	RNAS Culdrose
	XV786	HS Harrier GR3 [S] <rf>	RN, Predannack Fire School
	XV798	HS Harrier GR1(mod)	Bristol Aero Collection, stored Kemble
	XV804	HS Harrier GR3 (9280M) [O]	RAF North Luffenham Training Area
	XV808	HS Harrier GR3 (9076M) [08]	SFDO, RNAS Culdrose
	XV810	HS Harrier GR3 (9038M) [K]	Privately owned, Bruntingthorpe
	XV814	DH106 Comet 4 (G-APDF) <ff>	Privately owned, Chipping Campden
	XV863	HS Buccaneer S2B (9115M/ 9139M/9145M) [S]	RAF Lossiemouth
	XV864	HS Buccaneer S2B (9234M)	MoD FSCTE, Manston
	XV865	HS Buccaneer S2B (9226M)	Privately owned, Duxford
	XV867	HS Buccaneer S2B <ff>	Highland Aircraft Preservation Group, Dalcross
	XW175	HS Harrier T4(VAAC)	DPA/AFD/QinetiQ, Boscombe Down
	XW198	WS Puma HC1	RAF No 230 Sqn, Aldergrove
	XW199	WS Puma HC1	RAF No 33 Sqn, Benson
	XW200	WS Puma HC1 (wreck)	RAF, stored Shawbury
	XW201	WS Puma HC1	RAF No 230 Sqn, Aldergrove
	XW202	WS Puma HC1	RAF No 230 Sqn, Aldergrove
	XW204	WS Puma HC1	RAF No 33 Sqn, Benson
	XW206	WS Puma HC1	RAF No 33 Sqn, Benson
	XW207	WS Puma HC1	RAF No 33 Sqn, Benson
	XW208	WS Puma HC1	RAF No 33 Sqn, Benson
	XW209	WS Puma HC1	RAF No 230 Sqn, Aldergrove
	XW210	WS Puma HC1 (comp XW215)	RAF No 230 Sqn, Aldergrove
	XW211	WS Puma HC1	RAF No 33 Sqn, Benson
	XW212	WS Puma HC1	RAF No 230 Sqn, Aldergrove
	XW213	WS Puma HC1	RAF No 230 Sqn, Aldergrove
	XW214	WS Puma HC1	RAF No 33 Sqn, Benson
	XW216	WS Puma HC1	DPA/Westland Helicopters, Yeovil
	XW217	WS Puma HC1	RAF No 230 Sqn, Aldergrove
	XW218	WS Puma HC1	RAF No 1563 Flt, Basrah, Iraq
	XW219	WS Puma HC1	RAF No 33 Sqn, Benson
	XW220	WS Puma HC1	RAF No 33 Sqn, Benson
	XW221	WS Puma HC1	*Crashed 19 July 2004, Basrah*
	XW222	WS Puma HC1	RAF No 33 Sqn, Benson
	XW223	WS Puma HC1	RAF No 33 Sqn, Benson
	XW224	WS Puma HC1	RAF No 230 Sqn, Aldergrove
	XW226	WS Puma HC1	RAF 1563 Flt, Basrah, Iraq
	XW227	WS Puma HC1	DPA/Westland Helicopters, Yeovil (on repair)
	XW229	WS Puma HC1	RAF No 230 Sqn, Aldergrove
	XW231	WS Puma HC1	RAF No 230 Sqn, Aldergrove
	XW232	WS Puma HC1	RAF No 1563 Flt, Basrah, Iraq
	XW234	WS Puma HC1	*Scrapped, 2004*

Serial	Type (other identity) [code]	Owner/operator, location or fate	Notes
XW235	WS Puma HC1	RAF No 230 Sqn, Aldergrove	
XW236	WS Puma HC1	RAF No 33 Sqn, Benson	
XW237	WS Puma HC1	RAF No 33 Sqn, Benson	
XW241	Sud SA330E Puma	QinetiQ Avionics & Sensors Dept, Farnborough	
XW264	HS Harrier T2 <ff>	Gloucestershire Avn Coll, stored Gloucester	
XW265	HS Harrier T4A (9258M) <ff>	No 2345 Sqn ATC, RAF Leuchars	
XW265	HS Harrier T4A (9258M) <rf>	DARA, St Athan	
XW267	HS Harrier T4 (9263M) [SA]	Territorial Army, Toton, Notts	
XW269	HS Harrier T4	Boscombe Down Aviation Collection	
XW270	HS Harrier T4 (fuselage)	Coventry University, instructional use	
XW271	HS Harrier T4 [71]	SFDO, RNAS Culdrose	
XW272	HS Harrier T4 (8783M) (fuselage) (comp XV281)	Marsh Lane Technical School, Preston	
XW276	Aérospatiale SA341 Gazelle (F-ZWRI)	Newark Air Museum, Winthorpe	
XW281	WS Scout AH1 (G-BYNZ) [T]	Privately owned, Wembury, Devon	
XW283	WS Scout AH1 [U]	RM, stored Yeovilton	
XW284	WS Scout AH1 [A] (fuselage)	*Currently not known*	
XW289	BAC Jet Provost T5A (G-BVXT/ G-JPVA) [73]	Kennet Aviation, North Weald	
XW290	BAC Jet Provost T5A (9199M) [41,MA]	RAF No 1 SoTT, Cosford	
XW292	BAC Jet Provost T5A (9128M) [32]	RAF No 1 SoTT, Cosford	
XW293	BAC Jet Provost T5 (G-BWCS) [Z]	Privately owned, Bournemouth	
XW294	BAC Jet Provost T5A (9129M) [45]	RAF No 1 SoTT, Cosford	
XW299	BAC Jet Provost T5A (9146M) [60,MB]	RAF No 1 SoTT, Cosford	
XW301	BAC Jet Provost T5A (9147M) [63,MC]	RAF No 1 SoTT, Cosford	
XW303	BAC Jet Provost T5A (9119M) [127]	RAF No 1 SoTT, Cosford	
XW304	BAC Jet Provost T5 (9172M) [MD]	RAF No 1 SoTT, Cosford	
XW309	BAC Jet Provost T5 (9179M) [V,ME]	RAF No 1 SoTT, Cosford	
XW311	BAC Jet Provost T5 (9180M) [W,MF]	RAF No 1 SoTT, Cosford	
XW312	BAC Jet Provost T5A (9109M) [64]	RAF No 1 SoTT, Cosford	
XW315	BAC Jet Provost T5A <ff>	Privately owned, Wolverhampton	
XW318	BAC Jet Provost T5A (9190M) [78,MG]	RAF No 1 SoTT, Cosford	
XW320	BAC Jet Provost T5A (9015M) [71]	RAF No 1 SoTT, Cosford	
XW321	BAC Jet Provost T5A (9154M) [62,MH]	RAF No 1 SoTT, Cosford	
XW323	BAC Jet Provost T5A (9166M) [86]	RAF Museum, Hendon	
XW324	BAC Jet Provost T5 (G-BWSG) [K]	Privately owned, North Weald	
XW325	BAC Jet Provost T5B (G-BWGF) [E]	Privately owned, Blackpool	
XW327	BAC Jet Provost T5A (9130M) [62]	RAF No 1 SoTT, Cosford	
XW328	BAC Jet Provost T5A (9177M) [75,MI]	RAF No 1 SoTT, Cosford	
XW330	BAC Jet Provost T5A (9195M) [82,MJ]	RAF No 1 SoTT, Cosford	
XW333	BAC Jet Provost T5A (G-BVTC)	Global Aviation, Humberside	
XW335	BAC Jet Provost T5A (9061M) [74]	RAF No 1 SoTT, Cosford	
XW351	BAC Jet Provost T5A (9062M) [31]	RAF No 1 SoTT, Cosford	
XW353	BAC Jet Provost T5A (9090M) [3]	RAF Cranwell, on display	
XW354	BAC Jet Provost T5A (XW355/ G-JPTV)	Privately owned, Sandtoft	
XW358	BAC Jet Provost T5A (9181M) [59,MK]	RAF No 1 SoTT, Cosford	
XW360	BAC Jet Provost T5A (9153M) [61,ML]	RAF No 1 SoTT, Cosford	
XW361	BAC Jet Provost T5A (9192M) [81,MM]	RAF No 1 SoTT, Cosford	
XW363	BAC Jet Provost T5A [36]	BAE Systems North West Heritage Group, Warton	
XW364	BAC Jet Provost T5A (9188M) [35,MN]	RAF No 1 SoTT, Cosford	
XW365	BAC Jet Provost T5A (9018M) [73]	RAF No 1 SoTT, Cosford	
XW366	BAC Jet Provost T5A (9097M) [75]	RAF No 1 SoTT, Cosford	

Notes	Serial	Type (other identity) [code]	Owner/operator, location or fate
	XW367	BAC Jet Provost T5A (9193M) [64,MO]	RAF No 1 SoTT, Cosford
	XW370	BAC Jet Provost T5A (9196M) [72,MP]	RAF No 1 SoTT, Cosford
	XW375	BAC Jet Provost T5A (9149M) [52]	RAF No 1 SoTT, Cosford
	XW404	BAC Jet Provost T5A (9049M)	DARA Training School, RAF St Athan
	XW405	BAC Jet Provost T5A (9187M) [J,MQ]	RAF No 1 SoTT, Cosford
	XW409	BAC Jet Provost T5A (9047M)	DARA Training School, RAF St Athan
	XW410	BAC Jet Provost T5A (9125M) [80,MR]	RAF No 1 SoTT, Cosford
	XW413	BAC Jet Provost T5A (9126M) [69]	RAF No 1 SoTT, Cosford
	XW416	BAC Jet Provost T5A (9191M) [84,MS]	RAF No 1 SoTT, Cosford
	XW418	BAC Jet Provost T5A (9173M) [MT]	RAF No 1 SoTT, Cosford
	XW419	BAC Jet Provost T5A (9120M) [125]	RAF No 1 SoTT, Cosford
	XW420	BAC Jet Provost T5A (9194M) [83,MU]	RAF No 1 SoTT, Cosford
	XW421	BAC Jet Provost T5A (9111M) [60]	RAF No 1 SoTT, Cosford
	XW422	BAC Jet Provost T5A (G-BWEB) [3]	Privately owned, Kemble
	XW423	BAC Jet Provost T5A (G-BWUW) [14]	Deeside College, Connah's Quay, Clwyd
	XW425	BAC Jet Provost T5A (9200M) [H,MV]	RAF No 1 SoTT, Cosford
	XW427	BAC Jet Provost T5A (9124M) [67]	RAF No 1 SoTT, Cosford
	XW430	BAC Jet Provost T5A (9176M) [77,MW]	RAF No 1 SoTT, Cosford
	XW432	BAC Jet Provost T5A (9127M) [76,MX]	RAF No 1 SoTT, Cosford
	XW433	BAC Jet Provost T5A (G-JPRO)	Global Aviation, Humberside
	XW434	BAC Jet Provost T5A (9091M) [78,MY]	RAF No 1 SoTT, Cosford
	XW436	BAC Jet Provost T5A (9148M) [68]	RAF No 1 SoTT, Cosford
	XW530	HS Buccaneer S2B	Buccaneer Service Station, Elgin
	XW541	HS Buccaneer S2B (8858M) <ff>	Privately owned, Mold
	XW544	HS Buccaneer S2B (8857M) [Y]	Privately owned, Bruntingthorpe
	XW547	HS Buccaneer S2B (9095M/ 9169M) [R]	RAF Museum, Hendon
	XW550	HS Buccaneer S2B <ff>	Privately owned, West Horndon, Essex
	XW563	SEPECAT Jaguar S (*XX822*/ 8563M)	RAF Coltishall, on display
	XW566	SEPECAT Jaguar B	Farnborough Air Sciences Trust, Farnborough
	XW616	WS Scout AH1	AAC Dishforth, instructional use
	XW630	HS Harrier GR3	RNAS Yeovilton, Fire Section
	XW635	Beagle D5/180 (G-AWSW)	Privately owned, Spanhoe Lodge
	XW664	HS Nimrod R1	RAF No 51 Sqn, Waddington
	XW665	HS Nimrod R1	RAF No 51 Sqn, Waddington
	XW666	HS Nimrod R1 <ff>	Aeroventure, Doncaster
	XW750	HS748 Series 107	DPA/AFD/QinetiQ, Boscombe Down
	XW763	HS Harrier GR3 (9002M/9041M) <ff>	Privately owned, Wigston, Leics
	XW768	HS Harrier GR3 (9072M) [N]	RAF No 1 SoTT, Cosford
	XW784	Mitchell-Procter Kittiwake I (G-BBRN) [VL]	Privately owned, Henstridge
	XW795	WS Scout AH1	Blessingbourne Museum, Fivemiletown, Co Tyrone, NI
	XW796	WS Scout AH1	Privately owned, Sproughton
	XW838	WS Lynx (TAD 009)	Army SEAE, Arborfield
	XW839	WS Lynx	The Helicopter Museum, Weston-super-Mare
	XW844	WS Gazelle AH1	DARA Fleetlands Apprentice School
	XW846	WS Gazelle AH1	AAC No 665 Sqn/5 Regt, Aldergrove
	XW847	WS Gazelle AH1 [H]	AAC No 665 Sqn/5 Regt, Aldergrove
	XW848	WS Gazelle AH1 [D]	AAC No 671 Sqn/2 Regt, Middle Wallop
	XW849	WS Gazelle AH1 [G]	RM No 847 Sqn, Yeovilton
	XW851	WS Gazelle AH1	RM, stored Shawbury
	XW852	WS Gazelle HCC4 (9331M)	RAF No 1 SoTT, Cosford
	XW854	WS Gazelle HT2 (G-CBSD) [46/CU]	Privately owned, Redhill

Serial	Type (other identity) [code]	Owner/operator, location or fate	Notes
XW855	WS Gazelle HCC4	RAF Museum, Hendon	
XW856	WS Gazelle HT2 (G-GAZL) [49/CU]	Privately owned, Addison Mains	
XW857	WS Gazelle HT2 (G-CBSB) [55/CU]	*Repainted as G-CBSB*	
XW858	WS Gazelle HT3 (G-DMSS) [C]	Privately owned, Murton, York	
XW860	WS Gazelle HT2 (TAD021)	Army SEAE, Arborfield	
XW861	WS Gazelle HT2 (G-BZFJ) [52/CU]	Privately owned, Goodwood	
XW862	WS Gazelle HT3 (G-CBKC) [D]	Privately owned, Stapleford Tawney	
XW863	WS Gazelle HT2 (TAD022) [42/CU]	Army SEAE, Arborfield	
XW864	WS Gazelle HT2 [54/CU]	FAA Museum, stored RNAS Yeovilton	
XW865	WS Gazelle AH1 [5C]	AAC No 29 Flt, BATUS, Suffield, Canada	
XW866	WS Gazelle HT3 (G-BXTH) [E]	Flightline Ltd, Southend	
XW870	WS Gazelle HT3 [F]	MoD FSCTE, Manston	
XW871	WS Gazelle HT2 (G-CBSC) [44/CU]	Privately owned, Goodwood	
XW887	WS Gazelle HT2 (G-CBFD) [FL]	*Crashed 18 November 2003, Doncaster*	
XW888	WS Gazelle AH1 (TAD017)	Army SEAE, Arborfield	
XW889	WS Gazelle AH1 (TAD018)	Army SEAE, Arborfield	
XW890	WS Gazelle HT2	RNAS Yeovilton, on display	
XW892	WS Gazelle AH1 (9292M) [C]	Privately owned, Sproughton	
XW893	WS Gazelle AH1 <ff>	Privately owned, East Garston, Bucks	
XW895	WS Gazelle HT2 (G-BXZD) [51/CU]	Privately owned, Barnard Castle	
XW897	WS Gazelle AH1	AAC No 663 Sqn/3 Regt, Wattisham	
XW898	WS Gazelle HT3 (G-CBXT) [G]	Privately owned, Redhill	
XW899	WS Gazelle AH1 [Z]	AAC No 658 Sqn/7 Regt, Netheravon	
XW900	WS Gazelle AH1 (TAD900)	Army SEAE, Arborfield	
XW902	WS Gazelle HT3 [H]	DPA/QinetiQ, Boscombe Down, spares use	
XW904	WS Gazelle AH1 [H]	AAC No 6(V) Flt/7 Regt, Shawbury	
XW906	WS Gazelle HT3 [J]	QinetiQ Boscombe Down, Apprentice School	
XW908	WS Gazelle AH1 [A]	AAC No 666(V) Sqn/7 Regt, Netheravon	
XW909	WS Gazelle AH1	AAC No 672 Sqn/9 Regt, Dishforth	
XW912	WS Gazelle AH1 (TAD019)	Army SEAE, Arborfield	
XW913	WS Gazelle AH1	AAC No 663 Sqn/3 Regt, Wattisham	
XW917	HS Harrier GR3 (8975M)	RAF Cottesmore, at main gate	
XW919	HS Harrier GR3 [W]	R. Military College of Science, Shrivenham	
XW922	HS Harrier GR3 (8885M)	MoD FSCTE, Manston	
XW923	HS Harrier GR3 (8724M) <ff>	RAF Wittering, Fire Section	
XW924	HS Harrier GR3 (9073M) [G]	RAF Cottesmore, preserved	
XW934	HS Harrier T4 [Y]	DPA, QinetiQ Farnborough (wfu)	
XX105	BAC 1-11/201AC (G-ASJD)	DPA, QinetiQ, Boscombe Down (wfu)	
XX108	SEPECAT Jaguar GR3	Imperial War Museum, Duxford	
XX109	SEPECAT Jaguar GR1 (8918M) [US]	City of Norwich Aviation Museum	
XX110	SEPECAT Jaguar GR1 (8955M) [EP]	RAF No 1 SoTT, Cosford	
XX110	SEPECAT Jaguar GR1 <R> (BAPC 169)	RAF No 1 SoTT, Cosford	
XX112	SEPECAT Jaguar GR3A [EA]	RAF No 6 Sqn, Coltishall	
XX115	SEPECAT Jaguar GR1 (8821M) (fuselage)	RAF No 1 SoTT, Cosford	
XX116	SEPECAT Jaguar GR3A [EO]	RAF No 6 Sqn, Coltishall	
XX117	SEPECAT Jaguar GR3A [PA]	RAF No 16(R) Sqn, Coltishall	
XX119	SEPECAT Jaguar GR3A (8898M) [GD]	RAF No 54 Sqn, Coltishall	
XX121	SEPECAT Jaguar GR1 [EQ]	Privately owned, Charlwood, Surrey	
XX139	SEPECAT Jaguar T4 [PT]	RAF No 16(R) Sqn, Coltishall	
XX140	SEPECAT Jaguar T2 (9008M) [D,JJ]	Privately owned, Charlwood, Surrey	
XX141	SEPECAT Jaguar T2A [T]	AMIF, RAFC Cranwell	
XX144	SEPECAT Jaguar T2A [U]	RAF, stored Shawbury	
XX145	SEPECAT Jaguar T2A	DPA/ETPS, Boscombe Down	
XX146	SEPECAT Jaguar T4 [GT]	RAF No 54 Sqn, Coltishall	
XX150	SEPECAT Jaguar T4 [PW]	RAF No 16(R) Sqn, Coltishall	
XX153	WS Lynx AH1	Museum of Army Flying, Middle Wallop	
XX154	HS Hawk T1	DPA/DARA, St Athan	
XX156	HS Hawk T1	RN FRADU, Culdrose	
XX157	HS Hawk T1A	RAF No 4 FTS/*208(R) Sqn*, Valley	
XX158	HS Hawk T1A	DPA/DARA, St Athan	

Notes	*Serial*	*Type (other identity) [code]*	*Owner/operator, location or fate*
	XX159	HS Hawk T1A	RAF/DARA, St Athan
	XX160	HS Hawk T1 [CP]	RAF No 100 Sqn, Leeming
	XX161	HS Hawk T1W	RAF No 4 FTS/*208(R) Sqn*, Valley
	XX162	HS Hawk T1	RAF Aviation Medicine Flt, Boscombe Down
	XX165	HS Hawk T1	RN FRADU, Culdrose
	XX167	HS Hawk T1W	RN FRADU, Culdrose
	XX168	HS Hawk T1	RN FRADU, Culdrose
	XX169	HS Hawk T1	RAF No 4 FTS/*208(R) Sqn*, Valley
	XX170	HS Hawk T1	RN FRADU, Culdrose
	XX171	HS Hawk T1	RN FRADU, Culdrose
	XX172	HS Hawk T1	RAF No 4 FTS/*208(R) Sqn*, Valley
	XX173	HS Hawk T1	RN FRADU, Culdrose
	XX174	HS Hawk T1	RAF No 4 FTS/*19(R) Sqn*, Valley
	XX175	HS Hawk T1	RAF, stored Shawbury
	XX176	HS Hawk T1W	RAF No 4 FTS/*19(R) Sqn*, Valley
	XX177	HS Hawk T1	RAF No 4 FTS/*208(R) Sqn*, Valley
	XX178	HS Hawk T1W	RN FRADU, Culdrose
	XX179	HS Hawk T1W	RAF *Red Arrows*, Scampton
	XX181	HS Hawk T1W	RAF No 4 FTS/*208(R) Sqn*, Valley
	XX184	HS Hawk T1	RN FRADU, Culdrose
	XX185	HS Hawk T1	RAF No 4 FTS/*208(R) Sqn*, Valley
	XX187	HS Hawk T1A	RAF No 4 FTS, Valley
	XX188	HS Hawk T1A [CF]	RAF No 100 Sqn, Leeming
	XX189	HS Hawk T1A	RAF No 4 FTS/*19(R) Sqn*, Valley
	XX190	HS Hawk T1A	RAF No 4 FTS/*208(R) Sqn*, Valley
	XX191	HS Hawk T1A [CC]	RAF No 100 Sqn/JFACTSU, Leeming
	XX194	HS Hawk T1A [CL]	RAF No 100 Sqn, Leeming
	XX195	HS Hawk T1W	RAF No 4 FTS/*208(R) Sqn*, Valley
	XX196	HS Hawk T1A	RAF No 4 FTS/*19(R) Sqn*, Valley
	XX198	HS Hawk T1A	RAF No 4 FTS/*208(R) Sqn*, Valley
	XX199	HS Hawk T1A	RAF No 4 FTS/*19(R) Sqn*, Valley
	XX200	HS Hawk T1A [CF]	RAF No 4 FTS/*208(R) Sqn*, Valley
	XX201	HS Hawk T1A	RAF No 4 FTS, Valley
	XX202	HS Hawk T1A	RAF No 4 FTS/*19(R) Sqn*, Valley
	XX203	HS Hawk T1A	RAF No 4 FTS/*208(R) Sqn*, Valley
	XX204	HS Hawk T1A	RAF No 4 FTS/*19(R) Sqn*, Valley
	XX205	HS Hawk T1A	RAF No 4 FTS/*19(R) Sqn*, Valley
	XX217	HS Hawk T1A	RAF No 4 FTS/*208(R) Sqn*, Valley
	XX218	HS Hawk T1A	RAF No 4 FTS/*19(R) Sqn*, Valley
	XX219	HS Hawk T1A	RAF No 4 FTS/*208(R) Sqn*, Valley
	XX220	HS Hawk T1A	RAF No 4 FTS, Valley
	XX221	HS Hawk T1A	RAF No 4 FTS/*19(R) Sqn*, Valley
	XX222	HS Hawk T1A [CI]	RAF No 100 Sqn, Leeming
	XX223	HS Hawk T1 <ff>	Privately owned, Charlwood, Surrey
	XX224	HS Hawk T1W	RN FRADU, Culdrose
	XX225	HS Hawk T1 [CS]	RAF No 100 Sqn, Leeming
	XX226	HS Hawk T1	RN FRADU, Culdrose
	XX226	HS Hawk T1 <R> (*XX263*/ BAPC 152)	*Repainted as XX227*
	XX227	HS Hawk T1 <R> (*XX226*/ BAPC 152)	RAF M&RU, Bottesford
	XX227	HS Hawk T1A	RAF *Red Arrows*, Scampton
	XX228	HS Hawk T1A [CG]	RAF No 100 Sqn, Leeming
	XX230	HS Hawk T1A	RAF No 4 FTS/*208(R) Sqn*, Valley
	XX231	HS Hawk T1W	RN FRADU, Culdrose
	XX232	HS Hawk T1	RAF No 4 FTS/*208(R) Sqn*, Valley
	XX233	HS Hawk T1	RAF *Red Arrows*, Scampton
	XX234	HS Hawk T1	RN FRADU, Culdrose
	XX235	HS Hawk T1W	RAF No 4 FTS/*208(R) Sqn*, Valley
	XX236	HS Hawk T1W	RAF No 4 FTS/*19(R) Sqn*, Valley
	XX237	HS Hawk T1	RAF *Red Arrows*, Scampton
	XX238	HS Hawk T1	RN FRADU, Culdrose
	XX239	HS Hawk T1W	RAF No 4 FTS/*19(R) Sqn*, Valley
	XX240	HS Hawk T1	RN FRADU, Culdrose
	XX242	HS Hawk T1	RAF *Red Arrows*, Scampton
	XX244	HS Hawk T1	RAF No 4 FTS/*208(R) Sqn*, Valley
	XX245	HS Hawk T1	RAF No 4 FTS/*208(R) Sqn*, Valley
	XX246	HS Hawk T1A	RAF No 4 FTS/*19(R) Sqn*, Valley
	XX246	HS Hawk T1A <rf>	RAF CTTS, St Athan
	XX247	HS Hawk T1A [CM]	RAF No 100 Sqn, Leeming
	XX248	HS Hawk T1A [CJ]	RAF No 100 Sqn, Leeming
	XX250	HS Hawk T1	RAF/DARA, St Athan

Serial	Type (other identity) [code]	Owner/operator, location or fate	Notes
XX253	HS Hawk T1A	RAF *Red Arrows*, Scampton	
XX254	HS Hawk T1A <ff>	RAF/DARA, St Athan	
XX254	HS Hawk T1A	DPA/BAE Systems, stored Scampton	
XX254	HS Hawk T1A <R>	Privately owned, Marlow, Bucks	
XX255	HS Hawk T1A	RAF No 4 FTS/*208(R) Sqn*, Valley	
XX256	HS Hawk T1A [CX]	RAF No 4 FTS/*208(R) Sqn*, Valley	
XX257	HS Hawk T1A (fuselage)	Privately owned, Charlwood, Surrey	
XX258	HS Hawk T1A	RAF No 4 FTS/*19(R) Sqn*, Valley	
XX260	HS Hawk T1A	RAF *Red Arrows*, Scampton	
XX261	HS Hawk T1A	RAF No 4 FTS/*208(R) Sqn*, Valley	
XX263	HS Hawk T1A	RAF No 4 FTS/*208(R) Sqn*, Valley	
XX263	HS Hawk T1 <R> (*XX253*/ BAPC 171)	RAF M&RU, Bottesford	
XX264	HS Hawk T1A	RAF *Red Arrows*, Scampton	
XX265	HS Hawk T1A [CK]	RAF No 100 Sqn/JFACTSU, Leeming	
XX266	HS Hawk T1A	RAF *Red Arrows*, Scampton	
XX278	HS Hawk T1A [CD]	RAF No 100 Sqn, Leeming	
XX280	HS Hawk T1A	RAF No 4 FTS/*19(R) Sqn*, Valley	
XX281	HS Hawk T1A	DPA/BAE Systems, Warton (on loan)	
XX283	HS Hawk T1W	RAF No 4 FTS/*19(R) Sqn*, Valley	
XX284	HS Hawk T1A [CA]	RAF No 100 Sqn, Leeming	
XX285	HS Hawk T1A [CB]	RAF No 100 Sqn, Leeming	
XX286	HS Hawk T1A	RAF No 4 FTS/*19(R) Sqn*, Valley	
XX287	HS Hawk T1A	RAF No 4 FTS/*19(R) Sqn*, Valley	
XX289	HS Hawk T1A	RAF No 4 FTS/*208(R) Sqn*, Valley	
XX290	HS Hawk T1W [CU]	RAF, stored Shawbury	
XX292	HS Hawk T1	RAF *Red Arrows*, Scampton	
XX294	HS Hawk T1	RAF *Red Arrows*, Scampton	
XX295	HS Hawk T1W	RAF No 4 FTS/*208(R) Sqn*, Valley	
XX296	HS Hawk T1	RAF, stored Shawbury	
XX299	HS Hawk T1W [CH]	RAF No 100 Sqn, Leeming	
XX301	HS Hawk T1A	RAF No 4 FTS/*208(R) Sqn*, Valley	
XX303	HS Hawk T1A	RAF No 4 FTS/*19(R) Sqn*, Valley	
XX304	HS Hawk T1A <ff>	*Sold abroad*	
XX304	HS Hawk T1A <rf>	Cardiff International Airport Fire Section	
XX306	HS Hawk T1A	RAF *Red Arrows*, Scampton	
XX307	HS Hawk T1	RAF No 4 FTS/*208(R) Sqn*, Valley	
XX308	HS Hawk T1	RAF *Red Arrows*, Scampton	
XX309	HS Hawk T1	RAF No 4 FTS/*208(R) Sqn*, Valley	
XX310	HS Hawk T1W	RAF No 4 FTS/*208(R) Sqn*, Valley	
XX311	HS Hawk T1	RAF No 4 FTS/*19(R) Sqn*, Valley	
XX312	HS Hawk T1W	RAF No 4 FTS/*208(R) Sqn*, Valley	
XX313	HS Hawk T1W [CE]	RAF No 100 Sqn, Leeming	
XX314	HS Hawk T1W [CN]	RAF No 100 Sqn, Leeming	
XX315	HS Hawk T1A	RAF No 4 FTS/*19(R) Sqn*, Valley	
XX316	HS Hawk T1A	RAF No 4 FTS/*19(R) Sqn*, Valley	
XX317	HS Hawk T1A [CH]	RAF No 4 FTS/*208(R) Sqn*, Valley	
XX318	HS Hawk T1A	DPA/BAE Systems, Warton (on loan)	
XX319	HS Hawk T1A	RAF No 4 FTS/*208(R) Sqn*, Valley	
XX320	HS Hawk T1A	RAF No 4 FTS, Valley	
XX321	HS Hawk T1A	RAF No 4 FTS/*19(R) Sqn*, Valley	
XX322	HS Hawk T1A	RAF No 4 FTS/*208(R) Sqn*, Valley	
XX323	HS Hawk T1A	RAF No 4 FTS/*19(R) Sqn*, Valley	
XX324	HS Hawk T1A	RAF No 4 FTS/*19(R) Sqn*, Valley	
XX325	HS Hawk T1A [CT]	RN FRADU, Culdrose	
XX326	HS Hawk T1A <ff>	RAF/DARA, St Athan	
XX326	HS Hawk T1A	DPA/BAE Systems, Brough (on rebuild)	
XX327	HS Hawk T1	RAF Aviation Medicine Flt, Boscombe Down	
XX329	HS Hawk T1A	RAF No 4 FTS/*19(R) Sqn*, Valley	
XX330	HS Hawk T1A	RAF No 4 FTS/*19(R) Sqn*, Valley	
XX331	HS Hawk T1A	RAF No 4 FTS/*19(R) Sqn*, Valley	
XX332	HS Hawk T1A	RAF No 4 FTS/*19(R) Sqn*, Valley	
XX335	HS Hawk T1A [CR]	RAF No 100 Sqn, Leeming	
XX337	HS Hawk T1A	RAF/DARA, St Athan	
XX338	HS Hawk T1	RAF No 4 FTS/*19(R) Sqn*, Valley	
XX339	HS Hawk T1A	RAF No 4 FTS/*19(R) Sqn*, Valley	
XX341	HS Hawk T1 ASTRA [1]	DPA/ETPS, Boscombe Down	
XX342	HS Hawk T1 [2]	DPA/ETPS, Boscombe Down	
XX343	HS Hawk T1 [3] (wreck)	Boscombe Down Aviation Collection	
XX344	HS Hawk T1 (8847M) (fuselage)	QinetiQ Farnborough Fire Section	
XX345	HS Hawk T1A	RAF No 4 FTS/*19(R) Sqn*, Valley	
XX346	HS Hawk T1A	RAF No 4 FTS/*19(R) Sqn*, Valley	

Notes	Serial	Type (other identity) [code]	Owner/operator, location or fate
	XX348	HS Hawk T1A	RAF No 4 FTS/*19(R) Sqn*, Valley
	XX349	HS Hawk T1W [CO]	RAF No 100 Sqn, Leeming
	XX350	HS Hawk T1A	RAF No 4 FTS/*19(R) Sqn*, Valley
	XX351	HS Hawk T1A [CQ]	RAF No 100 Sqn, Leeming
	XX370	WS Gazelle AH1	AAC/DARA, Fleetlands
	XX371	WS Gazelle AH1	AAC No 12 Flt, Brüggen
	XX372	WS Gazelle AH1	AAC No 654 Sqn/4 Regt, Wattisham
	XX375	WS Gazelle AH1	AAC No 8 Flt, Credenhill
	XX378	WS Gazelle AH1 [Q]	AAC No 671 Sqn/2 Regt, Middle Wallop
	XX379	WS Gazelle AH1	AAC, stored Shawbury
	XX380	WS Gazelle AH1 [A]	RM No 847 Sqn, Yeovilton
	XX381	WS Gazelle AH1 [C]	RM No 847 Sqn, Yeovilton
	XX382	WS Gazelle HT3 (G-BZYB) [M]	Privately owned, Tadcaster
	XX383	WS Gazelle AH1 [D]	AAC No 666(V) Sqn/7 Regt, Netheravon
	XX384	WS Gazelle AH1	AAC/DARA, stored Fleetlands
	XX385	WS Gazelle AH1	RAF No 7 Sqn, Odiham
	XX386	WS Gazelle AH1	AAC No 12 Flt, Brüggen
	XX387	WS Gazelle AH1 (TAD 014)	Army SEAE, Arborfield
	XX388	WS Gazelle AH1 <ff>	Privately owned, East Garston, Bucks
	XX389	WS Gazelle AH1	AAC No 654 Sqn/4 Regt, Wattisham
	XX392	WS Gazelle AH1	AAC No 3(V) Flt/7 Regt, Leuchars
	XX393	WS Gazelle AH1 (fuselage)	Privately owned, East Garston, Bucks
	XX394	WS Gazelle AH1	AAC, stored Shawbury
	XX396	WS Gazelle HT3 (8718M) [N]	ATF, RAFC Cranwell
	XX398	WS Gazelle AH1	AAC No 3 Regt, Wattisham
	XX399	WS Gazelle AH1 [V]	AAC No 671 Sqn/2 Regt, Middle Wallop
	XX403	WS Gazelle AH1 [U]	AAC No 671 Sqn/2 Regt, Middle Wallop
	XX405	WS Gazelle AH1	AAC No 665 Sqn/5 Regt, Aldergrove
	XX406	WS Gazelle HT3 (G-CBSH) [P]	Privately owned, Redhill
	XX409	WS Gazelle AH1	AAC, stored Shawbury
	XX411	WS Gazelle AH1	Aeroventure, Doncaster
	XX411	WS Gazelle AH1 <rf>	FAA Museum, RNAS Yeovilton
	XX412	WS Gazelle AH1 [B]	RM No 847 Sqn, Yeovilton
	XX413	WS Gazelle AH1 <ff>	Privately owned, East Garston, Bucks
	XX414	WS Gazelle AH1 [V]	AAC No 671 Sqn/2 Regt, Middle Wallop
	XX416	WS Gazelle AH1	AAC No 9 Regt, Dishforth
	XX417	WS Gazelle AH1	AAC No 667 Sqn, Middle Wallop
	XX418	WS Gazelle AH1	Privately owned, East Garston, Bucks
	XX419	WS Gazelle AH1	AAC No 654 Sqn/4 Regt, Wattisham
	XX431	WS Gazelle HT2 (9300M) [43/CU]	RAF Shawbury, for display
	XX432	WS Gazelle AH1	AAC/DARA, stored Fleetlands
	XX433	WS Gazelle AH1 <ff>	Privately owned, East Garston, Bucks
	XX435	WS Gazelle AH1 [V]	AAC No 658 Sqn/7 Regt, Netheravon
	XX436	WS Gazelle HT2 (G-CBSE) [39/CU]	Privately owned, Redhill
	XX437	WS Gazelle AH1	AAC No 663 Sqn/3 Regt, Wattisham
	XX438	WS Gazelle AH1	AAC No 663 Sqn/3 Regt, Wattisham
	XX439	WS Gazelle AH1	AAC, stored Shawbury
	XX440	WS Gazelle AH1 (G-BCHN)	DARA Fleetlands Apprentice School
	XX442	WS Gazelle AH1 [E]	AAC, Wattisham
	XX443	WS Gazelle AH1 [Y]	AAC Stockwell Hall, Middle Wallop, instructional use
	XX444	WS Gazelle AH1	AAC Wattisham, instructional use
	XX445	WS Gazelle AH1 [T]	AAC No 658 Sqn/7 Regt, Netheravon
	XX447	WS Gazelle AH1 [D1]	AAC No 671 Sqn/2 Regt, Middle Wallop
	XX448	WS Gazelle AH1	AAC No 4 Regt, Wattisham
	XX449	WS Gazelle AH1	AAC No 654 Sqn/4 Regt, Wattisham
	XX450	WS Gazelle AH1 [D]	Privately owned, East Garston, Bucks
	XX453	WS Gazelle AH1	AAC No 4 Regt, Wattisham
	XX454	WS Gazelle AH1 (TAD 023) (fuselage)	Army SEAE, Arborfield
	XX455	WS Gazelle AH1	AAC/DARA, stored Fleetlands
	XX456	WS Gazelle AH1	AAC No 3(V) Flt/7 Regt, Leuchars
	XX457	WS Gazelle AH1 <ff>	Jet Avn Preservation Grp, Long Marston
	XX460	WS Gazelle AH1	AAC No 663 Sqn/3 Regt, Wattisham
	XX462	WS Gazelle AH1 [W]	AAC No 658 Sqn/7 Regt, Netheravon
	XX467	HS Hunter T66B/T7 (XL605/ G-TVII) [86]	Privately owned, Exeter
	XX475	HP137 Jetstream T2 (N1036S)	DPA/QinetiQ, stored Boscombe Down
	XX476	HP137 Jetstream T2 (N1037S) [561/CU]	RN No 750 Sqn, Culdrose
	XX477	HP137 Jetstream T1 (G-AXXS/ 8462M) <ff>	Privately owned, Askern, Doncaster

Serial	*Type (other identity) [code]*	*Owner/operator, location or fate*	*Notes*
XX478	HP137 Jetstream T2 (G-AXXT) [564/CU]	RN No 750 Sqn, Culdrose	
XX479	HP137 Jetstream T2 (G-AXUR)	RN, Predannack Fire School	
XX481	HP137 Jetstream T2 (G-AXUP) [560/CU]	RN No 750 Sqn, Culdrose	
XX482	SA Jetstream T1 [J]	RAF, stored Shawbury	
XX483	SA Jetstream T2 <ff>	Dumfries & Galloway Avn Mus, Dumfries	
XX484	SA Jetstream T2 [566/CU]	RN No 750 Sqn, Culdrose	
XX486	SA Jetstream T2 [569/CU]	RN No 750 Sqn, Culdrose	
XX487	SA Jetstream T2 [568/CU]	RN No 750 Sqn, Culdrose	
XX488	SA Jetstream T2 [562/CU]	RN No 750 Sqn, Culdrose	
XX491	SA Jetstream T1 [K]	RNAS Culdrose, spares use	
XX492	SA Jetstream T1 [A]	Newark Air Museum, Winthorpe	
XX493	SA Jetstream T1 [L]	*Scrapped, May 2004*	
XX494	SA Jetstream T1 [B]	RAF, stored Shawbury	
XX495	SA Jetstream T1 [C]	RAF, stored Shawbury	
XX496	SA Jetstream T1 [D]	RAF Museum, Cosford	
XX497	SA Jetstream T1 [E]	RAF, stored Shawbury	
XX498	SA Jetstream T1 [F]	*Scrapped, May 2004*	
XX499	SA Jetstream T1 [G]	RAF, stored Shawbury	
XX500	SA Jetstream T1 [H]	RNAS Culdrose, spares use	
XX510	WS Lynx HAS2 [69/DD]	SFDO, RNAS Culdrose	
XX513	SA Bulldog T1 (G-CCMI) [10]	Privately owned, Meppershall	
XX515	SA Bulldog T1 (G-CBBC) [4]	Privately owned, Blackbushe	
XX518	SA Bulldog T1 (G-UDOG) [S]	Privately owned, North Weald	
XX520	SA Bulldog T1 (9288M) [A]	No 172 Sqn ATC, Haywards Heath	
XX521	SA Bulldog T1 (G-CBEH) [H]	Privately owned, East Dereham, Norfolk	
XX522	SA Bulldog T1 (G-DAWG) [06]	Privately owned, Sleap	
XX524	SA Bulldog T1 (G-DDOG) [04]	Privately owned, North Weald	
XX525	SA Bulldog T1 (G-CBJJ) [8]	Privately owned, Norwich	
XX528	SA Bulldog T1 (G-BZON) [D]	Privately owned, Carlisle	
XX530	SA Bulldog T1 (XX637/9197M) [F]	Rolls-Royce, Renfrew	
XX534	SA Bulldog T1 (G-EDAV) [B]	Privately owned, Tollerton	
XX537	SA Bulldog T1 (G-CBCB) [C]	Privately owned, Elstree	
XX538	SA Bulldog T1 (G-TDOG) [O]	Privately owned, Shobdon	
XX539	SA Bulldog T1 [L]	Privately owned, Wellesbourne Mountford	
XX543	SA Bulldog T1 (G-CBAB) [F]	Privately owned, Duxford	
XX546	SA Bulldog T1 (G-WINI) [03]	Privately owned, Blackbushe	
XX549	SA Bulldog T1 (G-CBID) [6]	Privately owned, White Waltham	
XX550	SA Bulldog T1 (G-CBBL) [Z]	Privately owned, Fenland	
XX551	SA Bulldog T1 (G-BZDP) [E]	Privately owned, RAF Lyneham	
XX554	SA Bulldog T1 (G-BZMD) [09]	Privately owned, Wellesbourne Mountford	
XX557	SA Bulldog T1	Privately owned, Paull, Yorks	
XX561	SA Bulldog T1 (G-BZEP) [7]	Privately owned, Biggin Hill	
XX611	SA Bulldog T1 (G-CBDK) [7]	Privately owned, Coventry	
XX612	SA Bulldog T1 (G-BZXC) [A,03]	Privately owned, Wellesbourne Mountford	
XX614	SA Bulldog T1 (G-GGRR) [V]	Privately owned, White Waltham	
XX619	SA Bulldog T1 (G-CBBW) [T]	Privately owned, Coventry	
XX621	SA Bulldog T1 (G-CBEF) [H]	Privately owned, Spanhoe Lodge	
XX622	SA Bulldog T1 (G-CBGX) [B]	Privately owned, Findon, Sussex	
XX623	SA Bulldog T1 [M]	Privately owned, Hurstbourne Tarrant	
XX624	SA Bulldog T1 (G-KDOG) [E]	Privately owned, North Weald	
XX625	SA Bulldog T1 (G-CBBR) [01,N]	Privately owned, Norwich	
XX626	SA Bulldog T1 (9290M) [W,02]	DARA Training School, RAF St Athan	
XX628	SA Bulldog T1 (G-CBFU) [9]	Privately owned, Faversham	
XX629	SA Bulldog T1 (G-BZXZ) [V]	Privately owned, Sleap	
XX630	SA Bulldog T1 (G-SIJW) [5]	Privately owned, Shenington	
XX631	SA Bulldog T1 (G-BZXS) [W]	Privately owned, Newtownards	
XX633	SA Bulldog T1 [X]	Privately owned, Mansfield	
XX634	SA Bulldog T1 [T]	Privately owned, Wellesbourne Mountford	
XX635	SA Bulldog T1 (8767M)	DARA Training School, RAF St Athan	
XX636	SA Bulldog T1 (G-CBFP) [Y]	Privately owned, Biggin Hill	
XX638	SA Bulldog T1 (G-DOGG)	Privately owned, Bourne Park, Hants	
XX653	SA Bulldog T1 [E]	DPA/QinetiQ, stored Boscombe Down	
XX654	SA Bulldog T1 [3]	RAF Museum, Cosford	
XX656	SA Bulldog T1 [C]	Privately owned, Wellesbourne Mountford	
XX658	SA Bulldog T1 (G-BZPS) [07]	Privately owned, Wellesbourne Mountford	
XX659	SA Bulldog T1 [E]	Privately owned, Hixon, Staffs	
XX664	SA Bulldog T1 (G-CBCT) [04]	Privately owned, Sleap	
XX665	SA Bulldog T1	No 2409 Sqn ATC, Halton	
XX667	SA Bulldog T1 (G-BZFN) [16]	Privately owned, Staverton	
XX668	SA Bulldog T1 (G-CBAN) [1]	Privately owned, Colerne	
XX669	SA Bulldog T1 (8997M) [B]	No 2409 Sqn ATC, Halton	

Notes	Serial	Type (other identity) [code]	Owner/operator, location or fate
	XX671	SA Bulldog T1 [D]	Privately owned, Wellesbourne Mountford
	XX672	SA Bulldog T1 [E]	Barry Technical College, Cardiff Airport
	XX686	SA Bulldog T1 (9291M) [5]	DARA Training School, RAF St Athan
	XX687	SA Bulldog T1 [F]	Barry Technical College, Cardiff Airport
	XX690	SA Bulldog T1 [A]	James Watt College, Greenock
	XX692	SA Bulldog T1 (G-BZMH) [A]	Privately owned, Wellesbourne Mountford
	XX694	SA Bulldog T1 (G-CBBS) [E]	Privately owned, Teesside
	XX695	SA Bulldog T1 (G-CBBT) [3]	Privately owned, Teesside
	XX698	SA Bulldog T1 (G-BZME) [9]	Privately owned, Breighton
	XX699	SA Bulldog T1 (G-CBCV) [F]	Privately owned, Wickenby
	XX700	SA Bulldog T1 (G-CBEK) [17]	Privately owned, Blackbushe
	XX702	SA Bulldog T1 (G-CBCR) [π]	Privately owned, Fenland
	XX705	SA Bulldog T1 [5]	QinetiQ Boscombe Down, Apprentice School
	XX707	SA Bulldog T1 (G-CBDS) [4]	Privately owned, Sleap
	XX711	SA Bulldog T1 (G-CBBU) [X]	Privately owned, Egginton
	XX713	SA Bulldog T1 (G-CBJK) [2]	Privately owned, Norwich
	XX720	SEPECAT Jaguar GR3A [GB]	RAF No 54 Sqn, Coltishall
	XX722	SEPECAT Jaguar GR1 (fuselage)	RAF St Athan, BDRT
	XX723	SEPECAT Jaguar GR3A [GQ]	RAF, stored St Athan
	XX724	SEPECAT Jaguar GR3A [GC]	RAF No 54 Sqn, Coltishall
	XX725	SEPECAT Jaguar GR3A [GU]	RAF No 54 Sqn, Coltishall
	XX725	SEPECAT Jaguar GR1 <R> (BAPC 150/*XX718*) [GU]	*To Oman*
	XX726	SEPECAT Jaguar GR1 (8947M) [EB]	RAF No 1 SoTT, Cosford
	XX727	SEPECAT Jaguar GR1 (8951M) [ER]	RAF No 1 SoTT, Cosford
	XX729	SEPECAT Jaguar GR3A	RAF/DARA, St Athan
	XX730	SEPECAT Jaguar GR1 (8952M) [EC]	RAF No 1 SoTT, Cosford
	XX733	SEPECAT Jaguar GR1B [EB] (wreck)	Privately owned, Faygate
	XX734	SEPECAT Jaguar GR1 (8816M)	Gatwick Aviation Museum, Charlwood
	XX736	SEPECAT Jaguar GR1 (9110M) <ff>	BAE Systems Brough
	XX737	SEPECAT Jaguar GR3A [EE]	RAF No 6 Sqn, Coltishall
	XX738	SEPECAT Jaguar GR3A [GG]	RAF/DARA, St Athan
	XX739	SEPECAT Jaguar GR1 (8902M) [I]	RAF No 1 SoTT, Cosford
	XX741	SEPECAT Jaguar GR1A [04]	RAF, stored Shawbury
	XX743	SEPECAT Jaguar GR1 (8949M) [EG]	RAF No 1 SoTT, Cosford
	XX744	SEPECAT Jaguar GR1	Privately owned, Sproughton
	XX745	SEPECAT Jaguar GR1A [GV]	DPA/QinetiQ, Boscombe Down
	XX746	SEPECAT Jaguar GR1 (8895M/ 9251M) [S]	RAF No 1 SoTT, Cosford
	XX747	SEPECAT Jaguar GR1 (8903M)	ATF, RAFC Cranwell
	XX748	SEPECAT Jaguar GR3A [GK]	RAF No 54 Sqn, Coltishall
	XX751	SEPECAT Jaguar GR1 (8937M) [10]	RAF No 1 SoTT, Cosford
	XX752	SEPECAT Jaguar GR3A [FC]	RAF No 41 Sqn, Coltishall
	XX753	SEPECAT Jaguar GR1 (9087M) <ff>	RAF M&RU, Bottesford
	XX756	SEPECAT Jaguar GR1 (8899M) [AM]	RAF No 1 SoTT, Cosford
	XX757	SEPECAT Jaguar GR1 (8948M) [CU]	RAF No 1 SoTT, Cosford
	XX761	SEPECAT Jaguar GR1 (8600M) <ff>	Boscombe Down Aviation Collection
	XX763	SEPECAT Jaguar GR1 (9009M)	DARA Training School, RAF St Athan
	XX764	SEPECAT Jaguar GR1 (9010M)	DARA Training School, RAF St Athan
	XX765	SEPECAT Jaguar ACT	RAF Museum, Cosford
	XX766	SEPECAT Jaguar GR3A [PE]	RAF/DARA, St Athan
	XX767	SEPECAT Jaguar GR3A [GE]	RAF No 54 Sqn, Coltishall
	XX818	SEPECAT Jaguar GR1 (8945M) [DE]	RAF No 1 SoTT, Cosford
	XX819	SEPECAT Jaguar GR1 (8923M) [CE]	RAF No 1 SoTT, Cosford
	XX821	SEPECAT Jaguar GR1 (8896M) [P]	AMIF, RAFC Cranwell
	XX824	SEPECAT Jaguar GR1 (9019M) [AD]	RAF No 1 SoTT, Cosford

Serial	Type (other identity) [code]	Owner/operator, location or fate	Notes
XX825	SEPECAT Jaguar GR1 (9020M) [BN]	RAF No 1 SoTT, Cosford	
XX826	SEPECAT Jaguar GR1 (9021M) [34,JH]	RAF No 1 SoTT, Cosford	
XX829	SEPECAT Jaguar T2A [GZ]	RAF, stored Shawbury	
XX830	SEPECAT Jaguar T2 <ff>	The Cockpit Collection, RAF Coltishall	
XX832	SEPECAT Jaguar T2A [EZ]	RAF, stored Shawbury	
XX833	SEPECAT Jaguar T2B	RAF AWC/FJWOEU, Coningsby	
XX835	SEPECAT Jaguar T4 [FY]	RAF No 41 Sqn, Coltishall	
XX836	SEPECAT Jaguar T2A [X]	RAF, stored Shawbury	
XX837	SEPECAT Jaguar T2 (8978M) [I]	RAF No 1 SoTT, Cosford	
XX838	SEPECAT Jaguar T4 [PR]	RAF No 16(R) Sqn, Coltishall	
XX840	SEPECAT Jaguar T4 [PS]	RAF/DARA, St Athan	
XX841	SEPECAT Jaguar T4 [PQ]	RAF No 16(R) Sqn, Coltishall	
XX842	SEPECAT Jaguar T2A [PX]	RAF No 16(R) Sqn, Coltishall	
XX845	SEPECAT Jaguar T4 [ET]	RAF No 6 Sqn, Coltishall	
XX846	SEPECAT Jaguar T4 [PV]	RAF Coltishall, wfu	
XX847	SEPECAT Jaguar T4 [PY]	RAF No 16(R) Sqn, Coltishall	
XX885	HS Buccaneer S2B (9225M/ G-HHAA)	The Old Flying Machine Company, Scampton	
XX888	HS Buccaneer S2B <ff>	Privately owned, Barnstaple	
XX889	HS Buccaneer S2B [T]	Gloucestershire Avn Coll, stored Gloucester	
XX892	HS Buccaneer S2B <ff>	Privately owned, Forres	
XX893	HS Buccaneer S2B <ff>	Privately owned, Desborough, Northants	
XX894	HS Buccaneer S2B [020/R]	Buccaneer Supporters Club, Bruntingthorpe	
XX895	HS Buccaneer S2B <ff>	Privately owned, Bicester	
XX897	HS Buccaneer S2B(mod)	Bournemouth Aviation Museum	
XX899	HS Buccaneer S2B <ff>	Midland Air Museum, Coventry	
XX900	HS Buccaneer S2B	British Aviation Heritage, Bruntingthorpe	
XX901	HS Buccaneer S2B	Yorkshire Air Museum, Elvington	
XX907	WS Lynx AH1	Westland Helicopters, Yeovil, Fire Section	
XX910	WS Lynx HAS2	The Helicopter Museum, Weston-super-Mare	
XX914	BAC VC10/1103 (8777M) <rf>	RAF Air Movements School, Brize Norton	
XX919	BAC 1-11/402AP (PI-C1121) <ff>	Boscombe Down Aviation Collection	
XX946	Panavia Tornado (P02) (8883M)	RAF Museum, Cosford	
XX947	Panavia Tornado (P03) (8797M)	Shoreham Airport, on display	
XX948	Panavia Tornado (P06) (8879M) [P]	*To Hermeskeil, Germany, October 2004*	
XX955	SEPECAT Jaguar GR1A [GK]	RAF, stored Shawbury	
XX956	SEPECAT Jaguar GR1 (8950M) [BE]	RAF No 1 SoTT, Cosford	
XX958	SEPECAT Jaguar GR1 (9022M) [BK,JG]	RAF No 1 SoTT, Cosford	
XX959	SEPECAT Jaguar GR1 (8953M) [CJ]	RAF No 1 SoTT, Cosford	
XX962	SEPECAT Jaguar GR1B (9257M) [E]	RAF No 1 SoTT, Cosford	
XX965	SEPECAT Jaguar GR1A (9254M) [C]	AMIF, RAFC Cranwell	
XX966	SEPECAT Jaguar GR1 (8904M) [EL,JJ]	RAF No 1 SoTT, Cosford	
XX967	SEPECAT Jaguar GR1 (9006M) [AC,JD]	RAF No 1 SoTT, Cosford	
XX968	SEPECAT Jaguar GR1 (9007M) [AJ,JE]	RAF No 1 SoTT, Cosford	
XX969	SEPECAT Jaguar GR1 (8897M) [01]	RAF No 1 SoTT, Cosford	
XX970	SEPECAT Jaguar GR3A [EH]	RAF No 6 Sqn, Coltishall	
XX974	SEPECAT Jaguar GR3 [FE]	RAF No 41 Sqn, Coltishall	
XX975	SEPECAT Jaguar GR1 (8905M) [07]	RAF No 1 SoTT, Cosford	
XX976	SEPECAT Jaguar GR1 (8906M) [BD]	RAF No 1 SoTT, Cosford	
XX977	SEPECAT Jaguar GR1 (9132M) [DL,05]	DARA, RAF St Athan, BDRT	
XX979	SEPECAT Jaguar GR1A (9306M) <rf>	RAF Coltishall, instructional use	
XZ101	SEPECAT Jaguar GR1A (9282M) [D]	DPA/QinetiQ Boscombe Down, GI use	

Notes	Serial	Type (other identity) [code]	Owner/operator, location or fate
	XZ103	SEPECAT Jaguar GR3A [FP]	RAF No 41 Sqn, Coltishall
	XZ104	SEPECAT Jaguar GR3A [FM]	RAF No 41 Sqn, Coltishall
	XZ106	SEPECAT Jaguar GR3A [FR]	RAF No 41 Sqn, Coltishall
	XZ107	SEPECAT Jaguar GR3A [FH]	RAF No 41 Sqn, Coltishall
	XZ109	SEPECAT Jaguar GR3A [EN]	RAF No 6 Sqn, Coltishall
	XZ112	SEPECAT Jaguar GR3A [GA]	RAF No 54 Sqn, Coltishall
	XZ113	SEPECAT Jaguar GR3	RAF AWC/FJWOEU, Coningsby
	XZ114	SEPECAT Jaguar GR1A [FB]	RAF No 6 Sqn(R), Coltishall
	XZ115	SEPECAT Jaguar GR3 [PD]	RAF/DARA, St Athan
	XZ117	SEPECAT Jaguar GR3 [EP]	RAF No 6 Sqn, Coltishall
	XZ118	SEPECAT Jaguar GR3 [FF]	RAF No 41 Sqn, Coltishall
	XZ119	SEPECAT Jaguar GR1A (9266M) [F]	AMIF, RAFC Cranwell
	XZ129	HS Harrier GR3 [ETS]	RN ETS, Yeovilton
	XZ130	HS Harrier GR3 (9079M) [A,HE]	RAF No 1 SoTT, Cosford
	XZ131	HS Harrier GR3 (9174M) <ff>	No 2156 Sqn ATC, Brierley Hill, W Midlands
	XZ132	HS Harrier GR3 (9168M) [C]	ATF, RAFC Cranwell
	XZ133	HS Harrier GR3 [10]	Imperial War Museum, Duxford
	XZ135	HS Harrier GR3 (8848M) <ff>	RAF M&RU, Bottesford
	XZ138	HS Harrier GR3 (9040M) <ff>	RAFC Cranwell, Trenchard Hall
	XZ145	HS Harrier T4 [45]	SFDO, RNAS Culdrose
	XZ146	HS Harrier T4 (9281M) [S]	RAF Wittering, on display
	XZ170	WS Lynx AH9	DPA/Westland Helicopters, Yeovil
	XZ171	WS Lynx AH7	AAC No 4 Regt, Wattisham
	XZ172	WS Lynx AH7	AAC No 653 Sqn/3 Regt, Wattisham
	XZ173	WS Lynx AH7	AAC No 661 Sqn/1 Regt, Gütersloh
	XZ174	WS Lynx AH7 <ff>	Westland Helicopters, Yeovil
	XZ175	WS Lynx AH7	AAC/DARA, stored Fleetlands
	XZ176	WS Lynx AH7	AAC No 655 Sqn/5 Regt, Aldergrove
	XZ177	WS Lynx AH7	AAC No 655 Sqn/5 Regt, Aldergrove
	XZ178	WS Lynx AH7	AAC No 653 Sqn/3 Regt, Wattisham
	XZ179	WS Lynx AH7	AAC No 655 Sqn/5 Regt, Aldergrove
	XZ180	WS Lynx AH7 [R]	RM No 847 Sqn, Yeovilton
	XZ181	WS Lynx AH1	AAC/DARA, stored Fleetlands
	XZ182	WS Lynx AH7	RM No 847 Sqn, Yeovilton
	XZ183	WS Lynx AH7	AAC/DARA, stored Fleetlands
	XZ184	WS Lynx AH7 [Z]	AAC No 655 Sqn/5 Regt, Aldergrove
	XZ185	WS Lynx AH7	AAC No 653 Sqn/3 Regt, Wattisham
	XZ187	WS Lynx AH7	Army SEAE, Arborfield
	XZ188	WS Lynx AH7	Army SEAE, Arborfield
	XZ190	WS Lynx AH7	AAC/DARA, stored Fleetlands
	XZ191	WS Lynx AH7 [A]	AAC No 671 Sqn/2 Regt, Middle Wallop
	XZ192	WS Lynx AH7	DPA/Westland Helicopters, Yeovil (on rebuild)
	XZ193	WS Lynx AH7 [I]	AAC No 671 Sqn/2 Regt, Middle Wallop
	XZ194	WS Lynx AH7	AAC No 4 Regt, Wattisham
	XZ195	WS Lynx AH7	AAC/DARA, stored Fleetlands
	XZ196	WS Lynx AH7	AAC No 653 Sqn/3 Regt, Wattisham
	XZ197	WS Lynx AH7 <ff>	AAC/DARA, stored Fleetlands
	XZ198	WS Lynx AH7	AAC/DARA, stored Fleetlands
	XZ203	WS Lynx AH7 [L]	AAC No 671 Sqn/2 Regt, Middle Wallop
	XZ205	WS Lynx AH7	AAC No 653 Sqn/3 Regt, Wattisham
	XZ206	WS Lynx AH7	AAC No 653 Sqn/3 Regt, Wattisham
	XZ207	WS Lynx AH7	Army SEAE, Arborfield
	XZ208	WS Lynx AH7	AAC No 669 Sqn/4 Regt, Wattisham
	XZ209	WS Lynx AH7	AAC No 655 Sqn/5 Regt, Aldergrove
	XZ210	WS Lynx AH7	AAC No 669 Sqn/4 Regt, Wattisham
	XZ211	WS Lynx AH7	AAC, Middle Wallop
	XZ212	WS Lynx AH7	AAC No 661 Sqn/1 Regt, Gütersloh
	XZ213	WS Lynx AH1 (TAD 213)	DARA Fleetlands Apprentice School
	XZ214	WS Lynx AH7	AAC No 657 Sqn, Odiham
	XZ215	WS Lynx AH7	AAC No 653 Sqn/3 Regt, Wattisham
	XZ216	WS Lynx AH7	AAC/DARA, Fleetlands
	XZ217	WS Lynx AH7	AAC No 669 Sqn/4 Regt, Wattisham
	XZ218	WS Lynx AH7	Privately owned, Sproughton
	XZ219	WS Lynx AH7	AAC No 669 Sqn/4 Regt, Wattisham
	XZ220	WS Lynx AH7	AAC No 653 Sqn/3 Regt, Wattisham
	XZ221	WS Lynx AH7	AAC No 659 Sqn/4 Regt, Wattisham
	XZ222	WS Lynx AH7	AAC No 657 Sqn, Odiham
	XZ228	WS Lynx HAS3S [425/KT]	RN/DARA, stored Fleetlands
	XZ229	WS Lynx HAS3S [634]	RN No 702 Sqn, Yeovilton
	XZ230	WS Lynx HAS3S [302]	RN/DARA, stored Fleetlands

Serial	Type (other identity) [code]	Owner/operator, location or fate	Notes
XZ232	WS Lynx HAS3S [334/SN]	RN No 815 Sqn, *Southampton* Flt, Yeovilton	
XZ233	WS Lynx HAS3(ICE) [644]	RN No 702 Sqn, Yeovilton	
XZ234	WS Lynx HAS3S [635]	RN No 702 Sqn, Yeovilton	
XZ235	WS Lynx HAS3S [633]	RN No 702 Sqn, Yeovilton	
XZ236	WS Lynx HMA8	DPA/Westland Helicopters, Yeovil	
XZ237	WS Lynx HAS3S [301]	RN No 815 Sqn, HQ Flt, Yeovilton	
XZ238	WS Lynx HAS3S(ICE) [434/EE]	RN No 815 Sqn, *Endurance* Flt, Yeovilton	
XZ239	WS Lynx HAS3S [425/KT]	RN No 815 Sqn, *Kent* Flt, Yeovilton	
XZ241	WS Lynx HAS3S(ICE) [435/EE]	*Crashed 8 February 2004, Antarctica*	
XZ243	WS Lynx HAS3 <ff>	RN	
XZ245	WS Lynx HAS3S [422]	RN No 815 Sqn, *Sutherland* Flt, Yeovilton	
XZ246	WS Lynx HAS3S(ICE) [435/EE]	RN No 815 Sqn, *Endurance* Flt, Yeovilton	
XZ248	WS Lynx HAS3S [638]	RN No 702 Sqn, Yeovilton	
XZ250	WS Lynx HAS3S [304]	RN No 702 Sqn, Yeovilton	
XZ252	WS Lynx HAS3S	RN MASU, Fleetlands	
XZ254	WS Lynx HAS3S [303]	RN No 815 Sqn, HQ Flt, Yeovilton	
XZ255	WS Lynx HMA8	RN/DARA, stored Fleetlands	
XZ257	WS Lynx HAS3S [640]	RN No 702 Sqn, Yeovilton	
XZ286	BAe Nimrod AEW3 <rf>	*Scrapped at Kinloss*	
XZ287	BAe Nimrod AEW3 (9140M) (fuselage)	RAF TSW, Stafford	
XZ290	WS Gazelle AH1	AAC No 665 Sqn/5 Regt, Aldergrove	
XZ291	WS Gazelle AH1	AAC No 12 Flt, Brüggen	
XZ292	WS Gazelle AH1	AAC No 654 Sqn/4 Regt, Wattisham	
XZ294	WS Gazelle AH1 [X]	AAC No 658 Sqn/7 Regt, Netheravon	
XZ295	WS Gazelle AH1	AAC No 12 Flt, Brüggen	
XZ296	WS Gazelle AH1	RAF No 7 Sqn, Odiham	
XZ298	WS Gazelle AH1	AAC No 663 Sqn/3 Regt, Wattisham	
XZ299	WS Gazelle AH1	Privately owned, Breighton	
XZ300	WS Gazelle AH1 [L] (wreck)	Army, Bramley, Hants	
XZ301	WS Gazelle AH1 [U]	AAC No 654 Sqn/4 Regt, Wattisham	
XZ303	WS Gazelle AH1	AAC No 6(V) Flt/7 Regt, Shawbury	
XZ304	WS Gazelle AH1	AAC No 6(V) Flt/7 Regt, Shawbury	
XZ305	WS Gazelle AH1 (TAD020)	AAC Middle Wallop, instructional use	
XZ307	WS Gazelle AH1	DARA Fleetlands Apprentice School	
XZ308	WS Gazelle AH1	AAC No 654 Sqn/4 Regt, Wattisham	
XZ309	WS Gazelle AH1	Privately owned, Hixon, Staffs	
XZ311	WS Gazelle AH1	AAC No 6(V) Flt/7 Regt, Shawbury	
XZ312	WS Gazelle AH1	AAC, stored Shawbury	
XZ313	WS Gazelle AH1	AAC No 667 Sqn, Middle Wallop	
XZ314	WS Gazelle AH1	AAC No 8 Flt, Credenhill	
XZ315	WS Gazelle AH1	Privately owned, Sproughton	
XZ316	WS Gazelle AH1 [B]	AAC No 666(V) Sqn/7 Regt, Netheravon	
XZ318	WS Gazelle AH1 (fuselage)	AAC/DARA, stored Fleetlands	
XZ320	WS Gazelle AH1	AAC No 665 Sqn/5 Regt, Aldergrove	
XZ321	WS Gazelle AH1	AAC/DARA, stored Fleetlands	
XZ322	WS Gazelle AH1 (9283M) [N]	DARA, RAF St Athan, BDRT	
XZ323	WS Gazelle AH1 [H]	AAC No 666(V) Sqn/7 Regt, Netheravon	
XZ324	WS Gazelle AH1	AAC No 3(V) Flt/7 Regt, Leuchars	
XZ325	WS Gazelle AH1 [T]	Army SEAE, Arborfield	
XZ326	WS Gazelle AH1	AAC No 665 Sqn/5 Regt, Aldergrove	
XZ327	WS Gazelle AH1	AAC No 3(V) Flt/7 Regt, Leuchars	
XZ328	WS Gazelle AH1 [C]	AAC No 666(V) Sqn/7 Regt, Netheravon	
XZ329	WS Gazelle AH1 (G-BZYD) [J]	Privately owned, East Garston, Bucks	
XZ330	WS Gazelle AH1 [Y]	AAC Stockwell Hall, Middle Wallop	
XZ331	WS Gazelle AH1	AAC No 654 Sqn/4 Regt, Wattisham	
XZ332	WS Gazelle AH1 [O]	Army SEAE, Arborfield	
XZ333	WS Gazelle AH1 [A]	Army SEAE, Arborfield	
XZ334	WS Gazelle AH1	AAC No 665 Sqn/5 Regt, Aldergrove	
XZ335	WS Gazelle AH1	AAC No 6(V) Flt/7 Regt, Shawbury	
XZ337	WS Gazelle AH1	AAC No 654 Sqn/4 Regt, Wattisham	
XZ338	WS Gazelle AH1 [Y]	AAC No 671 Sqn/2 Regt, Middle Wallop	
XZ340	WS Gazelle AH1 [5B]	AAC No 29 Flt, BATUS, Suffield, Canada	
XZ341	WS Gazelle AH1	AAC No 665 Sqn/5 Regt, Aldergrove	
XZ342	WS Gazelle AH1	AAC No 8 Flt, Credenhill	
XZ343	WS Gazelle AH1	AAC, Wattisham	
XZ344	WS Gazelle AH1 [Y]	AAC No 658 Sqn/7 Regt, Netheravon	
XZ345	WS Gazelle AH1 [M]	AAC No 671 Sqn/2 Regt, Middle Wallop	
XZ346	WS Gazelle AH1	AAC, stored Shawbury	
XZ347	WS Gazelle AH1	AAC No 663 Sqn/3 Regt, Wattisham	
XZ348	WS Gazelle AH1 (wreck)	AAC/DARA, stored Fleetlands	
XZ349	WS Gazelle AH1 [G1]	AAC No 671 Sqn/2 Regt, Middle Wallop	

Notes	Serial	Type (other identity) [code]	Owner/operator, location or fate
	XZ355	SEPECAT Jaguar GR3A [FJ]	RAF/DARA, St Athan
	XZ356	SEPECAT Jaguar GR3A [GF]	RAF No 54 Sqn, Coltishall
	XZ357	SEPECAT Jaguar GR3A [FK]	RAF/DARA, St Athan
	XZ358	SEPECAT Jaguar GR1A (9262M) [L]	AMIF, RAFC Cranwell
	XZ360	SEPECAT Jaguar GR3 [FN]	RAF No 41 Sqn, Coltishall
	XZ361	SEPECAT Jaguar GR3 [FT]	RAF, stored Shawbury
	XZ363	SEPECAT Jaguar GR1A <R> (*XX824*/BAPC 151) [A]	RAF M&RU, Bottesford
	XZ364	SEPECAT Jaguar GR3A [GJ]	RAF No 54 Sqn, Coltishall
	XZ366	SEPECAT Jaguar GR3A [FS]	RAF No 41 Sqn, Coltishall
	XZ367	SEPECAT Jaguar GR3 [GP]	RAF Coltishall, instructional use
	XZ368	SEPECAT Jaguar GR1 [8900M] [E]	RAF No 1 SoTT, Cosford
	XZ369	SEPECAT Jaguar GR3A	RAF/DARA, St Athan
	XZ370	SEPECAT Jaguar GR1 (9004M) [JB]	RAF No 1 SoTT, Cosford
	XZ371	SEPECAT Jaguar GR1 (8907M) [AP]	RAF No 1 SoTT, Cosford
	XZ372	SEPECAT Jaguar GR3 [ED]	RAF No 41 Sqn, Coltishall
	XZ374	SEPECAT Jaguar GR1 (9005M) [JC]	RAF No 1 SoTT, Cosford
	XZ375	SEPECAT Jaguar GR1A (9255M) <ff>	The Cockpit Collection, RAF Coltishall
	XZ377	SEPECAT Jaguar GR3A [EG]	RAF No 6 Sqn, Coltishall
	XZ378	SEPECAT Jaguar GR1A [EP]	RAF, stored Shawbury
	XZ382	SEPECAT Jaguar GR1 (8908M) [AE]	Privately owned, Bruntingthorpe
	XZ383	SEPECAT Jaguar GR1 (8901M) [AF]	RAF No 1 SoTT, Cosford
	XZ384	SEPECAT Jaguar GR1 (8954M) [BC]	RAF No 1 SoTT, Cosford
	XZ385	SEPECAT Jaguar GR3A [PC]	RAF No 16(R) Sqn, Coltishall
	XZ389	SEPECAT Jaguar GR1 (8946M) [BL]	RAF No 1 SoTT, Cosford
	XZ390	SEPECAT Jaguar GR1 (9003M) [35,JA]	RAF No 1 SoTT, Cosford
	XZ391	SEPECAT Jaguar GR3A [EB]	RAF No 6 Sqn, Coltishall
	XZ392	SEPECAT Jaguar GR3A [PF]	RAF/DARA, St Athan
	XZ394	SEPECAT Jaguar GR3 [GN]	RAF/DARA, St Athan
	XZ396	SEPECAT Jaguar GR3A [EM]	RAF No 6 Sqn, Coltishall
	XZ398	SEPECAT Jaguar GR3A [FA]	RAF No 41 Sqn, Coltishall
	XZ399	SEPECAT Jaguar GR3A [EJ]	RAF No 6 Sqn, Coltishall
	XZ400	SEPECAT Jaguar GR3A [GR]	RAF No 54 Sqn, Coltishall
	XZ431	HS Buccaneer S2B (9233M) <ff>	Phoenix Aviation, Bruntingthorpe
	XZ439	BAe Sea Harrier FA2	Privately owned, Sproughton
	XZ440	BAe Sea Harrier FA2 [717]	RN No 899 Sqn, Yeovilton
	XZ455	BAe Sea Harrier FA2 [001] (wreck)	Privately owned, Sproughton
	XZ457	BAe Sea Harrier FA2	Boscombe Down Aviation Collection
	XZ459	BAe Sea Harrier FA2	RN/DARA, stored St Athan
	XZ492	BAe Sea Harrier FA2 (wreck)	Privately owned, Faygate
	XZ493	BAe Sea Harrier FRS1 (comp XV760) [001/N]	FAA Museum, RNAS Yeovilton
	XZ493	BAe Sea Harrier FRS1 <ff>	RN Yeovilton, Fire Section
	XZ494	BAe Sea Harrier FA2	Privately owned, Sproughton
	XZ497	BAe Sea Harrier FA2 [126]	RN SHOPS, Yeovilton
	XZ499	BAe Sea Harrier FA2 [003]	FAA Museum, stored Yeovilton
	XZ559	Slingsby T61F Venture T2 (G-BUEK)	Privately owned, Tibenham
	XZ570	WS61 Sea King HAS5(mod)	RN, stored *HMS Sultan*, Gosport
	XZ571	WS61 Sea King HAS6 [016/L]	RN, stored *HMS Sultan*, Gosport
	XZ574	WS61 Sea King HAS6 [829/CU]	RN No 771 Sqn, Culdrose
	XZ575	WS61 Sea King HU5	DPA/AFD/QinetiQ, Boscombe Down
	XZ576	WS61 Sea King HAS6	RN, stored *HMS Sultan*, Gosport
	XZ578	WS61 Sea King HU5SAR [708/PW]	RN No 771 Sqn, Prestwick
	XZ579	WS61 Sea King HAS6 [707/PW]	RN, stored *HMS Sultan*, Gosport
	XZ580	WS61 Sea King HC6 [ZB]	RN No 846 Sqn, Yeovilton
	XZ581	WS61 Sea King HAS6 [69/CU]	RN, stored *HMS Sultan*, Gosport
	XZ585	WS61 Sea King HAR3 [A]	RAF No 22 Sqn, C Flt, Valley
	XZ586	WS61 Sea King HAR3 [B]	RAF No 202 Sqn, E Flt, Leconfield
	XZ587	WS61 Sea King HAR3	RAF HMF, St Mawgan
	XZ588	WS61 Sea King HAR3 [D]	RAF No 78 Sqn, Mount Pleasant
	XZ589	WS61 Sea King HAR3	RAF No 203(R) Sqn, St Mawgan
	XZ590	WS61 Sea King HAR3	RAF HMF, St Mawgan

Serial	Type (other identity) [code]	Owner/operator, location or fate	Notes
XZ591	WS61 Sea King HAR3 [G]	RAF No 202 Sqn, E Flt, Leconfield	
XZ592	WS61 Sea King HAR3	RAF No 202 Sqn, A Flt, Boulmer	
XZ593	WS61 Sea King HAR3	RAF HMF, St Mawgan	
XZ594	WS61 Sea King HAR3 [J]	RAF No 202 Sqn, D Flt, Lossiemouth	
XZ595	WS61 Sea King HAR3	RAF No 22 Sqn, C Flt, Valley	
XZ596	WS61 Sea King HAR3 [L]	RAF No 203(R) Sqn, St Mawgan	
XZ597	WS61 Sea King HAR3	RAF No 202 Sqn, A Flt, Boulmer	
XZ598	WS61 Sea King HAR3	RAF/DARA, Fleetlands	
XZ599	WS61 Sea King HAR3	RAF HMF, St Mawgan	
XZ605	WS Lynx AH7 [Y]	AAC No 669 Sqn/4 Regt, Wattisham	
XZ606	WS Lynx AH7	AAC No 667 Sqn, Middle Wallop	
XZ607	WS Lynx AH7	AAC No 659 Sqn/4 Regt, Wattisham	
XZ608	WS Lynx AH7	AAC No 657 Sqn, Odiham	
XZ609	WS Lynx AH7	AAC/DARA, Fleetlands	
XZ611	WS Lynx AH7	AAC No 4 Regt, Wattisham	
XZ612	WS Lynx AH7 [N]	RM No 847 Sqn, Yeovilton	
XZ613	WS Lynx AH7 [F]	AAC/DARA, stored Fleetlands	
XZ614	WS Lynx AH7 [X]	RM No 847 Sqn, Yeovilton	
XZ615	WS Lynx AH7	AAC No 667 Sqn, Middle Wallop	
XZ616	WS Lynx AH7	AAC No 657 Sqn, Odiham	
XZ617	WS Lynx AH7	AAC No 669 Sqn/4 Regt, Wattisham	
XZ630	Panavia Tornado GR1 (8976M)	RAF Halton, on display	
XZ631	Panavia Tornado GR1	DPA/BAE Systems, Warton	
XZ641	WS Lynx AH7	AAC No 655 Sqn/5 Regt, Aldergrove	
XZ642	WS Lynx AH7	AAC No 669 Sqn/4 Regt, Wattisham	
XZ643	WS Lynx AH7	AAC No 669 Sqn/4 Regt, Wattisham	
XZ645	WS Lynx AH7	AAC No 4 Regt, Wattisham	
XZ646	WS Lynx AH7	RM No 847 Sqn, Yeovilton	
XZ646	WS Lynx AH7 (really XZ649)	QinetiQ Structures Dept, Farnborough	
XZ647	WS Lynx AH7 [Z]	AAC No 671 Sqn/2 Regt, Middle Wallop	
XZ648	WS Lynx AH7	AAC No 653 Sqn/3 Regt, Wattisham	
XZ651	WS Lynx AH7	AAC No 657 Sqn, Odiham	
XZ652	WS Lynx AH7 [T]	AAC No 671 Sqn/2 Regt, Middle Wallop	
XZ653	WS Lynx AH7	AAC No 659 Sqn/4 Regt, Wattisham	
XZ654	WS Lynx AH7	AAC/DARA, Fleetlands	
XZ655	WS Lynx AH7 [A]	AAC No 671 Sqn/2 Regt, Middle Wallop	
XZ661	WS Lynx AH1	AAC No 653 Sqn/3 Regt, Wattisham	
XZ663	WS Lynx AH7	AAC/DARA, stored Fleetlands	
XZ666	WS Lynx AH7	Army SEAE, Arborfield	
XZ669	WS Lynx AH7	AAC No 655 Sqn/5 Regt, Aldergrove	
XZ670	WS Lynx AH7	AAC No 669 Sqn/4 Regt, Wattisham	
XZ671	WS Lynx AH7 <ff>	Westland Helicopters, Yeovil, instructional use	
XZ672	WS Lynx AH7	AAC, Wattisham	
XZ673	WS Lynx AH7	AAC No 655 Sqn/5 Regt, Aldergrove	
XZ674	WS Lynx AH7	AAC No 655 Sqn/5 Regt, Aldergrove	
XZ675	WS Lynx AH7 [E]	AAC No 653 Sqn/3 Regt, Wattisham	
XZ676	WS Lynx AH7 [N]	AAC No 671 Sqn/2 Regt, Middle Wallop	
XZ677	WS Lynx AH7	AAC No 655 Sqn/5 Regt, Aldergrove	
XZ678	WS Lynx AH7	AAC No 669 Sqn/4 Regt, Wattisham	
XZ679	WS Lynx AH7	AAC No 4 Regt, Wattisham	
XZ680	WS Lynx AH7	AAC No 657 Sqn, Odiham	
XZ689	WS Lynx HMA8 [363/MA]	RN No 815 Sqn, *Marlborough* Flt, Yeovilton	
XZ690	WS Lynx HMA8 [404/IR]	RN No 815 Sqn, *Iron Duke* Flt, Yeovilton	
XZ691	WS Lynx HMA8 [410/GC]	RN No 815 Sqn, *Gloucester* Flight, Yeovilton	
XZ692	WS Lynx HMA8 [306]	RN AMG, Yeovilton	
XZ693	WS Lynx HAS3S [639]	RN No 702 Sqn, Yeovilton	
XZ694	WS Lynx HAS3S [444]	RN No 815 Sqn, *Montrose* Flt Yeovilton	
XZ695	WS Lynx HMA8 [417]	RN No 815 Sqn, *Nottingham* Flt Yeovilton	
XZ696	WS Lynx HAS3S [335/CF]	RN No 815 Sqn, *Cardiff* Flt, Yeovilton	
XZ697	WS Lynx HMA8 [437/GT]	RN No 815 Sqn, *Grafton* Flt, Yeovilton	
XZ698	WS Lynx HMA8 [348]	RN No 815 Sqn, *Chatham* Flt, Yeovilton	
XZ699	WS Lynx HAS3 [303]	FAA Museum, stored Yeovilton	
XZ719	WS Lynx HMA8 [360/MC]	RN No 815 Sqn, *Manchester* Flt, Yeovilton	
XZ720	WS Lynx HAS3S [407]	RN No 815 Sqn, *York* Flt, Yeovilton	
XZ721	WS Lynx HMA8 [302]	RN No 815 Sqn, HQ Flt, Yeovilton	
XZ722	WS Lynx HMA8 [474/RM]	RN No 815 Sqn, *Richmond* Flt, Yeovilton	
XZ723	WS Lynx HMA8 [671]	RN No 702 Sqn, Yeovilton	
XZ724	WS Lynx HAS3S [426/PD]	*Crashed 8 December 2004, off The Lizard*	
XZ725	WS Lynx HMA8 [361/NF]	RN AMG, Yeovilton	
XZ726	WS Lynx HMA8 [319]	RN No 815 Sqn OEU, Yeovilton	

Notes	Serial	Type (other identity) [code]	Owner/operator, location or fate
	XZ727	WS Lynx HAS3S [631]	RN No 702 Sqn, Yeovilton
	XZ728	WS Lynx HMA8 [MM]	RNAS Yeovilton, for display
	XZ729	WS Lynx HMA8	RN No 815 Sqn, Yeovilton
	XZ730	WS Lynx HAS3S [632]	RN No 702 Sqn, Yeovilton
	XZ731	WS Lynx HMA8 [307]	RN/DARA, stored Fleetlands
	XZ732	WS Lynx HMA8 [348/CM]	RN/DARA, Fleetlands
	XZ733	WS Lynx HAS3S [411/EB]	RN No 815 Sqn, *Edinburgh* Flt, Yeovilton
	XZ735	WS Lynx HAS3S [350/CL]	RN No 815 Sqn, *Cumberland* Flt, Yeovilton
	XZ736	WS Lynx HMA8 [437/GTi]	RN MASU, Fleetlands
	XZ920	WS61 Sea King HU5 [707/PW]	RN No 771 Sqn, Prestwick
	XZ921	WS61 Sea King HAS6 [269/N]	RN, stored *HMS Sultan*, Gosport
	XZ922	WS61 Sea King HAS6CR [ZA]	RN No 848 Sqn, Yeovilton
	XZ930	WS Gazelle HT3 [Q]	RN AESS, *HMS Sultan*, Gosport
	XZ933	WS Gazelle HT3 [T]	DPA/QinetiQ, Boscombe Down, spares use
	XZ934	WS Gazelle HT3 (G-CBSI) [U]	Privately owned, Redhill
	XZ935	WS Gazelle HCC4	RAF No 1 SoTT, Cosford
	XZ936	WS Gazelle HT2 [6]	DPA/ETPS, Boscombe Down
	XZ937	WS Gazelle HT2 (G-CBKA) [Y]	Privately owned, Stapleford Tawney
	XZ938	WS Gazelle HT2 [45/CU]	*Currently not known*
	XZ939	WS Gazelle HT2 [9]	DPA/ETPS, Boscombe Down
	XZ940	WS Gazelle HT2 (G-CBBV) [O]	Privately owned, Redhill
	XZ941	WS Gazelle HT2 [B]	DARA Training School, RAF St Athan, BDRT
	XZ942	WS Gazelle HT2 [42/CU]	AAC, Middle Wallop, instructional use
	XZ964	BAe Harrier GR3 [D]	Royal Engineers Museum, Chatham
	XZ966	BAe Harrier GR3 (9221M) [G]	MoD FSCTE, Manston
	XZ968	BAe Harrier GR3 (9222M) [3G]	Muckleborough Collection, Weybourne
	XZ969	BAe Harrier GR3 [69]	RN, Predannack Fire School
	XZ971	BAe Harrier GR3 (9219M) [G]	HQ DS&DC, Donnington, Shropshire, on display
	XZ987	BAe Harrier GR3 (9185M) [C]	RAF Stafford, at main gate
	XZ990	BAe Harrier GR3 <ff>	No 1220 Sqn ATC, March, Cambs
	XZ990	BAe Harrier GR3 <rf>	RAF Wittering, derelict
	XZ991	BAe Harrier GR3 (9162M) [3A]	DARA, RAF St Athan, BDRT
	XZ993	BAe Harrier GR3 (9240M) (fuselage)	DARA, RAF St Athan, fire training
	XZ994	BAe Harrier GR3 (9170M) [U]	RAF Air Movements School, Brize Norton
	XZ995	BAe Harrier GR3 (G-CBGK/ 9220M) [3G]	Privately owned, Lowestoft
	XZ996	BAe Harrier GR3 [96]	SFDO, RNAS Culdrose
	XZ997	BAe Harrier GR3 (9122M) [V]	RAF Museum, Hendon
	ZA101	BAe Hawk 100 (G-HAWK)	DPA/BAE Systems, Warton
	ZA105	WS61 Sea King HAR3 [Q]	RAF No 203(R) Sqn, St Mawgan
	ZA110	BAe Jetstream T2 (F-BTMI) [563/CU]	RN No 750 Sqn, Culdrose
	ZA111	BAe Jetstream T2 (9Q-CTC) [565/CU]	RN No 750 Sqn, Culdrose
	ZA126	WS61 Sea King HC6 [504/CU]	RN AMG, Yeovilton (conversion)
	ZA127	WS61 Sea King HAS6 [509/CU]	RN, stored *HMS Sultan*, Gosport
	ZA128	WS61 Sea King HAS6 [010]	RN, stored *HMS Sultan*, Gosport
	ZA129	WS61 Sea King HAS6 [502/CU]	Westland Helicopters, Yeovil (spares recovery)
	ZA130	WS61 Sea King HU5 [709/PW]	RN No 771 Sqn, Culdrose
	ZA131	WS61 Sea King HAS6 [271/N]	RN, stored *HMS Sultan*, Gosport
	ZA133	WS61 Sea King HAS6 [831/CU]	RN No 771 Sqn, Culdrose
	ZA134	WS61 Sea King HU5 [825/CU]	RN No 771 Sqn, Culdrose
	ZA135	WS61 Sea King HAS6 [705/CU]	RN AMG, Culdrose
	ZA136	WS61 Sea King HAS6 [018/L]	RN, AESS, *HMS Sultan*, Gosport (wreck)
	ZA137	WS61 Sea King HU5 [820/CU]	RN No 771 Sqn, Culdrose
	ZA142	BAe VC10 K2 (G-ARVI) [C]	*Scrapped at St Athan, May 2004*
	ZA147	BAe VC10 K3 (5H-MMT) [F]	RAF No 101 Sqn, Brize Norton
	ZA148	BAe VC10 K3 (5Y-ADA) [G]	RAF No 101 Sqn, Brize Norton
	ZA149	BAe VC10 K3 (5X-UVJ) [H]	RAF No 101 Sqn, Brize Norton
	ZA150	BAe VC10 K3 (5H-MOG)	RAF No 101 Sqn, Brize Norton
	ZA166	WS61 Sea King HU5 [828/CU]	RN No 771 Sqn, Culdrose
	ZA167	WS61 Sea King HU5 [822/CU]	RN No 771 Sqn, Culdrose
	ZA168	WS61 Sea King HAS6 [830/CU]	RN No 771 Sqn, Culdrose
	ZA169	WS61 Sea King HAS6 [515/CW]	RN No 771 Sqn, Culdrose
	ZA170	WS61 Sea King HAS5	RN, stored *HMS Sultan*, Gosport

Serial	Type (other identity) [code]	Owner/operator, location or fate	Notes
ZA175	BAe Sea Harrier FA2	Norfolk & Suffolk Avn Museum, Flixton	
ZA176	BAe Sea Harrier FA2	Newark Air Museum, Winthorpe	
ZA195	BAe Sea Harrier FA2	FAA Museum, stored RNAS Yeovilton	
ZA250	BAe Harrier T52 (G-VTOL)	Brooklands Museum, Weybridge	
ZA254	Panavia Tornado F2 (9253M) (fuselage)	*Currently not known*	
ZA267	Panavia Tornado F2 (9284M)	RAF Marham, instructional use	
ZA291	WS61 Sea King HC4 [WX]	RN No 848 Sqn, Yeovilton	
ZA292	WS61 Sea King HC4 [ZR]	DPA/Westland Helicopters, Yeovil	
ZA293	WS61 Sea King HC4 [WO]	RN No 848 Sqn, Yeovilton	
ZA295	WS61 Sea King HC4 [WR]	RN No 848 Sqn, Yeovilton	
ZA296	WS61 Sea King HC4 [B]	RN No 845 Sqn, Yeovilton	
ZA297	WS61 Sea King HC4 [C]	RN No 845 Sqn, Yeovilton	
ZA298	WS61 Sea King HC4 [WW]	RN No 848 Sqn, Yeovilton	
ZA299	WS61 Sea King HC4 [D]	RN No 845 Sqn, Yeovilton	
ZA310	WS61 Sea King HC4 [WY]	RN No 848 Sqn, Yeovilton	
ZA312	WS61 Sea King HC4 [ZS]	RN No 848 Sqn, Yeovilton	
ZA313	WS61 Sea King HC4 [M]	RN No 845 Sqn, Yeovilton	
ZA314	WS61 Sea King HC4 [F]	RN No 845 Sqn, Yeovilton	
ZA319	Panavia Tornado GR1	Army, Bicester, on display	
ZA320	Panavia Tornado GR1 (9314M) [TAW]	RAF No 1 SoTT, Cosford	
ZA322	Panavia Tornado GR1 (9334M) [TAC]	RAF Marham, Fire Section	
ZA323	Panavia Tornado GR1 [TAZ]	RAF No 1 SoTT, Cosford	
ZA324	Panavia Tornado GR1 [TAY]	RAF Lossiemouth, BDRT	
ZA325	Panavia Tornado GR1 [TAX]	RAF No 1 SoTT, Cosford	
ZA326	Panavia Tornado GR1P	DPA/AFD/QinetiQ, Boscombe Down	
ZA327	Panavia Tornado GR1	BAE Systems, Warton (spares use)	
ZA328	Panavia Tornado GR1	BAE Systems, Warton (spares use)	
ZA353	Panavia Tornado GR1 [B-53]	DPA/AFD/QinetiQ, Boscombe Down	
ZA354	Panavia Tornado GR1	BAE Systems, Warton (spares use)	
ZA355	Panavia Tornado GR1 [TAA]	RAF Lossiemouth, WLT	
ZA356	Panavia Tornado GR1 <ff>	RAF Marham, instructional use	
ZA357	Panavia Tornado GR1 [TTV]	RAF No 1 SoTT, Cosford	
ZA358	Panavia Tornado GR1	*Scrapped at Chesterfield, 2004*	
ZA359	Panavia Tornado GR1	BAE Systems Warton, Overseas Customer Training Centre	
ZA360	Panavia Tornado GR1 <ff>	RAF Marham, instructional use	
ZA361	Panavia Tornado GR1 [TD]	RAF Marham, Fire Section	
ZA362	Panavia Tornado GR1 [TR]	RAF, Lossiemouth, wfu	
ZA365	Panavia Tornado GR4 [AJ-Y]	RAF No 617 Sqn, Lossiemouth	
ZA367	Panavia Tornado GR4 [FW]	RAF No 12 Sqn, Lossiemouth	
ZA369	Panavia Tornado GR4A [U]	RAF No 2 Sqn, Marham	
ZA370	Panavia Tornado GR4A [DB]	RAF No 31 Sqn, Marham	
ZA371	Panavia Tornado GR4A [C]	RAF No 2 Sqn, Marham	
ZA372	Panavia Tornado GR4A [E]	RAF No 2 Sqn, Marham	
ZA373	Panavia Tornado GR4A [H]	RAF No 2 Sqn, Marham	
ZA375	Panavia Tornado GR1 (9335M) [AJ-W]	RAF Marham, Fire Section	
ZA393	Panavia Tornado GR4 [FE]	RAF/DARA, St Athan	
ZA395	Panavia Tornado GR4A [N]	RAF No 2 Sqn, Marham	
ZA398	Panavia Tornado GR4A [S]	RAF No 1 Sqn, Lossiemouth	
ZA399	Panavia Tornado GR1 [AJ-C]	RAF/DARA, St Athan, BDRT	
ZA400	Panavia Tornado GR4A [T]	RAF No 2 Sqn, Marham	
ZA401	Panavia Tornado GR4A [XIII]	RAF No 13 Sqn, Marham	
ZA402	Panavia Tornado GR4A	DPA/BAE Systems, Warton	
ZA404	Panavia Tornado GR4A [W]	RAF No 2 Sqn, Marham	
ZA405	Panavia Tornado GR4A [Y]	RAF No 2 Sqn, Marham	
ZA406	Panavia Tornado GR4 [FU]	RAF No 12 Sqn, Lossiemouth	
ZA407	Panavia Tornado GR1 (9336M) [AJ-N]	RAF Marham, on display	
ZA409	Panavia Tornado GR1 [VII]	RAF Lossiemouth, wfu	
ZA410	Panavia Tornado GR4 [DX]	RAF/DARA, St Athan	
ZA411	Panavia Tornado GR1 [TT]	RAF/DARA, stored St Athan	
ZA412	Panavia Tornado GR4 [TT]	RAF No 15(R) Sqn, Lossiemouth	
ZA446	Panavia Tornado GR4 [A]	RAF No 9 Sqn, Marham	
ZA447	Panavia Tornado GR4 [DE]	RAF No 31 Sqn, Marham	
ZA449	Panavia Tornado GR4 [AJ-N]	RAF/DARA, St Athan	
ZA450	Panavia Tornado GR1 [TH]	RAF No 1 SoTT, Cosford	
ZA452	Panavia Tornado GR4 [DF]	RAF/DARA, St Athan	
ZA453	Panavia Tornado GR4 [FH]	RAF No 12 Sqn, Lossiemouth	
ZA456	Panavia Tornado GR4	DPA/AFD/QinetiQ, Boscombe Down	

Notes	Serial	Type (other identity) [code]	Owner/operator, location or fate
	ZA457	Panavia Tornado GR1 [AJ-J]	RAF Museum, Hendon
	ZA458	Panavia Tornado GR4 [DG]	RAF No 31 Sqn, Marham
	ZA459	Panavia Tornado GR4 [F]	RAF No 15(R) Sqn, Lossiemouth
	ZA461	Panavia Tornado GR4 [AC]	RAF No 9 Sqn, Marham
	ZA462	Panavia Tornado GR4 [AJ-P]	RAF No 617 Sqn, Lossiemouth
	ZA463	Panavia Tornado GR4 [TL]	RAF Lossiemouth, WLT
	ZA465	Panavia Tornado GR1 [FF]	Imperial War Museum, Duxford
	ZA466	Panavia Tornado GR1 <ff>	*Scrapped at Chesterfield*
	ZA469	Panavia Tornado GR4 [TM]	RAF No 15(R) Sqn, Lossiemouth
	ZA470	Panavia Tornado GR4 [BQ]	RAF No 14 Sqn, Lossiemouth
	ZA472	Panavia Tornado GR4 [AE]	RAF/DARA, St Athan
	ZA473	Panavia Tornado GR4 [BH]	RAF No 14 Sqn, Lossiemouth
	ZA474	Panavia Tornado GR1	RAF Lossiemouth, wfu
	ZA475	Panavia Tornado GR1	RAF Lossiemouth, on display
	ZA491	Panavia Tornado GR4 [DL]	*Crashed 22 July 2004, North Sea*
	ZA492	Panavia Tornado GR4 [BO]	RAF No 14 Sqn, Lossiemouth
	ZA541	Panavia Tornado GR4 [III]	RAF No 2 Sqn, Marham
	ZA542	Panavia Tornado GR4 [DM]	RAF No 31 Sqn, Marham
	ZA543	Panavia Tornado GR4 [FO]	RAF No 12 Sqn, Lossiemouth
	ZA544	Panavia Tornado GR4 [FZ]	RAF No 12 Sqn, Lossiemouth
	ZA546	Panavia Tornado GR4 [AG]	RAF No 9 Sqn, Marham
	ZA547	Panavia Tornado GR4 [FF]	RAF No 12 Sqn, Lossiemouth
	ZA548	Panavia Tornado GR4 [T]	RAF No 15(R) Sqn, Lossiemouth
	ZA549	Panavia Tornado GR4 [AJ-Z]	RAF No 617 Sqn, Lossiemouth
	ZA550	Panavia Tornado GR4 [DD]	RAF No 31 Sqn, Marham
	ZA551	Panavia Tornado GR4 [AX]	RAF No 9 Sqn, Marham
	ZA552	Panavia Tornado GR4 [TX]	RAF No 15(R) Sqn, Lossiemouth
	ZA553	Panavia Tornado GR4 [DI]	RAF No 31 Sqn, Marham
	ZA554	Panavia Tornado GR4 [BF]	RAF No 14 Sqn, Lossiemouth
	ZA556	Panavia Tornado GR4 [AJ-C]	RAF No 617 Sqn, Lossiemouth
	ZA556	Panavia Tornado GR1 <R> (*ZA368*/BAPC 155) [Z]	RAF M&RU, Bottesford
	ZA557	Panavia Tornado GR4 [TJ]	RAF No 15(R) Sqn, Lossiemouth
	ZA559	Panavia Tornado GR4 [AD]	RAF No 2 Sqn, Marham
	ZA560	Panavia Tornado GR4 [BC]	RAF No 14 Sqn, Lossiemouth
	ZA562	Panavia Tornado GR4 [TO]	RAF No 15(R) Sqn, Lossiemouth
	ZA563	Panavia Tornado GR4 [AG]	RAF/DARA, St Athan
	ZA564	Panavia Tornado GR4 [DK]	RAF No 31 Sqn, Marham
	ZA585	Panavia Tornado GR4 [AH]	RAF No 9 Sqn, Marham
	ZA587	Panavia Tornado GR4 [AJ-M]	RAF No 617 Sqn, Lossiemouth
	ZA588	Panavia Tornado GR4 [BB]	RAF No 14 Sqn, Lossiemouth
	ZA589	Panavia Tornado GR4 [DN]	RAF/DARA, St Athan
	ZA591	Panavia Tornado GR4 [DJ]	RAF No 31 Sqn, Marham
	ZA592	Panavia Tornado GR4 [BJ]	RAF/DARA, St Athan
	ZA594	Panavia Tornado GR4 [TS]	RAF No 15(R) Sqn, Lossiemouth
	ZA595	Panavia Tornado GR4 [VIII]	RAF/DARA, St Athan
	ZA596	Panavia Tornado GR4 [BL]	RAF No 14 Sqn, Lossiemouth
	ZA597	Panavia Tornado GR4 [AJ-O]	RAF No 617 Sqn, Lossiemouth
	ZA598	Panavia Tornado GR4 [TW]	RAF No 15(R) Sqn, Lossiemouth
	ZA600	Panavia Tornado GR4	RAF No 13 Sqn, Marham
	ZA601	Panavia Tornado GR4 [TE]	RAF No 15(R) Sqn, Lossiemouth
	ZA602	Panavia Tornado GR4 [XIII]	RAF No 13 Sqn, Marham
	ZA604	Panavia Tornado GR4 [TY]	RAF No 15(R) Sqn, Lossiemouth
	ZA606	Panavia Tornado GR4 [BD]	RAF No 14 Sqn, Lossiemouth
	ZA607	Panavia Tornado GR4 [AB]	RAF No 9 Sqn, Marham
	ZA608	Panavia Tornado GR4	RAF/DARA, St Athan
	ZA609	Panavia Tornado GR4	RAF AWC/FJWOEU, Coningsby
	ZA611	Panavia Tornado GR4 [TK]	RAF No 15(R) Sqn, Lossiemouth
	ZA612	Panavia Tornado GR4 [TZ]	RAF No 15(R) Sqn, Lossiemouth
	ZA613	Panavia Tornado GR4 [AN]	RAF No 9 Sqn, Marham
	ZA614	Panavia Tornado GR4 [DO]	RAF No 31 Sqn, Marham
	ZA634	Slingsby T61F Venture T2 (G-BUHA) [C]	Privately owned, Saltby
	ZA670	B-V Chinook HC2 (N37010)	RAF No 1310 Flt, Basrah, Iraq
	ZA671	B-V Chinook HC2 (N37011)	RAF No 7 Sqn, Odiham
	ZA673	B-V Chinook HC2 (N37016)	RAF No 18 Sqn, Odiham
	ZA674	B-V Chinook HC2 (N37019)	RAF/DARA, Fleetlands
	ZA675	B-V Chinook HC2 (N37020)	RAF No 7 Sqn, Odiham
	ZA676	B-V Chinook HC1 (N37021/9230M) [FG] (wreck)	AAC, Wattisham
	ZA677	B-V Chinook HC2 (N37022)	RAF/DARA, Fleetlands
	ZA678	B-V Chinook HC1 (N37023/9229M) [EZ] (wreck)	RAF Odiham, BDRT

Serial	Type (other identity) [code]	Owner/operator, location or fate	Notes
ZA679	B-V Chinook HC2 (N37025)	RAF No 18 Sqn, Odiham	
ZA680	B-V Chinook HC2 (N37026)	RAF No 27 Sqn, Odiham	
ZA681	B-V Chinook HC2 (N37027)	RAF No 7 Sqn, Odiham	
ZA682	B-V Chinook HC2 (N37029)	RAF No 18 Sqn, Odiham	
ZA683	B-V Chinook HC2 (N37030)	RAF No 1310 Flt, Basrah, Iraq	
ZA684	B-V Chinook HC2 (N37031)	RAF No 7 Sqn, Odiham	
ZA704	B-V Chinook HC2 (N37033)	RAF No 18 Sqn, Odiham	
ZA705	B-V Chinook HC2 (N37035)	RAF/DARA, Fleetlands	
ZA707	B-V Chinook HC2 (N37040)	RAF No 27 Sqn, Odiham	
ZA708	B-V Chinook HC2 (N37042)	RAF No 78 Sqn, Mount Pleasant, FI	
ZA709	B-V Chinook HC2 (N37043)	RAF No 7 Sqn, Odiham	
ZA710	B-V Chinook HC2 (N37044)	RAF No 27 Sqn, Odiham	
ZA711	B-V Chinook HC2 (N37046)	RAF No 7 Sqn, Odiham	
ZA712	B-V Chinook HC2 (N37047)	RAF No 27 Sqn, Odiham	
ZA713	B-V Chinook HC2 (N37048)	RAF No 18 Sqn, Odiham	
ZA714	B-V Chinook HC2 (N37051)	RAF No 18 Sqn, Odiham	
ZA717	B-V Chinook HC1 (N37056/9238M) (wreck)	Trenchard Hall, RAF Cranwell, instructional use	
ZA718	B-V Chinook HC2 (N37058) [BN]	RAF No 1310 Flt, Basrah, Iraq	
ZA720	B-V Chinook HC2 (N37060)	RAF/DARA, Fleetlands	
ZA726	WS Gazelle AH1 [F1]	AAC No 671 Sqn/2 Regt, Middle Wallop	
ZA728	WS Gazelle AH1 [E]	RM No 847 Sqn, Yeovilton	
ZA729	WS Gazelle AH1	AAC Wattisham, BDRT	
ZA731	WS Gazelle AH1	AAC No 29 Flt, BATUS, Suffield, Canada	
ZA733	WS Gazelle AH1	DARA Fleetlands Apprentice School	
ZA734	WS Gazelle AH1	Privately owned, Hixon, Staffs	
ZA735	WS Gazelle AH1	Army SEAE, Arborfield	
ZA736	WS Gazelle AH1	AAC No 29 Flt, BATUS, Suffield, Canada	
ZA737	WS Gazelle AH1	Museum of Army Flying, Middle Wallop	
ZA766	WS Gazelle AH1	AAC No 665 Sqn/5 Regt, Aldergrove	
ZA768	WS Gazelle AH1 [F] (wreck)	AAC/DARA, stored Fleetlands	
ZA769	WS Gazelle AH1 [K]	Army SEAE, Arborfield	
ZA771	WS Gazelle AH1	AAC No 654 Sqn/4 Regt, Wattisham	
ZA772	WS Gazelle AH1	AAC, Middle Wallop	
ZA773	WS Gazelle AH1 [F]	AAC No 666(V) Sqn/7 Regt, Netheravon	
ZA774	WS Gazelle AH1	AAC/DARA, stored Fleetlands	
ZA775	WS Gazelle AH1	AAC No 665 Sqn/5 Regt, Aldergrove	
ZA776	WS Gazelle AH1 [F]	RM No 847 Sqn, Yeovilton	
ZA804	WS Gazelle HT3 [I]	DPA/QinetiQ Boscombe Down, spares use	
ZA934	WS Puma HC1 [BZ]	RAF No 1563 Flt, Basrah, Iraq	
ZA935	WS Puma HC1	RAF No 230 Sqn, Aldergrove	
ZA936	WS Puma HC1	RAF No 1563 Flt, Basrah, Iraq	
ZA937	WS Puma HC1	RAF No 230 Sqn, Aldergrove	
ZA938	WS Puma HC1	RAF No 33 Sqn, Benson	
ZA939	WS Puma HC1	RAF No 230 Sqn, Aldergrove	
ZA940	WS Puma HC1	RAF No 33 Sqn, Benson	
ZA947	Douglas Dakota C3 [AI]	RAF BBMF, Coningsby	
ZB500	WS Lynx 800 (G-LYNX/ZA500)	The Helicopter Museum, Weston-super-Mare	
ZB506	WS61 Sea King Mk 4X	DPA/AFD/QinetiQ, Boscombe Down	
ZB507	WS61 Sea King HC4	RN No 848 Sqn, Yeovilton	
ZB601	BAe Harrier T4 (fuselage)	RNAS Yeovilton, Fire Section	
ZB603	BAe Harrier T8 [724]	RN No 899 Sqn, Yeovilton	
ZB604	BAe Harrier T8 [722]	RN No 899 Sqn, Yeovilton	
ZB615	SEPECAT Jaguar T2A	DPA/AFD/QinetiQ, Boscombe Down	
ZB625	WS Gazelle HT3 [N]	DPA/AFD/QinetiQ, Boscombe Down	
ZB646	WS Gazelle HT2 (G-CBGZ) [59/CU]	Privately owned, Knebworth	
ZB647	WS Gazelle HT2 (G-CBSF) [40/CU]	*Repainted as G-CBSF*	
ZB649	WS Gazelle HT2 (G-SIVJ) [VL]	*Repainted as G-SIVJ*	
ZB665	WS Gazelle AH1	AAC No 665 Sqn/5 Regt, Aldergrove	
ZB666	WS Gazelle AH1 <ff>	Privately owned, Sproughton	
ZB667	WS Gazelle AH1	AAC No 665 Sqn/5 Regt, Aldergrove	
ZB668	WS Gazelle AH1 (TAD 015)	Army SEAC, Arborfield	
ZB669	WS Gazelle AH1	AAC No 665 Sqn/5 Regt, Aldergrove	
ZB670	WS Gazelle AH1	AAC/DARA, stored Fleetlands	
ZB671	WS Gazelle AH1 [2]	AAC No 29 Flt, BATUS, Suffield, Canada	
ZB672	WS Gazelle AH1	Army Training Regiment, Winchester	
ZB673	WS Gazelle AH1 [P]	AAC No 671 Sqn/2 Regt, Middle Wallop	
ZB674	WS Gazelle AH1	AAC No 665 Sqn/5 Regt, Aldergrove	

Notes	Serial	Type (other identity) [code]	Owner/operator, location or fate
	ZB677	WS Gazelle AH1	AAC No 29 Flt, BATUS, Suffield, Canada
	ZB678	WS Gazelle AH1	AAC/DARA, stored Fleetlands
	ZB679	WS Gazelle AH1	AAC No 665 Sqn/5 Regt, Aldergrove
	ZB682	WS Gazelle AH1	AAC/DARA, stored Fleetlands
	ZB683	WS Gazelle AH1	AAC No 665 Sqn/5 Regt, Aldergrove
	ZB684	WS Gazelle AH1	RAF Air Movements School, Brize Norton
	ZB685	WS Gazelle AH1	Privately owned, Sproughton
	ZB686	WS Gazelle AH1 <ff>	AAC Middle Wallop, instructional use
	ZB688	WS Gazelle AH1 [H]	AAC No 671 Sqn/2 Regt, Middle Wallop
	ZB689	WS Gazelle AH1	AAC No 665 Sqn/5 Regt, Aldergrove
	ZB690	WS Gazelle AH1	AAC No 665 Sqn/5 Regt, Aldergrove
	ZB691	WS Gazelle AH1	AAC No 654 Sqn/4 Regt, Wattisham
	ZB692	WS Gazelle AH1	AAC No 654 Sqn/4 Regt, Wattisham
	ZB693	WS Gazelle AH1	AAC No 665 Sqn/5 Regt, Aldergrove
	ZD230	BAC Super VC10 K4 (G-ASGA) [K]	RAF No 101 Sqn, Brize Norton
	ZD234	BAC Super VC10 (G-ASGF/ 8700M)	RAF Brize Norton, tanker simulator
	ZD235	BAC Super VC10 K4 (G-ASGG) [L]	*Scrapped at St Athan, 7 January 2004*
	ZD240	BAC Super VC10 K4 (G-ASGL) [M]	RAF No 101 Sqn, Brize Norton
	ZD241	BAC Super VC10 K4 (G-ASGM) [N]	RAF No 101 Sqn, Brize Norton
	ZD242	BAC Super VC10 K4 (G-ASGP) [P]	RAF No 101 Sqn, Brize Norton
	ZD249	WS Lynx HAS3S [637]	RN No 702 Sqn, Yeovilton
	ZD250	WS Lynx HAS3S [630]	RN No 702 Sqn, Yeovilton
	ZD251	WS Lynx HAS3S [636]	RN No 702 Sqn, Yeovilton
	ZD252	WS Lynx HMA8 [671]	RN/DARA, stored Fleetlands
	ZD254	WS Lynx HAS3S [635]	RN No 702 Sqn, Yeovilton
	ZD255	WS Lynx HAS3S [444/MR]	RN No 815 Sqn, *Montrose* Flt, Yeovilton
	ZD257	WS Lynx HMA8 [308]	RN No 815 Sqn, HQ Flt, Yeovilton
	ZD258	WS Lynx HMA8 (*XZ258*) [345/NC]	RN No 815 Sqn, *Newcastle* Flt, Yeovilton
	ZD259	WS Lynx HMA8 [361/NF]	RN No 815 Sqn, *Norfolk* Flt, Yeovilton
	ZD260	WS Lynx HMA8 [375/SM]	RN No 815 Sqn, *Somerset* Flt, Yeovilton
	ZD261	WS Lynx HMA8 [437/GT]	RN No 815 Sqn, *Grafton* Flt, Yeovilton
	ZD262	WS Lynx HMA8 [420/EX]	RN AMG, Yeovilton
	ZD263	WS Lynx HAS3S [305]	RN No 815 Sqn, HQ Flt, Yeovilton
	ZD264	WS Lynx HAS3S [634]	RN No 702 Sqn, Yeovilton
	ZD265	WS Lynx HMA8 [306]	RN No 815 Sqn, HQ Flt, Yeovilton
	ZD266	WS Lynx HMA8	DPA/AFD/QinetiQ, Boscombe Down
	ZD267	WS Lynx HMA8	RN/DARA, stored Fleetlands
	ZD268	WS Lynx HMA8 [317]	RN No 815 Sqn OEU, Yeovilton
	ZD272	WS Lynx AH7 [H]	AAC No 671 Sqn/2 Regt, Middle Wallop
	ZD273	WS Lynx AH7	AAC/DARA, Fleetlands
	ZD274	WS Lynx AH7	AAC No 655 Sqn/5 Regt, Aldergrove
	ZD276	WS Lynx AH7 [X]	AAC/DARA, Fleetlands
	ZD277	WS Lynx AH7	AAC No 653 Sqn/3 Regt, Wattisham
	ZD278	WS Lynx AH7 [A]	AAC No 655 Sqn/5 Regt, Aldergrove
	ZD279	WS Lynx AH7	RN/DARA, stored Fleetlands
	ZD280	WS Lynx AH7	AAC No 655 Sqn/5 Regt, Aldergrove
	ZD281	WS Lynx AH7 [K]	AAC No 671 Sqn/2 Regt, Middle Wallop
	ZD282	WS Lynx AH7 [L]	RM No 847 Sqn, Yeovilton
	ZD283	WS Lynx AH7	AAC No 653 Sqn/3 Regt, Wattisham
	ZD284	WS Lynx AH7	AAC/DARA, Fleetlands
	ZD285	WS Lynx AH7	DPA/AFD/QinetiQ, Boscombe Down
	ZD318	BAe Harrier GR7A	DPA/BAE Systems, Warton
	ZD319	BAe Harrier GR7	DPA/BAE Systems, Warton
	ZD320	BAe Harrier GR9	DPA/BAE Systems, Warton
	ZD321	BAe Harrier GR7 [02]	RAF No 4 Sqn, Cottesmore
	ZD322	BAe Harrier GR7 [03]	RAF No 1 Sqn, Cottesmore
	ZD323	BAe Harrier GR7 [04]	RAF No 1 Sqn, Cottesmore
	ZD327	BAe Harrier GR7A [08A]	RAF No 1 Sqn, Cottesmore
	ZD328	BAe Harrier GR7 [09]	RAF No 1 Sqn, Cottesmore
	ZD329	BAe Harrier GR7 [10]	RAF HOCU/No 20(R) Sqn, Wittering
	ZD330	BAe Harrier GR7 [11]	RAF HOCU/No 20(R) Sqn, Wittering
	ZD346	BAe Harrier GR7A [13A]	RAF No 3 Sqn, Cottesmore
	ZD347	BAe Harrier GR7A [14A]	RAF No 3 Sqn, Cottesmore
	ZD348	BAe Harrier GR7A [15A]	RAF, No 1 Sqn Cottesmore
	ZD350	BAe Harrier GR5 (9189M) <ff>	Privately owned, Sproughton
	ZD351	BAe Harrier GR7 [18]	RAF HOCU/No 20(R) Sqn, Wittering
	ZD352	BAe Harrier GR7 [19]	DPA/AFD/QinetiQ, Boscombe Down
	ZD353	BAe Harrier GR5 (fuselage)	BAE Systems, Brough
	ZD354	BAe Harrier GR7 [21]	RAF HOCU/No 20(R) Sqn, Wittering
	ZD375	BAe Harrier GR7 [23]	RAF No 1 Sqn, Cottesmore
	ZD376	BAe Harrier GR7A [24A]	RAF No 3 Sqn, Cottesmore

Serial	Type (other identity) [code]	Owner/operator, location or fate	Notes
ZD378	BAe Harrier GR7A [26A]	RAF, Cottesmore	
ZD379	BAe Harrier GR7 [27]	RAF No 4 Sqn, Cottesmore	
ZD380	BAe Harrier GR7 [28]	RAF No 20(R) Sqn, Wittering	
ZD401	BAe Harrier GR7 [30]	RAF No 1 Sqn, Cottesmore	
ZD402	BAe Harrier GR7 [31]	RAF HOCU/No 20(R) Sqn, Wittering	
ZD403	BAe Harrier GR7A [32A]	RAF AWC/FJWOEU, Coningsby	
ZD404	BAe Harrier GR7A [33A]	RAF No 4 Sqn, Cottesmore	
ZD405	BAe Harrier GR7A [34A]	RAF No 3 Sqn, Cottesmore	
ZD406	BAe Harrier GR7 [35]	RAF HOCU/No 20(R) Sqn, Wittering	
ZD407	BAe Harrier GR7 [36]	RAF HOCU/No 20(R) Sqn, Wittering	
ZD408	BAe Harrier GR7A [37A]	RAF No 3 Sqn, Cottesmore	
ZD409	BAe Harrier GR7 [38]	RAF No 4 Sqn, Cottesmore	
ZD410	BAe Harrier GR7 [39]	RAF HOCU/No 20(R) Sqn, Wittering	
ZD411	BAe Harrier GR7A [40A]	RAF No 4 Sqn, Cottesmore	
ZD412	BAe Harrier GR5 (fuselage)	RAF/DARA, St Athan, instructional use	
ZD431	BAe Harrier GR7A [43A]	RAF No 3 Sqn, Cottesmore	
ZD433	BAe Harrier GR7A [45A]	RAF No 3 Sqn, Cottesmore	
ZD435	BAe Harrier GR7 [47]	RAF No 1 Sqn, Cottesmore	
ZD436	BAe Harrier GR7A [48A]	RAF No 3 Sqn, Cottesmore	
ZD437	BAe Harrier GR7A [49A]	RAF No 4 Sqn, Cottesmore	
ZD438	BAe Harrier GR7 [50]	RAF No 4 Sqn, Cottesmore	
ZD461	BAe Harrier GR7A [51A]	RAF No 3 Sqn, Cottesmore	
ZD462	BAe Harrier GR7 (9302M) [52]	RAF St Athan, BDRT	
ZD463	BAe Harrier GR7 [53]	RAF AWC/FJWOEU, Coningsby	
ZD465	BAe Harrier GR7A [55A]	RAF No 4 Sqn, Cottesmore	
ZD466	BAe Harrier GR7 [56]	RAF No 3 Sqn, Cottesmore	
ZD467	BAe Harrier GR7 [57]	RAF No 1 Sqn, Cottesmore	
ZD468	BAe Harrier GR7 [58]	RAF HOCU/No 20(R) Sqn, Wittering	
ZD469	BAe Harrier GR7A [59A]	RAF No 3 Sqn, Cottesmore	
ZD470	BAe Harrier GR7 [60]	RAF No 1 Sqn, Cottesmore	
ZD476	WS61 Sea King HC4 [WU]	RN No 848 Sqn, Yeovilton	
ZD477	WS61 Sea King HC4 [H]	RN No 845 Sqn, Yeovilton	
ZD478	WS61 Sea King HC4 [VX]	RN No 846 Sqn, Yeovilton	
ZD479	WS61 Sea King HC4 [WV]	RN No 848 Sqn, Yeovilton	
ZD480	WS61 Sea King HC4 [E]	RN No 845 Sqn, Yeovilton	
ZD559	WS Lynx AH5X	DPA/AFD/QinetiQ, Boscombe Down	
ZD560	WS Lynx AH7	DPA/ETPS, Boscombe Down	
ZD565	WS Lynx HMA8 [307]	RN No 815 Sqn, HQ Flt, Yeovilton	
ZD566	WS Lynx HMA8 [670]	RN AMG, Yeovilton	
ZD574	B-V Chinook HC2 (N37077)	RAF No 1310 Flt, Basrah, Iraq	
ZD575	B-V Chinook HC2 (N37078)	RAF No 1310 Flt, Basrah, Iraq	
ZD578	BAe Sea Harrier FA2 [000,122]	RNAS Yeovilton, at main gate	
ZD579	BAe Sea Harrier FA2 [715/R]	RN No 899 Sqn, Yeovilton	
ZD580	BAe Sea Harrier FA2	Privately owned, Sproughton	
ZD581	BAe Sea Harrier FA2 [124]	RN, Predannack Fire School	
ZD582	BAe Sea Harrier FA2	RN SHOPS, Yeovilton	
ZD607	BAe Sea Harrier FA2	RAF St Athan, BDRT	
ZD608	BAe Sea Harrier FA2 [731]	RN/DARA, St Athan (spares recovery)	
ZD610	BAe Sea Harrier FA2 [001]	RN No 801 Sqn, Yeovilton	
ZD611	BAe Sea Harrier FA2	RNAS Culdrose Fire Section	
ZD612	BAe Sea Harrier FA2	RN ETS, Yeovilton	
ZD613	BAe Sea Harrier FA2 [122/R]	RN SHOPS, Yeovilton	
ZD614	BAe Sea Harrier FA2	Privately owned, Sproughton	
ZD615	BAe Sea Harrier FA2	RN/DARA, stored St Athan	
ZD620	BAe 125 CC3	RAF No 32(The Royal) Sqn, Northolt	
ZD621	BAe 125 CC3	RAF No 32(The Royal) Sqn, Northolt	
ZD625	WS61 Sea King HC4 [F]	RN No 845 Sqn, Yeovilton	
ZD626	WS61 Sea King HC4 [ZZ]	RN No 848 Sqn, Yeovilton	
ZD627	WS61 Sea King HC4 [VR]	RN No 846 Sqn, Yeovilton	
ZD630	WS61 Sea King HAS6 [012/L]	RN, stored *HMS Sultan*, Gosport	
ZD631	WS61 Sea King HAS6 [66] (fuselage)	RN, Predannack Fire School	
ZD633	WS61 Sea King HAS6 [014/L]	RN, stored *HMS Sultan*, Gosport	
ZD634	WS61 Sea King HAS6 [503]	RN, stored *HMS Sultan*, Gosport	
ZD636	WS61 Sea King AEW7 [182/CU]	RN No 849 Sqn, HQ Flt, Culdrose	
ZD637	WS61 Sea King HAS6 [700/PW]	RN, stored *HMS Sultan*, Gosport	
ZD667	BAe Harrier GR3 (9201M) [67]	SFDO, RNAS Culdrose	
ZD668	BAe Harrier GR3 (G-CBCU) [3E]	Privately owned, Lowestoft	
ZD670	BAe Harrier GR3 [3A]	Privately owned, South Molton, Devon	
ZD703	BAe 125 CC3	RAF No 32(The Royal) Sqn, Northolt	
ZD704	BAe 125 CC3	RAF No 32(The Royal) Sqn, Northolt	
ZD707	Panavia Tornado GR4	RAF/DARA, St Athan	
ZD708	Panavia Tornado GR4	DPA/BAE Systems, Warton	

Notes	Serial	Type (other identity) [code]	Owner/operator, location or fate
	ZD709	Panavia Tornado GR4 [DH]	RAF No 31 Sqn, Marham
	ZD710	Panavia Tornado GR1 <ff>	Privately owned, Barnstaple
	ZD711	Panavia Tornado GR4 [II]	RAF No 2 Sqn, Marham
	ZD712	Panavia Tornado GR4	RAF/DARA, St Athan
	ZD713	Panavia Tornado GR4 [AJ-F]	RAF No 617 Sqn, Lossiemouth
	ZD714	Panavia Tornado GR4 [AJ-W]	RAF No 617 Sqn, Lossiemouth
	ZD715	Panavia Tornado GR4	RAF No 15(R) Sqn, Lossiemouth
	ZD716	Panavia Tornado GR4 [AJ]	RAF No 9 Sqn, Marham
	ZD719	Panavia Tornado GR4 [BS]	RAF No 14 Sqn, Lossiemouth
	ZD720	Panavia Tornado GR4 [TA]	RAF No 15(R) Sqn, Lossiemouth
	ZD739	Panavia Tornado GR4	RAF AWC/FJWOEU, Coningsby
	ZD740	Panavia Tornado GR4 [DR]	RAF No 14 Sqn, Lossiemouth
	ZD741	Panavia Tornado GR4 [BZ]	RAF No 14 Sqn, Lossiemouth
	ZD742	Panavia Tornado GR4 [FY]	RAF No 15(R) Sqn, Lossiemouth
	ZD743	Panavia Tornado GR4 [TQ]	RAF No 15(R) Sqn, Lossiemouth
	ZD744	Panavia Tornado GR4 [FD]	RAF Lossiemouth, WLT
	ZD745	Panavia Tornado GR4	RAF AWC/FJWOEU, Coningsby
	ZD746	Panavia Tornado GR4 [TH]	RAF No 15(R) Sqn, Lossiemouth
	ZD747	Panavia Tornado GR4 [AL]	RAF No 9 Sqn, Marham
	ZD748	Panavia Tornado GR4 [FC]	RAF No 12 Sqn, Lossiemouth
	ZD749	Panavia Tornado GR4 [AP]	RAF No 13 Sqn, Marham
	ZD788	Panavia Tornado GR4 [BE]	RAF No 14 Sqn, Lossiemouth
	ZD789	Panavia Tornado GR1 <ff>	RAF, stored Shawbury
	ZD790	Panavia Tornado GR4 [FM]	RAF/DARA, St Athan
	ZD792	Panavia Tornado GR4 [AJ-G]	RAF/DARA, St Athan
	ZD793	Panavia Tornado GR4	RAF No 15(R) Sqn, Lossiemouth
	ZD810	Panavia Tornado GR4 [TD]	RAF No 15(R) Sqn, Lossiemouth
	ZD811	Panavia Tornado GR4	RAF/DARA, St Athan
	ZD812	Panavia Tornado GR4 [TU]	RAF No 15(R) Sqn, Lossiemouth
	ZD842	Panavia Tornado GR4 [TV]	RAF No 15(R) Sqn, Lossiemouth
	ZD843	Panavia Tornado GR4 [TG]	RAF No 15(R) Sqn, Lossiemouth
	ZD844	Panavia Tornado GR4 [AJ-A]	RAF No 617 Sqn, Lossiemouth
	ZD847	Panavia Tornado GR4 [AA]	RAF No 9 Sqn, Marham
	ZD848	Panavia Tornado GR4 [AE]	DPA/BAE Systems, Warton
	ZD849	Panavia Tornado GR4 [FG]	RAF No 12 Sqn, Lossiemouth
	ZD850	Panavia Tornado GR4 [AJ-T]	RAF/DARA, St Athan
	ZD851	Panavia Tornado GR4 [FP]	RAF No 12 Sqn, Lossiemouth
	ZD890	Panavia Tornado GR4	RAF No 2 Sqn, Marham
	ZD892	Panavia Tornado GR4 [TG]	RAF, stored St Athan
	ZD895	Panavia Tornado GR4 [TI]	RAF No 15(R) Sqn, Lossiemouth
	ZD899	Panavia Tornado F2	DPA, Boscombe Down, spares use
	ZD902	Panavia Tornado F2A(TIARA)	DPA/AFD/QinetiQ, Boscombe Down
	ZD903	Panavia Tornado F2 (comp ZE728) (fuselage)	*Scrapped*
	ZD906	Panavia Tornado F2 (comp ZE294) <ff>	RAF Leuchars, BDRT
	ZD932	Panavia Tornado F2 (comp ZE255) (fuselage)	RAF St Athan, BDRT
	ZD934	Panavia Tornado F2 (comp ZE786) <ff>	RAF Leeming, GI use
	ZD935	Panavia Tornado F2 (comp ZE793) <ff>	*Scrapped*
	ZD936	Panavia Tornado F2 (comp ZE251) <ff>	Boscombe Down Aviation Collection
	ZD938	Panavia Tornado F2 (comp ZE295) <ff>	RAF, stored Shawbury
	ZD939	Panavia Tornado F2 (comp ZE292) <ff>	RAF Cosford, instructional use
	ZD940	Panavia Tornado F2 (comp ZE288) (fuselage)	*Scrapped*
	ZD948	Lockheed TriStar KC1 (G-BFCA)	RAF No 216 Sqn, Brize Norton
	ZD949	Lockheed TriStar K1 (G-BFCB)	RAF No 216 Sqn, Brize Norton
	ZD950	Lockheed TriStar KC1 (G-BFCC)	RAF No 216 Sqn, Brize Norton
	ZD951	Lockheed TriStar K1 (G-BFCD)	RAF No 216 Sqn, Brize Norton
	ZD952	Lockheed TriStar KC1 (G-BFCE)	RAF No 216 Sqn, Brize Norton
	ZD953	Lockheed TriStar KC1 (G-BFCF)	RAF No 216 Sqn, Brize Norton
	ZD980	B-V Chinook HC2 (N37082)	RAF No 27 Sqn, Odiham
	ZD981	B-V Chinook HC2 (N37083)	RAF/DARA, Fleetlands
	ZD982	B-V Chinook HC2 (N37085)	RAF No 18 Sqn, Odiham
	ZD983	B-V Chinook HC2 (N37086)	RAF No 18 Sqn, Odiham
	ZD984	B-V Chinook HC2 (N37088)	RAF No 7 Sqn, Odiham
	ZD990	BAe Harrier T8 [721]	RN No 899 Sqn, Yeovilton
	ZD991	BAe Harrier T8 (9228M) [722/VL]	Privately owned, Sproughton

Serial	Type (other identity) [code]	Owner/operator, location or fate	Notes
ZD993	BAe Harrier T8 [723/VL]	RN No 899 Sqn, Yeovilton	
ZD996	Panavia Tornado GR4A [I]	DPA/AFD/QinetiQ, Boscombe Down	
ZE116	Panavia Tornado GR4A [X]	RAF No 13 Sqn, Marham	
ZE154	Panavia Tornado F3 (comp ZD901) [LT]	RAF F3 OCU/No 56(R) Sqn, Leuchars	
ZE155	Panavia Tornado F3	DPA/BAE Systems, Warton	
ZE156	Panavia Tornado F3 [GA]	RAF No 43 Sqn, Leuchars	
ZE157	Panavia Tornado F3 [TY]	RAF/DARA, St Athan	
ZE158	Panavia Tornado F3	RAF No 111 Sqn, Leuchars	
ZE159	Panavia Tornado F3 [UV]	RAF No 111 Sqn, Leuchars	
ZE160	Panavia Tornado F3 [TX]	RAF F3 OCU/No 56(R) Sqn, Leuchars	
ZE161	Panavia Tornado F3 [GB]	RAF No 43 Sqn, Leuchars	
ZE162	Panavia Tornado F3 [UR]	RAF No 111 Sqn, Leuchars	
ZE163	Panavia Tornado F3 (comp ZG753) [TW]	RAF/DARA, St Athan	
ZE164	Panavia Tornado F3 [GD]	RAF No 43 Sqn, Leuchars	
ZE165	Panavia Tornado F3 [GE]	RAF No 43 Sqn, Leuchars	
ZE167	Panavia Tornado F3 (MM7234)	*Scrapped, November 2004*	
ZE168	Panavia Tornado F3 [DN]	RAF No 11 Sqn, Leeming	
ZE199	Panavia Tornado F3 [TV]	RAF F3 OCU/No 56(R) Sqn, Leuchars	
ZE200	Panavia Tornado F3 [DB]	RAF No 11 Sqn, Leeming	
ZE201	Panavia Tornado F3 [UL]	RAF No 25 Sqn, Leeming	
ZE202	Panavia Tornado F3 (MM55056)	RAF/DARA, St Athan	
ZE203	Panavia Tornado F3 [DE]	RAF/DARA, St Athan	
ZE204	Panavia Tornado F3 [UJ]	RAF No 25 Sqn, Leeming	
ZE205	Panavia Tornado F3 (MM55061)	RAF/DARA, St Athan	
ZE206	Panavia Tornado F3 [UI]	DPA/BAE Systems, Warton	
ZE207	Panavia Tornado F3 [GC]	RAF No 43 Sqn, Leuchars	
ZE208	Panavia Tornado F3 (MM55060)	RAF/DARA, St Athan	
ZE209	Panavia Tornado F3 [AX]	RAF/EADS, Munich, Germany	
ZE250	Panavia Tornado F3 [TR]	RAF F3 OCU/No 56(R) Sqn, Leuchars	
ZE251	Panavia Tornado F3 (comp ZD936) [UF]	RAF No 111 Sqn, Leuchars	
ZE252	Panavia Tornado F3 (MM7225)	*Scrapped, November 2004*	
ZE253	Panavia Tornado F3 [AC]	RAF/EADS, Munich, Germany	
ZE254	Panavia Tornado F3 (comp ZD941) [UD]	RAF No 25 Sqn, Leeming	
ZE255	Panavia Tornado F3 (comp ZD932) [UC]	RAF No 25 Sqn, Leeming	
ZE256	Panavia Tornado F3 [TP]	RAF Leuchars, instructional use	
ZE257	Panavia Tornado F3 [UB]	RAF No 43 Sqn, Leuchars	
ZE258	Panavia Tornado F3 (comp ZD905) [F]	RAF No 1435 Flt, Mount Pleasant, FI	
ZE287	Panavia Tornado F3 [TO]	RAF No 11 Sqn, Leeming	
ZE288	Panavia Tornado F3 (comp ZD940) [HA]	RAF No 111 Sqn, Leuchars	
ZE289	Panavia Tornado F3 [VX]	RAF No 111 Sqn, Leuchars	
ZE290	Panavia Tornado F3 [AG]	RAF/DARA, stored St Athan	
ZE291	Panavia Tornado F3 [D]	RAF No 1435 Flt, Mount Pleasant, FI	
ZE292	Panavia Tornado F3 (comp ZD939) [YY]	RAF No 25 Sqn, Leeming	
ZE293	Panavia Tornado F3 [GZ]	RAF No 43 Sqn, Leuchars	
ZE294	Panavia Tornado F3 (comp ZD906) [DD]	RAF No 11 Sqn, Leeming	
ZE295	Panavia Tornado F3 (comp ZD938) [DC]	RAF/DARA, St Athan	
ZE338	Panavia Tornado F3 [YV]	RAF No 43 Sqn, Leuchars	
ZE339	Panavia Tornado F3 <ff>	RAF/DARA, stored St Athan	
ZE340	Panavia Tornado F3 (*ZE758*/ 9298M) [GO]	RAF No 1 SoTT, Cosford	
ZE341	Panavia Tornado F3 [DF]	RAF/DARA, St Athan	
ZE342	Panavia Tornado F3	RAF/DARA, St Athan	
ZE343	Panavia Tornado F3 (comp ZD900) [TI]	RAF F3 OCU/No 56(R) Sqn, Leuchars	
ZE350	McD F-4J(UK) Phantom (9080M) <ff>	Privately owned, Ingatestone, Essex	
ZE352	McD F-4J(UK) Phantom (9086M) <ff>	Privately owned, Preston, Lancs	
ZE356	McD F-4J(UK) Phantom (9060M) [Q]	*Scrapped at Waddington, 23 March 2004*	
ZE360	McD F-4J(UK) Phantom (9059M) [O]	MoD FSCTE, Manston	

Notes	Serial	Type (other identity) [code]	Owner/operator, location or fate
	ZE368	WS61 Sea King HAR3 [R]	RAF No 78 Sqn, Mount Pleasant, FI
	ZE369	WS61 Sea King HAR3	RAF/HMF, St Mawgan
	ZE370	WS61 Sea King HAR3 [T]	RAF No 202 Sqn, D Flt, Lossiemouth
	ZE375	WS Lynx AH9	AAC No 661 Sqn/1 Regt, Gütersloh
	ZE376	WS Lynx AH9	AAC/DARA, stored Fleetlands
	ZE378	WS Lynx AH7	AAC/DARA, Fleetlands
	ZE379	WS Lynx AH7	AAC/DARA, stored Fleetlands
	ZE380	WS Lynx AH9	AAC No 659 Sqn/4 Regt, Wattisham
	ZE381	WS Lynx AH7 [X]	AAC No 671 Sqn/2 Regt, Middle Wallop
	ZE382	WS Lynx AH9	AAC No 661 Sqn/1 Regt, Gütersloh
	ZE395	BAe 125 CC3	RAF No 32(The Royal) Sqn, Northolt
	ZE396	BAe 125 CC3	RAF No 32(The Royal) Sqn, Northolt
	ZE410	Agusta A109A (AE-334)	AAC No 8 Flt, Credenhill
	ZE411	Agusta A109A (AE-331)	AAC No 8 Flt, Credenhill
	ZE412	Agusta A109A	AAC No 8 Flt, Credenhill
	ZE413	Agusta A109A	AAC No 8 Flt, Credenhill
	ZE418	WS61 Sea King AEW7 [186/R]	RN No 849 Sqn, A Flt, Culdrose
	ZE420	WS61 Sea King AEW7 [189]	RN No 849 Sqn, A Flt, Culdrose
	ZE422	WS61 Sea King AEW7	RN HMF, St Mawgan (conversion)
	ZE425	WS61 Sea King HC4 [VP]	RN No 846 Sqn, Yeovilton
	ZE426	WS61 Sea King HC4 [WW]	RN AMG, Yeovilton
	ZE427	WS61 Sea King HC4 [WZ]	RN No 848 Sqn, Yeovilton
	ZE428	WS61 Sea King HC4 [VS]	RN No 846 Sqn, Yeovilton
	ZE432	BAC 1-11/479FU (DQ-FBV)	DPA/ETPS, Boscombe Down
	ZE433	BAC 1-11/479FU (DQ-FBQ)	DPA/FR Aviation, Bournemouth
	ZE438	BAe Jetstream T3 [76]	RN FONA/Heron Flight, Yeovilton
	ZE439	BAe Jetstream T3 [77]	RN FONA/Heron Flight, Yeovilton
	ZE440	BAe Jetstream T3 [78]	RN, stored Shawbury
	ZE441	BAe Jetstream T3 [79]	RN FONA/Heron Flight, Yeovilton
	ZE449	SA330L Puma HC1 (9017M/PA-12)	RAF No 33 Sqn, Benson
	ZE477	WS Lynx 3	The Helicopter Museum, Weston-super-Mare
	ZE495	Grob G103 Viking T1 (BGA3000) [VA]	RAF No 622 VGS, Upavon
	ZE496	Grob G103 Viking T1 (BGA3001) [VB]	RAF ACCGS/No 643 VGS, Syerston
	ZE498	Grob G103 Viking T1 (BGA3003) [VC]	RAF No 614 VGS, Wethersfield
	ZE499	Grob G103 Viking T1 (BGA3004) [VD]	RAF No 615 VGS, Kenley
	ZE501	Grob G103 Viking T1 (BGA3006) [VE]	Privately owned
	ZE502	Grob G103 Viking T1 (BGA3007) [VF]	RAF ACCGS/No 643 VGS, Syerston
	ZE503	Grob G103 Viking T1 (BGA3008) [VG]	RAF No 625 VGS, Hullavington
	ZE504	Grob G103 Viking T1 (BGA3009) [VH]	RAF No 621 VGS, Hullavington
	ZE520	Grob G103 Viking T1 (BGA3010) [VJ]	RAF No 625 VGS, Hullavington
	ZE521	Grob G103 Viking T1 (BGA3011) [VK]	RAF No 626 VGS, Predannack
	ZE522	Grob G103 Viking T1 (BGA3012) [VL]	RAF No 621 VGS, Hullavington
	ZE524	Grob G103 Viking T1 (BGA3014) [VM]	RAF No 625 VGS, Hullavington
	ZE526	Grob G103 Viking T1 (BGA3016) [VN]	RAF No 662 VGS, Arbroath
	ZE527	Grob G103 Viking T1 (BGA3017) [VP]	RAF No 626 VGS, Predannack
	ZE528	Grob G103 Viking T1 (BGA3018) [VQ]	RAF No 614 VGS, Wethersfield
	ZE529	Grob G103 Viking T1 (BGA3019) (comp ZE655) [VR]	RAF No 614 VGS, Wethersfield
	ZE530	Grob G103 Viking T1 (BGA3020) [VS]	RAF No 611 VGS, Watton
	ZE531	Grob G103 Viking T1 (BGA3021) [VT]	RAF No 615 VGS, Kenley
	ZE532	Grob G103 Viking T1 (BGA3022) [VU]	RAF No 614 VGS, Wethersfield
	ZE533	Grob G103 Viking T1 (BGA3023) [VV]	RAF No 622 VGS, Upavon

Serial	*Type (other identity) [code]*	*Owner/operator, location or fate*	*Notes*
ZE534	Grob G103 Viking T1 (BGA3024) [VW]	Privately owned	
ZE550	Grob G103 Viking T1 (BGA3025) [VX]	RAF No 614 VGS, Wethersfield	
ZE551	Grob G103 Viking T1 (BGA3026) [VY]	RAF No 614 VGS, Wethersfield	
ZE552	Grob G103 Viking T1 (BGA3027) [VZ]	RAF No 621 VGS, Hullavington	
ZE553	Grob G103 Viking T1 (BGA3028) [WA]	RAF No 615 VGS, Kenley	
ZE554	Grob G103 Viking T1 (BGA3029) [WB]	RAF No 611 VGS, Watton	
ZE555	Grob G103 Viking T1 (BGA3030) [WC]	RAF No 625 VGS, Hullavington	
ZE556	Grob G103 Viking T1 (BGA3031) [WD]	RAF CGMF, Syerston (damaged)	
ZE557	Grob G103 Viking T1 (BGA3032) [WE]	RAF No 622 VGS, Upavon	
ZE558	Grob G103 Viking T1 (BGA3033) [WF]	RAF No 615 VGS, Kenley	
ZE559	Grob G103 Viking T1 (BGA3034) [WG]	RAF No 661 VGS, Kirknewton	
ZE560	Grob G103 Viking T1 (BGA3035) [WH]	RAF No 661 VGS, Kirknewton	
ZE561	Grob G103 Viking T1 (BGA3036) [WJ]	RAF No 631 VGS, Sealand	
ZE562	Grob G103 Viking T1 (BGA3037) [WK]	RAF No 626 VGS, Predannack	
ZE563	Grob G103 Viking T1 (BGA3038) [WL]	RAF No 621 VGS, Hullavington	
ZE564	Grob G103 Viking T1 (BGA3039) [WN]	RAF ACCGS/No 643 VGS, Syerston	
ZE584	Grob G103 Viking T1 (BGA3040) [WP]	RAF No 631 VGS, Sealand	
ZE585	Grob G103 Viking T1 (BGA3041) [WQ]	RAF No 626 VGS, Predannack	
ZE586	Grob G103 Viking T1 (BGA3042) [WR]	RAF No 631 VGS, Sealand	
ZE587	Grob G103 Viking T1 (BGA3043) [WS]	RAF No 611 VGS, Watton	
ZE589	Grob G103 Viking T1 (BGA3045) <ff>	RAFGSA, Halton	
ZE590	Grob G103 Viking T1 (BGA3046) [WT]	RAF No 661 VGS, Kirknewton	
ZE591	Grob G103 Viking T1 (BGA3047) [WU]	RAF No 631 VGS, Sealand	
ZE592	Grob G103 Viking T1 (BGA3048) [WV]	RAF No 621 VGS, Hullavington	
ZE593	Grob G103 Viking T1 (BGA3049) [WW]	RAF, stored CGMF Syerston	
ZE594	Grob G103 Viking T1 (BGA3050) [WX]	RAF ACCGS/No 643 VGS, Syerston	
ZE595	Grob G103 Viking T1 (BGA3051) [WY]	RAF No 622 VGS, Upavon	
ZE600	Grob G103 Viking T1 (BGA3052) [W7]	RAF No 622 VGS, Upavon	
ZE601	Grob G103 Viking T1 (BGA3053) [XA]	RAF No 611 VGS, Watton	
ZE602	Grob G103 Viking T1 (BGA3054) [XB]	RAF No 621 VGS, Hullavington	
ZE603	Grob G103 Viking T1 (BGA3055) [XC]	RAF CGMF, Syerston	
ZE604	Grob G103 Viking T1 (BGA3056) [XD]	RAF ACCGS/No 643 VGS, Syerston	
ZE605	Grob G103 Viking T1 (BGA3057) [XE]	RAF, stored CGMF Syerston	
ZE606	Grob G103 Viking T1 (BGA3058) [XF]	RAF No 615 VGS, Kenley	
ZE607	Grob G103 Viking T1 (BGA3059) [XG]	RAF, stored CGMF Syerston	
ZE608	Grob G103 Viking T1 (BGA3060) [XH]	RAF, stored CGMF Syerston	

Notes	Serial	Type (other identity) [code]	Owner/operator, location or fate
	ZE609	Grob G103 Viking T1 (BGA3061) [XJ]	RAF CGMF, Syerston
	ZE610	Grob G103 Viking T1 (BGA3062) [XK]	RAF No 615 VGS, Kenley
	ZE611	Grob G103 Viking T1 (BGA3063) [XL]	RAF No 611 VGS, Watton
	ZE613	Grob G103 Viking T1 (BGA3065) [XM]	RAF No 662 VGS, Arbroath
	ZE614	Grob G103 Viking T1 (BGA3066) [XN]	RAF No 611 VGS, Watton
	ZE625	Grob G103 Viking T1 (BGA3067) [XP]	RAF No 625 VGS, Hullavington
	ZE626	Grob G103 Viking T1 (BGA3068) [XQ]	RAF No 626 VGS, Predannack
	ZE627	Grob G103 Viking T1 (BGA3069) [XR]	RAF No 631 VGS, Sealand
	ZE628	Grob G103 Viking T1 (BGA3070) [XS]	RAF ACCGS/No 643 VGS, Syerston
	ZE629	Grob G103 Viking T1 (BGA3071) [XT]	RAF CGMF, Syerston
	ZE630	Grob G103 Viking T1 (BGA3072) [XU]	RAF No 662 VGS, Arbroath
	ZE631	Grob G103 Viking T1 (BGA3073) [XV]	RAF No 662 VGS, Arbroath
	ZE632	Grob G103 Viking T1 (BGA3074) [XW]	RAF No 631 VGS, Sealand
	ZE633	Grob G103 Viking T1 (BGA3075) [XX]	RAF No 614 VGS, Wethersfield
	ZE635	Grob G103 Viking T1 (BGA3077) [XY]	Privately owned, Newark
	ZE636	Grob G103 Viking T1 (BGA3078) [XZ]	RAF CGMF, Syerston
	ZE637	Grob G103 Viking T1 (BGA3079) [YA]	RAF No 622 VGS, Upavon
	ZE650	Grob G103 Viking T1 (BGA3080) [YB]	RAF No 622 VGS, Upavon
	ZE651	Grob G103 Viking T1 (BGA3081) [YC]	RAF No 661 VGS, Kirknewton
	ZE652	Grob G103 Viking T1 (BGA3082) [YD]	RAF ACCGS/No 643 VGS, Syerston
	ZE653	Grob G103 Viking T1 (BGA3083) [YE]	RAF No 661 VGS, Kirknewton
	ZE656	Grob G103 Viking T1 (BGA3086) [YH]	RAF No 625 VGS, Hullavington
	ZE657	Grob G103 Viking T1 (BGA3087) [YJ]	RAF ACCGS/No 643 VGS, Syerston
	ZE658	Grob G103 Viking T1 (BGA3088) [YK]	RAF No 611 VGS, Watton
	ZE677	Grob G103 Viking T1 (BGA3090) [YM]	RAF No 621 VGS, Hullavington
	ZE678	Grob G103 Viking T1 (BGA3091) [YN]	RAF, stored CGMF Syerston
	ZE679	Grob G103 Viking T1 (BGA3092) [YP]	RAF No 622 VGS, Upavon
	ZE680	Grob G103 Viking T1 (BGA3093) [YQ]	RAF No 662 VGS, Arbroath
	ZE681	Grob G103 Viking T1 (BGA3094) [YR]	RAF CGMF, Syerston (damaged)
	ZE682	Grob G103 Viking T1 (BGA3095) [YS]	RAF No 662 VGS, Arbroath
	ZE683	Grob G103 Viking T1 (BGA3096) [YT]	RAF No 661 VGS, Kirknewton
	ZE684	Grob G103 Viking T1 (BGA3097) [YU]	RAF ACCGS/No 643 VGS, Syerston
	ZE685	Grob G103 Viking T1 (BGA3098) [YV]	RAF No 631 VGS, Sealand
	ZE686	Grob G103 Viking T1 (BGA3099)	DPA/Slingsby Kirkbymoorside
	ZE690	BAe Sea Harrier FA2 [713]	RN No 899 Sqn, Yeovilton
	ZE691	BAe Sea Harrier FA2	Privately owned, Sproughton
	ZE692	BAe Sea Harrier FA2 [718]	RN No 899 Sqn, Yeovilton
	ZE693	BAe Sea Harrier FA2 [714]	RN No 899 Sqn, Yeovilton
	ZE694	BAe Sea Harrier FA2 [N]	RN SHOPS, Yeovilton
	ZE695	BAe Sea Harrier FA2 [718]	Privately owned, Sproughton

Serial	Type (other identity) [code]	Owner/operator, location or fate	Notes
ZE696	BAe Sea Harrier FA2 [124/R]	RN SHOPS, Yeovilton	
ZE697	BAe Sea Harrier FA2 [006]	RN, stored St Athan	
ZE698	BAe Sea Harrier FA2 [001]	RN SHOPS, Yeovilton, wfu	
ZE700	BAe 146 CC2 (G-6-021)	RAF No 32(The Royal) Sqn, Northolt	
ZE701	BAe 146 CC2 (G-6-029)	RAF No 32(The Royal) Sqn, Northolt	
ZE704	Lockheed TriStar C2 (N508PA)	RAF No 216 Sqn, Brize Norton	
ZE705	Lockheed TriStar C2 (N509PA)	RAF No 216 Sqn, Brize Norton	
ZE706	Lockheed TriStar C2A (N503PA)	RAF No 216 Sqn, Brize Norton	
ZE728	Panavia Tornado F3 (comp ZD903)	RAF No 25 Sqn, Leeming	
ZE729	Panavia Tornado F3 (comp ZD933) [DH]	RAF No 11 Sqn, Leeming	
ZE730	Panavia Tornado F3 (MM7204)	RAF/DARA, stored St Athan	
ZE731	Panavia Tornado F3 [YP]	RAF No 111 Sqn, Leuchars	
ZE734	Panavia Tornado F3 [DA]	RAF No 11 Sqn, Leeming	
ZE735	Panavia Tornado F3	RAF F3 OCU/No 56(R) Sqn, Leuchars	
ZE736	Panavia Tornado F3 (comp ZD937) [HC]	RAF/DARA, St Athan	
ZE737	Panavia Tornado F3	RAF/DARA, St Athan	
ZE755	Panavia Tornado F3	RAF/DARA, St Athan	
ZE756	Panavia Tornado F3	RAF/DARA, stored St Athan	
ZE757	Panavia Tornado F3 [YJ]	RAF No 25 Sqn, Leeming	
ZE758	Panavia Tornado F3 [DO]	RAF No 11 Sqn, Leeming	
ZE760	Panavia Tornado F3 (MM7206) [AP]	RAF Coningsby, on display	
ZE761	Panavia Tornado F3 (MM7203)	DPA/BAE Systems, Warton	
ZE762	Panavia Tornado F3 (MM7207)	RAF/DARA, stored St Athan	
ZE763	Panavia Tornado F3 [DG]	RAF No 11 Sqn, Leeming	
ZE764	Panavia Tornado F3 [YD]	RAF No 111 Sqn, Leuchars	
ZE785	Panavia Tornado F3 [YC]	RAF AWC/FJWOEU, Coningsby	
ZE786	Panavia Tornado F3 (comp ZD934) [TF]	RAF F3 OCU/No 56(R) Sqn, Leuchars	
ZE787	Panavia Tornado F3 (MM7205)	RAF/DARA, St Athan	
ZE788	Panavia Tornado F3 [GL]	RAF No 43 Sqn, Leuchars	
ZE790	Panavia Tornado F3 [DK]	RAF No 11 Sqn, Leeming	
ZE791	Panavia Tornado F3 [XY]	RAF No 111 Sqn, Leuchars	
ZE792	Panavia Tornado F3 (MM7211)	RAF/DARA, stored St Athan	
ZE793	Panavia Tornado F3 (comp ZD935) [TE]	RAF F3 OCU/No 56(R) Sqn, Leuchars	
ZE794	Panavia Tornado F3	RAF No 25 Sqn, Leeming	
ZE808	Panavia Tornado F3 [XV]	RAF No 25 Sqn, Leeming	
ZE810	Panavia Tornado F3 [GM]	RAF No 43 Sqn, Leuchars	
ZE811	Panavia Tornado F3 (MM7208)	*Scrapped, November 2004*	
ZE812	Panavia Tornado F3 [XR]	RAF/DARA, St Athan	
ZE831	Panavia Tornado F3 [XQ]	RAF No 25 Sqn, Leeming	
ZE832	Panavia Tornado F3 (MM7202) [XP]	RAF/DARA, St Athan	
ZE834	Panavia Tornado F3 [XO]	RAF No 111 Sqn, Leuchars	
ZE835	Panavia Tornado F3 (MM7209)	RAF/DARA, St Athan	
ZE837	Panavia Tornado F3 (MM55057) [TD]	RAF F3 OCU/No 56(R) Sqn, Leuchars	
ZE838	Panavia Tornado F3 [GH]	RAF No 43 Sqn, Leuchars	
ZE839	Panavia Tornado F3 [XK]	RAF No 25 Sqn, Leeming	
ZE887	Panavia Tornado F3 [DJ]	RAF No 11 Sqn, Leeming	
ZE888	Panavia Tornado F3 [TC]	RAF/DARA, St Athan	
ZE889	Panavia Tornado F3 [XH]	RAF F3 OCU/No 56(R) Sqn, Leuchars	
ZE907	Panavia Tornado F3 [XI]	RAF No 11 Sqn, Leeming	
ZE908	Panavia Tornado F3 [TB]	RAF F3 OCU/No 56(R) Sqn, Leuchars	
ZE911	Panavia Tornado F3 (MM7226)	*Scrapped, October 2004*	
ZE934	Panavia Tornado F3 [TA]	RAF/DARA, St Athan	
ZE936	Panavia Tornado F3 [XF]	RAF No 111 Sqn, Leuchars	
ZE941	Panavia Tornado F3 [KT]	RAF F3 OCU/No 56(R) Sqn, Leuchars	
ZE942	Panavia Tornado F3 [XE]	RAF AWC/FJWOEU, Coningsby	
ZE961	Panavia Tornado F3 [XD]	RAF No 25 Sqn, Leeming	
ZE962	Panavia Tornado F3 [XC]	RAF No 111 Sqn, Leuchars	
ZE963	Panavia Tornado F3 [YT]	RAF F3 OCU/No 56(R) Sqn, Leuchars	
ZE964	Panavia Tornado F3 [XT]	RAF F3 OCU/No 56(R) Sqn, Leuchars	
ZE965	Panavia Tornado F3 [WT]	RAF/DARA, St Athan	
ZE966	Panavia Tornado F3 [VT]	RAF/DARA, St Athan	
ZE967	Panavia Tornado F3 [UT]	RAF Leuchars, at main gate	
ZE968	Panavia Tornado F3 [HB]	RAF No 111 Sqn, Leuchars	
ZE969	Panavia Tornado F3 [XA]	RAF No 25 Sqn, Leeming	
ZE982	Panavia Tornado F3 [VV]	RAF No 25 Sqn, Leeming	
ZE983	Panavia Tornado F3 [WY]	RAF No 111 Sqn, Leuchars	

Notes	Serial	Type (other identity) [code]	Owner/operator, location or fate
	ZF115	WS61 Sea King HC4 (wreck)	RN, stored *HMS Sultan*, Gosport
	ZF116	WS61 Sea King HC4 [WP]	RN No 848 Sqn, Yeovilton
	ZF117	WS61 Sea King HC4 [J]	RN No 845 Sqn, Yeovilton
	ZF118	WS61 Sea King HC4 [M]	RN AMG, Yeovilton
	ZF119	WS61 Sea King HC4 [VW]	RN No 846 Sqn, Yeovilton
	ZF120	WS61 Sea King HC4 [K]	RN No 845 Sqn, Yeovilton
	ZF121	WS61 Sea King HC4 [VT]	RN No 846 Sqn, Yeovilton
	ZF122	WS61 Sea King HC4 [VU]	RN No 846 Sqn, Yeovilton
	ZF123	WS61 Sea King HC4 [WQ]	RN No 848 Sqn, Yeovilton
	ZF124	WS61 Sea King HC4 [L]	RN No 845 Sqn, Yeovilton
	ZF135	Shorts Tucano T1	RAF, stored Shawbury
	ZF136	Shorts Tucano T1	RAF, stored Shawbury
	ZF137	Shorts Tucano T1	RAF No 1 FTS/*207(R) Sqn*, Linton-on-Ouse
	ZF138	Shorts Tucano T1	RAF No 1 FTS, Linton-on-Ouse
	ZF139	Shorts Tucano T1	RAF No 1 FTS, Linton-on-Ouse
	ZF140	Shorts Tucano T1	RAF No 1 FTS, Linton-on-Ouse
	ZF141	Shorts Tucano T1	RAF, stored Shawbury
	ZF142	Shorts Tucano T1	RAF No 1 FTS, Linton-on-Ouse
	ZF143	Shorts Tucano T1	RAF No 1 FTS, Linton-on-Ouse
	ZF144	Shorts Tucano T1	RAF No 1 FTS, Linton-on-Ouse
	ZF145	Shorts Tucano T1	RAF No 1 FTS, Linton-on-Ouse
	ZF160	Shorts Tucano T1	RAF, stored Shawbury
	ZF161	Shorts Tucano T1	RAF No 1 FTS, Linton-on-Ouse
	ZF162	Shorts Tucano T1	RAF, stored Shawbury
	ZF163	Shorts Tucano T1	RAF, stored Shawbury
	ZF164	Shorts Tucano T1	RAF, stored Shawbury
	ZF165	Shorts Tucano T1	RAF, stored Shawbury
	ZF166	Shorts Tucano T1	RAF, stored Shawbury
	ZF167	Shorts Tucano T1 (fuselage)	Shorts, Belfast
	ZF168	Shorts Tucano T1	RAF, stored Shawbury
	ZF169	Shorts Tucano T1	RAF, stored Shawbury
	ZF170	Shorts Tucano T1	RAF No 1 FTS, Linton-on-Ouse
	ZF171	Shorts Tucano T1	RAF No 1 FTS, Linton-on-Ouse
	ZF172	Shorts Tucano T1	RAF No 1 FTS, Linton-on-Ouse
	ZF200	Shorts Tucano T1	RAF, stored Shawbury
	ZF201	Shorts Tucano T1	RAF, stored Shawbury
	ZF202	Shorts Tucano T1	RAF, stored Shawbury
	ZF203	Shorts Tucano T1	RAF, stored Shawbury
	ZF204	Shorts Tucano T1	RAF No 1 FTS, Linton-on-Ouse
	ZF205	Shorts Tucano T1	RAF No 1 FTS, Linton-on-Ouse
	ZF206	Shorts Tucano T1	RAF, stored Shawbury
	ZF207	Shorts Tucano T1	RAF No 1 FTS/*207(R) Sqn*, Linton-on-Ouse
	ZF208	Shorts Tucano T1	RAF No 1 FTS, Linton-on-Ouse
	ZF209	Shorts Tucano T1	RAF No 1 FTS, Linton-on-Ouse
	ZF210	Shorts Tucano T1	RAF No 1 FTS, Linton-on-Ouse
	ZF211	Shorts Tucano T1	RAF, stored Shawbury
	ZF212	Shorts Tucano T1	RAF, stored Shawbury
	ZF238	Shorts Tucano T1	RAF No 1 FTS, Linton-on-Ouse
	ZF239	Shorts Tucano T1	RAF No 1 FTS, Linton-on-Ouse
	ZF240	Shorts Tucano T1	RAF No 1 FTS, Linton-on-Ouse
	ZF241	Shorts Tucano T1	RAF No 1 FTS/*72(R) Sqn*, Linton-on-Ouse
	ZF242	Shorts Tucano T1	RAF No 1 FTS, Linton-on-Ouse
	ZF243	Shorts Tucano T1	RAF No 1 FTS, Linton-on-Ouse
	ZF244	Shorts Tucano T1	RAF No 1 FTS/*72(R) Sqn*, Linton-on-Ouse
	ZF245	Shorts Tucano T1	RAF, stored Shawbury
	ZF263	Shorts Tucano T1	RAF, stored Shawbury
	ZF264	Shorts Tucano T1	RAF No 1 FTS, Linton-on-Ouse
	ZF265	Shorts Tucano T1	RAF, stored Shawbury
	ZF266	Shorts Tucano T1	RAF, stored Shawbury
	ZF267	Shorts Tucano T1	RAF, stored Shawbury
	ZF268	Shorts Tucano T1	RAF No 1 FTS, Linton-on-Ouse
	ZF269	Shorts Tucano T1	RAF No 1 FTS/*72(R) Sqn*, Linton-on-Ouse
	ZF284	Shorts Tucano T1	RAF, stored Shawbury
	ZF285	Shorts Tucano T1	RAF, stored Shawbury
	ZF286	Shorts Tucano T1	RAF No 1 FTS, Linton-on-Ouse
	ZF287	Shorts Tucano T1	RAF No 1 FTS, Linton-on-Ouse
	ZF288	Shorts Tucano T1	RAF, stored Shawbury
	ZF289	Shorts Tucano T1	RAF No 1 FTS, Linton-on-Ouse
	ZF290	Shorts Tucano T1	RAF No 1 FTS, Linton-on-Ouse
	ZF291	Shorts Tucano T1	RAF No 1 FTS, Linton-on-Ouse
	ZF292	Shorts Tucano T1	RAF No 1 FTS/*207(R) Sqn*, Linton-on-Ouse
	ZF293	Shorts Tucano T1	RAF No 1 FTS/*72(R) Sqn*, Linton-on-Ouse
	ZF294	Shorts Tucano T1	RAF No 1 FTS, Linton-on-Ouse

Serial	Type (other identity) [code]	Owner/operator, location or fate	Notes
ZF295	Shorts Tucano T1	RAF No 1 FTS/*207(R) Sqn*, Linton-on-Ouse	
ZF315	Shorts Tucano T1	RAF, stored Shawbury	
ZF317	Shorts Tucano T1	RAF No 1 FTS, Linton-on-Ouse	
ZF318	Shorts Tucano T1	RAF, stored Shawbury	
ZF319	Shorts Tucano T1	RAF No 1 FTS, Linton-on-Ouse	
ZF320	Shorts Tucano T1	RAF No 1 FTS, Linton-on-Ouse	
ZF338	Shorts Tucano T1	RAF No 1 FTS, Linton-on-Ouse	
ZF339	Shorts Tucano T1	RAF No 1 FTS, Linton-on-Ouse	
ZF340	Shorts Tucano T1	RAF, stored Shawbury	
ZF341	Shorts Tucano T1	RAF No 1 FTS/*207(R) Sqn*, Linton-on-Ouse	
ZF342	Shorts Tucano T1	RAF No 1 FTS, Linton-on-Ouse	
ZF343	Shorts Tucano T1	RAF No 1 FTS, Linton-on-Ouse	
ZF344	Shorts Tucano T1	RAF No 1 FTS, Linton-on-Ouse	
ZF345	Shorts Tucano T1	RAF No 1 FTS/*207(R) Sqn*, Linton-on-Ouse	
ZF346	Shorts Tucano T1	RAF, stored Shawbury	
ZF347	Shorts Tucano T1	RAF No 1 FTS, Linton-on-Ouse	
ZF348	Shorts Tucano T1	RAF, stored Shawbury	
ZF349	Shorts Tucano T1	RAF No 1 FTS, Linton-on-Ouse	
ZF350	Shorts Tucano T1	RAF, stored Shawbury	
ZF372	Shorts Tucano T1	RAF, stored Shawbury	
ZF373	Shorts Tucano T1	RAF, stored Shawbury	
ZF374	Shorts Tucano T1	RAF No 1 FTS/*72(R) Sqn*, Linton-on-Ouse	
ZF375	Shorts Tucano T1	RAF No 1 FTS, Linton-on-Ouse	
ZF376	Shorts Tucano T1	RAF, stored Shawbury	
ZF377	Shorts Tucano T1	RAF No 1 FTS, Linton-on-Ouse	
ZF378	Shorts Tucano T1	RAF No 1 FTS, Linton-on-Ouse	
ZF379	Shorts Tucano T1	RAF, stored Shawbury	
ZF380	Shorts Tucano T1	RAF, stored Shawbury	
ZF405	Shorts Tucano T1	RAF No 1 FTS, Linton-on-Ouse	
ZF406	Shorts Tucano T1	RAF No 1 FTS, Linton-on-Ouse	
ZF407	Shorts Tucano T1	RAF No 1 FTS, Linton-on-Ouse	
ZF408	Shorts Tucano T1	RAF, stored Shawbury	
ZF409	Shorts Tucano T1	RAF No 1 FTS, Linton-on-Ouse	
ZF410	Shorts Tucano T1	RAF, stored Shawbury	
ZF411	Shorts Tucano T1	RAF, stored Shawbury	
ZF412	Shorts Tucano T1	RAF, stored Shawbury	
ZF413	Shorts Tucano T1	RAF No 1 FTS, Linton-on-Ouse	
ZF414	Shorts Tucano T1	RAF No 1 FTS, Linton-on-Ouse	
ZF415	Shorts Tucano T1	RAF, stored Shawbury	
ZF416	Shorts Tucano T1	RAF No 1 FTS, Linton-on-Ouse	
ZF417	Shorts Tucano T1	RAF No 1 FTS, Linton-on-Ouse	
ZF418	Shorts Tucano T1	RAF No 1 FTS, Linton-on-Ouse	
ZF445	Shorts Tucano T1	RAF No 1 FTS/*207(R) Sqn*, Linton-on-Ouse	
ZF446	Shorts Tucano T1	RAF No 1 FTS, Linton-on-Ouse	
ZF447	Shorts Tucano T1	RAF, stored Shawbury	
ZF448	Shorts Tucano T1	RAF No 1 FTS, Linton-on-Ouse	
ZF449	Shorts Tucano T1	RAF, stored Shawbury	
ZF450	Shorts Tucano T1	RAF, stored Shawbury	
ZF483	Shorts Tucano T1	RAF No 1 FTS/*72(R) Sqn*, Linton-on-Ouse	
ZF484	Shorts Tucano T1	RAF, stored Shawbury	
ZF485	Shorts Tucano T1 (G-BULU)	RAF No 1 FTS, Linton-on-Ouse	
ZF486	Shorts Tucano T1	RAF, stored Shawbury	
ZF487	Shorts Tucano T1	RAF, stored Shawbury	
ZF488	Shorts Tucano T1	RAF, stored Shawbury	
ZF489	Shorts Tucano T1	RAF No 1 FTS, Linton-on-Ouse	
ZF490	Shorts Tucano T1	RAF, stored Shawbury	
ZF491	Shorts Tucano T1	RAF No 1 FTS, Linton-on-Ouse	
ZF492	Shorts Tucano T1	RAF No 1 FTS, Linton-on-Ouse	
ZF510	Shorts Tucano T1	DPA/AFD/QinetiQ, Boscombe Down	
ZF511	Shorts Tucano T1	DPA/AFD/QinetiQ, Boscombe Down	
ZF512	Shorts Tucano T1	RAF No 1 FTS, Linton-on-Ouse	
ZF513	Shorts Tucano T1	RAF No 1 FTS, Linton-on-Ouse	
ZF514	Shorts Tucano T1	RAF, stored Shawbury	
ZF515	Shorts Tucano T1	RAF No 1 FTS/*72(R) Sqn*, Linton-on-Ouse	
ZF516	Shorts Tucano T1	RAF, stored Shawbury	
ZF534	BAe EAP	Loughborough University	
ZF537	WS Lynx AH9	AAC No 672 Sqn/9 Regt, Dishforth	
ZF538	WS Lynx AH9	AAC No 659 Sqn/4 Regt, Wattisham	
ZF539	WS Lynx AH9	AAC/DARA, Fleetlands	
ZF540	WS Lynx AH9	AAC No 661 Sqn/1 Regt, Gütersloh	
ZF557	WS Lynx HMA8 [318]	RN No 815 Sqn OEU, Yeovilton	
ZF558	WS Lynx HMA8	DPA/Westland Helicopters, Yeovil	

Notes	Serial	Type (other identity) [code]	Owner/operator, location or fate
	ZF560	WS Lynx HMA8 [338/CT]	RN No 815 Sqn, *Campbeltown* Flt, Yeovilton
	ZF562	WS Lynx HMA8 [365]	RN No 815 Sqn, *Argyll* Flt, Yeovilton
	ZF563	WS Lynx HMA8 [361/NF]	RN No 815 Sqn, *Norfolk* Flt, Yeovilton
	ZF573	PBN 2T Islander CC2A (G-SRAY)	RAF Northolt Station Flight
	ZF579	BAC Lightning F53	Gatwick Aviation Museum, Charlwood
	ZF580	BAC Lightning F53	BAE Systems Samlesbury, at main gate
	ZF581	BAC Lightning F53	BAE Systems, Rochester, on display
	ZF582	BAC Lightning F53 <ff>	Bournemouth Aviation Museum
	ZF583	BAC Lightning F53	Solway Aviation Society, Carlisle
	ZF584	BAC Lightning F53	Ferranti Ltd, South Gyle, Edinburgh
	ZF587	BAC Lightning F53 <ff>	Lashenden Air Warfare Museum, Headcorn
	ZF588	BAC Lightning F53 [L]	East Midlands Airport Aeropark
	ZF590	BAC Lightning F53 <rf>	*Currently not known*
	ZF592	BAC Lightning F53	City of Norwich Aviation Museum
	ZF593	BAC Lightning F53 (fuselage)	*Currently not known*
	ZF594	BAC Lightning F53	North-East Aircraft Museum, Usworth
	ZF595	BAC Lightning T55 (fuselage)	Privately owned, Grainthorpe, Lincs
	ZF596	BAC Lightning T55 <ff>	BAe North-West Heritage Group Warton
	ZF622	Piper PA-31 Navajo Chieftain 350 (N3548Y)	DPA/AFD/QinetiQ, Boscombe Down
	ZF641	EHI-101 [PP1]	SFDO, RNAS Culdrose
	ZF649	EHI-101 Merlin [PP5]	RN AESS, *HMS Sultan*, Gosport
	ZG101	EHI-101 (mock-up) [GB]	Westland Helicopters/Agusta, Yeovil
	ZG471	BAe Harrier GR7 [61]	RAF/DARA, St Athan
	ZG472	BAe Harrier GR7 [62]	RAF No 1 Sqn, Cottesmore
	ZG474	BAe Harrier GR7 [64]	RAF No 1 Sqn, Cottesmore
	ZG477	BAe Harrier GR9 [67]	DPA/BAE Systems, Warton (conversion)
	ZG478	BAe Harrier GR9 [68]	DPA/BAE Systems, Warton (conversion)
	ZG479	BAe Harrier GR7 [69]	RAF HOCU/No 20(R) Sqn, Wittering
	ZG480	BAe Harrier GR9 [70]	DPA/BAE Systems, Warton (conversion)
	ZG500	BAe Harrier GR7 [71]	RAF No 3 Sqn, Cottesmore
	ZG501	BAe Harrier GR9 [72]	RAF No 20(R) Sqn, Wittering
	ZG502	BAe Harrier GR9 [73]	DPA/BAE Systems, Warton (conversion)
	ZG503	BAe Harrier GR9 [74]	DPA/BAE Systems, Warton
	ZG504	BAe Harrier GR7 [75]	RAF No 4 Sqn, Cottesmore
	ZG505	BAe Harrier GR9 [76]	DPA/BAE Systems, Warton (conversion)
	ZG506	BAe Harrier GR7 [77]	RAF No 1 Sqn, Cottesmore
	ZG507	BAe Harrier GR7 [78]	RAF HMF, Wittering (on rebuild)
	ZG508	BAe Harrier GR9 [79]	DPA/BAE Systems, Warton (conversion)
	ZG509	BAe Harrier GR7 [80]	RAF/DARA, St Athan
	ZG510	BAe Harrier GR9 [81]	DPA/BAE Systems, Warton (conversion)
	ZG511	BAe Harrier GR9 [82]	DPA/BAE Systems, Warton (conversion)
	ZG512	BAe Harrier GR7 [83]	RAF HOCU/No 20(R) Sqn, Wittering
	ZG530	BAe Harrier GR7 [84]	RAF No 4 Sqn, Cottesmore
	ZG531	BAe Harrier GR7 [85]	RAF No 4 Sqn, Cottesmore
	ZG705	Panavia Tornado GR4A [J]	RAF No 13 Sqn, Marham
	ZG706	Panavia Tornado GR1A [E]	RAF/DARA, stored St Athan
	ZG707	Panavia Tornado GR4A [B]	RAF No 13 Sqn, Marham
	ZG709	Panavia Tornado GR4A [V]	RAF No 13 Sqn, Marham
	ZG711	Panavia Tornado GR4A [O]	RAF No 2 Sqn, Marham
	ZG712	Panavia Tornado GR4A [F]	RAF Marham, WLT
	ZG713	Panavia Tornado GR4A [G]	RAF No 13 Sqn, Marham
	ZG714	Panavia Tornado GR4A [Q]	RAF No 13 Sqn, Marham
	ZG726	Panavia Tornado GR4A [K]	DPA/AFD/QinetiQ, Boscombe Down
	ZG727	Panavia Tornado GR4A [L]	RAF No 617 Sqn, Lossiemouth
	ZG728	Panavia Tornado F3 (MM7229)	RAF/DARA, St Athan
	ZG729	Panavia Tornado GR4A [M]	RAF No 13 Sqn, Marham
	ZG730	Panavia Tornado F3 (MM7230)	RAF/DARA, St Athan
	ZG731	Panavia Tornado F3	RAF AWC/FJWOEU, Coningsby
	ZG732	Panavia Tornado F3 (MM7227) [WU]	RAF F3 OCU/No 56(R) Sqn, Leuchars
	ZG733	Panavia Tornado F3 (MM7228)	*Scrapped, November 2004*
	ZG734	Panavia Tornado F3 (MM7231)	RAF/DARA, stored St Athan
	ZG735	Panavia Tornado F3 (MM7232)	RAF/DARA, stored St Athan
	ZG750	Panavia Tornado GR4 [DY]	RAF No 13 Sqn, Marham
	ZG751	Panavia Tornado F3 [WP]	RAF/DARA, St Athan (damaged)
	ZG752	Panavia Tornado GR4 [TW]	RAF No 15(R) Sqn, Lossiemouth
	ZG753	Panavia Tornado F3 [HH]	RAF No 111 Sqn, Leuchars
	ZG754	Panavia Tornado GR4 [TP]	RAF No 15(R) Sqn, Lossiemouth
	ZG755	Panavia Tornado F3 [DL]	RAF No 11 Sqn, Leeming

Serial	Type (other identity) [code]	Owner/operator, location or fate	Notes
ZG756	Panavia Tornado GR4 [BX]	RAF No 14 Sqn, Lossiemouth	
ZG757	Panavia Tornado F3 [GN]	RAF No 43 Sqn, Leuchars	
ZG768	Panavia Tornado F3 (MM7233)	RAF/DARA, stored St Athan	
ZG769	Panavia Tornado GR4	RAF/DARA, St Athan (damaged)	
ZG770	Panavia Tornado F3 [WK]	RAF F3 OCU/No 56(R) Sqn, Leuchars	
ZG771	Panavia Tornado GR4 [AZ]	RAF No 9 Sqn, Marham	
ZG772	Panavia Tornado F3 [C]	RAF No 1435 Flt, Mount Pleasant, FI	
ZG773	Panavia Tornado GR4	DPA/BAE Systems, Warton	
ZG774	Panavia Tornado F3 [WI]	RAF No 25 Sqn, Leeming	
ZG775	Panavia Tornado GR4 [FB]	RAF No 12 Sqn, Lossiemouth	
ZG776	Panavia Tornado F3 [WH]	RAF No 111 Sqn, Leuchars	
ZG777	Panavia Tornado GR4 [TC]	RAF No 15(R) Sqn, Lossiemouth	
ZG778	Panavia Tornado F3 [WG]	RAF No 1435 Flt, Mount Pleasant, FI	
ZG779	Panavia Tornado GR4 [FA]	RAF No 12 Sqn, Lossiemouth	
ZG780	Panavia Tornado F3 [WF]	RAF No 25 Sqn, Leeming	
ZG791	Panavia Tornado GR4 [AJ-T]	RAF No 617 Sqn, Lossiemouth	
ZG792	Panavia Tornado GR4 [AJ-G]	RAF/DARA, St Athan	
ZG793	Panavia Tornado F3 [DM]	RAF No 11 Sqn, Leeming	
ZG794	Panavia Tornado GR4 [TN]	RAF No 15(R) Sqn, Lossiemouth	
ZG795	Panavia Tornado F3 [WD]	RAF F3 OCU/No 56(R) Sqn, Leuchars	
ZG796	Panavia Tornado F3 [WC]	RAF Leuchars, for display	
ZG797	Panavia Tornado F3 [GF]	RAF No 43 Sqn, Leuchars	
ZG798	Panavia Tornado F3 [GQ]	RAF No 43 Sqn, Leuchars	
ZG799	Panavia Tornado F3	RAF/DARA, St Athan	
ZG816	WS61 Sea King HAS6 [014/L]	RN, stored *HMS Sultan*, Gosport	
ZG817	WS61 Sea King HAS6 [702/PW]	RN AESS, *HMS Sultan*, Gosport	
ZG818	WS61 Sea King HAS6 [707/PW]	RN, stored *HMS Sultan*, Gosport	
ZG819	WS61 Sea King HAS6 [265/N]	RN AESS, *HMS Sultan*, Gosport	
ZG820	WS61 Sea King HC4 [A]	RN No 845 Sqn, Yeovilton	
ZG821	WS61 Sea King HC4 [WQ]	RN No 848 Sqn, Yeovilton	
ZG822	WS61 Sea King HC4 [VN]	RN No 846 Sqn, Yeovilton	
ZG844	PBN 2T Islander AL1 (G-BLNE)	AAC No 1 Flt/5 Regt, Aldergrove	
ZG845	PBN 2T Islander AL1 (G-BLNT)	AAC No 1 Flt/5 Regt, Aldergrove	
ZG846	PBN 2T Islander AL1 (G-BLNU)	AAC No 1 Flt/5 Regt, Aldergrove	
ZG847	PBN 2T Islander AL1 (G-BLNV)	AAC No 1 Flt/5 Regt, Aldergrove	
ZG848	PBN 2T Islander AL1 (G-BLNY)	AAC No 1 Flt/5 Regt, Aldergrove	
ZG857	BAe Harrier GR7	RAF AWC/FJWOEU, Coningsby	
ZG858	BAe Harrier GR7 [90]	RAF No 1 Sqn, Wittering	
ZG859	BAe Harrier GR7 [91]	RAF No 4 Sqn, Cottesmore	
ZG860	BAe Harrier GR9	DPA/BAE Systems, Warton (conversion)	
ZG862	BAe Harrier GR9 [94]	DPA/BAE Systems, Warton (conversion)	
ZG875	WS61 Sea King HAS6 [013/L]	RN, stored *HMS Sultan*, Gosport (damaged)	
ZG879	Powerchute Raider Mk 1	DPA/Powerchute, Hereford	
ZG884	WS Lynx AH9	AAC No 672 Sqn/9 Regt, Dishforth	
ZG885	WS Lynx AH9	AAC No 672 Sqn/9 Regt, Dishforth	
ZG886	WS Lynx AH9	AAC No 661 Sqn/1 Regt, Gütersloh	
ZG887	WS Lynx AH9	*Crashed 9 September 2004, Namest, Czech Republic*	
ZG888	WS Lynx AH9	AAC No 672 Sqn/9 Regt, Dishforth	
ZG889	WS Lynx AH9	AAC No 672 Sqn/9 Regt, Dishforth	
ZG914	WS Lynx AH9	AAC No 661 Sqn/1 Regt, Gütersloh	
ZG915	WS Lynx AH9	AAC No 672 Sqn/9 Regt, Dishforth	
ZG916	WS Lynx AH9	AAC No 672 Sqn/9 Regt, Dishforth	
ZG917	WS Lynx AH9	AAC No 672 Sqn/9 Regt, Dishforth	
ZG918	WS Lynx AH9	AAC/DARA, stored Fleetlands	
ZG919	WS Lynx AH9	AAC No 659 Sqn/4 Regt, Wattisham	
ZG920	WS Lynx AH9	AAC No 659 Sqn/4 Regt, Wattisham	
ZG921	WS Lynx AH9	AAC No 659 Sqn/4 Regt, Wattisham	
ZG922	WS Lynx AH9	AAC/DARA, stored Fleetlands	
ZG923	WS Lynx AH9	AAC No 653 Sqn/3 Regt, Wattisham	
ZG969	Pilatus PC-9 (HB-HQE)	BAE Systems Warton	
ZG989	PBN 2T Islander ASTOR (G-DLRA)	DPA/PBN, Bembridge	
ZG993	PBN 2T Islander AL1 (G-BOMD)	AAC No 1 Flight/5 Regt, Aldergrove	
ZG994	PBN 2T Islander AL1 (G-BPLN) (fuselage)	Britten-Norman, stored Bembridge	
ZG995	BN Defender AL1 (G-SURV)	AAC, Basrah, Iraq	
ZG996	BN Defender AL1 (G-BWPR)	AAC, Basrah, Iraq	
ZG997	BN Defender AL1 (G-BWPV)	AAC, Basrah, Iraq	
ZH101	Boeing E-3D Sentry AEW1	RAF No 8 Sqn/No 23 Sqn, Waddington	
ZH102	Boeing E-3D Sentry AEW1	RAF No 8 Sqn/No 23 Sqn, Waddington	
ZH103	Boeing E-3D Sentry AEW1	RAF No 8 Sqn/No 23 Sqn, Waddington	

Notes	Serial	Type (other identity) [code]	Owner/operator, location or fate
	ZH104	Boeing E-3D Sentry AEW1	RAF No 8 Sqn/No 23 Sqn, Waddington
	ZH105	Boeing E-3D Sentry AEW1	RAF No 8 Sqn/No 23 Sqn, Waddington
	ZH106	Boeing E-3D Sentry AEW1	RAF No 8 Sqn/No 23 Sqn, Waddington
	ZH107	Boeing E-3D Sentry AEW1	RAF No 8 Sqn/No 23 Sqn, Waddington
	ZH115	Grob G109B Vigilant T1 [TA]	RAF No 635 VGS, Samlesbury
	ZH116	Grob G109B Vigilant T1 [TB]	RAF No 618 VGS, Odiham
	ZH117	Grob G109B Vigilant T1 [TC]	RAF No 642 VGS, Linton-on-Ouse
	ZH118	Grob G109B Vigilant T1 [TD]	RAF No 612 VGS, Abingdon
	ZH119	Grob G109B Vigilant T1 [TE]	RAF No 632 VGS, Ternhill
	ZH120	Grob G109B Vigilant T1 [TF]	RAF No 633 VGS, Cosford
	ZH121	Grob G109B Vigilant T1 [TG]	RAF No 633 VGS, Cosford
	ZH122	Grob G109B Vigilant T1 [TH]	RAF No 664 VGS, Newtownards
	ZH123	Grob G109B Vigilant T1 [TJ]	RAF No 637 VGS, Little Rissington
	ZH124	Grob G109B Vigilant T1 [TK]	RAF No 642 VGS, Linton-on-Ouse
	ZH125	Grob G109B Vigilant T1 [TL]	RAF No 613 VGS, Halton
	ZH126	Grob G109B Vigilant T1 (D-KGRA) [TM]	RAF No 637 VGS, Little Rissington
	ZH127	Grob G109B Vigilant T1 (D-KEEC) [TN]	RAF No 642 VGS, Linton-on-Ouse
	ZH128	Grob G109B Vigilant T1 [TP]	RAF No 624 VGS, Chivenor RMB
	ZH129	Grob G109B Vigilant T1 [TQ]	RAF No 635 VGS, Samlesbury
	ZH139	BAe Harrier GR7 <R> (BAPC 191/ *ZD472*)	RAF M&RU, Bottesford
	ZH141	AS355F-1 Twin Squirrel HCC1 (G-OILX)	RAF No 32(The Royal) Sqn, Northolt
	ZH144	Grob G109B Vigilant T1 [TR]	RAF No 636 VGS, Aberporth
	ZH145	Grob G109B Vigilant T1 [TS]	RAF ACCGS/No 644 VGS, Syerston
	ZH146	Grob G109B Vigilant T1 [TT]	RAF No 664 VGS, Newtownards
	ZH147	Grob G109B Vigilant T1 [TU]	RAF No 636 VGS, Aberporth
	ZH148	Grob G109B Vigilant T1 [TV]	RAF No 613 VGS, Halton
	ZH184	Grob G109B Vigilant T1 [TW]	RAF No 632 VGS, Ternhill
	ZH185	Grob G109B Vigilant T1 [TX]	RAF ACCGS/No 644 VGS, Syerston
	ZH186	Grob G109B Vigilant T1 [TY]	RAF No 613 VGS, Halton
	ZH187	Grob G109B Vigilant T1 [TZ]	RAF No 633 VGS, Cosford
	ZH188	Grob G109B Vigilant T1 [UA]	RAF No 612 VGS, Abingdon
	ZH189	Grob G109B Vigilant T1 [UB]	RAF No 624 VGS, Chivenor RMB
	ZH190	Grob G109B Vigilant T1 [UC]	RAF No 663 VGS, Kinloss
	ZH191	Grob G109B Vigilant T1 [UD]	RAF No 616 VGS, Henlow
	ZH192	Grob G109B Vigilant T1 [UE]	RAF No 635 VGS, Samlesbury
	ZH193	Grob G109B Vigilant T1 [UF]	RAF No 612 VGS, Abingdon
	ZH194	Grob G109B Vigilant T1 [UG]	RAF No 624 VGS, Chivenor RMB
	ZH195	Grob G109B Vigilant T1 [UH]	RAF No 642 VGS, Linton-on-Ouse
	ZH196	Grob G109B Vigilant T1 [UJ]	RAF No 618 VGS, Odiham
	ZH197	Grob G109B Vigilant T1 [UK]	RAF No 618 VGS, Odiham
	ZH200	BAe Hawk 200	BAE Systems Warton, Overseas Customer Training Centre
	ZH205	Grob G109B Vigilant T1 [UL]	RAF No 634 VGS, St Athan
	ZH206	Grob G109B Vigilant T1 [UM]	RAF No 635 VGS, Samlesbury
	ZH207	Grob G109B Vigilant T1 [UN]	RAF No 632 VGS, Ternhill
	ZH208	Grob G109B Vigilant T1 [UP]	RAF No 645 VGS, Topcliffe
	ZH209	Grob G109B Vigilant T1 [UQ]	RAF No 634 VGS, St Athan
	ZH211	Grob G109B Vigilant T1 [UR]	RAF ACCGS/No 644 VGS, Syerston
	ZH247	Grob G109B Vigilant T1 [US]	RAF No 618 VGS, Odiham
	ZH248	Grob G109B Vigilant T1 [UT]	RAF No 637 VGS, Little Rissington
	ZH249	Grob G109B Vigilant T1 [UU]	RAF No 633 VGS, Cosford
	ZH257	B-V CH-47C Chinook (AE-520/ 9217M) (fuselage)	*To the USA, October 2004*
	ZH263	Grob G109B Vigilant T1 [UV]	RAF No 632 VGS, Ternhill
	ZH264	Grob G109B Vigilant T1 [UW]	RAF No 616 VGS, Henlow
	ZH265	Grob G109B Vigilant T1 [UX]	RAF No 645 VGS, Topcliffe
	ZH266	Grob G109B Vigilant T1 [UY]	RAF No 635 VGS, Samlesbury
	ZH267	Grob G109B Vigilant T1 [UZ]	RAF No 645 VGS, Topcliffe
	ZH268	Grob G109B Vigilant T1 [SA]	RAF No 612 VGS, Abingdon
	ZH269	Grob G109B Vigilant T1 [SB]	RAF No 645 VGS, Topcliffe
	ZH270	Grob G109B Vigilant T1 [SC]	RAF No 616 VGS, Henlow
	ZH271	Grob G109B Vigilant T1 [SD]	RAF No 637 VGS, Little Rissington
	ZH278	Grob G109B Vigilant T1 (D-KAIS) [SF]	RAF No 633 VGS, Cosford
	ZH279	Grob G109B Vigilant T1 (D-KNPS) [SG]	RAF No 613 VGS, Halton
	ZH536	PBN 2T Islander CC2 (G-BSAH)	RAF Northolt Station Flight
	ZH540	WS61 Sea King HAR3A [U]	RAF No 22 Sqn, B Flt, Wattisham
	ZH541	WS61 Sea King HAR3A [V]	RAF HMF, St Mawgan

Serial	Type (other identity) [code]	Owner/operator, location or fate	Notes
ZH542	WS61 Sea King HAR3A [W]	RAF No 22 Sqn, A Flt, Chivenor RMB	
ZH543	WS61 Sea King HAR3A [X]	RAF/DPA Westlands, Yeovil	
ZH544	WS61 Sea King HAR3A	RAF No 22 Sqn, B Flt, Wattisham	
ZH545	WS61 Sea King HAR3A [Z]	RAF No 22 Sqn, A Flt, Chivenor RMB	
ZH552	Panavia Tornado F3 [ST]	RAF F3 OCU/No 56(R) Sqn, Leuchars	
ZH553	Panavia Tornado F3 [RT]	RAF No 11 Sqn, Leeming	
ZH554	Panavia Tornado F3	RAF AWC/FJWOEU, Coningsby	
ZH555	Panavia Tornado F3 (fuselage)	RAF/DARA, St Athan	
ZH556	Panavia Tornado F3 [HT]	RAF No 111 Sqn, Leuchars	
ZH557	Panavia Tornado F3 [NT]	RAF No 11 Sqn, Leeming	
ZH559	Panavia Tornado F3 [MT]	RAF No 43 Sqn, Leuchars	
ZH588	Eurofighter Typhoon (DA2)	DPA/BAE Systems, Warton	
ZH590	Eurofighter Typhoon (DA4)	DPA/BAE Systems, Warton	
ZH653	BAe Harrier T10	DPA/BAE Systems, Warton	
ZH654	BAe Harrier T10	DPA/QinetiQ, stored Boscombe Down (wreck)	
ZH655	BAe Harrier T10 [Q]	RAF/DARA, St Athan	
ZH656	BAe Harrier T10 [104]	RAF HOCU/No 20(R) Sqn, Wittering	
ZH657	BAe Harrier T10 [105]	RAF No 1 Sqn, Cottesmore	
ZH658	BAe Harrier T10 [106]	RAF HOCU/No 20(R) Sqn, Wittering	
ZH659	BAe Harrier T10 [107]	RAF No 4 Sqn, Cottesmore	
ZH660	BAe Harrier T10 [108]	RAF HOCU/No 20(R) Sqn, Wittering	
ZH661	BAe Harrier T10 [109]	RAF HOCU/No 20(R) Sqn, Wittering	
ZH662	BAe Harrier T10 [110]	RAF HOCU/No 20(R) Sqn, Wittering	
ZH663	BAe Harrier T12 [111]	DPA/BAE Systems, Warton (conversion)	
ZH664	BAe Harrier T12 [112]	RAF HOCU/No 20(R) Sqn, Wittering	
ZH665	BAe Harrier T12 [113]	DPA/BAE Systems, Warton (conversion)	
ZH763	BAC 1-11/539GL (G-BGKE)	DPA/AFD/QinetiQ, Boscombe Down	
ZH775	B-V Chinook HC2 (N7424J)	RAF/DARA, Fleetlands	
ZH776	B-V Chinook HC2 (N7424L)	RAF No 27 Sqn, Odiham	
ZH777	B-V Chinook HC2 (N7424M)	RAF No 1310 Flt, Basrah, Iraq	
ZH796	BAe Sea Harrier FA2 [712]	RN No 899 Sqn, Yeovilton	
ZH797	BAe Sea Harrier FA2 [000/N]	RN No 801 Sqn, Yeovilton	
ZH798	BAe Sea Harrier FA2 [002]	RN No 801 Sqn, Yeovilton	
ZH799	BAe Sea Harrier FA2 [730]	RN/DARA, stored St Athan	
ZH800	BAe Sea Harrier FA2 [719]	RN No 899 Sqn, Yeovilton	
ZH801	BAe Sea Harrier FA2 [716/R]	RN SHOPS, Yeovilton	
ZH802	BAe Sea Harrier FA2 [711]	RN No 899 Sqn, Yeovilton	
ZH803	BAe Sea Harrier FA2 [004]	RN No 801 Sqn, Yeovilton	
ZH804	BAe Sea Harrier FA2 [730/R]	RN SHOPS, Yeovilton	
ZH806	BAe Sea Harrier FA2 [007/N]	RN No 801 Sqn, Yeovilton	
ZH807	BAe Sea Harrier FA2 [711] (wreck)	RN/DARA, stored St Athan	
ZH808	BAe Sea Harrier FA2 [003/N]	RN No 801 Sqn, Yeovilton	
ZH809	BAe Sea Harrier FA2	RN No 899 Sqn, Yeovilton	
ZH810	BAe Sea Harrier FA2 [125]	RN SHOPS, Yeovilton	
ZH811	BAe Sea Harrier FA2 [005/N]	RN No 801 Sqn, Yeovilton	
ZH812	BAe Sea Harrier FA2 [716]	RN No 899 Sqn, Yeovilton	
ZH813	BAe Sea Harrier FA2 [006/N]	RN No 801 Sqn, Yeovilton	
ZH814	Bell 212HP (G-BGMH)	AAC No 7 Flt, Brunei	
ZH815	Bell 212HP (G-BGCZ)	AAC No 7 Flt, Brunei	
ZH816	Bell 212HP (G-BGMG)	AAC No 7 Flt, Brunei	
ZH821	EHI-101 Merlin HM1	DPA/Westland Helicopters, Yeovil	
ZH822	EHI-101 Merlin HM1	RN/DARA, stored Fleetlands	
ZH823	EHI-101 Merlin HM1	DPA/Westland Helicopters, stored Yeovil	
ZH824	EHI-101 Merlin HM1	DPA/AFD/QinetiQ, Boscombe Down	
ZH825	EHI-101 Merlin HM1 [583]	RN/DARA, stored Fleetlands	
ZH826	EHI-101 Merlin HM1	RN/DARA, stored Fleetlands	
ZH827	EHI-101 Merlin HM1	RN/DARA, stored Fleetlands	
ZH828	EHI-101 Merlin HM1 [013/CU]	RN No 820 Sqn, Culdrose	
ZH829	EHI-101 Merlin HM1	DPA/AFD/QinetiQ, Boscombe Down	
ZH830	EHI-101 Merlin HM1	DPA/AFD/QinetiQ, Boscombe Down	
ZH831	EHI-101 Merlin HM1 [583]	RN No 824 Sqn, Culdrose	
ZH832	EHI-101 Merlin HM1	DPA/AFD/QinetiQ, Boscombe Down	
ZH833	EHI-101 Merlin HM1 [500]	RN No 829 Sqn, Culdrose	
ZH834	EHI-101 Merlin HM1 [538/CU]	RN No 700 OEU, Culdrose	
ZH835	EHI-101 Merlin HM1	DPA/Westland Helicopters, Yeovil	
ZH836	EHI-101 Merlin HM1 [582/CU]	DPA/Westland Helicopters, Yeovil	
ZH837	EHI-101 Merlin HM1 [582/CU]	RN No 824 Sqn, Culdrose	
ZH838	EHI-101 Merlin HM1 [539/CU]	RN No 700 OEU, Culdrose	
ZH839	EHI-101 Merlin HM1 [581/CU]	RN No 824 Sqn, Culdrose	
ZH840	EHI-101 Merlin HM1 [537/CU]	RN AMG, Culdrose	
ZH841	EHI-101 Merlin HM1 [012/CU]	RN No 820 Sqn, Culdrose	
ZH842	EHI-101 Merlin HM1	DPA/Westland Helicopters, Yeovil	

Notes	Serial	Type (other identity) [code]	Owner/operator, location or fate
	ZH843	EHI-101 Merlin HM1 [533/CU]	DPA/Westland Helicopters, Yeovil
	ZH844	EHI-101 Merlin HM1	RN FSAIU, Yeovilton (damaged)
	ZH845	EHI-101 Merlin HM1 [535/CU]	DPA/Westland Helicopters, Yeovil
	ZH846	EHI-101 Merlin HM1 [587/CU]	RN No 824 Sqn, Culdrose
	ZH847	EHI-101 Merlin HM1 [585]	RN No 824 Sqn, Culdrose
	ZH848	EHI-101 Merlin HM1 [388/LA]	RN AMG, Culdrose
	ZH849	EHI-101 Merlin HM1 [265/R]	RN AMG, Culdrose
	ZH850	EHI-101 Merlin HM1 [462/WM]	RN No 829 Sqn, *Westminster* Flt, Culdrose
	ZH851	EHI-101 Merlin HM1 [457]	RN No 829 Sqn, *Lancaster* Flt, Culdrose
	ZH852	EHI-101 Merlin HM1 [583/CU]	RN AMG, Culdrose
	ZH853	EHI-101 Merlin HM1	RN AMG, Culdrose
	ZH854	EHI-101 Merlin HM1 [580/CU]	RN AMG, Culdrose
	ZH855	EHI-101 Merlin HM1 [587/CU]	RN AMG, Culdrose
	ZH856	EHI-101 Merlin HM1 [267/R]	RN No 814 Sqn, Culdrose
	ZH857	EHI-101 Merlin HM1 [268/R]	RN No 814 Sqn, Culdrose
	ZH858	EHI-101 Merlin HM1 [415]	RN No 829 Sqn, *Monmouth* Flt, Culdrose
	ZH859	EHI-101 Merlin HM1	*Crashed 30 March 2004, Culdrose*
	ZH860	EHI-101 Merlin HM1 [269/R]	RN No 814 Sqn, Culdrose
	ZH861	EHI-101 Merlin HM1 [586]	RN No 824 Sqn, Culdrose
	ZH862	EHI-101 Merlin HM1 [010/CU]	RN No 820 Sqn, Culdrose
	ZH863	EHI-101 Merlin HM1 [270]	RN No 814 Sqn, Culdrose
	ZH864	EHI-101 Merlin HM1 [011/CU]	RN No 820 Sqn, Culdrose
	ZH865	Lockheed C-130J-30 Hercules C4 (N130JA)	DPA/AFD/QinetiQ, Boscombe Down
	ZH866	Lockheed C-130J-30 Hercules C4 (N130JE)	RAF Lyneham Transport Wing
	ZH867	Lockheed C-130J-30 Hercules C4 (N130JJ)	RAF Lyneham Transport Wing
	ZH868	Lockheed C-130J-30 Hercules C4 (N130JN)	RAF Lyneham Transport Wing
	ZH869	Lockheed C-130J-30 Hercules C4 (N130JV)	RAF Lyneham Transport Wing
	ZH870	Lockheed C-130J-30 Hercules C4 (*N73235*/N78235)	RAF Lyneham Transport Wing
	ZH871	Lockheed C-130J-30 Hercules C4 (N73238)	DPA/AFD/QinetiQ, Boscombe Down
	ZH872	Lockheed C-130J-30 Hercules C4 (N4249Y)	RAF Lyneham Transport Wing
	ZH873	Lockheed C-130J-30 Hercules C4 (N4242N)	RAF Lyneham Transport Wing
	ZH874	Lockheed C-130J-30 Hercules C4 (N41030)	RAF Lyneham Transport Wing
	ZH875	Lockheed C-130J-30 Hercules C4 (N4099R)	RAF Lyneham Transport Wing
	ZH876	Lockheed C-130J-30 Hercules C4 (N4080M)	RAF Lyneham Transport Wing
	ZH877	Lockheed C-130J-30 Hercules C4 (N4081M)	RAF Lyneham Transport Wing
	ZH878	Lockheed C-130J-30 Hercules C4 (N73232)	RAF Lyneham Transport Wing
	ZH879	Lockheed C-130J-30 Hercules C4 (N4080M)	RAF Lyneham Transport Wing
	ZH880	Lockheed C-130J Hercules C5 (N73238)	DPA/AFD/QinetiQ, Boscombe Down
	ZH881	Lockheed C-130J Hercules C5 (N4081M)	RAF Lyneham Transport Wing
	ZH882	Lockheed C-130J Hercules C5 (N4099R)	RAF Lyneham Transport Wing
	ZH883	Lockheed C-130J Hercules C5 (N4242N)	RAF Lyneham Transport Wing
	ZH884	Lockheed C-130J Hercules C5 (N4249Y)	RAF Lyneham Transport Wing
	ZH885	Lockheed C-130J Hercules C5 (N41030)	RAF Lyneham Transport Wing
	ZH886	Lockheed C-130J Hercules C5 (N73235)	RAF Lyneham Transport Wing
	ZH887	Lockheed C-130J Hercules C5 (N4187W)	RAF Lyneham Transport Wing
	ZH888	Lockheed C-130J Hercules C5 (N4187)	RAF Lyneham Transport Wing
	ZH889	Lockheed C-130J Hercules C5 (N4099R)	RAF Lyneham Transport Wing

Serial	Type (other identity) [code]	Owner/operator, location or fate	Notes
ZH890	Grob G109B Vigilant T1 [SE]	RAF No 663 VGS, Kinloss	
ZH891	B-V Chinook HC2A (N20075)	RAF/DARA, Fleetlands	
ZH892	B-V Chinook HC2A (N2019V) [BL]	RAF No 18 Sqn, Odiham	
ZH893	B-V Chinook HC2A (N2025L)	RAF No 27 Sqn, Odiham	
ZH894	B-V Chinook HC2A (N2026E)	RAF No 18 Sqn, Odiham	
ZH895	B-V Chinook HC2A (N2034K)	RAF No 18 Sqn, Odiham	
ZH896	B-V Chinook HC2A (N2038G)	DPA/AFD/QinetiQ, Boscombe Down	
ZH897	B-V Chinook HC3 (N2045G)	DPA/AFD/QinetiQ, Boscombe Down	
ZH898	B-V Chinook HC3 (N2057Q)	DPA, stored Boscombe Down	
ZH899	B-V Chinook HC3 (N2057R)	DPA, stored Boscombe Down	
ZH900	B-V Chinook HC3 (N2060H)	DPA, stored Boscombe Down	
ZH901	B-V Chinook HC3 (N2060M)	DPA, stored Boscombe Down	
ZH902	B-V Chinook HC3 (N2064W)	DPA, stored Boscombe Down	
ZH903	B-V Chinook HC3 (N20671)	DPA, stored Boscombe Down	
ZH904	B-V Chinook HC3 (N2083K)	Boeing, Philadelphia, for RAF	
ZJ100	BAe Hawk 102D	BAE Systems Warton	
ZJ117	EHI-101 Merlin HC3	DPA/Westland Helicopters, Yeovil	
ZJ118	EHI-101 Merlin HC3 [B]	DPA/Westland Helicopters, Yeovil	
ZJ119	EHI-101 Merlin HC3 [C]	DPA/Westland Helicopters, Yeovil	
ZJ120	EHI-101 Merlin HC3 [D]	RAF No 28 Sqn, Benson	
ZJ121	EHI-101 Merlin HC3 [E]	RAF No 28 Sqn, Benson	
ZJ122	EHI-101 Merlin HC3 [F]	RAF No 28 Sqn, Benson	
ZJ123	EHI-101 Merlin HC3 [G]	RAF No 28 Sqn, Benson	
ZJ124	EHI-101 Merlin HC3 [H]	RAF No 28 Sqn, Benson	
ZJ125	EHI-101 Merlin HC3 [J]	RAF No 28 Sqn, Benson	
ZJ126	EHI-101 Merlin HC3 [K]	RAF No 28 Sqn, Benson	
ZJ127	EHI-101 Merlin HC3 [L]	RAF No 28 Sqn, Benson	
ZJ128	EHI-101 Merlin HC3 [M]	DPA/Westland Helicopters, Yeovil	
ZJ129	EHI-101 Merlin HC3 [N]	RAF No 28 Sqn, Benson	
ZJ130	EHI-101 Merlin HC3 [O]	RAF No 28 Sqn, Benson	
ZJ131	EHI-101 Merlin HC3 [P]	RAF No 28 Sqn, Benson	
ZJ132	EHI-101 Merlin HC3 [Q]	RAF No 28 Sqn, Benson	
ZJ133	EHI-101 Merlin HC3 [R]	RAF No 28 Sqn, Benson	
ZJ134	EHI-101 Merlin HC3 [S]	RAF No 28 Sqn, Benson	
ZJ135	EHI-101 Merlin HC3 [T]	RAF No 28 Sqn, Benson	
ZJ136	EHI-101 Merlin HC3 [U]	RAF No 28 Sqn, Benson	
ZJ137	EHI-101 Merlin HC3 [W]	RAF No 28 Sqn, Benson	
ZJ138	EHI-101 Merlin HC3 [X]	RAF No 28 Sqn, Benson	
ZJ139	AS355F-1 Twin Squirrel HCC1 (G-NUTZ)	RAF No 32(The Royal) Sqn, Northolt	
ZJ140	AS355F-1 Twin Squirrel HCC1 (G-FFHI)	RAF No 32(The Royal) Sqn, Northolt	
ZJ164	AS365N-2 Dauphin 2 (G-BTLC)	RN/Bond Helicopters, Plymouth	
ZJ165	AS365N-2 Dauphin 2 (G-NTOO)	RN/Bond Helicopters, Plymouth	
ZJ166	WAH-64 Apache AH1 (N9219G)	DPA/Westland Helicopters, Yeovil	
ZJ167	WAH-64 Apache AH1 (N3266B)	AAC, stored Shawbury	
ZJ168	WAH-64 Apache AH1 (N3123T)	AAC, stored Shawbury	
ZJ169	WAH-64 Apache AH1 (N3114H)	DPA/Westland Helicopters, Yeovil	
ZJ170	WAH-64 Apache AH1 (N3065U)	AAC, stored Shawbury	
ZJ171	WAH-64 Apache AH1 (N3266T)	DPA/AFD/QinetiQ, Boscombe Down	
ZJ172	WAH-64 Apache AH1	AAC, stored Shawbury	
ZJ173	WAH-64 Apache AH1 (N3266W)	AAC, stored Shawbury	
ZJ174	WAH-64 Apache AH1	AAC, stored Shawbury	
ZJ175	WAH-64 Apache AH1 (N3218V)	DPA/Westland Helicopters, Yeovil	
ZJ176	WAH-64 Apache AH1	DPA/Westland Helicopters, Yeovil	
ZJ177	WAH-64 Apache AH1	AAC, stored Shawbury	
ZJ178	WAH-64 Apache AH1	DPA/Westland Helicopters, Yeovil	
ZJ179	WAH-64 Apache AH1	DPA/Westland Helicopters, Yeovil	
ZJ180	WAH-64 Apache AH1	DPA/Westland Helicopters, Yeovil	
ZJ181	WAH-64 Apache AH1	AAC, stored Shawbury	
ZJ182	WAH-64 Apache AH1	AAC, stored Shawbury	
ZJ183	WAH-64 Apache AH1	AAC No 664 Sqn/9 Regt, Dishforth	
ZJ184	WAH-64 Apache AH1	DPA/Westland Helicopters, Yeovil	
ZJ185	WAH-64 Apache AH1	AAC No 664 Sqn/9 Regt, Dishforth	
ZJ186	WAH-64 Apache AH1	AAC, stored Shawbury	
ZJ187	WAH-64 Apache AH1	DPA/Westland Helicopters, Yeovil	
ZJ188	WAH-64 Apache AH1	DPA/Westland Helicopters, Yeovil	
ZJ189	WAH-64 Apache AH1	AAC, stored Shawbury	
ZJ190	WAH-64 Apache AH1	AAC, stored Shawbury	
ZJ191	WAH-64 Apache AH1	AAC, stored Shawbury	
ZJ192	WAH-64 Apache AH1	AAC, stored Shawbury	
ZJ193	WAH-64 Apache AH1	DPA/Westland Helicopters, Yeovil	

Notes	Serial	Type (other identity) [code]	Owner/operator, location or fate
	ZJ194	WAH-64 Apache AH1	AAC, stored Shawbury
	ZJ195	WAH-64 Apache AH1	AAC, stored Shawbury
	ZJ196	WAH-64 Apache AH1	AAC No 664 Sqn/9 Regt, Dishforth
	ZJ197	WAH-64 Apache AH1	AAC, stored Shawbury
	ZJ198	WAH-64 Apache AH1	AAC, stored Shawbury
	ZJ199	WAH-64 Apache AH1	AAC, stored Shawbury
	ZJ200	WAH-64 Apache AH1	AAC, stored Shawbury
	ZJ202	WAH-64 Apache AH1	AAC, stored Shawbury
	ZJ203	WAH-64 Apache AH1	AAC, stored Shawbury
	ZJ204	WAH-64 Apache AH1	AAC No 664 Sqn/9 Regt, Dishforth
	ZJ205	WAH-64 Apache AH1	DPA/AFD/QinetiQ, Boscombe Down
	ZJ206	WAH-64 Apache AH1	AAC No 673 Sqn/2 Regt, Middle Wallop
	ZJ207	WAH-64 Apache AH1	AAC No 673 Sqn/2 Regt, Middle Wallop
	ZJ208	WAH-64 Apache AH1	AAC No 656 Sqn/9 Regt, Dishforth
	ZJ209	WAH-64 Apache AH1	AAC No 664 Sqn/9 Regt, Dishforth
	ZJ210	WAH-64 Apache AH1	DPA/Westland Helicopters, Yeovil
	ZJ211	WAH-64 Apache AH1	AAC No 673 Sqn/2 Regt, Middle Wallop
	ZJ212	WAH-64 Apache AH1	AAC No 673 Sqn/2 Regt, Middle Wallop
	ZJ213	WAH-64 Apache AH1	AAC No 673 Sqn/2 Regt, Middle Wallop
	ZJ214	WAH-64 Apache AH1	AAC No 673 Sqn/2 Regt, Middle Wallop
	ZJ215	WAH-64 Apache AH1	DPA/Westland Helicopters, Yeovil
	ZJ216	WAH-64 Apache AH1	AAC No 673 Sqn/2 Regt, Middle Wallop
	ZJ217	WAH-64 Apache AH1	AAC No 673 Sqn/2 Regt, Middle Wallop
	ZJ218	WAH-64 Apache AH1	AAC No 673 Sqn/2 Regt, Middle Wallop
	ZJ219	WAH-64 Apache AH1	AAC No 673 Sqn/2 Regt, Middle Wallop
	ZJ220	WAH-64 Apache AH1	AAC No 673 Sqn/2 Regt, Middle Wallop
	ZJ221	WAH-64 Apache AH1	AAC No 673 Sqn/2 Regt, Middle Wallop
	ZJ222	WAH-64 Apache AH1	AAC, stored Shawbury
	ZJ223	WAH-64 Apache AH1	AAC No 656 Sqn/9 Regt, Dishforth
	ZJ224	WAH-64 Apache AH1	AAC No 656 Sqn/9 Regt, Dishforth
	ZJ225	WAH-64 Apache AH1	AAC No 656 Sqn/9 Regt, Dishforth
	ZJ226	WAH-64 Apache AH1	DPA/Westland Helicopters, Yeovil
	ZJ227	WAH-64 Apache AH1	AAC No 656 Sqn/9 Regt, Dishforth
	ZJ228	WAH-64 Apache AH1	AAC No 656 Sqn/9 Regt, Dishforth
	ZJ229	WAH-64 Apache AH1	AAC No 656 Sqn/9 Regt, Dishforth
	ZJ230	WAH-64 Apache AH1	AAC No 664 Sqn/9 Regt, Dishforth
	ZJ231	WAH-64 Apache AH1	AAC No 664 Sqn/9 Regt, Dishforth
	ZJ232	WAH-64 Apache AH1	AAC No 664 Sqn/9 Regt, Dishforth
	ZJ233	WAH-64 Apache AH1	AAC No 656 Sqn/9 Regt, Dishforth
	ZJ234	Bell 412EP Griffin HT1 (G-BWZR) [S]	DHFS No 60(R) Sqn, RAF Shawbury
	ZJ235	Bell 412EP Griffin HT1 (G-BXBF) [I]	DHFS No 60(R) Sqn, RAF Shawbury
	ZJ236	Bell 412EP Griffin HT1 (G-BXBE) [X]	DHFS No 60(R) Sqn, RAF Shawbury
	ZJ237	Bell 412EP Griffin HT1 (G-BXFF) [T]	DHFS No 60(R) Sqn, RAF Shawbury
	ZJ238	Bell 412EP Griffin HT1 (G-BXHC) [Y]	DHFS No 60(R) Sqn, RAF Shawbury
	ZJ239	Bell 412EP Griffin HT1 (G-BXFH) [R]	DHFS No 60(R) Sqn, RAF Shawbury
	ZJ240	Bell 412EP Griffin HT1 (G-BXIR) [U]	DHFS No 60(R) Sqn/SARTU, RAF Valley
	ZJ241	Bell 412EP Griffin HT1 (G-BXIS) [L]	DHFS No 60(R) Sqn/SARTU, RAF Valley
	ZJ242	Bell 412EP Griffin HT1 (G-BXDK) [E]	DHFS No 60(R) Sqn, RAF Shawbury
	ZJ243	AS350BA Squirrel HT2 (G-BWZS)	DHFS, RAF Shawbury
	ZJ244	AS350BA Squirrel HT2 (G-BXMD)	School of Army Aviation/No 670 Sqn, Middle Wallop
	ZJ245	AS350BA Squirrel HT2 (G-BXME)	School of Army Aviation/No 670 Sqn, Middle Wallop
	ZJ246	AS350BA Squirrel HT2 (G-BXMJ)	School of Army Aviation/No 670 Sqn, Middle Wallop
	ZJ247	AS350BA Squirrel HT2 (G-BXNB)	School of Army Aviation/No 670 Sqn, Middle Wallop
	ZJ248	AS350BA Squirrel HT2 (G-BXNE)	School of Army Aviation/No 670 Sqn, Middle Wallop
	ZJ249	AS350BA Squirrel HT2 (G-BXNJ)	School of Army Aviation/No 670 Sqn, Middle Wallop
	ZJ250	AS350BA Squirrel HT2 (G-BXNY)	School of Army Aviation/No 670 Sqn, Middle Wallop
	ZJ251	AS350BA Squirrel HT2 (G-BXOG)	DHFS, RAF Shawbury

Serial	Type (other identity) [code]	Owner/operator, location or fate	Notes
ZJ252	AS350BA Squirrel HT2 (G-BXOK)	School of Army Aviation/No 670 Sqn, Middle Wallop	
ZJ253	AS350BA Squirrel HT2 (G-BXPG)	School of Army Aviation/No 670 Sqn, Middle Wallop	
ZJ254	AS350BA Squirrel HT2 (G-BXPJ)	School of Army Aviation/No 670 Sqn, Middle Wallop	
ZJ255	AS350BB Squirrel HT1 (G-BXAG)	DHFS, RAF Shawbury	
ZJ256	AS350BB Squirrel HT1 (G-BXCE)	DHFS, RAF Shawbury	
ZJ257	AS350BB Squirrel HT1 (G-BXDJ)	DHFS, RAF Shawbury	
ZJ258	AS350BB Squirrel HT1 (G-BXEO)	Crashed 14 December 2005, Ternhill	
ZJ259	AS350BB Squirrel HT1 (G-BXFJ)	DHFS, RAF Shawbury	
ZJ260	AS350BB Squirrel HT1 (G-BXGB)	DHFS, RAF Shawbury	
ZJ261	AS350BB Squirrel HT1 (G-BXGJ)	DHFS, RAF Shawbury	
ZJ262	AS350BB Squirrel HT1 (G-BXHB)	DHFS, RAF Shawbury	
ZJ263	AS350BB Squirrel HT1 (G-BXHK)	DHFS, RAF Shawbury	
ZJ264	AS350BB Squirrel HT1 (G-BXHW)	DHFS, RAF Shawbury	
ZJ265	AS350BB Squirrel HT1 (G-BXHX)	DHFS, RAF Shawbury	
ZJ266	AS350BB Squirrel HT1 (G-BXIL)	DHFS, RAF Shawbury	
ZJ267	AS350BB Squirrel HT1 (G-BXIP)	DHFS, RAF Shawbury	
ZJ268	AS350BB Squirrel HT1 (G-BXJE)	DHFS, RAF Shawbury	
ZJ269	AS350BB Squirrel HT1 (G-BXJN)	DHFS, RAF Shawbury	
ZJ270	AS350BB Squirrel HT1 (G-BXJR)	DHFS, RAF Shawbury	
ZJ271	AS350BB Squirrel HT1 (G-BXKE)	DHFS, RAF Shawbury	
ZJ272	AS350BB Squirrel HT1 (G-BXKN)	DHFS, RAF Shawbury	
ZJ273	AS350BB Squirrel HT1 (G-BXKP)	DHFS, RAF Shawbury	
ZJ274	AS350BB Squirrel HT1 (G-BXKR)	DHFS, RAF Shawbury	
ZJ275	AS350BB Squirrel HT1 (G-BXLB)	DHFS, RAF Shawbury	
ZJ276	AS350BB Squirrel HT1 (G-BXLE)	DHFS, RAF Shawbury	
ZJ277	AS350BB Squirrel HT1 (G-BXLH)	DHFS, RAF Shawbury	
ZJ278	AS350BB Squirrel HT1 (G-BXMB)	DHFS, RAF Shawbury	
ZJ279	AS350BB Squirrel HT1 (G-BXMC)	DHFS, RAF Shawbury	
ZJ280	AS350BB Squirrel HT1 (G-BXMI)	DHFS, RAF Shawbury	
ZJ514	BAE Systems Nimrod MRA4 (XV251) [PA-4]	DPA/BAE Systems, Woodford (conversion)	
ZJ515	BAE Systems Nimrod MRA4 (XV258) [PA-5]	DPA/BAE Systems, Woodford (conversion)	
ZJ516	BAE Systems Nimrod MRA4 (XV247) [PA-1]	DPA/BAE Systems, Warton	
ZJ517	BAE Systems Nimrod MRA4 (XV242) [PA-3]	DPA/BAE Systems, Woodford (conversion)	
ZJ518	BAE Systems Nimrod MRA4 (XV234) [PA-2]	DPA/BAE Systems, Warton	
ZJ519	BAE Systems Nimrod MRA4 (XZ284) [PA-6]	DPA/BAE Systems, Woodford (conversion)	
ZJ520	BAE Systems Nimrod MRA4 (XV233) [PA-7]	DPA/BAE Systems, Woodford (conversion)	
ZJ521	BAE Systems Nimrod MRA4 [PA-8]	BAE Systems, for RAF	
ZJ522	BAE Systems Nimrod MRA4 [PA-9]	BAE Systems, for RAF	
ZJ523	BAE Systems Nimrod MRA4 [PA-10]	BAE Systems, for RAF	
ZJ524	BAE Systems Nimrod MRA4 [PA-11]	BAE Systems, for RAF	
ZJ525	BAE Systems Nimrod MRA4 [PA-12]	BAE Systems, for RAF	
ZJ526	BAE Systems Nimrod MRA4 [PA-13]	BAE Systems, for RAF	
ZJ527	BAE Systems Nimrod MRA4 [PA-14]	BAE Systems, for RAF	
ZJ528	BAE Systems Nimrod MRA4 [PA-15]	BAE Systems, for RAF	
ZJ529	BAE Systems Nimrod MRA4 [PA-16]	BAE Systems, for RAF	
ZJ530	BAE Systems Nimrod MRA4 [PA-17]	BAE Systems, for RAF	
ZJ531	BAE Systems Nimrod MRA4 [PA-18]	BAE Systems, for RAF	
ZJ583	Meteor Mirach	RNAS Culdrose	
ZJ584	Meteor Mirach	RNAS Culdrose	
ZJ585	Meteor Mirach	RNAS Culdrose	
ZJ587	Meteor Mirach	RNAS Culdrose	
ZJ591	Meteor Mirach	RNAS Culdrose	
ZJ593	Meteor Mirach	RNAS Culdrose	
ZJ600	Meteor Mirach	RN	

Notes	Serial	Type (other identity) [code]	Owner/operator, location or fate
	ZJ601	Meteor Mirach	RN
	ZJ602	Meteor Mirach	RN
	ZJ605	Meteor Mirach	RN
	ZJ608	Meteor Mirach	RN
	ZJ609	Meteor Mirach	RNAS Culdrose
	ZJ610	Meteor Mirach	RNAS Culdrose
	ZJ612	Meteor Mirach	RNAS Culdrose
	ZJ613	Meteor Mirach	RNAS Culdrose
	ZJ614	Meteor Mirach	RNAS Culdrose
	ZJ615	Meteor Mirach	RNAS Culdrose
	ZJ617	Meteor Mirach	RNAS Culdrose
	ZJ635	AS355F-1 Twin Squirrel (G-NEXT)	DPA/ETPS, Boscombe Down
	ZJ645	D-BD Alpha Jet (98+62)	DPA/ETPS, Boscombe Down
	ZJ646	D-BD Alpha Jet (98+55)	DPA/AFD/QinetiQ, Boscombe Down
	ZJ647	D-BD Alpha Jet (98+71)	DPA/ETPS, Boscombe Down
	ZJ648	D-BD Alpha Jet (98+09)	DPA/AFD/QinetiQ, Boscombe Down
	ZJ649	D-BD Alpha Jet (98+73)	DPA/AFD/QinetiQ, Boscombe Down
	ZJ650	D-BD Alpha Jet (98+35)	DPA/AFD/QinetiQ, Boscombe Down
	ZJ651	D-BD Alpha Jet (41+42)	DPA/QinetiQ Boscombe Down, spares use
	ZJ652	D-BD Alpha Jet (41+09)	DPA/QinetiQ Boscombe Down, spares use
	ZJ653	D-BD Alpha Jet (40+22)	DPA/QinetiQ Boscombe Down, spares use
	ZJ654	D-BD Alpha Jet (41+02)	DPA/QinetiQ Boscombe Down, spares use
	ZJ655	D-BD Alpha Jet (41+19)	DPA/QinetiQ Boscombe Down, spares use
	ZJ656	D-BD Alpha Jet (41+40)	DPA/QinetiQ Boscombe Down, spares use
	ZJ657	Meteor Mirach	RNAS Culdrose
	ZJ658	Meteor Mirach	RNAS Culdrose
	ZJ659	Meteor Mirach	RNAS Culdrose
	ZJ660	Meteor Mirach	RNAS Culdrose
	ZJ661	Meteor Mirach	RNAS Culdrose
	ZJ662	Meteor Mirach	RNAS Culdrose
	ZJ687	BAE Systems Hawk 115	*To Canada as 155221, 2 August 2004*
	ZJ688	BAE Systems Hawk 115	*To Canada as 155222, 2 August 2004*
	ZJ690	Bombardier Sentinel R1 (C-GJRG)	Bombardier, for RAF
	ZJ691	Bombardier Sentinel R1 (C-FZVM)	DPA/BAE Systems, Chester
	ZJ692	Bombardier Sentinel R1 (C-FZWW)	DPA/BAE Systems, Chester
	ZJ693	Bombardier Sentinel R1 (C-FZXC)	DPA/BAE Systems, Chester
	ZJ694	Bombardier Sentinel R1 (C-FZYL)	DPA/BAE Systems, Chester
	ZJ695	Eurofighter Training Rig	RAF No 1 SoTT, Cosford
	ZJ696	Eurofighter Training Rig	RAF No 1 SoTT, Cosford
	ZJ697	Eurofighter Training Rig	RAF No 1 SoTT, Cosford
	ZJ698	Eurofighter Training Rig	RAF No 1 SoTT, Cosford
	ZJ699	Eurofighter Typhoon (PT001)	DPA/BAE Systems, Warton
	ZJ700	Eurofighter Typhoon (PS002)	DPA/BAE Systems, Warton
	ZJ702	FR Falconet	For Army
	ZJ703	Bell 412EP Griffin HAR2 (G-CBST) [*Spades*, 3]	RAF No 84 Sqn, Akrotiri
	ZJ704	Bell 412EP Griffin HAR2 (G-CBWT) [*Clubs*, 4]	RAF No 84 Sqn, Akrotiri
	ZJ705	Bell 412EP Griffin HAR2 (G-CBXL) [*Hearts*, 5]	RAF No 84 Sqn, Akrotiri
	ZJ706	Bell 412EP Griffin HAR2 (G-CBYR) [*Diamonds*, 6]	RAF No 84 Sqn, Akrotiri
	ZJ707	Bell 412EP Griffin HT1 (G-CBUB) [O]	DHFS No 60(R) Sqn, RAF Shawbury
	ZJ708	Bell 412EP Griffin HT1 (G-CBVP) [K]	Bell Helicopters, for RAF
	ZJ721	Meteor Mirach	RNAS Culdrose
	ZJ722	Meteor Mirach	RNAS Culdrose
	ZJ723	Meteor Mirach	RNAS Culdrose
	ZJ724	Meteor Mirach	RNAS Culdrose
	ZJ725	Meteor Mirach	DPA/QinetiQ/RN
	ZJ726	Meteor Mirach	DPA/QinetiQ/RN
	ZJ727	Meteor Mirach	DPA/QinetiQ/RN
	ZJ728	Meteor Mirach	DPA/QinetiQ/RN
	ZJ729	Meteor Mirach	DPA/QinetiQ/RN
	ZJ730	Meteor Mirach	DPA/QinetiQ/RN
	ZJ731	Meteor Mirach	DPA/QinetiQ/RN
	ZJ732	Meteor Mirach	DPA/QinetiQ/RN
	ZJ733	Meteor Mirach	DPA/QinetiQ/RN
	ZJ734	Meteor Mirach	DPA/QinetiQ/RN
	ZJ735	Meteor Mirach	DPA/QinetiQ/RN
	ZJ736	Meteor Mirach	DPA/QinetiQ/RN
	ZJ737	Meteor Mirach	DPA/QinetiQ/RN

Serial	Type (other identity) [code]	Owner/operator, location or fate	Notes
ZJ738	Meteor Mirach	DPA/QinetiQ/RN	
ZJ739	Meteor Mirach	DPA/QinetiQ/RN	
ZJ740	Meteor Mirach	DPA/QinetiQ/RN	
ZJ741	Meteor Mirach	DPA/QinetiQ/RN	
ZJ742	Meteor Mirach	DPA/QinetiQ/RN	
ZJ743	Meteor Mirach	DPA/QinetiQ/RN	
ZJ744	Meteor Mirach	DPA/QinetiQ/RN	
ZJ745	Meteor Mirach	DPA/QinetiQ/RN	
ZJ746	Meteor Mirach	DPA/QinetiQ/RN	
ZJ747	Meteor Mirach	DPA/QinetiQ/RN	
ZJ748	Meteor Mirach	DPA/QinetiQ/RN	
ZJ749	Meteor Mirach	DPA/QinetiQ/RN	
ZJ750	Meteor Mirach	DPA/QinetiQ/RN	
ZJ751	Meteor Mirach	DPA/QinetiQ/RN	
ZJ752	Meteor Mirach	DPA/QinetiQ/RN	
ZJ753	Meteor Mirach	DPA/QinetiQ/RN	
ZJ754	Meteor Mirach	DPA/QinetiQ/RN	
ZJ755	Meteor Mirach	DPA/QinetiQ/RN	
ZJ756	Meteor Mirach	DPA/QinetiQ/RN	
ZJ757	Meteor Mirach	DPA/QinetiQ/RN	
ZJ758	Meteor Mirach	DPA/QinetiQ/RN	
ZJ759	Meteor Mirach	DPA/QinetiQ/RN	
ZJ760	Meteor Mirach	DPA/QinetiQ/RN	
ZJ761	Meteor Mirach	DPA/QinetiQ/RN	
ZJ762	Meteor Mirach	DPA/QinetiQ/RN	
ZJ763	Meteor Mirach	DPA/QinetiQ/RN	
ZJ764	Meteor Mirach	DPA/QinetiQ/RN	
ZJ765	Meteor Mirach	DPA/QinetiQ/RN	
ZJ766	Meteor Mirach	DPA/QinetiQ/RN	
ZJ767	Meteor Mirach	DPA/QinetiQ/RN	
ZJ768	Meteor Mirach	DPA/QinetiQ/RN	
ZJ769	Meteor Mirach	DPA/QinetiQ/RN	
ZJ770	Meteor Mirach	DPA/QinetiQ/RN	
ZJ771	Meteor Mirach	DPA/QinetiQ/RN	
ZJ772	Meteor Mirach	DPA/QinetiQ/RN	
ZJ773	Meteor Mirach	DPA/QinetiQ/RN	
ZJ774	Meteor Mirach	DPA/QinetiQ/RN	
ZJ775	Meteor Mirach	DPA/QinetiQ/RN	
ZJ776	Meteor Mirach	DPA/QinetiQ/RN	
ZJ800	Eurofighter Typhoon T1 (BT001) [AC]	RAF No 17(R) Sqn, Warton	
ZJ801	Eurofighter Typhoon T1 (BT002) [BJ[	RAF No 29(R) Sqn, Warton	
ZJ802	Eurofighter Typhoon T1 (BT003) [AB]	RAF No 17(R) Sqn, Warton	
ZJ803	Eurofighter Typhoon T1 (BT004) [AA]	RAF No 17(R) Sqn, Warton	
ZJ804	Eurofighter Typhoon T1 (BT005)	DPA/BAE Systems, for RAF	
ZJ805	Eurofighter Typhoon T1 (BT006) [AD]	RAF No 17(R) Sqn, Warton	
ZJ806	Eurofighter Typhoon T1 (BT007) [BE]	RAF No 29(R) Sqn, Warton	
ZJ807	Eurofighter Typhoon T1 (BT008) [BF]	RAF No 29(R) Sqn, Warton	
ZJ808	Eurofighter Typhoon T1 (BT009) [BG]	RAF No 29(R) Sqn, Warton	
ZJ809	Eurofighter Typhoon T1 (BT010) [BH]	RAF No 29(R) Sqn, Warton	
ZJ810	Eurofighter Typhoon T1 (BT011) [BI]	RAF No 29(R) Sqn, Warton	
ZJ811	Eurofighter Typhoon T1 (BT012)	DPA/BAE Systems, for RAF	
ZJ812	Eurofighter Typhoon T1 (BT013)	DPA/BAE Systems, for RAF	
ZJ813	Eurofighter Typhoon T1 (BT014)	DPA/BAE Systems, for RAF	
ZJ814	Eurofighter Typhoon T1 (BT015)	DPA/BAE Systems, for RAF	
ZJ815	Eurofighter Typhoon T1 (BT016)	DPA/BAE Systems, for RAF	
ZJ906	WS Lynx 100	*To R Malaysian Navy as M501-3, 19 August 2004*	
ZJ910	Eurofighter Typhoon F2 (BS0001)	DPA/BAE Systems, Warton	
ZJ911	Eurofighter Typhoon F2 (BS0002)	DPA/BAE Systems, Warton	
ZJ912	Eurofighter Typhoon F2 (BS0003)	DPA/BAE Systems, Warton	
ZJ913	Eurofighter Typhoon F2 (BS0004)	DPA/BAE Systems, Warton	
ZJ914	Eurofighter Typhoon F2 (BS0005)	DPA/BAE Systems, for RAF	
ZJ915	Eurofighter Typhoon F2 (BS0006)	DPA/BAE Systems, for RAF	

Notes	Serial	Type (other identity) [code]	Owner/operator, location or fate
	ZJ916	Eurofighter Typhoon F2 (BS0007)	DPA/BAE Systems, for RAF
	ZJ917	Eurofighter Typhoon F2 (BS0008)	DPA/BAE Systems, for RAF
	ZJ918	Eurofighter Typhoon F2 (BS0009)	DPA/BAE Systems, for RAF
	ZJ919	Eurofighter Typhoon F2 (BS0010)	DPA/BAE Systems, for RAF
	ZJ920	Eurofighter Typhoon F2 (BS0011)	DPA/BAE Systems, for RAF
	ZJ921	Eurofighter Typhoon F2 (BS0012)	DPA/BAE Systems, for RAF
	ZJ922	Eurofighter Typhoon F2 (BS0013)	DPA/BAE Systems, for RAF
	ZJ923	Eurofighter Typhoon F2 (BS0014)	DPA/BAE Systems, for RAF
	ZJ924	Eurofighter Typhoon F2 (BS0015)	DPA/BAE Systems, for RAF
	ZJ925	Eurofighter Typhoon F2 (BS0016)	DPA/BAE Systems, for RAF
	ZJ926	Eurofighter Typhoon F2 (BS0017)	DPA/BAE Systems, for RAF
	ZJ927	Eurofighter Typhoon F2 (BS0018)	DPA/BAE Systems, for RAF
	ZJ928	Eurofighter Typhoon F2 (BS0019)	DPA/BAE Systems, for RAF
	ZJ929	Eurofighter Typhoon F2 (BS0020)	DPA/BAE Systems, for RAF
	ZJ930	Eurofighter Typhoon F2 (BS0021)	DPA/BAE Systems, for RAF
	ZJ931	Eurofighter Typhoon F2 (BS0022)	DPA/BAE Systems, for RAF
	ZJ932	Eurofighter Typhoon F2 (BS0023)	DPA/BAE Systems, for RAF
	ZJ933	Eurofighter Typhoon F2 (BS0024)	DPA/BAE Systems, for RAF
	ZJ934	Eurofighter Typhoon F2 (BS0025)	DPA/BAE Systems, for RAF
	ZJ935	Eurofighter Typhoon F2 (BS0026)	DPA/BAE Systems, for RAF
	ZJ936	Eurofighter Typhoon F2 (BS0027)	DPA/BAE Systems, for RAF
	ZJ937	Eurofighter Typhoon F2 (BS0028)	DPA/BAE Systems, for RAF
	ZJ938	Eurofighter Typhoon F2 (BS0029)	DPA/BAE Systems, for RAF
	ZJ939	Eurofighter Typhoon F2 (BS0030)	DPA/BAE Systems, for RAF
	ZJ940	Eurofighter Typhoon F2 (BS0031)	DPA/BAE Systems, for RAF
	ZJ941	Eurofighter Typhoon F2 (BS0032)	DPA/BAE Systems, for RAF
	ZJ942	Eurofighter Typhoon F2 (BS0033)	DPA/BAE Systems, for RAF
	ZJ943	Eurofighter Typhoon F2 (BS0034)	DPA/BAE Systems, for RAF
	ZJ944	Eurofighter Typhoon F2 (BS0035)	DPA/BAE Systems, for RAF
	ZJ945	Eurofighter Typhoon F2 (BS0036)	DPA/BAE Systems, for RAF
	ZJ951	BAE Systems Hawk 120D	BAE Systems, Warton
	ZJ954	SA330H Puma HC1 (SAAF 144)	DPA/Westland Helicopters, Yeovil
	ZJ955	SA330H Puma HC1 (SAAF 148)	DPA/Eurocopter, for RAF
	ZJ956	SA330H Puma HC1 (SAAF 172)	DPA/Eurocopter, for RAF
	ZJ957	SA330H Puma HC1 (SAAF 169)	DPA/Eurocopter, for RAF
	ZJ958	SA330H Puma (SAAF 173)	DPA, stored DSDC Llangennech
	ZJ959	SA330H Puma (SAAF 184)	DPA, stored DSDC Llangennech
	ZJ960	Grob G109B Vigilant T1 (D-KSMU) [SH]	RAF No 663 VGS, Kinloss
	ZJ961	Grob G109B Vigilant T1 (D-KLCW) [SJ]	RAF ACCGS/No 644 VGS, Syerston
	ZJ962	Grob G109B Vigilant T1 (D-KBEU) [SK]	RAF No 613 VGS, Halton
	ZJ963	Grob G109B Vigilant T1 (D-KMSN) [SL]	RAF No 616 VGS, Henlow
	ZJ964	Bell 212HP (G-BJGV) [A]	AAC No 25 Flt, Belize
	ZJ965	Bell 212HP (G-BJGU) [B]	AAC No 25 Flt, Belize
	ZJ966	Bell 212HP (G-BJJO) [C]	AAC No 25 Flt, Belize
	ZJ967	Grob G109B Vigilant T1 (G-DEWS) [SM]	RAF ACCGS/No 644 VGS, Syerston
	ZJ968	Grob G109B Vigilant T1 (N109BT) [SN]	RAF No 616 VGS, Henlow
	ZJ969	Bell 212 (G-BGLJ)	AAC No 671 Sqn/2 Regt, Middle Wallop
	ZJ971	WS Lynx 120	*To Oman as 757, 27 October 2004*
	ZJ972	WS Lynx 120	Westland Helicopters, for Oman as 758
	ZJ973	WS Lynx 120	*To Oman as 759, 24 June 2004*
	ZJ974	WS Lynx 120	*To Oman as 760, 24 June 2004*
	ZJ975	WS Lynx 120	*To Oman as 761, 24 June 2004*
	ZJ976	WS Lynx 120	*To Oman as 762, 19 August 2004*
	ZJ977	WS Lynx 120	*To Oman as 763, 27 October 2004*
	ZJ978	WS Lynx 120	Westland Helicopters, for Oman as 764
	ZJ979	WS Lynx 120	Westland Helicopters, for Oman as 765
	ZJ980	WS Lynx 120	Westland Helicopters, for Oman as 766
	ZJ981	WS Lynx 120	Westland Helicopters, for Oman as 767
	ZJ982	WS Lynx 120	Westland Helicopters, for Oman as 768
	ZJ983	WS Lynx 120	Westland Helicopters, for Oman as 769
	ZJ984	WS Lynx 120	Westland Helicopters, for Oman as 770
	ZJ985	WS Lynx 120	Westland Helicopters, for Oman as 771
	ZJ986	WS Lynx 120	Westland Helicopters, for Oman as 772
	ZJ987	WS Lynx 110	Westland Helicopters, for Thai Navy as 2313
	ZJ988	WS Lynx 110	Westland Helicopters, for Thai Navy as 2314

Serial	Type (other identity) [code]	Owner/operator, location or fate	Notes
ZJ989	BAE Systems Eagle 0 UAV	DPA/BAE Systems, Warton	
ZJ990	EHI-101 Merlin Mk512	Westland Helicopters, for Denmark as M-501	
ZJ991	EHI-101 Merlin Mk512	Westland Helicopters, for Denmark as M-502	
ZJ992	EHI-101 Merlin Mk512	Westland Helicopters, for Denmark as M-503	
ZJ993	EHI-101 Merlin Mk512	Westland Helicopters, for Denmark as M-504	
ZJ994	EHI-101 Merlin Mk512	Westland Helicopters, for Denmark as M-505	
ZJ995	EHI-101 Merlin Mk512	Westland Helicopters, for Denmark as M-506	
ZJ996	EHI-101 Merlin Mk512	Westland Helicopters, for Denmark as M-507	
ZJ997	EHI-101 Merlin Mk512	Westland Helicopters, for Denmark as M-508	
ZJ998	EHI-101 Merlin Mk512	Westland Helicopters, for Denmark as M-509	
ZJ999	EHI-101 Merlin Mk512	Westland Helicopters, for Denmark as M-510	
ZK001	EHI-101 Merlin Mk512	Westland Helicopters, for Denmark as M-511	
ZK002	EHI-101 Merlin Mk512	Westland Helicopters, for Denmark as M-512	
ZK003	EHI-101 Merlin Mk512	Westland Helicopters, for Denmark as M-513	
ZK004	EHI-101 Merlin Mk512	Westland Helicopters, for Denmark as M-514	
ZK005	Grob G109B Vigilant T1 (OH-797) [SP]	RAF ACCGS/No 644 VGS, Syerston	
ZK006	Generic Fast Jet Training Aid <Sim>	RAF No 1 SoTT, Cosford	
ZK007	Pressure Refuelling Trainer	RAF No 1 SoTT, Cosford	
ZK008	Pressure Refuelling Trainer	RAF No 1 SoTT, Cosford	
ZK009	Mission Technologies Buster 1-1000 UAV	DPA	
ZK010	BAE Systems Hawk 128	Reservation for RAF	
ZK011	BAE Systems Hawk 128	Reservation for RAF	
ZK012	BAE Systems Hawk 128	Reservation for RAF	
ZK013	BAE Systems Hawk 128	Reservation for RAF	
ZK014	BAE Systems Hawk 128	Reservation for RAF	
ZK015	BAE Systems Hawk 128	Reservation for RAF	
ZK016	BAE Systems Hawk 128	Reservation for RAF	
ZK017	BAE Systems Hawk 128	Reservation for RAF	
ZK018	BAE Systems Hawk 128	Reservation for RAF	
ZK019	BAE Systems Hawk 128	Reservation for RAF	
ZK020	BAE Systems Hawk 128	Reservation for RAF	
ZK021	BAE Systems Hawk 128	Reservation for RAF	
ZK022	BAE Systems Hawk 128	Reservation for RAF	
ZK023	BAE Systems Hawk 128	Reservation for RAF	
ZK024	BAE Systems Hawk 128	Reservation for RAF	
ZK025	BAE Systems Hawk 128	Reservation for RAF	
ZK026	BAE Systems Hawk 128	Reservation for RAF	
ZK027	BAE Systems Hawk 128	Reservation for RAF	
ZK028	BAE Systems Hawk 128	Reservation for RAF	
ZK029	BAE Systems Hawk 128	Reservation for RAF	
ZK030	BAE Systems Hawk 128	Reservation for RAF	
ZK031	BAE Systems Hawk 128	Reservation for RAF	
ZK032	BAE Systems Hawk 128	Reservation for RAF	
ZK033	BAE Systems Hawk 128	Reservation for RAF	
ZK034	BAE Systems Hawk 128	Reservation for RAF	
ZK035	BAE Systems Hawk 128	Reservation for RAF	
ZK036	BAE Systems Hawk 128	Reservation for RAF	
ZK037	BAE Systems Hawk 128	Reservation for RAF	
ZK038	BAE Systems Hawk 128	Reservation for RAF	
ZK039	BAE Systems Hawk 128	Reservation for RAF	
ZK040	BAE Systems Hawk 128	Reservation for RAF	
ZK041	BAE Systems Hawk 128	Reservation for RAF	
ZK042	BAE Systems Hawk 128	Reservation for RAF	
ZK043	BAE Systems Hawk 128	Reservation for RAF	
ZK044	BAE Systems Hawk 128	Reservation for RAF	

Notes	Serial	Type (other identity) [code]	Owner/operator, location or fate
	ZK100	Westland Lynx Mk8 <Sim>	For Royal Navy
	ZK102	Lockheed-Martin Desert Hawk	For Army
	ZK103	EADS Scorpio Mk 6 UAV	For Army
	ZK104	EADS Quadrocopter UAV	For Army
	ZK201	Meggitt Banshee	For Army
	ZK202	Meggitt Banshee	For Army
	ZK203	Meggitt Banshee	For Army
	ZK204	Meggitt Banshee	For Army
	ZK450	Beech super King Air B200 (G-RAFJ)	Reservation for SERCO/RAF
	ZK451	Beech super King Air B200 (G-RAFK)	Reservation for SERCO/RAF
	ZK452	Beech super King Air B200 (G-RAFL)	Reservation for SERCO/RAF
	ZK453	Beech super King Air B200 (G-RAFM)	Reservation for SERCO/RAF
	ZK454	Beech super King Air B200 (G-RAFN)	Reservation for SERCO/RAF
	ZK455	Beech super King Air B200 (G-RAFO)	Reservation for SERCO/RAF
	ZK456	Beech super King Air B200 (G-RAFP)	Reservation for serco/RAF
	ZK531	BAe Hawk T53 (LL-5306)	DPA/BAE Systems, Warton
	ZK532	BAe Hawk T53 (LL-5315)	DPA/BAE Systems, Warton
	ZK533	BAe Hawk T53 (LL-5317)	DPA/BAE Systems, Brough
	ZK534	BAe Hawk T53 (LL-5319)	DPA/BAE Systems, Warton
	ZK535	BAe Hawk T53 (LL-5320)	DPA/BAE Systems, Warton
	ZM400	Airbus A400M	Reservation for RAF
	ZM401	Airbus A400M	Reservation for RAF
	ZM402	Airbus A400M	Reservation for RAF
	ZM403	Airbus A400M	Reservation for RAF
	ZM404	Airbus A400M	Reservation for RAF
	ZM405	Airbus A400M	Reservation for RAF
	ZM406	Airbus A400M	Reservation for RAF
	ZM407	Airbus A400M	Reservation for RAF
	ZM408	Airbus A400M	Reservation for RAF
	ZM409	Airbus A400M	Reservation for RAF
	ZM410	Airbus A400M	Reservation for RAF
	ZM411	Airbus A400M	Reservation for RAF
	ZM412	Airbus A400M	Reservation for RAF
	ZM413	Airbus A400M	Reservation for RAF
	ZM414	Airbus A400M	Reservation for RAF
	ZM415	Airbus A400M	Reservation for RAF
	ZM416	Airbus A400M	Reservation for RAF
	ZM417	Airbus A400M	Reservation for RAF
	ZM418	Airbus A400M	Reservation for RAF
	ZM419	Airbus A400M	Reservation for RAF
	ZM420	Airbus A400M	Reservation for RAF
	ZM421	Airbus A400M	Reservation for RAF
	ZM422	Airbus A400M	Reservation for RAF
	ZM423	Airbus A400M	Reservation for RAF
	ZM424	Airbus A400M	Reservation for RAF
	ZT800	WS Super Lynx Mk 300	DPA/Westland Helicopters, Yeovil
	ZZ171	Boeing C-17A Globemaster III (00-201/N171UK)	RAF No 99 Sqn, Brize Norton
	ZZ172	Boeing C-17A Globemaster III (00-202/N172UK)	RAF No 99 Sqn, Brize Norton
	ZZ173	Boeing C-17A Globemaster III (00-203/N173UK)	RAF No 99 Sqn, Brize Norton
	ZZ174	Boeing C-17A Globemaster III (00-204/N174UK)	RAF No 99 Sqn, Brize Norton
	ZZ175	Boeing C-17A Globemaster III	Reservation for RAF (2009)

Westland Lysander R9125 is displayed in the RAF Museum's Battle of Britain Hall.

De Havilland Hornet Moth W9385 is painted in World War 2 Coastal Command colours.

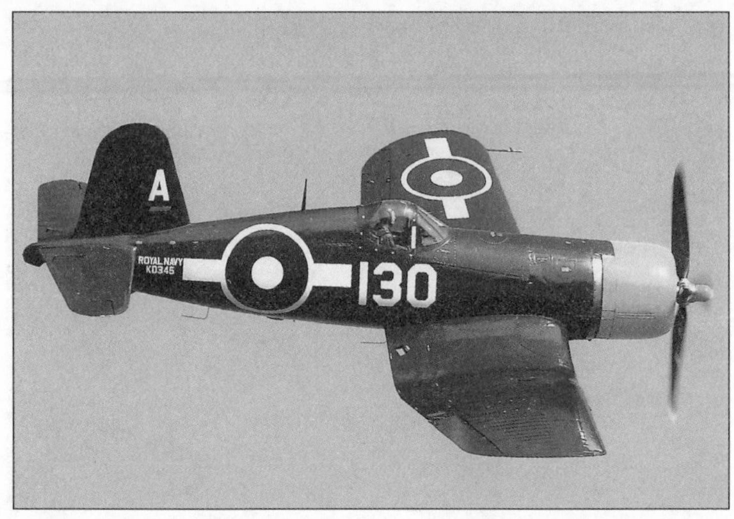

The Fighter Collection's Goodyear FG-1D Corsair flies from the IWM airfield at Duxford.

A rare Hawker Tempest II PR536 on display in the RAF Museum at Hendon.

Spitfire FR XVIII SM845 is owned by the Silver Victory Collection at Duxford.

The Royal Navy Historic Flight's Hawker Sea Fury FB11 VR930 landing at RNAS Yeovilton.

Former RAF Chipmunk T10 WK549/G-BTWF is privately owned at Breighton.

Delta Jets' Hawker Hunter T7B WV318 taking off from its home base at Kemble.

Hawker Sea Hawk FGA6 WV908 was first flown in September 2004 after a long restoration.

De Havilland Aviation's Vampire T11 WZ507 is based at Bournemouth.

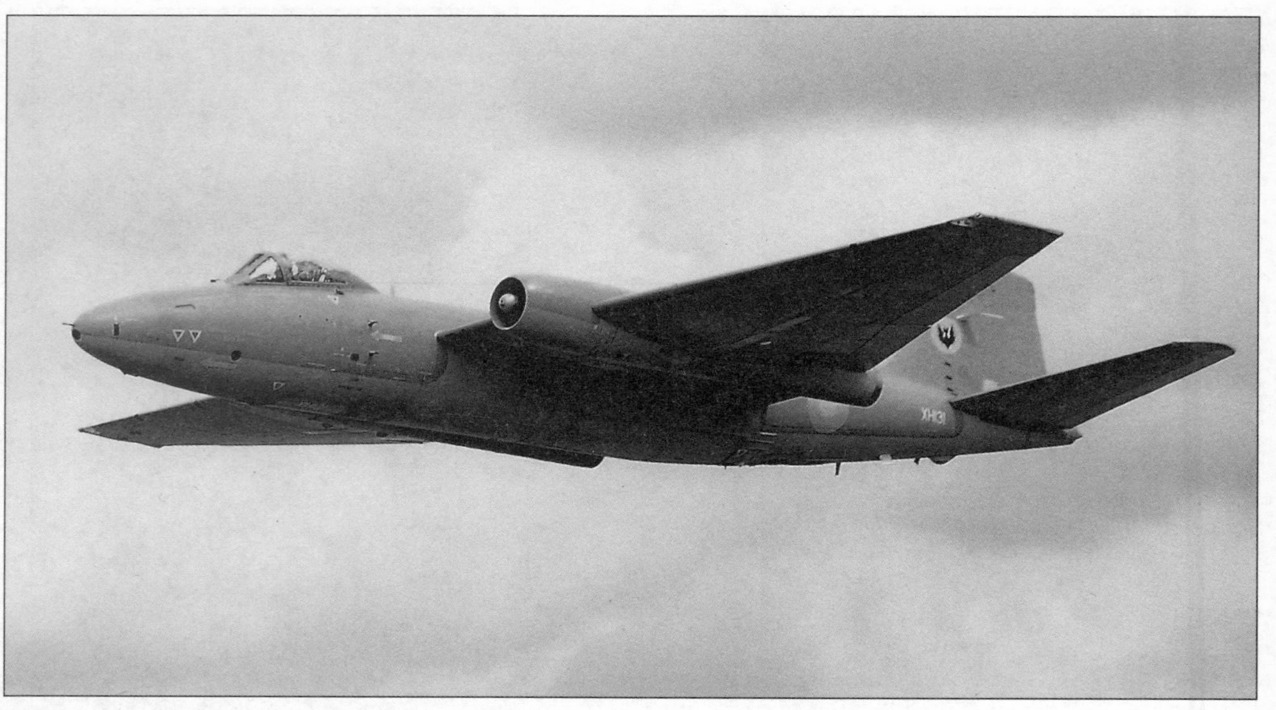

This English Electric Canberra PR9 XH131 is operated by No 39(1PRU) Squadron at Marham.

The Army Air Corps Historic Flight's Sud Alouette AH2 and Westland Scout AH1 XT626.

A former RNZAF Westland Wasp HAS1 XT787 is flown by Kennet Aviation at North Weald.

Hawker Siddeley Hawk T1W XX314 is based at RAF Leeming with No 100 Squadron.

Flown by 815 Naval Air Squadron, this Westland Lynx HAS3S XZ237, is with the Headquarters Flight.

The RAF Battle of Britain Memorial Flight's Coningsby based Douglas Dakota C3 ZA947.

BAe Harrier T8 ZB603, here operated by 899 Naval Air Squadron from RNAS Yeovilton.

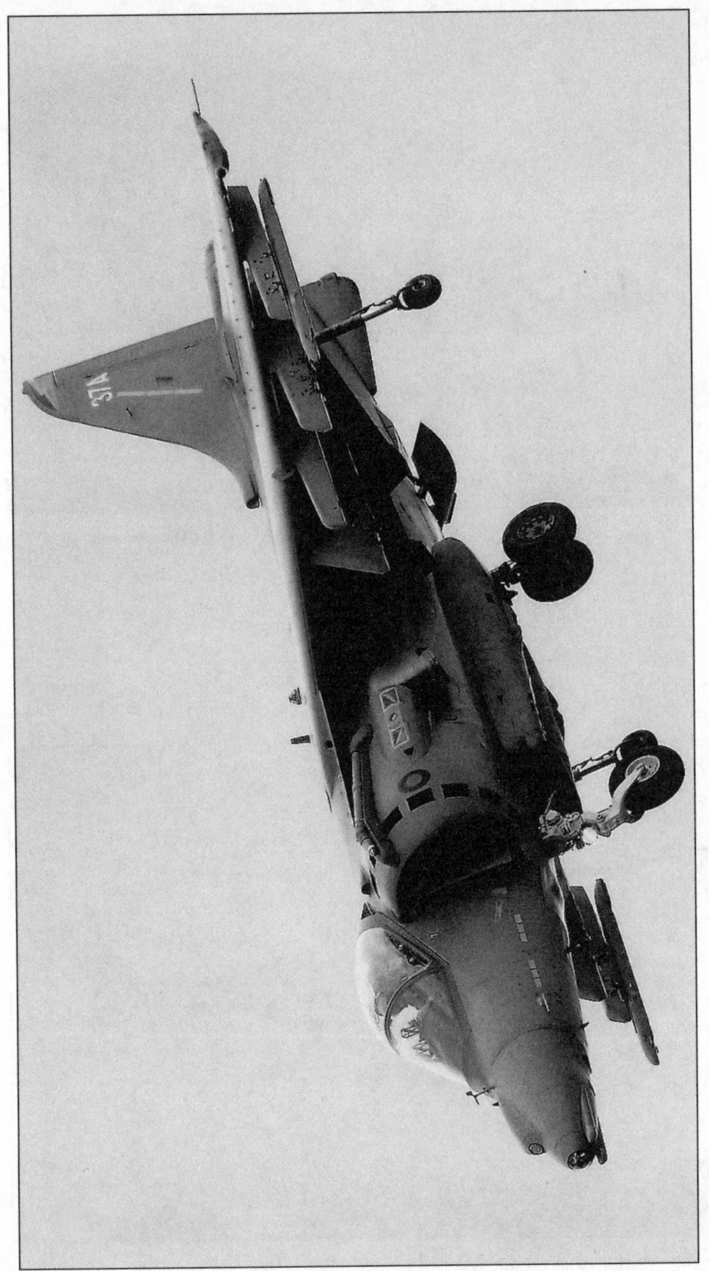

Based at RAF Cottesmore, this BAe Harrier GR7A ZD408 wears the markings of No 4 Squadron.

Panavia Tornado GR4 ZD843 is flown by No 15 (Reserve) Squadron from RAF Lossiemouth.

EH101 Merlin HC3 ZJ136 of No 28 Squadron is based at RAF Benson.

Civil Registered Aircraft in UK Military Service

Serial	Type (other identity) [code]	Owner/operator, location or fate	Notes
G-BONT	Slingsby T.67M Firefly 2	HCS/DEFTS, Middle Wallop	
G-BUUA	Slingsby T.67M Firefly 2	HCS/DEFTS, Middle Wallop	
G-BUUB	Slingsby T.67M Firefly 2	HCS/DEFTS, Middle Wallop	
G-BUUC	Slingsby T.67M Firefly 2	HCS/DEFTS, Middle Wallop	
G-BUUK	Slingsby T.67M Firefly 2	HCS/DEFTS, Middle Wallop	
G-BVHC	Grob G.115D-2 Heron	Shorts Bros/RN No 727 Sqn, Plymouth	
G-BVHD	Grob G.115D-2 Heron	Shorts Bros/RN No 727 Sqn, Plymouth	
G-BVHF	Grob G.115D-2 Heron	Shorts Bros/RN No 727 Sqn, Plymouth	
G-BVHG	Grob G.115D-2 Heron	Shorts Bros/RN No 727 Sqn, Plymouth	
G-BWXA	Slingsby T.67M Firefly 260	HCS/DEFTS, Barkston Heath	
G-BWXB	Slingsby T.67M Firefly 260	HCS/DEFTS, Barkston Heath	
G-BWXC	Slingsby T.67M Firefly 260	HCS/DEFTS, Barkston Heath	
G-BWXD	Slingsby T.67M Firefly 260	HCS/DEFTS, Barkston Heath	
G-BWXE	Slingsby T.67M Firefly 260	HCS/DEFTS, Barkston Heath	
G-BWXF	Slingsby T.67M Firefly 260	HCS/DEFTS, Barkston Heath	
G-BWXG	Slingsby T.67M Firefly 260	HCS/DEFTS, Barkston Heath	
G-BWXH	Slingsby T.67M Firefly 260	HCS/DEFTS, Barkston Heath	
G-BWXI	Slingsby T.67M Firefly 260	HCS/DEFTS, Barkston Heath	
G-BWXJ	Slingsby T.67M Firefly 260	HCS/DEFTS, Barkston Heath	
G-BWXK	Slingsby T.67M Firefly 260	HCS/DEFTS, Barkston Heath	
G-BWXL	Slingsby T.67M Firefly 260	HCS/DEFTS, Barkston Heath	
G-BWXM	Slingsby T.67M Firefly 260	HCS/DEFTS, Barkston Heath	
G-BWXN	Slingsby T.67M Firefly 260	HCS/DEFTS, Barkston Heath	
G-BWXO	Slingsby T.67M Firefly 260	HCS/DEFTS, Barkston Heath	
G-BWXR	Slingsby T.67M Firefly 260	HCS/DEFTS, Barkston Heath	
G-BWXS	Slingsby T.67M Firefly 260	HCS/DEFTS, Barkston Heath	
G-BWXT	Slingsby T.67M Firefly 260	HCS/DEFTS, Barkston Heath	
G-BWXU	Slingsby T.67M Firefly 260	HCS/DEFTS, Barkston Heath	
G-BWXV	Slingsby T.67M Firefly 260	HCS/DEFTS, Barkston Heath	
G-BWXW	Slingsby T.67M Firefly 260	HCS/DEFTS, Barkston Heath	
G-BWXX	Slingsby T.67M Firefly 260	HCS/DEFTS, Barkston Heath	
G-BWXY	Slingsby T.67M Firefly 260	HCS/DEFTS, Barkston Heath	
G-BWXZ	Slingsby T.67M Firefly 260	HCS/DEFTS, Barkston Heath	
G-BYUA	Grob G.115E Tutor	Bombardier/Cambridge UAS/ University of London AS, Wyton	
G-BYUB	Grob G.115E Tutor	Bombardier/CFS/East Midlands Universities AS, Cranwell	
G-BYUC	Grob G.115E Tutor	Bombardier/CFS/East Midlands Universities AS, Cranwell	
G-BYUD	Grob G.115E Tutor	Bombardier/Universities of Glasgow & Strathclyde AS, Glasgow	
G-BYUE	Grob G.115E Tutor	Bombardier/CFS/East Midlands Universities AS, Cranwell	
G-BYUF	Grob G.115E Tutor	Bombardier/University of Birmingham AS, Cosford	
G-BYUG	Grob G.115E Tutor	Bombardier/University of Birmingham AS, Cosford	
G-BYUH	Grob G.115E Tutor	Bombardier/Bristol UAS, Colerne	
G-BYUI	Grob G.115E Tutor	Bombardier/Liverpool UAS/Manchester and Salford Universities AS, Woodvale	
G-BYUJ	Grob G.115E Tutor	Bombardier/Southampton UAS, Boscombe Down	
G-BYUK	Grob G.115E Tutor	Bombardier/University of Birmingham AS, Cosford	
G-BYUL	Grob G.115E Tutor	Bombardier/Southampton UAS, Boscombe Down	
G-BYUM	Grob G.115E Tutor	Bombardier/Southampton UAS, Boscombe Down	
G-BYUN	Grob G.115E Tutor	Bombardier/University of Wales AS, St Athan	
G-BYUO	Grob G.115E Tutor	Bombardier/University of London AS, Wyton	
G-BYUP	Grob G.115E Tutor	Bombardier/East Lowlands UAS/ Aberdeen, Dundee & St Andrews UAS, Leuchars	

Notes	Serial	Type (other identity) [code]	Owner/operator, location or fate
	G-BYUR	Grob G.115E Tutor	Bombardier//East Lowlands UAS/ Aberdeen, Dundee & St Andrews UAS, Leuchars
	G-BYUS	Grob G.115E Tutor	Bombardier/University of Wales AS, St Athan
	G-BYUT	Grob G.115E Tutor	Bombardier/University of Wales AS, St Athan
	G-BYUU	Grob G.115E Tutor	Bombardier/East Lowlands UAS/ Aberdeen, Dundee & St Andrews UAS, Leuchars
	G-BYUV	Grob G.115E Tutor	Bombardier/Oxford UAS, Benson
	G-BYUW	Grob G.115E Tutor	Bombardier/East Lowlands UAS/ Aberdeen, Dundee & St Andrews UAS, Leuchars
	G-BYUX	Grob G.115E Tutor	Bombardier/Liverpool UAS/Manchester and Salford UniversAities AS, Woodvale
	G-BYUY	Grob G.115E Tutor	Bombardier/East Lowlands UAS/ Aberdeen, Dundee & St Andrews UAS, Leuchars
	G-BYUZ	Grob G.115E Tutor	Bombardier/Liverpool UAS/Manchester and Salford Universities AS, Woodvale
	G-BYVA	Grob G.115E Tutor	Bombardier/CFS/East Midlands Universities AS, Cranwell
	G-BYVB	Grob G.115E Tutor	Bombardier/East Lowlands UAS/ Aberdeen, Dundee & St Andrews UAS, Leuchars
	G-BYVC	Grob G.115E Tutor	Bombardier/Cambridge UAS/University of London AS, Wyton
	G-BYVD	Grob G.115E Tutor	Bombardier/Cambridge UAS/University of London AS, Wyton
	G-BYVE	Grob G.115E Tutor	Bombardier/Cambridge UAS/University of London AS, Wyton
	G-BYVF	Grob G.115E Tutor	Bombardier/RN No 727 Sqn, Plymouth
	G-BYVG	Grob G.115E Tutor	Bombardier/Yorkshire Universities AS, Church Fenton
	G-BYVH	Grob G.115E Tutor	Bombardier/East Lowlands UAS/ Aberdeen, Dundee & St Andrews UAS, Leuchars
	G-BYVI	Grob G.115E Tutor	Bombardier/Universities of Glasgow & Strathclyde AS, Glasgow
	G-BYVJ	Grob G.115E Tutor	Bombardier/University of Birmingham AS, Cosford
	G-BYVK	Grob G.115E Tutor	Bombardier/RN No 727 Sqn, Plymouth
	G-BYVL	Grob G.115E Tutor	Bombardier/Oxford UAS, Benson
	G-BYVM	Grob G.115E Tutor	Bombardier/Universities of Glasgow & Strathclyde AS, Glasgow
	G-BYVN	Grob G.115E Tutor	Bombardier/Bristol UAS, Colerne
	G-BYVO	Grob G.115E Tutor	Bombardier/Cambridge UAS/University of London AS, Wyton
	G-BYVP	Grob G.115E Tutor	Bombardier/Oxford UAS, Benson
	G-BYVR	Grob G.115E Tutor	Bombardier/CFS/East Midlands Universities AS, Cranwell
	G-BYVS	Grob G.115E Tutor	Bombardier/Northumbrian Universities AS, Leeming
	G-BYVT	Grob G.115E Tutor	Bombardier/Cambridge UAS/University of London AS, Wyton
	G-BYVU	Grob G.115E Tutor	Bombardier/Oxford UAS, Benson
	G-BYVV	Grob G.115E Tutor	Bombardier/Northumbrian Universities AS, Leeming
	G-BYVW	Grob G.115E Tutor	Bombardier/University of Wales AS, St Athan
	G-BYVX	Grob G.115E Tutor	Bombardier/Yorkshire Universities AS, Church Fenton
	G-BYVY	Grob G.115E Tutor	Bombardier/University of Birmingham AS, Cosford
	G-BYVZ	Grob G.115E Tutor	Bombardier/Yorkshire Universities AS, Church Fenton
	G-BYWA	Grob G.115E Tutor	Bombardier/Oxford UAS, Benson
	G-BYWB	Grob G.115E Tutor	Bombardier/CFS/East Midlands Universities AS, Cranwell
	G-BYWC	Grob G.115E Tutor	Bombardier/Bristol UAS, Colerne
	G-BYWD	Grob G.115E Tutor	Bombardier/Liverpool UAS/Manchester and Salford Universities AS, Woodvale

Serial	Type (other identity) [code]	Owner/operator, location or fate	Notes
G-BYWE	Grob G.115E Tutor	Bombardier/Bristol UAS, Colerne	
G-BYWF	Grob G.115E Tutor	Bombardier/CFS/East Midlands Universities AS, Cranwell	
G-BYWG	Grob G.115E Tutor	Bombardier/Bristol UAS, Colerne	
G-BYWH	Grob G.115E Tutor	Bombardier/Northumbrian Universities AS, Leeming	
G-BYWI	Grob G.115E Tutor	Bombardier/Cambridge UAS/University of London AS, Wyton	
G-BYWJ	Grob G.115E Tutor	Bombardier/Liverpool UAS/Manchester and Salford Universities AS, Woodvale	
G-BYWK	Grob G.115E Tutor	Bombardier/Yorkshire Universities AS, Church Fenton	
G-BYWL	Grob G.115E Tutor	Bombardier/Liverpool UAS/Manchester and Salford Universities AS, Woodvale	
G-BYWM	Grob G.115E Tutor	Bombardier/RN No 727 Sqn, Plymouth	
G-BYWN	Grob G.115E Tutor	Bombardier/Liverpool UAS/Manchester and Salford Universities AS, Woodvale	
G-BYWO	Grob G.115E Tutor	Bombardier/Yorkshire Universities AS, Church Fenton	
G-BYWP	Grob G.115E Tutor	Bombardier/Yorkshire Universities AS, Church Fenton	
G-BYWR	Grob G.115E Tutor	Bombardier/Cambridge UAS/University of London AS, Wyton	
G-BYWS	Grob G.115E Tutor	Bombardier/Yorkshire Universities AS, Church Fenton	
G-BYWT	Grob G.115E Tutor	Bombardier/Northumbrian Universities AS, Leeming	
G-BYWU	Grob G.115E Tutor	Bombardier/Cambridge UAS/University of London AS, Wyton	
G-BYWV	Grob G.115E Tutor	Bombardier/Yorkshire Universities AS, Church Fenton	
G-BYWW	Grob G.115E Tutor	Bombardier/CFS/East Midlands Universities AS, Cranwell	
G-BYWX	Grob G.115E Tutor	Bombardier/Bristol UAS, Colerne	
G-BYWY	Grob G.115E Tutor	Bombardier/CFS/East Midlands Universities AS, Cranwell	
G-BYWZ	Grob G.115E Tutor	Bombardier/CFS/East Midlands Universities AS, Cranwell	
G-BYXA	Grob G.115E Tutor	Bombardier/Liverpool UAS/Manchester and Salford Universities AS, Woodvale	
G-BYXB	Grob G.115E Tutor	Bombardier/Southampton UAS, Boscombe Down	
G-BYXC	Grob G.115E Tutor	Bombardier/CFS/East Midlands Universities AS, Cranwell	
G-BYXD	Grob G.115E Tutor	Bombardier/CFS/East Midlands Universities AS, Cranwell	
G-BYXE	Grob G.115E Tutor	Bombardier/Yorkshire Universities AS, Church Fenton	
G-BYXF	Grob G.115E Tutor	Bombardier/University of Birmingham AS, Cosford	
G-BYXG	Grob G.115E Tutor	Bombardier/Cambridge UAS/University of London AS, Wyton	
G-BYXH	Grob G.115E Tutor	Bombardier/University of Wales AS, St Athan	
G-BYXI	Grob G.115E Tutor	Bombardier/Liverpool UAS/Manchester and Salford Universities AS, Woodvale	
G-BYXJ	Grob G.115E Tutor	Bombardier/Southampton UAS, Boscombe Down	
G-BYXK	Grob G.115E Tutor	Bombardier/RN No 727 Sqn, Plymouth	
G-BYXL	Grob G.115E Tutor	Bombardier/University of Birmingham AS, Cosford	
G-BYXM	Grob G.115E Tutor	Bombardier/CFS/East Midlands Universities AS, Cranwell	
G-BYXN	Grob G.115E Tutor	Bombardier/CFS/East Midlands Universities AS, Cranwell	
G-BYXO	Grob G.115E Tutor	Bombardier/University of Birmingham AS, Cosford	
G-BYXP	Grob G.115E Tutor	Bombardier/Cambridge UAS/University of London AS, Wyton	
G-BYXR	Grob G.115E Tutor	Bombardier/Oxford UAS, Benson	
G-BYXS	Grob G.115E Tutor	Bombardier/RN No 727 Sqn, Plymouth	
G-BYXT	Grob G.115E Tutor	Bombardier/Cambridge UAS/University of London AS, Wyton	

Civil Registered Aircraft in UK Military Service

Notes	Serial	Type (other identity) [code]	Owner/operator, location or fate
	G-BYXX	Grob G.115E Tutor	Bombardier/Liverpool UAS/Manchester and Salford Universities AS, Woodvale
	G-BYXY	Grob G.115E Tutor	Bombardier/Cambridge UAS/University of London AS, Wyton
	G-BYXZ	Grob G.115E Tutor	Bombardier/CFS/East Midlands Universities AS, Cranwell
	G-BYYA	Grob G.115E Tutor	Bombardier/Northumbrian Universities AS, Leeming
	G-BYYB	Grob G.115E Tutor	Bombardier/CFS/East Midlands Universities AS, Cranwell
	G-FFRA	Dassault Falcon 20DC (N902FR)	FR Aviation, Teesside
	G-FRAE	Dassault Falcon 20E (N910FR)	FR Aviation, Bournemouth
	G-FRAF	Dassault Falcon 20E (N911FR)	FR Aviation, Bournemouth
	G-FRAH	Dassault Falcon 20DC (N900FR)	FR Aviation, Teesside
	G-FRAI	Dassault Falcon 20E (N901FR)	FR Aviation, Teesside
	G-FRAJ	Dassault Falcon 20E (N903FR)	FR Aviation, Teesside
	G-FRAK	Dassault Falcon 20DC (N905FR)	FR Aviation, Bournemouth
	G-FRAL	Dassault Falcon 20DC (N904FR)	FR Aviation, Bournemouth
	G-FRAM	Dassault Falcon 20DC (N907FR)	FR Aviation, Bournemouth
	G-FRAO	Dassault Falcon 20DC (N906FR)	FR Aviation, Bournemouth
	G-FRAP	Dassault Falcon 20DC (N908FR)	FR Aviation, Teesside
	G-FRAR	Dassault Falcon 20DC (N909FR)	FR Aviation, Teesside
	G-FRAS	Dassault Falcon 20C (117501)	FR Aviation, Teesside
	G-FRAT	Dassault Falcon 20C (117502)	FR Aviation, Teesside
	G-FRAU	Dassault Falcon 20C (117504)	FR Aviation, Teesside
	G-FRAW	Dassault Falcon 20ECM (117507)	FR Aviation, Teesside
	G-FRBA	Dassault Falcon 20C	FR Aviation, Bournemouth
	G-RAFJ	Beech Super King Air B200 (ZK450 reserved)	SERCO/RAF No 3 FTS/45 (R) Sqn, Cranwell
	G-RAFK	Beech Super King Air B200 (ZK451 reserved)	SERCO/RAF No 3 FTS/45 (R) Sqn, Cranwell
	G-RAFL	Beech Super King Air B200 (ZK452 reserved)	SERCO/RAF No 3 FTS/45 (R) Sqn, Cranwell
	G-RAFM	Beech Super King Air B200 (ZK453 reserved)	SERCO/RAF No 3 FTS/45 (R) Sqn, Cranwell
	G-RAFN	Beech Super King Air B200 (ZK454 reserved)	SERCO/RAF No 3 FTS/45 (R) Sqn, Cranwell
	G-RAFO	Beech Super King Air B200 (ZK455 reserved)	SERCO/RAF No 3 FTS/45 (R) Sqn, Cranwell
	G-RAFP	Beech Super King Air B200 (ZK456 reserved)	SERCO/RAF No 3 FTS/45 (R) Sqn, Cranwell

In the markings of No 17(R) Squadron, Eurofighter Typhoon T1 ZJ803 is with TOEU at Warton.

RAF Maintenance Command/ Support Command/Logistics Command 'M' number Cross-reference

1764M/K4972
2015M/K5600
2292M/K8203
2361M/K6035
3118M/H5199/(BK892)
3858M/X7688
4354M/BL614
4552M/T5298
5377M/EP120
5405M/LF738
5466M/*BN230*/(LF751)
5690M/MK356
5718M/BM597
5758M/DG202
6457M/ML427
6490M/LA255
6640M/RM694
6850M/TE184
6944M/RW386
6946M/RW388
6948M/DE673
6960M/MT847
7008M/EE549
7014M/N6720
7015M/NL985
7035M/*K2567*/(DE306)
7060M/VF301
7090M/EE531
7118M/LA198
7119M/LA226
7150M/PK683
7154M/WB188
7174M/VX272
7175M/VV106
7200M/VT812
7241M/TE311/*(MK178*)
7243M/TE462
7245M/RW382
7246M/TD248
7256M/TB752
7257M/TB252
7279M/TB752
7281M/TB252
7288M/PK724
7293M/RW393
7323M/VV217
7325M/R5868
7326M/VN485
7362M/475081/(VP546)
7416M/WN907
7421M/WT660
7422M/WT684
7428M/WK198
7432M/WZ724
7438M/*18671*/(WP905)
7443M/WX853
7458M/WX905
7464M/XA564
7470M/XA553
7473M/XE946
7491M/WT569
7496M/WT612
7499M/WT555
7510M/WT694
7525M/WT619
7530M/WT648
7532M/WT651
7533M/WT680
7544M/WN904
7548M/PS915
7556M/WK584
7564M/XE982
7570M/XD674
7582M/WP190
7583M/WP185
7602M/WE600
7605M/WS692
7606M/WV562
7607M/TJ138
7615M/WV679
7616M/WW388
7618M/WW442
7622M/WV606
7631M/VX185
7641M/XA634
7645M/WD293
7648M/XF785
7673M/WV332
7688M/WW421
7693M/WV483
7694M/WV486
7696M/WV493
7698M/WV499
7704M/TW536
7705M/WL505
7706M/WB584
7709M/WT933
7711M/PS915
7712M/WK281
7715M/XK724
7716M/WS776
7718M/WA577
7719M/WK277
7729M/WB758
7737M/XD602
7741M/VZ477
7750M/*WK864*/(WL168)
7751M/WL131
7755M/WG760
7758M/PM651
7759M/PK664
7761M/XH318
7762M/XE670
7764M/XH318
7770M/*XF506*/(WT746)
7793M/XG523
7796M/WJ676
7798M/XH783
7806M/TA639
7809M/XA699
7816M/WG763
7817M/TX214
7825M/WK991
7827M/XA917
7829M/XH992
7839M/WV781
7841M/WV783
7851M/WZ706
7854M/XM191
7855M/XK416
7859M/XP283
7860M/XL738
7862M/XR246
7863M/*XP248*
7864M/XP244
7865M/TX226
7866M/XH278
7868M/WZ736
7869M/WK935
7872M/*WZ826*/(XD826)
7881M/WD413
7882M/XD525
7883M/XT150
7891M/XM693
7894M/XD818
7895M/WF784
7898M/XP854
7900M/WA576
7906M/WH132
7917M/WA591
7920M/WL360
7923M/XT133
7928M/XE849
7930M/WH301
7931M/RD253
7932M/WZ744
7933M/XR220
7937M/WS843
7938M/XH903
7939M/XD596
7940M/XL764
7955M/XH767
7957M/XF545
7959M/WS774
7960M/WS726
7961M/WS739
7964M/WS760
7965M/WS792
7967M/WS788
7971M/XK699
7973M/WS807
7976M/XK418
7979M/XM529
7980M/XM561
7982M/XH892
7983M/XD506
7984M/XN597
7986M/WG777
7988M/XL149
7990M/XD452
7997M/XG452
7998M/*XM515*/(XD515)
8005M/WG768
8009M/XG518
8010M/XG547
8012M/VS562
8016M/XT677
8017M/XL762
8018M/XN344
8021M/XL824
8022M/XN341
8027M/XM555
8032M/XH837
8033M/XD382
8034M/XL703
8041M/XF690
8043M/XF836
8046M/XL770
8049M/WE168
8050M/XG329
8052M/WH166
8054AM/XM410
8054BM/XM417
8055AM/XM402
8055BM/XM404
8056M/XG337
8057M/XR243
8063M/WT536
8070M/EP120
8072M/PK624
8073M/TB252
8075M/RW382
8078M/XM351
8080M/XM480
8081M/XM468
8082M/XM409
8084M/XM369
8086M/TB752
8092M/WK654
8094M/WT520
8101M/WH984
8102M/WT486
8103M/WR985
8106M/WR982
8114M/WL798
8117M/WR974
8118M/WZ549
8119M/WR971
8121M/XM474
8124M/WZ572
8128M/WH775
8131M/WT507
8140M/XJ571
8142M/XJ560
8147M/XR526
8151M/WV795
8153M/WV903
8154M/WV908
8155M/WV797
8156M/XE339
8158M/XE369
8160M/XD622
8161M/XE993
8162M/WM913
8163M/XP919
8164M/*WN105*/(WF299)
8165M/WH791
8169M/WH364
8173M/XN685
8176M/WH791
8177M/*WM311*/(WM224)
8179M/XN928
8183M/*XN972*/(XN962)
8184M/WT520
8186M/WR977
8187M/WH791
8189M/*WD615* (WD646)
8190M/XJ918
8192M/XR658
8196M/XE920
8198M/WT339
8203M/XD377
8205M/XN819
8206M/WG419
8207M/WD318
8208M/WG303
8209M/WG418
8210M/WG471

8211M/WK570
8213M/WK626
8215M/WP869
8216M/WP927
8218M/WB645
8229M/XM355
8230M/XM362
8234M/XN458
8235M/XN549
8236M/XP573
8237M/XS179
8238M/XS180
8344M/WH960
8350M/WH840
8352M/XN632
8355M/*KG374*/(KN645)
8357M/WK576
8359M/WF825
8361M/WB670
8362M/WG477
8364M/WG464
8365M/XK421
8366M/XG454
8367M/XG474
8368M/XF926
8369M/WE139
8370M/N1671
8371M/XA847
8372M/K8042
8373M/P2617
8375M/NX611
8376M/RF398
8377M/R9125
8378M/*T9707*
8379M/DG590
8380M/Z7197
8382M/VR930
8383M/K9942
8384M/X4590
8385M/N5912
8386M/NV778
8387M/T6296
8388M/XL993
8389M/VX573
8392M/SL674
8394M/WG422
8395M/WF408
8396M/XK740
8399M/WR539
8401M/XP686
8406M/XP831
8407M/XP585
8408M/XS186
8409M/XS209
8410M/XR662
8413M/XM192
8414M/XM173
8417M/XM144
8422M/XM169
8427M/XM172
8429M/XH592
8434M/XM411
8436M/XN554
8437M/WG362
8439M/WZ846
8440M/WD935
8442M/XP411
8453M/XP745
8458M/XP672
8459M/XR650
8460M/XP680
8462M/XX477
8463M/XP355
8464M/XJ758
8465M/W1048
8466M/L-866
8467M/WP912
8468M/MM5701/(BT474)
8470M/584219
8471M/701152
8472M/120227/(VN679)
8473M/WP190
8474M/494083
8475M/360043/(PJ876)
8476M/24
8477M/4101/(DG200)
8478M/10639
8479M/730301
8481M/191614
8482M/112372/(VK893)
8483M/420430
8484M/5439
8485M/997
8486M/BAPC 99
8487M/J-1172
8488M/WL627
8491M/WJ880
8493M/XR571
8494M/XP557
8495M/XR672
8501M/XP640
8502M/XP686
8507M/XS215
8508M/XS218
8509M/XT141
8514M/XS176
8535M/XN776
8538M/XN781
8545M/XN726
8546M/XN728
8548M/WT507
8549M/WT534
8554M/TG511
8561M/XS100
8563M/*XX822*/(XW563)
8565M/*WT720*/(E-408)
8566M/XV279
8570M/XR954
8573M/XM708
8575M/XP542
8576M/XP502
8578M/XR534
8582M/XE874
8583M/BAPC 94
8585M/XE670
8586M/XE643
8588M/XR681
8589M/XR700
8590M/XM191
8591M/XA813
8595M/XH278
8598M/WP270
8600M/XX761
8602M/*PF179*/(XR541)
8606M/XP530
8608M/XP540
8610M/XL502
8611M/WF128
8618M/*XS111*/(XP504)
8620M/XP534
8621M/XR538
8624M/*XR991*/(XS102)
8627M/XP558
8628M/XJ380
8630M/WG362
8631M/XR574
8633M/3W-17/MK732
8634M/WP314
8640M/XR977
8642M/XR537
8645M/XD163
8648M/XK526
8653M/XS120
8655M/XN126
8656M/XP405
8657M/VZ634
8661M/XJ727
8662M/XR458
8666M/XE793
8668M/WJ821
8671M/XJ435
8672M/XP351
8673M/XD165
8676M/XL577
8679M/XF526
8680M/XF527
8681M/XG164
8682M/XP404
8687M/XJ639
8693M/WH863
8696M/WH773
8700M/ZD234
8702M/XG196
8703M/VW453
8706M/XF383
8708M/XF509
8709M/XG209
8710M/XG274
8711M/XG290
8713M/XG225
8718M/XX396
8719M/XT257
8722M/WJ640
8724M/XW923
8726M/XP299
8727M/XR486
8728M/WT532
8729M/WJ815
8733M/XL318
8736M/XF375
8739M/XH170
8740M/WE173
8741M/XW329
8743M/WD790
8746M/XH171
8749M/XH537
8751M/XT255
8753M/WL795
8762M/WH740
8763M/WH665
8764M/XP344
8767M/XX635
8768M/A-522
8769M/A-528
8770M/XL623
8771M/XM602
8772M/WR960
8777M/XX914
8778M/XM598
8779M/XM607
8780M/WK102
8781M/WE982
8782M/XH136
8783M/XW272
8785M/XS642
8789M/XK970
8792M/XP345
8793M/XP346
8794M/XP398
8796M/XK943
8797M/XX947
8799M/WV787
8800M/XG226
8805M/XT772
8807M/XL587
8810M/XJ825
8816M/XX734
8818M/XK527
8820M/VP952
8821M/XX115
8822M/VP957
8828M/XS587
8830M/XF515
8831M/XG160
8832M/*XG168*/(XG172)
8833M/XL569
8834M/*XL571*
8836M/XL592
8838M/*34037*/(429356)
8839M/*69*/(XG194)
8840M/XG252
8841M/XE606
8847M/XX344
8848M/XZ135
8852M/XV337
8853M/XT277
8855M/XT284
8857M/XW544
8858M/XW541
8863M/XG154
8867M/XK532
8868M/WH775
8869M/WH957
8870M/WH964
8871M/WJ565
8873M/XR453
8874M/XE597
8875M/XE624
8876M/*VM791*/(XA312)
8880M/XF435
8881M/XG254
8883M/XX946
8884M/VX275
8885M/XW922
8886M/XA243
8888M/XA231
8889M/XN239
8890M/WT532
8892M/XL618
8895M/XX746
8896M/XX821
8897M/XX969
8898M/XX119
8899M/XX756
8900M/XZ368
8901M/XZ383
8902M/XX739
8903M/XX747
8904M/XX966
8905M/XX975
8906M/XX976
8907M/XZ371
8908M/XZ382
8909M/XV784
8910M/XL160
8911M/XH673
8918M/XX109
8920M/XT469
8921M/XT466
8922M/XT467
8923M/XX819
8924M/XP701
8925M/XP706
8931M/XV779
8932M/XR718
8934M/XR749
8935M/XR713
8937M/XX751
8938M/WV746
8941M/XT456

8942M/XN185
8943M/XE799
8944M/WZ791
8945M/XX818
8946M/XZ389
8947M/XX726
8948M/XX757
8949M/XX743
8950M/XX956
8951M/XX727
8952M/XX730
8953M/XX959
8954M/XZ384
8955M/XX110
8957M/XN582
8958M/XN501
8961M/XS925
8967M/XV263
8969M/XR753
8972M/XR754
8973M/XS922
8974M/XM473
8975M/XW917
8976M/XZ630
8978M/XX837
8983M/XM478
8984M/XN551
8985M/WK127
8986M/XV261
8987M/XM358
8990M/XM419
8995M/XM425
8996M/XM414
8997M/XX669
8998M/XT864
9002M/XW763
9003M/XZ390
9004M/XZ370
9005M/XZ374
9006M/XX967
9007M/XX968
9008M/XX140
9009M/XX763
9010M/XX764
9011M/XM412
9012M/XN494
9014M/XN584
9015M/XW320
9017M/ZE449
9018M/XW365
9019M/XX824
9020M/XX825
9021M/XX826
9022M/XX958
9026M/XP629
9027M/XP556
9028M/XP563
9029M/XS217
9031M/XP688
9032M/XR673
9033M/XS181
9036M/XM350
9038M/XV810
9039M/XN586
9040M/XZ138
9041M/XW763
9042M/XL954
9044M/XS177
9045M/XN636
9046M/XM349
9047M/XW409
9048M/XM403
9049M/XW404
9052M/WJ717
9055M/XT770
9056M/XS488
9059M/ZE360
9061M/XW335
9062M/XW351
9066M/XV582
9067M/XV586
9070M/XV581
9072M/XW768
9073M/XW924
9075M/XV753
9076M/XV808
9078M/XV752
9079M/XZ130
9080M/ZE350
9086M/ZE352
9087M/XX753
9090M/XW353
9091M/XW434
9092M/XH669
9093M/WK124
9095M/XW547
9096M/WV322
9097M/XW366
9098M/XV406
9103M/XV411
9109M/XW312
9110M/XX736
9111M/XW421
9113M/*XV498*
9115M/XV863
9117M/XV161
9118M/XV253
9119M/XW303
9120M/XW419
9122M/XZ997
9123M/XT773
9124M/XW427
9125M/XW410
9126M/XW413
9127M/XW432
9128M/XW292
9129M/XW294
9130M/XW327
9131M/*DD931*
9132M/XX977
9133M/*413573*
9134M/XT288
9136M/XT891
9137M/XN579
9139M/XV863
9140M/XZ287
9141M/XV118
9143M/XN589
9144M/XV353
9145M/XV863
9146M/XW299
9147M/XW301
9148M/XW436
9149M/XW375
9150M/*FX760*
9151M/XT907
9152M/XV424
9153M/XW360
9154M/XW321
9155M/WL679
9162M/XZ991
9163M/XV415
9166M/XW323
9167M/XV744
9168M/XZ132
9169M/XW547
9170M/XZ994
9172M/XW304
9173M/XW418
9174M/XZ131
9175M/P1344
9176M/XW430
9177M/XW328
9179M/XW309
9180M/XW311
9181M/XW358
9185M/XZ987
9187M/XW405
9188M/XW364
9189M/ZD350
9190M/XW318
9191M/XW416
9192M/XW361
9193M/XW367
9194M/XW420
9195M/XW330
9196M/XW370
9197M/*XX530*/(XX637)
9198M/XS641
9199M/XW290
9200M/XW425
9201M/ZD667
9203M/*3066*
9205M/*E449*
9206M/F6314
9207M/8417/18
9208M/F938
9210M/MF628
9211M/733682
9212M/*KL216*/(45-49295)
9213M/N5182
9215M/XL164
9216M/XL190
9218M/XL563
9219M/XZ971
9220M/XZ995
9221M/XZ966
9222M/XZ968
9224M/XL568
9225M/XX885
9226M/XV865
9227M/XB812
9229M/ZA678
9230M/ZA676
9233M/XZ431
9234M/XV864
9236M/WV318
9237M/XF445
9238M/ZA717
9239M/7198/18
9241M/XS639
9242M/XH672
9246M/XS714
9247M/XV420
9248M/WB627
9249M/WV396
9250M/162068
9251M/XX746
9253M/ZA254
9254M/XX965
9255M/XZ375
9257M/XX962
9258M/XW265
9259M/XS710
9260M/XS734
9261M/*W2068*
9262M/XZ358
9263M/XW267
9264M/XS735
9265M/WK585
9266M/XZ119
9267M/XW269
9268M/XR529
9269M/XT914
9270M/XZ145
9272M/XS486
9273M/XS726
9274M/XS738
9275M/XS729
9276M/XS733
9277M/XT601
9278M/XS643
9279M/XT681
9280M/XV804
9281M/XZ146
9282M/XZ101
9283M/XZ322
9284M/ZA267
9285M
9286M
9287M
9288M/XX520
9289M
9290M/XX626
9291M/XX686
9292M/
9293M/
9294M/
9295M/
9296M/
9297M/
9298M/ZE340
9299M
9300M/XX431
9301M
9302M/ZD462
9303M/XV709
9304M
9305M
9306M/XX979
9307M
9308M
9309M
9310M
9311M
9312M
9313M
9314M/ZA320
9315M
9316M
9317M/ZA450
9318M
9319M
9320M
9321M
9322M
9323M
9324M/XV659
9325M/XV710
9326M/XV653
9327M
9328M
9329M
9330M
9331M/XW852
9332M/XZ935
9333M
9334M/ZA322
9335M/ZA375
9336M/ZA407
9337M
9338M
9339M
9340M
9341M
9342M/XR498
9343M/XR506

A pair of Westland Sea King HAS6CRs, XZ580 and XZ922, operateing with 846 Naval Air Squadron.

RN Landing Platform and Shore Station Code-letters

Code	Deck Letters	Vessel Name & Pennant No	Vessel Type & Unit
	AB	HMS *Albion* (L14)	Assault
—	AS	RFA *Argus* (A135)	Aviation Training ship
365/6	AY	HMS *Argyll* (F231)	Type 23 (815 Sqn)
—	BD	RFA *Sir Bedivere* (L3004)	Landing ship
—	BV	RFA *Black Rover* (A273)	Fleet tanker
335	CF	HMS *Cardiff* (D108)	Type 42 (815 Sqn)
350/1	CL	HMS *Cumberland* (F85)	Type 22 (815 Sqn)
348	CM	HMS *Chatham* (F87)	Type 22 (815 Sqn)
388	CT	HMS *Campbeltown* (F86)	Type 22 (815 Sqn)
—	CU	RNAS Culdrose (HMS *Seahawk*)	
412/3	CW	HMS *Cornwall* (F99)	Type 22 (815 Sqn)
—	DC	HMS *Dumbarton Castle* (P265)	Patrol ship
—	DG	RFA *Diligence* (A132)	Maintenance
411	EB	HMS *Edinburgh* (D97)	Type 42 (815 Sqn)
434/5	EE	HMS *Endurance* (A171)	Ice Patrol (815 Sqn)
420	EX	HMS *Exeter* (D89)	Type 42 (815 Sqn)
—	FA	RFA *Fort Austin* (A386)	Support ship
—	FE	RFA *Fort Rosalie* (A385)	Support ship
—	FL	DARA Fleetlands	
410	GC	HMS *Gloucester* (D96)	Type 42 (815 Sqn)
—	GD	RFA *Sir Galahad* (L3005)	Landing ship
—	GT	HMS *Grafton* (F80)	Type 23
—	GV	RFA *Gold Rover* (A271)	Fleet tanker
—	GY	RFA *Grey Rover* (A269)	Fleet tanker
404	IR	HMS *Iron Duke* (F234)	Type 23 (815 Sqn)
425	KT	HMS *Kent* (F78)	Type 23 (815 Sqn)
—	L	HMS *Illustrious* (R06)	Carrier
457	LA	HMS *Lancaster* (F229)	Type 23 (829 Sqn)
—	LC	HMS *Leeds Castle* (P258)	Fishery protection
332	LP	HMS *Liverpool* (D92)	Type 42 (815 Sqn)
363/4	MA	HMS *Marlborough* (F233)	Type 23 (815 Sqn)
360	MC	HMS *Manchester* (D95)	Type 42 (815 Sqn)
415	MM	HMS *Monmouth* (F235)	Type 23 (829 Sqn)
444	MR	HMS *Montrose* (F236)	Type 23 (815 Sqn)
—	N	HMS *Invincible* (R05)	Carrier
372	NL	HMS *Northumberland* (F238)	Type 23 (815 Sqn)
417	NM	HMS *Nottingham* (D91)	Type 42 (815 Sqn)
—	O	HMS *Ocean* (L12)	Helicopter carrier
426	PD	HMS *Portland* (F79)	Type 23 (815 Sqn)
—	R	HMS *Ark Royal* (R07)	Carrier
474	RM	HMS *Richmond* (F239)	Type 23 (815 Sqn)
427	SB	HMS *St Albans* (F83)	Type 23 (815 Sqn)
355	SM	HMS *Somerset* (F82)	Type 23 (815 Sqn)
334	SN	HMS *Southampton* (D90)	Type 42 (815 Sqn)
422	SU	HMS *Sutherland* (F81)	Type 23 (815 Sqn)
—	TM	RFA *Sir Tristram* (L3505)	Landing ship
—	VL	RNAS Yeovilton (HMS *Heron*)	
462	WM	HMS *Westminster* (F237)	Type 23 (829 Sqn)
407	YK	HMS *York* (D98)	Type 42 (815 Sqn)
—	—	HMS *Bulwark* (L15)	Assault
—	—	HMS *Daring* (D32)	Type 45
—	—	HMS *Dauntless* (D33)	Type 45
—	—	HMS *Diamond* (D34)	Type 45
—	—	RFA *Cardigan Bay* (L3009)	Landing ship
—	—	RFA *Fort Victoria* (A387)	Stores ship
—	—	RFA *Fort George* (A388)	Stores ship
—	—	RFA *Largs Bay* (L3006)	Landing ship
—	—	RFA *Lyme Bay* (L3007)	Landing ship
—	—	RFA *Mounts Bay* (L3008)	Landing ship
—	—	RFA *Wave Knight* (A389)	Fleet tanker
—	—	RFA *Wave Ruler* (A390)	Fleet tanker

Painted in admiral's barge colours, this Sea Harrier FA2 ZH809 was flown by 899 NAS in 2004.

Ships' Numeric Code – Deck Letters Analysis

	0	1	2	3	4	5	6	7	8	9
33			LP		SN	CF				
34									CM	
35	CL	CL				SM				
36	MC						AY			
37			NL							
38									CT	
40					IR			YK		
41	GC	EB	CW	CW		MM		NM		
42	EX		SU			KT	PD	SB		
43					EE	EE				
44					MR					
45								LA		
46			WM							
47					RM					

RN Code – Squadron – Base – Aircraft Cross-check

Deck/Base Code Numbers	*Letters*	*Unit*	*Location*	*Aircraft Type(s)*
000 — 006	N	801 Sqn	Yeovilton	Sea Harrier FA2
010 — 020	CU	820 Sqn	Culdrose	Merlin HM1
180 — 182	CU	849 Sqn HQ Flt	Culdrose	Sea King AEW7
183 — 185	N	849 Sqn B Flt	Culdrose	Sea King AEW7
186 — 188	R	849 Sqn A Flt	Culdrose	Sea King AEW7
264 — 274	R	814 Sqn	Culdrose	Merlin HM1
300 — 308	VL	815 Sqn	Yeovilton	Lynx HAS3/HMA8
318 — 319	VL	815 Sqn OEU	Yeovilton	Lynx HMA8
332 — 479	*	815 Sqn	Yeovilton	Lynx HAS3/HMA8
500 — 515	CU	829 Sqn	Culdrose	Merlin HM1
535 — 541	CU	700M OEU	Culdrose	Merlin HM1
560 — 573	CU	750 Sqn	Culdrose	Jetstream T2
576 — 579	-	FONA	Yeovilton	Jetstream T3
580 — 585	CU	824 Sqn	Culdrose	Merlin HM1
630 — 648	VL	702 Sqn	Yeovilton	Lynx HAS3
670 — 676	VL	702 Sqn	Yeovilton	Lynx HMA8
700 — 709	PW	771 Sqn	Prestwick	Sea King HAS6
710 — 719	VL	899 Sqn	Yeovilton	Sea Harrier FA2
720 — 724	VL	899 Sqn	Yeovilton	Harrier T8
730 — 731	VL	899 Sqn	Yeovilton	Sea Harrier FA2
820 — 831	CU	771 Sqn	Culdrose	Sea King HU5/HAS6

*See foregoing separate ships' Deck Letters Analysis
Note that only the 'last two' digits of the Code are worn by some aircraft types, especially helicopters.

Royal Air Force Squadron Markings

This table gives brief details of the markings worn by aircraft of RAF squadrons. While this may help to identify the operator of a particular machine, it may not always give the true picture. For example, from time to time aircraft are loaned to other units while others (such as those with No 4 FTS at Valley) wear squadron marks but are actually operated on a pool basis. Squadron badges are usually located on the front fuselage.

Squadron	*Type(s) operated*	*Base(s)*	*Distinguishing marks & other comments*
No 1 Sqn	Harrier GR7/GR7A/T10	RAF Cottesmore	Badge: A red & white winged number 1 on a white diamond. Tail fin has a red stripe with the badge repeated on it.
No 2 Sqn	Tornado GR4/GR4A	RAF Marham	Badge: A wake knot on a white circular background flanked on either side by black and white triangles. Tail fin has a black stripe with white triangles and the badge repeated on it. Codes are single letters inside a white triangle on the tail.
No 3 Sqn	Harrier GR7/GR7A/T10 Typhoon T1/F2 (from 2006)	RAF Cottesmore	Badge: A blue cockatrice on a white circular background flanked by two green bars edged with yellow. Tail fin has a green stripe edged with yellow.
No 4 Sqn	Harrier GR7/GR7A/T10	RAF Cottesmore	Badge: A yellow lightning flash inside a red and black circle flanked by bars on either side repeating this design. Tail fin has a yellow lightning flash on a red and black stripe.
No 6 Sqn	Jaguar GR3/T2A	RAF Coltishall	Badge: A red winged can opener inside a circle edged in red. Tail has a light blue bar with red diagonal lines. Aircraft are coded E*.
No 7 Sqn	Chinook HC2/ Gazelle AH1	RAF Odiham	Badge (on tail): A blue badge containing the seven stars of Ursa Major ('The Plough') in yellow. Aircraft are coded E*. Aircraft pooled with No 18 Sqn and No 27 Sqn.
No 8 Sqn	Sentry AEW1	RAF Waddington	Badge (on tail): A grey, sheathed, Arabian dagger. Aircraft pooled with No 23 Sqn.
No 9 Sqn	Tornado GR4	RAF Marham	Badge: A green bat on a black circular background, flanked by yellow and green horizontal stripes. The green bat also appears on the tail, edged in yellow. Aircraft are coded A*.
No 10 Sqn	VC10 C1K	RAF Brize Norton	Badge (on tail): A yellow arrow with red wings.
No 11 Sqn	Tornado F3 (Disbanding 10/05)	RAF Leeming	Roundel is superimposed over a yellow diamond on a black background. Badge (on tail): Two black eagles in flight.
No 12 Sqn	Tornado GR4	RAF Lossiemouth	Roundel is superimposed on a green chevron. Tail fin has a black & white horizontal stripe with the squadron badge, a fox's head on a white circle, in the middle. Aircraft are coded F*.
No 13 Sqn	Tornado GR4/GR4A	RAF Marham	A yellow lightning flash on a green and blue background on the nose. Badge (on tail): A lynx's head over a dagger on a white shield.

Squadron	Type(s) operated	Base(s)	Distinguishing marks & other comments
No 14 Sqn	Tornado GR4	RAF Lossiemouth	Badge: A red cross on a white circle, with wings either side, flanked by blue diamonds on a white background. The blue diamonds are repeated horizontally across the tail. Aircraft are coded B*.
No 15(R) Sqn [NTOCU]	Tornado GR4	RAF Lossiemouth	Roman numerals XV appear in white on the tail. Aircraft are either coded T* or TA*.
No 16(R) Sqn	Jaguar GR3A/T4 (Disbanding 03/05)	RAF Coltishall	Badge: Two keys crossed on a black circle. On the tail is a black circle containing the 'Saint' emblem from the 60's TV series.
No 17(R) Sqn [TOEU]	Typhoon T1/F2	Warton	Badge (on tail): A gauntlet on a black and white shield. Roundel is flanked by two white bars which have a pair of jagged black lines running along them horizontally. Aircraft are coded A*.
No 18 Sqn	Chinook HC2	RAF Odiham	Badge (on tail): A red winged horse on a black circle. Aircraft are coded B*. Aircraft pooled with No 7 Sqn and No 27 Sqn.
No 19(R) Sqn	Hawk T1/T1A/T1W	RAF Valley	Badge (on tail): A fish flanked by two wings on a yellow circle. Aircraft also carry black and white checks either side of the roundel on the fuselage. Aircraft pooled with No 208(R) Sqn; part of No 4 FTS.
No 20(R) Sqn [HOCU]	Harrier GR7/GR7A/T10	RAF Wittering	Badge: An eagle in a white circle flanked by a white stripe on a blue background. On the tail is a stripe made up of black, yellow, green and red triangles.
No 22 Sqn	Sea King HAR3/HAR3A	A Flt: RMB Chivenor B Flt: Wattisham C Flt: RAF Valley	Badge: A black pi symbol in front of a white Maltese cross on a red circle.
No 23 Sqn	Sentry AEW1	RAF Waddington	Badge (on tail): A red eagle preying on a yellow falcon. Aircraft pooled with No 8 Sqn.
No 24 Sqn	Hercules C1/C3/C4/C5	RAF Lyneham	No squadron markings carried. Aircraft pooled with No 30 Sqn, No 47 Sqn, No 57(R) Sqn and No 70 Sqn.
No 25 Sqn	Tornado F3	RAF Leeming	Badge (on tail): A hawk on a gauntlet.
No 27 Sqn	Chinook HC2	RAF Odiham	Badge (on tail): An dark green elephant on a green circle, flanked by green and dark green stripes. Aircraft pooled with No 7 Sqn and No 18 Sqn.
No 28 Sqn	Merlin HC3	RAF Benson	Badge: A winged horse above white two crosses on a red shield.
No 29 Sqn [TOCU]	Typhoon T1/F2	Warton	Badge (on tail): An eagle in flight, preying on a buzzard, with three red Xs across the top. The roundel is flanked by two white bars outlined by a red line, each containing three red Xs. Aircraft are coded B*.
No 30 Sqn	Hercules C1/C3/C4/C5	RAF Lyneham	No squadron markings carried. Aircraft pooled with No 24 Sqn, No 47 Sqn, No 57(R) Sqn and No 70 Sqn.

RAF Squadron Markings

Squadron	*Type(s) operated*	*Base(s)*	*Distinguishing marks & other comments*
No 31 Sqn	Tornado GR4	RAF Marham	Badge: A gold, five-pointed star on a yellow circle flanked by yellow and green checks. The star is repeated on the tail. Aircraft are coded D*.
No 32 (The Royal) Sqn	BAe 125 CC3/146 CC2/ Twin Squirrel HCC1	RAF Northolt	No squadron markings carried but aircraft carry a distinctive livery with a blue flash along the middle of the fuselage and a red tail.
No 33 Sqn	Puma HC1	RAF Benson	Badge: A stag's head.
No 39 (1 PRU) Sqn	Canberra PR9/T4	RAF Marham	Badge (on tail): A winged bomb on a light blue circle. Aircraft are coded A*.
No 41 Sqn	Jaguar GR3A/T4	RAF Coltishall	Badge: A red, double armed cross, flanked by red and white horizontal stipes. Stripes repeated on tail. Aircraft are coded F*.
No 42(R) Sqn [NOCU]	Nimrod MR2	RAF Kinloss	No squadron markings usually carried. Aircraft pooled with No 120 Sqn, No 201 Sqn and No 206 Sqn.
No 43 Sqn	Tornado F3	RAF Leuchars	Badge (on tail): A black and red gamecock in a band of black and white squares.
No 45(R) Sqn	Raytheon Beech Super King Air B200	RAF Cranwell	No squadron markings usually carried. Part of No 3 FTS.
No 47 Sqn	Hercules C1/C3/C4/C5	RAF Lyneham	No squadron markings usually carried. Aircraft pooled with No 24 Sqn, 30 Sqn, No 57(R) Sqn and No 70 Sqn.
No 51 Sqn	Nimrod R1	RAF Waddington	Badge (on tail): A red goose in flight.
No 54 Sqn	JaguarGR3A/T4	RAF Coltishall	Badge: A blue lion on a yellow shield, flanked by blue and yellow checks. A stripe of blue and yellow checks also appears on the tail. Aircraft are coded G*.
No 55(R) Sqn	Dominie T1	RAF Cranwell	Badge (on tail): A blue fist holding an arrow on a white circle. Part of No 3 FTS.
No 56(R) Sqn [F3OCU]	Tornado F3	RAF Leuchars	Badge (on tail): A gold phoenix rising from red flames. The tail fin has a stripe made up of red and white checks.
No 60(R) Sqn	Griffin HT1	RAF Shawbury [DHFS] & RAF Valley [SARTU]	No squadron markings usually carried.
No 70 Sqn	Hercules C1/C3/C4/C5	RAF Lyneham	No squadron markings usually carried. Aircraft pooled with No 24 Sqn, No 30 Sqn and No 47 Sqn.
No 72(R) Sqn	Tucano T1	RAF Linton-on-Ouse	Badge: A black swift in flight on a red disk, flanked by blue bars edged with red. The blue bars edged with red also flank the roundel on the fuselage; part of No 1 FTS
No 78 Sqn	Chinook HC2/ Sea King HAR3	RAF Mount Pleasant	Badge: A yellow, heraldic tiger with two tails, on a black circle. The badge appears on the tail of the Chinook and by the cockpit on the Sea King.
No 84 Sqn	Griffin HAR2	RAF Akrotiri	Badge (on tail): A scorpion on a playing card symbol (diamonds, clubs etc.). Aircraft carry a vertical blue stripe through the roundel on the fuselage.

Squadron	Type(s) operated	Base(s)	Distinguishing marks & other comments
No 99 Sqn	Globemaster III	RAF Brize Norton	Badge (on tail): A black puma leaping.
No 100 Sqn	Hawk T1/T1A	RAF Leeming	Badge (on tail): A skull in front of two bones crossed. Aircraft are usually coded C*. Incorporates the Joint Forward Air Control Training and Standards Unit (JFACTSU)
No 101 Sqn	VC10 K3/K4	RAF Brize Norton	Badge (on tail): A lion behind a castle turret.
No 111 Sqn	Tornado F3	RAF Leuchars	Badge (on tail): A cross in front of crossed swords on a light grey circle, flanked by a stripe of darker grey.
No 120 Sqn	Nimrod MR2	RAF Kinloss	No squadron markings usually carried. Aircraft pooled with No 42(R) Sqn, No 201 Sqn and No 206 Sqn.
No 201 Sqn	Nimrod MR2	RAF Kinloss	No squadron markings usually carried. Aircraft pooled with No 42(R) Sqn, No 120 Sqn and No 206 Sqn.
No 202 Sqn	Sea King HAR3	A Flt: RAF Boulmer D Flt: RAF Lossiemouth E Flt: RAF Leconfield	Badge: A mallard alighting on a white circle.
No 203(R) Sqn	Sea King HAR3	RAF St Mawgan	Badge: A green sea horse on a white circle.
No 206 Sqn	Nimrod MR2	RAF Kinloss	No squadron markings usually carried. Aircraft pooled with No 42(R) Sqn, No 120 Sqn and No 201 Sqn.
No 207(R) Sqn	Tucano T1	RAF Linton-on-Ouse	Badge: A red winged lion on a white disk. The roundel on the fuselage is flanked by red bars edged with yellow; part of No 1 FTS
No 208(R) Sqn	Hawk T1/T1A/T1W	RAF Valley	Badge (on tail): A Sphinx inside a white circle, flanked by flashes of yellow. Aircraft also carry blue and yellow bars either side of the roundel on the fuselage and a blue and yellow chevron on the nose. Aircraft pooled with No 19(R) Sqn; part of No 4 FTS.
No 216 Sqn	TriStar K1/KC1/C2/C2A	RAF Brize Norton	Badge (on tail): An eagle in flight with a bomb in its claws.
No 230 Sqn	Puma HC1	RAF Aldergrove	Badge: A tiger in front of a palm tree on a black pentagon.
No 617 Sqn	Tornado GR4	RAF Lossiemouth	Badge: Dam breached, flanked on either side by red lightning flashes on a black background. Tail fin is black with a red lightning flash. Aircraft are coded AJ-*.
No 1312 Flt	VC10 K3/K4 / Hercules C1/C3	RAF Mount Pleasant, FI	Badge (on tail): A red Maltese cross on a white Hercules (LTW) circle, flanked by red and white horizontal bars.
No 1435 Flt	Tornado F3	RAF Mount Pleasant, FI	Badge (on tail): A red Maltese cross on a white circle, flanked by red and white horizontal bars.
No 1563 Flt	Puma HC1 / Chinook HC2	Basrah, Iraq	No squadron markings carried. Part of Joint Helicopter Force (Iraq).

University Air Squadrons/ Air Experience Flights

UAS aircraft carry squadron badges and markings, usually on the tail. Squadron crests all consist of a white circle surrounded by a blue circle, topped with a red crown and having a yellow scroll beneath. Each differs by the motto on the scroll, the UAS name running around the blue circle and by the contents at the centre and it is the latter which are described below. All AEFs come under the administration of local UASs and these are listed here.

UAS	*Base(s)*	*Marks*
Aberdeen, Dundee & St Andrews UAS	RAF Leuchars	A red lion holding a stone turret between its paws above a crown.
University of Birmingham AS/No 8 AEF	RAF Cosford	A blue griffon with two heads.
Bristol UAS/No 3 AEF	RAF Colerne	A sailing ship on water.
Cambridge UAS/No 5 AEF	RAF Wyton	A heraldic lion in front of a red badge.
East Lowlands UAS/ No 12 AEF	RAF Leuchars	An open book in front of a white diagonal cross edged in blue.
East Midlands Universities AS/No 7 AEF	RAF Cranwell	A yellow quiver, full of arrows.
Universities of Glasgow No 4 AEF/ Strathclyde AS	Glasgow	A bird of prey in flight, holding a branch in its beak, in front of an upright sword.
Liverpool UAS	RAF Woodvale	A bird atop an open book, holding a branch in its beak.
University of London AS/No 6 AEF	RAF Wyton	A globe superimposed over an open book.
Manchester and Salford Universities AS/ No 10 AEF	RAF Woodvale	A bird of prey with a green snake in its beak.
Northumbrian Universities AS/No 11 AEF	RAF Leeming	A white cross on a blue background.
Oxford UAS	RAF Benson	An open book in front of crossed swords.
Southampton UAS/No 2 AEF No 2 AEF	Boscombe Down	A red stag in front of a stone pillar.
University of Wales AS/No 1 AEF	DARA St Athan	A red Welsh dragon in front of an open book, clasping a sword. Some aircraft have the dragon in front of white and green squares.
Yorkshire Universities AS/No 9 AEF	RAF Church Fenton	An open book in front of a Yorkshire rose with leaves,

Fleet Air Arm Squadron Markings

This table gives brief details of the markings worn by aircraft of FAA squadrons. Squadron badges, when worn, are usually located on the front fuselage. All FAA squadron badges comprise a crown atop a circle edged in gold braid and so the badge details below list only what appears in the circular part.

Squadron	*Type(s) operated*	*Base(s)*	*Distinguishing marks & other comments*
No 700M OEU	Merlin HM1	RNAS Culdrose	Badge: A pair of gold scales on a background of blue and white waves, flanked by two bees.
No 702 Sqn	Lynx HAS3/HMA8	RNAS Yeovilton	Badge: A Lynx rearing up in front of a circle comprising alternate dark blue and white sectors.
No 727 Sqn	Heron/Tutor	Plymouth	Badge: The head of Britannia wearing a gold helmet on a background of blue and white waves.
No 750 Sqn	Jetstream T2	RNAS Culdrose	Badge: A Greek runner bearing a torch & sword on a background of blue and white waves.
No 771 Sqn	Sea King HU5/HAS6	RNAS Culdrose & Prestwick	Badge: Three bees on a background of blue and white waves.
No 801 Sqn	Sea Harrier FA2	RNAS Yeovilton	Badge: A winged trident on a white background. On the tail is a white winged trident and there are black & white checks upon the rudder.
No 814 Sqn	Merlin HM1	RNAS Culdrose	Badge: A winged tiger mask on a background of dark blue and white waves.
No 815 Sqn	Lynx HAS3/HMA8	RNAS Yeovilton	Badge: A winged, gold harpoon on a background of blue and white waves.
No 820M Sqn	Merlin HM1	RNAS Culdrose	Badge: A flying fish on a background of blue and white waves.
No 824 Sqn	Merlin HM1	RNAS Culdrose	Badge: A heron on a background of blue and white waves.
No 829 Sqn	Merlin HM1	RNAS Culdrose	Badge: A kingfisher hovering on a background of blue and white waves
No 845 Sqn	Sea King HC4	RNAS Yeovilton	Badge: A dragonfly on a background of blue and white waves.
No 846 Sqn	Sea King HC4	RNAS Yeovilton	Badge: A swordsman riding a winged horse whilst attacking a serpent on a background of blue and white waves. Aircraft are usually coded V*.
No 847 Sqn	Gazelle AH1 & Lynx AH7	RNAS Yeovilton	Badge: A gold sea lion on a blue background.
No 848 Sqn	Sea King HC4	RNAS Yeovilton	Badge: Inside a red circle, a hawk in flight with a torpedo in its claws above white and blue waves. Aircraft are usually coded W*.
No 849 Sqn	Sea King AEW7	RNAS Culdrose	Badge: A winged streak of lightning with an eye in front on a background of blue and white waves.
No 899 Sqn	Harrier T8 & Sea Harrier FA2	RNAS Yeovilton	Badge: A winged gauntlet on a background of blue and white waves beneath a cloudy sky. On the tail is a winged gauntlet edged in black.

Historic Aircraft in Overseas Markings

Some *historic, classic and warbird* aircraft carry the markings of overseas air arms and can be seen in the UK, mainly preserved in museums and collections or taking part in air shows.

Notes	*Serial*	*Type (other identity)*	*Owner/operator, location*
	ARGENTINA		
	-	Bell UH-1H Iroquois (AE-406/ *998-8888*) [Z]	RAF Valley, instructional use
	0729	Beech T-34C Turbo Mentor	FAA Museum, stored RNAS Yeovilton
	0767	Aermacchi MB339AA	Rolls-Royce Heritage Trust, stored Derby
	A-515	FMA IA58 Pucara (ZD485)	RAF Museum, Cosford
	A-517	FMA IA58 Pucara (G-BLRP)	Privately owned, Channel Islands
	A-522	FMA IA58 Pucara (8768M)	FAA Museum, at NE Aircraft Museum, Usworth
	A-528	FMA IA58 Pucara (8769M)	Norfolk & Suffolk Avn Museum, Flixton
	A-533	FMA IA58 Pucara (ZD486) <ff>	Boscombe Down Museum
	A-549	FMA IA58 Pucara (ZD487)	Imperial War Museum, Duxford
	AE-409	Bell UH-1H Iroquois [656]	Museum of Army Flying, Middle Wallop
	AE-422	Bell UH-1H Iroquois	FAA Museum, stored RNAS Yeovilton
	AUSTRALIA		
	A2-4	Supermarine Seagull V (VH-ALB)	RAF Museum, Hendon
	A16-199	Lockheed Hudson IIIA (G-BEOX) [SF-R]	RAF Museum, Hendon
	A17-48	DH82A Tiger Moth (G-BPHR)	Privately owned, Netherthorpe
	A19-144	Bristol 156 Beaufighter XIc (JM135/A8-324)	The Fighter Collection, Duxford
	A79-808	DH115 Vampire T33	De Havilland Aviation, Swansea
	A92-480	GAF Jindivik 4A (A92-LLAN-1)	QinetiQ Llanbedr, on display
	A92-664	GAF Jindivik 4A	Privately owned, Llanbedr
	A92-708	GAF Jindivik 4A	Bristol Aero Collection, stored Kemble
	N6-766	DH115 Sea Vampire T22 (XG766/ G-SPDR)	De Havilland Aviation, Swansea
	BELGIUM		
	FT-36	Lockheed T-33A	Dumfries & Galloway Avn Mus, Dumfries
	H-50	Noorduyn AT-16 Harvard IIB (OO-DAF)	Privately owned, Brasschaat, Belgium
	HD-75	Hanriot HD1 (G-AFDX)	RAF Museum, Hendon
	IF-68	Hawker Hunter F6 <ff>	Privately owned, Market Drayton
	K-16	Douglas C-53D Skytrooper (OT-CWG/N49G)	Air Dakota, Brussels, Belgium
	L-44	Piper L-18C Super Cub (OO-SPQ)	BSD Aeroclub FBA, Bierset, Belgium
	L-47	Piper L-18C Super Cub (OO-SPG)	BSD Aeroclub FBA, Bierset, Belgium
	L-57	Piper L-18C Super Cub (OO-GDH)	BSD Aeroclub FBA, Bierset, Belgium
	L-156	Piper L-18C Super Cub (OO-LGB)	BSD Aeroclub FBA, Bierset, Belgium
	V-18	Stampe SV-4B (OO-GWD)	Antwerp Stampe Centre, Antwerp-Deurne, Belgium
	V-29	Stampe SV-4B (OO-GWB)	Antwerp Stampe Centre, Antwerp-Deurne, Belgium
	BOLIVIA		
	FAB184	SIAI-Marchetti SF.260W (G-SIAI)	Privately owned, Booker
	BOTSWANA		
	OJ1	BAC Strikemaster 83 (ZG805/ G-BXFU)	Global Aviation, Humberside
	BRAZIL		
	1317	Embraer T-27 Tucano	Shorts, Belfast (engine test bed)
	BURKINA FASO		
	BF-8431	SIAI-Marchetti SF.260 (G-NRRA) [31]	Privately owned, Oaksey Park
	CANADA		
	622	Piasecki HUP-3 Retriever (51-16622/N6699D)	The Helicopter Museum, Weston-super-Mare

Serial	Type (other identity)	Owner/operator, location	Notes
920	VS Stranraer (CF-BXO) [Q-N]	RAF Museum, Hendon	
3349	NA64 Yale (G-BYNF)	Privately owned, Duxford	
5450	Hawker Hurricane XII (G-TDTW)	Hawker Restorations Ltd, Milden	
5487	Hawker Hurricane II (G-CBOE)	Privately owned, Thruxton	
9754	Consolidated PBY-5A Catalina (VP-BPS) [P]	Privately owned, Lee-on-Solent	
9893	Bristol 149 Bolingbroke IVT	Imperial War Museum store, Duxford	
9940	Bristol 149 Bolingbroke IVT	Royal Scottish Mus'm of Flight, E Fortune	
15195	Fairchild PT-19A Cornell	RAF Museum Reserve Collection, Stafford	
16693	Auster J/1N Alpha (G-BLPG) [693]	Privately owned, Clacton	
18013	DHC1 Chipmunk 22 (G-TRIC) [013]	The Shuttleworth Collection, Old Warden	
18393	Avro Canada CF-100 Canuck 4B (G-BCYK)	Imperial War Museum, Duxford	
18671	DHC1 Chipmunk 22 (WP905/ 7438M/G-BNZC) [671]	Privately owned, Old Warden	
20310	CCF T-6J Harvard IV (G-BSBG) [310]	Privately owned, Tatenhill	
21261	Lockheed T-33A-N Silver Star (G-TBRD)	Golden Apple Operations/OFMC, Duxford	
21417	Canadair CT-133 Silver Star	Yorkshire Air Museum, Elvington	
23140	Canadair CL-13 Sabre [AX] <rf>	Midland Air Museum, Coventry	
23380	Canadair CL-13 Sabre <rf>	RAF Millom Museum, Haverigg	
FJ777	Boeing-Stearman PT-13D Kaydet(42-17786/G-BRTK)	Privately owned, Old Warden	

CHINA

Serial	Type (other identity)	Owner/operator, location	Notes
2632016	Nanchang CJ-6A Chujiao (G-BXZB) (also wears *2632019*)	Privately owned, Hibaldstow	
2751219	Nanchang CJ-6A Chujiao (G-BVVG) [68]	Privately owned, White Waltham	

CZECH REPUBLIC

Serial	Type (other identity)	Owner/operator, location	Notes
3677	Letov S-102 (MiG-15) (613677)	Royal Scottish Mus'm of Flight, E Fortune	
3794	Letov S-102 (MiG-15) (623794)	Imperial War Museum, stored Duxford	
9147	Mil Mi-4	The Helicopter Museum, Weston-super-Mare	

DENMARK

Serial	Type (other identity)	Owner/operator, location	Notes
A-011	SAAB A-35XD Draken	Privately owned, Grainthorpe, Lincs	
AR-107	SAAB S-35XD Draken	Newark Air Museum, Winthorpe	
E-402	Hawker Hunter F51	Farnborough Air Sciences Trust, Farnborough	
E-419	Hawker Hunter F51	North-East Aircraft Museum, Usworth	
E-420	Hawker Hunter F51 (G-9-442)	Privately owned, Walton-on-Thames	
E-421	Hawker Hunter F51	Brooklands Museum, Weybridge	
E-423	Hawker Hunter F51 (G-9-444)	SWWAPS, Lasham	
E-424	Hawker Hunter F51 (G-9-445)	Aeroventure, Doncaster	
ET-272	Hawker Hunter T7 <ff>	Boulton Paul Association, Wolverhampton	
ET-273	Hawker Hunter T7 <ff>	Aeroventure, Doncaster	
K-682	Douglas C-47A Skytrain (OY-BPB)	Foreningen For Flyvende Mus, Vaerløse, Denmark	
L-866	Consolidated PBY-6A Catalina (8466M)	RAF Museum, Cosford	
R-756	Lockheed F-104G Starfighter	Midland Air Museum, Coventry	
S-881	Sikorsky S-55C	The Helicopter Museum, Weston-super-Mare	
S-882	Sikorsky S-55C	Paintball Adventure West, Lulsgate	
S-887	Sikorsky S-55C	Privately owned, Marksbury, Somerset	

ECUADOR

Serial	Type (other identity)	Owner/operator, location	Notes
FAE259	BAC Strikemaster 80 (G-UPPI) [T59]	Privately owned, Swansea	

EGYPT

Serial	Type (other identity)	Owner/operator, location	Notes
764	Mikoyan MiG-21SPS <ff>	Privately owned, Northampton	
771	WS61 Sea King 47 (WA.826)	RN AESS, *HMS Sultan*, Gosport	
773	WS61 Sea King 47 (WA.823)	RN AESS, *HMS Sultan*, Gosport	
774	WS61 Sea King 47 (WA.822)	RN AESS, *HMS Sultan*, Gosport	
775	WS61 Sea King 47 (WA.824)	RN AESS, *HMS Sultan*, Gosport	
776	WS61 Sea King 47 (WA.825)	RN AESS, *HMS Sultan*, Gosport	
0446	Mikoyan MiG-21UM <ff>	Thameside Aviation Museum, Tilbury	
7907	Sukhoi Su-7 <ff>	Robertsbridge Aviation Society, Mayfield	

Notes	*Serial*	*Type (other identity)*	*Owner/operator, location*
	FINLAND		
	GN-101	Folland Gnat F1 (XK741)	Midland Air Museum, Coventry
	VI-3	Valtion Viima 2 (OO-EBL)	Privately owned, Brasschaat, Belgium
	FRANCE		
	1/4513	Spad XIII <R> (G-BFYO/*S3398*)	American Air Museum, Duxford
	06	Dewoitine D27 (290/F-AZJD)	The Old Flying Machine Company, Duxford
	20	MH1521C1 Broussard (G-BWGG) [315-SQ]	Privately owned, Rednal
	37	Nord 3400 (G-ZARA) [MAB]	Privately owned, Boston
	57	Dassault Mystère IVA [8-MT]	Imperial War Museum, Duxford
	67	SNCAN 1101 Noralpha (F-GMCY) [CY]	Privately owned, la Ferté-Alais, France
	70	Dassault Mystère IVA	Midland Air Museum, Coventry
	78	Nord 3202 (G-BIZK)	Privately owned, Little Snoring
	79	Dassault Mystère IVA [2-EG]	Norfolk & Suffolk Avn Museum, Flixton
	82	Curtiss Hawk 75 (G-CCVH)	The Fighter Collection, Duxford
	83	Dassault Mystère IVA [8-MS]	Newark Air Museum, Winthorpe
	83	Morane-Saulnier MS.733 Alcyon (F-AZKS)	Privately owned, Montlucon, France
	84	Dassault Mystère IVA [8-NF]	Lashenden Air Warfare Museum, Headcorn
	85	Dassault Mystère IVA [8-MV]	British Aviation Heritage, Bruntingthorpe
	101	Dassault Mystère IVA [8-MN]	Bomber County Aviation Museum, Hemswell
	104	MH1521M Broussard (F-GHFG) [307-FG]	Privately owned, France
	105	Nord N2501F Noratlas (F-AZVM) [62-SI]	Le Noratlas de Provence, Aix les Milles, France
	121	Dassault Mystère IVA	City of Norwich Aviation Museum
	128	Morane-Saulnier MS.733 Alcyon (F-BMMY)	Privately owned, St Cyr, France
	143	Morane-Saulnier MS733 Alcyon (G-MSAL)	The Squadron, North Weald
	146	Dassault Mystère IVA [8-MC]	North-East Aircraft Museum, Usworth
	185	MH1521M Broussard (G-BWLR)	Privately owned, Glos
	282	Dassault MD311 Flamant (F-AZFX) [316-KY]	Memorial Flt Association, la Ferté-Alais, France
	316	MH1521M Broussard (F-GGKR) [315-SN]	The Old Flying Machine Company, Duxford
	318	Dassault Mystère IVA [8-NY]	Dumfries & Galloway Avn Mus, Dumfries
	319	Dassault Mystère IVA [8-ND]	Rebel Air Museum, Andrewsfield
	354	Morane-Saulnier MS315E-D2 (G-BZNK)	Privately owned, Hemswell
	538	Dassault Mirage IIIE [3-QH]	Yorkshire Air Museum, Elvington
	1058	SO1221 Djinn (FR108) [CDL]	The Helicopter Museum, Weston-super-Mare
	17473	Lockheed T-33A	Midland Air Museum, Coventry
	42157	NA F-100D Super Sabre [11-ML]	North-East Aviation Museum, Usworth
	63938	NA F-100F Super Sabre [11-MU]	Lashenden Air Warfare Museum, Headcorn
	121748	Grumman F8F-2P Bearcat (F-AZRJ) [5834/P]	Privately owned, Anemasse, France
	125716	Douglas AD-4N Skyraider (F-AZFN) [22-DG]	Privately owned, Etampes, France
	126965	Douglas AD-4NA Skyraider (OO-FOR)	Privately owned, Braaschaat, Belgium
	133704	CV F4U-7 Corsair (125541/ F-AZYS)	Privately owned, Cuers, France
	141406	Douglas C-47A Skytrain (F-AZTE) [E]	Privately owned, la Ferté-Alais, France
	517545	NA T-28S Fennec (N14113) [CD-113]	Privately owned, Duxford
	517692	NA T-28S Fennec (F-AZFV/ G-TROY) [142]	Privately owned, Duxford
	18-5395	Piper L-18C Super Cub (52-2436/ G-CUBJ) [CDG]	Privately owned, Breighton
	C850	Salmson 2A2 <R>	Barton Aviation Heritage Society, Barton
	MS824	Morane-Saulnier Type N <R> (G-AWBU)	Privately owned, Compton Abbas

Serial	Type (other identity)	Owner/operator, location	Notes
GERMANY			
-	Fieseler Fi103R-IV (V-1) (BAPC 91)	Lashenden Air Warfare Museum, Headcorn	
-	Focke-Achgelis Fa330A-1 (8469M)	RAF Museum, Cosford	
-	Fokker Dr1 Dreidekker <R> (G-BVGZ)	Privately owned, Breighton	
-	Fokker Dr1 Dreidekker <R> (BAPC 88)	FAA Museum, RNAS Yeovilton	
-	Messerschmitt Bf109 <R> (*6357*/ BAPC 74) [6]	Kent Battle of Britain Museum, Hawkinge	
1	Hispano HA 1.112M1L Buchon (C4K-102/G-BWUE)	Privately owned, Breighton	
3	SNCAN 1101 Noralpha (G-BAYV)	Barton Aviation Heritage Society, Barton	
6	Messerschmitt Bf109G-2/Trop (10639/8478M/G-USTV)	RAF Museum, Hendon	
8	Focke Wulf Fw190 <R> (G-WULF)	Privately owned, Halfpenny Green	
9	Focke Wulf Fw190 <R> (G-CCFW)	Privately owned, Kemble	
14	Messerschmitt Bf109 <R> (BAPC 67)	Kent Battle of Britain Museum, Hawkinge	
14	SNCAN 1101 Noralpha (G-BSMD)	Privately owned, Prestwick	
152/17	Fokker Dr1 Dreidekker <R> (G-ATJM)	Privately owned, East Garston, Bucks	
210/16	Fokker EIII (BAPC 56)	Science Museum, South Kensington	
214	SPP Yak C-11 (G-DYAK)	Classic Aviation Company, Hannover, Germany	
422/15	Fokker EIII <R> (G-AVJO)	Privately owned, Compton Abbas	
425/17	Fokker Dr1 Dreidekker <R> (BAPC 133)	Kent Battle of Britain Museum, Hawkinge	
626/8	Fokker DVII <R> (N6268)	Blue Max Movie Aircraft Museum, Booker	
764	Mikoyan MiG-21SPS <ff>	Privately owned, Booker	
959	Mikoyan MiG-21SPS	Midland Air Museum, Coventry	
1190	Messerschmitt Bf109E-3 [4]	Imperial War Museum, Duxford	
1480	Messerschmitt Bf109 <R> (BAPC 66) [6]	Kent Battle of Britain Museum, Hawkinge	
1801/18	Bowers Fly Baby 1A (G-BNPV)	Privately owned, Chessington	
1803/18	Bowers Fly Baby 1A (G-BUYU)	Privately owned, Chessington	
1983	Messerschmitt Bf109E-3 (G-EMIL)	Privately owned, Surrey	
2088	Fieseler Fi156A Storch (G-STCH)	Privately owned, Surrey	
2100	Focke-Wulf Fw189A-1 (G-BZKY) [V7+1H]	Privately owned, Sandown	
3523	Messerschmitt Bf109E-7	Privately owned, Lancing	
4101	Messerschmitt Bf109E-3 (DG200/ 8477M) [12]	RAF Museum, Hendon	
4477	CASA 1.131E Jungmann (G-RETA) [GD+EG]	The Shuttleworth Collection, Old Warden	
6234	Junkers Ju87R-4 (G-STUK)	Privately owned, Surrey	
7198/18	LVG CVI (G-AANJ/9239M)	RAF Museum, Hendon	
7485	Messerschmitt Bf109F-4	Charleston Aviation Services, Colchester	
8147	Messerschmitt Bf109F-4	Charleston Aviation Services, Colchester	
8417/18	Fokker DVII (9207M)	RAF Museum, Hendon	
12802	Antonov An-2T (D-FOFM)	Privately owned, Lahr, Germany	
15458	Messerschmitt Bf109F-4	Charleston Aviation Services, Colchester	
100143	Focke-Achgelis Fa330A-1	Imperial War Museum, Duxford	
100502	Focke-Achgelis Fa330A-1	The Real Aeroplane Company, Breighton	
100509	Focke-Achgelis Fa330A-1	Science Museum, stored Wroughton	
100545	Focke-Achgelis Fa330A-1	Fleet Air Arm Museum, stored RNAS Yeovilton	
100549	Focke-Achgelis Fa330A-1	Lashenden Air Warfare Museum, Headcorn	
110451	Fieseler Fi156D Storch (G-STOR)	Privately owned, Surrey	
112372	Messerschmitt Me262A-2a (AM.51/VK893/8482M) [4]	RAF Museum, Hendon	
120227	Heinkel He162A-2 Salamander (VN679/AM.65/8472M) [2]	RAF Museum, Hendon	
120235	Heinkel He162A-1 Salamander (AM.68)	Imperial War Museum, Lambeth	
191316	Messerschmitt Me163B Komet	Science Museum, South Kensington	
191454	Messerschmitt Me163B Komet <R> (BAPC 271)	The Shuttleworth Collection, Old Warden	
191614	Messerschmitt Me163B Komet (8481M)	RAF Museum Restoration Centre, Cosford	
191659	Messerschmitt Me163B Komet (8480M) [15]	Royal Scottish Mus'm of Flight, E Fortune	

Notes	Serial	Type (other identity)	Owner/operator, location
	191660	Messerschmitt Me163B Komet (AM.214) [3]	Imperial War Museum, Duxford
	211028	Focke Wulf Fw190D-9 (G-DORA)	Privately owned, Surrey
	280020	Flettner Fl282/B-V20 Kolibri (frame only)	Midland Air Museum, Coventry
	360043	Junkers Ju88R-1 (PJ876/8475M) [D5+EV]	RAF Museum, Hendon
	420430	Messerschmitt Me410A-1/U2 (AM.72/8483M) [3U+CC]	RAF Museum, Cosford
	475081	Fieseler Fi156C-7 Storch (VP546/ AM.101/7362M)[GM+AK]	RAF Museum, Cosford
	494083	Junkers Ju87D-3 (8474M) [RI+JK]	RAF Museum, Hendon
	584219	Focke Wulf Fw190F-8/U1 (AM.29/8470M) [38]	RAF Museum, Hendon
	701152	Heinkel He111H-23 (8471M) [NT+SL]	RAF Museum, Hendon
	730301	Messerschmitt Bf110G-4 (AM.34/ 8479M) [D5+RL]	RAF Museum, Hendon
	733682	Focke Wulf Fw190A-8/R7 (AM.75/ 9211M)	Imperial War Museum, Lambeth
	2+1	Focke Wulf Fw190 <R> (G-SYFW) [7334]	Privately owned, Guernsey, CI
	22+35	Lockheed F-104G Starfighter	SWWAPS, Lasham
	22+57	Lockheed F-104G Starfighter	Privately owned, Grainthorpe, Lincs
	2E+RA	Fieseler Fi-156C-2 Storch (NX436FS)	Privately owned, North Weald
	4+1	Focke Wulf Fw190 <R> (G-BSLX)	Privately owned, Norwich
	4V+GH	Amiot AAC1/Ju52 (Port.AF 6316) [9]	Imperial War Museum, Duxford
	6G+ED	Slepcev Storch (G-BZOB) [5447]	Privately owned, Little Gransden
	58+89	Dornier Do28D-2 Skyservant (D-ICDY)	Moosreiner Consulting, Hamburg, Germany
	96+21	Mil Mi-24D (406)	Imperial War Museum, Duxford
	96+26	Mil Mi-24D (429)	The Helicopter Museum, Weston-super-Mare
	97+04	Putzer Elster B (G-APVF)	Privately owned, Breighton
	98+14	Sukhoi Su-22M-4	The Old Flying Machine Company, stored Scampton
	99+24	NA OV-10B Bronco (F-AZKM)	Privately owned, Montelimar, France
	99+26	NA OV-10B Bronco (G-BZGL)	Privately owned, Duxford
	99+32	NA OV-10B Bronco (G-BZGK)	Privately owned, Duxford
	AZ+JU	CASA 3.52L (F-AZJU)	Amicale J-B Salis, la Ferté-Alais, France
	BU+CC	CASA 1.131E Jungmann (G-BUCC)	Privately owned, Goodwood
	BU+CK	CASA 1.131E Jungmann (G-BUCK)	Privately owned, White Waltham
	CC+43	Pilatus P-2 (G-CJCI)	Privately owned, Norwich
	CF+HF	Morane-Saulnier MS502 (EI-AUY)	Imperial War Museum, Duxford
	CW+BG	CASA 1.131E Jungmann (G-BXBD) [50,483]	Privately owned, Kemble
	D5397/17	Albatros DVA <R> (G-BFXL)	FAA Museum, RNAS Yeovilton
	ES+BH	Messerschmitt Bf108B-2 (D-ESBH)	Messerschmitt Stiftung, Germany
	FI+S	Morane-Saulnier MS505 (G-BIRW)	Royal Scottish Mus'm of Flight, E Fortune
	FM+BB	Messerschmitt Bf109G-6 (D-FMBB)	Messerschmitt Stiftung, Germany
	GL+SU	Bücker Bü181B-1 Bestmann (G-GLSU)	Privately owned, Surrey
	JA+120	Canadair CL-13 Sabre 4 (MM19607)	Privately owned
	KG+EM	Nord 1002 (G-ETME)	Privately owned, Booker
	LG+03	Bücker Bü133C Jungmeister (G-AEZX)	Privately owned, Milden
	LG+0I	Bücker Bü133C Jungmeister (G-AYSJ)	The Fighter Collection, Duxford
	NJ+C11	Nord 1002 (G-ATBG)	Privately owned, Sutton Bridge
	S4+A07	CASA 1.131E Jungmann (G-BWHP)	Privately owned, Yarcombe, Devon
	S5+B06	CASA 1.131E Jungmann 2000 (G-BSFB)	Privately owned, Stretton, Cheshire
	TA+RC	Morane-Saulnier MS505 (G-BPHZ)	Historic Aircraft Collection, Duxford
	GHANA		
	G-102	SA122 Bulldog	Privately owned, Hurstbourne Tarrant
	G-108	SA122 Bulldog (G-BCUP)	Privately owned, Hurstbourne Tarrant

Serial	Type (other identity)	Owner/operator, location	Notes
GREECE			
51-6171	NA F-86D Sabre	North-East Aircraft Museum, Usworth	
52-6541	Republic F-84F Thunderflash [541]	North-East Aircraft Museum, Usworth	
63-8418	Northrop F-5A	Martin-Baker Ltd, Chalgrove, Fire Section	
HONG KONG			
HKG-5	SA128 Bulldog (G-BULL)	Privately owned, Old Sarum	
HKG-6	SA128 Bulldog (G-BPCL)	Privately owned, North Weald	
HKG-11	Slingsby T.67M Firefly 200 (G-BYRY)	Privately owned, Tibenham	
HKG-13	Slingsby T.67M Firefly 200 (G-BXKW)	Privately owned, Tibenham	
HUNGARY			
501	Mikoyan MiG-21PF	Imperial War Museum, Duxford	
INDIA			
Q497	EE Canberra T4 (WE191) (fuselage)	Dumfries & Galloway Avn Mus, Dumfries	
INDONESIA			
LL-5313	BAe Hawk T53	BAE Systems, Brough	
IRAQ			
333	DH115 Vampire T55 <ff>	Aeroventure, Doncaster	
ITALY			
MM5701	Fiat CR42 (BT474/8468M) [13-95]	RAF Museum, Hendon	
MM52801	Fiat G46-3B (G-BBII) [4-97]	Privately owned, Sandown	
MM53692	CCF T-6G Texan	RAeS Medway Branch, Rochester	
MM53774	Fiat G59-4B (I-MRSV) [181]	Privately owned, Parma, Italy	
MM54099	NA T-6G Texan (G-BRBC) [RR-56]	Privately owned, Chigwell	
MM54-2372	Piper L-21B Super Cub	Privately owned, Kesgrave, Suffolk	
W7	Avia FL3 (G-AGFT)	Privately owned, Sandtoft	
JAPAN			
-	Yokosuka MXY 7 Ohka II (BAPC 159)	Defence School, Chattenden	
24	Kawasaki Ki100-1B (8476M/ BAPC 83)	RAF Museum, Hendon	
3685	Mitsubishi A6M3-2 Zero	Imperial War Museum, Duxford	
5439	Mitsubishi Ki46-III (8484M/ BAPC 84)	RAF Museum, Cosford	
15-1585	Yokosuka MXY 7 Ohka II (BAPC 58)	Science Museum, at FAA Museum, RNAS Yeovilton	
997	Yokosuka MXY 7 Ohka II (8485M/ BAPC 98)	Gr Manchester Mus of Science & Industry	
I-13	Yokosuka MXY 7 Ohka II (8486M/ BAPC 99)	RAF Museum, Cosford	
JORDAN			
408	SA125 Bulldog (G-BDIN)	Privately owned, RAF Wittering	
417	SA125A Bulldog (G-CCZE)	Privately owned, RAF Wittering	
418	SA125A Bulldog (G-CCZF)	Privately owned, RAF Wittering	
420	SA125 Bulldog (G-DISA)	Privately owned, RAF Wittering	
MEXICO			
EPC-152	Mudry/CAARP CAP-10B (G-CCXC) [52]	Privately owned, Hatch	
MYANMAR			
UB424	VS361 Spitfire IX (UB425)	Historic Flying Ltd, Duxford	
UB441	VS361 Spitfire IX (ML119)	Privately owned, Rochester	
NETHERLANDS			
16-218	Consolidated PBY-5A Catalina (2459/PH-PBY)	Neptune Association, Lelystad, The Netherlands	
174	Fokker S-11 Instructor (E-31/ G-BEPV)	Privately owned, Elstree	
204	Lockheed SP-2H Neptune [V]	RAF Museum, Cosford	
A-12	DH82A Tiger Moth (PH-TYG)	Privately owned, Gilze-Rijen, The Netherlands	

Notes	Serial	Type (other identity)	Owner/operator, location
	B-64	Noorduyn AT-16 Harvard IIB (PH-LSK)	Privately owned, Gilze-Rijen, The Netherlands
	B-71	Noorduyn AT-16 Harvard IIB (PH-MLM)	Privately owned, Gilze-Rijen, The Netherlands
	B-118	Noorduyn AT-16 Harvard IIB (PH-IIB)	Privately owned, Gilze-Rijen, The Netherlands
	E-14	Fokker S-11 Instructor (PH-AFS)	Privately owned, Lelystad, The Netherlands
	E-15	Fokker S-11 Instructor (G-BIYU)	Privately owned, Bagby
	E-18	Fokker S-11 Instructor (PH-HTC)	Dukes of Brabant AF, Eindhoven, The Netherlands
	E-20	Fokker S-11 Instructor (PH-GRB)	Privately owned, Gilze-Rijen, The Netherlands
	E-27	Fokker S-11 Instructor (PH-HOL)	Privately owned, Lelystad, The Netherlands
	E-32	Fokker S-11 Instructor (PH-HOI)	Privately owned, Gilze-Rijen, The Netherlands
	E-36	Fokker S-11 Instructor (PH-ACG)	Privately owned, Lelystad, The Netherlands
	E-39	Fokker S-11 Instructor (PH-HOG)	Privately owned, Lelystad, The Netherlands
	G-29	Beech D18S (N5369X)	KLu Historic Flt, Gilze-Rijen, The Netherlands
	MK732	VS 361 Spitfire LF IXC (8633M/ PH-OUQ) [3W-17]	KLu Historic Flight, Lelystad, The Netherlands
	N-202	Hawker Hunter F6 [10] <ff>	Privately owned, Eaglescott
	N-250	Hawker Hunter F6 (G-9-185) <ff>	Imperial War Museum, Duxford
	N-268	Hawker Hunter FGA78 (Qatar QA-10)	Yorkshire Air Museum, Elvington
	N-315	Hawker Hunter T7 (XM121)	Jet Avn Preservation Grp, Long Marston
	N5-149	NA B-25J Mitchell (44-29507/ *HD346*/N320SQ) [232511]	Duke of Brabant AF, Eindhoven, The Netherlands
	R-55	Piper L-18C Super Cub (52-2466/ G-BLMI)	Privately owned, White Waltham
	R-109	Piper L-21B Super Cub (54-2337/ PH-GAZ)	Privately owned, Gilze-Rijen, The Netherlands
	R-122	Piper L-21B Super Cub (54-2412/ PH-PPW)	Privately owned, Gilze-Rijen, The Netherlands
	R-137	Piper L-21B Super Cub (54-2427/ PH-PSC)	Privately owned, Gilze-Rijen, The Netherlands
	R-151	Piper L-21B Super Cub (54-2441/ G-BIYR)	Privately owned, Dunkeswell
	R-156	Piper L-21B Super Cub (54-2446/ G-ROVE)	Privately owned, Headcorn
	R-163	Piper L-21B Super Cub (54-2453/ G-BIRH)	Privately owned, Lee-on-Solent
	R-167	Piper L-21B Super Cub (54-2457/ G-LION)	Privately owned, Turweston, Bucks
	R-177	Piper L-21B Super Cub (54-2467/ PH-KNR)	Privately owned, Gilze-Rijen, The Netherlands
	R-181	Piper L-21B Super Cub (54-2471/ PH-GAU)	Privately owned, Gilze-Rijen, The Netherlands
	R-345	Piper J-3C Cub (PH-UCS)	Privately owned, The Netherlands
	S-9	DHC2 L-20A Beaver (PH-DHC)	KLu Historic Flt, Gilze-Rijen, The Netherlands
	NEW ZEALAND		
	NZ3909	WS Wasp HAS1 (XT782)	Kennet Aviation, North Weald
	NZ6361	BAC Strikemaster 87 (OJ5/ G-BXFP)	Privately owned, Chalgrove
	NORTH KOREA		
	-	WSK Lim-2 (MiG-15) (01420/ G-BMZF)	FAA Museum, RNAS Yeovilton
	NORTH VIETNAM		
	1211	WSK Lim-5 (MiG-17F) (G-MIGG)	Privately owned, Bournemouth
	NORWAY		
	423/427	Gloster Gladiator I (L8032/ G-AMRK/*N2308*)	The Shuttleworth Collection, Old Warden
	848	Piper L-18C Super Cub (LN-ACL) [FA-N]	Privately owned, Norway

Serial	Type (other identity)	Owner/operator, location	Notes
56321	SAAB S91B Safir (G-BKPY) [U-AB]	Newark Air Museum, Winthorpe	
OMAN			
853	Hawker Hunter FR10 (XF426)	RAF Museum, Hendon	
POLAND			
05	WSK SM-2 (Mi-2) (1005)	The Helicopter Museum, Weston-super-Mare	
309	WSK SBLim-2A (MiG-15UTI) <ff>	Royal Scottish Mus'm of Flight, E Fortune	
408	WSK-PZL Mielec TS-11 Iskra (1H-0408)	Midland Air Museum, Coventry	
1018	WSK-PZL Mielec TS-11 Iskra (1H-1018/G-ISKA)	Privately owned, Bruntingthorpe	
1120	WSK Lim-2 (MiG-15bis)	RAF Museum, Cosford	
PORTUGAL			
85	Isaacs Fury II (G-BTPZ)	Privately owned, Ormskirk	
1360	OGMA/DHC1 Chipmunk T20 (G-BYYU) (fuselage)	Privately owned, Little Staughton	
1365	OGMA/DHC1 Chipmunk T20 (G-DHPM)	Privately owned, Spanhoe Lodge	
1372	OGMA/DHC1 Chipmunk T20 (HB-TUM)	Privately owned, Switzerland	
1377	DHC1 Chipmunk 22 (G-BARS)	Privately owned, Yeovilton	
1741	CCF Harvard IV (G-HRVD)	Privately owned, Bruntingthorpe	
1747	CCF T-6J Harvard IV (*20385*/ G-BGPB)	The Aircraft Restoration Co, Duxford	
QATAR			
QA12	Hawker Hunter FGA78 <ff>	Privately owned, Cwmbran	
QP30	WS Lynx Mk 28 (G-BFDV/TD 013)	Army SEAE, Arborfield	
QP31	WS Lynx Mk 28	DARA Fleetlands Apprentice School	
QP32	WS Lynx Mk 28 (TD 016)	AAC Stockwell Hall, Middle Wallop	
RUSSIA (& FORMER SOVIET UNION)			
-	Mil Mi-24V (3532424810853)	Privately owned, Hawarden	
-	Mil Mi-24D (3532464505029)	BAE Systems, Rochester	
1	SPP Yak C-11 (G-BZMY)	Privately owned, North Weald	
01	Yakovlev Yak-52 (9311709/ G-YKSZ)	Privately owned, White Waltham	
02	Yakovlev Yak-52 (888615/G-CBLJ)	Privately owned, North Weald	
2	Yakovlev Yak-18T (RA-02933)	Privately owned, Wickenby	
2	Yakovlev Yak-52 (9311708/ G-YAKS)	Privately owned, North Weald	
03	Mil Mi-24D (3532461715415)	Privately owned, Hawarden	
03	Yakovlev Yak-9UM (0470403/ F-AZYJ)	Privately owned, Dijon, France	
03	Yakovlev Yak-52 (899803/ G-YAKR)	Privately owned, North Weald	
04	Yakovlev Yak-52 (9211612/ RA-22521)	Privately owned, Wellesbourne Mountford	
05	Yakovlev Yak-50 (832507/YL-CBH)	Privately owned, Hawarden	
07	Mikoyan MiG-23ML (024003607)	Newark Air Museum, Winthorpe	
07	WSK SM-1 (Mi-1) (Czech. 2007)	The Helicopter Museum, Weston-super-Mare	
07	Yakovlev Yak-18M (G-BMJY)	Privately owned, East Garston, Bucks	
09	Yakovlev Yak-52 (9411809/ G-BVMU)	Privately owned, Shipdham	
9	Polikarpov Po-2 (ZK-POZ)	The Shuttleworth Collection, Old Warden	
10	Yakovlev Yak-50 (801810/G-BTZB)	Privately owned, Abingdon/Halton	
10	Yakovlev Yak-52 (822710/ G-CBMD)	Privately owned, Headcorn	
11	SPP Yak C-11 (G-YCII)	Privately owned, Duxford	
12	LET L-29 Delfin (194555/ ES-YLM/G-DELF)	Privately owned, Manston	
14	Yakovlev Yak-52 (899404/ G-CCCP)	Privately owned, Navestock	
18	LET L-29S Delfin (591771/YL-PAF)	Privately owned, Hawarden	
19	Yakovlev Yak-52 (811202/YL-CBI)	Privately owned, Hawarden	
20	Lavochkin La-11	The Fighter Collection, Duxford	
20	Yakovlev Yak-52 (790404/YL-CBJ)	Privately owned, Hawarden	
23	Mikoyan MiG-27D (83712515040)	Privately owned, Hawarden	

Notes	*Serial*	*Type (other identity)*	*Owner/operator, location*
	26	Yakovlev Yak-52 (9111306/ G-BVXK)	Privately owned, White Waltham
	27	SPP Yak C-11 (G-OYAK)	Privately owned, North Weald
	31	Yakovlev Yak-52 (9111311/ G-YAKV)	Privately owned, Rendcomb
	33	Yakovlev Yak-50 (853206/G-YAKZ)	Privately owned, Compton Abbas
	35	Sukhoi Su-17M-3 (25102)	Privately owned, Hawarden
	36	LET/Yak C-11 (G-KYAK)	Privately owned, North Weald
	36	SPP Yak C-11 (G-IYAK)	Privately owned, Sleap
	42	Yakovlev Yak-52 (833901/G-LENA)	Privately owned, Compton Abbas
	43	Yakovlev Yak-52 (877601/ G-BWSV)	Privately owned, North Weald
	46	Yakovlev Yak-50 (825905/ G-GYAK)	Privately owned, North Weald
	48	Yakovlev Yak-52 (9111413/ G-CBSN)	Privately owned, Manston
	49	Yakovlev Yak-50 (822305/ G-YAKU)	Privately owned, Compton Abbas
	50	Yakovlev Yak-50 (812101/ G-CBPM)	Privately owned, High Cross
	50	Yakovlev Yak-50 (822305/ G-BXNO)	Privately owned, Denham
	50	Yakovlev Yak-52 (9111415/ G-CBRW)	Privately owned, White Waltham
	51	LET L-29S Delfin (491273/YL-PAG)	Privately owned, Hawarden
	52	Yakovlev Yak-52 (800708/ G-CBPY)	Privately owned, Sherburn-in-Elmet
	52	Yakovlev Yak-52 (878202/ G-BWVR)	Privately owned, Barton
	54	Sukhoi Su-17M (69004)	Privately owned, Hawarden
	55	Yakovlev Yak-52 (9111505/ G-BVOK)	Intrepid Aviation, North Weald
	56	Yakovlev Yak-52 (811504)	Privately owned, Hawarden
	56	Yakovlev Yak-52 (9111506/ RA-44516)	Privately owned, White Waltham
	61	Yakovlev Yak-50 (842710/ G-YAKM)	Privately owned, Compton Abbas
	66	Yakovlev Yak-52 (855905/ G-YAKN)	Privately owned, Compton Abbas
	67	Yakovlev Yak-52 (822013/ G-CBSL)	Privately owned, Leicester
	69	Hawker Hunter FGA9 (8839M/ XG194)	RAF North Luffenham Training Area
	69	Yakovlev Yak-52 (855509/LY-ALS)	Privately owned, Little Gransden
	69	Yakovlev Yak-52 (888712/ G-CCSU)	Privately owned,
	69	Yakovlev Yak-52 (899413/ G-XYAK)	Privately owned, Compton Abbas
	71	Mikoyan MiG-27M (61912507006)	Newark Air Museum, Winthorpe
	72	Yakovlev Yak-52 (9111608/ G-BXAV)	Privately owned, Halfpenny Green
	74	Yakovlev Yak-52 (877404/ G-LAOK) [JA-74, IV-62]	Privately owned, Tollerton
	74	Yakovlev Yak-52 (888802/G-BXID)	Privately owned, Kemble
	93	Yakovlev Yak-50 (853001/G-JYAK)	Privately owned, North Weald
	96	Yakovlev Yak-55M (901103/ G-YKSS)	Privately owned, Headcorn
	98	Yakovlev Yak-52 (888911/ G-CBRU)	Privately owned, Rochester
	100	Yakovlev Yak-52 (866904/G-YAKI)	Privately owned, Popham
	101	Yakovlev Yak-52 (866915/ G-CDBW)	Privately owned, Rochester
	112	Yakovlev Yak-52 (822610/LY-AFB)	Privately owned, Little Gransden
	139	Yakovlev Yak-52 (833810/ G-BWOD)	Privately owned, Sywell
	503	Mikoyan MiG-21SMT (G-BRAM)	Farnborough Air Sciences Trust, Farnborough
	1342	Yakovlev Yak-1 (G-BTZD)	Privately owned, St Leonards-on-Sea
	1-12	Yakovlev Yak-52 (9011013/ RA-02293)	Privately owned, Halfpenny Green
	1870710	Ilyushin Il-2 (G-BZVW)	Privately owned, Sandtoft
	1878576	Ilyushin Il-2 (G-BZVX)	Privately owned, Sandtoft
	(RK858)	VS361 Spitfire LF IX	The Fighter Collection, Duxford

Serial	Type (other identity)	Owner/operator, location	Notes
(SM639)	VS361 Spitfire LF IX	Privately owned, Catfield	
SAUDI ARABIA			
1112	BAC Strikemaster 80 (G-FLYY)	Privately owned, Hawarden	
1120	BAC Strikemaster 80A	Privately owned, Hawarden	
1125	BAC Strikemaster 80A	Privately owned, Bentwaters	
1133	BAC Strikemaster 80A (G-BESY)	Imperial War Museum, Duxford	
1206	AB.206A JetRanger	Privately owned, Shoreham	
1207	AB.206A JetRanger	Privately owned, Shoreham	
55-713	BAC Lightning T55 (ZF598)	Midland Air Museum, Coventry	
SOUTH AFRICA			
91	Westland Wasp HAS1 (pod)	Privately owned, Oaksey Park	
92	Westland Wasp HAS1 (G-BYCX)	Privately owned, Chiseldon	
221	DH115 Vampire T55 <ff>	Privately owned, Hemel Mempstead	
6130	Lockheed Ventura II (AJ469)	RAF Museum, stored Cosford	
7429	NA AT-6D Harvard III (D-FASS)	Privately owned, Germany	
SOUTH VIETNAM			
24550	Cessna L-19E Bird Dog (G-PDOG) [GP]	Privately owned, Lincs	
SPAIN			
B.2I-27	CASA 2.111B (He111H-16) (B.2I-103)	Imperial War Museum, stored Duxford	
C.4E-88	Messerschmitt Bf109E	Privately owned, East Garston, Bucks	
E.3B-114	CASA 1.131E Jungmann (G-BJAL)	Privately owned, Breighton	
E.3B-143	CASA 1.131E Jungmann (G-JUNG)	Privately owned, White Waltham	
E.3B-153	CASA 1.131E Jungmann (G-BPTS) [781-75]	Privately owned, Duxford	
E.3B-336	CASA 1.131E Jungmann (G-BUTA)	Privately owned, Breighton	
E.3B-350	CASA 1.131E Jungmann (G-BHPL) [05-97]	Privately owned, Kemble	
(E.3B-369)	CASA 1.131E Jungmann (G-BPDM) [781-32]	Privately owned, Heighington	
E.3B-521	CASA 1.131E Jungmann [781-3]	RAF Museum, Hendon	
EM-01	DH60G Moth (G-AAOR)	Privately owned, Rendcomb	
ES.1-4	Bücker Bü133 Jungmeister	Privately owned, Breighton	
ES.1-16	CASA 1.133L Jungmeister	Privately owned, Stretton, Cheshire	
SWEDEN			
081	CFM 01 Tummelisa <R> (SE-XIL)	Privately owned, Karlstad, Sweden	
05108	DH60 Moth	Privately owned, Langham	
17239	SAAB B-17A (SE-BYH) [7-J]	Flygvapenmuseum, Linköping, Sweden	
28693	DH100 Vampire FB6 (J-1184/ SE-DXY) [9-G]	Scandinavian Historic Flight, North Weald	
29640	SAAB J-29F [20-08]	Midland Air Museum, Coventry	
29670	SAAB J-29F (SE-DXB) [10-R]	Flygvapenmuseum/F10 Wing, Angelholm, Sweden	
32028	SAAB 32A Lansen (G-BMSG)	Privately owned, Cranfield	
34066	Hawker Hunter F58 (J-4089/ SE-DXA) [9-G]	Scandinavian Historic Flight, North Weald	
35075	SAAB J-35J Draken [40]	Imperial War Museum, Duxford	
35515	SAAB J-35F Draken [49]	Irvin-GQ, Llangeinor	
A14	Thulin A/Bleriot XI (SE-XMC)	Privately owned, Karlstad, Sweden	
SWITZERLAND			
A-10	CASA 1.131E Jungmann (G-BECW)	Privately owned, Rochester	
A-12	Bücker Bu131B Jungmann (G-CCHY)	Privately owned, Booker	
A-50	CASA 1.131E Jungmann (G-CBCE)	Privately owned, Breighton	
A-57	CASA 1.131E Jungmann (G-BECT)	Privately owned, Goodwood	
A-125	Pilatus P-2 (G-BLKZ)	Privately owned, Duxford	
A-701	Junkers Ju52/3m (HB-HOS)	Ju-Air, Dubendorf, Switzerland	
A-702	Junkers Ju52/3m (HB-HOT)	Ju-Air, Dubendorf, Switzerland	
A-703	Junkers Ju52/3m (HB-HOP)	Ju-Air, Dubendorf, Switzerland	
A-806	Pilatus P3-03 (G-BTLL)	Privately owned, stored Headcorn	
C-552	EKW C-3605 (G-DORN)	Privately owned, Bournemouth	
C-558	EKW C-3605	Privately owned, Spanhoe	
J-1008	DH100 Vampire FB6	Mosquito Aircraft Museum, London Colney	
J-1172	DH100 Vampire FB6 (8487M)	RAF Museum Reserve Collection, Stafford	
J-1573	DH112 Venom FB50 (G-VICI)	Source Classic Jet Flight, Bournemouth	

Notes	Serial	Type (other identity)	Owner/operator, location
	J-1605	DH112 Venom FB50 (G-BLID)	Gatwick Aviation Museum, Charlwood, Surrey
	J-1629	DH112 Venom FB50	Air Atlantique Classic Flight, Coventry
	J-1632	DH112 Venom FB50 (G-VNOM)	Kennet Aviation, North Weald
	J-1649	DH112 Venom FB50	Air Atlantique Classic Flight, Coventry
	J-1704	DH112 Venom FB54	RAF Museum, Cosford
	J-1712	DH112 Venom FB54 <ff>	North West Aviation Heritage, Hooton Park
	J-1758	DH112 Venom FB54 (N203DM)	Privately owned, stored North Weald
	J-4015	Hawker Hunter F58 (J-4040/ HB-RVS)	Privately owned, Altenrhein, Switzerland
	J-4021	Hawker Hunter F58 (G-HHAC)	Hawker Hunter Aviation Ltd, Scampton
	J-4031	Hawker Hunter F58 (G-BWFR)	Hawker Hunter Aviation Ltd, Scampton
	J-4058	Hawker Hunter F58 (G-HHAD)	Hawker Hunter Aviation Ltd, Scampton
	J-4066	Hawker Hunter F58 (G-HHAE)	Hawker Hunter Aviation Ltd, Scampton
	J-4072	Hawker Hunter F58 (G-HHAB)	Hawker Hunter Aviation Ltd, Scampton
	J-4081	Hawker Hunter F58 (G-HHAF)	Hawker Hunter Aviation Ltd, Scampton
	J-4083	Hawker Hunter F58 (G-EGHH)	Privately owned, Bournemouth
	J-4086	Hawker Hunter F58 (HB-RVU)	Privately owned, Altenrhein, Switzerland
	J-4090	Hawker Hunter F58 (G-SIAL)	The Old Flying Machine Company, Scampton
	J-4091	Hawker Hunter F58	British Aviation Heritage, Bruntingthorpe
	J-4201	Hawker Hunter T68 (HB-RVR)	Privately owned, Altenrhein, Switzerland
	J-4205	Hawker Hunter T68 (HB-RVP)	Privately owned, Altenrhein, Switzerland
	U-80	Bücker Bü133D Jungmeister (G-BUKK)	Privately owned, Kendford
	U-99	Bücker Bü133C Jungmeister (G-AXMT)	Privately owned, Breighton
	U-110	Pilatus P-2 (G-PTWO)	Privately owned, Earls Colne
	V-54	SE3130 Alouette II (G-BVSD)	Privately owned, Glos
	USA		
	-	Noorduyn AT-16 Harvard IIB (KLu B-168)	American Air Museum, Duxford
	001	Ryan ST-3KR Recruit (G-BYPY)	Privately owned, Duxford
	14	Boeing-Stearman A75N-1 Kaydet (G-ISDN)	Privately owned, Kemble
	23	Fairchild PT-23 (N49272)	Privately owned, RAF Cosford
	27	NA SNJ-7 Texan (90678/G-BRVG)	Privately owned, Goodwood
	43	Noorduyn AT-16 Harvard IIB (43-13064/G-AZSC) [SC]	Privately owned, North Weald
	44	Boeing-Stearman D75N-1 Kaydet (42-15852/G-RJAH)	Privately owned, Rendcomb
	49	Curtiss P-40M Kittyhawk (43-5802/ G-KITT/*P8196*)	The Fighter Collection, Duxford
	85	WAR P-47 Thunderbolt <R> (G-BTBI)	Privately owned, Perth
	112	Boeing-Stearman PT-13D Kaydet (42-17397/G-BSWC)	Privately owned, Staverton
	379	Boeing-Stearman PT-13D Kaydet (42-14865/G-ILLE)	Privately owned, Tibenham
	441	Boeing-Stearman N2S-4 Kaydet (30010/G-BTFG)	Privately owned, Manston
	540	Piper L-4H Grasshopper (43-29877/G-BCNX)	Privately owned, Monewden
	578	Boeing-Stearman N2S-5 Kaydet (N1364V)	Privately owned, North Weald
	628	Beech D17S (44-67761/N18V)	Privately owned, stored East Garston, Bucks
	718	Boeing-Stearman PT-13D Kaydet (42-17555/N5345N)	Privately owned, Tibenham
	744	Boeing-Stearman A75N-1 Kaydet (42-16532/OO-USN)	Privately owned, Wevelgem, Belgium
	854	Ryan PT-22 Recruit (42-17378/ G-BTBH)	Privately owned, Old Warden
	855	Ryan PT-22 Recruit (41-15510/ N56421)	Privately owned, RAF Cosford
	897	Aeronca 11AC Chief (G-BJEV) [E]	Privately owned, English Bicknor, Glos
	1102	Boeing-Stearman N2S-5 Kaydet (G-AZLE)	Privately owned, Tongham
	1164	Beech D18S (G-BKGL)	The Aircraft Restoration Co, Duxford
	1180	Boeing-Stearman N2S-3 Kaydet (3403/G-BRSK)	Privately owned, Morley

Serial	*Type (other identity)*	*Owner/operator, location*	*Notes*
2807	NA T-6G Texan (49-3072/G-BHTH) [V-103]	Privately owned, Shoreham	
6136	Boeing-Stearman A75N-1 Kaydet (42-16136/G-BRUJ) [205]	Privately owned, Liverpool	
6771	Republic F-84F Thunderstreak (BAF FU-6)	RAF Museum, stored Cosford	
7797	Aeronca L-16A (47-0797/G-BFAF)	Privately owned, Finmere	
8084	NA AT-6D Harvard III (42-85068/ LN-AMY)	The Old Flying Machine Company, Duxford	
8178	NA F-86A Sabre (48-0178/ G-SABR) [FU-178]	Golden Apple Operations/ARC, Duxford	
8242	NA F-86A Sabre (48-0242) [FU-242]	American Air Museum, Duxford	
01532	Northrop F-5E Tiger II <R>	RAF Alconbury on display	
02538	Fairchild PT-19B (N33870)	Privately owned, Greenham Common	
07539	Boeing-Stearman N2S-3 Kaydet (N63590) [143]	Privately owned, Billericay	
14286	Lockheed T-33A (51-4286)	American Air Museum, Duxford	
O-14419	Lockheed T-33A (51-4419)	Midland Air Museum, Coventry	
14863	NA AT-6D Harvard III (41-33908/ G-BGOR)	Privately owned, Rednal	
15154	Bell OH-58A Kiowa (70-15154)	R. Military College of Science, Shrivenham	
15445	Piper L-18C Super Cub (51-15445/ G-BLGT)	Privately owned, Dunkeswell	
15990	Bell AH-1F Hueycobra (67-19590)	Museum of Army Flying, stored Middle Wallop	
16445	Bell AH-1F Hueycobra (69-16445)	R. Military College of Science, Shrivenham	
16506	Hughes OH-6A Cayuse (67-16506)	The Helicopter Museum, Weston-super-Mare	
16579	Bell UH-1H Iroquois (66-16579)	The Helicopter Museum, Weston-super-Mare	
16718	Lockheed T-33A (51-6718)	City of Norwich Aviation Museum	
17962	Lockheed SR-71A (64-17962)	American Air Museum, Duxford	
18263	Boeing-Stearman PT-17 Kaydet (41-8263/N38940) [822]	Privately owned, Tibenham	
19252	Lockheed T-33A (51-9252)	Tangmere Military Aviation Museum	
20249	Noorduyn AT-16 Harvard IIB (PH-KLU) [XS-249]	Privately owned, Lelystad, The Netherlands	
21605	Bell UH-1H Iroquois (72-21605)	American Air Museum, Duxford	
21714	Grumman F8F-2P Bearcat (121714/G-RUMM) [201-B]	The Fighter Collection, Duxford	
24538	Kaman HH-43F Huskie (62-4535)	Midland Air Museum, Coventry	
24541	Cessna L-19E Bird Dog (F-GFVE)	Privately owned, Redhill	
24568	Cessna L-19E Bird Dog (LN-WNO)	Army Aviation Norway, Kjeller, Norway	
28521	CCF Harvard IV (G-TVIJ) [TA-521]	Privately owned, Woodchurch, Kent	
30861	NA TB-25J Mitchell (44-30861/ N9089Z)	Privately owned, North Weald	
31145	Piper L-4B Grasshopper (43-1145/ G-BBLH) [26-G]	Privately owned, Biggin Hill	
31171	NA B-25J Mitchell (44-31171/ N7614C)	American Air Museum, Duxford	
31430	Piper L-4B Grasshopper (43-1430/ G-BHVV)	Privately owned, Rochester	
31952	Aeronca O-58B Defender (G-BRPR)	Privately owned, Earls Colne	
34037	NA TB-25N Mitchell (44-29366/ N9115Z/8838M)	RAF Museum, Hendon	
37414	McD F-4C Phantom (63-7414)	Midland Air Museum, Coventry	
39624	Wag Aero Sport Trainer (G-BVMH) [39-D]	Privately owned, Temple Bruer	
40467	Grumman F6F-5K Hellcat (80141/ G-BTCC) [19]	The Fighter Collection, Duxford	
41386	Thomas-Morse S4 Scout <R> (G-MJTD)	Privately owned, Lutterworth	
42165	NA F-100D Super Sabre (54-2165) [VM]	American Air Museum, Duxford	
42174	NA F-100D Super Sabre (54-2174) [UH]	Midland Air Museum, Coventry	
42196	NA F-100D Super Sabre (54-2196)	Norfolk & Suffolk Avn Museum, Flixton	
46214	Grumman TBM-3E Avenger (69327/CF-KCG) [X-3]	American Air Museum, Duxford	
48846	Boeing B-17G Fortress (44-8846/ F-AZDX) [DS-M]	Assoc Fortresse Toujours Volant, Paris, France	

Notes	Serial	Type (other identity)	Owner/operator, location
	53319	Grumman TBM-3R Avenger (G-BTDP) [319-RB]	Privately owned, North Weald
	54433	Lockheed T-33A (55-4433)	Norfolk & Suffolk Avn Museum, Flixton
	54439	Lockheed T-33A (55-4439)	North-East Aircraft Museum, Usworth
	58811	NA B-25J Mitchell (45-8811/ F-AZID) [HD]	Privately owned, Athens, Greece
	60312	McD F-101F Voodoo (56-0312)	Midland Air Museum, Coventry
	60689	Boeing B-52D Stratofortress (56-0689)	American Air Museum, Duxford
	63000	NA F-100D Super Sabre (54-2212) [FW-000]	USAF Croughton, Oxon, at gate
	63319	NA F-100D Super Sabre (54-2269) [FW-319]	RAF Lakenheath, on display
	63428	Republic F-105G Thunderchief (62-4428)	USAF Croughton, Oxon, at gate
	66692	Lockheed U-2CT (56-6692)	American Air Museum, Duxford
	70270	McD F-101B Voodoo (57-270) (fuselage)	Midland Air Museum, Coventry
	80425	Grumman F7F-3P Tigercat (N7235C/G-RUMT) [WT-14]	The Fighter Collection, Duxford
	82062	DHC U-6A Beaver (58-2062)	Midland Air Museum, Coventry
	91822	Republic F-105D Thunderchief (59-1822)	American Air Museum, Duxford
	93542	CCF Harvard IV (G-BRLV) [LTA-542]	Privately owned, North Weald
	96995	CV F4U-4 Corsair (OE-EAS) [BR-37]	Tyrolean Jet Services, Innsbruck, Austria
	97264	CV F4U-4 Corsair (F-AZVJ) [403]	Flying Legend, Dijon, France
	111836	NA AT-6C Harvard IIA (41-33262/ G-TSIX) [JZ-6]	The Real Aeroplane Company, Breighton
	111989	Cessna L-19A Bird Dog (51-11989/ N33600)	Museum of Army Flying, Middle Wallop
	114700	NA T-6G Texan (51-14700/ G-TOMC)	Privately owned, Netherthorpe
	115042	NA T-6G Texan (51-15042/ G-BGHU) [TA-042]	Privately owned, Headcorn
	115227	NA T-6G Texan (51-15227/ G-BKRA)	Privately owned, Staverton
	115302	Piper L-18C Super Cub (51-15302/ G-BJTP) [TP]	Privately owned, Defford
	115684	Piper L-21A Supèr Cub (51-15684/ G-BKVM) [DC]	Privately owned, Strubby
	124143	Douglas AD-4NA Skyraider (F-AZDP) [205-RM]	Amicale J-B Salis, la Ferté-Alais, France
	124485	Boeing B-17G Fortress (44-85784/ G-BEDF) [DF-A]	B-17 Preservation Ltd, Duxford
	124724	CV F4U-5NL Corsair (F-AZEG) [22]	Amicale J-B Salis, la Ferté-Alais, France
	126922	Douglas AD-4NA Skyraider (G-RADR) [402-AK]	Kennet Aviation, North Weald
	126956	Douglas AD-4NA Skyraider (F-AZDQ) [3-RM]	Aéro Retro, St Rambert d'Albon, France
	127002	Douglas AD-4NA Skyraider (F-AZHK) [618-G]	Privately owned, Cuers, France
	133704	CV F4U-5NL Corsair (124541/ F-AZYS) [14.F.6]	Privately owned, Le Castellet, France
	134076	NA AT-6D Harvard III (41-34671/ F-AZSC) [TA076]	Privately owned, Yvetot, France
	138179	NA T-28A Trojan (OE-ESA) [BA]	Tyrolean Jet Services, Innsbruck, Austria
	140547	NA T-28C Trojan (N2800Q)	Privately owned
	146289	NA T-28C Trojan (N99153) [2W]	Norfolk & Suffolk Aviation Museum, Flixton
	150225	WS58 Wessex 60 (G-AWOX) [123]	Privately owned, Lulsgate
	151632	NA TB-25N Mitchell (44-30925/ G-BWGR)	Privately owned, Sandtoft
	155529	McD F-4S Phantom (ZE359) [AJ-114]	American Air Museum, Duxford
	155848	McD F-4S Phantom [WT-11]	Royal Scottish Mus'm of Flight, E Fortune
	159233	HS AV-8A Harrier [CG-33]	Imperial War Museum North, Salford Quays
	162068	McD AV-8B Harrier II (9250M) (fuselage)	RAF Cottesmore BDRT
	162071	McD AV-8B Harrier II (fuselage)	Rolls-Royce, Filton
	162730	McD AV-8B Harrier II (fuselage)	RAF/DARA, St Athan

Serial	Type (other identity)	Owner/operator, location	Notes
162958	McD AV-8B Harrier II (fuselage)	QinetiQ, Boscombe Down	
162964	McD AV-8B Harrier II (fuselage)	BAE Systems, Warton	
163177	McD AV-8B Harrier II (fuselage)	BAE Systems, Warton	
163205	McD AV-8B Harrier II (fuselage)	BAE Systems, Warton	
217786	Boeing-Stearman PT-17 Kaydet (41-8169/CF-EQS) [25]	American Air Museum, Duxford	
219993	Bell P-39Q Airacobra (42-19993/ N793QG)	The Fighter Collection, Duxford	
224319	Douglas C-47B Skytrain (44-77047/ G-AMSN) <ff>	Privately owned, Sussex	
226413	Republic P-47D Thunderbolt (45-49192/N47DD) [ZU-N]	American Air Museum, Duxford	
226671	Republic P-47M Thunderbolt (G-THUN) [MX-X]	The Fighter Collection, Duxford	
231983	Boeing B-17G Fortress (44-83735/ F-BDRS) [IY-G]	American Air Museum, Duxford	
234539	Fairchild PT-19B Cornell (42-34539/N50429) [63]	Privately owned, Dunkeswell	
236657	Piper L-4A Grasshopper (42-36657/G-BGSJ) [72-D]	Privately owned, Langport	
237123	Waco CG-4A Hadrian (BAPC 157) (fuselage)	Yorkshire Air Museum, Elvington	
238410	Piper L-4A Grasshopper (42-38410/G-BHPK) [44-A]	Privately owned, Tibenham	
243809	Waco CG-4A Hadrian (BAPC 185)	Museum of Army Flying, Middle Wallop	
252983	Schweizer TG-3A (42-52983/ N66630)	American Air Museum, Duxford	
314887	Fairchild Argus III (43-14887/ G-AJPI)	Privately owned, Eelde, The Netherlands	
315211	Douglas C-47A (43-15211/ N1944A) [J8-Z]	Privately owned, Kemble	
315509	Douglas C-47A (43-15509/ G-BHUB) [W7-S]	American Air Museum, Duxford	
329405	Piper L-4H Grasshopper (43-29405/G-BCOB) [23-A]	Privately owned, South Walsham	
329417	Piper L-4A Grasshopper (42-38400/G-BDHK)	Privately owned, Coleford	
329471	Piper L-4H Grasshopper (43-29471/G-BGXA) [44-F]	Privately owned, Martley, Worcs	
329601	Piper L-4H Grasshopper (43-29601/G-AXHR) [44-D]	Privately owned, Nayland	
329854	Piper L-4H Grasshopper (43-29854/G-BMKC) [44-R]	Privately owned, Newtownards	
329934	Piper L-4H Grasshopper (43-29934/G-BCPH) [72-B]	Privately owned, Thatcham	
330238	Piper L-4H Grasshopper (43-30238/G-LIVH) [24-A]	Privately owned, Barton	
330485	Piper L-4H Grasshopper (43-30485/G-AJES) [44-C]	Privately owned, Shifnal	
343251	Boeing-Stearman N2S-5 Kaydet (43517/G-NZSS) [27]	Privately owned, Kidlington	
411622	NA P-51D Mustang (44-74427/ F-AZSB) [G4-C]	Amicale J-B Salis, la Ferté-Alais, France	
413317	NA P-51D Mustang (44-74409/ N51RT) [VF-B]	RAF Museum, Hendon	
413573	NA P-51D Mustang (44-73415/ 9133M/N6526D) [B6-V]	RAF Museum, Cosford	
413704	NA P-51D Mustang (44-73149/ G-BTCD) [B7-H]	The Old Flying Machine Company, Duxford	
414151	NA P-51D Mustang (44-73140/ NL314BG) [HO-M]	Privately owned, Greenham Common	
414419	NA P-51D Mustang (45-15118/ G-MSTG) [LH-F]	Privately owned, Hardwick, Norfolk	
414450	NA P-51D Mustang (44-73877/ N167F) [B6-S]	Scandinavian Historic Flight, North Weald	
434602	Douglas A-26B Invader (44-34602/ N167B) [BC-602]	Scandinavian Historic Flight, North Weald	
435710	Douglas A-26C Invader (44-35710/ OO-INV)	Historic Invader Avn, Schiphol, The Netherlands	
442268	Noorduyn AT-16 Harvard IIB (KF568/LN-TEX) [TA-268]	Scandinavian Historic Flight, Oslo, Norway	
454467	Piper L-4J Grasshopper (45-4467/G-BILI) [44-J]	Privately owned, White Waltham	

Notes	*Serial*	*Type (other identity)*	*Owner/operator, location*
	454537	Piper L-4J Grasshopper (45-4537/ G-BFDL) [04-J]	Privately owned, Shempston Farm, Lossiemouth
	461748	Boeing B-29A Superfortress (44-61748/G-BHDK) [Y]	American Air Museum, Duxford
	463209	NA P-51D Mustang <R> (BAPC 255) [WZ-S]	American Air Museum, Duxford
	463864	NA P-51D Mustang (44-63864/ G-CBNM) [HL-W]	The Fighter Collection, Duxford
	472035	NA P-51D Mustang (44-72035/ G-SIJJ)	Privately owned, North Weald
	472216	NA P-51D Mustang (44-72216/ G-BIXL) [HO-M]	Privately owned, East Garston, Bucks
	472218	CAC-18 Mustang 22 (A68-192/ G-HAEC) [WZ-I]	Privately owned, Woodchurch, Kent
	472218	NA P-51D Mustang (44-73979) [WZ-I]	Imperial War Museum, Lambeth
	472773	NA P-51D Mustang (44-72773/ G-SUSY) [QP-M]	Privately owned, Sywell
	474425	NA P-51D Mustang (44-74425/ NL11T) [OC-G]	Dutch Mustang Flt, Lelystad, The Netherlands
	474923	NA P-51D Mustang (44-74923/ N6395)	Privately owned, Lelystad, The Netherlands
	479744	Piper L-4H Grasshopper (44-79744/G-BGPD) [49-M]	Privately owned, Marsh, Bucks
	479766	Piper L-4H Grasshopper (44-79766/G-BKHG) [63-D]	Privately owned, Frogland Cross
	480015	Piper L-4H Grasshopper (44-80015/G-AKIB) [44-M]	Privately owned, Bodmin
	480133	Piper L-4J Grasshopper (44-80133/G-BDCD) [44-B]	Privately owned, Slinfold
	480321	Piper L-4J Grasshopper (44-80321/G-FRAN) [44-H]	Privately owned, Rayne, Essex
	480480	Piper L-4J Grasshopper (44-80480/G-BECN) [44-E]	Privately owned, Kersey, Suffolk
	480551	Piper L-4J Grasshopper (44-80551/LN-KLT) [43-S]	Scandinavian Historic Flight, Oslo, Norway
	480636	Piper L-4J Grasshopper (44-80636/G-AXHP) [58-A]	Privately owned, Spanhoe
	480723	Piper L-4J Grasshopper (44-80723/G-BFZB) [E5-J]	Privately owned, Egginton
	480752	Piper L-4J Grasshopper (44-80752/G-BCXJ) [39-E]	Privately owned, Old Sarum
	483868	Boeing B-17G Fortress (44-83868/N5237V) [A-N]	RAF Museum, Hendon
	486893	NA B-25J Mitchell (N6123C)	Tyrolean Jet Services, Innsbruck, Austria
	493209	NA T-6G Texan (49-3209/ G-DDMV/*41*)	Privately owned, Duxford
	511701A	Beech C-45H (51-11701/G-BSZC) [AF258]	Privately owned, Bryngwyn Bach
	607327	PA-18 Super Cub 95 (G-ARAO) [09-L]	Privately owned, Denham
	2106449	NA P-51C Mustang (43-25147/ N51PR/G-PSIC) [HO-W]	The Fighter Collection, Duxford
	00195700	Cessna F.150G (G-OIDW)	Privately owned, Halfpenny Green
	3-1923	Aeronca O-58B Defender (43-1923/G-BRHP)	Privately owned, Chiseldon
	18-2001	Piper L-18C Super Cub (52-2401/ G-BIZV)	Privately owned, Croydon, Cambs
	39-139	Beech YC-43 Traveler (N295BS)	Dukes of Brabant AF, Eindhoven, The Netherlands
	41-33275	NA AT-6C Texan (G-BICE) [CE]	Privately owned, Monewden
	42-12417	Noorduyn AT-16 Harvard IIB (Klu. B-163)	Covert Forces Museum, Harrington, Northants
	42-35870	Taylorcraft DCO-65 (G-BWLJ) [129]	Privately owned, Nayland
	42-58678	Taylorcraft DF-65 (G-BRIY) [IY]	Privately owned, Carlisle
	42-78044	Aeronca 11AC Chief (G-BRXL)	Privately owned, Thurrock
	42-84555	NA AT-6D Harvard III (FAP.1662/ G-ELMH) [EP-H]	Privately owned, Hardwick, Norfolk
	42-93510	Douglas C-47A Skytrain [CM] <ff>	Privately owned, Kew
	43-9628	Douglas A-20G Havoc <ff>	Privately owned, Hinckley, Leics
	44-4315	Bell P-63C Kingcobra	Privately owned, Redhill
	44-4368	Bell P-63C Kingcobra	Privately owned, Redhill
	44-13954	NA P-51D Mustang (G-UAKE)	Mustang Restoration Co Ltd, Coventry

Serial	Type (other identity)	Owner/operator, location	Notes
44-14574	NA P-51D Mustang (fuselage)	East Essex Aviation Museum, Clacton	
44-51228	Consolidated B-24M Liberator [RE-N]	American Air Museum, Duxford	
44-79609	Piper L-4H Grasshopper (G-BHXY) [PR]	Privately owned, Bodmin	
44-80594	Piper L-4J Grasshopper (G-BEDJ)	Privately owned, White Waltham	
44-80647	Piper L-4J Grasshopper (D-EGAF)	The Vintage Aircraft Co, Fürstenwalde, Germany	
44-83184	Fairchild UC-61K Argus III (G-RGUS)	Privately owned, Snitterby	
46-11042	Wolf WII <R> (G-BMZX) [7]	Privately owned, Kilrush, Eire	
51-9036	Lockheed T-33A	Newark Air Museum, Winthorpe	
51-15319	Piper L-18C Super Cub (G-FUZZ) [A-319]	Privately owned, Elvington	
51-15555	Piper L-18C Super Cub (G-OSPS)	Privately oened, Weston, Eire	
54-005	NA F-100D Super Sabre (54-2163)	Dumfries & Galloway Avn Mus, Dumfries	
54-223	NA F-100D Super Sabre (54-2223)	Newark Air Museum, Winthorpe	
54-2447	Piper L-21B Super Cub (G-SCUB)	Privately owned, Anwick	
63-699	McD F-4C Phantom (63-7699) [CG]	Midland Air Museum, Coventry	
64-17657	Douglas A-26A Invader (N99218) <ff>	Privately owned, Catfield	
65-777	McD F-4C Phantom (63-7419) [LN]	RAF Lakenheath, on display	
67-120	GD F-111E Aardvark (67-0120) [UH]	American Air Museum, Duxford	
68-0060	GD F-111E Aardvark <ff>	Dumfries & Galloway Avn Mus, Dumfries	
72-1447	GD F-111F Aardvark <ff>	American Air Museum, Duxford	
72-448	GD F-111E Aardvark (68-0011) [LN]	RAF Lakenheath, on display	
76-020	McD F-15A Eagle (76-0020) [BT]	American Air Museum, Duxford	
76-124	McD F-15B Eagle (76-0124) [LN]	RAF Lakenheath, instructional use	
77-259	Fairchild A-10A Thunderbolt (77-0259) [AR]	American Air Museum, Duxford	
80-219	Fairchild GA-10A Thunderbolt (80-0219) [AR]	RAF Alconbury, on display	
92-048	McD F-15A Eagle (74-0131) [LN]	RAF Lakenheath, on display	
146-11083	Wolf WII <R> (G-BNAI) [5]	Privately owned, Haverfordwest	
H-57	Piper L-4A Grasshopper (42-36375/G-AKAZ)	Privately owned, Duxford	

YUGOSLAVIA

Serial	Type (other identity)	Owner/operator, location	Notes
23194	Soko G-2A Galeb (YU-YAG)	Privately owned, Biggin Hill	
23196	Soko G-2A Galeb (YU-YAC)	Privately owned, Biggin Hill	
30139	Soko P-2 Kraguj [139]	Privately owned, Biggin Hill	
30140	Soko P-2 Kraguj (G-RADA) [140]	Privately owned, Biggin Hill	
30146	Soko P-2 Kraguj (G-BSXD) [146]	Privately owned, Elstree	
30149	Soko P-2 Kraguj (G-SOKO) [149]	Privately owned, Bournemouth	
30151	Soko P-2 Kraguj [151]	Privately owned, Sopley, Hants	

The RAF Museum's Messerschmitt Bf 109E w/n 4101 is displayed in the Battle of Britain Hall.

Morane Saulnier MS505 TA-RC is operated by the Historic Aircraft Collection at Duxford.

Colourful Fokker DVII 8417/18 is an exhibit in the RAFM's Milestones of Flight Exhibition.

Kennet Aviation's North Weald based Douglas AD-4NA Skyraider 126922.

Ferocious Frankie, the Old Flying Machine Company's NA P-51D Mustang 413704.

Irish Military Aircraft Markings

Serial	Type (other identity)	Owner/operator, location	Notes
34	Miles M14A Magister (N5392)	IAC, stored Baldonnel	
141	Avro 652A Anson C19	IAC, stored Baldonnel	
161	VS509 Spitfire T9 (G-CCCA)	Historic Flying Ltd, Duxford	
164	DHC1 Chipmunk T20	IAC, stored Baldonnel	
168	DHC1 Chipmunk T20	IAC No 1 Operations Wing, Baldonnel	
172	DHC1 Chipmunk T20	IAC, stored Baldonnel	
173	DHC1 Chipmunk T20	South East Aviation Enthusiasts, Dromod	
176	DH104 Dove 4 (VP-YKF)	South East Aviation Enthusiasts, Waterford	
177	Percival P56 Provost T51 (G-BLIW)	Privately owned, Shoreham	
181	Percival P56 Provost T51	Privately owned, Thatcham	
183	Percival P56 Provost T51	IAC stored, Baldonnel	
184	Percival P56 Provost T51	South East Aviation Enthusiasts, Waterford	
187	DH115 Vampire T55	South East Aviation Enthusiasts, Waterford	
189	Percival P56 Provost T51 (comp XF846)	IAC Baldonnel Fire Section	
191	DH115 Vampire T55	IAC Museum, Baldonnel	
192	DH115 Vampire T55	South East Aviation Enthusiasts, Waterford	
195	Sud SA316 Alouette III (F-WJDH)	IAC No 302 Sqn/3 Operations Wing, Baldonnel	
196	Sud SA316 Alouette III (F-WKQB)	IAC No 302 Sqn/3 Operations Wing, Baldonnel	
197	Sud SA316 Alouette III	IAC No 302 Sqn/3 Operations Wing, Baldonnel	
198	DH115 Vampire T11 (XE977)	IAC, stored Baldonnel	
199	DHC1 Chipmunk T22	IAC, stored Baldonnel	
203	Reims-Cessna FR172H	IAC No 104 Sqn/1 Operations Wing, Baldonnel	
205	Reims-Cessna FR172H	IAC No 104 Sqn/1 Operations Wing, Baldonnel	
206	Reims-Cessna FR172H	IAC No 104 Sqn/1 Operations Wing, Baldonnel	
207	Reims-Cessna FR172H	IAC, stored Waterford	
208	Reims-Cessna FR172H	IAC No 104 Sqn/1 Operations Wing, Baldonnel	
210	Reims-Cessna FR172H	IAC No 104 Sqn/1 Operations Wing, Baldonnel	
211	Sud SA316 Alouette III	IAC No 302 Sqn/3 Operations Wing, Baldonnel	
212	Sud SA316 Alouette III	IAC No 302 Sqn/3 Operations Wing, Baldonnel	
213	Sud SA316 Alouette III	IAC No 302 Sqn/3 Operations Wing, Baldonnel	
214	Sud SA316 Alouette III	IAC No 302 Sqn/3 Operations Wing, Baldonnel	
215	Fouga CM170 Super Magister	IAC Baldonnel, on display	
216	Fouga CM170 Super Magister	Carlow Institute of Technology, instructional use	
217	Fouga CM170 Super Magister (F-WVKO)	IAC 3 Operations Wing, Baldonnel	
218	Fouga CM170 Super Magister	IAC, stored Baldonnel	
219	Fouga CM170 Super Magister	IAC, stored Baldonnel	
220	Fouga CM170 Super Magister	Cork University, instructional use	
222	SIAI SF-260WE Warrior	IAC Flying Training School, Baldonnel	
225	SIAI SF-260WE Warrior	IAC Flying Training School, Baldonnel	
226	SIAI SF-260WE Warrior	IAC Flying Training School, Baldonnel	
227	SIAI SF-260WE Warrior	IAC Flying Training School, Baldonnel	
229	SIAI SF-260WE Warrior	IAC Flying Training School, Baldonnel	
230	SIAI SF-260WE Warrior	IAC Flying Training School, Baldonnel	
231	SIAI SF-260WE Warrior	IAC Flying Training School, Baldonnel	
240	Beech Super King Air 200MR	IAC No 102 Sqn/1 Operations Wing, Baldonnel	
241	Aérospatiale SA342L Gazelle	IAC No 303 Sqn/3 Operations Wing, Baldonnel	
244	Aérospatiale SA365F Dauphin II (F-ZKBZ)	IAC, stored Baldonnel	

Notes	Serial	Type (other identity)	Owner/operator, location
	245	Aérospatiale SA365F Dauphin II (F-ZKBJ)	IAC No 301 Sqn/3 Operations Wing, Baldonnel
	246	Aérospatiale SA365F Dauphin II (F-ZKBP)	IAC No 301 Sqn/3 Operations Wing, Baldonnel
	247	Aérospatiale SA365F Dauphin II (F-ZKBW)	IAC No 301 Sqn/3 Operations Wing, Baldonnel
	251	Grumman G1159C Gulfstream IV (N17584)	IAC No 102 Sqn/1 Operations Wing, Baldonnel
	252	Airtech CN.235 MPA Persuader	IAC No 101 Sqn/1 Operations Wing, Baldonnel
	253	Airtech CN.235 MPA Persuader	IAC No 101 Sqn/1 Operations Wing, Baldonnel
	254	PBN-2T Defender 4000 (G-BWPN)	IAC No 106 Sqn/1 Operations Wing, Baldonnel
	255	AS355N Twin Squirrel (G-BXEV)	IAC No 106 Sqn/1 Operations Wing, Baldonnel
	256	Eurocopter EC135T-1 (G-BZRM)	IAC No 106 Sqn/1 Operations Wing, Baldonnel
	258	Gates Learjet 45 (N5009T)	IAC No 102 Sqn/1 Operations Wing, Baldonnel
	260	Pilatus PC-9M (HB-HQS)	IAC Flying Training School, Baldonnel
	261	Pilatus PC-9M (HB-HQT)	IAC Flying Training School, Baldonnel
	262	Pilatus PC-9M (HB-HQU)	IAC Flying Training School, Baldonnel
	263	Pilatus PC-9M (HB-HQV)	IAC Flying Training School, Baldonnel
	264	Pilatus PC-9M (HB-HQW)	IAC Flying Training School, Baldonnel
	265	Pilatus PC-9M (HB-HQX)	IAC Flying Training School, Baldonnel
	266	Pilatus PC-9M (HB-HQY)	IAC Flying Training School, Baldonnel
	267	Pilatus PC-9M (HB-HQZ)	IAC Flying Training School, Baldonnel

Taking off from Fairford during RIAT 04, this Fouga Magister MT48 remains in service.

Overseas Military Aircraft Markings

Aircraft included in this section are a selection of those likely to be seen visiting UK civil and military airfields on transport flights, exchange visits, exercises and for air shows. It is not a comprehensive list of *all* aircraft operated by the air arms concerned.

ALGERIA
Force Aérienne Algérienne/ Al Quwwat al Jawwiya al Jaza'eriya

Lockheed C-130H Hercules
7T-WHE (4935)
7T-WHF (4934)
7T-WHI (4930)
7T-WHJ (4928)
7T-WHQ (4926)
7T-WHR (4924)
7T-WHS (4912)
7T-WHT (4911)
7T-WHY (4913)
7T-WHZ (4914)

Lockheed C-130H-30 Hercules
7T-WHA (4997)
7T-WHB (5224)
7T-WHD (4987)
7T-WHL (4989)
7T-WHM (4919)
7T-WHN 4894)
7T-WHO (4897)
7T-WHP (4921)

Grumman G.1159C Gulfstream IVSP
Ministry of Defence, Boufarik
7T-VPC (1418)
7T-VPM (1421)
7T-VPR (1288)
7T-VPS (1291)

Gulfstream Aerospace Gulfstream V
Ministry of Defence, Boufarik
7T-VPG (617)

AUSTRALIA
Royal Australian Air Force

Boeing 707-338C/368C*
33 Sqn, Amberley
A20-261*
A20-623
A20-624
A20-629

Boeing 737-7DT
34 Sqn, Canberra
A36-001
A36-002

Canadair CL.604 Challenger
34 Sqn, Canberra
A37-001
A37-002
A37-003

Lockheed C-130H Hercules
36 Sqn, Richmond, NSW
A97-001
A97-002
A97-003
A97-004
A97-005
A97-006
A97-007
A97-008
A97-009
A97-010
A97-011
A97-012

Lockheed C-130J-30 Hercules II
37 Sqn, Richmond, NSW
A97-440
A97-441
A97-442
A97-447
A97-448
A97-449
A97-450
A97-464
A97-465
A97-466
A97-467
A97-468

Lockheed P-3 Orion
10/11 Sqns, Maritime Patrol Group, Edinburgh, NSW

A9-656	AP-3C	11 Sqn
A9-657	P-3W	11 Sqn
A9-658	P-3W	10 Sqn
A9-659	P-3W	11 Sqn
A9-660	AP-3C	10 Sqn
A9-661	AP-3C	10 Sqn
A9-662	P-3W	11 Sqn
A9-663	P-3W	11 Sqn
A9-664	P-3W	11 Sqn
A9-665	AP-3C	10 Sqn
A9-751	P-3C	11 Sqn
A9-752	AP-3C	10 Sqn
A9-753	P-3C	10 Sqn
A9-755	P-3C	10 Sqn
A9-756	P-3C	11 Sqn
A9-757	P-3C	10 Sqn
A9-758	P-3C	10 Sqn
A9-759	AP-3C	10 Sqn
A9-760	AP-3C	10 Sqn

AUSTRIA
Öesterreichische Luftstreitkräfte

Lockheed C-130K Hercules
Fliegerregiment III
Transportstaffel, Linz
8T-CA
8T-CB
8T-CC

Northrop F-5E Tiger II
Fliegerregiment II
2 Staffel/Uberwg, Graz
J-3004
J-3005
J-3030
J-3033
J-3038
J-3052
J-3057
J-3065

SAAB 35ÖE Draken
Fliegerregiment II
1 Staffel/Uberwg, Zeltweg;
2 Staffel/Uberwg, Graz

01	(351401)	1 Staffel
02	(351402)	1 Staffel
03	(351403)	1 Staffel
04	(351404)	1 Staffel
05	(351405)	1 Staffel
06	(351406)	1 Staffel
07	(351407)	1 Staffel
08	(351408)	1 Staffel
09	(351409)	1 Staffel
10	(351410)	1 Staffel
11	(351411)	1 Staffel
12	(351412)	1 Staffel
13	(351413)	2 Staffel
14	(351414)	2 Staffel
15	(351415)	2 Staffel
16	(351416)	2 Staffel
18	(351418)	2 Staffel
19	(351419)	2 Staffel
20	(351420)	2 Staffel
21	(351421)	2 Staffel
22	(351422)	2 Staffel
23	(351423)	2 Staffel
24	(351424)	2 Staffel

SAAB 105ÖE
Fliegerregiment III
Dusenstaffel, Linz

(yellow)
B (105402)
D (105404)
E (105405)
G (105407)
I (105409)
J (105410)

(green)
B (105412)
D (105414)
GF-16 (105416)
GG-17 (105417)

(red)
B (105422)
C (105423)

D (105424)
E (105425)
F (105426)
G (105427)
H (105428)
I (105429)
J (105430)
(blue)
A (105431)
B (105432)
C (105433)
D (105434)
E (105435)
F (105436)
G (105437)
I (105439)
J (105440)

Short SC7 Skyvan 3M
Fliegerregiment I
Flachenstaffel, Tulln
5S-TA
5S-TB

BAHRAIN
BAE RJ.85/RJ.100*
Bahrain Defence Force
A9C-BDF*
A9C-HWR

Boeing 747SP-21
Bahrain Amiri Flt
A9C-HMH

Boeing 747-4P8
Bahrain Amiri Flt
A9C-HMK

Grumman G.1159 Gulfstream IITT/G.1159C Gulfstream IV-SP
Govt of Bahrain
A9C-BAH Gulfstream IV-SP
A9C-BG Gulfstream IITT

BELGIUM
Belgische Luchtmacht
D-BD Alpha Jet E
7/11 Smaldeel (1 Wg), Bevekom
AT-01
AT-02
AT-03
AT-05
AT-06
AT-08
AT-10
AT-11
AT-12
AT-13
AT-14
AT-15
AT-17
AT-18
AT-19
AT-20
AT-21
AT-22
AT-23
AT-24
AT-25
AT-26
AT-27
AT-28
AT-29
AT-30
AT-31
AT-32
AT-33

Airbus A.310-322
21 Smaldeel (15 Wg), Melsbroek
CA-01
CA-02

Dassault Falcon 900B
21 Smaldeel (15 Wg), Melsbroek
CD-01

Embraer ERJ.135LR/ ERJ.145LR*
21 Smaldeel (15 Wg), Melsbroek
CE-01
CE-02
CE-03*
CE-04*

Lockheed C-130H Hercules
20 Smaldeel (15 Wg), Melsbroek
CH-01
CH-02
CH-03
CH-04
CH-05
CH-07
CH-08
CH-09
CH-10
CH-11
CH-12

Dassault Falcon 20E
21 Smaldeel (15 Wg), Melsbroek
CM-01
CM-02

General Dynamics F-16
(MLU aircraft are marked with a *)
1,350 Smaldeel (2 Wg), Florennes [FS];
31,349 Smaldeel, OCU (10 Wg), Kleine-Brogel [BL]

FA-56	F-16A*	10 Wg
FA-57	F-16A*	2 Wg
FA-58	F-16A*	2 Wg
FA-65	F-16A*	10 Wg
FA-66	F-16A*	2 Wg
FA-67	F-16A*	2 Wg
FA-68	F-16A*	2 Wg
FA-69	F-16A*	2 Wg
FA-70	F-16A*	10 Wg
FA-71	F-16A*	2 Wg
FA-72	F-16A*	2 Wg
FA-74	F-16A*	10 Wg
FA-76	F-16A*	2 Wg
FA-77	F-16A*	2 Wg
FA-81	F-16A*	2 Wg
FA-82	F-16A*	10 Wg
FA-83	F-16A*	10 Wg
FA-84	F-16A*	2 Wg
FA-86	F-16A*	10 Wg
FA-87	F-16A*	10 Wg
FA-88	F-16A*	2 Wg
FA-89	F-16A*	2 Wg
FA-91	F-16A*	2 Wg
FA-92	F-16A*	2 Wg
FA-94	F-16A*	10 Wg
FA-95	F-16A*	2 Wg
FA-97	F-16A*	10 Wg
FA-98	F-16A*	10 Wg
FA-99	F-16A*	10 Wg
FA-100	F-16A*	2 Wg
FA-101	F-16A*	2 Wg
FA-102	F-16A*	2 Wg
FA-103	F-16A*	2 Wg
FA-104	F-16A*	2 Wg
FA-106	F-16A*	10 Wg
FA-107	F-16A*	2 Wg
FA-108	F-16A*	2 Wg
FA-109	F-16A*	2 Wg
FA-110	F-16A*	10 Wg
FA-111	F-16A*	10 Wg
FA-112	F-16A*	2 Wg
FA-114	F-16A*	10 Wg
FA-115	F-16A*	2 Wg
FA-116	F-16A*	10 Wg
FA-117	F-16A*	2 Wg
FA-118	F-16A*	10 Wg
FA-119	F-16A*	10 Wg
FA-120	F-16A*	2 Wg
FA-121	F-16A*	2 Wg
FA-123	F-16A*	10 Wg
FA-124	F-16A*	10 Wg
FA-125	F-16A*	2 Wg
FA-126	F-16A*	2 Wg
FA-127	F-16A*	2 Wg
FA-128	F-16A*	2 Wg
FA-129	F-16A*	10 Wg
FA-130	F-16A*	2 Wg
FA-131	F-16A	2 Wg
FA-132	F-16A*	2 Wg
FA-133	F-16A	2 Wg
FA-134	F-16A*	10 Wg
FA-135	F-16A*	2 Wg
FA-136	F-16A*	10 Wg
FB-01	F-16B*	2 Wg
FB-02	F-16B	OCU
FB-04	F-16B	2 Wg
FB-05	F-16B*	2 Wg
FB-08	F-16B*	10 Wg
FB-09	F-16B*	2 Wg
FB-10	F-16B*	2 Wg
FB-12	F-16B	2 Wg
FB-14	F-16B*	10 Wg
FB-15	F-16B*	OCU
FB-17	F-16B*	OCU
FB-18	F-16B*	2 Wg
FB-20	F-16B*	2 Wg
FB-21	F-16B*	2 Wg
FB-22	F-16B*	OCU
FB-23	F-16B*	10 Wg
FB-24	F-16B*	OCU

Fouga CM170 Magister
Fouga Flight/7 Smaldeel (1 Wg), Bevekom
MT-04
MT-13
MT-14
MT-26
MT-34
MT-35
MT-37
MT-40
MT-48

Westland Sea King Mk48/48A*
40 Smaldeel, Koksijde
RS-01
RS-02
RS-03*
RS-04
RS-05

SIAI Marchetti SF260M/SF260D*
Ecole de Pilotage Elementaire (5 Sm/1 Wg), Bevekom
ST-02
ST-03
ST-04
ST-06
ST-12
ST-15
ST-16
ST-17
ST-18
ST-19
ST-20
ST-22
ST-23
ST-24
ST-25
ST-26
ST-27
ST-30
ST-31
ST-32
ST-34
ST-35
ST-36
ST-40*
ST-41*
ST-42*
ST-43*
ST-44*
ST-45*
ST-46*
ST-47*
ST-48*

Aviation Légère de la Force Terrestre/Belgische Landmacht

Sud SA318C/SE3130* Alouette II
16 BnHLn, Bierset;
SLV, Brasschaat

A-22*	16 BnHLn
A-37	16 BnHLn
A-41	16 BnHLn
A-43	SLV
A-44	SLV
A-47	16 BnHLn
A-49	SLV
A-50	16 BnHLn
A-53	16 BnHLn
A-54	16 BnHLn
A-55	SLV
A-57	16 BnHLn
A-59	16 BnHLn
A-61	SLV
A-62	16 BnHLn
A-64	SLV
A-65	SLV
A-66	SLV
A-68	16 BnHLn
A-69	16 BnHLn
A-70	SLV
A-72	16 BnHLn
A-74	16 BnHLn
A-77	SLV
A-78	SLV
A-79	SLV

Britten-Norman BN-2A/ BN-2B-21* Islander
SLV, Brasschaat

B-01	LA
B-02*	LB
B-04*	LD
B-08*	LH
B-09*	LI
B-10*	LJ
B-12	LL

Agusta A109HA/HO*
17 BnHATk, Bierset;
18 BnHATk, Bierset;
SLV, Brasschaat

H-01*	SLV
H-02*	SLV
H-04*	SLV
H-05*	18 BnHATk
H-06*	17 BnHATk
H-07*	17 BnHATk
H-11*	18 BnHATk
H-17*	17 BnHATk
H-18*	18 BnHATk
H-20	18 BnHATk
H-21	18 BnHATk
H-22	17 BnHATk
H-24	17 BnHATk
H-25	18 BnHATk
H-26	18 BnHATk
H-27	18 BnHATk
H-28	17 BnHATk
H-29	18 BnHATk
H-30	18 BnHATk
H-31	18 BnHATk
H-32	18 BnHATk
H-33	18 BnHATk
H-35	18 BnHATk
H-36	17 BnHATk
H-37	18 BnHATk
H-38	17 BnHATk
H-39	18 BnHATk
H-40	18 BnHATk
H-41	SLV
H-42	SLV
H-43	17 BnHATk
H-44	17 BnHATk
H-45	17 BnHATk
H-46	17 BnHATk

Force Navale Belge/Belgische Zeemacht

Sud SA316B Alouette III
Koksijde Heli Flight

M-1	(OT-ZPA)
M-2	(OT-ZPB)
M-3	(OT-ZPC)

Gendarmerie/Rijkswacht

Cessna 182 Skylane
Luchsteundetachment, Melsbroek

G-01	C.182Q
G-04	C.182R

MDH MD.520N
Luchsteundetachment, Melsbroek
G-14
G-15

MDH MD.900 Explorer
Luchsteundetachment, Melsbroek
G-10
G-11
G-12

BOTSWANA

Botswana Defence Force

Grumman G.1159C Gulfstream IV
VIP Sqn, Sir Seretse Kharma IAP
OK-1

Lockheed C-130B Hercules
Z10 Sqn, Thebephatshwa
OM-1
OM-2
OM-3

BRAZIL

Força Aérea Brasileira

Boeing KC-137
2° GT 2° Esq, Galeão
2401
2402
2403
2404

Lockheed C-130 Hercules
1° GT, 1° Esq, Galeão;
1° GTT, 1° Esq, Afonsos

2451	C-130E	1° GTT
2453	C-130E	1° GTT
2454	C-130E	1° GTT
2456	C-130E	1° GTT
2458	SC-130E	1° GT
2459	SC-130E	1° GT
2461	KC-130H	1° GT
2462	KC-130H	1° GT
2463	C-130H	1° GT
2464	C-130H	1° GT
2465	C-130H	1° GT
2466	C-130H	1° GT
2467	C-130H	1° GT
2470	C-130H	1° GT
2471	C-130H	1° GT
2472	C-130H	1° GT
2473	C-130H	
2474	C-130H	1° GT
2475	C-130H	1° GT
2476	C-130H	
2477	C-130H	1° GT
2478	C-130H	1° GT
2479	C-130H	1° GT

BRUNEI

Airbus A.340
Brunei Govt, Bandar Seri Bergawan
V8-BKH A.340-212

Boeing 747-430
Brunei Govt, Bandar Seri Bergawan
V8-ALI

Boeing 767-27GER
Brunei Govt, Bandar Seri Bergawan
V8-MHB

Gulfstream Aerospace Gulfstream V
Brunei Govt, Bandar Seri Bergawan
V8-001

BULGARIA
Bulgarsky Voenno-Vazdushni Sily

Antonov An-30
16 TAP, Sofia/Dobroslavtzi
055

Pilatus PC.XII/45
16 TAP, Sofia/Dobroslavtzi
020

Bulgarian Govt

Dassault Falcon 2000
Bulgarian Govt, Sofia
LZ-OOI

Tupolev Tu-134A-3
Bulgarian Govt, Sofia
LZ-TUG

Tupolev Tu-154M
Bulgarian Govt, Sofia
LZ-BTQ
LZ-BTZ

BURKINA FASO

Boeing 727-14
Govt of Burkina Faso, Ouagadougou
XT-BBE

CAMEROON

Grumman G.1159A Gulfstream III
Govt of Cameroon, Yaounde
TJ-AAW

CANADA
Canadian Forces

Lockheed CC-130 Hercules
CC-130E/CC-130E(SAR)*
413 Sqn, Greenwood (SAR) (14 Wing);
424 Sqn, Trenton (SAR) (8 Wing);
426 Sqn, Trenton (8 Wing);
429 Sqn, Trenton (8 Wing);
435 Sqn, Winnipeg (17 Wing);
436 Sqn, Trenton (8 Wing)

130305*	8 Wing
130306*	14 Wing
130307	8 Wing
130308*	8 Wing
130310*	8 Wing
130311*	8 Wing
130313	8 Wing
130314*	14 Wing
130315*	14 Wing
130316	8 Wing
130317	8 Wing
130319	8 Wing
130320	8 Wing
130323	8 Wing
130324*	8 Wing
130325	8 Wing
130326	8 Wing
130327	8 Wing
130328	8 Wing

CC-130H/CC-130H(T)*

130332	17 Wing
130333	17 Wing
130334	8 Wing
130335	8 Wing
130336	17 Wing
130337	8 Wing
130338*	17 Wing
130339*	17 Wing
130340*	17 Wing
130341*	17 Wing
130342*	17 Wing

CC-130H-30

130343	8 Wing
130344	8 Wing

Lockheed CP-140 Aurora/ CP-140A Arcturus*
404/405/415 Sqns, Greenwood (14 Wing);
407 Sqn, Comox (19 Wing)

140101	407 Sqn
140102	407 Sqn
140103	407 Sqn
140104	14 Wing
140105	407 Sqn
140106	14 Wing
140107	14 Wing
140108	14 Wing
140109	14 Wing
140110	14 Wing
140111	14 Wing
140112	14 Wing
140113	407 Sqn
140114	14 Wing
140115	14 Wing
140116	407 Sqn
140117	14 Wing
140118	14 Wing
140119*	14 Wing
140120*	14 Wing
140121*	14 Wing

De Havilland Canada CT-142
402 Sqn, Winnipeg (17 Wing)

142803	CT-142
142804	CT-142
142805	CT-142
142806	CT-142

Canadair CC-144 Challenger
412 Sqn, Ottawa (8 Wing)

144601	CC-144A
144614	CC-144B
144615	CC-144B
144616	CC-144B
144617	CC-144C
144618	CC-144C

Airbus CC-150 Polaris (A310-304/A310-304F*)
437 Sqn, Trenton (8 Wing)

15001	216
15002*	212
15003*	202
15004*	205
15005*	204

CHILE
Fuerza Aérea de Chile

Boeing 707
Grupo 10, Santiago

902	707-351C
903	707-330B
904	707-358C

Boeing 737
Grupo 10, Santiago

921	737-58N
922	737-330

Extra EA-300L
Los Halcones

132	[6]
145	[2]
146	[3]
147	[4]
148	[5]
149	[1]

Grumman G.1159C Gulfstream IV
Grupo 10, Santiago
911

Lockheed C-130B/H Hercules
Grupo 10, Santiago

994	C-130B
995	C-130H
996	C-130H
997	C-130B
998	C-130B

CROATIA

Canadair CL.601 Challenger
Croatian Govt, Zagreb
9A-CRO
9A-CRT

CZECH REPUBLIC
Ceske Vojenske Letectvo

Aero L-39/L-59 Albatros
221.TL/22 zL, Náměšt;
LS, Pardubice

0103	L-39C	LS
0105	L-39C	LS
0106	L-39C	LS
0107	L-39C	LS
0108	L-39C	LS
0113	L-39C	LS
0115	L-39C	LS
0440	L-39C	LS
0441	L-39C	LS
0444	L-39C	LS
0445	L-39C	LS
0448	L-39C	LS
2341	L-39ZA	221.TL/22 zL
2344	L-39ZA	221.TL/22 zL
2347	L-39ZA	221.TL/22 zL
2350	L-39ZA	221.TL/22 zL
2415	L-39ZA	221.TL/22 zL
2418	L-39ZA	221.TL/22 zL
2421	L-39ZA	221.TL/22 zL
2424	L-39ZA	221.TL/22 zL
2427	L-39ZA	221.TL/22 zL
2430	L-39ZA	221.TL/22 zL
2433	L-39ZA	221.TL/22 zL
2436	L-39ZA	221.TL/22 zL
3903	L-39ZA	221.TL/22 zL
4605	L-39C	LS
4606	L-39C	LS

5013 L-39ZA 221.TL/22 zL
5015 L-39ZA 221.TL/22 zL
5017 L-39ZA 221.TL/22 zL
5019 L-39ZA 221.TL/22 zL

Aero L-159A ALCA/L-159B*
212.TL/21.zTL, Cáslav;
LZO, Praha/Kbely
5831* LZO
5832* LZO
6001 212.TL/21.zTL
6002 212.TL/21.zTL
6003 212.TL/21.zTL
6004 212.TL/21.zTL
6005 212.TL/21.zTL
6006 212.TL/21.zTL
6007 212.TL/21.zTL
6008 212.TL/21.zTL
6009 212.TL/21.zTL
6010 212.TL/21.zTL
6011 212.TL/21.zTL
6012 212.TL/21.zTL
6013 212.TL/21.zTL
6014 212.TL/21.zTL
6015 212.TL/21.zTL
6016 212.TL/21.zTL
6017 212.TL/21.zTL
6018 212.TL/21.zTL
6019 212.TL/21.zTL
6020 212.TL/21.zTL
6021 212.TL/21.zTL
6022 212.TL/21.zTL
6023 212.TL/21.zTL
6024 212.TL/21.zTL
6025 212.TL/21.zTL
6026 212.TL/21.zTL
6027 212.TL/21.zTL
6028 212.TL/21.zTL
6029 212.TL/21.zTL
6030 212.TL/21.zTL
6031 212.TL/21.zTL
6032 212.TL/21.zTL
6033 212.TL/21.zTL
6034 212.TL/21.zTL
6035 212.TL/21.zTL
6036 212.TL/21.zTL
6037 212.TL/21.zTL
6038 212.TL/21.zTL
6039 212.TL/21.zTL
6040 212.TL/21.zTL
6041 212.TL/21.zTL
6042 212.TL/21.zTL
6043
6044
6045
6046 212.TL/21.zTL
6047 212.TL/21.zTL
6048 212.TL/21.zTL
6049 212.TL/21.zTL
6050 212.TL/21.zTL
6051
6052
6053 212.TL/21.zTL
6054
6055
6057
6058 212.TL/21.zTL
6059 212.TL/21.zTL
6060 212.TL/21.zTL
6061 212.TL/21.zTL
6062 212.TL/21.zTL
6063 212.TL/21.zTL
6064
6065
6066
6067
6068
6069
6070
6071
6072
6073*

Antonov An-24V
241.smdl/24.zDL,
Praha/Kbely
7109
7110

Antonov An-26/
An-26Z-1M*
241.smdl/24.zDL,
Praha/Kbely
2408
2409
2507
3209*
4201

Antonov An-30FG
241.smdl/24.zDL,
Praha/Kbely
1107

Canadair CL.601-3A
Challenger
241.smdl/24.zDL,
Praha/Kbely
5105

LET 410 Turbolet
241.smdl/24.zDL,
Praha/Kbely
0503 L-410MA
0712 L-410UVP-S
0731 L-410UVP
0926 L-410UVP-T
0928 L-410UVP-T
0929 L-410UVP-T
1132 L-410UVP-T
1134 L-410UVP
1504 L-410UVP
1523 L-410FG
1525 L-410FG
1526 L-410FG
2312 L-410UVP-E
2601 L-410UVP-E
2602 L-410UVP-E
2710 L-410UVP-E

Mikoyan MiG-21MF/
MiG-21UM*
211.TL/21.zTL, Cáslav;
LZO, Ceske Budejovice
2105 211.TL/21.zTL
2205 211.TL/21.zTL
2500 211.TL/21.zTL
2614 211.TL/21.zTL
3186* 211.TL/21.zTL
3746* 211.TL/21.zTL
4003 211.TL/21.zTL
4017 211.TL/21.zTL
4175 211.TL/21.zTL
4307 LZO
4405 211.TL/21.zTL
5031* 211.TL/21.zTL
5203 LZO
5210 211.TL/21.zTL
5212 211.TL/21.zTL
5213 211.TL/21.zTL
5214 211.TL/21.zTL
5301 211.TL/21.zTL
5302 211.TL/21.zTL
5303 211.TL/21.zTL
5304 211.TL/21.zTL
5305 211.TL/21.zTL
5508 211.TL/21.zTL
5512 211.TL/21.zTL
5581 211.TL/21.zTL
5603 211.TL/21.zTL
7701 211.TL/21.zTL
7802 211.TL/21.zTL
9011* 211.TL/21.zTL
9332* 211.TL/21.zTL
9333* 211.TL/21.zTL
9341* 211.TL/21.zTL
9399* 211.TL/21.zTL
9410 211.TL/21.zTL
9414 211.TL/21.zTL
9707 211.TL/21.zTL
9711 211.TL/21.zTL
9801 211.TL/21.zTL
9802 LZO
9804 211.TL/21.zTL
9805 211.TL/21.zTL

Mil Mi-17
232.vrl/23.zVrL, Perov
0803
0805
0809
0811
0816
0818
0819
0822
0825
0828
0830
0831
0832
0833
0834
0835
0836
0837
0839
0840
0848
0849
0850

Mil Mi-24/Mi-35
231.lbvr/23.zVrL, Perov
0103 Mi-24D
0214 Mi-24D
0217 Mi-24D
0218 Mi-24D
0219 Mi-24D
0220 Mi-24D
0701 Mi-24V1
0702 Mi-24V1
0703 Mi-24V1
0705 Mi-24V1
0709 Mi-24V1
0710 Mi-24V1
0788 Mi-24V1
0789 Mi-24V1
0790 Mi-24V1
0812 Mi-24V1
0815 Mi-24V1
0816 Mi-24V1

0834 Mi-24V2
0835 Mi-24V2
0836 Mi-24V2
0837 Mi-24V2
0838 Mi-24V2
0839 Mi-24V2
4010 Mi-24D
4011 Mi-24D
6050 Mi-24DU
7353 Mi-35
7354 Mi-35
7355 Mi-35
7356 Mi-35
7357 Mi-35
7358 Mi-35

SAAB JAS 39 Gripen
JAS 39C
9234
9235
9236
9237
9238
9239
9240
9241
9242
9243
9244
9245
JAS 39C
9819820

Tupolev Tu-154
241.smdl/24.zDL,
Praha/Kbely
0601 Tu-154B-2
1003 Tu-154M
1016 Tu-154M

Yakovlev Yak-40
241.smdl/24.zDL,
Praha/Kbely
0260 Yak-40
1257 Yak-40K

DENMARK
Flyvevåbnet
Lockheed C-130J-30 Hercules II
Eskadrille 721, Aalborg
B-536
B-537
B-538

Canadair CL.604 Challenger
Eskadrille 721, Aalborg
C-080
C-168
C-172

General Dynamics F-16
(MLU aircraft are marked with a *)
Eskadrille 726, Aalborg;
Eskadrille 727, Skrydstrup;
Eskadrille 730, Skrydstrup
E-004 F-16A* Esk 730
E-005 F-16A* Esk 726
E-007 F-16A* Esk 726
E-008 F-16A* Esk 726
E-011 F-16A* Esk 727
E-016 F-16A* Esk 726
E-017 F-16A* Esk 730
E-018 F-16A* Esk 730
E-024 F-16A* Esk 730
E-070 F-16A* Esk 730
E-074 F-16A Esk 730
E-075 F-16A* Esk 730
E-107 F-16A* Esk 726
E-180 F-16A Esk 730
E-182 F-16A* Esk 730
E-184 F-16A Esk 727
E-187 F-16A* Esk 730
E-188 F-16A* Esk 730
E-189 F-16A* Esk 726
E-190 F-16A* Esk 730
E-191 F-16A Esk 730
E-192 F-16A* Esk 730
E-193 F-16A* Esk 727
E-194 F-16A* Esk 730
E-195 F-16A* Esk 726
E-196 F-16A* Esk 727
E-197 F-16A* Esk 730
E-198 F-16A* Esk 726
E-199 F-16A* Esk 730
E-200 F-16A Esk 727
E-202 F-16A* Esk 730
E-203 F-16A* Esk 730
E-596 F-16A* Esk 730
E-597 F-16A* Esk 730
E-598 F-16A* Esk 726
E-599 F-16A* Esk 727
E-600 F-16A* Esk 730
E-601 F-16A* Esk 726
E-602 F-16A* Esk 730
E-603 F-16A* Esk 730
E-604 F-16A* Esk 726
E-605 F-16A* Esk 730
E-606 F-16A* Esk 730
E-607 F-16A* Esk 730
E-608 F-16A* Esk 726
E-609 F-16A* Esk 726
E-610 F-16A* Esk 730
E-611 F-16A* Esk 726
ET-022 F-16B* Esk 730
ET-197 F-16B Esk 727
ET-198 F-16B* Esk 727
ET-199 F-16B* Esk 730
ET-204 F-16B* Esk 726
ET-206 F-16B* Esk 730
ET-207 F-16B* Esk 730
ET-208 F-16B Esk 730
ET-210 F-16B* Esk 727
ET-612 F-16B* Esk 726
ET-613 F-16B* Esk 727
ET-614 F-16B* Esk 726
ET-615 F-16B* Esk 726

SAAB T-17 Supporter
Eskadrille 721, Aalborg;
Flyveskolen, Karup (FLSK)
T-401 FLSK
T-402 Esk 721
T-403 FLSK
T-404 FLSK
T-405 FLSK
T-407 Esk 721
T-408 FLSK
T-409 FLSK
T-410 FLSK
T-411 FLSK
T-412 FLSK
T-413 FLSK
T-414 Esk 721
T-415 FLSK
T-417 FLSK
T-418 Esk 721
T-419 FLSK
T-420 Esk 721
T-421 FLSK
T-423 FLSK
T-425 FLSK
T-426 FLSK
T-427 FLSK
T-428 FLSK
T-429 FLSK
T-430 FLSK
T-431 Esk 721
T-432 FLSK

Sikorsky S-61A Sea King
Eskadrille 722, Vaerløse
Detachments at:
Aalborg, Ronne, Skrydstrup
U-240
U-275
U-276
U-277
U-278
U-279
U-280
U-481

Søvaernets Flyvetjaeneste (Navy)
Westland Lynx Mk 80/90B
Eskadrille 728, Karup
S-134 Mk 90B
S-142 Mk 90B
S-170 Mk 90B
S-175 Mk 80
S-181 Mk 90B
S-191 Mk 90B
S-249 Mk 90B
S-256 Mk 90B

Haerens Flyvetjaeneste (Army)
Hughes 500M
Eskadrille 724, Vandel
H-201
H-202
H-203
H-205
H-206
H-207
H-209
H-211
H-213
H-244
H-245
H-246

Aérospatiale AS.550C-2 Fennec
Eskadrille 724, Vandel
P-090
P-234
P-254
P-275
P-276
P-287
P-288
P-319
P-320
P-339
P-352
P-369

EGYPT
Al Quwwat al-Jawwiya il Misriya
Lockheed C-130H/ C-130H-30* Hercules
16 Sqn, Cairo West
1271/SU-BAB
1272/SU-BAC
1273/SU-BAD
1274/SU-BAE
1275/SU-BAF
1277/SU-BAI
1278/SU-BAJ
1279/SU-BAK
1280/SU-BAL
1281/SU-BAM
1282/SU-BAN
1283/SU-BAP
1284/SU-BAQ
1285/SU-BAR
1286/SU-BAS
1287/SU-BAT
1288/SU-BAU
1289/SU-BAV
1290/SU-BEW
1291/SU-BEX
1292/SU-BEY
1293/SU-BKS*
1294/SU-BKT*
1295/SU-BKU*
1296
1297
1298

Egyptian Govt
Airbus A.340-211
Egyptian Govt, Cairo
SU-GGG

Boeing 707-366C
Egyptian Govt, Cairo
SU-AXJ

Grumman G.1159A Gulfstream III/ G.1159C Gulfstream IV/ G.1159C Gulftream IV-SP/ Gulfstream 400
Egyptian Air Force/Govt, Cairo
SU-BGM Gulfstream IV
SU-BGU Gulfstream III
SU-BGV Gulfstream III
SU-BNC Gulfstream IV
SU-BND Gulfstream IV
SU-BNO Gulfstream IV-SP
SU-BNP Gulfstream IV-SP
SU-BPE Gulfstream 400

FINLAND
Suomen Ilmavoimat
Fokker F.27 Friendship
Tukilentolaivue, Jyväskylä/Tikkakoski
FF-1 F.27-100
FF-3 F.27-400M

Gates Learjet 35A
Tukilentolaivue, Jyväskylä/Tikkakoski;
Tukilentolaivue (Det.), Kuopio/Rissala*
LJ-1*
LJ-2
LJ-3

McDonnell Douglas F-18 Hornet
Hävittäjälentolaivue 11, Roveniemi;
Hävittäjälentolaivue 21, Tampere/Pirkkala;
Hävittäjälentolaivue 31, Kuopio/Rissala;
Koelentokeskus, Halli
F-18C Hornet
HN-401 HavLLv 31
HN-402 HavLLv 21
HN-403 HavLLv 31
HN-404 HavLLv 11
HN-405 HavLLv 31
HN-406 HavLLv 11
HN-407 HavLLv 21
HN-408 HavLLv 31
HN-409 HavLLv 31
HN-410 HavLLv 31
HN-411 HavLLv 21
HN-412 HavLLv 21
HN-413 HavLLv 21
HN-414 KoelntK
HN-415 HavLLv 21
HN-416 HavLLv 21
HN-417 HavLLv 21
HN-418 HavLLv 31
HN-419 HavLLv 11
HN-420 HavLLv 11
HN-421 HavLLv 21
HN-422 HavLLv 31
HN-423 HavLLv 21
HN-424 HavLLv 31
HN-425 HavLLv 21
HN-426 HavLLv 31
HN-427 HavLLv 21
HN-428 HavLLv 31
HN-429 HavLLv 11
HN-431 HavLLv 31
HN-432 HavLLv 31
HN-433 HavLLv 21
HN-434 HavLLv 31
HN-435 HavLLv 31
HN-436 HavLLv 21
HN-437 HavLLv 31
HN-438 HavLLv 31
HN-439 HavLLv 21
HN-440 HavLLv 11
HN-441 HavLLv 21
HN-442 HavLLv 31
HN-443 HavLLv 31
HN-444 HavLLv 31
HN-445 HavLLv 21
HN-446 HavLLv 31
HN-447 HavLLv 11
HN-448 HavLLv 11
HN-449 HavLLv 21
HN-450 HavLLv 21
HN-451 HavLLv 21
HN-452 HavLLv 21
HN-453 HavLLv 21
HN-454 HavLLv 31
HN-455 HavLLv 31
HN-456 HavLLv 21
HN-457 HavLLv 11
F-18D Hornet
HN-461 KoelntK
HN-462 KoelntK
HN-463 HavLLv 21
HN-464 HavLLv 11
HN-465 HavLLv 31
HN-466 HavLLv 11
HN-467 HavLLv 31

FRANCE
Armée de l'Air
Aérospatiale SN601 Corvette
CEV, Cazaux
1 MV
2 MW
10 MX

Aérospatiale TB-30 Epsilon
**Cartouche Dorée*, (EPAA 00.315) Cognac;
EPAA 00.315, Cognac;
SOCATA, Tarbes
Please note: A large number of these machines are kept in temporary storage at Chateaudun
1 315-UA
2 315-UB
3 FZ SOCATA
4 315-UC
5 315-UD
6 315-UE
7 315-UF
8 315-UG
9 315-UH
10 315-UI
12 315-UK
13 315-UL
14 315-UM
15 315-UN
16 315-UO
17 315-UP
19 315-UR
20 315-US
21 315-UT
24 315-UW
25 315-UX
26 315-UY
27 315-UZ
28 315-VA
29 315-VB
30 315-VC
31 315-VD
32 315-VE
33 315-VF
34 315-VG
35 315-VH
36 315-VI
37 315-VJ
38 315-VK
39 315-VL
40 315-VM
41 315-VN
42 315-VO
43 315-VP
44 315-VQ
45 315-VR
46 315-VS
47 315-VT
48 315-VU
50 315-VW
52 315-VX
54 315-VZ
56 315-WA
57 F-ZVLB
61 315-WD
62 315-WE
63 315-WF
64 315-WG

65	315-WH
66	315-WI
67	315-WJ
68	315-WK
69	315-WL
70	315-WM
72	315-WO
73	315-WP
74	315-WQ
75	315-WR
76	315-WS
77	315-WT
78	315-WU
79	315-WV
80	315-WW
81	315-WX
82	315-WY
83	315-WZ
84	315-XA
85	315-XB
86	315-XC
87	315-XD
88	315-XE
89	315-XF
90	315-XG
91	315-XH
92	F-SEXI [1]*
93	315-XJ
94	315-XK
95	315-XL
96	315-XM
97	315-XN
98	315-XO
99	315-XP
100	F-SEXQ [2]*
101	315-XR
102	315-XS
103	315-XT
104	315-XU
105	F-SEXV [4]*
106	315-XW
107	315-XX
108	315-XY
109	315-XZ
110	315-YA
111	315-YB
112	315-YC
113	315-YD
114	315-YE
115	315-YF
116	315-YG
117	F-SEYH [3]*
118	315-YI
119	315-YJ
120	315-YK
121	315-YL
122	315-YM
123	315-YN
124	315-YO
125	315-YP
126	315-YQ
127	315-YR
128	315-YS
129	315-YT
130	315-YU
131	315-YV
132	315-YW
133	315-YX
134	315-YY
135	315-YZ
136	315-ZA
137	315-ZB
138	315-ZC
139	315-ZD
140	315-ZE
141	315-ZF
142	315-ZG
143	315-ZH
144	315-ZI
145	315-ZJ
146	315-ZK
149	315-ZM
150	315-ZN
152	315-ZO
153	315-ZP
154	315-ZQ
155	315-ZR
158	315-ZS
159	315-ZT

Airbus A.310-304

ET 03.060 *Esterel*, Paris/Charles de Gaulle

418	F-RADC
421	F-RADA
422	F-RADB

Airbus A.319CJ-115

ETEC 00.065, Villacoublay

1485	F-RBFA
1556	F-RBFB

Airbus A.340-311

ET 03.060 *Esterel*, Paris/Charles de Gaulle

013
058

Airtech CN-235M-200

ET 00.042 *Ventoux*, Mont-de-Marsan;
ETL 01.062 *Vercours*, Creil;
ETOM 00.052 *La Tontouta*, Noumea;
ETOM 00.082 *Maine*, Faaa-Tahiti

045	62-IB	01.062
065	82-IC	00.082
066	52-ID	00.052
071	62-IE	01.062
072	82-IF	00.082
105	52-IG	00.052
107	52-IH	00.052
111	62-II	01.062
114	62-IJ	01.062
123	62-IM	01.062
128	62-IK	00.042
129	62-IL	01.062
137	62-IN	01.062
141	62-IO	01.062
152	62-IP	01.062
156	62-IQ	01.062
158	62-IR	01.062
160	62-IS	01.062
165	62-IT	01.062

Boeing C-135 Stratotanker

ERV 00.093 *Bretagne*, Istres

470	C-135FR	93-CA
471	C-135FR	93-CB
472	C-135FR	93-CC
474	C-135FR	93-CE
475	C-135FR	93-CF
497	KC-135R	93-CM
525	KC-135R	93-CN
574	KC-135R	93-CP
735	C-135FR	93-CG
736	C-135FR	93-CH
737	C-135FR	93-CI
738	C-135FR	93-CJ
739	C-135FR	93-CK
740	C-135FR	93-CL

Boeing E-3F Sentry

EDCA 00.036, Avord

201	36-CA
202	36-CB
203	36-CC
204	36-CD

CASA 212-300 Aviocar

CEV, Cazaux & Istres

377	MO
378	MP
386	MQ

Cessna 310

CEV, Cazaux & Istres

187	310N	BJ
188	310N	BK
190	310N	BL
193	310N	BG
194	310N	BH
242	310K	AW
244	310K	AX
513	310N	BE
693	310N	BI
820	310Q	CL
981	310Q	BF

D-BD Alpha Jet

AMD-BA, Istres;
CEAM (EC 02.330), Mont-de-Marsan;
CEV, Cazaux & Istres;
CITac 00.339 *Aquitaine*, Luxeuil;
EAC 00.314, Tours;
EC 01.002 *Cicogne*, Dijon;
EC 01.007 *Provence* & EC 02.007 *Argonne*, St Dizier;
EPNER, Istres;
ERS 01.091 *Gascogne*, Mont-de-Marsan;
ETO 01.008 *Saintonge* & ETO 02.008 *Nice*, Cazaux;
GI 00.312, Salon de Provence;
Patrouille de France (PDF) (EPAA 20.300), Salon de Provence

01	F-ZJTS	CEV
E1		CEV
E3		
E4		
E5	314-LV	00.314
E7	7-PF	02.007
E8		CEV
E9	8-MJ	01.008
E10	314-LK	00.314
E11	7-PX	02.007
E12		CEV
E13		
E14	314-TP	00.314
E15	8-NO	02.008
E17	314-LW	00.314
E18	8-NN	02.008
E19	330-AH	CEAM
E20	339-DI	00.339
E21	330-AL	CEAM

E22		
E23	314-UG	00.314
E24	314-TJ	00.314
E25		
E26	314-LS	00.314
E28	8-NK	02.008
E29	314-TM	00.314
E30	7-PV	02.007
E31	F-TERK	*PDF* [8]
E32		
E33	8-MZ	01.008
E34	8-MF	01.008
E35	314-LF	00.314
E36	314-UF	00.314
E37	8-NI	02.008
E38	8-MQ	01.008
E41	F-TERA	*PDF* [0]
E42		
E43	314-LI	00.314
E44	314-LP	00.314
E45	314-TF	00.314
E46	F-TERN	*PDF* [7]
E47	314-TR	00.314
E48	8-MH	01.008
E49	314-TA	00.314
E51	314-TH	00.314
E52		
E53	314-TC	00.314
E55	314-UC	00.314
E58	314-TK	00.314
E59	314-LY	00.314
E60		EPNER
E61	314-LQ	00.314
E63	314-LN	00.314
E64	314-TL	00.314
E65	8-MD	01.008
E66	8-ME	01.008
E67	314-TB	00.314
E68	339-DK	00.339
E69	314-TO	00.314
E72	314-LA	00.314
E73		
E74	8-MS	01.008
E75	F-TERW	*PDF* [9]
E76	8-MR	01.008
E79	330-AH	CEAM
E80		CEV
E81	314-LX	00.314
E82	8-NB	02.008
E83	7-PU	02.007
E84	314-UK	00.314
E85	8-MT	01.008
E86	8-NS	02.008
E87		
E88	314-LL	00.314
E89	314-LM	00.314
E90	8-NF	02.008
E91	2-EL	01.002
E92	330-AK	CEAM
E93		
E94	F-TERH	*PDF* [1]
E95	8-NM	02.008
E96	314-LC	00.314
E97	8-NT	02.008
E98	314-TT	00.314
E99		
E100		EPNER
E101	8-NQ	02.008
E102	8-MY	01.008
E103	314-UA	00.314
E104		
E105	8-NU	02.008
E106	8-NA	02.008
E107	312-RT	00.312
E108		
E109	8-NJ	02.008
E110	8-NG	02.008
E112	DA	01.091
E113	314-UB	00.314
E114	314-TU	00.314
E115	8-NW	02.008
E116		
E117	F-TERI	*PDF*
E118	339-DN	00.339
E119	8-MI	01.008
E120	F-TERG	*PDF* [6]
E121	8-NE	02.008
E122	F-TERD	*PDF*
E123	8-ML	01.008
E124	314-TE	00.314
E125	314-LG	00.314
E126	314-LU	00.314
E127	314-TV	00.314
E128		
E129		
E130	312-RU	00.312
E131	312-RV	00.312
E132	314-LZ	00.314
E133	8-MN	01.008
E134	F-TERM	*PDF* [2]
E135	F-TERX	*PDF* [4]
E136	314-TN	00.314
E137	314-LJ	00.314
E138	314-LT	00.314
E139	8-ND	02.008
E140	314-UD	00.314
E141	7-PJ	02.007
E142	314-LB	00.314
E143	312-RS	00.312
E144		
E145		
E146	7-PW	02.007
E147	8-NH	02.008
E148	8-MG	01.008
E149	8-MO	01.008
E150	8-NC	02.008
E151	8-MC	01.008
E152	314-LO	00.314
E153	314-TG	00.314
E154	339-DF	00.339
E155	8-NP	02.008
E156	314-TI	00.314
E157		
E158		
E159	7-PP	02.007
E160	F-TERC	*PDF* [3]
E161		
E162	314-TZ	00.314
E163	F-TERB	*PDF*
E164	8-MB	01.008
E165	F-TERE	*PDF* [5]
E166	314-TX	00.314
E167	314-UH	00.314
E168	314-TS	00.314
E169	314-LE	00.314
E170	314-UN	00.314
E171	314-LR	00.314
E173	314-LH	00.314
E176	8-MA	01.008

Dassault Falcon 20

CEV, Cazaux & Istres;
CITac 00.339 *Aquitaine*, Luxeuil;
ETEC 00.065, Villacoublay

22	CS	CEV
79	CT	CEV
86	CG	CEV
93	F-RAED	00.065
96	CB	CEV
104	CW	CEV
124	CC	CEV
131	CD	CEV
138	CR	CEV
167	(F-RAEB)	00.065
182	339-JA	00.339
188	CX	CEV
252	CA	CEV
263	CY	CEV
288	CV	CEV
291	65-EG	00.065
342	F-RAEC	00.065
375	CZ	CEV
422	F-RAEH	00.065
451	339-JC	00.339
483	339-JI	00.339

Dassault Falcon 50

ETEC 00.065, Villacoublay

5	F-RAFI
27	(F-RAFK)
34	(F-RAFL)
78	F-RAFJ

Dassault Falcon 900

ETEC 00.065, Villacoublay

02	(F-RAFP)
004	(F-RAFQ)

Dassault Mirage IVP

ERS 01.091 *Gascogne*, Mont-de-Marsan

25	AX
53	BZ
59	CF
61	CH
62	CI

Dassault Mirage F.1

CEAM (EC 02.330), Mont-de-Marsan;
CEV, Cazaux & Istres;
EC 01.030 *Alsace* & EC 02.030 *Normandie Niemen*, Colmar;
ER 01.033 *Belfort*, ER 02.033 *Savoie* & EC 03.033 *Lorraine*, Reims;

Mirage F.1CT

219	30-SN	01.030
220	30-QK	02.030
221	30-SY	01.030
223	30-SA	01.030
225	330-AJ	CEAM
226		
227	330-AP	CEAM
228	30-QT	02.030
229		
230	33-FH	03.033
231		
232	33-FK	02.033
233	30-QG	02.030
234	30-SI	01.030
235	30-SK	01.030
236	30-SB	01.030
237	30-SM	01.030
238		
239	30-QD	02.030
241	30-QA	02.030
242	30-QV	02.030
243	30-QJ	02.030

244	30-QH	02.030
245	30-SX	01.030
246	33-FX	03.033
248	30-QC	02.030
251	33-FM	03.033
252	33-FN	03.033
253	30-SJ	01.030
254		
255		
256	30-SL	01.030
257	30-SF	01.030
258	33-FO	03.033
259	30-QZ	02.030
260	30-SR	01.030
261	30-SY	01.030
262	30-SE	01.030
264	33-FX	03.033
265	33-FQ	03.033
267	30-QU	02.030
268		
271	30-QQ	02.030
272	30-QL	02.030
273	33-FG	03.033
274	30-QR	02.030
275	33-FY	03.033
278	30-SG	01.030
279	30-SC	01.030
280	30-SD	01.030
281	33-FI	03.033
283	30-SV	01.030

Mirage F.1B

501		
502	33-FR	03.033
504	33-FV	03.033
505		
507	33-FE	03.033
509	33-FS	03.033
510		
511	33-FT	03.033
512	33-FL	03.033
513	33-FA	03.033
514	33-FZ	03.033
516	33-FP	03.033
517	33-FB	03.033
518	33-FF	03.033
519	33-FC	03.033
520	33-FD	03.033

Mirage F.1CR

602		CEV
603	33-CB	01.033
604	33-CF	01.033
605	33-CO	01.033
606	33-NP	02.033
607	33-ND	02.033
608	33-NG	02.033
610	33-NQ	02.033
611	33-CN	01.033
612	33-NJ	02.033
613	33-CC	01.033
614	33-NR	02.033
615	33-NZ	02.033
616	33-NM	02.033
617	33-NO	02.033
620	33-CT	01.033
622	33-NH	02.033
623	33-CM	01.033
624	33-NY	02.033
627	33-NT	02.033
628	33-NB	02.033
630	33-CU	01.033
631	33-NS	02.033
632	33-CL	01.033
634	33-CK	01.033
635	33-CG	01.033
636	33-NL	02.033
637	33-CP	01.033
638	33-NX	02.033
640	33-NV	02.033
641	33-CD	01.033
642	330-AO	CEAM
643	33-CK	01.033
645	33-CH	01.033
646	33-NW	02.033
647	33-CQ	01.033
648	33-NT	02.033
649	330-AB	CEAM
650	33-CJ	01.033
651	33-NB	02.033
653	33-CV	01.033
654	33-CS	01.033
655	33-NG	02.033
656	33-NK	02.033
657		
658	33-CW	01.033
659	33-CA	01.033
660	33-CY	01.033
661	33-NE	02.033
662	33-NA	02.033

Dassault Mirage 2000B

AMD-BA, Istres;
CEAM (EC 02.330), Mont-de-Marsan;
CEV, Cazaux & Istres;
EC 02.002 *Côte d'Or*, Dijon;
EC 01.005 *Vendée* & EC 02.005 *Ile de France*, Orange;
EC 01.012 *Cambrésis* & EC 02.012 *Picardie*, Cambrai

501	(BX1)	CEV
502		
504		CEV
505	5-OY	02.005
506	5-OD	02.005
507	5-OR	02.005
508		
509	5-OP	02.005
510	5-OQ	02.005
512	5-OU	02.005
513	5-OI	02.005
514	5-OE	02.005
515	5-OG	02.005
516	5-OL	02.005
518	5-OM	02.005
519	5-OW	02.005
520	5-OS	02.005
521	5-ON	02.005
522	5-OV	02.005
523	5-OA	02.005
524	12-YR	01.012
525	12-YP	01.012
526	12-KO	02.012
527	5-OB	02.005
528	5-OT	02.005
529	12-KJ	02.012
530	12-YM	01.012

Dassault Mirage 2000C/ 2000-5F*

CEAM (EC 02.330), Mont-de-Marsan;
CEV, Istres;
EC 01.002 *Cigognes* & EC 02.002 *Côte d'Or*, Dijon;
EC 01.005 *Vendée* & EC 02.005 *Ile de France*, Orange;
EC 01.012 *Cambrésis* & EC 02.012 *Picardie*, Cambrai;
EC 04.033 *Vexin*, Djibouti

01*		CEV
1		
2		CEV
3	5-NN	01.005
4	5-NB	01.005
5	5-NT	01.005
8	5-NF	01.005
9	5-OJ	02.005
11	5-NJ	01.005
12	5-NV	01.005
13	5-NM	01.005
14	5-NW	01.005
15	5-NA	01.005
16	5-NE	01.005
17	5-NR	01.005
18	5-NP	01.005
19	5-OX	02.005
20	5-NQ	01.005
21		
22	5-ND	01.005
25	5-NU	01.005
27	5-OH	02.005
28		
29	5-NO	01.005
30	5-OF	02.005
32	5-NS	01.005
34	5-NH	01.005
35	5-NL	01.005
36	5-OC	02.005
37	5-OO	02.005
38*	2-FK	02.002
40*	2-FG	02.002
41*	2-EJ	01.002
42*		
43*	330-AA	CEAM
44*	2-EQ	01.002
45*	2-EF	01.002
46*	2-EN	01.002
47*	2-EP	01.002
48*	2-FX	02.002
49*	2-FF	02.002
51*	330-AS	CEAM
52*	2-FC	02.002
53*	2-FA	02.002
54*	2-FY	02.002
55*		
56*	2-EG	01.002
57*	2-ET	01.002
58*	2-FO	02.002
59*	2-EV	01.002
61*	2-EM	01.002
62*	2-ED	01.002
63*	2-FQ	02.002
64	330-AQ	CEAM
65*	2-EK	01.002
66*	2-FD	02.002
67*	2-FL	02.002
68*	2-FM	02.002
69*	2-FP	02.002
70*	2-EH	01.002
71*		
72*	2-EE	01.002
73*	2-ES	01.002
74*	2-EU	01.002
76*	2-EB	01.002
77*	330-AX	CEAM
78*	2-EC	01.002

79	12-YF	01.012
80	12-YJ	01.012
81	12-KP	02.012
82	12-KS	02.012
83	12-YL	01.012
85	33-LD	04.033
86	12-KA	02.012
87	12-KN	02.012
88	12-KI	02.012
89	12-YQ	01.012
90	12-YS	01.012
91	12-KL	02.012
92	330-AW	CEAM
93	12-KK	02.012
94	12-YI	01.012
95	12-KM	02.012
96	12-YB	01.012
97	12-YT	01.012
98	12-YU	01.012
99		
100	12-YG	01.012
101	12-KE	02.012
102	12-KR	02.012
103	12-YN	01.012
104	12-KG	02.012
105	12-YF	01.012
106		
107	12-KQ	02.012
108	12-YD	01.012
109	12-KF	02.012
111	12-KN	02.012
112	12-YC	01.012
113	12-YO	01.012
114	12-YK	01.012
115	12-KH	02.012
116	12-YD	01.012
117		
118	12-YE	01.012
119	12-KD	02.012
120	12-YP	01.012
121	12-KC	02.012
122	12-YA	01.012
123	12-YH	01.012
124	12-KB	02.012
X7		CEV

Dassault Mirage 2000D

AMD-BA, Istres;
CEAM (EC 02.330), Mont-de-Marsan;
CEV, Istres;
EC 01.003 *Navarre*, EC 02.003 *Champagne* & EC 03.003 *Ardennes*, Nancy;
EC 04.033 *Vexin*, Djibouti

601	3-IS	01.003
602	3-JY	02.003
603	3-IM	01.003
604	3-IN	01.003
605	3-XE	03.003
606	3-XX	03.003
607		CEV
609	3-JP	02.003
610	3-JW	02.003
611		
612	3-JK	02.003
613	3-XU	03.003
614	3-JB	02.003
615	3-JA	02.003
616	3-JS	02.003
617	3-XA	03.003
618	3-JF	02.003
619	3-JE	02.003
620	3-IM	01.003
622		
623	3-IB	01.003
624	3-IW	01.003
625	3-JC	02.003
626	3-XH	03.003
627	3-JL	02.003
628	3-XF	03.003
629	3-XO	03.003
630	3-XD	03.003
631	3-JO	02.003
632	3-XJ	03.003
634	3-IL	01.003
635	3-XP	03.003
636	3-JJ	02.003
637	3-XC	03.003
638	3-IJ	01.003
639	330-AZ	CEAM
640	3-IR	01.003
641	3-XG	03.003
642	3-JB	02.003
643	3-JD	02.003
644	3-IU	01.003
645	3-XL	03.003
646	3-IC	01.003
647	3-IO	01.003
648		
649		
650	3-IA	01.003
651	3-JV	02.003
652	3-XN	03.003
653	3-IE	01.003
654	3-IT	01.003
655		
657	3-JM	02.003
658	3-JN	02.003
659	3-XR	03.003
660	3-ID	01.003
661	3-IH	01.003
662	3-IP	01.003
664	3-JU	02.003
665	3-XT	03.003
666	3-IK	01.003
667	3-JX	02.003
668	330-AR	CEAM
669	3-XV	03.003
670	3-IQ	01.003
671	3-XK	03.003
672	3-JQ	02.003
673		
674	3-IR	01.003
675	3-JI	02.003
676		CEV
677	3-JT	01.003
678	330-AG	CEAM
679	3-JX	01.003
680	3-XM	03.003
681	3-IG	01.003
682	3-JR	02.003
683	3-JT	02.003
684	3-IF	01.003
685	3-XZ	03.003
686	3-JH	02.003

Dassault Mirage 2000N

CEAM (EC 02.330), Mont-de-Marsan;
CEV, Istres;
EC 01.004 *Dauphiné* & EC 02.004 *Lafayette*, Luxeuil;
EC 03.004 *Limousin*, Istres

301		CEV
303	4-CL	03.004
304	4-CK	03.004
305	4-CS	03.004
306	4-BL	02.004
307	4-CH	03.004
309	4-AO	01.004
310	4-CE	03.004
311	4-AF	01.004
312	4-CN	03.004
313	4-CR	03.004
314	4-AX	01.004
315	4-BF	02.004
316	4-BH	02.004
317	4-BP	02.004
319	4-AC	01.004
320	4-CD	03.004
322	4-CP	03.004
323	4-CV	03.004
324	4-CX	03.004
325	4-CC	03.004
326	4-AS	01.004
327	4-CJ	03.004
329	4-AU	01.004
330	4-AT	01.004
331	4-BO	02.004
332	4-BN	02.004
333	4-AB	01.004
334	330-AV	CEAM
335	4-CI	03.004
336	4-BI	02.004
337	4-AK	01.004
338	4-CG	03.004
339	4-AD	01.004
340	4-AA	01.004
341	4-AF	01.004
342	4-BA	02.004
343	4-AH	01.004
344	4-BV	02.004
345	4-BU	02.004
348	4-AL	01.004
349	4-BM	02.004
350	4-AJ	01.004
351	4-AQ	01.004
353	4-BD	02.004
354	4-BJ	02.004
355	4-AE	01.004
356	4-BX	02.004
357	4-CO	03.004
358	4-BQ	02.004
359	4-BG	02.004
360	4-CB	03.004
361		
362	4-CU	03.004
363	4-BK	02.004
364	4-BB	02.004
365	4-BE	02.004
366		
367	4-AS	01.004
368	4-AR	01.004
369	4-AG	01.004
370	4-CA	03.004
371	4-AV	01.004
372	4-BR	02.004
373	4-CF	03.004
374	4-BS	02.004
375	4-CL	03.004

Dassault Rafale-B

AMD-BA, Istres;
CEV, Istres

301	CEV
302	CEV
303	
304	
305	

B01 CEV

Dassault Rafale-C
AMD-BA, Istres;
CEV, Istres
101 CEV
C01 CEV

DHC-6 Twin Otter 200/300*
ET 00.042 *Ventoux*, Mont-de-Marsan;
GAM 00.056 *Vaucluse*, Evreux

292	CC	00.056
298	CD	00.056
300	CE	00.056
730*	CA	00.042
742*	CB	00.042
745*	CV	00.042
790*	CW	00.042

Embraer EMB.121AA/ AN* Xingu
EAT 00.319, Avord

054	YX
055*	YZ
064	YY
066*	ZA
69*	
070*	ZC
072	YA
073	YB
075	YC
076	YD
77*	ZD
078	YE
080	YF
082	YG
083*	ZE
084	YH
086	YI
089	YJ
090*	ZF
091	YK
092	YL
095	YM
096	YN
098	YO
099	YP
101	YR
102	YS
103	YT
105	YU
107	YV
108	YW
111	YQ

Embraer EMB.312F Tucano
GI 00.312, Salon de Provence

438	312-UW
439	312-UY
456	312-JA
457	312-JB
458	312-JC
459	312-JD
460	312-JE
461	312-JF
462	312-JG
463	312-JH
464	312-JI
466	312-JK
467	312-JL
468	312-JM
469	312-JN
470	312-JO
471	312-JP
472	312-JQ
473	312-JR
474	312-JS
475	312-JT
477	312-JU
478	312-JV
479	312-JX
480	312-JY
481	312-JZ
483	312-UB
484	312-UC
485	312-UD
486	312-UE
487	312-UF
488	312-UG
489	312-UH
490	312-UI
491	312-UJ
492	312-UK
493	312-UL
494	312-UM
495	312-UN
496	312-UO
497	312-UP
498	312-UQ
499	312-UR
500	312-US
501	312-UT
503	312-UV
504	312-UX

Eurocopter AS.332 Super Puma/AS.532 Cougar
EH 03.067 *Parisis*, Villacoublay;
EH 05.067 *Alpilles*, Aix-en-Provence;
ETOM 00.082 *Maine*, Faaa-Tahiti;
GAM 00.056 *Vaucluse*, Evreux;
CEAM, Mont-de-Marsan

2014	AS.332C	PN	05.067
2057	AS.332C	PO	00.082
2093	AS.332L	PP	05.067
2233	AS.332L-1	67-FY	03.067
2235	AS.332L-1	67-FZ	03.067
2244	AS.332C	PM	00.082
2342	AS.532UL	FX	00.056
2369	AS.532UL	FW	00.056
2375	AS.532UL	FV	00.056
2377	AS.332L-1	67-FU	03.067
2461	AS.532A-2	IH	CEAM

Lockheed C-130H/ C-130H-30* Hercules
ET 02.061 *Franche-Comté*, Orléans

4588	61-PM
4589	61-PN
5114	61-PA
5116	61-PB
5119	61-PC
5140	61-PD
5142*	61-PE
5144*	61-PF
5150*	61-PG
5151*	61-PH
5152*	61-PI
5153*	61-PJ
5226*	61-PK
5227*	61-PL

SEPECAT Jaguar
CEV, Cazaux & Istres;
CEAM (EC 02.330), Mont-de-Marsan;
CITac 00.339 *Aquitaine*, Luxeuil;
EC 01.007 *Provence*, St Dizier

Jaguar A

A99	7-HC	01.007
A104	7-HM	01.007
A120	7-HL	01.007
A128	7-HP	01.007
A129	7-HD	01.007
A133	7-HB	01.007
A135	7-HF	01.007
A137	7-HQ	01.007
A138	7-HV	01.007
A140	7-HI	01.007
A141	7-HU	01.007
A144	7-HA	01.007
A145	7-HG	01.007
A148	7-HN	01.007
A150	7-HE	01.007
A151	7-HJ	01.007
A153	7-HK	01.007
A154	7-HO	01.007
A157	7-HH	01.007
A158	7-HT	01.007
A160	7-HS	01.007

Jaguar E

E3	339-WF	00.339
E6	7-HR	01.007
E10	339-WL	00.339
E12	339-WI	00.339
E19	339-WG	00.339
E22	7-HX	01.007
E29	339-WJ	00.339
E32	7-HW	01.007
E35	7-HY	01.007
E37	7-HZ	01.007

SOCATA TBM 700
CEV, Cazaux & Istres;
ETM 00.040 *Moselle*, Metz;
ETE 00.043 *Médoc*, Bordeaux;
ETE 00.044 *Mistral*, Villacoublay;
ETEC 00.065, Villacoublay;
EdC 00.070, Chateaudun

33	XA	00.043
35	XB	00.043
70	XC	00.043
77	XD	00.040
78	XE	00.044
80	XF	00.040
93	XL	00.043
94	65-XG	00.070
95	65-XH	00.065
103	XI	00.040

104 XJ 00.044
105 XK 00.065
106 MN CEV
110 XP 00.040
111 XM 00.065
117 XN 00.040
125 65-XO 00.065
131 XQ 00.065
146 XR 00.065
147 XS 00.065

Transall C-160F/C-160NG GABRIEL*/C-160R

CEAM (EET 06.330), Mont-de-Marsan;
CEV, Cazaux & Istres;
EET 01.054 *Dunkerque*, Metz;
ET 01.061 *Touraine* & ET 03.061 *Poitou*, Orléans;
ET 01.064 *Bearn* & ET 02.064 *Anjou*, Evreux;
ETOM 00.050 *Réunion*, St Denis;
ETOM 00.055 *Ouessant*, Dakar;
ETOM 00.058 *Guadeloupe*, Pointe-à-Pitre;
ETOM 00.088 *Larzac*, Djibouti

RA02 C-160R 61-MI 01.061
RA04 C-160R 61-MS 01.061
RA06 C-160R 61-ZB 03.061
R1 C-160R 61-MA 01.061
R2 C-160R 61-MB 01.061
R3 C-160R 61-MC 00.058
R4 C-160R 61-MD 01.061
R5 C-160R 61-ME 01.061
R11 C-160R 61-MF 01.061
R12 C-160R 61-MG 01.061
R13 C-160R 61-MH 00.050
R15 C-160R 61-MJ 01.061
R17 C-160R 61-ML 01.061
R18 C-160R 61-MM 01.061
R42 C-160R 61-MN 01.061
R43 C-160R 61-MO 01.061
R44 C-160R 61-MP 01.061
R45 C-160R 61-MQ 01.061
R46 C-160R 61-MR 01.061
R48 C-160R 61-MT 01.061
R49 C-160F 59-MU CEV
R51 C-160R 61-MW 01.061
R52 C-160R 61-MX 01.061
R53 C-160R 61-MY 01.061
R54 C-160R 61-MZ 01.061
R55 C-160R 61-ZC 03.061
R86 C-160R 61-ZD 03.061
R87 C-160R 61-ZE 00.050
R88 C-160R 61-ZF 03.061
R89 C-160R 61-ZG 03.061
R90 C-160R 61-ZH 03.061
R91 C-160R 61-ZI 03.061
R92 C-160R 61-ZJ 03.061
R93 C-160R 61-ZK 03.061
R94 C-160R 61-ZL 03.061
R95 C-160R 61-ZM 03.061
R96 C-160R 61-ZN 03.061
R97 C-160R 61-ZO 03.061
R98 C-160R 61-ZP 03.061
R99 C-160R 61-ZQ 03.061
R100 C-160R 61-ZR 03.061
R153 C-160R 61-ZS 03.061
R154 C-160R 61-ZT 03.061
R157 C-160R 61-ZW 03.061
R158 C-160R 61-ZX 03.061
R159 C-160R 61-ZY 03.061
R160 C-160R 61-ZZ 03.061
R201 C-160R 64-GA 01.064
R202 C-160R 64-GB 02.064
R203 C-160R 64-GC 01.064
R204 C-160R 64-GD 02.064
R205 C-160R 64-GE 01.064
R206 C-160R 64-GF 02.064
R207 C-160R 64-GG 01.064
R208 C-160R 64-GH 02.064
R210 C-160R 64-GJ 02.064
R211 C-160R 64-GK 01.064
R212 C-160R 64-GL 02.064
R213 C-160R 64-GM 01.064
R214 C-160R 64-GN 02.064
R215 C-160R 64-GO 01.064
F216 C-160NG* 54-GT 01.054
R217 C-160R 64-GQ 01.064
R218 C-160R 64-GR 02.064
F221 C-160NG* GS 01.054
R223 C-160R 64-GW 01.064
R224 C-160R 64-GX 02.064
R225 C-160R 64-GY 01.064
R226 C-160R 64-GZ 02.064

Aéronavale/Marine Aérospatiale SA.321G Super Frelon

32 Flottille, Hyères & Lanvéoc/Poulmic

101
106
118
134
137
144
148
160
162
163
165

Dassault-Breguet Atlantique 2

21 Flottille, Nimes/Garons;
23 Flottille, Lorient/ Lann Bihoué

1 21F
2 23F
3 23F
4 21F
5 21F
6 23F
7 21F
8 23F
9 21F
10 23F
11 23F
12 23F
13 21F
14 21F
15 23F
16 23F
17 21F
18 21F
19 23F
20 21F
21 23F
22 23F
23 21F
24 21F
25 21F
26 23F
27 23F
28 21F

Dassault Falcon 10(MER)
ES 57, Landivisiau
32
101
129
133
143
185

Dassault Falcon 20G Guardian
25 Flottille, Papeete & Tontouta
48
65
72
77
80

Dassault Falcon 50 SURMAR
24 Flottille, Lorient/Lann Bihoué
7
30
36
132

Dassault Rafale-M
12 Flottille, Landivisiau;
AMD-BA, Istres;
CEV, Istres
M01 CEV
M02 CEV
1 CEV
2 12F
3
4 12F
5 12F
6 12F
7 12F
8 12F
9 12F
10 12F

Dassault Super Etendard
11 Flottille, Landivisiau;
17 Flottille, Landivisiau;
CEV, Cazaux & Istres
1 17F
2 11F
3 11F
4 11F
6 17F
8 17F
10 11F
11 17F
12 11F
13 17F
14 17F
15 17F
16 11F
17 11F
18 17F
19 11F
23 17F
24 11F
25 17F
28 11F
30 11F
31 17F
32 11F
33 11F
35 11F
37 11F
38 11F
39 11F
41 11F
43 17F
44 17F
45 11F
46 17F
47 11F
48 17F
49 17F
50 11F
51 17F
52 11F
55 11F
57 11F
59 17F
61 17F
62 11F
64 11F
65 17F
66 11F
68 CEV
69 11F
71 11F

Embraer EMB.121AN Xingu
24 Flottille, Lorient/Lann Bihoué;
28 Flottille, Hyères
30 24F
47 24F
65 28F
67 24F
68 24F
71 28F
74 24F
79 24F
81 24F
85 28F
87 24F

Eurocopter SA.365/ AS.565 Panther
35 Flottille, Hyères, (with detachments at Cherbourg, La Rochelle & Le Touquet)
36 Flottille, Hyères
17 SA.365N 35F
19 SA.365N 35F
24 SA.365N 35F
57 SA.365N 35F
81 SA.365N 35F
91 SA.365N 35F
157 SA.365N 35F
313 SA.365F1 35F
318 SA.365F1 35F
322 SA.365F1 35F
355 AS.565MA 36F
362 AS.565MA 35F
436 AS.565MA 36F
452 AS.565MA 36F
453 AS.565MA 35F
466 AS.565MA 36F
482 AS.565MA 36F
486 AS.565MA 36F
503 AS.565MA 35F
505 AS.565MA 36F
506 AS.565MA 35F
507 AS.565MA 36F
511 AS.565MA 36F
519 AS.565MA 36F
522 AS.565MA 36F
524 AS.565MA 36F
542 AS.565MA 36F

Nord 262E Frégate
24 Flottille, Lorient/Lann Bihoué;
28 Flottille, Hyères;
ERCE, Hyères;
ES 10, Hyères;
ES 55, Aspretto
45 28F
46 28F
51 28F
53 28F
60 28F
63 28F
69 28F
70 28F
71 28F
72 28F
73 28F
75 24F
79 28F
100 28F

Northrop Grumman E-2C Hawkeye
4 Flottille, Lorient/Lann Bihoué
1 (165455)
2 (165456)
3 (166417)

Westland Lynx HAS2(FN)/HAS4(FN)*
31 Flottille, Hyères;
34 Flottille, Lanvéoc/Poulmic;
CEPA, Hyères;
260 CEPA
263 34F
264 31F
265 34F
266 31F
267 31F
269 34F
270 31F
271 34F
272 34F
273 34F
274 34F
275 31F
276 34F
620 31F
621 31F
622 34F
623 34F
624 31F
625 34F
627 34F
801* 31F
802* 31F
804* 31F
806* 34F
807* 34F
808* 34F
810* 34F
811* 31F
812* 31F
813* 34F
814* 31F

Aviation Legére de l'Armée de Terre (ALAT)

Cessna F.406 Caravan II
EAAT, Rennes
0008 ABM
0010 ABN

SOCATA TBM 700
EAAT, Rennes
99 ABO
100 ABP
115 ABQ
136 ABR
139 ABS
156 ABT
159 ABU
160 ABV

French Govt

Aérospatiale AS.355F-1 Twin Ecureuil
Douanes Francaises
F-ZBAC (5026)
F-ZBEF (5236)
F-ZBEJ (5003)
F-ZBEK (5298)
F-ZBEL (5299)

Beech Super King Air B200
Sécurité Civile
F-ZBEM
F-ZBFJ 98
F-ZBFK 96
F-ZBMB B97

Cessna F.406 Caravan II
Douanes Francaises
F-ZBAB (0025)
F-ZBBB (0039)
F-ZBCE (0042)
F-ZBCF (0077)
F-ZBCG (0066)
F-ZBCH (0075)
F-ZBCI (0070)
F-ZBCJ (0074)
F-ZBEP (0006)
F-ZBES (0017)
F-ZBFA (0001)
F-ZBGA (0086)
F-ZBGB (0090)

Dassault Falcon 20
AVDEF, Nimes/Garons
F-GPAA Falcon 20ECM
F-GPAB Falcon 20E

Fokker F-27-600
Sécurité Civile
F-ZBFF 71 (10432)
F-ZBFG 72 (10440)

GERMANY
Luftwaffe, Marineflieger

Airbus A.310-304/MRTT*
1/FBS, Köln-Bonn
10+21
10+22
10+23
10+24*
10+25*
10+26*
10+27*

Canadair CL601-1A Challenger
3/FBS, Köln-Bonn
12+02
12+03
12+04
12+05
12+06
12+07

Eurofighter EF.2000/ EF.2000T*
EADS, Manching;
JG-73 *Steinhoff*, Laage;
TsLw-1, Kaufbeuren;
WTD-61, Ingolstadt
30+02* JG-73
30+03* JG-73
30+04* JG-73
30+05* JG-73
30+06
30+07
30+08
30+09
30+10* JG-73
30+11
30+12
30+13
30+14* JG-73
30+15
30+16
30+17* JG-73
30+18
30+19
30+20*
30+21
30+22
30+23
30+24*
30+25
98+03* EADS
98+29 WTD-61
98+30 WTD-61
98+31* TsLw-1

McD F-4F Phantom
Fluglehrzentrum F-4F, Hopsten;
JG-71 *Richthofen*, Wittmundhaven;
JG-74 *Molders*, Neuburg/ Donau;
TsLw-1, Kaufbeuren;
WTD-61, Ingolstadt
37+01 FIZ F-4F
37+03 JG-71
37+04 TsLw-1
37+11 FIZ F-4F
37+13 JG-74
37+14 TsLw-1
37+15 WTD-61
37+16 WTD-61
37+17 FIZ F-4F
37+22 JG-71
37+26 JG-71
37+28 JG-71
37+32 FIZ F-4F
37+39 JG-71
37+48 JG-71
37+55 JG-71
37+61 JG-74
37+63 JG-71
37+65 JG-71
37+71 JG-74
37+75 FIZ F-4F
37+76 JG-71
37+77 JG-71
37+78 JG-71
37+79 JG-71
37+81 JG-74
37+82 JG-71
37+83 FIZ F-4F
37+84 JG-71
37+85 JG-71
37+86 JG-71
37+88 FIZ F-4F
37+89 JG-71
37+92 JG-74
37+93 FIZ F-4F
37+94 JG-74
37+96 FIZ F-4F
37+98 JG-71
38+00 JG-71
38+01 JG-71
38+02 JG-74
38+03 FIZ F-4F
38+05 FIZ F-4F
38+06 JG-74
38+07 JG-71
38+09 JG-74
38+10 JG-74
38+12 JG-71
38+13 WTD-61
38+14 JG-71
38+16 JG-74
38+17 JG-74
38+18 JG-74
38+20 FIZ F-4F
38+24 JG-74
38+26 JG-74
38+27 JG-71
38+28 JG-74
38+29 JG-74
38+30 JG-71
38+31 JG-74
38+32 FIZ F-4F
38+33 JG-74
38+36 JG-71
38+37 JG-74
38+39 JG-74
38+40 FIZ F-4F
38+42 JG-71
38+43 FIZ F-4F
38+44 JG-71
38+45 JG-71
38+46 JG-71
38+48 JG-71
38+49 JG-71
38+50 FIZ F-4F
38+53 JG-74
38+54 JG-71
38+55 JG-71
38+56 JG-71
38+57 JG-74
38+58 JG-71
38+60 JG-74
38+61 FIZ F-4F
38+62 FIZ F-4F
38+64 JG-71
38+66 FIZ F-4F
38+67 JG-71
38+68 JG-74
38+69 FIZ F-4F
38+70 JG-74
38+73 FIZ F-4F
38+74 JG-71
38+75 JG-71

Panavia Tornado Strike/ Trainer[1]/ECR[2]
AkG-51 *Immelmann*, Schleswig/Jagel;
EADS, Manching;
GAFTTC, Holloman AFB, USA;
JbG-31 *Boelcke*, Nörvenich;
JbG-32, Lechfeld;
JbG-33, Büchel;
JbG-38 *Ostfriesland*, Jever;
MFG-2, Eggebek;
TsLw-1, Kaufbeuren;
WTD-61, Ingolstadt

43+01[1] JbG-38
43+02[1] JbG-38
43+04[1] JbG-38
43+05[1] TsLw-3
43+07[1] TsLw-3
43+08[1] JbG-32
43+10[1] JbG-38
43+13 EADS
43+15[1] JbG-38
43+17[1] JbG-38
43+18 GAFTTC
43+20 JbG-31
43+23[1] JbG-33
43+25 JbG-31
43+27 JbG-31
43+28 JbG-32
43+29[1] JbG-31
43+31[1] JbG-31
43+33[1] JbG-32
43+34 TsLw-1
43+35[1] AkG-51
43+37[1] JbG-32
43+38 JbG-31
43+41 JbG-31
43+42[1] GAFTTC
43+43[1] JbG-31
43+45[1] JbG-32
43+46 AkG-51
43+47 AkG-51
43+48 AkG-51
43+50 AkG-51
43+52 JbG-38
43+53 JbG-33
43+54 JbG-31
43+55 MFG-2
43+57 GAFTTC
43+58 JbG-33
43+59 TsLw-1
43+60
43+62 JbG-33
43+63 JbG-32
43+64 JbG-33
43+65 JbG-38
43+67 JbG-38
43+68 JbG-32
43+69 JbG-31
43+70 JbG-33
43+71 JbG-38
43+72 JbG-38
43+73 AkG-51
43+75 GAFTTC
43+76 JbG-38
43+77 GAFTTC
43+78 TsLw-1
43+79 AkG-51
43+81 AkG-51
43+82 AkG-51
43+85 JbG-33
43+86 JbG-33
43+87 MFG-2
43+90[1] JbG-38
43+91[1] GAFTTC
43+92[1] JbG-31
43+94[1] JbG-38
43+96 AkG-51
43+97[1] GAFTTC
43+98 AkG-51
44+00 JbG-31
44+01[1] JbG-33
44+02 GAFTTC
44+04 AkG-51
44+06 AkG-51
44+07 JbG-32
44+08 JbG-38
44+09 JbG-33
44+11 JbG-33
44+12 GAFTTC
44+13 TsLw-1
44+15 AkG-51
44+16[1] JbG-31
44+17 AkG-51
44+19 JbG-31
44+20[1] GAFTTC
44+21 JbG-31
44+23 JbG-33
44+25[1] JbG-38
44+26 JbG-33
44+27 JbG-33
44+29 JbG-31
44+30 JbG-31
44+32 JbG-38
44+33 JbG-33
44+34 AkG-51
44+35 JbG-31
44+37[1] JbG-38
44+38[1] GAFTTC
44+39[1] GAFTTC
44+41 JbG-31
44+42 AkG-51
44+43 JbG-31
44+44 JbG-31
44+46 JbG-33
44+48 JbG-33
44+50 AkG-51
44+52 JbG-31
44+54 JbG-33
44+55 JbG-38
44+57 JbG-31
44+58 JbG-31
44+59 GAFTTC
44+60 GAFTTC
44+61 AkG-51
44+62 JbG-31
44+63 JbG-33
44+64 AkG-51
44+65 AkG-51
44+66 JbG-38
44+68 AkG-51
44+69 AkG-51
44+70 JbG-31
44+71 JbG-31
44+72[1] JbG-33
44+73[1] GAFTTC
44+75[1] JbG-31
44+76 JbG-31
44+77 GAFTTC
44+78 JbG-31
44+79 JbG-33
44+80 JbG-31
44+81 GAFTTC
44+83 JbG-33
44+84 JbG-33
44+85 JbG-33
44+86 AkG-51
44+87 AkG-51
44+88 AkG-51
44+89 JbG-32
44+90 JbG-38
44+91 JbG-33
44+92 JbG-38
44+94 JbG-33
44+95 JbG-38
44+96 JbG-31
44+97 JbG-38
45+00 JbG-38
45+01 GAFTTC
45+02 MFG-2
45+03 GAFTTC
45+04 JbG-33
45+06 AkG-51
45+07 JbG-33
45+08 JbG-33
45+09 GAFTTC
45+10 JbG-32
45+11 GAFTTC
45+12[1] MFG-2
45+13[1] MFG-2
45+14[1] JbG-38
45+15[1] GAFTTC
45+16[1] JbG-38
45+17 GAFTTC
45+19 JbG-33
45+20 AkG-51
45+21 JbG-33
45+22 JbG-33
45+23 JbG-31
45+24 JbG-33
45+25 AkG-51
45+28 MFG-2
45+30 MFG-2
45+31 MFG-2
45+33 MFG-2
45+34 MFG-2
45+35 MFG-2
45+36 MFG-2
45+37 JbG-33
45+38 MFG-2
45+39 MFG-2
45+40 MFG-2
45+41 MFG-2
45+42 MFG-2
45+43 MFG-2
45+44 MFG-2
45+45 MFG-2
45+46 JbG-33
45+47 MFG-2
45+49 MFG-2
45+50 JbG-33
45+51 AkG-51
45+52 JbG-33
45+53 JbG-33
45+54 GAFTTC
45+55 GAFTTC
45+56 MFG-2
45+57 AkG-51
45+59 MFG-2
45+61[1] GAFTTC
45+60[1] AkG-51
45+64 TsLw-1
45+66 MFG-2
45+67 AkG-51
45+68 MFG-2
45+69 JbG-33
45+70[1] JbG-31
45+71 MFG-2
45+72 MFG-2
45+73[1] GAFTTC

45+74 TsLw-1
45+76 JbG-38
45+77[1] JbG-31
45+78 JbG-33
45+79 JbG-31
45+81 JbG-31
45+82 JbG-31
45+84 AkG-51
45+85 AkG-51
45+86 JbG-33
45+87 JbG-33
45+88 JbG-31
45+89 JbG-38
45+90 JbG-31
45+91 AkG-51
45+92 JbG-31
45+93 AkG-51
45+94 JbG-33
45+95 JbG-31
45+98 GAFTTC
45+99[1] GAFTTC
46+00[1] GAFTTC
46+01 GAFTTC
46+02 JbG-33
46+04[1] GAFTTC
46+05[1] MFG-2
46+07[1] GAFTTC
46+08[1] GAFTTC
46+09[1] GAFTTC
46+10 WTD-61
46+11 MFG-2
46+14 AkG-51
46+15 MFG-2
46+18 JbG-33
46+19 MFG-2
46+20 MFG-2
46+21 AkG-51
46+22 MFG-2
46+23[2] JbG-32
46+24[2] JbG-32
46+25[2] JbG-32
46+26[2] JbG-32
46+27[2] JbG-32
46+28[2] JbG-32
46+29[2] JbG-32
46+30[2] JbG-32
46+31[2] JbG-32
46+32[2] JbG-32
46+33[2] JbG-32
46+34[2] JbG-32
46+35[2] JbG-32
46+36[2] JbG-32
46+37[2] JbG-32
46+38[2] JbG-32
46+39[2] JbG-32
46+40[2] WTD-61
46+41[2] JbG-32
46+42[2] JbG-32
46+43[2] JbG-32
46+44[2] JbG-32
46+45[2] JbG-32
46+46[2] JbG-32
46+47[2] JbG-32
46+48[2] JbG-32
46+49[2] JbG-32
46+50[2] JbG-32
46+51[2] JbG-32
46+52[2] JbG-32
46+53[2] JbG-32
46+54[2] GAFTTC
46+55[2] JbG-32
46+56[2] JbG-32
46+57[2] JbG-32
98+59 WTD-61
98+60 WTD-61
98+77 WTD-61
98+79[2] WTD-61

Transall C-160D
LTG-61, Landsberg;
LTG-62, Wunstorf;
LTG-63, Hohn;
WTD-61, Ingolstadt
50+06 LTG-63
50+07 LTG-61
50+08 LTG-63
50+09 LTG-62
50+10 LTG-62
50+17 LTG-62
50+29 LTG-62
50+33 LTG-61
50+34 LTG-63
50+35 LTG-62
50+36 LTG-62
50+37 LTG-62
50+38 LTG-62
50+40 LTG-61
50+41 LTG-62
50+42 LTG-62
50+44 LTG-61
50+45 LTG-63
50+46 LTG-62
50+47 LTG-61
50+48 LTG-61
50+49 LTG-63
50+50 LTG-63
50+51 LTG-61
50+52 LTG-62
50+53 LTG-61
50+54 LTG-62
50+55 LTG-63
50+56 LTG-63
50+57 LTG-62
50+58 LTG-62
50+59 LTG-63
50+60 LTG-62
50+61 LTG-63
50+62 LTG-62
50+64 LTG-61
50+65 LTG-62
50+66 LTG-61
50+67 LTG-63
50+68 LTG-61
50+69 LTG-63
50+70 LTG-62
50+71 LTG-63
50+72 LTG-63
50+73 LTG-63
50+74 LTG-61
50+75 LTG-63
50+76 LTG-63
50+77 LTG-63
50+78 LTG-62
50+79 LTG-62
50+81 LTG-62
50+82 LTG-62
50+83 LTG-62
50+84 LTG-61
50+85 LTG-63
50+86 LTG-61
50+87 LTG-63
50+88 LTG-61
50+89 LTG-62
50+90 LTG-62
50+91 LTG-62
50+92 LTG-61
50+93 LTG-61
50+94 LTG-63
50+95 LTG-63
50+96 LTG-61
50+97 LTG-62
50+98 LTG-61
50+99 LTG-61
51+00 LTG-62
51+01 LTG-62
51+02 WTD-61
51+03 LTG-62
51+04 LTG-61
51+05 LTG-62
51+06 LTG-63
51+07 LTG-62
51+08 WTD-61
51+09 LTG-63
51+10 LTG-63
51+11 LTG-62
51+12 LTG-63
51+13 LTG-63
51+14 WTD-61
51+15 LTG-61

Dornier Do.228/Do.228LM*
MFG-3, Nordholz;
WTD-61, Ingolstadt
57+01* MFG-3
57+02* MFG-3
57+03 MFG-3
57+04* MFG-3
98+78 WTD-61

Lockheed P-3C Orion
MFG-3, Nordholz
60+01
60+02
60+03
60+04
60+05
60+06
60+07
60+08

Breguet Br.1150 Atlantic *Elint
MFG-3, Nordholz
61+03*
61+04
61+05
61+06*
61+08
61+09
61+10
61+11
61+12
61+13
61+14
61+15
61+16
61+17
61+18*
61+19*
61+20

Eurocopter AS.532U-2 Cougar
3/FBS, Berlin-Tegel
82+01
82+02
82+03

Westland Lynx Mk88/ Super Lynx Mk88A*
MFG-3, Nordholz
83+02*

83+03*
83+04*
83+05*
83+06*
83+07*
83+09*
83+10*
83+11*
83+12*
83+13*
83+15*
83+17
83+18*
83+19*
83+20*
83+21*
83+22*
83+23*
83+24*
83+25*
83+26*

Westland Sea King HAS41
MFG-5, Kiel-Holtenau
89+50
89+51
89+52
89+53
89+54
89+55
89+56
89+57
89+58
89+60
89+61
89+62
89+63
89+64
89+65
89+66
89+67
89+68
89+69
89+70
89+71

NH Industries NH.90
98+90
98+91

Heeresfliegertruppe
Eurocopter AS.665 Tiger
WTD-61, Ingolstadt
74+05
74+07
74+08
74+09
74+10
98+12
98+13
98+14
98+23
98+25
98+26
98+27

Eurocopter EC.135P-1
HFWS, Bückeburg
82+51
82+52
82+53
82+54
82+55
82+56
82+57
82+58
82+59
82+60
82+61
82+62
82+63
82+64
82+65

MBB Bo.105
HFR-35, Mendig;
HFUS-1, Holzdorf;
HFUS-7, Mendig;
HFUS-10, Laupheim;
HFUS-14, Celle;
HFVAS-100, Celle;
HFVS-910, Bückeburg;
HFWS, Bückeburg;
KHR-26, Roth;
KHR-36, Fritzlar;
TsLw-3, Fassberg;
WTD-61, Ingolstadt
80+01 Bo.105M HFR-35
80+05 Bo.105M HFR-35
80+07 Bo.105M HFWS
80+08 Bo.105M HFUS-10
80+18 Bo.105M
80+26 Bo.105M HFUS-7
80+27 Bo.105M HFR-35
80+33 Bo.105M HFR-35
80+40 Bo.105M HFUS-10
80+47 Bo.105M KHR-26
80+59 Bo.105M HFR-35
80+61 Bo.105M HFUS-1
80+66 Bo.105M
80+79 Bo.105M HFR-35
80+86 Bo.105M HFUS-1
80+88 Bo.105M HFUS-1
80+90 Bo.105M HFUS-1
80+91 Bo.105M HFR-35
80+92 Bo.105M HFR-35
80+97 Bo.105M HFR-35
86+01 Bo.105P
86+02 Bo.105P HFVS-910
86+03 Bo.105P HFWS
86+04 Bo.105P KHR-36
86+05 Bo.105P HFWS
86+06 Bo.105P HFWS
86+07 Bo.105P HFWS
86+08 Bo.105P HFWS
86+09 Bo.105P HFWS
86+10 Bo.105P
86+11 Bo.105P KHR-36
86+12 Bo.105P HFWS
86+13 Bo.105P HFWS
86+14 Bo.105P HFVAS-100
86+15 Bo.105P HFUS-14
86+16 Bo.105P HFWS
86+17 Bo.105P HFVS-910
86+18 Bo.105P KHR-26
86+19 Bo.105P KHR-26
86+20 Bo.105P HFWS
86+21 Bo.105P HFVAS-100
86+22 Bo.105P HFWS
86+23 Bo.105P TsLw-3
86+24 Bo.105P HFVS-910
86+25 Bo.105P HFVAS-100
86+26 Bo.105P HFVS-910
86+27 Bo.105P KHR-26
86+28 Bo.105P HFWS
86+29 Bo.105P HFUS-14
86+30 Bo.105P KHR-26
86+31 Bo.105P HFUS-14
86+32 Bo.105P KHR-26
86+33 Bo.105P KHR-26
86+34 Bo.105P HFUS-1
86+35 Bo.105P KHR-26
86+36 Bo.105P KHR-36
86+37 Bo.105P
86+38 Bo.105P KHR-36
86+39 Bo.105P HFVAS-100
86+41 Bo.105P HFVAS-100
86+42 Bo.105P KHR-26
86+43 Bo.105P HFUS-14
86+44 Bo.105P KHR-26
86+45 Bo.105P HFUS-14
86+46 Bo.105P HFVAS-100
86+47 Bo.105P HFVAS-100
86+48 Bo.105P HFVAS-100
86+49 Bo.105P KHR-36
86+50 Bo.105P KHR-36
86+51 Bo.105P KHR-36
86+52 Bo.105P
86+53 Bo.105P KHR-36
86+54 Bo.105P HFUS-14
86+55 Bo.105P HFUS-14
86+56 Bo.105P KHR-36
86+57 Bo.105P HFUS-14
86+58 Bo.105P KHR-36
86+59 Bo.105P HFVAS-100
86+60 Bo.105P HFWS
86+61 Bo.105P KHR-26
86+62 Bo.105P HFVS-910
86+63 Bo.105P KHR-26
86+64 Bo.105P KHR-26
86+65 Bo.105P KHR-26
86+66 Bo.105P HFVS-910
86+67 Bo.105P HFVAS-100
86+68 Bo.105P KHR-36
86+69 Bo.105P KHR-26
86+70 Bo.105P HFVAS-100
86+71 Bo.105P KHR-36
86+72 Bo.105P KHR-36
86+73 Bo.105P KHR-36
86+74 Bo.105P KHR-36
86+75 Bo.105P KHR-36
86+76 Bo.105P KHR-26
86+77 Bo.105P HFUS-1
86+78 Bo.105P KHR-26
86+80 Bo.105P
86+81 Bo.105P KHR-36
86+83 Bo.105P HFUS-14
86+84 Bo.105P KHR-26
86+85 Bo.105P HFUS-1
86+86 Bo.105P HFVAS-100
86+87 Bo.105P HFUS-14
86+88 Bo.105P HFUS-14
86+89 Bo.105P HFUS-1
86+90 Bo.105P KHR-26
86+91 Bo.105P KHR-26
86+92 Bo.105P KHR-36
86+93 Bo.105P HFVS-910
86+94 Bo.105P KHR-26
86+95 Bo.105P HFUS-1
86+96 Bo.105P KHR-26
86+97 Bo.105P KHR-36
86+98 Bo.105P HFR-35
86+99 Bo.105P TsLw-3
87+00 Bo.105P KHR-26
87+01 Bo.105P KHR-26
87+02 Bo.105P KHR-26
87+03 Bo.105P TsLw-3
87+04 Bo.105P KHR-36
87+06 Bo.105P KHR-36
87+07 Bo.105P KHR-26
87+08 Bo.105P HFWS
87+09 Bo.105P KHR-36

87+10 Bo.105P KHR-26
87+11 Bo.105P KHR-36
87+12 Bo.105P KHR-36
87+13 Bo.105P KHR-36
87+14 Bo.105P KHR-36
87+15 Bo.105P KHR-36
87+16 Bo.105P KHR-36
87+17 Bo.105P KHR-36
87+18 Bo.105P HFVAS-100
87+19 Bo.105P TsLw-3
87+20 Bo.105P KHR-26
87+21 Bo.105P TsLw-3
87+22 Bo.105P HFUS-10
87+23 Bo.105P HFVAS-100
87+24 Bo.105P HFUS-7
87+25 Bo.105P KHR-26
87+26 Bo.105P HFUS-1
87+27 Bo.105P HFUS-14
87+28 Bo.105P HFUS-1
87+29 Bo.105P HFVS-910
87+30 Bo.105P HFUS-14
87+31 Bo.105P
87+32 Bo.105P HFWS
87+33 Bo.105P KHR-26
87+34 Bo.105P KHR-26
87+35 Bo.105P KHR-26
87+36 Bo.105P HFWS
87+37 Bo.105P KHR-26
87+38 Bo.105P KHR-36
87+39 Bo.105P KHR-36
87+41 Bo.105P KHR-36
87+42 Bo.105P KHR-36
87+43 Bo.105P KHR-36
87+44 Bo.105P KHR-36
87+45 Bo.105P HFUS-1
87+46 Bo.105P KHR-36
87+47 Bo.105P HFUS-14
87+48 Bo.105P HFVAS-100
87+49 Bo.105P HFWS
87+50 Bo.105P KHR-26
87+51 Bo.105P HFVAS-100
87+52 Bo.105P HFUS-1
87+53 Bo.105P KHR-26
87+55 Bo.105P HFVS-910
87+56 Bo.105P KHR-26
87+57 Bo.105P KHR-26
87+58 Bo.105P HFWS
87+59 Bo.105P KHR-36
87+60 Bo.105P KHR-36
87+61 Bo.105P KHR-36
87+62 Bo.105P HFWS
87+63 Bo.105P HFWS
87+64 Bo.105P HFWS
87+65 Bo.105P KHR-36
87+66 Bo.105P KHR-36
87+67 Bo.105P HFVAS-100
87+68 Bo.105P HFWS
87+69 Bo.105P KHR-26
87+70 Bo.105P HFR-35
87+71 Bo.105P KHR-26
87+72 Bo.105P
87+73 Bo.105P HFWS
87+74 Bo.105P KHR-36
87+75 Bo.105P KHR-26
87+76 Bo.105P HFUS-7
87+77 Bo.105P
87+78 Bo.105P
87+79 Bo.105P
87+80 Bo.105P HFUS-1
87+81 Bo.105P HFUS-14
87+82 Bo.105P HFUS-14
87+83 Bo.105P
87+84 Bo.105P HFVS-910
87+85 Bo.105P HFR-35
87+86 Bo.105P KHR-26
87+87 Bo.105P HFR-35
87+88 Bo.105P KHR-26
87+89 Bo.105P KHR-36
87+90 Bo.105P HFWS
87+91 Bo.105P HFR-35
87+92 Bo.105P KHR-26
87+94 Bo.105P KHR-26
87+95 Bo.105P KHR-26
87+96 Bo.105P KHR-26
87+97 Bo.105P KHR-26
87+98 Bo.105P KHR-26
87+99 Bo.105P KHR-36
88+01 Bo.105P KHR-36
88+02 Bo.105P KHR-36
88+03 Bo.105P KHR-36
88+04 Bo.105P KHR-36
88+05 Bo.105P HFVS-910
88+06 Bo.105P KHR-36
88+07 Bo.105P HFVAS-100
88+08 Bo.105P KHR-36
88+09 Bo.105P HFR-35
88+10 Bo.105P HFVS-910
88+11 Bo.105P KHR-36
88+12 Bo.105P HFVAS-100
98+28 Bo.105C WTD-61

Sikorsky/VFW
CH-53G/CH-53GS*
HFWS, Bückeburg;
MTHR-15, Rheine-Bentlage;
MTHR-25, Laupheim;
TsLw-3, Fassberg;
WTD-61, Ingolstadt

84+01* WTD-61
84+02 WTD-61
84+05 HFWS
84+06 MTHR-15
84+09 TsLw-3
84+10 HFWS
84+11 HFWS
84+12 MTHR-15
84+13 HFWS
84+14 HFWS
84+15* MTHR-25
84+16 HFWS
84+17 MTHR-25
84+18 HFWS
84+19 TsLw-3
84+21 HFWS
84+22 MTHR-15
84+23
84+24 MTHR-15
84+25*
84+26 MTHR-15
84+27 HFWS
84+28 MTHR-25
84+29
84+30*
84+31 MTHR-15
84+32 MTHR-25
84+33
84+34 MTHR-15
84+35
84+36 WTD-61
84+37 HFWS
84+38 MTHR-25
84+39 MTHR-15
84+40 MTHR-25
84+41 HFWS
84+42* MTHR-25
84+43 MTHR-25
84+44 MTHR-25
84+45* MTHR-25
84+46 MTHR-15
84+47 MTHR-25
84+48 MTHR-25
84+49 HFWS
84+50 HFWS
84+51* MTHR-25
84+52* MTHR-25
84+53 MTHR-25
84+54 MTHR-25
84+55 MTHR-25
84+56
84+57 HFWS
84+58 MTHR-25
84+59 MTHR-25
84+60 MTHR-25
84+62* MTHR-25
84+63 MTHR-25
84+64* MTHR-25
84+65
84+66* MTHR-25
84+67* MTHR-15
84+68 MTHR-15
84+69 MTHR-15
84+70 MTHR-15
84+71 MTHR-15
84+72 MTHR-15
84+73 MTHR-15
84+74 MTHR-15
84+75 MTHR-15
84+76 HFWS
84+77 MTHR-15
84+78 MTHR-15
84+79* MTHR-15
84+80 MTHR-15
84+82 MTHR-15
84+83 MTHR-15
84+84 MTHR-15
84+85* MTHR-25
84+86 MTHR-15
84+87 MTHR-15
84+88 MTHR-15
84+89 MTHR-15
84+90 MTHR-15
84+91* MTHR-15
84+92 MTHR-15
84+94
84+95 MTHR-25
84+96 MTHR-25
84+97 MTHR-25
84+98* MTHR-15
84+99 MTHR-15
85+00* HFWS
85+01
85+02
85+03 MTHR-15
85+04 MTHR-15
85+05 MTHR-25
85+06 MTHR-15
85+07* HFWS
85+08 MTHR-15
85+10*
85+11 MTHR-25
85+12* MTHR-15

GHANA

Ghana Air Force

Fokker F-28 Fellowship 3000
VIP Flight, Accra
G-530

Grumman G.1159A Gulfstream III
VIP Flight, Accra
G-540

GREECE
Ellinikí Polemiki Aeroporía
Embraer ERJ-135BJ Legacy/ERJ.145H/ ERJ.135LR
356 MTM/112 PM, Elefsís;
380 Mira/112 PM, Elefsís
135L-484 ERJ-135BJ 356 MTM
145-209 ERJ-135LR 356 MTM
145-374 ERJ-145H 380 Mira
145-671 ERJ-145H 380 Mira
145-729 ERJ-145H 380 Mira
145-757 ERJ-145H 380 Mira

Gulfstream Aerospace Gulfstream V
356 MTM/112 PM, Elefsís
678

Lockheed C-130H Hercules
356 MTM/112 PM, Elefsís
**ECM*
741*
742
743
744
745
746
747*
749
751
752

Lockheed F-16C/F-16D* Fighting Falcon
330 Mira/111 PM, Nea Ankhialos;
340 Mira/115 PM, Souda
341 Mira/111 PM, Nea Ankhialos;
345 Mira/115 PM, Souda
346 MAPK/110 PM, Larissa;
347 Mira/111 PM, Nea Ankhialos
046 341 Mira
047 347 Mira
048 341 Mira
049 347 Mira
050 341 Mira
051 347 Mira
052 341 Mira
053 347 Mira
054 341 Mira
055 347 Mira
056 341 Mira
057 347 Mira
058 341 Mira
059 347 Mira
060 341 Mira
061 347 Mira
062 341 Mira
063 347 Mira
064 341 Mira
065 347 Mira
066 341 Mira
067 347 Mira
068 341 Mira
069 347 Mira
070 341 Mira
071 347 Mira
072 341 Mira
073 347 Mira
074 341 Mira
075 341 Mira
076 341 Mira
077* 341 Mira
078* 347 Mira
079* 347 Mira
080* 341 Mira
081* 341 Mira
082* 341 Mira
083* 347 Mira
084* 341 Mira
110 330 Mira
111 330 Mira
112 346 MAPK
113 330 Mira
114 346 MAPK
115 330 Mira
116 330 Mira
117 330 Mira
118 346 MAPK
119 330 Mira
120 330 Mira
121 330 Mira
122 346 MAPK
124 346 MAPK
125 330 Mira
126 346 MAPK
127 330 Mira
128 346 MAPK
129 330 Mira
130 346 MAPK
132 346 MAPK
133 330 Mira
134 346 MAPK
136 346 MAPK
138 346 MAPK
139 330 Mira
140 346 MAPK
141 330 Mira
143 346 MAPK
144* 330 Mira
145* 330 Mira
146* 346 MAPK
147* 330 Mira
148* 346 MAPK
149* 330 Mira
500 340/345 Mira
501 340/345 Mira
502 340/345 Mira
503 340/345 Mira
504 340/345 Mira
505 340/345 Mira
506 340/345 Mira
507 340/345 Mira
508 340/345 Mira
509 340/345 Mira
510 340/345 Mira
511 340/345 Mira
512 340/345 Mira
513 340/345 Mira
514 340/345 Mira
515 340/345 Mira
516 340/345 Mira
517 340/345 Mira
518 340/345 Mira
519 340/345 Mira
520 340/345 Mira
521 340/345 Mira
522 340/345 Mira
523 340/345 Mira
524 340/345 Mira
525 340/345 Mira
526 340/345 Mira
527 340/345 Mira
528 340/345 Mira
529 340/345 Mira
530 340/345 Mira
531 340/345 Mira
532 340/345 Mira
533 340/345 Mira
534 340/345 Mira
535 340/345 Mira
536 340/345 Mira
537 340/345 Mira
538 340/345 Mira
539 340/345 Mira
600* 340/345 Mira
601* 340/345 Mira
602* 340/345 Mira
603* 340/345 Mira
604* 340/345 Mira
605* 340/345 Mira
606* 340/345 Mira
607* 340/345 Mira
608* 340/345 Mira
609* 340/345 Mira
610* 340/345 Mira
611* 340/345 Mira
612* 340/345 Mira
613* 340/345 Mira
614* 340/345 Mira
615* 340/345 Mira
616* 340/345 Mira
617* 340/345 Mira
618* 340/345 Mira
619* 340/345 Mira

HUNGARY
Magyar Honvédseg Repülö Csapatai
Antonov An-26
89 VSD, Szolnok
110
405
406
407
603

Mikoyan MiG-29/29UB*
59 HRO, Kecskemét
01
02
03
04
05
06
07
08
09
10
11
12
14
15
16
18
19
20
21

23
24*
25*
26*
27*
28*
29*

ISRAEL
Heyl ha'Avir
Boeing 707
120 Sqn, Tel Aviv

120	RC-707
128	RC-707
137	RC-707
140	KC-707
242	VC-707
248	KC-707
250	KC-707
255	EC-707
260	KC-707
264	RC-707
272	VC-707
275	KC-707
290	KC-707

Lockheed C-130 Hercules
103 Sqn & 131 Sqn, Tel Aviv

102	C-130H
106	C-130H
208	C-130E
305	C-130E
309	C-130E
310	C-130E
313	C-130E
314	C-130E
316	C-130E
420	KC-130H
427	C-130H
428	C-130H
435	C-130H
436	C-130H
522	KC-130H
545	KC-130H

Israeli Govt
Hawker 800XP
Israeli Govt, Tel Aviv
4X-COV

ITALY
Aeronautica Militare Italiana
Aeritalia G222/C-27J
9ª Brigata Aerea, Pratica di Mare: 8° Gruppo & 71° Gruppo;
46ª Brigata Aerea, Pisa: 2° Gruppo & 98° Gruppo;
RSV, Pratica di Mare

G222AAA

CSX62144	RS-44	RSV

G222RM

MM62139	14-20	8
MM62140	14-21	8
MM62141	14-22	8

G222TCM

MM62117	46-25	2
MM62122	46-23	2
MM62124	46-88	98
MM62125	14-24	8
MM62136	46-97	98
MM62137	46-95	98
MM62145	46-50	8
MM62152	RS-45	RSV
MM62153X	RS-46	RSV
MM62154	46-54	8

G222VS

MM62107		71

C-27J

MMCSX62127		Alenia

Aeritalia-EMB AMX/AMX-T*
32° Stormo, Amendola: 13° Gruppo & 101° Gruppo;
51° Stormo, Istrana: 103° Gruppo & 132° Gruppo;
RSV, Pratica di Mare

MMX595		Alenia
MMX596		Alenia
MMX597		Alenia
MMX599		Alenia
MM7089		
MM7090		
MM7092	RS-14	RSV
MM7093		
MM7094	3-37	
MM7096		
MM7097	3-36	
MM7098	3-35	
MM7099		
MM7100	32-66	101
MM7101	51-25	103
MM7103		
MM7104	51-26	103
MM7106		
MM7107		
MM7110		
MM7111		
MM7112		
MM7115	2-12	
MM7116	32-11	13
MM7117	3-34	
MM7118	2-11	
MM7119		
MM7120	51-52	132
MM7122		3-32
MM7123		
MM7124		
MM7125	RS-11	RSV
MM7126		
MM7127	3-24	
MM7128		
MM7129	66	101
MM7130		
MM7131	2-19	
MM7132	51-12	103
MM7133	2-18	
MM7134	51-07	103
MM7135		
MM7138		
MM7139	51-24	103
MM7140	51-26	103
MM7141		
MM7142		
MM7143	51-20	103
MM7144	51-41	132
MM7145	51-44	132
MM7146		
MM7147	32-04	13
MM7148	51-50	132
MM7149		
MM7150		
MM7151	51-54	132
MM7152	51-03	103
MM7153	32-60	101
MM7154		
MM7155	51-45	132
MM7156	32-02	13
MM7157	32-06	13
CSX7158	RS-12	RSV
MM7159	51-11	103
MM7160	32-14	13
MM7161	2-21	
MM7162	51-01	103
MM7163	32-23	13
MM7164	51-37	132
MM7165	51-45	132
MM7166	32-10	13
MM7167	2-01	
MM7168	51-30	132
MM7169	32-26	13
MM7170	51-35	132
MM7171		
MM7172	51-37	132
MM7173	51-21	103
MM7174	51-04	103
MM7175	51-42	132
MM7176	2-20	
MM7177	32-25	13
MM7178	32-24	13
MM7179	51-02	103
MM7180	32-20	13
MM7182	51-16	103
MM7183	32-22	13
MM7184	51-33	132
MM7185		
MM7186	51-05	103
MM7189		
MM7190	32-17	13
MM7191	32-01	13
MM7192	51-31	132
MM7193	51-23	103
MM7194	32-07	13
MM7195		
MM7196	32-13	13
MM7197	32-21	13
MM7198		
MM55024*	15	RSV
MM55025*	RS-16	RSV
MM55026*	32-43	101
MM55027*		
MM55029*	32-50	101
MM55030*	32-41	101
MM55031*	32-40	101
MM55034*	RS-18	RSV
MM55035*		
MM55036*	32-51	101
MM55037*	32-64	101
MM55038*	32-53	101
MM55039*	32-54	101
MM55040*	32-52	101
MM55041*	32-55	101
MM55042*	32-56	101
MM55043*	32-65	101
MM55044*	32-57	101
MM55046*	32-47	101
MM55047*	32-45	101
MM55048*	32-44	101
MM55049*	32-46	101
MM55050*	32-43	101
MM55051*	32-42	101

Aermacchi MB339A/ MB339CD*
61° Stormo, Lecce:
212° Gruppo &
213° Gruppo;
Aermacchi, Venegono;
Frecce Tricolori [FT]
(313° Gruppo), Rivolto
(MB339A/PAN);
RSV, Pratica di Mare

MMX606*		RSV
MM54440	61-00	
MM54441	61-71	
MM54442	61-112	
MM54443	61-50	
MM54445	61-25	
MM54446	61-01	
MM54447	61-02	
MM54450	61-115	
MM54451	61-116	
MM54452		
CX54453	Aermacchi	
MM54455	61-07	
MM54456	61-10	
MM54457	61-11	
MM54458	61-12	
MM54459	61-13	
MM54460	61-14	
MM54462	61-16	
MM54463	61-17	
MM54467	61-23	
MM54468	61-24	
MM54471	61-27	
MM54472	61-30	
MM54473	8	[FT]
MM54475	10	[FT]
MM54477	9	[FT]
MM54478	7	[FT]
MM54479	3	[FT]
MM54480	2	[FT]
MM54482	6	[FT]
MM54483	61-102	
MM54484	61-101	
MM54485	1	[FT]
MM54486	5	[FT]
MM54487	61-31	
MM54488	61-32	
MM54489	61-33	
MM54490	61-34	
MM54491	61-35	
MM54492	61-36	
MM54493	61-37	
MM54494	61-40	
MM54496	61-42	
MM54498	61-44	
MM54499	61-45	
MM54500		[FT]
MM54503	61-51	
MM54504	61-52	
MM54505	0	[FT]
MM54506	61-54	
MM54507	61-55	
MM54508	61-56	
MM54509	61-57	
MM54510	61-60	
MM54511	61-61	
MM54512	61-62	
MM54514	61-64	
MM54515	61-65	
MM54516	61-66	
MM54517		[FT]
MM54518	61-70	
MM54532		
MM54533	61-72	
MM54534	61-73	
MM54535	61-74	
MM54536		[FT]
MM54537		
MM54538	61-75	
MM54539	61-76	
MM54541	61-100	
MM54542		[FT]
MM54543	4	[FT]
MM54545	61-84	
MM54546		[FT]
MM54547		[FT]
MM54548	61-90	
MM54549	61-107	
MM54550	61-110	
MM54551		[FT]
MM55052	6	[FT]
MM55053	61-97	
MM55054	61-15	
MM55055	61-20	
MM55058	61-41	
MM55059	61-26	
MM55062*	61-128	
MM55063*	RS-27	RSV
MM55064*	61-130	
MM55065*	61-131	
MM55066*	61-132	
MM55067*	61-133	
MM55068*	61-134	
MM55069*	61-135	
MM55070*	61-136	
MM55072*	61-140	
MM55073*	61-141	
MM55074*	61-142	
MM55075*	61-143	
MM55076*	61-144	
MM55077*	RS-28	RSV
MM55078*	RS-29	RSV
MM55079*		
MM55080*	61-	
MM55081*		
MM55082*	61-	
CSX55083*	RS-30	RSV
MM55084*	61-	
MM55085*	61-	
MM55086*	61-	
MM55087*		
MM55088*		
MM55089*		
MM55090*		
MM55091*		

Aermacchi M346
Aermacchi, Venegono
MMCSX615
MMCSX616

Airbus A.319CJ-115
31° Stormo, Roma-Ciampino:
306° Gruppo
MM62173
MM62174
MM62209

Boeing 707-328B/-3F5C*
9ª Brigata Aerea,
Pratica di Mare:
8° Gruppo;

MM62148	14-01
MM62149	14-02
MM62150*	14-03
MM62151*	14-04

Breguet Br.1150 Atlantic
41° Stormo, Catania:
88° Gruppo

MM40108	41-70
MM40109	41-71
MM40110	41-72
MM40111	41-73
MM40113	41-74
MM40114	41-76
MM40115	41-77
MM40116	41-01
MM40117	41-02
MM40118	41-03
MM40119	41-04
MM40120	41-05
MM40121	41-06
MM40122	41-07
MM40123	41-10
MM40124	41-11
MM40125	41-12

Dassault Falcon 50
31° Stormo, Roma-Ciampino:
93° Gruppo
MM62020
MM62021
MM62026
MM62029

Dassault Falcon 900EX
31° Stormo, Roma-Ciampino:
93° Gruppo
MM62171
MM62172
MM62210

Eurofighter EF.2000/ EF.2000B*
4° Stormo, Grosseto:
9° Gruppo & 20° Gruppo;
Alenia, Torino/Caselle;
RSV, Pratica di Mare

MMX602	RS-01	RSV
MMX603		Alenia
MMX614*		Alenia
CSX7235		Alenia
CSX55092*		Alenia
MM55093*	4-1	9
MM55094*	4-3	9
MM55095*	4-23	20
MM55096*	4-4	9
MM55097*		
MM55098*		
MM55099*		
MM55100*		
MM55101*		

Lockheed C-130J/C-130J-30 Hercules II
46ª Brigata Aerea, Pisa:
2° Gruppo & 50° Gruppo
C-130J

MM62175	46-40	2
MM62175	46-40	2
MM62176	46-41	2
MM62177	46-42	2
MM62178	46-43	2
MM62179	46-44	2
MM62180	46-45	2
MM62181	46-46	50
MM62182	46-47	50
MM62183	46-48	50
MM62184	46-49	50
MM62185	46-50	50

MM62186	46-51	50

C-130J-30

MM62187	46-53	50
MM62188	46-54	50
MM62189	46-55	50
MM62190	46-56	50
MM62191	46-57	50
MM62192	46-58	50
MM62193	46-59	50
MM62194		
MM62195		
MM62196		

Lockheed (GD) F-16A-ADF/F-16B*

5° Stormo, Cervia:
23° Gruppo
37° Stormo, Trapani:
18° Gruppo

MM7236		18
MM7238		23
MM7239		23
MM7240		
MM7241		
MM7242		
MM7243		23
MM7244		23
MM7245		23
MM7246		18
MM7247		18
MM7248		18
MM7249		18
MM7250		
MM7251		23
MM7252		23
MM7253		
MM7254		
MM7255		
MM7256		
MM7257		
MM7258		
MM7259		
MM7260		
MM7261		
MM7262		
MM7263		
MM7264		18
MM7265		18
MM7266*		18
MM7267*		18
MM7268*		23
MM7269*		23

Panavia Tornado Strike/ Trainer[1]/ECR[2]

6° Stormo, Ghedi:
102° Gruppo &
154° Gruppo;
50° Stormo, Piacenza:
155° Gruppo;
156° Gruppo Autonomo,
Gioia del Colle;
RSV, Pratica di Mare

MM7002	6-10	154
MM7003	6-23	154
MM7004	36-46	156
MM7005[2]	36-43	156
MM7006	6-16	154
MM7007	36-37	156
MM7008		
MM7009	6-09	154
MM7011		
MM7013	36-40	156
MM7014		
MM7015	50-53	155
MM7016	36-45	156
MM7018	6-46	102
MM7019[2]	50-05	155
MM7020[2]	50-21	155
MM7021[2]	50-01	155
MM7022		
MM7023	6-13	154
MM7024	36-41	156
MM7025	6-43	102
MM7026	6-44	102
MM7027[2]	50-51	155
MM7028		
MM7029	6-22	154
MM7030[2]	50-04	155
MM7031	6-21	154
MM7033	50-50	155
MM7034		
MM7035	36-47	156
MM7036[2]	50-..	155
MM7037	6-47	102
MM7038		
MM7039	6-02	154
CMX7040	RS-01	RSV
MM7041	6-36	102
MM7042	36-57	156
MM7043	6-30	154
MM7044	36-51	156
MM7046[2]	6-06	154
MM7047[2]	50-43	155
MM7048		Alenia
MM7049	6-34	102
MM7050	36-44	156
MM7051	50-45	155
MM7052		
MM7053[2]	50-07	155
MM7054[2]	50-40	155
MM7055	50-42	155
MM7056	36-50	156
MM7057	36-54	156
MM7058		
MM7059	50-47	155
MM7061	6-01	154
MM7062[2]	50-44	155
MM7063		Alenia
MM7064	6-26	154
MM7065	6-25	154
MM7066		
MM7067		
CSX7068[2]		Alenia
MM7070[2]	50-46	155
MM7071	6-35	102
MM7072		
MM7073[2]	36-42	156
MM7075	36-53	156
MM7078	50-02	155
CMX7079[2]		Alenia
MM7080	6-33	102
MM7081	6-11	154
MM7082[2]	6-14	154
MM7083	6-37	102
MM7084	6-36	102
CMX7085	36-50	Alenia
MM7086	36-35	156
MM7087	6-36	102
MM7088	6-18	154
MM55000[1]	6-51	102
MM55001[1]	6-42	102
MM55002[1]	6-52	102
MM55003[1]	6-..	154
MM55004[1]	6-53	102
MM55005[1]	6-40	102
MM55006[1]	6-44	102
MM55007[1]	36-55	156
MM55008[1]	6-45	102
MM55009[1]	36-56	156
MM55010[1]	6-42	102
MM55011[1]		

Piaggio P-180AM Avanti

9ª Brigata Aerea,
Pratica di Mare:
71° Gruppo;
36° Stormo, Gioia del Colle:
636ª SC;
RSV, Pratica di Mare

MM62159		636
MM62160	54	RSV
MM62161		71
MM62162		71
MM62163		71
CSX62164		RSV
MM62199		71
MM62200	9-01	71
MM62201		71
MM62202		71
MM62203		71
MM62204	9-02	71
MM62205		71
MM62206		

Guardia di Finanza

Aérospatiale ATR.42-400MP

2° Gruppo EM,
Pratica di Mare

MM62165	GF-13
MM62166	GF-14

Marina Militare Italiana

McDonnell Douglas AV-8B/TAV-8B Harrier II+

Gruppo Aerei Imbarcarti,
Taranto/Grottaglie

AV-8B

MM7199	1-03
MM7200	1-04
MM7201	1-05
MM7212	1-06
MM7213	1-07
MM7214	1-08
MM7215	1-09
MM7217	1-11
MM7218	1-12
MM7219	1-13
MM7220	1-14
MM7221	1-15
MM7222	1-16
MM7223	1-18
MM7224	1-19

TAV-8B

MM55032	1-01
MM55033	1-02

Italian Govt

Dassault Falcon 200

Italian Govt/Soc. CAI,
Roma/Ciampino

I-CNEF
I-SOBE

Dassault Falcon 900

Italian Govt/Soc. CAI,
Roma/Ciampino

I-DIES
I-FICV
I-NUMI

IVORY COAST
Grumman G.1159C Gulfstream IV
Ivory Coast Govt, Abidjan
TU-VAD

JAPAN
Japan Air Self Defence Force
Boeing 747-47C
701st Flight Sqn, Chitose
20-1101
20-1102

JORDAN
Al Quwwat al Jawwiya al Malakiya al Urduniya
Extra EA-300S
Royal Jordanian Falcons, Amman
JY-RNA
JY-RNC
JY-RND
JY-RNE
JY-RNG
JY-RNL

Lockheed C-130H Hercules
3 Sqn, Al Matar AB/Amman
344
345
346
347

Jordanian Govt
Airbus A.340-211
Jordanian Govt, Amman
JY-ABH

Boeing 737-7BC
Jordanian Govt, Amman
VP-BFA

Canadair CL.604 Challenger
Jordanian Govt, Amman
JY-ONE
JY-TWO

Lockheed L.1011 TriStar 500
Jordanian Govt, Amman
JY-HKJ

KAZAKHSTAN
Boeing 767-2DXER
Govt of Kazakhstan, Almaty
UN-B6701

Tupolev Tu-154B-2
Govt of Kazakhstan, Almaty
UN-85464

KENYA
Kenyan Air Force
Fokker 70ER
308

KUWAIT
Al Quwwat al Jawwiya al Kuwaitiya
Lockheed L100-30 Hercules
41 Sqn, Kuwait International
KAF 323
KAF 324
KAF 325

Kuwaiti Govt
Airbus A.300C4-620
Kuwaiti Govt, Safat
9K-AHI

Airbus A.310-308
Kuwaiti Govt, Safat
9K-ALD

Airbus A.330-212
Kuwaiti Govt, Safat
9K-AKD

Gulfstream Aerospace Gulfstream V
Kuwaiti Govt/Kuwait Airways, Safat
9K-AJD
9K-AJE
9K-AJF

KYRGYZSTAN
Tupolev Tu-134A-3
Govt of Kyrgyzstan, Bishkek
EX-65119

Tupolev Tu-154B/Tu-154M
Govt of Kyrgyzstan, Bishkek

EX-85294	Tu-154B
EX-85718	Tu-154M
EX-85762	Tu-154M

LITHUANIA
Karines Oro Pajegos
Antonov An-26RV
Transporto Eskadrile, Siauliai-Zokniai
03
04
05

LET 410 Turbolet
Transporto Eskadrile, Siauliai-Zokniai
01
02

Lithuanian Govt
Lockheed L.1329 Jetstar 731
Lithuanian Govt, Vilnius
LY-AMB

LUXEMBOURG
NATO
Boeing CT-49A
NAEW&CF, Geilenkirchen
LX-N19997
LX-N19999
LX-N20000
LX-N20199

Boeing E-3A
NAEW&CF, Geilenkirchen
LX-N90442
LX-N90443
LX-N90444
LX-N90445
LX-N90446
LX-N90447
LX-N90448
LX-N90449
LX-N90450
LX-N90451
LX-N90452
LX-N90453
LX-N90454
LX-N90455
LX-N90456
LX-N90458
LX-N90459

MALAYSIA
Royal Malaysian Air Force/ Tentera Udara Diraja Malaysia
Boeing 737-7H6
2 Sqn, Simpang
M53–01

Bombardier BD.700-1A10 Global Express
2 Sqn, Simpang
M48-02

Lockheed C-130 Hercules
14 Sqn, Labuan;
20 Sqn, Subang

M30-01	C-130H(MP)	20 Sqn
M30-02	C-130H	14 Sqn
M30-03	C-130H	14 Sqn
M30-04	C-130H-30	20 Sqn
M30-05	C-130H	14 Sqn
M30-06	C-130H	14 Sqn
M30-07	C-130T	20 Sqn
M30-08	C-130H(MP)	20 Sqn
M30-09	C-130H(MP)	20 Sqn
M30-10	C-130H-30	20 Sqn
M30-11	C-130H-30	20 Sqn
M30-12	C-130H-30	20 Sqn
M30-14	C-130H-30	20 Sqn
M30-15	C-130H-30	20 Sqn
M30-16	C-130H-30	20 Sqn

MALTA
Bombardier Learjet 60
Govt of Malta, Luqa
9H-AEE

MEXICO
Fuerza Aérea Mexicana
Boeing 757-225
8º Grupo Aéreo, Mexico City

TP-01	(XC-UJM)

MOROCCO
Force Aérienne Royaume Marocaine/ Al Quwwat al Jawwiya al Malakiya Marakishiya
Airtech CN.235M-100
Escadrille de Transport, Rabat

023	CNA-MA
024	CNA-MB
025	CNA-MC
026	CNA-MD
027	CNA-ME
028	CNA-MF
031	CNA-MG

CAP-231/CAP-232
Marche Verte
CAP-231

09	CN-ABL

22	CN-ABM
23	CN-ABN
24	CN-ABO

CAP-232

28	CNA-BP
29	CN-ABQ
31	CN-ABR
36	CNA-BS
37	CNA-BT
41	CN-ABU
42	CN-ABV

Lockheed C-130H Hercules
Escadrille de Transport, Rabat

4535	CN-AOA
4551	CN-AOC
4581	CN-AOE
4583	CN-AOF
4713	CN-AOG
4717	CN-AOH
4733	CN-AOI
4738	CN-AOJ
4739	CN-AOK
4742	CN-AOL
4875	CN-AOM
4876	CN-AON
4877	CN-AOO
4888	CN-AOP
4892	CN-AOQ
4907	CN-AOR
4909	CN-AOS
4940	CN-AOT

Govt of Morocco

Boeing 707-138B
Govt of Morocco, Rabat
CNA-NS

Cessna 560 Citation V
Govt of Morocco, Rabat
CNA-NW

Dassault Falcon 50
Govt of Morocco, Rabat
CN-ANO

Grumman G.1159 Gulfstream IITT/ G.1159A Gulfstream III
Govt of Morocco, Rabat

CNA-NL	Gulfstream IITT
CNA-NU	Gulfstream III
CNA-NV	Gulfstream III

NAMIBIA

Dassault Falcon 900B
Namibian Govt, Windhoek
V5-NAM

NETHERLANDS

Koninklijke Luchtmacht

Agusta-Bell AB.412SP
303 Sqn, Leeuwarden
R-01
R-02
R-03

Boeing-Vertol CH-47D Chinook
298 Sqn, Soesterberg
D-101
D-102
D-103
D-104
D-105
D-106
D-661
D-662
D-663
D-664
D-665
D-666
D-667

Eurocopter AS.532U-2 Cougar
300 Sqn, Gilze-Rijen
S-400
S-419
S-433
S-438
S-440
S-441
S-442
S-444
S-445
S-447
S-450
S-453
S-454
S-456
S-457
S-458
S-459

Fokker 50
334 Sqn, Eindhoven
U-05
U-06

Fokker 60UTA-N
334 Sqn, Eindhoven
U-01
U-02
U-03
U-04

General Dynamics F-16
TGp/306/311/312 Sqns, Volkel;
313 Sqn, Twenthe;
322/323 Sqns, Leeuwarden

J-001	F-16AM	322 Sqn
J-002	F-16AM	323 Sqn
J-003	F-16AM	306 Sqn
J-004	F-16AM	322 Sqn
J-005	F-16AM	323 Sqn
J-006	F-16AM	306 Sqn
J-008	F-16AM	323 Sqn
J-009	F-16AM	323 Sqn
J-010	F-16AM	323 Sqn
J-011	F-16AM	311 Sqn
J-013	F-16AM	322 Sqn
J-014	F-16AM	322 Sqn
J-015	F-16AM	313 Sqn
J-016	F-16AM	323 Sqn
J-017	F-16AM	312 Sqn
J-018	F-16AM	323 Sqn
J-019	F-16AM	323 Sqn
J-020	F-16AM	313 Sqn
J-021	F-16AM	312 Sqn
J-055	F-16AM	322 Sqn
J-057	F-16AM	323 Sqn
J-058	F-16AM	313 Sqn
J-060	F-16AM	323 Sqn
J-061	F-16AM	312 Sqn
J-062	F-16AM	322 Sqn
J-063	F-16AM	322 Sqn
J-064	F-16BM	322 Sqn
J-065	F-16BM	313 Sqn
J-066	F-16BM	TGp
J-067	F-16BM	313 Sqn
J-068	F-16BM	322 Sqn
J-135	F-16AM	311 Sqn
J-136	F-16AM	313 Sqn
J-137	F-16AM	322 Sqn
J-138	F-16AM	313 Sqn
J-139	F-16AM	323 Sqn
J-141	F-16AM	313 Sqn
J-142	F-16AM	323 Sqn
J-143	F-16AM	313 Sqn
J-144	F-16AM	322 Sqn
J-145	F-16AM	313 Sqn
J-146	F-16AM	323 Sqn
J-192	F-16AM	311 Sqn
J-193	F-16AM	312 Sqn
J-194	F-16AM	323 Sqn
J-196	F-16AM	323 Sqn
J-197	F-16AM	311 Sqn
J-198	F-16AM	322 Sqn
J-199	F-16AM	312 Sqn
J-201	F-16AM	312 Sqn
J-202	F-16AM	312 Sqn
J-203	F-16AM	311 Sqn
J-204	F-16AM	323 Sqn
J-205	F-16AM	322 Sqn
J-207	F-16AM	311 Sqn
J-208	F-16BM	312 Sqn
J-209	F-16BM	313 Sqn
J-210	F-16BM	323 Sqn
J-211	F-16BM	322 Sqn
J-251	F-16AM	306 Sqn
J-253	F-16AM	311 Sqn
J-254	F-16AM	306 Sqn
J-255	F-16AM	306 Sqn
J-257	F-16AM	312 Sqn
J-267	F-16BM	306 Sqn
J-269	F-16BM	313 Sqn
J-270	F-16BM	306 Sqn
J-360	F-16AM	323 Sqn
J-362	F-16AM	323 Sqn
J-363	F-16AM	323 Sqn
J-364	F-16AM	313 Sqn
J-365	F-16AM	311 Sqn
J-366	F-16AM	313 Sqn
J-367	F-16AM	322 Sqn
J-368	F-16BM	306 Sqn
J-369	F-16BM	306 Sqn
J-508	F-16AM	313 Sqn
J-509	F-16AM	313 Sqn
J-510	F-16AM	312 Sqn
J-511	F-16AM	313 Sqn
J-512	F-16AM	313 Sqn
J-513	F-16AM	323 Sqn
J-514	F-16AM	313 Sqn
J-515	F-16AM	323 Sqn
J-516	F-16AM	311 Sqn
J-616	F-16AM	313 Sqn
J-617	F-16AM	311 Sqn
J-619	F-16AM	323 Sqn
J-620	F-16AM	313 Sqn
J-622	F-16AM	323 Sqn
J-623	F-16AM	323 Sqn
J-624	F-16AM	311 Sqn
J-627	F-16AM	311 Sqn
J-628	F-16AM	313 Sqn
J-630	F-16AM	311 Sqn
J-631	F-16AM	311 Sqn
J-632	F-16AM	311 Sqn
J-633	F-16AM	322 Sqn
J-635	F-16AM	312 Sqn

J-636 F-16AM 306 Sqn
J-637 F-16AM 312 Sqn
J-638 F-16AM 311 Sqn
J-640 F-16AM 312 Sqn
J-641 F-16AM 311 Sqn
J-642 F-16AM 311 Sqn
J-643 F-16AM 322 Sqn
J-644 F-16AM 322 Sqn
J-646 F-16AM 312 Sqn
J-647 F-16AM 311 Sqn
J-648 F-16AM 311 Sqn
J-649 F-16BM 306 Sqn
J-650 F-16BM 323 Sqn
J-652 F-16BM 306 Sqn
J-653 F-16BM 312 Sqn
J-654 F-16BM 312 Sqn
J-655 F-16BM 306 Sqn
J-656 F-16BM 306 Sqn
J-657 F-16BM 306 Sqn
J-864 F-16AM
J-866 F-16AM 312 Sqn
J-867 F-16AM 313 Sqn
J-868 F-16AM 311 Sqn
J-869 F-16AM 322 Sqn
J-870 F-16AM 313 Sqn
J-871 F-16AM 312 Sqn
J-872 F-16AM 311 Sqn
J-873 F-16AM 322 Sqn
J-874 F-16AM 312 Sqn
J-875 F-16AM 313 Sqn
J-876 F-16AM 311 Sqn
J-877 F-16AM 322 Sqn
J-878 F-16AM 322 Sqn
J-879 F-16AM 306 Sqn
J-881 F-16AM 323 Sqn
J-882 F-16BM 306 Sqn
J-884 F-16BM 306 Sqn
J-885 F-16BM 323 Sqn

Grumman G-1159C Gulfstream IV
334 Sqn, Eindhoven
V-11

Lockheed C-130H-30 Hercules
334 Sqn, Eindhoven
G-273
G-275

MDH AH-64D Apache Longbow
301 Sqn, Gilze-Rijen;
302 Sqn, Gilze-Rijen
Q-01 302 Sqn
Q-02 302 Sqn
Q-03 302 Sqn
Q-04 301 Sqn
Q-05 302 Sqn
Q-06 302 Sqn
Q-07 302 Sqn
Q-08 302 Sqn
Q-09 301 Sqn
Q-10 301 Sqn
Q-11
Q-12
Q-13 302 Sqn
Q-14 301 Sqn
Q-15 301 Sqn
Q-16 301 Sqn
Q-17 301 Sqn
Q-18 301 Sqn
Q-19 301 Sqn
Q-21 301 Sqn
Q-22 302 Sqn
Q-23 301 Sqn
Q-24 301 Sqn
Q-25 301 Sqn
Q-26 302 Sqn
Q-27
Q-28
Q-29 301 Sqn
Q-30 302 Sqn

McDonnell Douglas DC-10*/KDC-10
334 Sqn, Eindhoven
T-235
T-255*
T-264

Pilatus PC-7
131 EMVO Sqn, Woensdrecht
L-01
L-02
L-03
L-04
L-05
L-06
L-07
L-08
L-09
L-10
L-11
L-12
L-13

Sud Alouette III
300 Sqn, Soesterberg
A-247
A-275
A-292
A-301

Marine Luchtvaart Dienst

Beech Super King Air 200
OVALK, Maastricht
PH-SBK

Westland SH-14D Lynx
HELIGRP (7 Sqn & 860 Sqn), De Kooij (7 Sqn operates 860 Sqn aircraft on loan)
261
262
264
265
267
268
269
270
271
276
277
280
281
283

Netherlands Govt

Fokker 70
Dutch Royal Flight, Schiphol
PH-KBX

NEW ZEALAND

Royal New Zealand Air Force

Boeing 757-2K2
40 Sqn, Whenuapai
NZ7571
NZ7572

Lockheed C-130H Hercules
40 Sqn, Whenuapai
NZ7001
NZ7002
NZ7003
NZ7004
NZ7005

Lockheed P-3K Orion
5 Sqn, Whenuapai
NZ4201
NZ4202
NZ4203
NZ4204
NZ4205
NZ4206

NIGERIA

Federal Nigerian Air Force

Lockheed C-130H/ C-130H-30* Hercules
88 MAG, Lagos
NAF-910
NAF-912
NAF-913
NAF-917*
NAF-918*

Nigerian Govt

Boeing 727-2N6
Federal Govt of Nigeria, Lagos
5N-FGN [001]

Dassault Falcon 900
Federal Govt of Nigeria, Lagos
5N-FGE
5N-FGO

Grumman G.1159 Gulfstream II/ G.1159A Gulfstream III
Federal Govt of Nigeria, Lagos
5N-AGV Gulfstream II
5N-FGP Gulfstream III

Gulfstream Aerospace Gulfstream V
Federal Govt of Nigeria, Lagos
5N-FGS

Hawker 1000
Federal Govt of Nigeria, Lagos
5N-FGR

NORWAY

Luftforsvaret

Bell 412SP
339 Skv, Bardufoss;
720 Skv, Rygge
139 339 Skv
140 720 Skv
141 720 Skv

142 720 Skv
143 339 Skv
144 339 Skv
145 720 Skv
146 339 Skv
147 720 Skv
148 339 Skv
149 339 Skv
161 339 Skv
162 339 Skv
163 720 Skv
164 720 Skv
165 720 Skv
166 720 Skv
167 720 Skv
194 720 Skv

Dassault Falcon 20 ECM
717 Skv, Rygge
041
053
0125

General Dynamics F-16
(MLU aircraft are marked with a *)
331 Skv, Bodø (*r/w/bl*);
332 Skv, Rygge (*y/bk*);
338 Skv, Ørland

272	F-16A*	332 Skv
273	F-16A*	332 Skv
275	F-16A*	338 Skv
276	F-16A	338 Skv
277	F-16A*	338 Skv
279	F-16A*	338 Skv
281	F-16A	332 Skv
282	F-16A*	338 Skv
284	F-16A*	338 Skv
285	F-16A*	338 Skv
286	F-16A*	338 Skv
288	F-16A*	338 Skv
289	F-16A*	332 Skv
291	F-16A*	338 Skv
292	F-16A*	338 Skv
293	F-16A*	338 Skv
295	F-16A*	338 Skv
297	F-16A*	338 Skv
298	F-16A*	338 Skv
299	F-16A*	331 Skv
302	F-16B*	332 Skv
304	F-16B*	338 Skv
305	F-16B*	338 Skv
306	F-16B*	332 Skv
658	F-16A*	338 Skv
659	F-16A*	338 Skv
660	F-16A*	331 Skv
661	F-16A*	338 Skv
662	F-16A*	332 Skv
663	F-16A*	331 Skv
664	F-16A*	331 Skv
665	F-16A*	332 Skv
666	F-16A*	
667	F-16A*	331 Skv
668	F-16A*	331 Skv
669	F-16A*	331 Skv
670	F-16A*	331 Skv
671	F-16A*	331 Skv
672	F-16A*	331 Skv
673	F-16A*	331 Skv
674	F-16A	331 Skv
675	F-16A*	331 Skv
677	F-16A*	331 Skv
678	F-16A*	331 Skv
680	F-16A*	331 Skv
681	F-16A*	338 Skv
682	F-16A*	331 Skv
683	F-16A*	331 Skv
686	F-16A*	331 Skv
687	F-16A*	331 Skv
688	F-16A*	331 Skv
689	F-16B*	332 Skv
690	F-16B*	338 Skv
691	F-16B*	338 Skv
692	F-16B*	332 Skv
693	F-16B*	338 Skv
711	F-16B*	338 Skv

Lockheed C-130H Hercules
335 Skv, Gardermoen
952
953
954
955
956
957

Lockheed P-3C Orion
333 Skv, Andøya
3296
3297
3298
3299

Lockheed P-3N Orion
333 Skv, Andøya
4576
6603

Northrop F-5A
Eye of the Tiger Project, Rygge
128
130
131
133
134
896
902

Northrop F-5B
Eye of the Tiger Project, Rygge
136
243
244
387
906
907
908
909

Westland Sea King Mk 43/ Mk 43A/Mk 43B
330 Skv:
A Flt, Bodø;
B Flt, Banak;
C Flt, Ørland;
D Flt, Sola

060	Mk 43
062	Mk 43
066	Mk 43
069	Mk 43
070	Mk 43
071	Mk 43B
072	Mk 43
073	Mk 43
074	Mk 43
189	Mk 43A
322	Mk 43B
329	Mk 43B
330	Mk 43B

Kystvakt (Coast Guard)
Westland Lynx Mk86
337 Skv, Bardufoss
207
216
228
232
237
350

OMAN
Royal Air Force of Oman
BAC 1-11/485GD
4 Sqn, Seeb
551
552
553

Lockheed C-130H Hercules
4 Sqn, Seeb
501
502
503

Omani Govt
Boeing 747-430
Govt of Oman, Seeb
A4O-OMN

Boeing 747SP-27
Govt of Oman, Seeb
A4O-SO
A4O-SP

Grumman G.1159C Gulfstream IV
Govt of Oman, Seeb
A4O-AB
A4O-AC

PAKISTAN
Pakistan Fiza'ya
Boeing 707-340C
68-19635 12 Sqn
68-19866 12 Sqn

Pakistani Govt
Boeing 737-33A
Govt of Pakistan, Karachi
AP-BEH

PERU
Fuerza Aérea Peruana
Douglas DC-8-62AF
370 (OB-1372)
371 (OB-1373)

POLAND
Sily Powietrzne RP
Antonov An-26
13 ELTR, Krakow/Balice
1310
1402
1403
1406
1407
1508
1509
1602

1603
1604

CASA 295M
13 ELTR, Krakow/Balice
011
012
013
014
015
016

Mikoyan MiG-29A/UB*
1 ELT, Minsk/Mazowiecki;
41 ELT, Malbork
01 41 ELT
02 41 ELT
04* 41 ELT
06 41 ELT
08 41 ELT
10 41 ELT
11 41 ELT
13 41 ELT
15* 1 ELT
18 41 ELT
19 41 ELT
22 41 ELT
24 41 ELT
26* 41 ELT
28* 1 ELT
32 41 ELT
38 1 ELT
40 1 ELT
42* 1 ELT
48* 41 ELT
54 1 ELT
56 1 ELT
59 1 ELT
64* 1 ELT
65 1 ELT
66 1 ELT
67 1 ELT
70 1 ELT
77 1 ELT
83 1 ELT
89 1 ELT
92 1 ELT
105 1 ELT
108 1 ELT
111 1 ELT
114 1 ELT
115 1 ELT
128 41 ELT
300 41 ELT
310 41 ELT
314 41 ELT
315 41 ELT
408* 41 ELT
800 41 ELT
5115 41 ELT

PZL M28 Bryza
13 ELTr, Balice;
LGPR, Bydgoszcz
0203 M28B-1 13 ELTr
0204 M28B-1 13 ELTr
0723 M28RL LGPR
1003 M28TD 13 ELTr

Tupolev Tu-154M
36 SPLT, Warszawa
101
102

Yakovlev Yak-40
36 SPLT, Warszawa
032
034
036
037
038
040
041
042
043
044
045
047
048

Lotnictwo Marynarki Wojennej
PZL M28 Bryza
1 DLMW, Gdynia/Babie Doly;
3 DLMW, Cewice/Siemirowice
0404 M28B-E 1 DLMW
0405 M28B-E 1 DLMW
0810 M28B-1R PZL
1006 M28B-1R 3 DLMW
1007 M28B-1 1 DLMW
1008 M28B-1R 3 DLMW
1017 M28B-1R 3 DLMW
1022 M28B-1R 3 DLMW
1114 M28B-1R 3 DLMW
1115 M28B-1R 3 DLMW
1116 M28B-1R 3 DLMW
1117 M28B-1 1 DLMW
1118 M28B-1 1 DLMW

PORTUGAL
Força Aérea Portuguesa
Aérospatiale SA.330C Puma
Esq 711, Lajes;
Esq 751, Montijo
19502 Esq 751
19503 Esq 751
19504 Esq 751
19505 Esq 751
19506 Esq 711
19508 Esq 711
19509 Esq 751
19511 Esq 711
19512 Esq 751
19513 Esq 711

CASA 212A/212ECM* Aviocar
Esq 401, Sintra;
Esq 501, Sintra;
Esq 502, Sintra;
Esq 711, Lajes
16501* Esq 501
16503 Esq 501
16504 Esq 501
16505 Esq 502
16506 Esq 502
16507 Esq 502
16508 Esq 502
16509 Esq 501
16510 Esq 401
16511 Esq 502
16512 Esq 401
16513 Esq 711
16514 Esq 711
16515 Esq 711
16517 Esq 711
16519 Esq 401
16520 Esq 711
16521* Esq 401
16522* Esq 401
16523* Esq 401
16524* Esq 401

CASA 212-300 Aviocar
Esq 401, Sintra
17201
17202

D-BD Alpha Jet
Esq 103, Beja;
Esq 301, Beja
15201
15202
15204
15205
15206
15208
15209
15210
15211
15213
15214
15215
15216
15217
15218
15219
15220
15221
15222
15223
15224
15225
15226
15227
15228
15229
15230
15231
15232
15233
15235
15236
15237
15238
15239
15240
15241
15242
15243
15244
15246
15247
15250

Dassault Falcon 20DC
Esq 504, Lisbon/Montijo
17103

Dassault Falcon 50
Esq 504, Lisbon/Montijo
17401
17402
17403

EHI EH-101
Esq 711, Lajes;
Esq 751, Montijo
19601

19602
19603
19604
19605
19606
19607
19608
19609
19610
19611
19612

Lockheed C-130H/ C-130H-30* Hercules
Esq 501, Lisbon/Montijo
16801*
16802*
16803
16804
16805
16806*

Lockheed (GD) F-16
(MLU aircraft are marked with a *)
Esq 201, Monte Real;
Esq 304, Monte Real

15101	F-16A	Esq 201
15102	F-16A	Esq 201
15103	F-16A	Esq 201
15104	F-16A	Esq 201
15105	F-16A	Esq 201
15106	F-16A	Esq 201
15107	F-16A	Esq 201
15108	F-16A	Esq 201
15109	F-16A	Esq 201
15110	F-16A	Esq 201
15112	F-16A	Esq 201
15113	F-16A	Esq 201
15114	F-16A	Esq 201
15115	F-16A	Esq 201
15116	F-16A	Esq 201
15117	F-16A	Esq 201
15118	F-16B	Esq 201
15119	F-16B	Esq 201
15120	F-16B	Esq 201
15121	F-16A*	Esq 201
15122	F-16A	Esq 304
15123	F-16A	Esq 304
15124	F-16A	Esq 304
15125	F-16A	Esq 304
15126	F-16A	Esq 304
15127	F-16A	Esq 304
15128	F-16A	Esq 304
15129	F-16A	Esq 304
15130	F-16A	Esq 304
15131	F-16A	Esq 304
15132	F-16A	Esq 304
15133	F-16A*	Esq 201
15134	F-16A	Esq 304
15135	F-16A	Esq 304
15136	F-16A	Esq 304
15137	F-16A	Esq 304
15138	F-16A*	Esq 201
15139	F-16B*	Esq 201
15140	F-16B	Esq 304
15141	F-16B	Esq 304

Lockheed P-3C/ P-3P Orion
Esq 601, Lisbon/Montijo

14801	P-3P
14802	P-3P
14803	P-3P
14804	P-3P
14805	P-3P
14806	P-3P
14807	P-3C
14808	P-3C
14809	P-3C
14810	P-3C
14811	P-3C

Marinha

Westland Super Lynx Mk 95
Esq de Helicopteros, Lisbon/Montijo
19201
19202
19203
19204
19205

QATAR

Airbus A.310-304
Qatari Govt, Doha
A7-AAF

Airbus A.319CJ-133
Qatari Govt, Doha
A7-HHJ

Airbus A.320-232
Qatari Govt, Doha
A7-AAG

Airbus A.340-211/-541*
Qatari Govt, Doha
A7-HHH*
A7-HHK

ROMANIA

Fortele Aeriene Romania

Lockheed C-130B Hercules
19 FMT, Bucharest/Otapeni
5927
5930
6150
6166

RUSSIA

Voenno-Vozdushniye Sily Rossiski Federatsii (Russian Air Force)

Sukhoi Su-27
TsAGI, Gromov Flight Institute, Zhukhovsky

595	Su-27P
597	Su-30
598	Su-27P

Russian Govt

Ilyushin Il-62M
Russian Govt, Moscow
RA-86466
RA-86467
RA-86468
RA-86536
RA-86537
RA-86540
RA-86553
RA-86554
RA-86559
RA-86561
RA-86710
RA-86711
RA-86712

Ilyushin Il-96-300
Russian Govt, Moscow
RA-96012
RA-96016

Tupolev Tu-134A
Russian Govt, Moscow
RA-65904

Tupolev Tu-154M
Russian Govt, Moscow;
Open Skies*
RA-85629
RA-85631
RA-85645
RA-85655*
RA-85659
RA-85666
RA-85843

SAUDI ARABIA

Al Quwwat al Jawwiya as Sa'udiya

BAe 125-800/-800B*
1 Sqn, Riyadh
HZ-105
HZ-109*
HZ-110*

Boeing 737-7DP/-8DP*
1 Sqn, Riyadh
HZ-101
HZ-102*

Boeing E-3A/KE-3A/ RE-3A Sentry
18 Sqn, Riyadh;
19 Sqn, Riyadh

1801	E-3A	18 Sqn
1802	E-3A	18 Sqn
1803	E-3A	18 Sqn
1804	E-3A	18 Sqn
1805	E-3A	18 Sqn
1811	KE-3A	18 Sqn
1812	KE-3A	18 Sqn
1813	KE-3A	18 Sqn
1814	KE-3A	18 Sqn
1815	KE-3A	18 Sqn
1816	KE-3A	18 Sqn
1818	KE-3A	18 Sqn
1901	RE-3A	19 Sqn

Lockheed C-130/L.100 Hercules
1 Sqn, Prince Sultan AB;
4 Sqn, Jeddah;
16 Sqn, Prince Sultan AB;
32 Sqn, Prince Sultan AB

111	VC-130H	1 Sqn
112	VC-130H	1 Sqn
451	C-130E	4 Sqn
452	C-130E	4 Sqn
455	C-130E	4 Sqn
461	C-130H	4 Sqn
462	C-130H	4 Sqn
463	C-130H	4 Sqn
464	C-130H	4 Sqn
465	C-130H	4 Sqn
466	C-130H	4 Sqn
467	C-130H	4 Sqn
468	C-130H	4 Sqn
471	C-130H-30	4 Sqn
472	C-130H	4 Sqn
473	C-130H	4 Sqn

474	C-130H	4 Sqn
475	C-130H	4 Sqn
476	C-130E	4 Sqn
477	C-130H	4 Sqn
1601	C-130H	16 Sqn
1602	C-130H	16 Sqn
1603	C-130H	16 Sqn
1604	C-130H	16 Sqn
1605	C-130H	16 Sqn
1606	C-130E	16 Sqn
1607	C-130E	16 Sqn
1608	C-130E	16 Sqn
1609	C-130E	16 Sqn
1611	C-130E	16 Sqn
1614	C-130H	16 Sqn
1615	C-130H	16 Sqn
1618	C-130H	16 Sqn
1619	C-130H	16 Sqn
1622	C-130H-30	16 Sqn
1623	C-130H-30	16 Sqn
1624	C-130H	16 Sqn
1625	C-130H	16 Sqn
1626	C-130H	16 Sqn
3201	KC-130H	32 Sqn
3202	KC-130H	32 Sqn
3203	KC-130H	32 Sqn
3204	KC-130H	32 Sqn
3205	KC-130H	32 Sqn
3206	KC-130H	32 Sqn
3207	KC-130H	32 Sqn
HZ-114	VC-130H	1 Sqn
HZ-115	VC-130H	1 Sqn
HZ-116	VC-130H	1 Sqn
HZ-117	L.100-30	1 Sqn
HZ-128	L.100-30	1 Sqn
HZ-129	L.100-30	1 Sqn

Saudi Govt

Airbus A.340-211
Royal Embassy of Saudi Arabia, Riyadh
HZ-124

Boeing 737-268
Saudi Royal Flight, Jeddah
HZ-HM4

Boeing 747-3G1
Saudi Royal Flight, Jeddah
HZ-HM1A

Boeing 747SP-68
Saudi Govt, Jeddah;
Saudi Royal Flight, Jeddah

HZ-AIF	Govt
HZ-AIJ	Royal Flight
HZ-HM1B	Royal Flight

Boeing MD-11
Saudi Royal Flight, Jeddah
HZ-AFA1
HZ-HM7

Canadair CL.604 Challenger
Saudi Royal Flight, Jeddah
HZ-AFA2

Dassault Falcon 900
Saudi Govt, Jeddah
HZ-AFT
HZ-AFZ

Grumman G.1159A Gulfstream III
Armed Forces Medical Services, Riyadh;
Saudi Govt, Jeddah

HZ-AFN	Govt
HZ-AFR	Govt
HZ-MS3	AFMS

Grumman G.1159C Gulfstream IV
Armed Forces Medical Services, Riyadh;
Saudi Govt, Jeddah

HZ-AFU	Govt
HZ-AFV	Govt
HZ-AFW	Govt
HZ-AFX	Govt
HZ-AFY	Govt
HZ-MS4	AFMS
HZ-MS5A	AFMS

Gulfstream Aerospace Gulfstream V
Armed Forces Medical Services, Riyadh
HZ-MS5

Lockheed C-130H/L.100 Hercules
Armed Forces Medical Services, Riyadh

HZ-MS6	L.100-30
HZ-MS7	C-130H
HZ-MS8	C-130H-30
HZ-MS09	L.100-30
HZ-MS019	C-130H

Lockheed L.1011 TriStar 500
Saudi Royal Flight, Jeddah
HZ-HM5
HZ-HM6

SINGAPORE

Republic of Singapore Air Force

Boeing KC-135R Stratotanker
750
751
752
753

Lockheed C-130 Hercules
122 Sqn, Paya Lebar

720	KC-130B
721	KC-130B
724	KC-130B
725	KC-130B
730	C-130H
731	C-130H
732	C-130H
733	C-130H
734	KC-130H
735	C-130H

SLOVAKIA

Slovenské Vojenske Letectvo

Aero L-39 Albatros
1 SLK/3 Letka, Sliač [SL]

0101	L-39C
0102	L-39C
0111	L-39C
0112	L-39C
0442	L-39C
0443	L-39C
0730	L-39V
0745	L-39V
1701	L-39ZA
1725	L-39ZA
1730	L-39ZA
4701	L-39ZA
4703	L-39ZA
4707	L-39ZA
4711	L-39ZA

Antonov An-24V
2 SBoLK/2 Letka, Malacky
2903
5605

Antonov An-26
2 SBoLK/2 Letka, Malacky
2506
3208

LET 410 Turbolet
1 SLK/3 Letka, Sliač [SL];
2 SBoLK/2 Letka, Malacky;
VLA, Košice

0730	L-410UVP	2 SBoLK
0927	L-410T	1 SLK
0930	L-410T	2 SBoLK
1133	L-410T	VLA
1203	L-410FG	2 SBoLK
1521	L-410FG	2 SBoLK
2311	L-410UVP	2 SBoLK

Mikoyan MiG-29A/UB*
1 SLK/1 & 2 Letka, Sliač [SL]
0619
0820
0921
1303*
2123
3709
3911
4401*
5113
5304*
5515
5817
6124
6425
6526
6627
6728
7501
8003
8605
9308

Slovak Govt

Tupolev Tu-154M
Slovak Govt, Bratislava/Ivanka
OM-BYO
OM-BYR

Yakovlev Yak-40
Slovak Govt, Bratislava/Ivanka
OM-BYE
OM-BYL

SLOVENIA
Slovene Army
LET 410UVP-E
15 Brigada, Ljubljana
L4-01

Pilatus PC-9M
15 Brigada, Ljubljana
L9-51
L9-53
L9-61
L9-62
L9-63
L9-64
L9-65
L9-66
L9-67
L9-68
L9-69

Slovenian Govt
Gates Learjet
Slovenian Govt, Ljubljana
S5-BAA Learjet 35A
S5-BAB Learjet 24D

SOUTH AFRICA
South African Air Force/ Suid Afrikaanse Lugmag
Boeing 707
60 Sqn, Waterkloof
1415 328C
1417 328C
1419 328C
1423 344C

Boeing 737-7ED
21 Sqn, Waterkloof
ZS-RSA

Dassault Falcon 900
21 Sqn, Waterkloof
ZS-NAN

Lockheed C-130B/ C-130BZ* Hercules
28 Sqn, Waterkloof
401
402*
403
404
405*
406*
407*
408*
409*

SPAIN
Ejército del Aire
Airbus A.310-304
Grupo 45, Torrejón
T.22-1 45-50
T.22-2 45-51

Airtech CN.235M-10 (T.19A)/ CN.235M-100 (T.19B)
Ala 35, Getafe
T.19A-01 35-60
T.19A-02 35-61
T.19B-03 35-21
T.19B-04 35-22
T.19B-05 35-23
T.19B-06 35-24
T.19B-07 35-25
T.19B-08 35-26
T.19B-09 35-27
T.19B-10 35-28
T.19B-11 35-29
T.19B-12 35-30
T.19B-13 35-31
T.19B-14 35-32
T.19B-15 35-33
T.19B-16 35-34
T.19B-17 35-35
T.19B-18 35-36
T.19B-19 35-37
T.19B-20 35-38

Boeing 707
47 Grupo Mixto, Torrejón
T.17-1 331B 45-10
T.17-2 331B 45-11
T.17-3 368C 45-12
TM.17-4 351C 408-21

CASA 101EB Aviojet
Grupo 54, Torrejón;
Grupo de Escuelas de Matacán (74);
AGA, San Javier (79);
Patrulla Aguila, San Javier*
E.25-01 79-01 [6]*
E.25-05 79-05
E.25-06 79-06
E.25-07 79-07
E.25-08 79-08 [4]*
E.25-09 79-09
E.25-10 79-10
E.25-11 79-11
E.25-12 79-12
E.25-13 79-13 [7]*
E.25-14 79-14 [2]*
E.25-15 79-15
E.25-16 79-16
E.25-17 74-40
E.25-18 74-42
E.25-19 79-19
E.25-20 79-20
E.25-21 79-21
E.25-22 79-22 [2]*
E.25-23 79-23 [4]*
E.25-24 79-24
E.25-25 79-25 [3]*
E.25-26 79-26
E.25-27 79-27
E.25-28 79-28
E.25-29 74-45
E.25-31 79-31
E.25-33 74-02
E.25-34 79-34
E.25-35 54-20
E.25-37 79-37
E.25-38 79-38
E.25-40 79-40
E.25-41 74-41
E.25-43 74-43
E.25-44 79-44
E.25-45 79-45
E.25-46 79-46
E.25-47 79-47
E.25-48 79-48
E.25-49 79-49
E.25-50 79-33
E.25-51 74-07
E.25-52 79-34
E.25-53 74-09
E.25-54 79-35
E.25-55 54-21
E.25-56 74-11
E.25-57 74-12
E.25-59 74-13
E.25-61 54-22
E.25-62 79-17
E.25-63 74-17
E.25-64 79-18
E.25-65 79-95
E.25-66 74-20
E.25-67 74-21
E.25-68 74-22
E.25-69 79-97
E.25-71 74-25
E.25-72 74-26
E.25-73 79-98
E.25-74 74-28
E.25-75 74-29
E.25-76 74-30
E.25-78 79-02
E.25-79 79-39
E.25-80 79-03
E.25-81 74-34
E.25-83 74-35
E.25-84 79-04
E.25-86 79-32 [5]*
E.25-87 79-29
E.25-88 74-39

CASA 212 Aviocar 212 (XT.12)/ 212A (T.12B)/ 212B (TR.12A)/ 212D (TE.12B)/ 212DE (TM.12D)/ 212E (T.12C)/ 212S (D.3A)/ 212S1 (D.3B)/ 212-200 (T.12D)/ 212-200 (TR.12D)
Ala 37, Villanubla;
Ala 46, Gando, Las Palmas;
47 Grupo Mixto, Torrejón;
CLAEX, Torrejón (54);
Ala 72, Alcantarilla;
Grupo Esc, Matacán (74);
AGA (Ala 79), San Javier;
403 Esc, Getafe;
801 Esc, Palma/ Son San Juan;
803 Esc, Cuatro Vientos;
INTA, Torrejón
D.3A-1 (801 Esc)
D.3A-2 (803 Esc)
D.3B-3 (803 Esc)
D.3B-4 (801 Esc)
D.3B-5 (801 Esc)
D.3B-6 (801 Esc)
D.3B-7 (803 Esc)
D.3B-8 (801 Esc)
XT.12A-1 54-10
TR.12A-4 403-02
TR.12A-5 403-03
TR.12A-6 403-04
TR.12A-8 403-06
T.12B-9 74-83
TE.12B-10 79-92
T.12B-12 74-82
T.12B-15 37-02
T.12B-16 74-71
T.12B-17 37-03
T.12B-18 46-31
T.12B-19 46-32
T.12B-20 37-04

T.12B-21	37-05
T.12B-22	37-06
T.12B-23	72-01
T.12B-24	54-12
T.12B-25	74-72
T.12B-26	72-02
T.12B-27	46-33
T.12B-28	72-03
T.12B-29	37-08
T.12B-30	74-73
T.12B-31	46-34
T.12B-33	72-04
T.12B-34	74-74
T.12B-36	37-10
T.12B-37	72-05
T.12B-39	74-75
TE.12B-40	79-93
TE.12B-41	79-94
T.12C-43	46-50
T.12C-44	37-50
T.12B-46	74-76
T.12B-47	72-06
T.12B-48	37-11
T.12B-49	72-07
T.12B-52	46-35
T.12B-53	46-36
T.12B-54	46-37
T.12B-55	46-38
T.12B-56	74-79
T.12B-57	72-08
T.12C-59	37-51
T.12C-60	37-52
T.12C-61	37-53
T.12B-63	37-14
T.12B-64	46-40
T.12B-65	74-80
T.12B-67	74-81
T.12B-69	37-16
T.12B-70	37-17
T.12B-71	37-18
TM.12D-72	
TM.12D-74	54-11
T.12D-75	403-07
TR.12D-76	37-60
TR.12D-77	37-61
TR.12D-78	37-62
TR.12D-79	37-63
TR.12D-80	37-64
TR.12D-81	37-65

CASA 295
Ala 35, Getafe;

T.21-01	35-39
T.21-02	35-40
T.21-03	35-41
T.21-04	35-42
T.21-05	35-43
T.21-06	35-44
T.21-07	35-45
T.21-08	
T.21-09	

Cessna 560 Citation VI
403 Esc, Getafe

TR.20-01	403-11
TR.20-02	403-12

Dassault Falcon 20D/E/F
47 Grupo Mixto, Torrejón

TM.11-1	20E	45-02
TM.11-2	20D	45-03
TM.11-3	20D	408-11
TM.11-4	20E	408-12

Dassault Falcon 900/900B*
Grupo 45, Torrejón

T.18-1	45-40
T.18-2	45-41
T.18-3*	45-42
T.18-4*	45-43
T.18-5*	45-44

Eurofighter EF.2000/ EF.2000B*
Ala 11, Morón;
CASA, Getafe

CE.16-01*	11-70
CE.16-02*	11-71
CE.16-03*	11-72
C.16-20	11-91

Fokker F.27M Friendship 400MPA
802 Esc, Gando, Las Palmas

D.2-01	802-10
D.2-02	802-11
D.2-03	802-12

Lockheed C-130H/ C-130H-30/KC-130H Hercules
311 Esc/312 Esc (Ala 31), Zaragoza

TL.10-01	C-130H-30	31-01
T.10-02	C-130H	31-02
T.10-03	C-130H	31-03
T.10-04	C-130H	31-04
TK.10-5	KC-130H	31-50
TK.10-6	KC-130H	31-51
TK.10-7	KC-130H	31-52
T.10-8	C-130H	31-05
T.10-9	C-130H	31-06
T.10-10	C-130H	31-07
TK.10-11	KC-130H	31-53
TK.10-12	KC-130H	31-54

Lockheed P-3A/P-3B/P-3M Orion
Grupo 22, Morón

P.3-01	P-3A	22-21
P.3-08	P-3B	22-31*
P.3-09	P-3M	22-32*
P.3-10	P-3B	22-33*
P.3-11	P-3B	22-34*
P.3-12	P-3B	22-35*

McDonnell Douglas F-18 Hornet
Ala 11, Morón;
Ala 12, Torrejón;
Ala 15, Zaragoza;
Esc 462, Gran Canaria

EF-18A/EF-18B* Hornet

CE.15-1	15-70*
CE.15-2	15-71*
CE.15-3	15-72*
CE.15-4	15-73*
CE.15-5	15-74*
CE.15-6	15-75*
CE.15-7	15-76*
CE.15-8	12-71*
CE.15-9	15-77*
CE.15-10	12-73*
CE.15-11	12-74*
CE.15-12	12-75*
C.15-13	12-01
C.15-14	15-01
C.15-15	15-02
C.15-16	15-03
C.15-18	15-05
C.15-20	15-07
C.15-21	15-08
C.15-22	15-09
C.15-23	15-10
C.15-24	15-11
C.15-25	15-12
C.15-26	15-13
C.15-27	15-14
C.15-28	15-15
C.15-29	15-16
C.15-30	15-17
C.15-31	15-18
C.15-32	15-19
C.15-33	15-20
C.15-34	15-21
C.15-35	15-22
C.15-36	15-23
C.15-37	15-24
C.15-38	15-25
C.15-39	15-26
C.15-40	15-27
C.15-41	15-28
C.15-43	15-30
C.15-44	12-02
C.15-45	12-03
C.15-46	12-04
C.15-47	15-31
C.15-48	12-06
C.15-49	12-07
C.15-50	12-08
C.15-51	12-09
C.15-52	12-10
C.15-53	12-11
C.15-54	12-12
C.15-55	12-13
C.15-56	12-14
C.15-57	12-15
C.15-58	12-16
C.15-59	12-17
C.15-60	12-18
C.15-61	12-19
C.15-62	12-20
C.15-64	12-22
C.15-65	12-23
C.15-66	12-24
C.15-67	15-33
C.15-68	12-26
C.15-69	12-27
C.15-70	12-28
C.15-72	12-30

F/A-18A Hornet

C.15-73	46-01
C.15-74	46-02
C.15-75	46-03
C.15-77	46-05
C.15-78	46-06
C.15-79	46-07
C.15-80	21-08
C.15-81	11-09
C.15-82	46-10
C.15-83	46-11
C.15-84	46-12
C.15-85	46-13
C.15-86	11-14
C.15-87	46-15
C.15-88	46-16
C.15-89	46-17
C.15-90	46-18
C.15-91	46-19
C.15-92	46-20
C.15-93	46-21

C.15-94 46-22
C.15-95 46-23
C.15-96 46-24

Arma Aérea de l'Armada Española

BAe/McDonnell Douglas EAV-8B/EAV-8B+/ TAV-8B Harrier II
Esc 009, Rota
EAV-8B
VA.1A-15 01-903
VA.1A-18 01-906
VA.1A-19 01-907
VA.1A-21 01-909
VA.1A-22 01-910
VA.1A-23 01-911
VA.1A-24 01-912
EAV-8B+
VA.1B-25 01-914
VA.1B-26 01-915
VA.1B-27 01-916
VA.1B-28 01-917
VA.1B-29 01-918
VA.1B-30 01-919
VA.1B-31 01-920
VA.1B-34
VA.1B-35 01-923
VA.1B-36 01-924
VA.1B-37 01-925
VA.1B-38 01-926
VA.1B-39 01-927
TAV-8B
VAE.1A-33 01-922

Cessna 550 Citation 2
Esc 004, Rota
U.20-1 01-405
U.20-2 01-406
U.20-3 01-407

SUDAN

Dassault Falcon 900B
Sudanese Govt, Khartoum
ST-PSA

SWEDEN
Svenska Flygvapnet

Grumman G.1159C Gulfstream 4 (Tp.102A/S.102B Korpen/ Tp.102C)
Flottiljer 17M, Stockholm/ Bromma & Malmslätt
Tp.102A
102001 021
S.102B Korpen
102002 022
102003 023
Tp.102C
102004 024

Lockheed C-130 Hercules (Tp.84)
Flottiljer 7, Såtenäs

84001	841	C-130E
84002	842	C-130E
84003	843	C-130H
84004	844	C-130H
84005	845	C-130H
84006	846	C-130H
84007	847	C-130H
84008	848	C-130H

Rockwell Sabreliner-40 (Tp.86)
FMV, Malmslätt
86001 861
86002 862

SAAB 37 Viggen
Flottiljer 4, Östersund/ Frösön;
Flottiljer 21, Luleå/Kallax;
FMV, Malmslätt

JA 37/JA 37D[D]/JA 37DI[I]

37325	25	F4
37326[I]	26	FMV
37331	31	F4
37341	41	F4
37343	43	F4
37347[D]	43	SAAB
37357	57	F4
37366	13	SAAB
37377	37	F4
37380	50	F4
37382	52	F4
37385	55	F4
37386[D]	46	F4
37388	58	F4
37390	60	F4
37398[I]	08	F4
37401[I]	01	F4
37406	26	F4
37412[D]	12	F4
37413[D]	13	F4
37414[I]	14	F4
37418[D]	18	F4
37421[I]	21	F4
37422[I]	22	F4
37424[I]	24	F4
37428[I]	28	F4
37436[I]	32	F4
37438[D]	38	F4
37439	01	F4
37440[I]	40	F4
37443[D]	43	F4
37444[I]	04	F4
37445[D]	45	F4
37446[I]	06	F4
37449[I]	49	F4

Sk 37/Sk 37E*

37801	80	F4
37807*	70	
37808*	71	
37809*	72	
37811*	73	
37813*	74	
37814*	76	
37817*	75	

AJSH 37

37901	51	
37903	53	
37911	33	
37913		
37916	37	FMV
37918	57	
37922	61	

AJSF 37

37950	48	F21
37951	50	F21
37954	54	F21
37957	56	F21
37958	58	F21
37971	62	F21
37974	64	F21
37976	66	F21

SAAB JAS 39 Gripen
Flottiljer 7, Såtenäs [G];
Flottiljer 10, Angelholm;
Flottiljer 17, Ronneby/ Kallinge;
Flottiljer 21, Luleå/ Kallax
FMV, Malmslätt

JAS 39

39-5	55	FMV

JAS 39A

39101	51	FMV
39103	103	FMV
39104	04	F7
39106	106	F10
39107	107	F7
39109	09	F7
39110	10	F7
39112	112	F7
39113	13	F7
39114	14	F7
39115	15	F7
39116	16	SAAB
39117	17	F7
39118	18	SAAB
39119	19	F7
39120	120	F7
39121	121	F7
39122	122	F7
39123	23	F7
39124	124	F7
39125	125	F21
39126	126	F17
39127	127	F7
39128	28	F7
39129	129	F7
39131	31	F7
39132	132	F17
39133	133	F7
39134	134	F7
39135	135	F17
39136	36	F17
39137	137	F10
39138	138	F17
39139	139	F17
39140	140	F17
39141	41	F17
39142	42	F21
39143	43	F17
39144	44	F10
39145	145	F21
39146	146	F17
39147	147	F17
39148	148	F17
39149	149	F7
39150	150	F17
39151	51	F7
39152	152	F17
39153	153	F21
39154	54	F7
39155	155	F17
39157	157	F17
39158	58	F7
39159	59	F7
39160	160	F7
39161	61	F7
39162	162	F17
39163	163	F17
39164	64	F17
39166	166	F17
39167	167	F17
39168	168	F10
39169	169	F17
39170	170	F17

39171	171	F17
39172	172	F17
39173	173	F17
39174	174	F17
39175	175	F17
39176	176	F7
39177	177	F17
39178	178	F17
39179	179	F7
39180	180	F17
39181	181	F21
39182	182	F7
39183	183	F17
39184	184	F17
39185	185	FMV
39186	186	F17
39187	187	F17
39188	188	F7
39189	189	FMV
39190	190	F17
39191	191	F17
39192	192	F7
39193	193	F21
39194	194	F21
39195	195	F21
39196	196	F21
39197	197	F21
39198	198	F21
39199	199	F21
39200	200	F21
39201	201	F21
39202	202	F21
39203	203	F21
39204	204	F21
39205	205	F21
39206	206	F21

JAS 39B

39800	56	FMV
39801	801	F7
39802	802	FMV
39803	803	F7
39804	804	F7
39805	805	F7
39806	806	F17
39807	807	F7
39808	808	F17
39809	809	F21
39810		
39811	811	FMV
39812		
39813	813	FMV
39814	814	FMV

JAS 39C

39-6	6	FMV
39208	208	SAAB
39209	209	FMV
39210	210	FMV
39211	211	SAAB
39212	212	FMV
39213		
39214		
39215	215	FMV
39216	216	FMV
39217		
39218		
39219		
39220		
39221	221	F17
39222		
39223		
39224	224	F17
39225	225	F17
39226		
39227		
39228	228	SAAB
39229		
39230		
39231		
39232		
39233		

SAAB SF.340 (OS.100 & Tp.100C)/SF.340AEW&C (S.100B & S.100D) Argus

Flottiljer 17, Ronneby/Kallinge;
Flottiljer 17M, Malmslätt;
Flottiljer 21, Luleå/Kallax

OS.100

100001	001	F17M

S.100B

100002	002	F17M
100005	005	F17M
100006	006	F17M
100007	007	F17M

Tp.100C

100008	008	F17
100009	009	F21

S.100D

100003	003	F17M
100004	004	F17M

Förvarsmaktens Helikopterflottilj

Aérospatiale AS.332M-1 Super Puma (Hkp.10)

1.HkpSkv, Lycksele & Östersund/Frösön
2.HkpSkv, Berga, Goteborg/Säve, & Ronneby/Kallinge;

10402	92	2.HkpSkv
10403	93	1.HkpSkv
10405	95	2.HkpSkv
10406	96	2.HkpSkv
10407	97	1.HkpSkv
10408	98	2.HkpSkv
10410	90	2.HkpSkv
10411	88	1.HkpSkv
10412	89	1.HkpSkv

MBB Bo.105CBS (Hkp.9A)

1.HkpSkv, Boden

09201	01
09202	02
09203	03
09204	04
09205	05
09206	06
09207	07
09208	08
09209	09
09210	10
09211	11
09212	12
09213	13
09214	14
09215	15
09216	16
09217	17
09218	18
09219	19
09220	20
09221	90

Vertol/Kawasaki-Vertol 107

2.HkpSkv, Berga, Goteborg/Säve, & Ronneby/Kallinge;
FMV (Flygvapnet), Malmslätt

Vertol 107-II-15 (Hkp.4B)

04061	61	2.HkpSkv
04063	63	2.HkpSkv
04064	64	2.HkpSkv

Kawasaki-Vertol KV.107-II-16 (Hkp.4C)

04065	65	2.HkpSkv
04067	67	2.HkpSkv
04068	68	2.HkpSkv
04069	69	2.HkpSkv
04070	70	2.HkpSkv
04071	71	2.HkpSkv
04072	72	FMV

Vertol 107-II-15 (Hkp.4D)

04073	73	2.HkpSkv
04074	74	2.HkpSkv
04075	75	2.HkpSkv
04076	76	2.HkpSkv

SWITZERLAND

Schweizerische Flugwaffe

(Most aircraft are pooled centrally. Some carry unit badges but these rarely indicate actual operators.)

Aérospatiale AS.332M-1/AS.532UL Super Puma

Lufttransport Staffel 3 (LtSt 3), Dübendorf;
Lufttransport Staffel 4 (LtSt 4), Dübendorf;
Lufttransport Staffel 5 (LtSt 5), Payerne;
Lufttransport Staffel 6 (LtSt 6), Alpnach;
Lufttransport Staffel 8 (LtSt 8), Alpnach
Detachments at Emmen, Meiringen & Sion

AS.332M-1

T-311
T-312
T-313
T-314
T-315
T-316
T-317
T-318
T-319
T-320
T-321
T-322
T-323
T-324
T-325

AS.532UL

T-331
T-332
T-333
T-334
T-335
T-336
T-337
T-338
T-339
T-340
T-341
T-342

Beechcraft Super King Air 350C
Koordinationsstelle für Luftaufnahmen, Dübendorf
T-721

Dassault Falcon 50
Gruppe Transport Flugzeuge, Dübendorf
T-783

Gates Learjet 35A
Gruppe Transport Flugzeuge, Dübendorf
T-781

McDonnell Douglas F/A-18 Hornet
Flieger Staffel 11 (FlSt 11), Meiringen;
Escadrille d'Aviation 17 (EdAv 17), Payerne;
Flieger Staffel 18 (FlSt 18), Payerne
F/A-18C
J-5001
J-5002
J-5003
J-5004
J-5005
J-5006
J-5007
J-5008
J-5009
J-5010
J-5011
J-5012
J-5013
J-5014
J-5015
J-5016
J-5017
J-5018
J-5019
J-5020
J-5021
J-5022
J-5023
J-5024
J-5025
J-5026
F/A-18D
J-5232
J-5233
J-5234
J-5235
J-5236
J-5237
J-5238

Northrop F-5 Tiger II
Armasuisse, Emmen;
Escadrille d'Aviation 6 (EdAv 6), Sion;
Flieger Staffel 8 (FlSt 8), Meiringen;
Flieger Staffel 11 (FlSt 11), Meiringen;
Flieger Staffel 19 (FlSt 19), Sion;
Instrumentation Flieger Staffel 14 (InstruFlSt 14), Dübendorf;
Patrouille Suisse, Emmen (*P. Suisse*)
F-5E
J-3001
J-3008 InstruFlSt 14
J-3014
J-3015
J-3024
J-3025
J-3036
J-3041
J-3043
J-3044
J-3047
J-3049
J-3054
J-3055
J-3056
J-3058
J-3060
J-3062
J-3063
J-3066
J-3067
J-3068
J-3069
J-3070
J-3072
J-3073
J-3074
J-3075
J-3076
J-3077
J-3079
J-3080 *P. Suisse*
J-3081 *P. Suisse*
J-3082 *P. Suisse*
J-3083 *P. Suisse*
J-3084 *P. Suisse*
J-3085 *P. Suisse*
J-3086 *P. Suisse*
J-3087 *P. Suisse*
J-3088 *P. Suisse*
J-3089 *P. Suisse*
J-3090 *P. Suisse*
J-3091 *P. Suisse*
J-3092
J-3093
J-3094
J-3095
J-3096
J-3097
J-3098
F-5F
J-3201
J-3202
J-3203
J-3204
J-3205
J-3206
J-3207
J-3208
J-3209
J-3210
J-3211
J-3212

SYRIA
Dassault Falcon 900
Govt of Syria, Damascus
YK-ASC

TUNISIA
Boeing 737-7HJ
Govt of Tunisia, Tunis
TS-IOO

TURKEY
Türk Hava Kuvvetleri

Boeing KC-135R Stratotanker
101 Filo, Incirlik
00325
00326
23539
23563
23567
72609
80110

Cessna 650 Citation VII
224 Filo, Ankara/Etimesut
004
005

Grumman G.1159C Gulfstream IV
224 Filo, Ankara/Etimesut
003
TC-ATA
TC-GAP

Lockheed C-130B Hercules
222 Filo, Erkilet
3496 (23496)
10960
10963
70527
80736

Lockheed C-130E Hercules
222 Filo, Erkilet
01468 12-468
01947
13186 12-186
13187
13188 12-188
13189
73-991

Transall C-160D
221 Filo, Erkilet
69-019
68-020
021
022
68-023
024
69-026
027
69-028 12-028
029
69-031
69-032
69-033
034
035 12-035
036
69-038
69-040

TUSAS-GD F-16C/F-16D*
Fighting Falcon
4 AJÜ, Mürted:
141 Filo, 142 Filo
& Öncel Filo;
5 AJÜ, Merzifon:
151 Filo & 152 Filo;
6 AJÜ, Bandirma:
161 Filo & 162 Filo;
8 AJÜ, Diyarbakir:
181 Filo & 182 Filo;
9 AJÜ, Balikesir:
191 Filo & 192 Filo

86-0066	Öncel Filo
86-0068	Öncel Filo
86-0069	Öncel Filo
86-0070	Öncel Filo
86-0071	Öncel Filo
86-0072	Öncel Filo
86-0191*	Öncel Filo
86-0192*	Öncel Filo
86-0193*	Öncel Filo
86-0194*	Öncel Filo
86-0195*	Öncel Filo
86-0196*	Öncel Filo
87-0002*	Öncel Filo
87-0003*	Öncel Filo
87-0009	Öncel Filo
87-0010	Öncel Filo
87-0011	Öncel Filo
87-0013	Öncel Filo
87-0014	Öncel Filo
87-0015	Öncel Filo
87-0016	Öncel Filo
87-0017	Öncel Filo
87-0018	Öncel Filo
87-0019	Öncel Filo
87-0020	Öncel Filo
87-0021	Öncel Filo
88-0013*	Öncel Filo
88-0014*	141 Filo
88-0015*	141 Filo
88-0019	Öncel Filo
88-0020	Öncel Filo
88-0021	Öncel Filo
88-0024	142 Filo
88-0025	141 Filo
88-0026	142 Filo
88-0027	Öncel Filo
88-0028	191 Filo
88-0029	142 Filo
88-0030	191 Filo
88-0031	Öncel Filo
88-0032	Öncel Filo
88-0033	141 Filo
88-0034	141 Filo
88-0035	141 Filo
88-0036	141 Filo
88-0037	141 Filo
89-0022	141 Filo
89-0023	141 Filo
89-0024	141 Filo
89-0025	141 Filo
89-0026	141 Filo
89-0027	141 Filo
89-0028	141 Filo
89-0030	141 Filo
89-0031	141 Filo
89-0032	141 Filo
89-0034	162 Filo
89-0035	162 Filo
89-0036	162 Filo
89-0037	162 Filo
89-0038	162 Filo
89-0039	162 Filo
89-0040	162 Filo
89-0041	162 Filo
89-0042*	141 Filo
89-0043*	162 Filo
89-0044*	162 Filo
89-0045*	182 Filo
90-0001	162 Filo
90-0004	162 Filo
90-0005	162 Filo
90-0006	162 Filo
90-0007	162 Filo
90-0008	162 Filo
90-0009	162 Filo
90-0010	162 Filo
90-0011	162 Filo
90-0012	161 Filo
90-0013	161 Filo
90-0014	161 Filo
90-0015	161 Filo
90-0016	161 Filo
90-0017	161 Filo
90-0018	161 Filo
90-0019	161 Filo
90-0020	162 Filo
90-0021	161 Filo
90-0022*	161 Filo
90-0023*	161 Filo
90-0024*	161 Filo
91-0001	161 Filo
91-0002	161 Filo
91-0003	161 Filo
91-0004	161 Filo
91-0005	161 Filo
91-0006	161 Filo
91-0007	161 Filo
91-0008	141 Filo
91-0010	141 Filo
91-0011	141 Filo
91-0012	141 Filo
91-0013	192 Filo
91-0014	141 Filo
91-0015	182 Filo
91-0016	182 Filo
91-0017	182 Filo
91-0018	182 Filo
91-0019	182 Filo
91-0020	182 Filo
91-0022*	141 Filo
91-0024*	141 Filo
92-0001	182 Filo
92-0002	182 Filo
92-0003	162 Filo
92-0004	182 Filo
92-0005	191 Filo
92-0006	182 Filo
92-0007	182 Filo
92-0008	191 Filo
92-0009	191 Filo
92-0010	182 Filo
92-0011	182 Filo
92-0012	182 Filo
92-0013	182 Filo
92-0014	182 Filo
92-0015	181 Filo
92-0016	182 Filo
92-0017	182 Filo
92-0018	181 Filo
92-0019	181 Filo
92-0020	181 Filo
92-0021	181 Filo
92-0022*	181 Filo
92-0023*	181 Filo
92-0024*	182 Filo
93-0001	181 Filo
93-0003	181 Filo
93-0004	181 Filo
93-0005	181 Filo
93-0006	181 Filo
93-0007	181 Filo
93-0008	181 Filo
93-0009	181 Filo
93-0010	181 Filo
93-0011	181 Filo
93-0012	181 Filo
93-0013	181 Filo
93-0014	181 Filo
93-0657	141 Filo
93-0658	
93-0659	151 Filo
93-0660	151 Filo
93-0661	151 Filo
93-0662	151 Filo
93-0663	151 Filo
93-0664	
93-0665	151 Filo
93-0666	
93-0667	151 Filo
93-0668	
93-0669	152 Filo
93-0670	
93-0671	
93-0672	152 Filo
93-0673	Öncel Filo
93-0674	192 Filo
93-0675	192 Filo
93-0676	192 Filo
93-0677	192 Filo
93-0678	192 Filo
93-0679	192 Filo
93-0680	192 Filo
93-0681	192 Filo
93-0682	192 Filo
93-0683	192 Filo
93-0684	192 Filo
93-0685	192 Filo
93-0686	192 Filo
93-0687	192 Filo
93-0688	192 Filo
93-0689	Öncel Filo
93-0690	192 Filo
93-0691*	
93-0692*	151 Filo
93-0693*	151 Filo
93-0694*	
93-0695*	192 Filo
93-0696*	192 Filo
94-0071	192 Filo
94-0072	191 Filo
94-0073	191 Filo
94-0074	191 Filo
94-0075	191 Filo
94-0076	191 Filo
94-0077	191 Filo
94-0078	191 Filo
94-0079	191 Filo
94-0080	191 Filo
94-0081	191 Filo
94-0082	191 Filo
94-0083	191 Filo
94-0084	191 Filo
94-0085	191 Filo
94-0086	191 Filo
94-0087	191 Filo
94-0088	
94-0089	152 Filo
94-0090	
94-0091	152 Filo

94-0092	
94-0093	
94-0094	Öncel Filo
94-0095	152 Filo
94-0096	152 Filo
94-0105*	191 Filo
94-0106*	191 Filo
94-0107*	191 Filo
94-0108*	151 Filo
94-0109*	152 Filo
94-0110*	152 Filo
94-1557*	152 Filo
94-1558*	Öncel Filo
94-1559*	152 Filo
94-1560*	151 Filo
94-1561*	191 Filo
94-1562*	192 Filo
94-1563*	192 Filo
94-1564*	191 Filo

TURKMENISTAN

BAe 1000B
Govt of Turkmenistan, Ashkhabad
EZ-B021

Boeing 757-23A
Govt of Turkmenistan, Ashkhabad
EZ-A010

UGANDA

Grumman G.1159C Gulfstream IV
Govt of Uganda, Entebbe
5X-UEF

UKRAINE

Ukrainian Air Force

Ilyushin Il-76MD
321 TAP, Uzin
78820
UR-76413
UR-76537
UR-76624
UR-76677
UR-76687
UR-76697
UR-76699

Ilyushin Il-62M
Govt of Ukraine, Kiev
UR-86527
UR-86528

Tupolev Tu-134
Govt of Ukraine, Kiev
UR-63982

UNITED ARAB EMIRATES

United Arab Emirates Air Force

Abu Dhabi

Lockheed C-130H/ L.100-30* Hercules
1211
1212
1213
1214
1215*
1216*

Dubai
311*
312*

Airbus A.319CJ-113X
Dubai Air Wing
A6-ESH

Antonov AN-124
UAE Govt
UR-ZYD

Boeing 737-2W8/7F0/7Z5/8EC/8EX
Govt of Abu Dhabi;
Govt of Dubai

A6-AIN	7Z5	Abu Dhabi
A6-AUH	8EX	Dubai
A6-DAS	7Z5	Abu Dhabi
A6-ESJ	2W8	Dubai
A6-HRS	7F0	Dubai
A6-LIW	7Z5	Dubai
A6-MRM	8EC	Dubai

Boeing 747-2B4BF/422/48E/4F6
Dubai Air Wing;
Govt of Abu Dhabi

A6-GDP	2B4BF	Dubai
A6-HRM	422	Dubai
A6-MMM	422	Dubai
A6-UAE	46E	Dubai
A6-YAS	4F6	Abu Dhabi

Boeing 747SP-31/ 747SP-Z5*
Govt of Dubai
A6-SMM
A6-SMR
A6-ZSN*

Boeing 767-341ER
Govt of Abu Dhabi
A6-SUL

Dassault Falcon 900
Govt of Abu Dhabi
A6-AUH

Grumman G.1159C Gulfstream IV
Dubai Air Wing
A6-HHH

YEMEN

Boeing 747SP-27
Govt of Yemen, Sana'a
7O-YMN

YUGOSLAVIA

Dassault Falcon 50
Govt of Yugoslavia, Belgrade
YU-BNA

Gates Learjet 25B/ Learjet 25D*
Govt of Yugoslavia, Belgrade
YU-BJG
YU-BKR*

French Air Force D-BD AlphaJet E103 is flown by EAC 00.314 from Tours.

This French Air Force Dassault Mirage IVP No 59 is due to be retired this year at Mont-de-Marsan.

Dassault Mirage 2000D No 637 is operated by French Air Force EC 03.003 at Nancy.

SOCATA TBM 700 No 160 taking off to return to its base at Rennes, France.

German Navy Breguet Br1150 Atlantic 61+14 is flown by MFG-3 at Nordholz.

US Military Aircraft Markings

All USAF aircraft have been allocated a fiscal year (FY) number since 1921. Individual aircraft are given a serial according to the fiscal year in which they are ordered. The numbers commence at 0001 and are prefixed with the year of allocation. For example F-15C Eagle 84-001 (84-0001) was the first aircraft ordered in 1984. The fiscal year (FY) serial is carried on the technical data block which is usually stencilled on the left-hand side of the aircraft just below the cockpit. The number displayed on the fin is a corruption of the FY serial. Most tactical aircraft carry the fiscal year in small figures followed by the last three or four digits of the serial in large figures. Large transport and tanker aircraft such as C-130s and KC-135s sometimes display a five-figure number commencing with the last digit of the appropriate fiscal year and four figures of the production number. An example of this is KC-135R 58-0128 which displays 80128 on its fin.

USN serials follow a straightforward numerical sequence which commenced, for the present series, with the allocation of 00001 to an SB2C Helldiver by the Bureau of Aeronautics in 1940. Numbers in the 166000 series are presently being issued. They are usually carried in full on the rear fuselage of the aircraft.

UK-based USAF Aircraft

The following aircraft are normally based in the UK. They are listed in numerical order of type with individual aircraft in serial number order, as depicted on the aircraft. The number in brackets is either the alternative presentation of the five-figure number commencing with the last digit of the fiscal year, or the fiscal year where a five-figure serial is presented on the aircraft. Where it is possible to identify the allocation of aircraft to individual squadrons by means of colours carried on fin or cockpit edge, this is also provided.

Notes	Type			
	McDonnell Douglas F-15C Eagle/F-15D Eagle/ F-15E Strike Eagle			
	LN: 48th FW, RAF Lakenheath:			
	492nd FS *bl*ue/white			
	493rd FS black/*y*ellow			
	494th FS *r*ed/white			
	00-3000	F-15E	*r*	
	00-3001	F-15E	*r*	
	00-3002	F-15E	*r*	
	00-3003	F-15E	*r*	
	00-3004	F-15E	*r*	
	01-2000	F-15E	*r*	
	01-2001	F-15E	*m*	[48th OG]
	01-2002	F-15E	*r*	
	01-2003	F-15E	*r*	
	01-2004	F-15E	*r*	
	83-0018	F-15C	*y*	
	84-0001	F-15C	*y*	
	84-0004	F-15C	*y*	
	84-0009	F-15C	*y*	
	84-0010	F-15C	*y*	
	84-0014	F-15C	*y*	
	84-0015	F-15C	*y*	
	84-0019	F-15C	*y*	
	84-0027	F-15C	*y*	
	84-0044	F-15D	*y*	[48th OSS]
	86-0147	F-15C	*y*	
	86-0154	F-15C	*y*	
	86-0156	F-15C	*y*	
	86-0159	F-15C	*y*	

Notes	Type			
	86-0160	F-15C	*y*	
	86-0163	F-15C	*y*	
	86-0164	F-15C	*y*	
	86-0165	F-15C	*y*	[493rd FS]
	86-0166	F-15C	*y*	
	86-0167	F-15C	*y*	
	86-0171	F-15C	*y*	
	86-0172	F-15C	*y*	
	86-0174	F-15C	*y*	
	86-0175	F-15C	*y*	
	86-0176	F-15C	*y*	
	86-0178	F-15C	*y*	
	86-0182	F-15D	*y*	
	91-0300	F-15E	*r*	
	91-0301	F-15E	*bl*	
	91-0302	F-15E	*bl*	
	91-0303	F-15E	*bl*	
	91-0304	F-15E	*bl*	
	91-0306	F-15E	*r*	
	91-0307	F-15E	*bl*	
	91-0308	F-15E	*bl*	
	91-0309	F-15E	*bl*	
	91-0310	F-15E	*r*	
	91-0311	F-15E	*bl*	
	91-0312	F-15E	*bl*	
	91-0313	F-15E	*m*	[48th OG]
	91-0314	F-15E	*r*	
	91-0315	F-15E	*r*	
	91-0316	F-15E	*r*	
	91-0317	F-15E	*r*	
	91-0318	F-15E	*r*	

Type				Notes
91-0320	F-15E	*r*		
91-0321	F-15E	*bl*		
91-0324	F-15E	*r*		
91-0326	F-15E	*r*		
91-0329	F-15E	*bl*		
91-0330	F-15E	*r*		
91-0331	F-15E	*r*		
91-0332	F-15E	*bl*		
91-0334	F-15E	*r*		
91-0335	F-15E	*r*		
91-0601	F-15E	*r*		
91-0602	F-15E	*r*		
91-0603	F-15E	*r*		
91-0604	F-15E	*r*		
91-0605	F-15E	*bl*		
92-0364	F-15E	*r*		
96-0201	F-15E	*bl*		
96-0202	F-15E	*bl*		
96-0204	F-15E	*bl*		
96-0205	F-15E	*bl*		
97-0217	F-15E	*bl*		
97-0218	F-15E	*m*	[48th FW]	
97-0219	F-15E	*bl*		
97-0220	F-15E	*bl*		
97-0221	F-15E	*bl*	[492nd FS]	
97-0222	F-15E	*bl*		
98-0131	F-15E	*bl*		
98-0132	F-15E	*bl*		
98-0133	F-15E	*bl*		
98-0134	F-15E	*bl*		
98-0135	F-15E	*bl*		

Sikorsky MH-53M
21st SOS/352nd SOG,
RAF Mildenhall

01630	(FY70)	
14994	(FY67)	
31649	(FY73)	
31652	(FY73)	
95784	(FY69)	
95795	(FY69)	
95796	(FY69)	

Lockheed C-130 Hercules
352nd SOG, RAF Mildenhall:
7th SOS* & 67th SOS,

Type			Notes
37814	(FY63)	C-130E	
61699	(FY86)	MC-130H*	
70126	(FY87)	MC-130P*	
70127	(FY87)	MC-130P*	
80193	(FY88)	MC-130H*	
80194	(FY88)	MC-130H*	
90280	(FY89)	MC-130H*	
95825	(FY69)	MC-130P	
95826	(FY69)	MC-130P	
95828	(FY69)	MC-130P	
95831	(FY69)	MC-130P	
95832	(FY69)	MC-130P	

Boeing KC-135R Stratotanker
351st ARS/100th ARW,
RAF Mildenhall [D] (*r/w/bl*)

00313	(FY60)	
00351	(FY60)	
10292	(FY61)	
14828	(FY64)	
14830	(FY64)	
14835	(FY64)	
23505	(FY62)	
23538	(FY62)	
23541	(FY62)	
23551	(FY62)	
23561	(FY62)	
23573	(FY62)	
23575	(FY62)	
38871	(FY63)	
38879	(FY63)	
38884	(FY63)	
72605	(FY57)	
80128	(FY58)	
91459	(FY59)	

UK-based US Navy Aircraft

Beech UC-12M Super King Air
Naval Air Facility, Mildenhall
3836 (163836)
3843 (163843)

European-based USAF Aircraft

These aircraft are normally based in Western Europe with the USAFE. They are shown in numerical order of type designation, with individual aircraft in serial number order as carried on the aircraft. Fiscal year (FY) details are also provided if necessary. The unit allocation and operating bases are given for most aircraft.

Notes *Type*

McDonnell Douglas C-9A Nightingale
86th AW, Ramstein, Germany:
76th AS
FY71
10876

Fairchild A-10A Thunderbolt II
SP: 52nd FW, Spangdahlem, Germany: 81st FS black/*y*ellow

80-0281	*y*	[81st FS]
81-0945	*y*	
81-0948	*y*	
81-0951	*y*	
81-0952	*m*	[52nd FW]
81-0954	*y*	
81-0956	*y*	
81-0962	*y*	
81-0963	*y*	
81-0966	*y*	
81-0976	*y*	
81-0978	*y*	
81-0980	*y*	
81-0983	*y*	
81-0984	*y*	
81-0985	*y*	
81-0988	*y*	
81-0991	*y*	
81-0992	*m*	[52nd OG]
82-0649	*y*	
82-0650	*y*	
82-0654	*y*	
82-0656	*y*	

Beech C-12D
US Embassy Flight, Budapest, Hungary
FY83
30495

Lockheed (GD) F-16C/F-16D*
AV: 31st FW, Aviano, Italy:
510th FS *pu*rple/white
555th FS *gree*n/yellow
SP: 52nd FW, Spangdahlem, Germany:
22nd FS *r*ed/white
23rd FS *bl*ue/white

87-0350	AV *gn*	
87-0351	AV *m*	[31st OSS]
87-0355	AV *pr*	
87-0359	AV *gn*	
88-0413	AV *pr*	[510th FS]
88-0425	AV *gn*	[16th AF]
88-0435	AV *gn*	
88-0443	AV *pr*	
88-0444	AV *pr*	
88-0446	AV *gn*	
88-0491	AV *pr*	
88-0525	AV *pr*	
88-0526	AV *gn*	
88-0529	AV *pr*	
88-0532	AV *gn*	
88-0535	AV *gn*	
88-0541	AV *pr*	
89-2001	AV *m*	[31st FW]
89-2009	AV *gn*	
89-2011	AV *pr*	
89-2016	AV *gn*	[16th AF]
89-2018	AV *gn*	
89-2023	AV *gn*	
89-2024	AV *gn*	
89-2026	AV *gn*	
89-2029	AV *pr*	
89-2030	AV *pr*	
89-2035	AV *gn*	[555th FS]
89-2038	AV *gn*	
89-2039	AV *gn*	
89-2041	AV *gn*	
89-2044	AV *gn*	
89-2046	AV *pr*	
89-2047	AV *pr*	
89-2049	AV *pr*	[USAFE]
89-2057	AV *pr*	
89-2068	AV *gn*	
89-2102	AV *gn*	
89-2118	AV *pr*	
89-2137	AV *pr*	[31st OG]
89-2178*	AV *pr*	
90-0709	AV *pr*	
90-0772	AV *gn*	
90-0773	AV *gn*	
90-0777*	AV *pr*	
90-0795*	AV *gn*	
90-0796*	AV *pr*	
90-0800*	AV *gn*	
90-0813	SP *r*	
90-0818	SP *r*	
90-0827	SP *r*	
90-0828	SP *r*	
90-0829	SP *r*	[22nd FS]
90-0831	SP *r*	
90-0833	SP *r*	
90-0843*	SP *r*	
90-0846*	SP *bl*	
91-0336	SP *r*	
91-0337	SP *r*	
91-0338	SP *r*	
91-0339	SP *r*	[22nd FS]
91-0340	SP *r*	
91-0341	SP *r*	
91-0342	SP *r*	
91-0343	SP *r*	
91-0344	SP *r*	
91-0351	SP *r*	
91-0352	SP *m*	[52nd FW]
91-0391	SP *r*	
91-0402	SP *bl*	
91-0403	SP *bl*	

Type			Notes
91-0405	SP *bl*		
91-0406	SP *bl*		
91-0407	SP *bl*		
91-0408	SP *r*		
91-0409	SP *bl*		
91-0410	SP *bl*		
91-0412	SP *bl*		
91-0414	SP *bl*		
91-0416	SP *bl*	[52nd OG]	
91-0417	SP *bl*		
91-0418	SP *bl*		
91-0419	SP *bl*		
91-0420	SP *bl*		
91-0421	SP *bl*		
91-0464*	SP *r*		
91-0472*	SP *bl*		
91-0474*	SP *bl*		
91-0481*	SP *bl*		
92-3915	SP *bl*		
92-3918	SP *bl*		
96-0080	SP *bl*	[23rd FS]	
96-0081	SP *bl*		
96-0082	SP *m*	[52nd FW]	
96-0083	SP *bl*		

Grumman C-20H Gulfstream IV
76th AS/86th AW, Ramstein, Germany
FY90
00300
FY92
20375

Gates C-21A Learjet
76th AS/86th AW, Ramstein, Germany
FY84
40068
40081
40082
40083
40084
40085
40086
40087
40108
40109
40110
40111
40112

Gulfstream Aerospace C-37A Gulfstream V
309th AS/86th AW, Chievres, Belgium
FY01
10076

Sikorsky HH-60G Blackhawk
56th RQS/85th Wing, Keflavik, Iceland [IS]

26109	(FY88)	
26205	(FY89)	
26206	(FY89)	
26208	(FY89)	
26212	(FY89)	

Lockheed C-130E Hercules
37th AS/86th AW, Ramstein, Germany [RS] (*bl/w*)

01260	(FY70)	
01264	(FY70)	
01271	(FY70)	
01274	(FY70)	[86th AW]
10935	(FY68)	
10943	(FY68)	[86th OG]
17681	(FY64)	
21835	(FY62)	
37865	(FY63)	
37879	(FY63)	
37885	(FY63)	
37887	(FY63)	
40496	(FY64)	
40499	(FY64)	
40502	(FY64)	
40527	(FY64)	

European-based US Navy Aircraft

Notes	Type

Lockheed P-3 Orion
VQ-2, NAF Rota, Spain

156519	[21]	EP-3E
156529	[24]	EP-3E
157316	[23]	EP-3E
157325	[25]	EP-3E
157326	[22]	EP-3E
159886	[886]	P-3C
161121	[15]	P-3C

Beech UC-12M Super King Air
NAF Rota, Spain

3839 (163839)	Rota
3842 (163842)	Rota

Fairchild C-26D
NAF Naples, Italy;
NAF Sigonella, Italy

900528	Sigonella
900530	Sigonella
900531	Naples
910502	Naples

Grumman C-20A Gulfstream III
CinCUSNFE
NAF Sigonella, Italy
830500

Sikorsky MH-53E Sea Stallion
HC-4, NAF Sigonella, Italy

162504	[HC-40]
162505	[HC-47]
162514	[HC-50]
162516	[HC-00]
163053	[HC-44]
163055	[HC-45]
163057	[HC-41]
163065	[HC-43]
164864	[HC-00]

European-based US Army Aircraft

Notes	Type

Bell UH-1H Iroquois
Combat Manoeuvre Training Centre, Hohenfels
FY72
21569
21632
21636
FY73
21668
21786
FY74
22330
22355
22370
22410
22448
22465

Beech C-12 Super King Air
'A' Co, 2nd Btn, 228th Avn Reg't, Heidelberg;
HQ/USEUCOM, Stuttgart;
'E' Co, 1st Btn, 214th Avn Reg't, Vicenza, Italy;
1st Military Intelligence Btn, Wiesbaden;
'B' Co, 1st Btn, 214th Avn Reg't, Wiesbaden
FY84

40153	C-12U	1st MIB
40156	C-12U	B/1-214th Avn
40157	C-12U	E/1-214th Avn
40158	C-12U	B/1-214th Avn
40160	C-12U	E/1-214th Avn
40161	C-12U	B/1-214th Avn
40162	C-12U	B/1-214th Avn
40163	C-12U	HQ/USEUCOM
40165	C-12U	B/1-214th Avn
40180	C-12U	HQ/USEUCOM

FY94

40315	C-12R	A/2-228th Avn
40316	C-12R	A/2-228th Avn
40318	C-12R	A/2-228th Avn
40319	C-12R	A/2-228th Avn

FY95

50091	C-12R	A/2-228th Avn

FY85

50147	RC-12K	1st MIB
50148	RC-12K	1st MIB
50149	RC-12K	1st MIB
50150	RC-12K	1st MIB
50152	RC-12K	1st MIB
50153	RC-12K	1st MIB
50155	RC-12K	1st MIB

Beech C-12J
HQ/USEUCOM, Stuttgart
FY86
60079

Cessna UC-35A Citation V
214th Avn Reg't, Wiesbaden
FY95
50123
50124
FY97
70101
70102
70105
FY99
90102

Boeing-Vertol CH-47D Chinook
'F' Co, 159th Avn Reg't Giebelstadt
FY87
70072
70073

Type	Notes
FY88	
80099	
80100	
80101	
80102	
80103	
80104	
80106	
FY89	
90138	
90139	
90140	
90141	
90142	
90143	
90144	
90145	

Bell OH-58D(I) Kiowa Warrior

1st Btn, 1st Cavalry Reg't, Budingen;
1st Btn, 4th Cavalry Reg't, Schweinfurt

FY90
00348 1-1st Cav
00371 1-1st Cav
00373 1-4th Cav
FY91
10540 1-1st Cav
10544 1-1st Cav
10564 1-1st Cav
FY92
20520 1-1st Cav
20545 1-1st Cav
FY93
30971 1-4th Cav
30996 1-4th Cav
30998 1-4th Cav
31002 1-4th Cav
31005 1-4th Cav
31006 1-4th Cav
31007 1-4th Cav
31008 1-4th Cav
FY94
40149 1-4th Cav
40150 1-4th Cav
40151 1-4th Cav
40152 1-1st Cav
40153 1-4th Cav
40154 1-4th Cav
40174 1-4th Cav
40175 1-1st Cav
40176 1-4th Cav
40178 1-1st Cav
40179 1-1st Cav
40180 1-1st Cav
FY89
90114 1-1st Cav
90116 1-1st Cav
90117 1-1st Cav

Sikorsky H-60 Black Hawk

2nd Btn, 1st Avn Reg't, Ansbach;
45th Medical Co, Ansbach;
'B' Co, 5th Btn, 158th Avn Reg't, Aviano;
'A' Co, 127th Divisional Avn Support Btn, Bad Kreuznach;
357th Avn Det/SHAPE, Chievres;
'B' Co, 70th Transportation Reg't, Coleman Barracks;
214th Avn Reg't, Coleman Barracks;
'A' Co, 3rd Btn, 158th Avn Reg't, Giebelstadt;
'B' Co, 3rd Btn, 158th Avn Reg't, Giebelstadt;
'A' Co, 5th Btn, 158th Avn Reg't, Giebelstadt;
'C' Co, 5th Btn, 158th Avn Reg't, Giebelstadt;
2nd Btn, 501st Avn Reg't, Hanau;
'B' Co, 7th Btn, 159th AVIM, Illesheim;
236th Medical Co (HA), Landstuhl;
6th Avn Co, Vicenza, Italy;
159th Medical Co, Wiesbaden

FY82
23675 UH-60A 45th Med Co
23685 UH-60A 159th Med Co
23692 UH-60A A/3-158th Avn
23693 UH-60A 45th Med Co
23729 UH-60A 236th Med Co
23735 UH-60A 236th Med Co
23737 UH-60A 236th Med Co
23738 UH-60A 159th Med Co
23745 UH-60A 236th Med Co
23750 UH-60A 159th Med Co
23751 UH-60A 159th Med Co
23752 UH-60A 236th Med Co
23753 UH-60A 159th Med Co
23754 UH-60A 45th Med Co
23755 UH-60A 236th Med Co
23756 UH-60A 159th Med Co
23757 UH-60A 214th Avn
FY83
23854 UH-60A A/5-158th Avn
23855 UH-60A 214th Avn
23868 UH-60A 214th Avn
23869 UH-60A 214th Avn
FY84
23951 UH-60A 45th Med Co
23970 UH-60A C/5-158th Avn
23975 UH-60A C/5-158th Avn
FY85
24391 UH-60A 45th Med Co
FY86
24498 UH-60A 2-501st Avn
24530 UH-60A 2-501st Avn
24531 UH-60A 45th Med Co
24532 UH-60A 236th Med Co
24538 UH-60A 214th Avn
24550 UH-60A 236th Med Co
24552 UH-60A 159th Med Co
24554 UH-60A C/5-158th Avn
24555 UH-60A
FY87
24579 UH-60A A/5-158th Avn
24581 UH-60A 159th Med Co
24583 UH-60A 357th Avn Det
24584 UH-60A 357th Avn Det
24589 UH-60A 214th Avn
24621 UH-60A 214th Avn
24628 UH-60A 159th Med Co
24634 UH-60A 159th Med Co
24642 UH-60A 214th Avn
24644 UH-60A 45th Med Co
24645 UH-60A 45th Med Co
24647 UH-60A 214th Avn
24650 UH-60A
24656 UH-60A 159th Med Co
24660 EH-60C 2-501st Avn
24664 EH-60A 2-501st Avn
26001 UH-60A 45th Med Co
26002 UH-60A 159th Med Co
26003 UH-60A B/5-158th Avn
26004 UH-60A 45th Med Co

Notes	Type		
	FY88		
	26019	UH-60A	214th Avn
	26020	UH-60A	236th Med Co
	26021	UH-60A	B/5-158th Avn
	26023	UH-60A	236th Med Co
	26025	UH-60A	214th Avn
	26026	UH-60A	B/5-158th Avn
	26027	UH-60A	214th Avn
	26028	UH-60A	C/5-158th Avn
	26031	UH-60A	236th Med Co
	26034	UH-60A	159th Med Co
	26037	UH-60A	B/7-159th AVIM
	26038	UH-60A	A/5-158th Avn
	26039	UH-60A	45th Med Co
	26040	UH-60A	236th Med Co
	26041	UH-60A	A/5-158th Avn
	26042	UH-60A	A/5-158th Avn
	26045	UH-60A	45th Med Co
	26050	UH-60A	159th Med Co
	26051	UH-60A	A/5-158th Avn
	26052	UH-60A	B/5-158th Avn
	26053	UH-60A	A/5-158th Avn
	26054	UH-60A	236th Med Co
	26055	UH-60A	236th Med Co
	26056	UH-60A	A/5-158th Avn
	26058	UH-60A	159th Med Co
	26063	UH-60A	B/5-158th Avn
	26067	UH-60A	B/5-158th Avn
	26068	UH-60A	236th Med Co
	26071	UH-60A	2-501st Avn
	26072	UH-60A	236th Med Co
	26075	UH-60A	159th Med Co
	26077	UH-60A	C/5-158th Avn
	26080	UH-60A	236th Med Co
	26085	UH-60A	236th Med Co
	26086	UH-60A	236th Med Co
	FY89		
	26138	UH-60A	159th Med Co
	26142	UH-60A	2-501st Avn
	26145	UH-60A	B/5-158th Avn
	26146	UH-60A	159th Med Co
	26151	UH-60A	159th Med Co
	26153	UH-60A	B/5-158th Avn
	26164	UH-60A	C/5-158th Avn
	26165	UH-60A	214th Avn
	FY95		
	26621	UH-60L	2-1st Avn
	26628	UH-60L	2-1st Avn
	26629	UH-60L	2-1st Avn
	26630	UH-60L	2-1st Avn
	26631	UH-60L	2-1st Avn
	26632	UH-60L	2-1st Avn
	26633	UH-60L	2-1st Avn
	26635	UH-60L	2-1st Avn
	26636	UH-60L	2-1st Avn
	26637	UH-60L	2-1st Avn
	26638	UH-60L	2-1st Avn
	26639	UH-60L	2-1st Avn
	26640	UH-60L	2-1st Avn
	26641	UH-60L	B/3-158th Avn
	26642	UH-60L	B/3-158th Avn
	26643	UH-60L	B/3-158th Avn
	26644	UH-60L	2-1st Avn
	26645	UH-60L	A/3-158th Avn
	26646	UH-60L	2-1st Avn
	26647	UH-60L	2-1st Avn
	26648	UH-60L	2-1st Avn
	26649	UH-60L	B/3-158th Avn
	26650	UH-60L	A/3-158th Avn
	26651	UH-60L	B/3-158th Avn
	26652	UH-60L	B/3-158th Avn
	26653	UH-60L	A/3-158th Avn
	26654	UH-60L	A/3-158th Avn

Notes	Type		
	26655	UH-60L	A/3-158th Avn
	FY96		
	26674	UH-60L	B/3-158th Avn
	26675	UH-60L	A/3-158th Avn
	26676	UH-60L	B/3-158th Avn
	26677	UH-60L	B/3-158th Avn
	26678	UH-60L	B/3-158th Avn
	26679	UH-60L	B/3-158th Avn
	26680	UH-60L	B/3-158th Avn
	26681	UH-60L	B/3-158th Avn
	26682	UH-60L	B/3-158th Avn
	26683	UH-60L	A/3-158th Avn
	26684	UH-60L	A/3-158th Avn
	26685	UH-60L	A/3-158th Avn
	26686	UH-60L	A/3-158th Avn
	26687	UH-60L	A/3-158th Avn
	26688	UH-60L	A/3-158th Avn
	26689	UH-60L	A/3-158th Avn
	26690	UH-60L	A/3-158th Avn
	26691	UH-60L	A/3-158th Avn
	26692	UH-60L	A/3-158th Avn
	FY97		
	26762	UH-60L	A/3-158th Avn
	26763	UH-60L	2-501st Avn
	26765	UH-60L	A/3-158th Avn
	26766	UH-60L	2-501st Avn
	26767	UH-60L	A/3-158th Avn
	FY98		
	26795	UH-60L	2-501st Avn
	26796	UH-60L	2-501st Avn
	26797	UH-60L	2-501st Avn
	26798	UH-60L	2-501st Avn
	26799	UH-60L	2-501st Avn
	26800	UH-60L	2-501st Avn
	26801	UH-60L	2-501st Avn
	26802	UH-60L	2-501st Avn
	26813	UH-60L	2-501st Avn
	26814	UH-60L	2-501st Avn
	FY01		
	26878	UH-60L	B/3-158th Avn
	26880	UH-60L	B/3-158th Avn
	26884	UH-60L	B/3-158th Avn
	26885	UH-60L	B/3-158th Avn
	26886	UH-60L	B/3-158th Avn
	26889	UH-60L	B/3-158th Avn
	FY02		
	26970	UH-60L	B/3-158th Avn
	FY03		
	26992	UH-60L	B/3-158th Avn

MDH AH-64 Apache

3rd Btn, 1st Avn Reg't, Illesheim;
2nd Btn, 6th Cavalry Reg't, Illesheim;
6th Btn, 6th Cavalry Reg't, Illesheim

AH-64A

Notes	Type	
	FY86	
	68940	3-1st Avn
	68942	3-1st Avn
	68943	3-1st Avn
	68946	3-1st Avn
	68948	3-1st Avn
	68951	3-1st Avn
	68952	3-1st Avn
	68955	3-1st Avn
	68956	3-1st Avn
	68957	3-1st Avn
	68959	3-1st Avn
	68960	3-1st Avn
	68961	3-1st Avn
	68981	3-1st Avn
	69026	3-1st Avn
	69030	3-1st Avn
	69032	3-1st Avn

Type		Notes
69037	3-1st Avn	
69048	3-1st Avn	
FY87		
70443	3-1st Avn	
70503	3-1st Avn	
AH-64D		
FY96		
05007	2-6th Cav	
05009	6-6th Cav	
05011	2-6th Cav	
05015	2-6th Cav	
05018	2-6th Cav	
05020	2-6th Cav	
05021	2-6th Cav	
05022	2-6th Cav	
FY99		
05101	2-6th Cav	
05109	2-6th Cav	
05114	2-6th Cav	
05120	2-6th Cav	
05143	2-6th Cav	
FY00		
05175	6-6th Cav	
05178	2-6th Cav	
05190	2-6th Cav	
05199	6-6th Cav	
05200	6-6th Cav	

Type		Notes
05204	6-6th Cav	
05205	6-6th Cav	
05206	6-6th Cav	
05207	6-6th Cav	
05208	6-6th Cav	
05209	6-6th Cav	
05210	6-6th Cav	
05212	6-6th Cav	
05213	6-6th Cav	
05214	6-6th Cav	
05215	6-6th Cav	
05216	2-6th Cav	
05217	6-6th Cav	
05218	6-6th Cav	
05220	6-6th Cav	
05225	6-6th Cav	
05226	6-6th Cav	
05231	6-6th Cav	
05232	6-6th Cav	
FY01		
05233	2-6th Cav	
05243	2-6th Cav	
05250	2-6th Cav	
05253	2-6th Cav	
05273	6-6th Cav	
05274	2-6th Cav	
05284	2-6th Cav	

RAF Lakenheath-based F-15E Strike Eagle 97-0222 of the 492nd FS, USAFE.

US-based USAF Aircraft

The following aircraft are normally based in the USA but are likely to be seen visiting the UK from time to time. The presentation is in numerical order of the type, commencing with the B-**1B** and concluding with the C-**141**. The aircraft are listed in numerical progression by the serial actually carried externally. Fiscal year information is provided, together with details of mark variations and in some cases operating units. Where base-code letter information is carried on the aircrafts' tails, this is detailed with the squadron/base data; for example the 7th Wing's B-1B 60105 carries the letters DY on its tail, thus identifying the Wing's home base as Dyess AFB, Texas.

Notes	*Type*		
	Rockwell B-1B Lancer		
	7th BW, Dyess AFB, Texas [DY]: 9th BS (*y/bk*) & 28th BS (*bl/w*);		
	28th BW, Ellsworth AFB, South Dakota [EL]: 34th BS (*bk/r*) & 37th BS (*bk/y*);		
	419th FLTS/412th TW, Edwards AFB, California [ED]		
	FY84		
	40049	412th TW	
	FY85		
	50059	7th BW	*bl/w*
	50060	28th BW	
	50061	7th BW	*bl/w*
	50064	7th BW	
	50065	7th BW	*bl/w*
	50066	28th BW	
	50068	412th TW	
	50069		
	50072	7th BW	*y/bk*
	50073	7th BW	*y/bk*
	50074	7th BW	
	50075	28th BW	
	50077	28th BW	
	50079	28th BW	
	50080	7th BW	*bl/w*
	50081	28th BW	*bk/y*
	50083	28th BW	*bk/y*
	50084	28th BW	
	50085	28th BW	*bk/y*
	50087	28th BW	*bk/y*
	50088	7th BW	*y/bk*
	50089	7th BW	*bl/w*
	50090	7th BW	
	50091	28th BW	*bk/y*
	FY86		
	60093	28th BW	
	60094	28th BW	
	60095		
	60097	7th BW	
	60098	7th BW	*bl/w*
	60099	28th BW	
	60100	7th BW	
	60101	7th BW	*bl/w*
	60102	28th BW	
	60103	7th BW	*y/bk*
	60104	28th BW	*bk/y*
	60105	7th BW	*bl/w*
	60107	7th BW	
	60108	7th BW	*bl/w*
	60109	7th BW	

Notes	*Type*		
	60110	7th BW	*bl/w*
	60111	28th BW	
	60112	7th BW	*y/bk*
	60113	28th BW	*bk/y*
	60115	28th BW	
	60116	28th BW	
	60117	7th BW	*bl/w*
	60118	28th BW	
	60119	7th BW	*bl/w*
	60120	7th BW	*y/bk*
	60121	28th BW	*bk/y*
	60122	7th BW	
	60123	7th BW	*y/bk*
	60124	7th BW	*y/bk*
	60125	28th BW	
	60126	7th BW	*bl/w*
	60127	28th BW	*bk/y*
	60129	28th BW	
	60130	7th BW	*bl/w*
	60132	7th BW	*bl/w*
	60133	7th BW	*bl/w*
	60134	28th BW	*bk/r*
	60135	7th BW	*bl/w*
	60136	7th BW	*bl/w*
	60137	7th BW	
	60138	28th BW	*bk/y*
	60139	28th BW	*bk/y*
	60140	7th BW	*y/bk*
	Northrop B-2 Spirit		
	419th FLTS/412th TW, Edwards AFB, California [ED];		
	509th BW, Whiteman AFB, Missouri [WM]: 325th BS, 393rd BS & 715th BS		
	(Names are given where known. Each begins *Spirit of ...*)		
	FY90		
	00040	509th BW	*Alaska*
	00041	509th BW	*Hawaii*
	FY92		
	20700	509th BW	*Florida*
	FY82		
	21066	509th BW	*America*
	21067	509th BW	*Arizona*
	21068	412th TW	*New York*
	21069	509th BW	*Indiana*
	21070	Northrop	*Ohio*
	21071	509th BW	*Mississippi*
	FY93		
	31085	509th BW	*Oklahoma*

Type			Notes
31086	509th BW	*Kitty Hawk*	
31087	509th BW	*Pennsylvania*	
31088	509th BW	*Louisiana*	
FY88			
80328	509th BW	*Texas*	
80329	509th BW	*Missouri*	
80330	509th BW	*California*	
80331	509th BW	*South Carolina*	
80332	509th BW	*Washington*	
FY89			
90127	509th BW	*Kansas*	
90128	509th BW	*Nebraska*	
90129	509th BW	*Georgia*	

Lockheed U-2

9th RW, Dyess AFB, Texas [BB]:
1st RS, 5th RS
& 99th RS (*bk/r*);
Lockheed, Palmdale

FY68			
68-10329	U-2S	9th RW	
68-10331	U-2S	9th RW	
68-10336	U-2S		
68-10337	U-2S	9th RW	
FY80			
80-1064	TU-2S	9th RW	
80-1065	TU-2S	9th RW	
80-1066	U-2S	9th RW	
80-1067	U-2S	Lockheed	
80-1068	U-2S	9th RW	
80-1069	U-2S	9th RW	
80-1070	U-2S	9th RW	
80-1071	U-2S	9th RW	
80-1073	U-2S	9th RW	
80-1074	U-2S	9th RW	
80-1076	U-2S	9th RW	
80-1077	U-2S	9th RW	
80-1078	TU-2S	9th RW	
80-1079	U-2S	9th RW	
80-1080	U-2S	9th RW	
80-1081	U-2S	9th RW	
80-1082	U-2S	9th RW	
80-1083	U-2S	9th RW	
80-1084	U-2S	9th RW	
80-1085	U-2S	9th RW	
80-1086	U-2S	9th RW	
80-1087	U-2S	9th RW	
80-1089	U-2S	9th RW	
80-1090	U-2S	9th RW	
80-1091	TU-2S	9th RW	
80-1092	U-2S	9th RW	
80-1093	U-2S	9th RW	
80-1094	U-2S	9th RW	
80-1096	U-2S	9th RW	
80-1099	U-2S	9th RW	

Boeing E-3 Sentry

552nd ACW, Tinker AFB,
Oklahoma [OK]:
960th AACS (*w*), 963rd AACS (*bk*),
964th AACS (*r*), 965th AACS (*y*)
& 966th AACS (*bl*);
961st AACS/18th Wg, Kadena AB,
Japan [ZZ] (*or*);
962nd AACS/3rd Wg, Elmendorf AFB,
Alaska [AK] (*gn*);

Type			Notes
FY80			
00137	E-3C	*gn*	
00138	E-3C	*y*	
00139	E-3C	*bk*	
FY81			
10004	E-3C	*bk*	
10005	E-3C	*bk*	
FY71			
11407	E-3B	*r*	
11408	E-3B	*w*	
FY82			
20006	E-3C	*y*	
20007	E-3C	*w*	
FY83			
30008	E-3C	*bk*	
30009	E-3C	*or*	
FY73			
31674	JE-3C	Boeing	
31675	E-3B	*gn*	
FY75			
50556	E-3B	*w*	
50557	E-3B	*w*	
50558	E-3B	*or*	
50559	E-3B	*bk*	
50560	E-3B	*y*	
FY76			
61604	E-3B	*r*	
61605	E-3B	*gn*	
61606	E-3B	*or*	
61607	E-3B	*bl*	
FY77			
70351	E-3B	*w*	
70352	E-3B	*r*	
70353	E-3B	*y*	
70355	E-3B	*gn*	
70356	E-3B	*y*	
FY78			
80576	E-3B	*r*	
80577	E-3B	*r*	
80578	E-3B	*or*	
FY79			
90001	E-3B	*r*	
90002	E-3B	*y*	
90003	E-3B	*bl*	

Boeing E-4B

1st ACCS/55th Wg, Offutt AFB,
Nebraska [OF]

31676	(FY73)	
31677	(FY73)	
40787	(FY74)	
50125	(FY75)	

Lockheed C-5 Galaxy

60th AMW, Travis AFB, California:
21st AS (*bk/gd*) & 22nd AS (*bk/bl*);
56th AS/97th AMW, Altus AFB,
Oklahoma (*r/y*);
137th AS/105th AW, Stewart AFB,
New York (*bl*);
155th AS/164th AW, Memphis,
Tennessee ANG (*r*);
68th AS/433rd AW AFRC, Kelly AFB,
Texas;
436th AW, Dover AFB, Delaware:
3rd AS (*y/r*) & 9th AS (*y/bl*);
337th AS/439th AW AFRC, Westover
ARB, Massachusetts (*bl/r*)

Notes	Type			
	FY70			
	00445	C-5A	433rd AW	
	00446	C-5A	439th AW	*bl/r*
	00447	C-5A	436th AW	*y*
	00448	C-5A	439th AW	*bl/r*
	00449	C-5A	60th AMW	*bk/gd*
	00451	C-5A	60th AMW	
	00452	C-5A	97th AMW	*r/y*
	00453	C-5A	433rd AW	
	00454	C-5A	97th AMW	*r/y*
	00455	C-5A	97th AMW	*r/y*
	00456	C-5A	433rd AW	
	00457	C-5A	60th AMW	*bk/gd*
	00459	C-5A	60th AMW	*bk/gd*
	00460	C-5A	105th AW	*bl*
	00461	C-5A	436th AW	*y*
	00462	C-5A	97th AMW	*r/y*
	00463	C-5A	97th AMW	*r/y*
	00464	C-5A	60th AMW	*bk/bl*
	00465	C-5A	97th AMW	*r/y*
	00466	C-5A	433rd AW	
	00467	C-5A	97th AMW	*r/y*
	FY83			
	31285	C-5B	436th AW	*y/r*
	FY84			
	40059	C-5B	436th AW	
	40060	C-5B	60th AMW	*bk/bl*
	40061	C-5B	436th AW	*y*
	40062	C-5B	60th AMW	*bk/gd*
	FY85			
	50001	C-5B	436th AW	*m*
	50002	C-5B	60th AMW	*bk/bl*
	50003	C-5B	436th AW	*y*
	50004	C-5B	60th AMW	*bk/bl*
	50005	C-5B	436th AW	*y*
	50006	C-5B	60th AMW	*bk/gd*
	50007	C-5B	436th AW	y/bl
	50008	C-5B	60th AMW	*bk/gd*
	50009	C-5B	436th AW	*y*
	50010	C-5B	60th AMW	*bk/gd*
	FY86			
	60011	C-5B	436th AW	*y/bl*
	60012	C-5B	60th AMW	*bk/bl*
	60013	C-5B	436th AW	*y*
	60014	C-5B	60th AMW	*bk/bl*
	60015	C-5B	436th AW	*y/r*
	60016	C-5B	60th AMW	*bk/bl*
	60017	C-5B	436th AW	*y*
	60018	C-5B	60th AMW	*bk/gd*
	60019	C-5B	436th AW	*y*
	60020	C-5B	436th AW	*y*
	60021	C-5B	60th AMW	*bk/gd*
	60022	C-5B	60th AMW	*bk/bl*
	60023	C-5B	436th AW	*y*
	60024	C-5B	60th AMW	*bk/bl*
	60025	C-5B	436th AW	*y*
	60026	C-5B	60th AMW	*bk/gd*
	FY66			
	68305	C-5A	433rd AW	
	FY87			
	70027	C-5B	436th AW	*y/bl*
	70028	C-5B	60th AMW	*bk/bl*
	70029	C-5B	436th AW	*y*
	70030	C-5B	60th AMW	*bk/bl*
	70031	C-5B	436th AW	*y*
	70032	C-5B	60th AMW	*bk/bl*
	70033	C-5B	436th AW	*y*
	70034	C-5B	60th AMW	*bk/gd*

Notes	Type			
	70035	C-5B	436th AW	*y*
	70036	C-5B	60th AMW	*bk/gd*
	70037	C-5B	436th AW	*y*
	70038	C-5B	60th AMW	*bk/bl*
	70039	C-5B	436th AW	*y*
	70040	C-5B	60th AMW	*bk/gd*
	70041	C-5B	436th AW	*y*
	70042	C-5B	60th AMW	*bk/gd*
	70043	C-5B	436th AW	*y/bl*
	70044	C-5B	60th AMW	*bk/gd*
	70045	C-5B	436th AW	*y*
	FY67			
	70167	C-5A	439th AW	*bl/r*
	70168	C-5A	433rd AW	
	70169	C-5A	105th AW	*bl*
	70173	C-5A	105th AW	*bl*
	70174	C-5A	105th AW	*bl*
	FY68			
	80211	C-5A	439th AW	*bl/r*
	80212	C-5A	105th AW	*bl*
	80213	C-5C	60th AMW	*bk/bl*
	80214	C-5A	433rd AW	
	80215	C-5A	439th AW	*bl/r*
	80216	C-5C	60th AMW	*bk/gd*
	80217	C-5A	97th AMW	*r/y*
	80219	C-5A	439th AW	*bl/r*
	80220	C-5A	433rd AW	
	80221	C-5A	433rd AW	
	80222	C-5A	439th AW	*bl/r*
	80223	C-5A	433rd AW	
	80224	C-5A	105th AW	*bl*
	80225	C-5A	105th AW	*bl*
	80226	C-5A	105th AW	*bl*
	FY69			
	90001	C-5A	60th AMW	*bk/gd*
	90002	C-5A	433rd AW	
	90003	C-5A	439th AW	*bl/r*
	90005	C-5A	439th AW	*bl/r*
	90006	C-5A	433rd AW	
	90007	C-5A	433rd AW	
	90008	C-5A	105th AW	*bl*
	90009	C-5A	105th AW	*bl*
	90010	C-5A	97th AMW	*r/y*
	90011	C-5A	439th AW	*bl/r*
	90012	C-5A	105th AW	*bl*
	90013	C-5A	439th AW	*bl/r*
	90014	C-5A	433rd AW	
	90015	C-5A	105th AW	*bl*
	90016	C-5A	433rd AW	
	90017	C-5A	439th AW	*bl/r*
	90018	C-5A	436th AW	
	90019	C-5A	439th AW	*bl/r*
	90020	C-5A	439th AW	*bl/r*
	90021	C-5A	105th AW	*bl*
	90022	C-5A	439th AW	*bl/r*
	90023	C-5A	105th AW	*bl*
	90024	C-5A	436th AW	*y*
	90025	C-5A	60th AMW	
	90026	C-5A	433rd AW	
	90027	C-5A	436th AW	*y*

Boeing E-8 J-STARS

116th ACW, Robins AFB, Georgia [WR]: 12th ACCS (*gn*), 16th ACCS (*bk*), 128th ACS/Georgia ANG (*r*) & 330th CTS (*y*);
Grumman, Melbourne, Florida

Type				Notes
FY00				
02000	E-8C	116th ACW		
FY90				
00175	E-8A	Grumman		
FY02				
20005	E-8C			
FY92				
23289	E-8C	116th ACW	*m*	
23290	E-8C	116th ACW	*bk*	
FY93				
30597	E-8C	116th ACW	*gn*	
31097	E-8C	116th ACW	*gn*	
FY94				
40284	E-8C	116th ACW	*gn*	
40285	E-8C	116th ACW	*bk*	
FY95				
50121	E-8C	116th ACW	*bk*	
50122	E-8C	116th ACW	*r*	
FY96				
60042	E-8C	116th ACW	*bk*	
60043	E-8C	116th ACW		
FY86				
60416	TE-8A	116th ACW	*y*	
60417	TE-8A	116th ACW	*y*	
FY97				
70100	E-8C	116th ACW	*gn*	
70200	E-8C	116th ACW	*bk*	
70201	E-8C	116th ACW	*bk*	
FY99				
90006	E-8C	116th ACW	*gn*	

McDonnell Douglas
C-9 Nightingale

86th AW, Ramstein, Germany:
76th AS;
99th AS/89th AW, Andrews AFB, Maryland;

Type			Notes
FY71			
10876	C-9A	76th AS	
FY73			
31681	C-9C	89th AW	
31682	C-9C	89th AW	
31683	C-9C	89th AW	

McDonnell Douglas
KC-10A Extender

60th AMW, Travis AFB, California:
6th ARS (*bk/bl*) & 9th ARS (*bk/r*);
305th AMW, McGuire AFB, New Jersey:
2nd ARS (*bl/r*) & 32nd ARS (*bl*)

Type			Notes
FY82			
20191	60th AMW	*bk/bl*	
20192	60th AMW	*bk/r*	
20193	60th AMW	*bk/bl*	
FY83			
30075	60th AMW	*bk/r*	
30076	60th AMW	*bk/bl*	
30077	60th AMW	*bk/r*	
30078	60th AMW	*bk/bl*	
30079	305th AMW	*bl/r*	
30080	60th AMW	*bk/bl*	
30081	305th AMW	*bl*	
30082	305th AMW	*bl*	
FY84			
40185	60th AMW	*bk/bl*	
40186	305th AMW	*bl/r*	
40187	60th AMW	*bk/bl*	
40188	305th AMW	*bl/r*	
40189	305th AMW	*bl*	
40190	305th AMW	*bl/r*	
40191	60th AMW	*bk/bl*	
40192	305th AMW	*bl/r*	
FY85			
50027	305th AMW	*bl/r*	
50028	305th AMW	*bl/r*	
50029	60th AMW	*bk/r*	
50030	305th AMW	*bl/r*	
50031	305th AMW	*bl/r*	
50032	305th AMW	*bl/r*	
50033	305th AMW	*bl*	
50034	305th AMW	*bl/r*	
FY86			
60027	305th AMW	*bl*	
60028	305th AMW	*bl/r*	
60029	60th AMW	*bk/r*	
60030	305th AMW	*bl/r*	
60031	60th AMW	*bk/r*	
60032	60th AMW	*bk/r*	
60033	60th AMW	*bk/r*	
60034	60th AMW	*bk/r*	
60035	305th AMW	*bl*	
60036	305th AMW	*bl*	
60037	60th AMW	*bk/r*	
60038	60th AMW	*bk/r*	
FY87			
70117	60th AMW	*bk/r*	
70118	60th AMW	*bk/bl*	
70119	60th AMW	*bk/r*	
70120	305th AMW	*bl*	
70121	305th AMW	*bl*	
70122	305th AMW	*bl/r*	
70123	305th AMW	*bl*	
70124	305th AMW	*bl/r*	
FY79			
90433	305th AMW	*bl*	
90434	305th AMW	*bl/r*	
91710	305th AMW	*bl/r*	
91711	305th AMW	*bl*	
91712	305th AMW	*bl/r*	
91713	305th AMW	*bl*	
91946	60th AMW	*bk/bl*	
91947	305th AMW	*bl*	
91948	60th AMW	*bk/bl*	
91949	305th AMW	*bl/r*	
91950	60th AMW	*bk/bl*	
91951	60th AMW	*bk/bl*	

McDonnell Douglas
C-17 Globemaster III

62nd AW, McChord AFB, Washington (*gn*):
4th AS, 7th AS, 8th AS & 10th AS;
58th AS/97th AMW, Altus AFB, Oklahoma (*r/y*);
172nd AW, Jackson Int'l Airport, Mississippi ANG:
183rd AS (*bl/gd*);
305th AMW, McGuire AFB, New Jersey (*bl*):
6th AS & 13th AS;
417th FLTS/412th TW, Edwards AFB, California [ED];

Notes	Type			
	437th AW, Charleston AFB, South Carolina (*y/bl*): 14th AS, 15th AS, 16th AS & 17th AS			
	FY00			
	00171	C-17A	62nd AW	
	00172	C-17A	62nd AW	
	00173	C-17A	62nd AW	
	00174	C-17A	62nd AW	
	00175	C-17A	62nd AW	
	00176	C-17A	437th AW	*y/bl*
	00177	C-17A	437th AW	*y/bl*
	00178	C-17A	62nd AW	
	00179	C-17A	62nd AW	
	00180	C-17A	62nd AW	
	00181	C-17A	62nd AW	
	00182	C-17A	62nd AW	
	00183	C-17A	62nd AW	
	00184	C-17A	62nd AW	
	00185	C-17A	62nd AW	
	FY90			
	00532	C-17A	437th AW	*y/bl*
	00533	C-17A	97th AMW	*r/y*
	00534	C-17A	437th AW	*y/bl*
	00535	C-17A	97th AMW	*r/y*
	FY01			
	10186	C-17A	62nd AW	
	10187	C-17A	62nd AW	
	10188	C-17A	437th AW	*y/bl*
	10189	C-17A	437th AW	*y/bl*
	10190	C-17A	437th AW	*y/bl*
	10191	C-17A	437th AW	*y/bl*
	10192	C-17A	437th AW	*y/bl*
	10193	C-17A	437th AW	*y/bl*
	10194	C-17A	437th AW	*y/bl*
	10195	C-17A	437th AW	*y/bl*
	10196	C-17A	437th AW	*y/bl*
	10197	C-17A	437th AW	*y/bl*
	FY02			
	21098	C-17A	437th AW	*y/bl*
	21099	C-17A	437th AW	*y/bl*
	21100	C-17A	437th AW	*y/bl*
	21101	C-17A	437th AW	*y/bl*
	21102	C-17A	437th AW	*y/bl*
	21103	C-17A	62nd AW	
	21104	C-17A	62nd AW	
	21105	C-17A	62nd AW	
	21106	C-17A	62nd AW	
	21107	C-17A	62nd AW	
	21108	C-17A	62nd AW	
	21109	C-17A	62nd AW	
	21110	C-17A	62nd AW	
	21111	C-17A	62nd AW	
	21112	C-17A	172nd AW	*bl/gd*
	FY92			
	23291	C-17A	62nd AW	
	23292	C-17A	437th AW	*y/bl*
	23293	C-17A	62nd AW	
	23294	C-17A	97th AMW	*r/y*
	FY93			
	30599	C-17A	97th AMW	*r/y*
	30600	C-17A	62nd AW	
	30601	C-17A	437th AW	*y/bl*
	30602	C-17A	97th AMW	*r/y*
	30603	C-17A	437th AW	*y/bl*
	30604	C-17A	437th AW	*y/bl*
	FY03			
	33113	C-17A	172nd AW	*bl/gd*

Notes	Type			
	33114	C-17A	172nd AW	*bl/gd*
	33115	C-17A	172nd AW	*bl/gd*
	33116	C-17A	172nd AW	*bl/gd*
	33117	C-17A	172nd AW	*bl/gd*
	33118	C-17A	172nd AW	*bl/gd*
	33119	C-17A	172nd AW	*bl/gd*
	33120	C-17A	62nd AW	*gn*
	33121	C-17A	412th TW	
	33122	C-17A	62nd AW	*gn*
	33123	C-17A	62nd AW	*gn*
	33124	C-17A	62nd AW	*gn*
	33125	C-17A	305th AMW	*bl*
	33126	C-17A	305th AMW	*bl*
	33127	C-17A	305th AMW	*bl*
	FY94			
	40065	C-17A	437th AW	*y/bl*
	40066	C-17A	437th AW	*y/bl*
	40067	C-17A	437th AW	*y/bl*
	40068	C-17A	437th AW	*y/bl*
	40069	C-17A	437th AW	*y/bl*
	40070	C-17A	437th AW	*y/bl*
	44128	C-17A	305th AMW	*bl*
	44129	C-17A	305th AMW	*bl*
	44130	C-17A	305th AMW	*bl*
	44131	C-17A		
	44132	C-17A		
	44133	C-17A		
	44134	C-17A		
	44134	C-17A		
	FY95			
	50102	C-17A	437th AW	*y/bl*
	50103	C-17A	437th AW	*y/bl*
	50104	C-17A	62nd AW	*gn*
	50105	C-17A	437th AW	*y/bl*
	50106	C-17A	437th AW	*y/bl*
	50107	C-17A	437th AW	*y/bl*
	FY96			
	60001	C-17A	437th AW	*y/bl*
	60002	C-17A	437th AW	*y/bl*
	60003	C-17A	437th AW	*y/bl*
	60004	C-17A	437th AW	*y/bl*
	60005	C-17A	437th AW	*y/bl*
	60006	C-17A	437th AW	*y/bl*
	60007	C-17A	437th AW	*y/bl*
	60008	C-17A	437th AW	*y/bl*
	FY87			
	70025	C-17A	412th TW	
	FY97			
	70041	C-17A	437th AW	*y/bl*
	70042	C-17A	437th AW	*y/bl*
	70043	C-17A	437th AW	*y/bl*
	70044	C-17A	437th AW	*y/bl*
	70045	C-17A	437th AW	*y/bl*
	70046	C-17A	437th AW	*y/bl*
	70047	C-17A	437th AW	*y/bl*
	70048	C-17A	437th AW	*y/bl*
	FY98			
	80049	C-17A	62nd AW	*gn*
	80050	C-17A	62nd AW	*gn*
	80051	C-17A	62nd AW	*gn*
	80052	C-17A	62nd AW	*gn*
	80053	C-17A	62nd AW	*gn*
	80054	C-17A	437th AW	*y/bl*
	80055	C-17A	62nd AW	*gn*
	80056	C-17A	62nd AW	*gn*
	80057	C-17A	62nd AW	*gn*
	FY88			
	80265	C-17A	697th AMW	*r/y*

Type				Notes
80266	C-17A	97th AMW	*r/y*	
FY99				
90058	C-17A	62nd AW	*gn*	
90059	C-17A	62nd AW	*gn*	
90060	C-17A	62nd AW	*gn*	
90061	C-17A	62nd AW	*gn*	
90062	C-17A	62nd AW	*gn*	
90063	C-17A	62nd AW	*gn*	
90064	C-17A	62nd AW	*gn*	
90165	C-17A	62nd AW	*gn*	
90166	C-17A	62nd AW	*gn*	
90167	C-17A	62nd AW	*gn*	
90168	C-17A	62nd AW	*gn*	
90169	C-17A	62nd AW	*gn*	
90170	C-17A	62nd AW	*gn*	
FY89				
91189	C-17A	437th AW	*y/bl*	
91190	C-17A	437th AW	*y/bl*	
91191	C-17A	437th AW	*y/bl*	
91192	C-17A	437th AW	*y/bl*	

Grumman C-20 Gulfstream III/IV

89th AW, Andrews AFB, Maryland:
99th AS;
OSAC/PAT, US Army, Andrews AFB, Maryland;
Pacific Flight Detachment, Hickam AFB, Hawaii

C-20B Gulfstream III

FY86
60201 89th AW
60202 89th AW
60203 89th AW
60204 89th AW
60206 89th AW
60403 89th AW

C-20C Gulfstream III

FY85
50049 89th AW
50050 89th AW

C-20E Gulfstream III

FY87
70139 Pacific Flt Det
70140 OSAC/PAT

C-20F Gulfstream IV

FY91
10108 OSAC/PAT

Boeing VC-25A

89th AW, Andrews AFB, Maryland
FY82
28000
FY92
29000

Boeing C-32

1st AS/89th AW, Andrews AFB, Maryland;
486th FLTS/46th TW, Eglin AFB, Florida & McGuire AFB, New Jersey

			Notes
FY00			
09001	C-32B	486th FLTS	
FY02			
24452	C-32B	486th FLTS	
25001	C-32B	486th FLTS	
FY98			
80001	C-32A	89th AW	
80002	C-32A	89th AW	
FY99			
90003	C-32A	89th AW	
90004	C-32A	89th AW	

Gulfstream Aerospace C-37A Gulfstream V

6th AMW, MacDill AFB, Florida:
310th AS;
15th ABW, Hickam AFB, Hawaii:
65th AS;
89th AW, Andrews AFB, Maryland:
99th AS;
OSAC/PAT, US Army, Andrews AFB, Maryland

FY01
10028 6th AMW
10029 6th AMW
10030 6th AMW
10065 15th ABW
FY02
21863 OSAC/PAT
FY04
41778 OSAC/PAT
FY97
70049 OSAC/PAT
70400 89th AW
70401 89th AW
FY99
90402 89th AW
90404 89th AW

IAI C-38A Astra

201st AS/113th FW, DC ANG, Andrews AFB, Maryland
FY94
41569
41570

Boeing C-40

15th ABW, Hickam AFB, Hawaii:
65th AS;
89th AW, Andrews AFB, Maryland:
1st AS;
201st AS/113th FW, DC ANG, Andrews AFB, Maryland

			Notes
FY01			
10005	C-40B	89th AW	
10015	C-40B	15th ABW	
10040	C-40B	89th AW	
FY02			
20201	C-40C	201st AS	
20202	C-40C	201st AS	
20203	C-40C	201st AS	
20204	C-40C	201st AS	

Boeing T-43A

562nd FTS/12th FTW, Randolph AFB, Texas [RA] (*bk/y*)
FY71
11404
11405
FY72
20288
FY73
31150
31151
31152

Notes	Type		
	31153		
	31154		
	31156		

Boeing B-52H Stratofortress

2nd BW, Barksdale AFB, Louisiana [LA]: 11th BS (*gd*), 20th BS (*bl*) & 96th BS (*r*);
23rd BS/5th BW, Minot AFB, North Dakota [MT] (*r/y*);
49th TES/53rd TEG, Barksdale AFB, Louisiana [OT];
93rd BS/917th Wg AFRC, Barksdale AFB, Louisiana [BD] (*y/bl*);
419th FLTS/412th TW Edwards AFB, California [ED]

FY60

Notes	Type		
	00001	2nd BW	*bl*
	00002	2nd BW	*gd*
	00003	93rd BS	*y/bl*
	00004	5th BW	*r/y*
	00005	5th BW	*r/y*
	00007	5th BW	*r/y*
	00008	2nd BW	*r*
	00009	5th BW	*r/y*
	00010	2nd BW	*r*
	00011	2nd BW	*gd*
	00012	2nd BW	*r*
	00013	2nd BW	*r*
	00014	2nd BW	*bl*
	00015	5th BW	*r/y*
	00016	2nd BW	*r*
	00017	2nd BW	*gd*
	00018	5th BW	*r/y*
	00019	2nd BW	*r*
	00020	2nd BW	*bl*
	00022	2nd BW	*r*
	00023	5th BW	*r/y*
	00024	5th BW	*r/y*
	00025	2nd BW	*bl*
	00026	5th BW	*r/y*
	00028	2nd BW	*r*
	00029	5th BW	*r/y*
	00030	2nd BW	*bl*
	00031	53rd TEG	
	00032	2nd BW	*gd*
	00033	5th BW	*r/y*
	00034	5th BW	*r/y*
	00035	2nd BW	*gd*
	00036	419th FLTS	
	00037	2nd BW	*r*
	00038	2nd BW	*gd*
	00041	93rd BS	*y/bl*
	00042	93rd BS	*y/bl*
	00043	2nd BW	*bl*
	00044	5th BW	*r/y*
	00045	93rd BS	*y/bl*
	00046	2nd BW	*bl*
	00047	5th BW	*r/y*
	00048	2nd BW	*gd*
	00049	2nd BW	*bl*
	00050	412th TW	
	00051	5th BW	*r/y*
	00052	2nd BW	*r*
	00053	2nd BW	*r*
	00054	2nd BW	*r*
	00055	5th BW	*r/y*
	00056	5th BW	*r/y*
	00057	2nd BW	*gd*
	00058	2nd BW	*gd*
	00059	2nd BW	*r*
	00060	5th BW	*r/y*
	00061	2nd BW	*gd*
	00062	2nd BW	*bl*

FY61

Notes	Type		
	10001	5th BW	*r/y*
	10002	2nd BW	*bl*
	10003	2nd BW	*gd*
	10004	2nd BW	*bl*
	10005	5th BW	*r/y*
	10006	2nd BW	*gd*
	10007	5th BW	*r/y*
	10008	93rd BS	*y/bl*
	10009	2nd BW	*r*
	10010	2nd BW	*bl*
	10011	2nd BW	*gd*
	10012	2nd BW	*gd*
	10013	2nd BW	*r*
	10014	5th BW	*r/y*
	10015	2nd BW	*gd*
	10016	2nd BW	*r*
	10017	93rd BS	*y/bl*
	10018	5th BW	*r/y*
	10019	2nd BW	*r*
	10020	2nd BW	*r*
	10021	93rd BS	*y/bl*
	10022	93rd BS	*y/bl*
	10023	2nd BW	*bl*
	10024	2nd BW	*r*
	10027	5th BW	*r/y*
	10028	2nd BW	*gd*
	10029	93rd BS	*y/bl*
	10031	2nd BW	*gd*
	10032	93rd BS	*y/bl*
	10034	5th BW	*r/y*
	10035	5th BW	*r/y*
	10036	2nd BW	*gd*
	10038	2nd BW	*gd*
	10039	2nd BW	*gd*
	10040	5th BW	*r/y*

Lockheed F-117A Nighthawk

49th FW, Holloman AFB, New Mexico [HO]: 8th FS (*y*) & 9th FS (*r*)
53rd Wg, Nellis AFB, Nevada [OT] (*gy/w*);
445th FLTS/412th TW, Edwards AFB, California [ED]

Notes	Type				
	79-783	(79-10783)	ED		
	79-784	(79-10784)	ED		
	80-786	(80-0786)	HO	*r*	
	80-787	(80-0787)	HO	*y*	
	80-788	(80-0788)	HO		
	80-789	(80-0789)	HO	*r*	
	80-790	(80-0790)	HO	*r*	
	80-791	(80-0791)	HO	*y*	
	81-794	(81-10794)	HO	*r*	
	81-795	(81-10795)	HO	*y*	
	81-796	(81-10796)	HO	*r*	[49th OG]
	81-797	(81-10797)	HO	*r*	
	81-798	(81-10798)	HO	*r*	[49th FW]
	82-799	(82-0799)	HO	*r*	
	82-800	(82-0800)	HO	*y*	[8th FS]

Type				Notes
82-801	(82-0801)	HO		
82-802	(82-0802)	HO *y*		
82-803	(82-0803)	HO *y*		
82-804	(82-0804)	HO *y*		
82-805	(82-0805)	HO *r*		
83-807	(83-0807)	HO *r*		
83-808	(83-0808)	HO *r*		
84-809	(84-0809)	HO *r*	[9th FS]	
84-810	(84-0810)	HO *r*		
84-811	(84-0811)	HO *r*		
84-812	(84-0812)	HO		
84-824	(84-0824)	HO *r*		
84-825	(84-0825)	HO *y*		
84-826	(84-0826)	HO *r*		
84-827	(84-0827)	HO *y*		
84-828	(84-0828)	HO *r*		
85-813	(85-0813)	HO *r*		
85-814	(85-0814)	HO *r*		
85-816	(85-0816)	HO *y*	[49th FW]	
85-817	(85-0817)	HO *y*		
85-818	(85-0818)	HO *y*		
85-819	(85-0819)	HO *y*	[49th FW]	
85-820	(85-0820)	HO *r*		
85-829	(85-0829)	HO *y*		
85-830	(85-0830)	HO *r*		
85-831	(85-0831)	ED		
85-832	(85-0832)	HO *y*		
85-833	(85-0833)	HO *r*		
85-834	(85-0834)	HO *y*		
85-835	(85-0835)	OT		
85-836	(85-0836)	HO *r*		
86-821	(86-0821)	HO *r*		
86-822	(86-0822)	HO		
86-823	(86-0823)	HO *r*		
86-837	(86-0837)	HO *y*		
86-838	(86-0838)	HO *y*		
86-839	(86-0839)	HO *y*		
86-840	(86-0840)	HO *r*		
88-841	(88-0841)	HO *r*	[9th FS]	
88-842	(88-0842)	HO *y*		
88-843	(88-0843)	HO *y*		

Lockheed C-130 Hercules

1st SOS/353rd SOG, Kadena AB, Japan;
3rd Wg, Elmendorf AFB, Alaska [AK]: 517th AS (*w*);
4th SOS/16th SOW, Hurlburt Field, Florida;
7th SOS/352nd SOG, RAF Mildenhall, UK;
8th SOS/16th SOW, Duke Field, Florida;
9th SOS/16th OG, Eglin AFB, Florida;
15th SOS/16th SOW, Hurlburt Field, Florida;
16th SOS/16th SOW, Hurlburt Field, Florida;
17th SOS/353rd SOG, Kadena AB, Japan;
37th AS/86th AW, Ramstein AB, Germany [RS] (*bl/w*);
39th RQS/920th RQW AFRC, Patrick AFB, Florida [FL];
41st ECS/55th Wg, Davis-Monthan AFB, Arizona [DM] (*bl*);
43rd AW, Pope AFB, North Carolina [FT]: 2nd AS (*gn/bl*) & 41st AS (*gn/or*);
43rd ECS/55th Wg, Davis-Monthan AFB, Arizona [DM] (*r*);
53rd WRS/403rd AW AFRC, Keesler AFB, Missouri;
58th SOW, Kirtland AFB, New Mexico: 550th SOS;
67th SOS/352nd SOG, RAF Mildenhall, UK;
71st RQS/347th Wg, Moody AFB, Georgia [MY] (*bl*);
79th RQS/55th Wg, Davis-Monthan AFB, Arizona [DM];
95th AS/440th AW AFRC, General Mitchell ARS, Wisconsin (*w/r*);
96th AS/934th AW AFRC, Minneapolis/St Paul, Minnesota (*pr*);
102nd RQS/106th RQW, Suffolk Field, New York ANG [LI];
105th AS/118th AW, Nashville, Tennessee ANG (*r*);
109th AS/133rd AW, Minneapolis/ St Paul, Minnesota ANG [MN] (*pr/bk*);
115th AS/146th AW, Channel Island ANGS, California ANG [CI] (*gn*);
122nd FS/159th FW, NAS New Orleans, Louisiana ANG [JZ];
130th AS/130th AW, Yeager Int'l Airport, Charleston West Virginia ANG [WV] (*pr/y*);
130th RQS/129th RQW, Moffet Field, California ANG [CA] (*bl*);
135th AS/135th AW, Martin State Airport, Maryland ANG [MD] (*bk/y*);
139th AS/109th AW, Schenectady, New York ANG [NY];
142nd AS/166th AW, New Castle County Airport, Delaware ANG [DE] (*bl*);
143rd AS/143rd AW, Quonset, Rhode Island ANG [RI] (*r*);
144th AS/176th CW, Kulis ANGB, Alaska ANG (*bk/y*);
154th TS/189th AW, Little Rock, Arkansas ANG (*r*);
156th AS/145th AW, Charlotte, North Carolina ANG [NC] (*bl*);
157th FS/169th FW, McEntire ANGS, South Carolina ANG [SC];
158th AS/165th AW, Savannah, Georgia ANG (*r*);
159th FS/125th FW, Jacksonville, Florida ANG;
164th AS/179th AW, Mansfield, Ohio ANG [OH] (*bl*);
165th AS/123rd AW, Standiford Field, Kentucky ANG [KY];
167th AS/167th AW, Martinsburg, West Virginia ANG [WV] (*r*);
169th AS/182nd AW, Peoria, Illinois ANG [IL];
171st AS/191st AW, Selfridge ANGB, Michigan ANG (*y/bk*);

Notes Type

180th AS/139th AW, Rosencrans Memorial Airport, Missouri ANG [XP] (*y*);
181st AS/136th AW, NAS Dallas, Texas ANG (*bl/w*);
185th AS/137th AW, Will Rogers World Airport, Oklahoma ANG [OK] (*bl*);
187th AS/153rd AW, Cheyenne, Wyoming ANG [WY];
189th AS/124th Wg, Boise, Idaho ANG [ID];
192nd AS/152nd AW, Reno, Nevada ANG [NV] (*w*);
193rd SOS/193rd SOW, Harrisburg, Pennsylvania ANG [PA];
198th AS/156th AW, San Juan, Puerto Rico ANG;
204th AS/154th Wg, Hickam AFB, Hawaii ANG [HH];
210th RQS/176th CW, Kulis ANGB, Alaska ANG [AK];
314th AW, Little Rock AFB, Arkansas: 48th AS (*y*), 53rd AS (*bk*) & 62nd AS (*bl*);
317th AG, Dyess AFB, Texas: 39th AS (*r*) & 40th AS (*bl*);
327th AS/913th AW AFRC, NAS Willow Grove, Pennsylvania (*bk*);
328th AS/914th AW AFRC, Niagara Falls, New York [NF] (*bl*);
357th AS/908th AW AFRC, Maxwell AFB, Alabama (*bl*);
374th AW, Yokota AB, Japan [YJ]: 36th AS (*r*);
412th TW Edwards AFB, California: 452nd FLTS [ED];
463rd AG Little Rock AFB, Arkansas [LK]: 50th AS (*r*) & 61st AS (*gn*);
645th Materiel Sqn, Palmdale, California [D4];
700th AS/94th AW AFRC, Dobbins ARB, Georgia [DB] (*bl*);
711th SOS/919th SOW AFRC, Duke Field, Florida;
731st AS/302nd AW AFRC, Peterson AFB, Colorado (*pr/w*);
757th AS/910th AW AFRC, Youngstown ARS, Ohio [YO] (*bl*);
758th AS/911th AW AFRC, Pittsburgh ARS, Pennsylvania (*bk/y*);
773rd AS/910th AW AFRC, Youngstown ARS, Ohio [YO] (*r*);
815th AS/403rd AW AFRC, Keesler AFB, Missouri [KT] (*r*);
LMTAS, Marietta, Georgia

FY90
00162 MC-130H 15th SOS
00163 AC-130U 4th SOS
00164 AC-130U 4th SOS
00165 AC-130U 4th SOS
00166 AC-130U 4th SOS
00167 AC-130U 4th SOS

FY80
00320 C-130H 158th AS *r*
00321 C-130H 158th AS *r*

Notes Type

00322 C-130H 158th AS *r*
00323 C-130H 158th AS *r*
00324 C-130H 158th AS *r*
00325 C-130H 158th AS *r*
00326 C-130H 158th AS *r*
00332 C-130H 158th AS *r*

FY90
01057 C-130H 204th AS
01058 C-130H 204th AS

FY70
01259 C-130E 43rd AW *gn/bl*
01260 C-130E 37th AS *bl/w*
01261 C-130E 43rd AW *gn/bl*
01262 C-130E 43rd AW *gn/or*
01263 C-130E 43rd AW *gn/or*
01264 C-130E 37th AS *bl/w*
01265 C-130E 43rd AW *gn/bl*
01266 C-130E 43rd AW *gn/bl*
01267 C-130E 43rd AW *gn/or*
01268 C-130E 43rd AW *gn/bl*
01270 C-130E 43rd AW *gn/bl*
01271 C-130E 37th AS *bl/w*
01272 C-130E 43rd AW *gn/bl*
01273 C-130E 43rd AW *gn/bl*
01274 C-130E 37th AS *bl/w*
01275 C-130E 43rd AW *gn/bl*
01276 C-130E 43rd AW *gn/bl*

FY90
01791 C-130H 164th AS *bl*
01792 C-130H 164th AS *bl*
01793 C-130H 164th AS *bl*
01794 C-130H 164th AS *bl*
01795 C-130H 164th AS *bl*
01796 C-130H 164th AS *bl*
01797 C-130H 164th AS *bl*
01798 C-130H 164th AS *bl*

FY00
01934 EC-130J LMTAS

FY90
02103 HC-130N 210th RQS
09107 C-130H 757th AS *bl*
09108 C-130H 757th AS *bl*

FY81
10626 C-130H 700th AS *bl*
10627 C-130H 700th AS *bl*
10628 C-130H 700th AS *bl*
10629 C-130H 700th AS *bl*
10630 C-130H 700th AS *bl*
10631 C-130H 700th AS *bl*

FY68
10935 C-130E 37th AS *bl/w*
10939 C-130E 43rd AW *gn/bl*
10941 C-130E 43rd AW *gn/bl*
10943 C-130E 37th AS *bl/w*
10948 C-130E 463rd AG *gn*

FY91
11231 C-130H 165th AS
11232 C-130H 165th AS
11233 C-130H 165th AS
11234 C-130H 165th AS
11235 C-130H 165th AS
11236 C-130H 165th AS
11237 C-130H 165th AS
11238 C-130H 165th AS
11239 C-130H 165th AS

FY01
11461 C-130J 115th AS *gn*
11462 C-130J 115th AS *gn*

Type			Notes
FY91			
11651	C-130H	165th AS	
11652	C-130H	165th AS	
11653	C-130H	165th AS	
FY61			
12358	C-130E	171st AS	*y/bk*
12367	C-130E	189th AS	
12369	C-130E	198th AS	
12370	C-130E	171st AS	*y/bk*
12372	C-130E	115th AS	*gn*
FY64			
14852	HC-130P	71st RQS	*bl*
14853	HC-130P	71st RQS	*bl*
14854	MC-130P	9th SOS	
14855	HC-130P	39th RQS	
14858	MC-130P	58th SOW	
14859	C-130E	16th SOW	
14860	HC-130P	79th RQS	
14861	WC-130H	53rd WRS	
14862	EC-130H	645th MS	
14863	HC-130P	71st RQS	*bl*
14864	HC-130P	39th RQS	
14865	HC-130P	71st RQS	*bl*
14866	WC-130H	53rd WRS	
17681	C-130E	37th AS	*bl/w*
FY91			
19141	C-130H	96th AS	*pr*
19142	C-130H	96th AS	*pr*
19143	C-130H	96th AS	*pr*
19144	C-130H	773rd AS	*r*
FY82			
20054	C-130H	144th AS	*bk/y*
20055	C-130H	144th AS	*bk/y*
20056	C-130H	144th AS	*bk/y*
20057	C-130H	144th AS	*bk/y*
20058	C-130H	144th AS	*bk/y*
20059	C-130H	144th AS	*bk/y*
20060	C-130H	144th AS	*bk/y*
20061	C-130H	144th AS	*bk/y*
FY02			
20314	C-130J	314th AW	*y*
FY92			
20253	AC-130U	4th SOS	
20547	C-130H	463rd AG	*r*
20548	C-130H	463rd AG	*r*
20549	C-130H	463rd AG	*r*
20550	C-130H	463rd AG	*r*
20551	C-130H	463rd AG	*r*
20552	C-130H	463rd AG	*r*
20553	C-130H	463rd AG	*r*
20554	C-130H	463rd AG	*r*
21094	LC-130H	139th AS	
21095	LC-130H	139th AS	
FY72			
21288	C-130E	374th AW	*r*
21289	C-130E	374th AW	*r*
21290	C-130E	374th AW	*r*
21291	C-130E	314th AW	*bk*
21292	C-130E	463rd AG	*gn*
21293	C-130E	463rd AG	*gn*
21294	C-130E	463rd AG	*gn*
21295	C-130E	314th AW	*bl*
21296	C-130E	314th AW	*bk*
21299	C-130E	374th AW	*r*
FY02			
21434	C-130J	143rd AS	*r*
FY92			
21451	C-130H	156th AS	*bl*

Type			Notes
21452	C-130H	156th AS	*bl*
21453	C-130H	156th AS	*bl*
21454	C-130H	156th AS	*bl*
FY02			
21463	C-130J	115th AS	*gn*
21464	C-130J	115th AS	*gn*
FY92			
21531	C-130H	187th AS	
21532	C-130H	187th AS	
21533	C-130H	187th AS	
21534	C-130H	187th AS	
21535	C-130H	187th AS	
21536	C-130H	187th AS	
21537	C-130H	187th AS	
21538	C-130H	187th AS	
FY62			
21784	C-130E	154th TS	*r*
21786	C-130E	189th AS	
21787	C-130E	154th TS	*r*
21788	C-130E	154th TS	*r*
21789	C-130E	314th AW	*bk*
21791	EC-130E	41st ECS	*bl*
21792	C-130E	463rd AG	*gn*
21793	C-130E	115th AS	*gn*
21798	C-130E	314th AW	*bk*
21799	C-130E	115th AS	*gn*
21801	C-130E	115th AS	*gn*
21804	C-130E	154th TS	*r*
21806	C-130E	327th AS	*bk*
21808	C-130E	314th AW	*bk*
21810	C-130E	314th AW	*bl*
21811	C-130E	115th AS	*gn*
21816	C-130E	314th AW	*bl*
21817	C-130E	189th AS	
21818	HC-130P	79th RQS	
21820	C-130E	171st AS	*y/bk*
21823	C-130E	43rd AW	
21824	C-130E	154th TS	*r*
21826	C-130E	115th AS	*gn*
21829	C-130E	171st AS	*y/bk*
21832	HC-130P	79th RQS	
21833	C-130E	115th AS	*gn*
21834	C-130E	374th AW	*r*
21835	C-130E	37th AS	*bl/w*
21836	HC-130P	79th RQS	
21837	C-130E	189th AS	
21839	C-130E	327th AS	*bk*
21842	C-130E	171st AS	*y/bk*
21843	MC-130E	711th SOS	
21844	C-130E	314th AW	*pr*
21846	C-130E	189th AS	
21847	C-130E	327th AS	*bk*
21848	C-130E	314th AW	*bk*
21849	C-130E	463rd AG	*gn*
21850	C-130E	314th AW	*bk*
21851	C-130E	115th AS	*gn*
21852	C-130E	327th AS	*bk*
21855	C-130E	374th AW	*r*
21856	C-130E	143rd AS	*r*
21857	EC-130E	43rd ECS	*r*
21858	C-130E	171st AS	*y/bk*
21859	C-130E	122nd FS	
21862	C-130E	115th AS	*gn*
21863	EC-130E		
21864	C-130E	189th AS	
FY92			
23021	C-130H	773rd AS	*r*
23022	C-130H	773rd AS	*r*

Notes	Type			
	23023	C-130H	773rd AS	*r*
	23024	C-130H	773rd AS	*r*
	23281	C-130H	328th AS	*bl*
	23282	C-130H	328th AS	*bl*
	23283	C-130H	328th AS	*bl*
	23284	C-130H	328th AS	*bl*
	23285	C-130H	328th AS	*bl*
	23286	C-130H	328th AS	*bl*
	23287	C-130H	328th AS	*bl*
	23288	C-130H	328th AS	*bl*
	FY02			
	28155	C-130J	815th AS	*r*
	FY83			
	30486	C-130H	139th AS	
	30487	C-130H	139th AS	
	30488	C-130H	139th AS	
	30489	C-130H	139th AS	
	30490	LC-130H	139th AS	
	30491	LC-130H	139th AS	
	30492	LC-130H	139th AS	
	30493	LC-130H	139th AS	
	FY93			
	31036	C-130H	463rd AG	*r*
	31037	C-130H	463rd AG	*r*
	31038	C-130H	463rd AG	*r*
	31039	C-130H	463rd AG	*r*
	31040	C-130H	463rd AG	*r*
	31041	C-130H	463rd AG	*r*
	31096	LC-130H	139th AS	
	FY83			
	31212	MC-130H	15th SOS	
	FY93			
	31455	C-130H	156th AS	*bl*
	31456	C-130H	156th AS	*bl*
	31457	C-130H	156th AS	*bl*
	31458	C-130H	156th AS	*bl*
	31459	C-130H	156th AS	*bl*
	31561	C-130H	156th AS	*bl*
	31562	C-130H	156th AS	*bl*
	31563	C-130H	156th AS	*bl*
	FY73			
	31580	EC-130H	43rd ECS	*r*
	31581	EC-130H	43rd ECS	*r*
	31582	C-130H	317th AG	*r*
	31583	EC-130H	43rd ECS	*r*
	31584	EC-130H	43rd ECS	*r*
	31585	EC-130H	41st ECS	*bl*
	31586	EC-130H	41st ECS	*bl*
	31587	EC-130H	41st ECS	*bl*
	31588	EC-130H	41st ECS	*bl*
	31590	EC-130H	43rd ECS	*r*
	31592	EC-130H	41st ECS	*bl*
	31594	EC-130H	41st ECS	*bl*
	31595	EC-130H	43rd ECS	*r*
	31597	C-130H	317th AG	*r*
	31598	C-130H	317th AG	*r*
	FY93			
	32041	C-130H	204th AS	
	32042	C-130H	204th AS	
	32104	HC-130N	210th RQS	
	32105	HC-130N	210th RQS	
	32106	HC-130N	210th RQS	
	37311	C-130H	731st AS	*pr/w*
	37312	C-130H	731st AS	*pr/w*
	37313	C-130H	731st AS	*pr/w*
	37314	C-130H	731st AS	*pr/w*
	FY63			
	37764	C-130E	463rd AG	*gn*

Notes	Type			
	37765	C-130E	314th AW	*bl*
	37767	C-130E	314th AW	*bl*
	37769	C-130E	327th AS	*bk*
	37770	C-130E	43rd AW	*pr*
	37776	C-130E	327th AS	*bk*
	37781	C-130E	463rd AG	*gn*
	37782	C-130E	143rd AS	*r*
	37784	C-130E	314th AW	*bl*
	37785	MC-130E	711th SOS	
	37786	C-130E	171st AS	*y/bk*
	37790	C-130E	374th AW	*r*
	37791	C-130E	314th AW	*bl*
	37792	C-130E	169th AS	
	37796	C-130E	314th AW	*bk*
	37799	C-130E	314th AW	*bl*
	37800	C-130E	169th AS	
	37804	C-130E	314th AW	*bl*
	37808	C-130E	463rd AG	*gn*
	37809	C-130E	463rd AG	*gn*
	37811	C-130E	143rd AS	*r*
	37812	C-130E	169th AS	
	37814	C-130E	67th SOS	
	37815	C-130E	193rd SOS	
	37816	C-130E	193rd SOS	
	37817	C-130E	463rd AG	*gn*
	37818	C-130E	169th AS	
	37819	C-130E	374th AW	*r*
	37821	C-130E	374th AW	*r*
	37823	C-130E	43rd AW	
	37824	C-130E	143rd AS	*r*
	37825	C-130E	169th AS	
	37826	C-130E	327th AS	*bk*
	37828	EC-130E	193rd SOS	
	37829	C-130E	463rd AG	*gn*
	37830	C-130E	314th AW	*bk*
	37831	C-130E	171st AS	*y/bk*
	37832	C-130E	327th AS	*bk*
	37833	C-130E	327th AS	*bk*
	37834	C-130E	327th AS	*bk*
	37835	C-130E	314th AW	*bk*
	37837	C-130E	374th AW	*r*
	37839	C-130E	463rd AG	*gn*
	37840	C-130E	143rd AS	*r*
	37841	C-130E	198th AS	
	37842	C-130E	39th RQS	
	37845	C-130E	463rd AG	
	37846	C-130E	314th AW	
	37847	C-130E	154th TS	*r*
	37848	C-130E	43rd AW	
	37849	C-130E	314th AW	*bl*
	37850	C-130E	374th AW	*r*
	37851	C-130E	198th AS	
	37852	C-130E	463rd AG	*gn*
	37853	C-130E	327th AS	*bk*
	37856	C-130E	463rd AG	*gn*
	37857	C-130E	463rd AG	*gn*
	37858	C-130E	169th AS	
	37859	C-130E	143rd AS	*r*
	37860	C-130E	314th AW	*bl*
	37861	C-130E	130th RQS	*bl*
	37864	C-130E	314th AW	*bl*
	37865	C-130E	37th AS	*bl/w*
	37866	C-130E	314th AW	*bk*
	37867	C-130E	327th AS	*bk*
	37868	C-130E	143rd AS	*r*
	37871	C-130E	374th AW	*r*
	37872	C-130E	169th AS	
	37874	C-130E	314th AW	*bk*

Type			Notes
37876	C-130E	463rd AG	*gn*
37877	C-130E	169th AS	
37879	C-130E	37th AS	*bl/w*
37880	C-130E	314th AW	*bl*
37882	C-130E	314th AW	*bk*
37883	C-130E	327th AS	*bk*
37884	C-130E	463rd AG	*gn*
37885	C-130E	37th AS	*bl/w*
37887	C-130E	37th AS	*bl/w*
37888	C-130E	463rd AG	*gn*
37889	C-130E	143rd AS	*r*
37890	C-130E	314th AW	*bl*
37892	C-130E	327th AS	*bk*
37893	C-130E	314th AW	*bk*
37894	C-130E	463rd AG	*gn*
37895	C-130E	171st AS	*y/bk*
37896	C-130E	314th AW	*bk*
37897	C-130E	171st AS	*y/bk*
37898	C-130E	8th SOS	
37899	C-130E	314th AW	*bl*
39810	C-130E	71st RQS	*bl*
39812	C-130E	314th AW	*bk*
39813	C-130E	171st AS	*y/bk*
39814	C-130E	314th AW	*bl*
39815	C-130E	198th AS	
39816	EC-130E	193rd SOS	
39817	EC-130E	193rd SOS	
FY84			
40204	C-130H	700th AS	*bl*
40205	C-130H	700th AS	*bl*
40206	C-130H	142nd AS	*bl*
40207	C-130H	142nd AS	*bl*
40208	C-130H	142nd AS	*bl*
40209	C-130H	142nd AS	*bl*
40210	C-130H	142nd AS	*bl*
40212	C-130H	142nd AS	*bl*
40213	C-130H	142nd AS	*bl*
40476	MC-130H	15th SOS	
FY64			
40495	C-130E	43rd AW	*n/or*
40496	C-130E	37th AS	*bl/w*
40498	C-130E	43rd AW	*gn/bl*
40499	C-130E	37th AS	*bl/w*
40502	C-130E	37th AS	*bl/w*
40504	C-130E	43rd AW	*gn/bl*
40510	C-130E	198th AS	
40512	C-130E	154th TS	*r*
40515	C-130E	198th AS	
40517	C-130E	43rd AW	*gn/bl*
40518	C-130E	463rd AG	*gn*
40519	C-130E	314th AW	*bl*
40520	C-130E	157th FS	
40521	C-130E	159th FS	
40523	MC-130E	8th SOS	
40525	C-130E	43rd AW	*gn/bl*
40526	C-130E	154th TS	*r*
40527	C-130E	37th AS	*bl/w*
40529	C-130E	43rd AW	*n/or*
40531	C-130E	43rd AW	*gn/bl*
40537	C-130E	43rd AW	*n/or*
40538	C-130E	314th AW	*bk*
40539	C-130E	43rd AW	*n/or*
40540	C-130E	43rd AW	*gn/bl*
40541	C-130E	314th AW	*bk*
40544	C-130E	198th AS	
40551	MC-130E	711th SOS	
40555	MC-130E	711th SOS	
40559	MC-130E	711th SOS	

Type			Notes
40561	MC-130E	711th SOS	
40562	MC-130E	711th SOS	
40565	MC-130E	711th SOS	
40566	MC-130E	8th SOS	
40567	MC-130E	8th SOS	
40568	MC-130E	8th SOS	
40571	MC-130E	711th SOS	
40572	MC-130E	8th SOS	
FY74			
41658	C-130H	3rd Wg	*w*
41659	C-130H	3rd Wg	*w*
41660	C-130H	3rd Wg	*w*
41661	C-130H	3rd Wg	*w*
41663	C-130H	317th AG	*bl*
41664	C-130H	3rd Wg	*w*
41665	C-130H	317th AG	*bl*
41666	C-130H	317th AG	*bl*
41667	C-130H	317th AG	*r*
41668	C-130H	3rd Wg	*w*
41669	C-130H	317th AG	*bl*
41670	C-130H	317th AG	*r*
41671	C-130H	317th AG	*bl*
41673	C-130H	317th AG	*bl*
41674	C-130H	317th AG	*r*
41675	C-130H	317th AG	*r*
41676	C-130H	3rd Wg	*m*
41677	C-130H	317th AG	*bl*
41679	C-130H	317th AG	*bl*
41680	C-130H	317th AG	*r*
41682	C-130H	3rd Wg	*w*
41684	C-130H	3rd Wg	*w*
41685	C-130H	3rd Wg	*w*
41687	C-130H	317th AG	*r*
41688	C-130H	317th AG	*bl*
41689	C-130H	317th AG	*bl*
41690	C-130H	3rd Wg	*w*
41691	C-130H	317th AG	*r*
41692	C-130H	3rd Wg	*w*
42061	C-130H	317th AG	*r*
42062	C-130H	3rd Wg	*w*
42063	C-130H	317th AG	*bl*
42065	C-130H	317th AG	*bl*
42066	C-130H	3rd Wg	*w*
42067	C-130H	317th AG	*r*
42069	C-130H	317th AG	*r*
42070	C-130H	3rd Wg	*w*
42071	C-130H	3rd Wg	*w*
42072	C-130H	317th AG	*bl*
42130	C-130H	317th AG	*r*
42131	C-130H	3rd Wg	*w*
42132	C-130H	317th AG	*r*
42133	C-130H	3rd Wg	*w*
42134	C-130H	317th AG	*r*
FY94			
46701	C-130H	167th AS	*r*
46702	C-130H	167th AS	*r*
46703	C-130H	167th AS	*r*
46704	C-130H	167th AS	*r*
46705	C-130H	167th AS	*r*
46706	C-130H	167th AS	*r*
46707	C-130H	167th AS	*r*
46708	C-130H	167th AS	*r*
47310	C-130H	731st AS	*pr/w*
47315	C-130H	731st AS	*pr/w*
47316	C-130H	731st AS	*pr/w*
47317	C-130H	731st AS	*pr/w*
47318	C-130H	731st AS	*pr/w*
47319	C-130H	731st AS	*pr/w*

Notes	Type			
	47320	C-130H	731st AS	*pr/w*
	47321	C-130H	731st AS	*pr/w*
	48151	C-130J	815th AS	*r*
	48152	C-130J	815th AS	*r*
	FY85			
	50011	MC-130H	15th SOS	
	50012	MC-130H	15th SOS	
	50035	C-130H	357th AS	*bl*
	50036	C-130H	357th AS	*bl*
	50037	C-130H	357th AS	*bl*
	50038	C-130H	357th AS	*bl*
	50039	C-130H	357th AS	*bl*
	50040	C-130H	773rd AS	*r*
	50041	C-130H	357th AS	*bl*
	50042	C-130H	357th AS	*bl*
	FY65			
	50962	EC-130H	43rd ECS	*r*
	50963	WC-130H	53rd WRS	
	50964	HC-130P	79th RQS	
	50966	WC-130H	53rd WRS	
	50967	WC-130H	53rd WRS	
	50968	WC-130H	53rd WRS	
	50970	HC-130P	39th RQS	
	50971	MC-130P	58th SOW	
	50973	HC-130P	71st RQS	*bl*
	50974	HC-130P	102nd RQS	
	50975	MC-130P	58th SOW	
	50976	HC-130P	39th RQS	
	50977	WC-130H	53rd WRS	
	50978	HC-130P	102nd RQS	
	50979	NC-130H	412th TW	
	50980	WC-130H	53rd WRS	
	50981	HC-130P	71st RQS	*bl*
	50982	HC-130P	71st RQS	*bl*
	50983	MC-130P	71st RQS	*bl*
	50984	WC-130H	53rd WRS	
	50985	WC-130H	53rd WRS	
	50986	HC-130P	71st RQS	*bl*
	50987	HC-130P	71st RQS	*bl*
	50988	HC-130P	71st RQS	*bl*
	50989	EC-130H	41st ECS	*bl*
	50991	MC-130P	9th SOS	
	50992	MC-130P	17th SOS	
	50993	MC-130P	17th SOS	
	50994	MC-130P	17th SOS	
	FY95			
	51001	C-130H	109th AS	*pr/bk*
	51002	C-130H	109th AS	*pr/bk*
	FY85			
	51361	C-130H	181st AS	*bl/w*
	51362	C-130H	181st AS	*bl/w*
	51363	C-130H	181st AS	*bl/w*
	51364	C-130H	181st AS	*bl/w*
	51365	C-130H	181st AS	*bl/w*
	51366	C-130H	181st AS	*bl/w*
	51367	C-130H	181st AS	*bl/w*
	51368	C-130H	181st AS	*bl/w*
	FY95			
	56709	C-130H	167th AS	*r*
	56710	C-130H	167th AS	*r*
	56711	C-130H	167th AS	*r*
	56712	C-130H	167th AS	*r*
	FY66			
	60212	HC-130P	130th RQS	*bl*
	60216	HC-130P	130th RQS	*bl*
	60217	MC-130P	9th SOS	
	60219	HC-130P	130th RQS	*bl*
	60220	MC-130P	17th SOS	

Notes	Type			
	60221	HC-130P	58th SOW	
	60222	HC-130P	102nd RQS	
	60223	MC-130P	9th SOS	
	60224	HC-130P	79th RQS	
	60225	MC-130P	9th SOS	
	FY86			
	60410	C-130H	758th AS	*bk/y*
	60411	C-130H	758th AS	*bk/y*
	60412	C-130H	758th AS	*bk/y*
	60413	C-130H	758th AS	*bk/y*
	60414	C-130H	758th AS	*bk/y*
	60415	C-130H	758th AS	*bk/y*
	60418	C-130H	758th AS	*bk/y*
	60419	C-130H	758th AS	*bk/y*
	FY96			
	61003	C-130H	109th AS	*pr/bk*
	61004	C-130H	109th AS	*pr/bk*
	61005	C-130H	109th AS	*pr/bk*
	61006	C-130H	109th AS	*pr/bk*
	61007	C-130H	109th AS	*pr/bk*
	61008	C-130H	109th AS	*pr/bk*
	FY86			
	61391	C-130H	180th AS	*y*
	61392	C-130H	180th AS	*y*
	61393	C-130H	180th AS	*y*
	61394	C-130H	180th AS	*y*
	61395	C-130H	180th AS	*y*
	61396	C-130H	180th AS	*y*
	61397	C-130H	180th AS	*y*
	61398	C-130H	180th AS	*y*
	61699	MC-130H	7th SOS	
	FY76			
	63300	LC-130R	139th AS	
	63302	LC-130R	139th AS	
	FY96			
	65300	WC-130J	53rd WRS	
	65301	WC-130J	53rd WRS	
	65302	WC-130J	53rd WRS	
	67322	C-130H	731st AS	*pr/w*
	67323	C-130H	731st AS	*pr/w*
	67324	C-130H	731st AS	*pr/w*
	67325	C-130H	731st AS	*pr/w*
	68153	C-130J	815th AS	*r*
	68154	C-130J	193rd SOS	
	FY87			
	70023	MC-130H	7th SOS	
	70024	MC-130H	15th SOS	
	70125	MC-130H	58th SOW	
	70126	MC-130H	58th SOW	
	70127	MC-130H	58th SOW	
	70128	AC-130U	4th SOS	
	FY97			
	71351	C-130J	135th AS	*bk/y*
	71352	C-130J	135th AS	*bk/y*
	71353	C-130J	135th AS	*bk/y*
	71354	C-130J	135th AS	*bk/y*
	71931	EC-130J	193rd SOS	
	75303	WC-130J	53rd WRS	
	75304	WC-130J	53rd WRS	
	75305	WC-130J	53rd WRS	
	75306	WC-130J	53rd WRS	
	FY87			
	79281	C-130H	95th AS	*w/r*
	79282	C-130H	95th AS	*w/r*
	79283	C-130H	96th AS	*pr*
	79284	C-130H	700th AS	*bl*
	79285	C-130H	95th AS	*w/r*
	79286	C-130H	357th AS	*bl*

Type				Notes
79287	C-130H	96th AS	pr	
79288	C-130H	758th AS	bk/y	
FY88				
80191	MC-130H	1st SOS		
80192	MC-130H	1st SOS		
80193	MC-130H	7th SOS		
80194	MC-130H	7th SOS		
80195	MC-130H	1st SOS		
80264	MC-130H	1st SOS		
FY78				
80806	C-130H	185th AS	bl	
80807	C-130H	185th AS	bl	
80808	C-130H	185th AS	bl	
80809	C-130H	185th AS	bl	
80810	C-130H	185th AS	bl	
80811	C-130H	185th AS	bl	
80812	C-130H	185th AS	bl	
80813	C-130H	185th AS	bl	
FY88				
81301	C-130H	130th AS	pr/y	
81302	C-130H	130th AS	pr/y	
81303	C-130H	130th AS	pr/y	
81304	C-130H	130th AS	pr/y	
81305	C-130H	130th AS	pr/y	
81306	C-130H	130th AS	pr/y	
81307	C-130H	130th AS	pr/y	
81308	C-130H	130th AS	pr/y	
FY98				
81355	C-130J	135th AS	bk/y	
81356	C-130J	135th AS	bk/y	
81357	C-130J	135th AS	bk/y	
81358	C-130J	135th AS	bk/y	
FY88				
81803	MC-130H	1st SOS		
FY98				
81932	EC-130J	193rd SOS		
FY88				
82101	HC-130N	102nd RQS		
82102	HC-130N	102nd RQS		
84401	C-130H	95th AS	w/r	
84402	C-130H	95th AS	w/r	
84403	C-130H	95th AS	w/r	
84404	C-130H	95th AS	w/r	
84405	C-130H	95th AS	w/r	
84406	C-130H	95th AS	w/r	
84407	C-130H	95th AS	w/r	
FY98				
85307	WC-130J	53rd WRS		
85308	WC-130J	53rd WRS		
FY89				
90280	MC-130H	7th SOS		
90281	MC-130H	15th SOS		
90282	MC-130H	15th SOS		
90283	MC-130H	15th SOS		
FY79				
90473	C-130H	192nd AS	w	
90474	C-130H	192nd AS	w	
90475	C-130H	192nd AS	w	
90476	C-130H	192nd AS	w	
90477	C-130H	192nd AS	w	
90478	C-130H	192nd AS	w	
90479	C-130H	192nd AS	w	
90480	C-130H	192nd AS	w	
FY89				
90509	AC-130U	4th SOS		
90510	AC-130U	4th SOS		
90511	AC-130U	4th SOS		
90512	AC-130U	4th SOS		

Type				Notes
90513	AC-130U	4th SOS		
90514	AC-130U	4th SOS		
91051	C-130H	105th AS	r	
91052	C-130H	105th AS	r	
91053	C-130H	105th AS	r	
91054	C-130H	105th AS	r	
91055	C-130H	105th AS	r	
91056	AC-130U			
91181	C-130H	105th AS	r	
91182	C-130H	105th AS	r	
91183	C-130H	105th AS	r	
91184	C-130H	105th AS	r	
91185	C-130H	105th AS	r	
91186	C-130H	105th AS	r	
91187	C-130H	105th AS	r	
91188	C-130H	105th AS	r	
FY99				
91431	C-130J	143rd AS	r	
91432	C-130J	143rd AS	r	
91433	C-130J	143rd AS	r	
91933	EC-130J	LMTAS		
95309	WC-130J	53rd WRS		
FY69				
95819	MC-130P	9th SOS		
95820	MC-130P	9th SOS		
95821	MC-130P	58th SOW		
95822	MC-130P	9th SOS		
95823	MC-130P	9th SOS		
95825	MC-130P	67th SOS		
95826	MC-130P	67th SOS		
95827	MC-130P	9th SOS		
95828	MC-130P	67th SOS		
95829	HC-130N	58th SOW		
95830	HC-130N	39th RQS		
95831	MC-130P	67th SOS		
95832	MC-130P	67th SOS		
95833	HC-130N	58th SOW		
96568	AC-130H	16th SOS		
96569	AC-130H	16th SOS		
96570	AC-130H	16th SOS		
96572	AC-130H	16th SOS		
96573	AC-130H	16th SOS		
96574	AC-130H	16th SOS		
96575	AC-130H	16th SOS		
96577	AC-130H	16th SOS		
FY89				
99101	C-130H	757th AS	bl	
99102	C-130H	757th AS	bl	
99103	C-130H	757th AS	bl	
99104	C-130H	757th AS	bl	
99105	C-130H	757th AS	bl	
99106	C-130H	757th AS	bl	

Boeing C-135/C-137

6th AMW, MacDill AFB, Florida:
91st ARS (*y/bl*);
15th ABW, Hickam AFB, Hawaii:
65th AS;
18th Wg, Kadena AB, Japan [ZZ]:
909th ARS (*w*);
19th ARG, Robins AFB, Georgia:
99th ARS (*y/bl*);
22nd ARW, McConnell AFB, Kansas:
344th ARS (*y/bk*), 349th ARS (*y/bl*)
350th ARS (*y/r*) & 384th ARS (*y/pr*);
55th Wg, Offutt AFB, Nebraska [OF]:
38th RS (*gn*), 45th RS (*bk*)
& 343rd RS;

Notes	Type
	88th ABW, Wright-Patterson AFB, Ohio; 92nd ARW, Fairchild AFB, Washington: 92nd ARS (*bk*), 93rd ARS (*bl*), 96th ARS (*gn*) & 97th ARS (*y*); 97th AMW, Altus AFB, Oklahoma: 55th ARS (*y/r*); 100th ARW, RAF Mildenhall, UK [D]: 351st ARS (*r/w/bl*); 106th ARS/117th ARW, Birmingham, Alabama ANG (*w/r*); 108th ARS/126th ARW, Scott AFB, Illinois ANG (*w/bl*); 108th ARW, McGuire AFB, New Jersey ANG: 141st ARS (*bk/y*) & 150th ARS (*bl*); 116th ARS/141st ARW, Fairchild AFB, Washington ANG (*gn/w*); 117th ARS/190th ARW, Forbes Field, Kansas ANG (*bl/y*); 121st ARW, Rickenbacker ANGB, Ohio ANG: 145th ARS & 166th ARS (*bl*); 126th ARS/128th ARW, Mitchell Field, Wisconsin ANG (*w/bl*); 127th ARS/184th ARW, McConnell AFB, Kansas ANG; 132nd ARS/101st ARW, Bangor, Maine ANG (*w/gn*); 133rd ARS/157th ARW, Pease ANGB, New Hampshire ANG (*bl*); 136th ARS/107th ARW, Niagara Falls, New York ANG (*bl*); 151st ARS/134th ARW, Knoxville, Tennessee ANG (*w/or*); 153rd ARS/186th ARW, Meridian, Mississippi ANG (*bk/gd*); 168th ARS/168th ARW, Eielson AFB, Alaska ANG (*bl/y*); 171st ARW, Greater Pittsburgh, Pennsylvania ANG: 146th ARS (*y/bk*) & 147th ARS (*bk/y*); 173rd ARS/155th ARW, Lincoln, Nebraska ANG (*r/w*); 174th ARS/185th ARW, Sioux City, Iowa ANG (*y/bk*); 191st ARS/151st ARW, Salt Lake City, Utah ANG (*bl/bk*); 196th ARS/163rd ARW, March ARB, California ANG (*bl/w*); 197th ARS/161st ARW, Phoenix, Arizona ANG; 203rd ARS/154th Wg, Hickam AFB, Hawaii ANG [HH] (*y/bk*); 319th ARW, Grand Forks AFB, North Dakota: 905th ARS (*bl*), 906th ARS (*y*), 911th ARS (*r*) & 912th ARS (*w*); 366th Wg, Mountain Home AFB, Idaho [MO]: 22nd ARS (*y/gn*); 412th TW, Edwards AFB, California [ED]: 452nd FLTS (*bl*); 434th ARW AFRC, Grissom AFB, Indiana: 72nd ARS (*bl*) & 74th ARS (*r/w*); 452nd AMW AFRC, March ARB, California: 336th ARS (*y*); 459th ARW AFRC, Andrews AFB, Maryland: 756th ARS (*y/bk*); 507th ARW AFRC, Tinker AFB, Oklahoma: 465th ARS (*bl/y*); 645th Materiel Sqn, Greenville, Texas; 916th ARW AFRC, Seymour Johnson AFB, North Carolina: 77th ARS (*gn*); 927th ARW AFRC, Selfridge ANGB, Michigan: 63rd ARS (*pr/w*); 939th ARW AFRC, Portland, Oregon: 64th ARS (*pr/y*); 940th ARW AFRC, McClellan AFB, California: 314th ARS (*or/bk*)

Notes	Type			
	FY60			
	0313	KC-135R	100th ARW	*r/w/bl*
	00314	KC-135R	434th ARW	*r/w*
	00315	KC-135R	126th ARS	*w/bl*
	00316	KC-135R	116th ARS	*gn/w*
	00318	KC-135R	203rd ARS	*y/bk*
	00319	KC-135R	22nd ARW	
	00320	KC-135R	319th ARW	*w*
	00321	KC-135R	319th ARW	
	00322	KC-135R	434th ARW	*bl*
	00323	KC-135R	203rd ARS	*y/bk*
	00324	KC-135R	319th ARW	
	00327	KC-135E	191st ARS	*bl/bk*
	00328	KC-135R	97th AMW	*y/r*
	00329	KC-135R	203rd ARS	*y/bk*
	00331	KC-135R	319th ARW	
	00332	KC-135R	6th AMW	*y/bl*
	00333	KC-135R	92nd AMW	*gn*
	00334	KC-135R	168th ARS	*bl/y*
	00335	KC-135T	22nd ARW	*y/bk*
	00336	KC-135T	18th Wg	*w*
	00337	KC-135T	92nd ARW	*m*
	00339	KC-135T	92nd ARW	*bl*
	00341	KC-135R	121st ARW	*bl*
	00342	KC-135T	319th ARW	*y*
	00343	KC-135T	19th ARG	*y/bl*
	00344	KC-135T	319th ARW	*r*
	00345	KC-135T	319th ARW	
	00346	KC-135T	92nd ARW	*bk*
	00347	KC-135R	121st ARW	*bl*
	00348	KC-135R	18th Wg	*w*
	00349	KC-135R	916th ARW	*gn*
	00350	KC-135R	97th AMW	*y/r*
	00351	KC-135R	100th ARW	*r/w/bl*
	00353	KC-135R	22nd ARW	
	00355	KC-135R	319th ARW	*y*
	00356	KC-135R	22nd ARW	*y/bl*
	00357	KC-135R	22nd ARW	*y*
	00358	KC-135R	136th ARS	*bl*
	00359	KC-135R	434th ARW	*r/w*
	00360	KC-135R	22nd ARW	*y/r*
	00362	KC-135R	22nd ARW	*y/r*
	00363	KC-135R	434th ARW	*bl*
	00364	KC-135R	434th ARW	*r/w*
	00365	KC-135R	127th ARS	
	00366	KC-135R	19th ARG	*y/bl*

Type *Notes*

00367 KC-135R 121st ARW *bl*
00372 C-135E 412th TW *bl*

FY61

10264 KC-135R 121st ARW *bl*
10266 KC-135R 173rd ARS *r/w*
10267 KC-135R 92nd ARW *y*
10268 KC-135E 940th ARW *or/bk*
10270 KC-135E 927th ARW *pr/w*
10271 KC-135E 927th ARW *pr/w*
10272 KC-135R 434th ARW *r/w*
10275 KC-135R 18th Wg *w*
10276 KC-135R 173rd ARS *r/w*
10277 KC-135R 127th ARS
10280 KC-135R 452nd AMW *y*
10281 KC-135E 197th ARS
10284 KC-135R 319th ARW *bl*
10288 KC-135R 92nd ARW *bk*
10290 KC-135R 203rd ARS *y/bk*
10292 KC-135R 100th ARW *r/w/bl*
10293 KC-135R 22nd ARW *y/r*
10294 KC-135R 92nd ARW
10295 KC-135R 319th ARW *bl*
10298 KC-135R 126th ARS *w/bl*
10299 KC-135R 319th ARW *bl*
10300 KC-135R 319th ARW
10302 KC-135R 22nd ARW *y*
10303 KC-135E 940th ARW *or/bk*
10304 KC-135R 92nd ARW *y*
10305 KC-135R 459th ARW *y/bk*
10306 KC-135R 319th ARW *bl*
10307 KC-135R 459th ARW *y/bk*
10308 KC-135R 97th AMW *y/r*
10309 KC-135R 126th ARS *w/bl*
10310 KC-135R 133rd ARS *bl*
10311 KC-135R 22nd ARW *y*
10312 KC-135R 319th ARW *r*
10313 KC-135R 916th ARW *gn*
10314 KC-135R 22nd ARW *y*
10315 KC-135R 319th ARW
10317 KC-135R 22nd ARW *y*
10318 KC-135R 6th AMW *y/bl*
10320 KC-135R 412th TW *bl*
10321 KC-135R 18th Wg *w*
10323 KC-135R 18th Wg *w*
10324 KC-135R 452nd AMW *y*
10330 EC-135E 412th TW *bl*
12662 RC-135S 55th Wg *bk*
12663 RC-135S 55th Wg *bk*
12666 NC-135W 645th MS
12667 WC-135W 55th Wg *bk*
12669 C-135C 412th TW *bl*
12670 OC-135B 55th Wg
12672 OC-135B 55th Wg

FY64

14828 KC-135R 100th ARW *r/w/bl*
14829 KC-135R
14830 KC-135R 100th ARW *r/w/bl*
14831 KC-135R 22nd ARW
14832 KC-135R 203rd ARS *y/bk*
14833 KC-135R 22nd ARW
14834 KC-135R 434th ARW *r/w*
14835 KC-135R 100th ARW *r/w/bl*

Type *Notes*

14836 KC-135R 6th AMW *y/bl*
14837 KC-135R 22nd ARW
14838 KC-135R 18th Wg *w*
14839 KC-135R 136th ARS *bl*
14840 KC-135R 121st ARW *bl*
14841 RC-135V 55th Wg *gn*
14842 RC-135V 55th Wg *gn*
14843 RC-135V 55th Wg *gn*
14844 RC-135V 55th Wg *gn*
14845 RC-135V 55th Wg *gn*
14846 RC-135V 55th Wg *gn*
14847 RC-135U 55th Wg *gn*
14848 RC-135V 55th Wg *gn*
14849 RC-135U 55th Wg *gn*

FY62

23498 KC-135R 319th ARW *y*
23499 KC-135R 22nd ARW *y*
23500 KC-135R 126th ARS *w/bl*
23502 KC-135R 319th ARW *bk*
23503 KC-135R 939th ARW *pr/y*
23504 KC-135R 319th ARW *y*
23505 KC-135R 100th ARW *r/w/bl*
23506 KC-135R 133rd ARS *bl*
23507 KC-135R 92nd ARW
23508 KC-135R 19th ARG *y/bl*
23509 KC-135R 916th ARW *gn*
23510 KC-135R 434th ARW *r/w*
23511 KC-135R 121st ARW *bl*
23512 KC-135R 126th ARS *w/bl*
23513 KC-135R 366th Wg *y/gn*
23514 KC-135R 203rd ARS *y/bk*
23515 KC-135R 133rd ARS *bl*
23516 KC-135R 319th ARW
23517 KC-135R 22nd ARW
23518 KC-135R 434th ARW *bl*
23519 KC-135R 22nd ARW
23520 KC-135R 6th AMW *y/bl*
23521 KC-135R 434th ARW *r/w*
23523 KC-135R 19th ARG *y/bl*
23524 KC-135R 106th ARS *w/r*
23526 KC-135R 173rd ARS *r/w*
23527 KC-135E 108th ARW *bl*
23528 KC-135R 22nd ARW
23529 KC-135R 18th Wg *w*
23530 KC-135R 434th ARW *bl*
23531 KC-135R 121st ARW *bl*
23533 KC-135R 319th ARW *bl*
23534 KC-135R 22nd ARW
23537 KC-135R 927th ARW *pr/w*
23538 KC-135R 100th ARW *r/w/bl*
23540 KC-135R 6th AMW *y/bl*
23541 KC-135R 100th ARW *r/w/bl*
23542 KC-135R 916th ARW *gn*
23543 KC-135R 459th ARW *y/bk*
23544 KC-135R 319th ARW
23545 KC-135R 22nd ARW
23546 KC-135R 6th AMW *y/bl*
23547 KC-135R 133rd ARS *bl*
23548 KC-135R 319th ARW *y*
23549 KC-135R 319th ARW *r*
23550 KC-135R 22nd ARW
23551 KC-135R 100th ARW *r/w/bl*
23552 KC-135R 319th ARW *r*
23553 KC-135R 97th AMW *y/r*
23554 KC-135R 19th ARG *y/bl*
23556 KC-135R 459th ARW *y/bk*
23557 KC-135R 927th ARW *pr/w*
23558 KC-135R 939th ARW *pr/y*

Notes	Type			
	23559	KC-135R	22nd ARW	*y/pr*
	23561	KC-135R	100th ARW	*r/w/bl*
	23562	KC-135R	319th ARW	*w*
	23564	KC-135R	22nd ARW	
	23565	KC-135R	6th AMW	*y/bl*
	23566	KC-135E	116th ARS	*gn/w*
	23568	KC-135R	97th AMW	*y/r*
	23569	KC-135R	22nd ARW	
	23571	KC-135R	168th ARS	*bl/y*
	23572	KC-135R	127th ARS	
	23573	KC-135R	100th ARW	*r/w/bl*
	23575	KC-135R	100th ARW	*r/w/bl*
	23576	KC-135R	133rd ARS	*bl*
	23577	KC-135R	916th ARW	*gn*
	23578	KC-135R	22nd ARW	
	23580	KC-135R	22nd ARW	
	23582	WC-135C	55th Wg	*bk*
	24125	RC-135W	55th Wg	*gn*
	24126	C-135B	108th ARW	*bk/y*
	24127	RC-135W	55th Wg	
	24128	RC-135S	55th Wg	
	24129	TC-135W	55th Wg	*gn*
	24130	RC-135W	55th Wg	*gn*
	24131	RC-135W	55th Wg	*gn*
	24132	RC-135W	55th Wg	*gn*
	24133	TC-135S	55th Wg	*bk*
	24134	RC-135W	55th Wg	*gn*
	24135	RC-135W	55th Wg	*gn*
	24138	RC-135W	55th Wg	*gn*
	24139	RC-135W	55th Wg	*gn*
	FY63			
	37976	KC-135R	319th ARW	
	37977	KC-135R	97th AMW	*y/r*
	37978	KC-135R	92nd ARW	*bk*
	37979	KC-135R	22nd ARW	
	37980	KC-135R		
	37981	KC-135R	136th ARS	*bl*
	37982	KC-135R	22nd ARW	
	37984	KC-135R	106th ARS	*w/r*
	37985	KC-135R	507th ARW	*bl/y*
	37987	KC-135R	319th ARW	
	37988	KC-135R	173rd ARS	*r/w*
	37991	KC-135R	173rd ARS	*r/w*
	37992	KC-135R	121st ARW	*bl*
	37993	KC-135R	121st ARW	*m*
	37995	KC-135R	22nd ARW	*y/bl*
	37996	KC-135R	434th ARW	*bl*
	37997	KC-135R	319th ARW	*bl*
	37999	KC-135R	92nd ARW	
	38000	KC-135R	22nd ARW	
	38002	KC-135R	22nd ARW	
	38003	KC-135R	6th AMW	*y/bl*
	38004	KC-135R	127th ARS	
	38006	KC-135R	97th AMW	*y/r*
	38007	KC-135R	106th ARS	*w/r*
	38008	KC-135R		
	38011	KC-135R	92nd ARW	*y*
	38012	KC-135R	319th ARW	*r*
	38013	KC-135R	121st ARW	*bl*
	38014	KC-135R	319th ARW	*bl*
	38015	KC-135R	168th ARS	*bl/y*
	38017	KC-135R	92nd ARW	*bk*
	38018	KC-135R	173rd ARS	*r/w*
	38019	KC-135R	97th AMW	*y/r*
	38020	KC-135R	6th AMW	*y/bl*
	38021	KC-135R	92nd ARW	
	38022	KC-135R	22nd ARW	*m*
	38023	KC-135R	197th ARS	

Notes	Type			
	38024	KC-135R	452nd AMW	*y*
	38025	KC-135R		
	38026	KC-135R	319th ARW	*y*
	38027	KC-135R	92nd ARW	*gn*
	38028	KC-135R	168th ARS	*bl/y*
	38029	KC-135R	126th ARS	*w/bl*
	38030	KC-135R	203rd ARS	*y/bk*
	38031	KC-135R	6th AMW	*y/bl*
	38032	KC-135R	434th ARW	*bl*
	38033	KC-135R	92nd ARW	
	38034	KC-135R	22nd ARW	
	38035	KC-135R	106th ARS	*w/r*
	38036	KC-135R	136th ARS	*bl*
	38037	KC-135R	6th AMW	*y/bl*
	38038	KC-135R	133rd ARS	*bl*
	38039	KC-135R	507th ARW	*bl/y*
	38040	KC-135R	6th AMW	*y/bl*
	38041	KC-135R	434th ARW	*bl*
	38043	KC-135R	168th ARS	*bl/y*
	38044	KC-135R	22nd ARW	
	38045	KC-135R	319th ARW	
	38050	NKC-135B	412th TW	*bl*
	38058	KC-135D	117th ARS	*bl/y*
	38059	KC-135D	117th ARS	*bl/y*
	38060	KC-135D	117th ARS	*bl/y*
	38061	KC-135D	117th ARS	*bl/y*
	38871	KC-135R	319th ARW	*y*
	38872	KC-135R	136th ARS	*bl*
	38873	KC-135R	6th AMW	*y/bl*
	38874	KC-135R	6th AMW	*y/bl*
	38875	KC-135R	127th ARS	
	38876	KC-135R	168th ARS	*bl/y*
	38877	KC-135R	97th AMW	*y/r*
	38878	KC-135R	97th AMW	*y/r*
	38879	KC-135R	100th ARW	*r/w/bl*
	38880	KC-135R	507th ARW	*bl/y*
	38881	KC-135R	97th AMW	*y/r*
	38883	KC-135R	18th ARW	*w*
	38884	KC-135R	100th ARW	*r/w/bl*
	38885	KC-135R	18th Wg	*w*
	38886	KC-135R	18th Wg	*w*
	38887	KC-135R	22nd ARW	
	38888	KC-135R	92nd ARW	
	39792	RC-135V	55th Wg	*gn*
	FY55			
	53132	NKC-135E	412th TW	*bl*
	53145	KC-135E	117th ARS	*bl/y*
	53146	KC-135E	108th ARW	*bk/y*
	FY56			
	63593	KC-135E	108th ARW	*bk/y*
	63606	KC-135E	132nd ARS	*w/gn*
	63609	KC-135E	151st ARS	*w/or*
	63611	KC-135E	171st ARW	*y/bk*
	63622	KC-135E	132nd ARS	*w/gn*
	63626	KC-135E	171st ARW	*y/bk*
	63630	KC-135E	171st ARW	*y/bk*
	63631	KC-135E	191st ARS	*bl/bk*
	63638	KC-135E	197th ARS	
	63640	KC-135E	132nd ARS	*w/gn*
	63641	KC-135E	117th ARS	*bl/y*
	63643	KC-135E	151st ARS	*w/or*
	63650	KC-135E	174th ARS	*y/bk*
	63654	KC-135E	132nd ARS	*w/gn*
	FY57			
	71419	KC-135R	19th ARG	*y/bl*
	71421	KC-135E	174th ARS	*y/bk*
	71422	KC-135E	927th ARW	*pr/w*
	71423	KC-135E	171st ARW	*bk/y*

	Type		Notes
71425	KC-135E	151st ARS	*w/or*
71426	KC-135E	197th ARS	
71427	KC-135R	127th ARS	
71428	KC-135R	196th ARS	*bl/w*
71429	KC-135E	117th ARS	*bl/y*
71430	KC-135R	133rd ARS	*bl*
71431	KC-135E	108th ARW	*bk/y*
71432	KC-135R	106th ARS	*w/r*
71433	KC-135E	197th ARS	
71434	KC-135E	174th ARS	*y/bk*
71435	KC-135R	18th Wg	*w*
71436	KC-135R	196th ARS	*bl/w*
71437	KC-135R	916th ARW	*gn*
71438	KC-135R	939th ARW	*pr/y*
71439	KC-135R	319th ARW	*bl*
71440	KC-135R	319th ARW	*r*
71441	KC-135E	108th ARS	*w/bl*
71443	KC-135E	132nd ARS	*w/gn*
71445	KC-135E	108th ARW	*bk/y*
71447	KC-135E	174th ARS	*y/bk*
71448	KC-135E	132nd ARS	*w/gn*
71450	KC-135E	132nd ARS	*w/gn*
71451	KC-135R	196th ARS	*bl/w*
71452	KC-135E	197th ARS	
71453	KC-135R	106th ARS	*w/r*
71454	KC-135R	319th ARW	
71455	KC-135E	151st ARS	*w/or*
71456	KC-135R	319th ARW	*y*
71458	KC-135E	108th ARS	*w/bl*
71459	KC-135R	196th ARS	*bl/w*
71460	KC-135E	117th ARS	*bl/y*
71461	KC-135R	173rd ARS	*r/w*
71462	KC-135R	121st ARW	*bl*
71463	KC-135E	117th ARS	*bl/y*
71464	KC-135E	108th ARW	*bk/y*
71465	KC-135E	151st ARS	*w/or*
71468	KC-135E	452nd AMW	*y*
71469	KC-135R	121st ARW	*bl*
71471	KC-135E	132nd ARS	*w/gn*
71472	KC-135R	434th ARW	*bl*
71473	KC-135R	19th ARG	*y/bl*
71474	KC-135R	18th Wg	*w*
71475	KC-135E	197th ARS	
71478	KC-135E	151st ARS	*w/or*
71479	KC-135E	459th ARW	*y/bk*
71480	KC-135E	108th ARS	*w/bl*
71482	KC-135E	108th ARS	*w/bl*
71483	KC-135R	92nd ARW	
71484	KC-135E	197th ARS	
71485	KC-135E	151st ARS	*w/or*
71486	KC-135R	18th Wg	*w*
71487	KC-135R	434th ARW	*bl*
71488	KC-135R	319th ARW	
71491	KC-135E	132nd ARS	*w/gn*
71492	KC-135E	151st ARS	*w/or*
71493	KC-135R	97th AMW	*y/r*
71494	KC-135E	108th ARS	*w/bl*
71495	KC-135E	197th ARS	
71496	KC-135E	197th ARS	
71497	KC-135E	191st ARS	*bl/bk*
71499	KC-135R	319th ARW	*r*
71501	KC-135E	174th ARS	*y/bk*
71502	KC-135R	22nd ARW	*s*
71503	KC-135E	151st ARS	*w/or*
71504	KC-135E	940th ARW	*or/bk*
71505	KC-135E	132nd ARS	*w/gn*
71506	KC-135R	6th AMW	*y/bl*
71507	KC-135E	108th ARW	*bk/y*

	Type		Notes
71508	KC-135R	203rd ARS	*y/bk*
71509	KC-135E	171st ARW	*bk/y*
71510	KC-135E	191st ARS	*bl/bk*
71512	KC-135R	459th ARW	*y/bk*
71514	KC-135R	126th ARS	*w/bl*
72589	KC-135E	412th TW	
72593	KC-135R	121st ARW	*bl*
72594	KC-135E	108th ARS	*w/bl*
72595	KC-135E	171st ARW	*bk/y*
72597	KC-135R	153rd ARS	*bk/gd*
72598	KC-135R	452nd AMW	*y*
72599	KC-135R	916th ARW	*gn*
72600	KC-135E	108th ARS	*w/bl*
72601	KC-135E	151st ARS	*w/or*
72602	KC-135E	108th ARW	*bl*
72603	KC-135R	452nd AMW	*y*
72604	KC-135E	171st ARW	*y/bk*
72605	KC-135R	100th ARW	*r/w/bl*
72606	KC-135E	108th ARW	*bl*
72607	KC-135E	171st ARW	*bk/y*
72608	KC-135E	174th ARS	*y/bk*
FY58			
80001	KC-135R	319th ARW	*w*
80003	KC-135E	108th ARS	*w/bl*
80004	KC-135R	153rd ARS	*bk/gd*
80005	KC-135E	117th ARS	*bl/y*
80006	KC-135E	191st ARS	*bl/bk*
80008	KC-135R	133rd ARS	*bl*
80009	KC-135R	126th ARS	*w/bl*
80010	KC-135R	153rd ARS	*bk/gd*
80011	KC-135R	22nd ARW	*y/bl*
80012	KC-135E	191st ARS	*bl/bk*
80013	KC-135E	117th ARS	*bl/y*
80014	KC-135E	117th ARS	*bl/y*
80015	KC-135R	939th ARW	*pr/y*
80016	KC-135R	92nd ARW	*y*
80017	KC-135E	171st ARW	*y/bk*
80018	KC-135R	22nd ARW	*y*
80020	KC-135E	171st ARW	*y/bk*
80021	KC-135R	127th ARS	
80023	KC-135R	136th ARS	*bl*
80024	KC-135E	171st ARW	*y/bk*
80027	KC-135R	319th ARW	*y*
80030	KC-135R	106th ARS	*w/r*
80032	KC-135E	108th ARW	*bl*
80034	KC-135R	6th AMW	*y/bl*
80035	KC-135R	22nd ARW	*y*
80036	KC-135R	92nd ARW	*bk*
80037	KC-135E	171st ARW	*bk/y*
80038	KC-135R	916th ARW	*gn*
80040	KC-135E	108th ARW	*bl*
80041	KC-135E	927th ARW	*pr/w*
80042	KC-135T	22nd ARW	
80043	KC-135E	191st ARS	*bl/bk*
80044	KC-135E	108th ARW	*bk/y*
80045	KC-135T	92nd ARW	*bl*
80046	KC-135T	92nd ARW	*bl*
80047	KC-135T	319th ARW	
80049	KC-135T	92nd ARW	*y*
80050	KC-135T	92nd ARW	*bk*
80051	KC-135R	507th ARW	*bl/y*
80052	KC-135R	452nd AMW	*y*
80054	KC-135T	92nd ARW	
80055	KC-135T	18th Wg	*w*
80056	KC-135R	153rd ARS	*bk/gd*
80057	KC-135R	116th ARS	*gn/w*
80058	KC-135R	939th ARW	*pr/y*
80059	KC-135R	153rd ARS	*bk/gd*

Notes	Type			
	80060	KC-135T	18th Wg	*w*
	80061	KC-135T	319th ARW	*r*
	80062	KC-135T	92nd ARW	*bc*
	80063	KC-135R	507th ARW	*bl/y*
	80064	KC-135E	940th ARW	*or/bk*
	80065	KC-135T	22nd ARW	
	80066	KC-135R	507th ARW	*bl/y*
	80067	KC-135E	116th ARS	*gn/w*
	80068	KC-135E	108th ARS	*w/bl*
	80069	KC-135T	92nd ARW	*bk*
	80071	KC-135T	22nd ARW	*y/bk*
	80072	KC-135T	18th Wg	*w*
	80073	KC-135R	106th ARS	*w/r*
	80074	KC-135T	92nd ARW	
	80075	KC-135R	459th ARW	*y/bk*
	80076	KC-135R	434th ARW	*r/w*
	80077	KC-135T	92nd ARW	*bk*
	80078	KC-135E	108th ARW	*bl*
	80079	KC-135R	507th ARW	*bl/y*
	80080	KC-135E	191st ARS	*bl/bk*
	80082	KC-135E	174th ARS	*y/bk*
	80083	KC-135R	121st ARW	*bl*
	80084	KC-135T	92nd ARW	*bl*
	80085	KC-135R	452nd AMW	*y*
	80086	KC-135T	92nd ARW	*gn*
	80087	KC-135E	108th ARW	*bl*
	80088	KC-135T	18th Wg	*w*
	80089	KC-135T	319th ARW	*w*
	80090	KC-135E	940th ARW	*or/bk*
	80092	KC-135R	127th ARS	
	80093	KC-135R	319th ARW	*r*
	80094	KC-135T	92nd ARW	*bk*
	80095	KC-135T	319th ARW	*w*
	80096	KC-135E	940th ARW	*or/bk*
	80098	KC-135R	133rd ARS	*bl*
	80099	KC-135T	92nd ARW	*bl*
	80100	KC-135R	92nd ARW	
	80102	KC-135R	939th ARW	*pr/y*
	80103	KC-135T	92nd ARW	*gn*
	80104	KC-135R	136th ARS	*bl*
	80106	KC-135R	106th ARS	*w/r*
	80107	KC-135E	116th ARS	*gn/w*
	80108	KC-135E	940th ARW	*or/bk*
	80109	KC-135R	153rd ARS	*bk/gd*
	80111	KC-135E	108th ARW	*bk/y*
	80112	KC-135T	92nd ARW	*y*
	80113	KC-135R	97th AMW	*y/r*
	80114	KC-135R	92nd ARW	*bl*
	80115	KC-135E	108th ARW	*bl*
	80116	KC-135E	197th ARS	
	80117	KC-135T	92nd ARW	*bl*
	80118	KC-135R	18th Wg	*w*
	80119	KC-135R	92nd ARW	
	80120	KC-135R	319th ARW	
	80121	KC-135R	507th ARW	*bl/y*
	80122	KC-135R	168th ARS	*bl/y*
	80123	KC-135R	18th Wg	*w*
	80124	KC-135R	22nd ARW	
	80125	KC-135T	92nd ARW	*bl*
	80126	KC-135R	22nd ARW	*y*
	80128	KC-135R	100th ARW	*r/w/bl*
	80129	KC-135T	92nd ARW	*bl*
	80130	KC-135R	126th ARS	*w/bl*
	FY88			
	86005	EC-137D	88th ABW	
	86008	EC-137D	88th ABW	
	FY59			
	91444	KC-135R	121st ARW	*bl*

Notes	Type			
	91445	KC-135E	174th ARS	*y/bk*
	91446	KC-135R	153rd ARS	*bk/gd*
	91447	KC-135E	927th ARW	*pr/w*
	91448	KC-135R	196th ARS	*bl/w*
	91450	KC-135R	196th ARS	*bl/w*
	91451	KC-135E	927th ARW	*pr/w*
	91453	KC-135R	121st ARW	*bl*
	91455	KC-135R	153rd ARS	*bk/gd*
	91456	KC-135E	108th ARW	*bk/y*
	91457	KC-135E	171st ARW	*bk/y*
	91458	KC-135R	121st ARW	*bl*
	91459	KC-135R	100th ARW	*r/w/bl*
	91460	KC-135T	92nd ARW	*gn*
	91461	KC-135R	168th ARS	*bl/y*
	91462	KC-135T	319th ARW	*bl*
	91463	KC-135R	173rd ARS	*r/w*
	91464	KC-135T	92nd ARW	*bk*
	91466	KC-135R	136th ARS	*bl*
	91467	KC-135T	92nd ARW	*bl*
	91468	KC-135T	92nd ARW	*bl*
	91469	KC-135R	459th ARW	*y/bk*
	91470	KC-135T	92nd ARW	*y*
	91471	KC-135T	92nd ARW	*y*
	91472	KC-135R	203rd ARS	*y/bk*
	91473	KC-135E	191st ARS	*bl/bk*
	91474	KC-135T	92nd ARW	*bk*
	91475	KC-135R	97th AMW	*y/r*
	91476	KC-135R	319th ARW	*r*
	91477	KC-135E	940th ARW	*or/bk*
	91478	KC-135R	153rd ARS	*bk/gd*
	91479	KC-135E	171st ARW	*y/bk*
	91480	KC-135T	92nd ARW	*gn*
	91482	KC-135R	319th ARW	
	91483	KC-135R	121st ARW	*bl*
	91484	KC-135E	171st ARW	*bk/y*
	91485	KC-135E	108th ARW	*bl*
	91486	KC-135R	22nd ARW	*y*
	91487	KC-135E	108th ARS	*w/bl*
	91488	KC-135R	6th AMW	*y/bl*
	91489	KC-135E	191st ARS	*bl/bk*
	91490	KC-135T	92nd ARW	*bk*
	91492	KC-135R	97th AMW	*y/r*
	91493	KC-135E	132nd ARS	*w/gn*
	91495	KC-135R	126th ARS	*w/bl*
	91496	KC-135E	171st ARW	*y/bk*
	91497	KC-135E	108th ARW	*bl*
	91498	KC-135R	127th ARS	
	91499	KC-135R	196th ARS	*bl/w*
	91500	KC-135R	197th ARS	
	91501	KC-135R	319th ARW	
	91502	KC-135R	319th ARW	*y*
	91503	KC-135E	108th ARW	*bk/y*
	91504	KC-135T	92nd ARW	*bk*
	91505	KC-135R	196th ARS	*bl/w*
	91506	KC-135E	116th ARS	*gn/w*
	91507	KC-135R	19th ARG	*y/bl*
	91508	KC-135R	92nd ARW	*bk*
	91509	KC-135R	196th ARS	*bl/w*
	91510	KC-135T	319th ARW	*r*
	91511	KC-135R	22nd ARW	
	91512	KC-135T	18th Wg	*w*
	91513	KC-135T	92nd ARW	*bl*
	91515	KC-135R	319th ARW	*r*
	91516	KC-135R	196th ARS	*bl/w*
	91517	KC-135R	97th AMW	*y/r*
	91519	KC-135R	116th ARS	*gn/w*
	91520	KC-135T	319th ARW	
	91521	KC-135R	168th ARS	*bl/y*

Type			Notes
91522	KC-135R	136th ARS *bl*	
91523	KC-135T	92nd ARW *bk*	

Lockheed C-141C Starlifter

445th AW AFRC, Wright-Patterson AFB, Ohio (*si*):
89th AS & 356th AS;
452nd AMW AFRC, March ARB, California (*or/y*):
729th AS & 730th AS

Type			Notes
FY64			
40620	445th AW	*si*	
40637	445th AW	*si*	
40645	445th AW	*si*	
FY65			
50229	452nd AMW	*or/y*	
50248	452nd AMW	*or/y*	
50249	445th AW	*si*	
50250	445th AW	*si*	
59414	452nd AMW	*or/y*	
FY66			
60132	445th AW	*si*	
60152	452nd AMW	*or/y*	
60177	445th AW	*si*	
67950	445th AW	*si*	
67953	445th AW	*si*	
67954	445th AW	*si*	
67959	445th AW	*si*	
FY67			
70031	445th AW	*si*	
70166	445th AW	*si*	

F-16C Fighting Falcon 89-2035 from the 555th FS, USAFE at Aviano, Italy.

Based at Ramstein, Germany, this C-20H Gulfstream IV 00300 is operated by the 86th AW.

Lockheed P-3 Orion
CinCLANT/VP-30, NAS Jacksonville, Florida;
CinCPAC/ETD, MCBH Kaneohe Bay, Hawaii;
CNO/VP-30, NAS Jacksonville, Florida;
NASC-FS, Point Mugu, California;
Navy Research Lab, Patuxent River, Maryland;
USNTPS, NAS Point Mugu, California;
VP-1, NAS Whidbey Island, Washington [YB];
VP-4, MCBH Kaneohe Bay, Hawaii [YD];
VP-5, NAS Jacksonville, Florida [LA];
VP-8, NAS Brunswick, Maine [LC];
VP-9, MCBH Kaneohe Bay, Hawaii [PD];
VP-10, NAS Brunswick, Maine [LD];
VP-16, NAS Jacksonville, Florida [LF];
VP-26, NAS Brunswick, Maine [LK];
VP-30, NAS Jacksonville, Florida [LL];
VP-40, NAS Whidbey Island, Washington [QE];
VP-45, NAS Jacksonville, Florida [LN];
VP-46, NAS Whidbey Island, Washington [RC];
VP-47, MCBH Kaneohe Bay, Hawaii [RD];
VP-62, NAS Jacksonville, Florida [LT];
VP-65, NAS Point Mugu, California [PG];
VP-66, NAS Willow Grove, Pennsylvania [LV];
VP-69, NAS Whidbey Island, Washington [PJ];
VP-92, NAS Brunswick, Maine [LY];
VP-94, NAS New Orleans, Louisiana [PZ];
VPU-1, NAS Brunswick, Maine;
VPU-2, MCBH Kaneohe Bay, Hawaii;
VQ-1, NAS Whidbey Island, Washington [PR];
VQ-2, NAF Rota, Spain;
VX-1, NAS Patuxent River, Maryland;
VX-20, Patuxent River, Maryland;
VX-30, NAS Point Mugu, California

148889		UP-3A	USNTPS
149674	[674]	NP-3D	NRL
149675		VP-3A	CinCPAC
149676		VP-3A	CNO
150499	[337]	NP-3D	VX-30
150515		VP-3A	VP-30
150521	[341]	NP-3D	VX-30
150522	[340]	NP-3D	VX-30
152141	[408]	P-3A	VP-1
152150	[150]	NP-3D	NRL
152165	[404]	P-3A	VP-1
153442	[442]	NP-3D	NRL
153443	[443]	NP-3D	USNTPS
154587	[587]	NP-3D	NRL
154589	[589]	NP-3D	NRL
156507	[PR-507]	EP-3E	VQ-1
156509	[LL-509]	P-3C	VP-30
156510	[LL-510]	P-3C	VP-30
156511	[PR-32]	EP-3E	VQ-1
156514	[PR-33]	EP-3E	VQ-1
156515	[515]	P-3C	VP-9
156517	[PR-34]	EP-3E	VQ-1
156519	[21]	EP-3E	VQ-2
156521	[PG-521]	P-3C	VP-65
156523	[LL-523]	P-3C	VP-30
156527	[PD-527]	P-3C	VP-9
156528	[PR-36]	EP-3E	VQ-1
156529	[24]	EP-3E	VQ-2
156530	[LL-530]	P-3C	VP-30
157312	[PG-312]	P-3C	VP-65
157313	[LF-313]	P-3C	VP-16
157316	[23]	EP-3E	VQ-2
157317	[LY-317]	P-3C	VP-92
157318	[PR-318]	EP-3E	VQ-1
157319	[LL-319]	P-3C	VP-30
157322	[RC-322]	P-3C	VP-46
157323	[PG-323]	P-3C	VP-65
157324	[YD-324]	P-3C	VP-4
157325	[25]	EP-3E	VQ-2
157326	[22]	EP-3E	VQ-2
157327	[LC-327]	P-3C	VP-8
157329	[329]	P-3C	VP-46
157330	[330]	P-3C	VP-1
157331	[LL-331]	P-3C	VP-30
158204	[204]	P-3C	VX-20
158206		P-3C	VPU-1
158209	[PD-209]	P-3C	VP-9
158210	[LD-210[	P-3C	VP-10
158214	[LL-214]	P-3C	VP-30
158215	[LL-215]	P-3C	VP-30
158216	[216]	P-3C	VP-46
158222	[LL-222]	P-3C	VP-30
158224	[LA-224]	P-3C	VP-5
158225	[225]	P-3C	VP-46
158226	[PJ-226]	P-3C	VP-69
158563	[LL-563]	P-3C	VP-30
158564	[564]	P-3C	VP-16
158565	[565]	P-3C	VP-92
158567	[567]	P-3C	VP-16
158568	[568]	P-3C	VP-26
158570	[02]	P-3C	VX-1
158571	[LL-571]	P-3C	VP-30
158573	[LL-573]	P-3C	VP-30
158574		P-3C	NASC-FS
158912	[912]	P-3C	VX-20
158914	[914]	P-3C	VP-1
158915	[915]	P-3C	VP-40
158916	[LL-37]	P-3C	VP-30
158917	[LL-917]	P-3C	VP-30
158918	[RD-918]	P-3C	VP-47
158919	[919]	P-3C	VP-5
158921	[921]	P-3C	VP-4
158922	[PD-922]	P-3C	VP-9
158923	[YD-923]	P-3C	VP-4
158924	[924]	P-3C	VP-16
158925	[925]	P-3C	VP-10
158926	[926]	P-3C	VP-10
158927	[927]	P-3C	VP-69
158929	[LN-929]	P-3C	VP-45
158931	[LA-931]	P-3C	VP-5
158932	[932]	P-3C	VP-45
158933	[933]	P-3C	VP-26
158934	[934]	P-3C	VP-40
158935	[LL-935]	P-3C	VP-30
159318	[318]	P-3C	VP-8
159320	[LD-320]	P-3C	VP-10
159322	[LL-322]	P-3C	VP-30
159323	[323]	P-3C	VP-1
159326	[YD-326]	P-3C	VP-4
159329	[329]	P-3C	VP-40
159503	[LA-503]	P-3C	VP-5
159504		P-3C	VPU-2
159506	[LK-506]	P-3C	VP-26
159507	[RD-507]	P-3C	VP-47
159512	[512]	P-3C	VP-16
159513	[LL-513]	P-3C	VP-30
159514	[LL-514]	P-3C	VP-30
159885	[PD-885]	P-3C	VP-9
159886	[886]	P-3C	VQ-2
159887		P-3C	NASC-FS
159889	[04]	P-3C	VX-1
159893		EP-3E	
159894	[894]	P-3C	VP-45
160283	[YD-283]	P-3C	VP-4
160284	[LL-284]	P-3C	VP-30

160286	[LK-286]	P-3C	VP-26
160287	[LL-287]	P-3C	VP-30
160288		P-3C	NASC-FS
160290	[290]	P-3C	VX-20
160291	[JA-05]	P-3C	VX-1
160292	[292]	P-3C	VPU-2
160293	[293]	P-3C	
160610	[PD-610]	P-3C	VP-9
160611	[PG-611]	P-3C	VP-65
160612	[PR-52]	P-3C	VQ-1
160761	[YD-761]	P-3C	VP-4
160762		P-3C	VPU-2
160763	[LF-763]	P-3C	VP-16
160764	[764]	EP-3E	
160765	[LF-765]	P-3C	VP-16
160766	[766]	P-3C	VPU-2
160767	[LV-767]	P-3C	VP-66
160768	[768]	P-3C	VP-46
160769	[769]	P-3C	VP-69
160770	[LF-770]	P-3C	VP-16
160999	[LL-999]	P-3C	VP-30
161001		P-3C	
161002	[LF-002]	P-3C	VP-16
161003	[PD-003]	P-3C	VP-9
161004	[LK-004]	P-3C	VP-26
161005	[JA-07]	P-3C	VX-1
161006	[006]	P-3C	VP-10
161007	[RC-007]	P-3C	VP-46
161008	[LL-008]	P-3C	VP-30
161009		P-3C	VP-10
161010	[LL-010]	P-3C	VP-30
161011	[011]	P-3C	VP-16
161012	[YD-012]	P-3C	VP-4
161013	[LT-013]	P-3C	VP-62
161014	[PG-014]	P-3C	VP-65
161121	[121]	P-3C	VP-45
161122	[226]	P-3C	VPU-1
161123		P-3C	
161124	[LF-124]	P-3C	VP-16
161125	[LV-125]	P-3C	VP-66
161126	[PR-50]	P-3C	VQ-1
161127		P-3C	
161128	[LL-128]	P-3C	VP-30
161129	[LV-129]	P-3C	VP-66
161130	[130]	P-3C	VP-40
161131	[PJ-131]	P-3C	VP-69
161132	[YD-132]	P-3C	VP-4
161329		P-3C	
161330	[LL-330]	P-3C	VP-30
161331	[LY-331]	P-3C	VP-92
161332	[PG-332]	P-3C	VP-65
161333	[PZ-333]	P-3C	VP-94
161334	[PZ-334]	P-3C	VP-94
161335	[PZ-335]	P-3C	VP-94
161336	[LY-336]	P-3C	VP-92
161337	[PZ-337]	P-3C	VP-94
161338	[LA-338]	P-3C	VP-5
161339	[339]	P-3C	VP-4
161340	[340]	P-3C	VP-10
161404	[LL-404]	P-3C	VP-30
161405	[405]	P-3C	VP-40
161406	[PR-406]	P-3C	VQ-1
161407	[PG-407]	P-3C	VP-65
161408	[LV-408]	P-3C	VP-66
161409	[LV-409]	P-3C	VP-66
161410		EP-3E	
161411	[LL-411]	P-3C	VP-30
161412	[412]	P-3C	VP-92
161413	[LL-413]	P-3C	VP-30
161414	[LA-414]	P-3C	VP-5
161415	[LL-415]	P-3C	VP-30
161585		P-3C	VPU-1
161586	[LL-586]	P-3C	VP-30
161587	[YD-587]	P-3C	VP-4
161588	[LL-588]	P-3C	VP-30
161589	[589]	P-3C	VX-1
161590	[LL-590]	P-3C	VP-30
161591	[PZ-591]	P-3C	VP-94
161592	[PZ-592]	P-3C	VP-94
161593	[LL-593]	P-3C	VP-30
161594	[LL-594]	P-3C	VP-30
161595	[LV-595]	P-3C	VP-66
161596	[LL-596]	P-3C	VP-30
161763	[RD-763]	P-3C	VP-47
161764	[764]	P-3C	VP-47
161765	[LF-765]	P-3C	VP-16
161766	[PJ-766]	P-3C	VP-69
161767	[767]	P-3C	VP-9
162314	[314]	P-3C	VP-40
162315	[315]	P-3C	VP-40
162316	[316]	P-3C	VP-16
162317	[YB-317]	P-3C	VP-1
162318	[318]	P-3C	VP-46
162770	[770]	P-3C	VP-40
162771	[RD-771]	P-3C	VP-47
162772	[772]	P-3C	VP-40
162773	[773]	P-3C	VP-1
162774	[774]	P-3C	VX-20
162775	[775]	P-3C	VP-45
162776	[776]	P-3C	VP-8
162777	[PD-777]	P-3C	VP-9
162778	[LK-778]	P-3C	VP-26
162998	[998]	P-3C	VP-46
162999	[999]	P-3C	VP-92
163000	[000]	P-3C	VP-45
163001	[LT-001]	P-3C	VP-62
163002	[LT-002]	P-3C	VP-62
163003	[PJ-003]	P-3C	VP-69
163004	[004]	P-3C	VP-92
163006	[LF-006]	P-3C	VP-16
163289	[YB-289]	P-3C	VP-1
163290	[YB-290]	P-3C	VP-1
163291	[LT-291]	P-3C	VP-62
163292	[LF-292]	P-3C	VP-16
163293	[LF-293]	P-3C	VP-16
163294	[294]	P-3C	VP-16
163295	[295]	P-3C	VP-69

Boeing E-6 Mercury
Boeing, McConnell AFB, Kansas;
VQ-3 & VQ-4, SCW-1, Tinker AFB, Oklahoma

162782	E-6B	VQ-4
162783	E-6B	VQ-3
162784	E-6B	VQ-3
163918	E-6B	VQ-3
163919	E-6B	VQ-3
163920	E-6B	VQ-3
164386	E-6A	VQ-3
164387	E-6B	VQ-3
164388	E-6A	VQ-4
164404	E-6B	VQ-4
164405	E-6A	VQ-4
164406	E-6B	VQ-3
164407	E-6A	VQ-4
164408	E-6A	VQ-4
164409	E-6B	VQ-4
164410	E-6A	VQ-4

McDonnell Douglas
C-9B Skytrain II/DC-9-32*
VMR-1, Cherry Point MCAS, North Carolina;
VR-46, Atlanta, Georgia [JS];
VR-52, Willow Grove NAS, Pennsylvania [JT];
VR-56, Norfolk NAS, Virginia [JU];

VR-57, North Island NAS, California [RX];
VR-61, Whidbey Island NAS, Washington [RS];

159113	[RX]	VR-57
159114	[RX]	VR-57
159115	[RS]	VR-61
159116	[RS]	VR-61
159117	[JU]	VR-56
159118	[JU]	VR-56
159119	[JU]	VR-56
159120	[JU]	VR-56
160046		VMR-1
160047		VMR-1
160048	[JT]	VR-52
160049	[JT]	VR-52
160050		VR-52
160051	[JT]	VR-52
161266	[JS]	VR-46
161529	[JS]	VR-46
161530	[JS]	VR-46
164605*	[RX]	VR-57
164606*	[RS]	VR-61
164607*	[RX]	VR-57
164608*	[RS]	VR-61

Grumman C-20D Gulfstream III/ C-20G Gulfstream IV*

MASD, NAF Washington, Maryland;
VR-1, NAF Washington, Maryland;
VR-48, NAF Washington, Maryland [JR];
VR-51, MCBH Kaneohe Bay, Hawaii [RG]

163691		VR-1
163692		VR-1
165093*	[JR]	VR-48
165094*	[JR]	VR-48
165151*	[RG]	VR-51
165152*	[RG]	VR-51
165153*		MASD

Gulfstream Aerospace C-37A Gulfstream V

VR-1, NAF Washington, Maryland;

166375	VR-1
166376	
166377	
166378	
166379	

Boeing C-40A Clipper

VR-58, Jacksonville NAS, Florida [JV];
VR-59, NAS Fort Worth JRB, Texas [RY]

165829	[JV]	VR-58
165830	[RY]	VR-59
165831	[RY]	VR-59
165832	[JV]	VR-58
165833	[RY]	VR-59
165834	[JV]	VR-58
165835		Boeing
165836		Boeing

Lockheed C-130 Hercules

VR-53, NAF Washington,Maryland [AX];
VR-54, New Orleans NAS, Louisiana [CW];
VR-55, NAS Point Mugu, California [RU];
VR-62, Brunswick NAS, Maine [JW];
VR-64, NAS Willow Grove, Pennsylvania [LU];
VMGR-152, Futenma MCAS, Japan [QD];
VMGR-234, NAS Fort Worth, Texas [QH];
VMGR-252, Cherry Point MCAS, North Carolina [BH];
VMGRT-253, Cherry Point MCAS, North Carolina [GR];
VMGR-352, MCAS Miramar, California [QB];
VMGR-452, Stewart Field, New York [NY];
VX-20, Patuxent River, Maryland

147572	[QB]	KC-130F	VMGR-352
147573	[QD]	KC-130F	VMGR-152
148246	[GR]	KC-130F	VMGRT-253
148247	[QB]	KC-130F	VMGR-352
148248	[QD]	KC-130F	VMGR-152
148249	[GR]	KC-130F	VMGRT-253
148891	[QB]	KC-130F	VMGR-352
148893	[QD]	KC-130F	VMGR-152
148894	[GR]	KC-130F	VMGRT-253
148896	[BH]	KC-130F	VMGR-252
148897	[BH]	KC-130F	VMGR-252
148898	[BH]	KC-130F	VMGR-252
148899	[QD]	KC-130F	VMGR-152
149788	[BH]	KC-130F	VMGR-252
149789	[QB]	KC-130F	VMGR-352
149791	[QB]	KC-130F	VMGR-352
149792	[QB]	KC-130F	VMGR-352
149795	[QB]	KC-130F	VMGR-352
149798	[QB]	KC-130F	VMGR-352
149799	[QD]	KC-130F	VMGR-152
149800	[QB]	KC-130F	VMGR-352
149803	[GR]	KC-130F	VMGRT-253
149806		KC-130F	VX-20
149807	[QD]	KC-130F	VMGR-152
149808		KC-130F	VX-20
149811	[BH]	KC-130F	VMGR-252
149812	[QD]	KC-130F	VMGR-152
149815	[QB]	KC-130F	VMGR-352
149816	[QD]	KC-130F	VMGR-152
150684	[GR]	KC-130F	VMGRT-253
150686	[BH]	KC-130F	VMGR-252
150689	[QB]	KC-130F	VMGR-352
150690	[QD]	KC-130F	VMGR-152
160013	[QD]	KC-130R	VMGR-152
160014	[QD]	KC-130R	VMGR-152
160015	[QB]	KC-130R	VMGR-352
160016	[QB]	KC-130R	VMGR-352
160017	[QB]	KC-130R	VMGR-352
160018	[QD]	KC-130R	VMGR-152
160019	[QD]	KC-130R	VMGR-152
160020	[QD]	KC-130R	VMGR-152
160022	[QB]	KC-130R	VMGR-352
160240	[QB]	KC-130R	VMGR-352
160625	[BH]	KC-130R	VMGR-252
160626	[BH]	KC-130R	VMGR-252
160627	[BH]	KC-130R	VMGR-252
160628	[QD]	KC-130R	VMGR-152
162308	[QH]	KC-130T	VMGR-234
162309	[QH]	KC-130T	VMGR-234
162310	[QH]	KC-130T	VMGR-234
162311	[QH]	KC-130T	VMGR-234
162785	[QH]	KC-130T	VMGR-234
162786	[QH]	KC-130T	VMGR-234
163022	[QH]	KC-130T	VMGR-234
163023	[QH]	KC-130T	VMGR-234
163310	[QH]	KC-130T	VMGR-234
163311	[NY]	KC-130T	VMGR-452
163591	[NY]	KC-130T	VMGR-452
163592	[NY]	KC-130T	VMGR-452
164105	[NY]	KC-130T	VMGR-452
164106	[NY]	KC-130T	VMGR-452
164180	[NY]	KC-130T	VMGR-452
164181	[NY]	KC-130T	VMGR-452
164441	[NY]	KC-130T	VMGR-452
164442	[NY]	KC-130T	VMGR-452
164597	[NY]	KC-130T-30	VMGR-452
164598	[QH]	KC-130T-30	VMGR-234
164762	[CW]	C-130T	VR-54
164763		C-130T	*Blue Angels*
164993	[LU]	C-130T	VR-64

164994	[AX]	C-130T	VR-53	165352	[NY]	KC-130T	VMGR-452
164995	[AX]	C-130T	VR-53	165353	[NY]	KC-130T	VMGR-452
164996	[AX]	C-130T	VR-53	165378	[RU]	C-130T	VR-55
164997	[AX]	C-130T	VR-53	165379	[RU]	C-130T	VR-55
164998	[AX]	C-130T	VR-53	165735	[BH]	KC-130J	VMGR-252
164999	[QH]	KC-130T	VMGR-234	165736	[QB]	KC-130J	VMGR-352
165000	[QH]	KC-130T	VMGR-234	165737	[BH]	KC-130J	VMGR-252
165158	[CW]	C-130T	VR-54	165738	[BH]	KC-130J	VMGR-252
165159	[CW]	C-130T	VR-54	165739	[BH]	KC-130J	VMGR-252
165160	[CW]	C-130T	VR-54	165809	[BH]	KC-130J	VMGR-252
165161	[LU]	C-130T	VR-64	165810	[BH]	KC-130J	VMGR-252
165162	[QH]	KC-130T	VMGR-234	165957	[BH]	KC-130J	VMGR-252
165163	[QH]	KC-130T	VMGR-234	166380	[BH]	KC-130J	VMGR-252
165313	[JW]	C-130T	VR-62	166381	[BH]	KC-130J	VMGR-252
165314	[JW]	C-130T	VR-62	166382	[BH]	KC-130J	VMGR-252
165315	[NY]	KC-130T	VMGR-452	166472	[BH]	KC-130J	VMGR-252
165316	[NY]	KC-130T	VMGR-452	166473	[BH]	KC-130J	VMGR-252
165348	[JW]	C-130T	VR-62	166511	[BH]	KC-130J	VMGR-252
165349	[JW]	C-130T	VR-62	166512	[BH]	KC-130J	VMGR-252
165350	[RU]	C-130T	VR-55	166513	[BH]	KC-130J	VMGR-252
165351	[RU]	C-130T	VR-55	166514	[BH]	KC-130J	VMGR-252

Boeing B-52H Stratofortress 00042 is flown by the 917th Wing of the AFRC from Barksdale, LA.

US-based US Coast Guard Aircraft

Gulfstream Aerospace C-37A Gulfstream V
USCG, Washington DC
01

Grumman Gulfstream IV
USCG, Washington DC
02

Lockheed C-130 Hercules
USCGS Barbers Point, Hawaii;
USCGS Clearwater, Florida;
USCGS Elizabeth City, North Carolina;
USCGS Kodiak, Alaska;
USCGS Sacramento, California

1500	HC-130H	Elizabeth City
1501	HC-130H	Elizabeth City
1502	HC-130H	Elizabeth City
1503	HC-130H	Elizabeth City
1504	HC-130H	Elizabeth City
1700	HC-130H	Sacramento
1701	HC-130H	Barbers Point
1702	HC-130H	Kodiak
1703	HC-130H	Sacramento
1704	HC-130H	Sacramento
1705	HC-130H	Clearwater
1706	HC-130H	Clearwater
1707	HC-130H	Kodiak
1708	HC-130H	Clearwater
1709	HC-130H	Kodiak
1710	HC-130H	Kodiak
1711	HC-130H	Kodiak
1712	HC-130H	Barbers Point
1713	HC-130H	Clearwater
1714	HC-130H	Barbers Point
1715	HC-130H	Kodiak
1716	HC-130H	Sacramento
1717	HC-130H	Clearwater
1718	HC-130H	Sacramento
1719	HC-130H	Clearwater
1720	HC-130H	Clearwater
1790	HC-130H	Clearwater
2001	C-130J	
2002	C-130J	
2003	C-130J	
2004	C-130J	
2005	C-130J	
2006	C-130J	

Aircraft in US Government or Military Services with Civil Registrations

BAe 125-800A (C-29A)
Federal Aviation Administration, Oklahoma
N94 (88-0269)
N95 (88-0270)
N96 (88-0271)
N97 (88-0272)
N98 (88-0273)
N99 (88-0274)

Gates LearJet 35A
Phoenix Aviation/Flight International/ US Navy, Naples
N20DK
N50FN
N88JA
N118FN
N710GS

156th AW Puerto Rico Air National Guard Lockheed C-130E Hercules 63-7851.

Military Aviation Sites on the Internet

The list below is not intended to be a complete list of military aviation sites on the Internet. The sites listed cover Museums, Locations, Air Forces, Companies and Organisations that are mentioned elsewhere in 'Military Aircraft Markings'. Sites listed are in English or contain sufficient English to be reasonably easily understood. Each site address is believed to be correct at the time of going to press. Additions are welcome, via the usual address found at the front of the book, or via e-mail to admin@aviation-links.co.uk. An up to date copy of this list is to be found at http://homepage.ntlworld.com/airnet/mam.html.

Name of site	*Internet Dial (all prefixed 'http://')*
MILITARY SITES – UK	
No 1 Sqn	www.raf-cott.demon.co.uk/1sqn.html
No 2 Sqn	www.rafmarham.co.uk/organisation/2squadron/2squadron.htm
No 4 Regiment Army Air Corps	www.4regimentaac.co.uk/
No 4 Sqn	www.raf-cott.demon.co.uk/4sqn.html
No 6 Flt	www.shawbury.raf.mod.uk/6fltaac.htm
No 6 Sqn	www.raf.mod.uk/rafcoltishall/squadrons/6Sqn.htm
No 7 Sqn	www.rafodiham.co.uk/structure/squadrons/7sqn/7sqn.htm
No 8 Sqn	www.users.globalnet.co.uk/~8sqnwad/
No 9 Sqn	www.rafmarham.co.uk/organisation/9squadron/9sqn_front.htm
No 10 Sqn	www.raf.mod.uk/rafbrizenorton/10squadron.html
No 12 Sqn	www.raf.mod.uk/raflossiemouth/sqn/pages/12.htm
No 13 Sqn	www.rafmarham.co.uk/organisation/13squadron/13squadron.htm
No 14 Sqn	www.raf.mod.uk/raflossiemouth/sqn/pages/14.htm
No 15 Sqn	www.xvsquadron.co.uk/
No 16(R) Sqn	www.raf.mod.uk/rafcoltishall/squadrons/16Sqn.htm
No 18 Sqn	www.rafodiham.co.uk/structure/squadrons/18sqn/18sqn.htm
No 19(R) Sqn	www.rafvalley.org/Flying/19Sqn/19Sqnindex.htm
No 20(R) Sqn	www.raf.mod.uk/rafwittering/sqn20.htm
No 23 Sqn	www.users.globalnet.co.uk/~23sqnwad/
No 24 Sqn	www.lyneham.raf.mod.uk/24sqn/xxiv.htm
No 27 Sqn	www.rafodiham.co.uk/structure/squadrons/27sqn/27sqn.htm
No 31 Sqn	www.rafmarham.co.uk/organisation/31squadron/31sqn.htm
No 39(1 PRU) Sqn	www.rafmarham.co.uk/organisation/39squadron/39squadron2.htm
No 41 Sqn	www.raf.mod.uk/rafcoltishall/squadrons/41Sqn.htm
No 42(R) Sqn	www.kinloss-raf.co.uk//42sqnintro.html
No 45(R) Sqn	www.cranwell.raf.mod.uk/3fts/45sqn/45sqn.htm
No 51 Sqn	website.lineone.net/~redgoose/
No 54 Sqn	www.raf.mod.uk/rafcoltishall/squadrons/54Sqn.htm
No 55(R) Sqn	www.cranwell.raf.mod.uk/3fts/55sqn/55sqn.htm
No 70 Sqn	70sqn.tripod.com/
No 99 Sqn	www.raf.mod.uk/rafbrizenorton/99squadron.html
No 101 Sqn	www.raf.mod.uk/rafbrizenorton/101squadron.html
No 120 Sqn	www.kinloss-raf.co.uk//120sqnintro.htm
No 201 Sqn	www.kinloss-raf.co.uk//201sqnintro.html
No 206 Sqn	www.kinloss.raf.mod.uk/opswing/ops206.htm
No 216 Sqn	www.raf.mod.uk/rafbrizenorton/216squadron.html
No 617 Sqn	www.raf.mod.uk/raflossiemouth/sqn/pages/617.htm
Aberdeen, Dundee and St Andrews UAS	dialspace.dial.pipex.com/town/way/gba87/adstauas/
The Army Air Corps	www.army.mod.uk/armyaircorps/info.htm
Blue Eagles Home Page	www.deltaweb.co.uk/eagles/
Cambridge University Air Squadron	www.srcf.ucam.org/cuas/
Defence Helicopter Flying School	www.shawbury.raf.mod.uk/dhfs.htm
East Midlands UAS	www.emuas.dial.pipex.com/
Fleet Air Arm	www.royal-navy.mod.uk/static/pages/145.html
JFACTSU	www.raf.mod.uk/jfactsu/
Liverpool University Air Squadron	www.sn63.dial.pipex.com/
Manchester & Salford Universities Air Sqn	www.masuas.dial.pipex.com/
Ministry of Defence	www.mod.uk/

Military Aviation Internet

Name of site	*Internet Dial (all prefixed 'http://')*
Northumbrian UAS	www.dur.ac.uk/nuas/DisplayPage.php3?path =welcome2.htm
Oxford University Air Sqn	users.ox.ac.uk/~ouairsqn/
QinetiQ	www.qinetiq.com/
RAF Benson	www.raf.mod.uk/rafbenson/index.htm
RAF Boulmer	www.rafboulmer.co.uk/
RAF Brize Norton	www.raf.mod.uk/rafbrizenorton/
RAF Church Fenton (unofficial)	www.rafchurchfenton.org.uk/
RAF College Cranwell	www.cranwell.raf.mod.uk/
RAF Cosford	www.raf.mod.uk/cosford/
RAF Kinloss	www.kinloss.raf.mod.uk/
RAF Leuchars	www.leuchars.raf.mod.uk/
RAF Lossiemouth	www.raf.mod.uk/raflossiemouth/
RAF Lyneham	www.lyneham.raf.mod.uk/
RAF Marham	www.rafmarham.co.uk/
RAF Northolt	www.rafnortholt.com/
RAF Northolt (unofficial)	www.fly.to/Northolt/
RAF Odiham	www.rafodiham.co.uk/
RAF Shawbury	www.shawbury.raf.mod.uk/
RAF Valley	www.rafvalley.org/
RAF Waddington	www.raf-waddington.com/
RAF Wittering	www.raf.mod.uk/rafwittering/
Red Arrows	www.raf.mod.uk/reds/redhome.html
Royal Air Force	www.raf.mod.uk/
Royal Auxiliary Air Force	www.rauxaf.mod.uk/
SAOEU	www.saoeu.org/
University of London Air Sqn	www.raf.mod.uk/ulas
Yorkshire UAS	www.yuas.dial.pipex.com/
MILITARY SITES – US	
Air Combat Command	www.acc.af.mil/
Air Force Reserve Command	www.afrc.af.mil/
Air National Guard	www.ang.af.mil/
Aviano Air Base	www.aviano.af.mil/
Liberty Wing Home Page (48th FW)	www.lakenheath.af.mil/
NASA	www.nasa.gov/
Ramstein Air Base	www.ramstein.af.mil/home.html
Spangdahlem Air Base	www.spangdahlem.af.mil/
USAF	www.af.mil/
USAF Europe	www.usafe.af.mil/
USAF World Wide Web Sites	www.af.mil/sites/
US Army	www.army.mil/
US Marine Corps	www.usmc.mil/
US Navy	www.navy.mil/
US Navy Patrol Squadrons (unofficial)	www.vpnavy.com/
MILITARY SITES – ELSEWHERE	
Armée de l'Air	www.defense.gouv.fr/air/
Aeronautica Militare	www.aeronautica.difesa.it
Austrian Armed Forces (in German)	www.bmlv.gv.at/
Belgian Air Force	www.mil.be/aircomp/index.asp?LAN=E
Canadian Forces	www.forces.ca/
Finnish Defence Force	www.mil.fi/english/
Forca Aerea Portuguesa	www.emfa.pt/
Frecce Tricolori	users.iol.it/gromeo/
German Marine	www.deutschemarine.de/
Greek Air Force	www.haf.gr/gea_uk/frame.htm
Irish Air Corps	www.military.ie/aircorps/index.html
Israeli Defence Force/Air Force	www.idf.il/
Luftforsvaret	www.mil.no/
Luftwaffe	www.luftwaffe.de/
NATO	www.nato.int/
Royal Australian Air Force	www.defence.gov.au/RAAF/
Royal Danish Air Force (in Danish)	www.ftk.dk/
Royal Netherlands AF	www.mindef.nl/english/rnlaf1.htm
Royal New Zealand AF	www.airforce.mil.nz/
Singapore Air Force	www.mindef.gov.sg/rsaf/
South African AF Site (unofficial)	www.saairforce.co.za/
Spanish Air Force	www.aire.org/
Swedish Air Force	www.mil.se/
Swedish Military Aviation (unofficial)	www.canit.se/%7Egriffon/aviation/
Swiss Armed Forces	www.vbs.admin.ch/internet/e/armee/
Turkish General Staff (Armed Forces)	www.tsk.mil.tr/

Name of site	Internet Dial (all prefixed 'http://')
AIRCRAFT & AERO ENGINE MANUFACTURERS	
BAE Systems	www.baesystems.com/
Bell Helicopter Textron	www.bellhelicopter.textron.com/index.html
Boeing	www.boeing.com/
Bombardier	www.bombardier.com/
Britten-Norman	www.britten-norman.com/
CFM International	www.cfm56.com/
Dassault	www.dassault-aviation.com/
EADS	www.eads.net/
Embraer	www.embraer.com/
General Electric	www.ge.com/
Gulfstream Aerospace	www.gulfstream.com/
Kaman Aerospace	www.kaman.com/
Lockheed Martin	www.lockheedmartin.com/
Lockheed Martin Aeronautics	www.lmaeronautics.com/palmdale/index.html
Raytheon	www.raytheon.com/rac/
Rolls-Royce	www.rolls-royce.com/
SAAB	www.saab.se/
Sikorsky	www.sikorsky.com/
Westland	www.whl.co.uk/
UK AVIATION MUSEUMS	
Aeroventure	www.aeroventure.org.uk/
Aviation Museums in Great Britain	www.rdg.ac.uk/AcaDepts/sn/wsn1/dept/av/gb.html
Bournemouth Aviation Museum	www.aviation-museum.co.uk/
Brooklands Museum	www.brooklandsmuseum.com/
City of Norwich Aviation Museum	www.cnam.co.uk/
de Havilland Aircraft Heritage Centre	www.hertsmuseums.org.uk/dehavilland/index.htm
Dumfries & Galloway Aviation Museum	www.dgam.co.uk/
Fleet Air Arm Museum	www.fleetairarm.com/
Gatwick Aviation Museum	www.gatwick-aviation-museum.co.uk/
The Helicopter Museum	www.helicoptermuseum.co.uk/
Imperial War Museum, Duxford	www.iwm.org.uk/duxford/
Imperial War Museum, Duxford (unofficial)	dspace.dial.pipex.com/town/square/rcy85/
The Jet Age Museum	www.jetagemuseum.org/
Lincs Aviation Heritage Centre	freespace.virgin.net/nick.tasker/ekirkby.htm
Midland Air Museum	www.midlandairmuseum.org.uk/
Museum of Army Flying	www.flying-museum.org.uk/
Museum of Berkshire Aviation	fly.to/MuseumofBerkshireAviation/
Museum of Flight, East Fortune	www.nms.ac.uk/flight/main.htm
Museum of Science & Industry, Manchester	www.msim.org.uk/
Newark Air Museum	www.newarkairmuseum.co.uk/
North East Aircraft Museum	www.neam.co.uk/
RAF Manston Spitfire & Hurricane Memorial	www.spitfire-museum.com/
RAF Museum, Hendon	www.rafmuseum.org.uk/
Science Museum, South Kensington	www.sciencemuseum.org.uk/
Yorkshire Air Museum, Elvington	www.yorkshireairmuseum.co.uk
AVIATION SOCIETIES	
Air Britain	www.air-britain.com/
Air North	www.airnorth.demon.co.uk/
Cleveland Aviation Society	homepage.ntlworld.com/phillip.charlton/ cashome.html
East London Aviation Society	www.westrowops.co.uk/newsletter/elas.htm
Friends of Leeming Aviation Group	www.screamin-leeming.co.uk/
Gilze-Rijen Aviation Society	www.gras-spotters.nl/
Royal Aeronautical Society	www.raes.org.uk/
St Athan Aviation Group	www.westrowops.co.uk/newsletter/stamu.htm
Scottish Air News	www.scottishairnews.co.uk/
Scramble (Dutch Aviation Society)	www.scramble.nl/
Solent Aviation Society	www.solent-aviation-society.co.uk/
Spitfire Society	www.spitfiresociety.demon.co.uk/
The Aviation Society Manchester	www.tasmanchester.com/
Ulster Aviation Society	www.d-n-a.net/users/dnetrAzQ/
Wolverhampton Aviation Group	www.wolverhamptonag.fsnet.co.uk/
OPERATORS OF HISTORIC AIRCRAFT	
The Aircraft Restoration Company	www.arc-duxford.co.uk/
Battle of Britain Memorial Flight	www.bbmf.co.uk/
Catalina Online	www.catalina.org.uk/
De Havilland Aviation	www.dehavilland.net/
Delta Jets	www.deltajets.ik.com/
Hunter Flying Club	www.hunterflyingclub.co.uk/

Military Aviation Internet

Names of sites	*Internet Dial (all prefixed 'http;//')*
Kennet Aircraft	www.airplane.demon.co.uk/
Old Flying Machine Company	www.ofmc.co.uk/
The Fighter Collection	www.fighter-collection.com/
The Real Aeroplane Company	www.realaero.com/
The Shuttleworth Collection	www.shuttleworth.org/
The Vulcan Operating Company	www.tvoc.co.uk/
SITES RELATING TO SPECIFIC TYPES OF MILITARY AIRCRAFT	
The 655 Maintenance & Preservation Society	www.jetman.dircon.co.uk/xm655/
The Avro Shackleton Page	www.home.aone.net.au/shack_one/
B-24 Liberator	www.b24bestweb.com/
EE Canberra	www.bywat.co.uk/
English Electric Lightning - Vertical Reality	www.aviation-picture-hangar.co.uk/Lightning.html
The Eurofighter site	www.eurofighter.org/
The ex FRADU Canberra Site	www.fradu-hunters.co.uk/canberra/
The ex FRADU Hunter Site	www.fradu-hunters.co.uk/
F-4 Phantom II Society	www.f4phantom.com/
F-16: The Complete Reference	www.f-16.net/
F-86 Web Page	f-86.tripod.com/
F-105 Thunderchief	www.geocities.com/Pentagon/7002/
The Gripen	www.gripen.com/
K5083 - Home Page (Hawker Hurricane)	www3.mistral.co.uk/k5083/
Lockheed C-130 Hercules	hometown.aol.com/SamC130/
Lockheed SR-71 Blackbird	www.wvi.com/~lelandh/sr-71~1.htm
The MiG-21 Page	www.topedge.com/panels/aircraft/sites/kraft/mig.htm
P-3 Orion Research Group	home.wxs.nl/~p3orin/
P-51 Mustang	www.p51.mustangsmustangs.com/
Scramble on the Web - SAAB Viggen Database	www.scramble.nl/viggen.htm
Thunder & Lightnings (Postwar British Aircraft)	www.thunder-and-lightnings.co.uk/
UK Apache Resource Centre	www.ukapache.com/
Vulcan 558 Club	www.vulcan558club.demon.co.uk/
Vulcan Restoration Trust	www.XL426.com
MISCELLANEOUS	
Aerodata	www.aerodata.biz/
Aeroflight	www.netlink.co.uk/users/aeroflt/
The AirNet Web Site	fly.to/AirNet/
The AirNet Web Site: Aviation Mailing Lists	homepage.ntlworld.com/airnet/lists.html
Air-Scene UK	www.f4aviation.co.uk
Chinese Military Aviation	www.concentric.net/~Jetfight/
Joseph F. Baugher's US Military Serials Site	home.att.net/%7Ejbaugher/
Military Aircraft Database	www.csd.uwo.ca/~pettypi/elevon/gustin_military/
Military Aviation	www.crakehal.demon.co.uk/aviation/aviation.htm
Military Aviation Review/MAP	www.mar.co.uk/
Pacific Aviation Database Organisation	www.gfiapac.co.uk/
Polish Aviation Site	aviation.pol.pl/
Russian Aviation Page	aeroweb.lucia.it/~agretch/RAP.html
Scramble on the Web - Air Show Reports	www.scramble.nl/airshows.htm
The Spotter's Nest	www.spotters.it/
Target Lock Military Aviation E-zine	http://www.targetlock.org.uk/
UK Military Aircraft Serials Resource Centre	www.serials.uk.com/
UK Military Spotting	www.thunder-and-lightnings.co.uk/spotting/